Foundations of Multithreaded, Parallel, and Distributed Programming

Foundations of Multithreaded, Parallel, and Distributed Programming

Gregory R. Andrews

University of Arizona

 Addison-Wesley

An imprint of Addison Wesley Longman, Inc.

Reading, Massachusetts • Menlo Park, California •
New York • Harlow, England • Don Mills, Ontario •
Sydney • Mexico City • Madrid • Amsterdam

Acquisions Editor: *Maite Suarez-Rivas*
Associate Editor: *Jason Miranda*
Project Manager: *Trillium Project Management*
Production Assistant: *Tracy Treeful*
Copyeditor: *Stephanie Magean*
Proofreader: *Trillium Project Management*
Cover Designer: *Night & Day Design*
Composition: *Chiron, Inc.*

Library of Congress Cataloging-in-Publication Data
Andrews, Gregory R.
   Foundations of multithreaded, parallel, and distributed programming / Gregory R. Andrews.
      p. cm.
   Includes bibliographical references.
   ISBN 0-201-35752-6
   1. Parallel programming (Computer science) 2. Electronic data processing—Distributed
processing. 3. Threads (Computer programs) I. Title: Multithreaded, parallel, and
distributed programming. II. Title.

QA76.58.A57 2000
004′.3--dc21

                             99-045285

Access the latest information about Addison-Wesley titles from our World Wide Web
site: www.awlonline.com

1 2 3 4 5 6 7 8 9 10 CRS 0302010099

Preface

Concurrent programming originated in 1962 with the invention of channels, which are independent device controllers that make it possible to have a CPU execute a new application program at the same time that I/O operations are being executed on behalf of other, suspended application programs. Hence, concurrent programming—the word *concurrent* means happening at the same time—was initially of concern to operating systems designers. In the late 1960s, hardware designers developed multiple processor machines. This presented not only a challenge for operating systems designers but also an opportunity that application programmers could exploit.

The first major concurrent programming challenge was to solve what is now called the critical section problem. It and related problems (dining philosophers, readers/writers, etc.) led to a spate of papers in the 1960s. To harness the challenge, people developed synchronization primitives such as semaphores and monitors to simplify the programmer's task. By the mid-1970s, people came to appreciate the necessity of using formal methods to help control the inherent complexity of concurrent programs.

Computer networks were introduced in the late 1970s and early 1980s. The Arpanet supported wide-area computing, and the Ethernet established local-area networks. Networks gave rise to distributed programming, which was a major topic of the 1980s and became even more important in the 1990s. The essence of distributed programming is that processes interact by means of message passing rather than by reading and writing shared variables.

Now, at the dawn of a new century, we have seen the emergence of massively parallel processing—in which tens, hundreds, or even thousands of processors are used to solve a single problem. We have also seen the emergence of client/server computing, the Internet, and the World Wide Web. Finally, we are beginning to see multiprocessor workstations and PCs. Concurrent hardware is more prevalent than ever, and concurrent programming is more relevant than ever.

This is my third book, another attempt to capture a part of the history of concurrent programming. My first book—*Concurrent Programming: Principles and Practice*, published in 1991—gives a broad, reference-level coverage of the period between 1960 and 1990. Because new problems, programming mechanisms, and formal methods were significant topics in those decades, the book focuses on them.

My second book—*The SR Programming Language: Concurrency in Practice*, published in 1993—summarizes my work with Ron Olsson in the late 1980s and early 1990s on a specific language that can be used to write concurrent programs for both shared- and distributed-memory machines. The SR book is pragmatic rather than formal, showing how to solve numerous problems in a single programming language.

This book is an outgrowth of my past and a reflection of what I think is important now and will be in the future. I have drawn heavily from material in the *Concurrent Programming* book, but I have completely rewritten every section that I have retained and have rewritten examples to use pseudo-C rather than SR. I have added new material throughout, especially on parallel scientific programming. I have also included case studies of the most important languages and software libraries, with complete sample programs. Finally, I have a new vision for the role of this book—in classrooms and in personal libraries.

A New Vision and Role

Parallel and distributed computing are today pervasive concepts. As usual in computer science, advances have been led by hardware designers, who keep building bigger, faster, more powerful computers and communication networks. For the most part, they are succeeding—witness the stock market!

New computers and networks create new challenges and opportunities, and for once software designers are no longer all that far behind. Consider Web browsers, Internet commerce, Pthreads, Java, MPI, and so on—and again, witness the stock market! These software products are specifically designed to take advantage of concurrency in hardware and applications. In short, much of the computing world is now concurrent!

Aspects of concurrent computing—whether multithreaded, parallel, or distributed—are now covered in almost every advanced course in computer science.

Reflecting the history of the topic, operating systems courses lead the way—covering topics like multithreading, communication protocols, and distributed file systems. Architecture courses cover multiprocessors and networks. Compilers courses cover compilation issues for parallel machines. Theory courses cover models for parallel computing. Algorithms courses cover parallel algorithms. Database courses cover locking and distributed databases. Graphics courses make use of parallelism for rendering and ray tracing. The list goes on. In addition, concurrent computing has become a fundamental tool in a wide range of science and engineering disciplines.

The main purpose of this book—as reflected in the title—is to lay the foundations for programming multithreaded, parallel, and distributed computations. The specific goal is to provide a text that can be used for, or to create, an advanced undergraduate/beginning graduate course. Whenever a topic in computing has become pervasive, as concurrency surely has, we have added foundation courses to provide students with basic knowledge of a topic. Similarly, whenever a topic has become well understood, as concurrency now is, we have migrated the topic to the core curriculum.

I have tried to cover those aspects of parallel and distributed computing that I think every computer science student should know. This includes basic principles, programming techniques, major applications, implementations, and performance issues. In addition, I have included case studies of many of the most important languages and software libraries: Pthreads (three chapters), Java (three chapters), CSP, Linda, MPI (two chapters), Ada, SR, and OpenMP. Each case study describes relevant parts of the language or library and then presents a complete sample program. (Sources for the programs are available on this book's Web site. In addition, I summarize several additional languages, models, and tools for parallel scientific computing in Chapter 12.

On the other hand, no single book can cover everything—and still be affordable—so students and instructors may wish to augment this text with others. The Historical Notes and the References at the end of each chapter describe additional material and provide pointers for further study. This book's Web pages provide further information and links to relevant material.

Content Overview

This book contains 12 chapters. Chapter 1 summarizes basic concepts of concurrency, hardware, and applications. Then it examines five representative applications: matrix multiplication, adaptive quadrature, Unix pipes, file systems, and distributed matrix multiplication. Each application is simple yet useful; together they illustrate the range of issues and five recurring programming styles. The last section of Chapter 1 summarizes the programming notation that is used in the text.

The remaining chapters are organized into three parts. Part 1 describes concurrent programming mechanisms that use shared variables, and hence that are directly suitable for shared-memory machines. Chapter 2 introduces fundamental concepts of processes and synchronization; the chapter uses a series of examples to illustrate the key points and ends with a discussion of the formal semantics of concurrency. Understanding the semantic concepts will help you understand parts of later chapters, but it should also be sufficient to refer back to them when necessary. Chapter 3 shows how to implement and use locks and barriers; it also describes data parallel algorithms and a parallel programming technique called a bag of tasks. Chapter 4 describes semaphores and gives numerous examples of how to use them. Semaphores were the first high-level concurrent programming mechanism and remain one of the most important. Chapter 5 covers monitors in detail. Monitors were introduced in a seminal 1974 paper, somewhat lost favor in the 1980s and early 1990s, but have regained importance with the Java language. Finally, Chapter 6 describes how to implement processes, semaphores, and monitors on both uniprocessors and multiprocessors.

Part 2 covers distributed programming, in which processes communicate and synchronize by means of messages. Chapter 7 describes message passing using **send** and **receive** primitives. It shows how to use these primitives to program filters (which have one-way communication), clients and servers (which have two-way communication), and interacting peers (which have back and forth communication). Chapter 8 examines two additional communication primitives: remote procedure call (RPC) and rendezvous. With these, a client process initiates a communication by issuing a **call**—which is implicitly a **send** followed by a **receive**; the communication is serviced either by a new process (RPC) or by a rendezvous with an existing process. Chapter 9 describes several paradigms for process interaction in distributed programs. These include three that are commonly used in parallel computations—manager/workers, heartbeat, and pipeline—as well as four that arise in distributed systems—probe/echo, broadcast, token passing, and replicated servers. Finally, Chapter 10 describes how to implement message passing, RPC, and rendezvous. That chapter also shows how to implement what is called a distributed shared memory, which supports a shared-memory programming model in a distributed environment.

Part 3 covers parallel programming, especially for high-performance scientific computations. (Many other kinds of parallel computations are described in earlier chapters and in the exercises of several chapters.) The goal of a parallel program is speedup—namely, to solve a problem faster by using multiple processors. Parallel programs are written using shared variables or message passing; hence they employ the techniques described in Parts 1 and 2. Chapter 11 examines the three major classes of scientific computing applications: grid, particle, and matrix computations. These arise in simulating (modeling) physical and biological systems; matrix computations are also used for such things as economic forecasting. Chapter 12 surveys the most important tools that are used to write parallel scientific computations: libraries (Pthreads, MPI, and OpenMP), parallelizing compilers, languages and models, and higher-level tools such as metacomputations.

The end of each chapter provides historical notes, references, and an extensive set of exercises. The historical notes summarize the origin and evolution of each topic and how the topics relate to each other. The notes also describe the papers and books listed in the reference section. The exercises explore the topics covered in each chapter and also introduce additional applications.

Classroom Use

I use this book each spring at the University of Arizona for a class of about 60 students. About half the students are undergraduates and half are graduates. Most are computer science majors; the class is an elective for them, but most majors end up taking it. The class is also taken each year by a few Ph.D. students from other departments who have an interest in computational science and parallel computing. Most of the undergraduates are simultaneously taking our undergraduate operating systems course; the CS graduate students have all had such a course and many have also taken our advanced operating systems course.

Our operating systems classes, like those elsewhere, examine the synchronization *needs* of operating systems, and explore how processes, synchronization, and other OS topics are implemented, mostly on single processor machines. My class shows how to *use* concurrency as a general programming tool in a broad range of applications. I look at programming techniques, higher-level concepts, parallel computing, and distributed computing. In a sense, my class is to an OS class somewhat like what a comparative programming languages class is to a compilers class.

In the first half of my class, I cover Chapter 2 in some detail but then go fairly rapidly through the other chapters in Part I, emphasizing topics not covered in the OS classes: the Test-and-Test-and-Set protocol, the Ticket Algorithm, barriers, passing the baton for semaphores, some of the monitor programming techniques, and the multiprocessor kernel. In addition, students are introduced to the Pthreads library and Java's threads and synchronized methods in homework assignments. I also include a parallel computing project after my lectures on barriers (drawing material from Chapter 11).

In the second half of my class I cover much of Part 2 of the book on distributed programming. We look at message passing, and how it is used to program both distributed systems and distributed parallel computations. Then we look at RPC and rendezvous, their realization in Java and Ada, and distributed systems applications. Finally, we look at each of the paradigms in Chapter 9, again using applications from parallel and distributed systems to motivate and illustrate them. Students are introduced to the MPI library in a homework assignment and again use Java.

During the term I give four homework assignments, two in-class exams, a parallel computing project, and a final project. (See the book's Web site for samples.) Each homework assignment consists of written problems from the exercises, as well as one or two programming problems. Graduate students are required to do all problems; undergraduates do two-thirds of the problems (of their choice). Exams are administered similarly: graduates do all problems, undergraduates choose a subset of the problems to answer. At Arizona we use SR in the earliest programming assignments, and students have the option of using SR for many of the later assignments, but they are encouraged to use Pthreads, Java, and MPI.

The parallel programming project addresses one of the problems in Chapter 11 (often a grid computation). Students write programs and do timing experiments on a small shared-memory multiprocessor. Graduate students implement harder algorithms and are also required to write a fairly detailed report on their experiments. The final project is a paper or programming project on some aspect of distributed computing. Students get to choose what they want to do, subject to my approval. Most students do implementation projects; many work in pairs. The students produce an amazing variety of interesting systems, and most include a graphical user interface.

Even though the students in my class have a wide range of backgrounds, almost all give the class an excellent evaluation. Undergraduates frequently remark on how well it meshes with their OS class; they like seeing concurrency from another perspective, learning about multiprocessors, and seeing a broad range of applications and tools. Graduate students remark on how the class ties together a variety of things they had heard something about, and also introduces them to the breadth of concurrent programming; many of them would, however, like to see more coverage of parallel computing. Eventually we hope to be able to offer separate classes for undergraduates and graduates. I would not change much for the undergraduate-only class, but I would cover slightly fewer topics in somewhat more depth. For the graduate version I would spend less time on material they were familiar with (Part 1) and more time on parallel applications and parallel computing tools (Part 3).

This book is ideally suited for classes that cover the range of concurrent programming mechanisms, tools, and applications. Almost all students will make use of *some* of what is covered here, but not many will do just parallel computing, just distributed systems, or just programming in Java. However, the book can also be used as a supplement to classes with a more specialized focus. For example, a parallel computing class might use this book together with one that covers parallel algorithms and applications.

Online Resources

The "home page" for the book is located at

```
http://www.cs.arizona.edu/people/greg/mpdbook
```

The Web site contains the source for the larger programs in the text, links to software and information on the languages and libraries described in the case studies, and a variety of other useful links. It also contains extensive information from my Arizona class, including the syllabus, lecture notes, and copies of homework assignments, projects, and exams. Information on this book is also available at

```
http://www.awlonline.com/cs
```

Despite my best efforts, this book no doubt contains errors, so there will be (too soon I'm sure) an errata page. Contact your Addison Wesley representative for information on obtaining a copy of the Instructor's Manual for this book. Other material will no doubt be added in the future.

Acknowledgments

I received many useful suggestions from the reviewers of earlier drafts of this book. Martti Tienari and his students at the University of Helsinki found several subtle errors. My most recent Ph.D. students, Vince Freeh and Dave Lowenthal, provided comments on new chapters and helped debug my thinking, if not my programs, over the past several years. The students in my spring 1999 class served as guinea pigs and found several embarrassing errors. Andy Bernat also provided feedback from his spring 1999 class at the University of Texas, El Paso. Thank you to the following reviewers for their invaluable feedback: Jaspal Subhlok (Carnegie Mellon University), Boleslaw Szymanski (Rensselaer

Polytechnic Institute), G.S. Stiles (Utah State University), Narsingh Deo (University of Central Florida), Janet Hartman (Illinois State University), Nan C. Schaller (Rochester Institute of Technology), and Mark Fienup (University of Northern Iowa).

The National Science Foundation has supported my research for many years, most recently through grants CCR-9415303 and ACR-9720738. A research infrastructure grant from the NSF (CDA-9500991), helped support the equipment used to prepare the book and test the programs.

Most importantly, I want to thank my wife, Mary, who once again put up with the thousands of hours I spent working on this book—despite having vowed "never again" after finishing the SR book.

Greg Andrews
Tucson, Arizona

Table of Contents

1

The Concurrent
Computing Landscape

Imagine the following scenario:

> Several cars want to drive from point A to point B. They can compete for space on the same road and end up either following each other or competing for positions (and having accidents!). Or they could drive in parallel lanes, thus arriving at about the same time without getting in each other's way. Or they could travel different routes, using separate roads.

This scenario captures the essence of concurrent computing: There are multiple tasks that need to be done (cars moving). Each can execute one at a time on a single processor (road), execute in parallel on multiple processors (lanes in a road), or execute on distributed processors (separate roads). However, tasks often need to synchronize to avoid collisions or to stop at traffic lights or stop signs.

This book is an "atlas" of concurrent computing. It examines the kinds of cars (processes), the routes they might wish to travel (applications), the patterns of roads (hardware), and the rules of the road (communication and synchronization). So load up the tank and get started.

In this chapter we describe the legend of the concurrent programming map. Section 1.1 introduces fundamental concepts. Sections 1.2 and 1.3 describe the kinds of hardware and applications that make concurrent programming both interesting and challenging. Sections 1.4 through 1.8 describe and illustrate five recurring programming styles: iterative parallelism, recursive parallelism, producers and consumers, clients and servers, and interacting peers. The last section defines the programming notation that is used in the examples and the remainder of the book.

Later chapters cover applications and programming techniques in detail. The chapters are organized into three parts—shared-variable programming, distributed (message-based) programming, and parallel programming. The introduction to each part and each chapter gives a road map, summarizing where we have been and where we are going.

1.1 The Essence of Concurrent Programming

A concurrent program contains two or more processes that work together to perform a task. Each process is a sequential program—namely, a sequence of statements that are executed one after another. Whereas a sequential program has a *single thread of control*, a concurrent program has *multiple threads of control*.

The processes in a concurrent program work together by *communicating* with each other. Communication is programmed using shared variables or message passing. When shared variables are used, one process writes into a variable that is read by another. When message passing is used, one process sends a message that is received by another.

Whatever the form of communication, processes also need to *synchronize* with each other. There are two basic kinds of synchronization: mutual exclusion and condition synchronization. *Mutual exclusion* is the problem of ensuring that *critical sections* of statements do not execute at the same time. *Condition synchronization* is the problem of delaying a process until a given condition is true. As an example, communication between a producer process and a consumer process is often implemented using a shared memory buffer. The producer writes into the buffer; the consumer reads from the buffer. Mutual exclusion is required to ensure that the producer and consumer do not access the buffer at the same time, and hence that a partially written message is not read prematurely. Condition synchronization is used to ensure that a message is not read by the consumer until after it has been written by the producer.

The history of concurrent programming has followed the same stages as other experimental areas of computer science. The topic arose due to opportunities presented by hardware developments and has evolved in response to technological changes. Over time, the initial, *ad hoc* approaches have coalesced into a collection of core principles and general programming techniques.

Concurrent programming originated in the 1960s within the context of operating systems. The motivation was the invention of hardware units called *channels* or *device controllers*. These operate independently of a controlling processor and allow an I/O operation to be carried out concurrently with continued execution of program instructions by the central processor. A channel communicates with the central processor by means of an *interrupt*—a hardware signal that says "stop what you are doing and start executing a different sequence of instructions."

The programming challenge—indeed the intellectual challenge—that resulted from the introduction of channels was that now parts of a program could execute in an unpredictable order. Hence, if one part of a program is updating the value of a variable, an interrupt might occur and lead to another part of the program trying to change the value of the variable. This specific problem came to be known as the *critical section problem*, which we cover in detail in Chapter 3.

Shortly after the introduction of channels, hardware designers conceived of multiprocessor machines. For a couple decades these were too expensive to be widely used, but now all large machines have multiple processors. Indeed, the largest machines have hundreds of processors and are often called *massively parallel processors*, or MPPs. Even most personal computers will soon have a few processors.

Multiprocessor machines allow different application programs to execute at the same time on different processors. They also allow a *single* application program to execute faster if it can be rewritten to use multiple processors. But how does one synchronize the activity of concurrent processes? How can one use multiple processors to make an application run faster?

To summarize, channels and multiprocessors provide both opportunities and challenges. When writing a concurrent program one has to make decisions about what kinds of processes to employ, how many to use, and how they should interact. These decisions are affected by the application and by the underlying hardware on which the program will run. Whatever choices are made, the key to developing a *correct* program is to ensure that process interaction is properly synchronized.

This book examines all aspects of concurrent programming. However, we focus on *imperative programs* with explicit concurrency, communication, and synchronization. In particular, the programmer has to specify the actions of each process and how they communicate and synchronize. This contrasts with *declarative programs*—e.g., functional or logic programs—in which concurrency is implicit and there is no reading and writing of a program state. In declarative programs, independent parts of the program may execute in parallel; they communicate and synchronize implicitly when one part depends on the results produced by another. Although the declarative approach is interesting and important—see Chapter 12 for more information—the imperative approach is much more widely used. In addition, to implement a declarative program on a traditional machine, one has to write an imperative program.

We also focus on concurrent programs in which process execution is *asynchronous*—namely, each process executes at its own rate. Such programs can be executed by interleaving the processes on a single processor or by executing the processes in parallel on a multiple instruction stream, multiple data stream (MIMD) multiprocessor. This class of machines includes shared-memory multiprocessors, distributed-memory multicomputers, and networks of work-stations—as described in the next section. Although we focus on asynchronous multiprocessing, we describe *synchronous* multiprocessing (SIMD machines) in Chapter 3 and the associated data-parallel programming style in Chapters 3 and 12.

1.2 Hardware Architectures

This section summarizes key attributes of modern computer architectures. The next section describes concurrent programming applications and how they make use of these architectures. We first describe single processors and cache memories. Then we examine shared-memory multiprocessors. Finally, we describe distributed-memory machines, which include multicomputers and networks of machines.

1.2.1 Processors and Caches

A modern single-processor machine contains several components: a central processing unit (CPU), primary memory, one or more levels of cache memory, secondary (disk) storage, and a variety of peripheral devices—display, keyboard, mouse, modem, CD, printer, etc. The key components with respect to the execution of programs are the CPU, cache, and memory. The relation between these is depicted in Figure 1.1.

The CPU fetches instructions from memory and decodes and executes them. It contains a control unit, arithmetic/logic unit (ALU), and registers. The control unit issues signals that control the actions of the ALU, memory system,

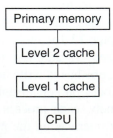

Figure 1.1   Processor, cache, and memory in a modern machine.

and external devices. The ALU implements the arithmetic and logical instructions defined by the processor's instruction set. The registers contain instructions, data, and the machine state (including the program counter).

A cache is a small, fast memory unit that is used to speed up program execution. It contains the contents of those memory locations that have recently been used by the processor. The rationale for cache memory is that most programs exhibit *temporal locality*, meaning that once they reference a memory location they are likely to do so again in the near future. For example, instructions inside loops are fetched and executed many times.

When a program attempts to read a memory location, the processor first looks in the cache. If the data is there—a cache *hit*—then it is read from the cache. If the data is not there—a cache *miss*—then the data is read from primary memory into both the processor and cache. Similarly, when data is written by a program, it is placed in the local cache and in the primary memory (or possibly just in the primary memory). In a *write through cache*, data is placed in memory immediately; in a *write back cache*, data is placed in memory later. The key point is that after a write, the contents of the primary memory might temporarily be *inconsistent* with the contents of the cache.

To increase the transfer rate (bandwidth) between caches and primary memory, an entry in a cache typically contains multiple, contiguous words of memory. These entries are called cache *lines* or *blocks*. Whenever there is a cache miss, the entire contents of a cache line are transferred between the memory and cache. This is effective because most programs exhibit *spatial locality*, meaning that when they reference one memory word they soon reference nearby memory words.

Modern processors typically contain two levels of cache. The level 1 cache is close to the processor; the level 2 cache is between the level 1 cache and the primary memory. The level 1 cache is smaller and faster than the level 2 cache, and it is often organized differently. For example, the level 1 cache is often *direct mapped* and the level 2 cache is often *set associative*.[1] Moreover, the level 1 cache often contains separate caches for instructions and data, whereas the level 2 cache is commonly *unified*, meaning that it contains both instructions and data.

To illustrate the speed differences between the levels of the memory hierarchy, registers can be accessed in one clock cycle because they are small and internal to the CPU. The contents of the level 1 cache can typically be accessed in one or two clock cycles. In contrast, it takes on the order of 10 clock cycles to

---

[1] In a direct-mapped cache, each memory address maps into one cache entry. In a set-associative cache, each memory address maps into a set of cache entries; the set size is typically two or four. Thus, if two memory addresses map into the same location, only the most recently referenced location can be in a direct-mapped cache, whereas both locations can be in a set-associative cache. On the other hand, a direct-mapped cache is faster because it is easier to decide if a word is in the cache.

access the level 2 cache and perhaps 50 to 100 clock cycles to access primary memory. There are similar size differences in the memory hierarchy: a CPU has a few dozen registers, a level 1 cache contains a few dozen kilobytes, a level 2 cache contains on the order of one megabyte, and primary memory contains tens to hundreds of megabytes.

1.2.2 Shared-Memory Multiprocessors

In a *shared-memory multiprocessor*, the processors and memory modules are connected by means of an *interconnection network*, as shown in Figure 1.2. The processors share the primary memory, but each processor has its own cache memory.

On a small multiprocessor with from two to 30 or so processors, the interconnection network is implemented by a memory bus or possibly a crossbar switch. Such a multiprocessor is called a UMA machine because there is a uniform memory access time between every processor and every memory location. UMA machines are also called *symmetric multiprocessors* (SMPs).

Large shared-memory multiprocessors—those having tens or hundreds of processors—have a hierarchically organized memory. In particular, the interconnection network is a tree-structured collection of switches and memories. Consequently, each processor has some memory that is close by and other memory that is farther away. This organization avoids the congestion that would occur if there were only a single shared bus or switch. Because it also leads to nonuniform memory access times, such a multiprocessor is called a NUMA machine.

On both UMA and NUMA machines, each processor has its own cache. If two processors reference different memory locations, the contents of these locations can safely be in the caches of the two processors. However, problems can arise when two processors reference the same memory location at about the

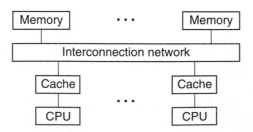

Figure 1.2   Structure of Shared-Memory Multiprocessors.

same time. If both processors just read the same location, each can load a copy of the data into its local cache. But if one processor writes into the location, there is a *cache consistency* problem: The cache of the other processor no longer contains the correct value. Hence, either the other cache needs to be updated with the new value or the cache entry needs to be invalidated. Every multiprocessor has to implement a cache consistency protocol in hardware. One method is to have each cache "snoop" on the memory address bus, looking for references to locations in its cache.

Writing also leads to a *memory consistency* problem: When is primary memory actually updated? For example, if one processor writes into a memory location and another processor later reads from that memory location, is the second processor guaranteed to see the new value? There are several different memory consistency models. *Sequential consistency* is the strongest model; it guarantees that memory updates will appear to occur in some sequential order, and that every processor will see the same order. *Processor consistency* is a weaker model; it ensures that the writes by each processor will occur in memory in the order they are issued by the processor, but writes issued by different processors might be seen in different orders by other processors. *Release consistency* is an even weaker model; it ensures only that the primary memory is updated at programmer-specified synchronization points.

The memory consistency problem presents tradeoffs between ease of programming and implementation overhead. The programmer intuitively expects sequential consistency, because a program reads and writes variables without regard to where the values are actually stored inside the machine. In particular, when a process assigns to a variable, the programmer expects the result of that assignment to be seen immediately by every other process in the program. On the other hand, sequential consistency is costly to implement and it makes a machine slower. This is because on each write, the hardware has to invalidate or update other caches and to update primary memory; moreover, these actions have to be *atomic* (indivisible). Consequently, multiprocessors typically implement a weaker memory consistency model and leave to programmers the task of inserting memory synchronization instructions. Compilers and libraries often take care of this so the application programmer does not have to do so.

As noted, cache lines often contain multiple words that are transferred to and from memory as a unit. Suppose variables x and y occupy one word each and that they are stored in adjacent memory words that map into the same cache line. Suppose some process is executing on processor 1 of a multiprocessor and reads and writes variable x. Finally, suppose another process is executing on processor 2 and reads and writes variable y. Then whenever processor 1 accesses variable x, the cache line on that processor will also contain a copy of variable y; a similar process will occur with processor 2.

The above scenario causes what is called *false sharing*: The processes do not actually share variables x and y, but the cache hardware treats the two variables as a unit. Consequently, when processor 1 updates x, the cache line containing both x and y in processor 2 has to be invalidated or updated. Similarly, when processor 2 updates y, the cache line containing x and y in processor 1 has to be invalidated or updated. Cache invalidations or updates slow down the memory system, so the program will run much more slowly than would be the case if the two variables were in separate cache lines. The key point is that the programmer would correctly think that the processes do not share variables when in fact the memory system has introduced sharing and overhead to deal with it.

To avoid false sharing, the programmer has to ensure that variables that are written by different processes are not in adjacent memory locations. One way to ensure this is to use *padding*—that is to declare dummy variables that take up space and separate actual variables from each other. This is an instance of a time/space tradeoff: waste some space in order to reduce execution time.

To summarize, multiprocessors employ caches to improve performance. However, the presence of a memory hierarchy introduces cache and memory consistency problems and the possibility of false sharing. Consequently, to get maximal performance on a given machine, the programmer has to know about the characteristics of the memory system and has to write programs to account for them. These issues will be revisited at relevant points in the remainder of the text.

1.2.3 *Distributed-Memory Multicomputers and Networks*

In a *distributed-memory multiprocessor*, there is again an interconnection network, but each processor has its own private memory. As shown in Figure 1.3, the location of the interconnection network and memory modules are reversed relative to their location in a shared-memory multiprocessor. The interconnection

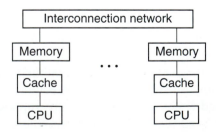

Figure 1.3   Structure of distributed-memory machines.

network supports *message passing* rather than memory reading and writing. Hence, the processors communicate with each other by sending and receiving messages. Each processor has its own cache, but because memory is not shared there are no cache or memory consistency problems.

A *multicomputer* is a distributed-memory multiprocessor in which the processors and network are physically close to each other (in the same cabinet). For this reason, a multicomputer is often called a *tightly coupled machine*. A multicomputer is used by one or at most a few applications at a time; each application uses a dedicated set of processors. The interconnection network provides a high-speed and high-bandwidth communication path between the processors. It is typically organized as a mesh or hypercube. (Hypercube machines were among the earliest examples of multicomputers.)

A *network system* is a distributed-memory multiprocessor in which nodes are connected by a local area communication network such as an Ethernet or by a long-haul network such as the Internet. Consequently, network systems are called *loosely coupled* multiprocessors. Again processors communicate by sending messages, but these take longer to deliver than in a multicomputer and there is more network contention. On the other hand, a network system is built out of commodity workstations and networks whereas a multicomputer often has custom components, especially for the interconnection network.

A network system that consists of a collection of workstations is often called a *network of workstations* (NOW) or a *cluster of workstations* (COW). These workstations execute a single application, separate applications, or a mixture of the two. A currently popular way to build an inexpensive distributed-memory multiprocessor is to construct what is called a *Beowulf machine*. A Beowulf machine is built out of basic hardware and free software, such as Pentium processor chips, network interface cards, disks, and the Linux operating system. (The name Beowulf refers to an Old English epic poem, the first masterpiece of English literature.)

Hybrid combinations of distributed- and shared-memory multiprocessors also exist. The nodes of the distributed-memory machine might be shared-memory multiprocessors rather than single processors. Or the interconnection network might support both message passing and mechanisms for direct access to remote memory (this is done in today's most powerful machines). The most general combination is a machine that supports what is called *distributed shared memory*—namely, a distributed implementation of the shared-memory abstraction. This makes the machines easier to program for many applications, but again raises the issues of cache and memory consistency. (Chapter 10 describes distributed shared memory and how to implement it entirely in software.)

1.3 Applications and Programming Styles

Concurrent programming provides a way to organize software that contains relatively independent parts. It also provides a way to make use of multiple processors. There are three broad, overlapping classes of applications—multithreaded systems, distributed systems, and parallel computations—and three corresponding kinds of concurrent programs.

Recall that a process is a sequential program that, when executed, has its own thread of control. Every concurrent program contains multiple processes, so every concurrent program has multiple threads. However, the term *multithreaded* usually means that a program contains more processes (threads) than there are processors to execute the threads. Consequently, the processes take turns executing on the processors. A multithreaded software system manages multiple independent activities such as the following:

- window systems on personal computers or workstations;

- time-shared and multiprocessor operating systems; and

- real-time systems that control power plants, spacecraft, and so on.

These systems are written as multithreaded programs because it is much easier to organize the code and data structures as a collection of processes than as a single, huge sequential program. In addition, each process can be scheduled and executed independently. For example, when the user clicks the mouse on a personal computer, a signal is sent to the process that manages the window into which the mouse currently points. That process (thread) can now execute and respond to the mouse click. In addition, applications in other windows can continue to execute in the background.

The second broad class of applications is distributed computing, in which components execute on machines connected by a local or global communication network. Hence the processes communicate by exchanging messages. Examples are as follows:

- file servers in a network;

- database systems for banking, airline reservations, and so on;

- Web servers on the Internet;

- enterprise systems that integrate components of a business; and

- fault-tolerant systems that keep executing despite component failures.

Distributed systems are written to off-load processing (as in file servers), to provide access to remote data (as in databases and the Web), to integrate and manage data that is inherently distributed (as in enterprise systems), or to increase reliability (as in fault-tolerant systems). Many distributed systems are organized as client/server systems. For example, a file server provides data files for processes executing on client machines. The components in a distributed system are often themselves multithreaded programs.

Parallel computing is the third broad class of applications. The goal is to solve a given problem faster or equivalently to solve a larger problem in the same amount of time. Examples of parallel computations are as follows:

* scientific computations that model and simulate phenomena such as the global climate, evolution of the solar system, or effects of a new drug;

* graphics and image processing, including the creation of special effects in movies; and

* large combinatorial or optimization problems, such as scheduling an airline business or modeling the economy.

These kinds of computations are large and compute-intensive. They are executed on parallel processors to achieve high performance, and there usually are as many processes (threads) as processors. Parallel computations are written as *data parallel programs*—in which each process does the same thing on its part of the data—or as *task parallel programs* in which different processes carry out different tasks.

We examine these as well as other applications in this book. Most importantly, we show how to program them. The processes (threads) in a multi-threaded program interact using shared variables. The processes in a distributed system communicate by exchanging messages or by invoking remote operations. The processes in a parallel computation interact using either shared variables or message passing, depending on the hardware on which the program will execute. Part 1 in this book shows how to write programs that use shared variables for communication and synchronization. Part 2 covers message passing and remote operations. Part 3 examines parallel programming in detail, with an emphasis on scientific computing.

Although there are many concurrent programming applications, they employ only a small number of solution patterns, or *paradigms*. In particular, there are five basic paradigms: (1) iterative parallelism, (2) recursive parallelism, (3) producers and consumers (pipelines), (4) clients and servers, and (5) interacting peers. Applications are programmed using one or more of these.

Iterative parallelism is used when a program has several, often identical processes, each of which contains one or more loops. Hence, each process is an iterative program. The processes in the program work together to solve a single problem; they communicate and synchronize using shared variables or message passing. Iterative parallelism occurs most frequently in scientific computations that execute on multiple processors.

Recursive parallelism can be used when a program has one or more recursive procedures and the procedure calls are independent, meaning that each works on different parts of the shared data. Recursion is often used in imperative languages, especially to implement divide-and-conquer or backtracking algorithms. Recursion is also the fundamental programming paradigm in symbolic, logic, and functional languages. Recursive parallelism is used to solve many combinatorial problems, such as sorting, scheduling (e.g., traveling salesperson), and game playing (e.g., chess).

Producers and consumers are communicating processes. They are often organized into a *pipeline* through which information flows. Each process in a pipeline is a *filter* that consumes the output of its predecessor and produces output for its successor. Filters occur at the application (shell) level in operating systems such as Unix, within operating systems themselves, and within application programs whenever one process produces output that is consumed (read) by another.

Clients and servers are the dominant interaction pattern in distributed systems, from local networks to the World Wide Web. A client process requests a service and waits to receive a reply. A server waits for requests from clients then acts upon them. A server can be implemented by a single process that handles one client request at a time, or it can be multithreaded to service client requests concurrently. Clients and servers are the concurrent programming generalization of procedures and procedure calls: a server is like a procedure, and clients call the server. However, when the client code and server code reside on different machines, a conventional procedure call—jump to subroutine and later return from subroutine—cannot be used. Instead one has to use a *remote procedure call* or a *rendezvous*, as described in Chapter 8.

Interacting peers is the final interaction paradigm. It occurs in distributed programs when there are several processes that execute basically the same code and that exchange messages to accomplish a task. Interacting peers are used to implement distributed parallel programs, especially those with iterative parallelism. They are also used to implement decentralized decision making in distributed systems. We describe several applications and communication patterns in Chapter 9.

The next five sections give examples that illustrate the use of each of these patterns. The examples also introduce the programming notation that we will be using throughout the text. (The notation is summarized in Section 1.9.) Many more examples are described in later chapters—either in the text or in the exercises.

1.4 Iterative Parallelism: Matrix Multiplication

An iterative sequential program is one that uses `for` or `while` loops to examine data and compute results. An iterative parallel program contains two or more iterative processes. Each process computes results for a subset of the data, then the results are combined.

As a simple example, consider the following problem from scientific computing. Given matrices `a` and `b`, assume that each matrix has `n` rows and columns, and that each has been initialized. The goal is to compute the matrix product of `a` and `b`, storing the result in the $n \times n$ matrix `c`. This requires computing n^2 inner products, one for each pair of rows and columns.

The matrices are shared variables, which we will declare as follows:

```
double a[n,n], b[n,n], c[n,n];
```

Assuming `n` has already been declared and initialized, this allocates storage for three arrays of double-precision floating point numbers. By default, the indices for the rows and columns range from `0` to `n-1`.

After initializing `a` and `b`, we can compute the matrix product by the following sequential program:

```
for [i = 0 to n-1] {
  for [j = 0 to n-1] {
    # compute inner product of a[i,*] and b[*,j]
    c[i,j] = 0.0;
    for [k = 0 to n-1]
      c[i,j] = c[i,j] + a[i,k]*b[k,j];
  }
}
```

Above, the outer loops (with indices `i` and `j`) iterate over each row and column. The inner loop (with index `k`) computes the inner product of row `i` of matrix `a` and column `j` of matrix `b`, and then stores the result in `c[i,j]`. The line that begins with a sharp character is a comment.

Matrix multiplication is an example of what is called an *embarrassingly parallel application*, because there are a multitude of operations that can be executed in parallel. Two operations can be executed in parallel if they are *independent*. Assume that the *read set* of an operation contains the variables it reads but does not alter and that the *write set* of an operation contains the variables that it alters (and possibly also reads). Two operations are independent if their write sets are disjoint. Informally, it is always safe for two processes to read variables that do not change. However, it is generally not safe for two processes to write into the same variable, or for one process to read a variable that the other writes. (We will examine this topic in detail in Chapter 2.)

For matrix multiplication, the computations of inner products are independent operations. In particular, lines 4 through 6 in the above program initialize an element of c then compute the value of that element. The innermost loop in the program reads a row of a and a column of b, and reads and writes one element of c. Hence, the read set for an inner product is a row of a and a column of b, and the write set is an element of c.

Since the write sets for pairs of inner products are disjoint, we could compute all of them in parallel. Alternatively, we could compute rows of results in parallel, columns of results in parallel, or blocks of rows or columns in parallel. Below we show how to program these parallel computations.

First consider computing rows of c in parallel. This can be programmed as follows using the co (concurrent) statement:

```
co [i = 0 to n-1] {   # compute rows in parallel
  for [j = 0 to n-1] {
    c[i,j] = 0.0;
    for [k = 0 to n-1]
      c[i,j] = c[i,j] + a[i,k]*b[k,j];
  }
}
```

The *only* syntactic difference between this program and the sequential program is that co is used in place of **for** in the outermost loop. However, there is an important semantic difference: The co statement specifies that its body should be executed *concurrently*—at least conceptually if not actually, depending on the number of processors—for each value of index variable i.

A different way to parallelize matrix multiplication is to compute the columns of c in parallel. This can be programmed as

```
co [j = 0 to n-1] {   # compute columns in parallel
  for [i = 0 to n-1] {
    c[i,j] = 0.0;
    for [k = 0 to n-1]
      c[i,j] = c[i,j] + a[i,k]*b[k,j];
  }
}
```

Here the outer two loops have been *interchanged*, meaning that the loop on i in the previous program has been interchanged with the loop on j. It is safe to interchange two loops as long as the bodies are independent and hence compute the same results, as they do here. (We examine this and related kinds of program transformations in Chapter 12.)

We can also compute all inner products in parallel. This can be programmed in several ways. First, we could use a single co statement with two indices:

```
co [i = 0 to n-1, j = 0 to n-1] { # all rows and
  c[i,j] = 0.0;                    # all columns
  for [k = 0 to n-1]
    c[i,j] = c[i,j] + a[i,k]*b[k,j];
}
```

The body of the above co statement is executed concurrently for each combination of values of i and j; hence the program specifies n^2 processes. (Again, whether or not the processes execute in parallel depends on the underlying implementation.) A second way to compute all inner products in parallel is to use nested co statements:

```
co [i = 0 to n-1] {      # rows in parallel then
  co [j = 0 to n-1] {   # columns in parallel
    c[i,j] = 0.0;
    for [k = 0 to n-1]
      c[i,j] = c[i,j] + a[i,k]*b[k,j];
  }
}
```

This specifies one process for each row (outer co statement) and then one process for each column (inner co statement). A third way to write the program would be to interchange the first two lines in the last program. The effect of all three programs is the same: Execute the inner loop for all n^2 combinations of i and j. The difference between the three programs is how the processes are specified, and hence when they are created.

Notice that in all the concurrent programs above, all we have done is to replace instances of **for** by co. However, we have done so only for index variables i and j. What about the innermost loop on index variable k? Can this **for** statement also be replaced by a co statement? The answer is "no," because the body of the inner loop both reads and writes variable c[i,j]. It is possible to compute an inner product—the **for** loop on k—using binary parallelism, but this is impractical on most machines (see the exercises at the end of this chapter).

Another way to specify any of the above parallel computations is to use a **process** declaration instead of a co statement. In essence, a **process** is a co statement that is executed "in the background." For example, the first concurrent program above—the one that computes rows of results in parallel—could be specified by the following program:

```
process row[i = 0 to n-1] { # rows in parallel
  for [j = 0 to n-1] {
    c[i,j] = 0.0;
    for [k = 0 to n-1]
      c[i,j] = c[ij] + a[i,k]*b[k,j];
  }
}
```

This declares an array of processes—`row[1]`, `row[2]`, etc.—one for each value of index variable `i`. The `n` processes are created and start executing when this declaration is encountered. If there are statements following the process declaration, they are executed concurrently with the processes, whereas any statements following a `co` statement are not executed until the `co` statement terminates. Process declarations cannot be nested within other declarations or statements, whereas `co` statements may be nested. (Process declarations and `co` statements are defined in detail in Section 1.9.)

The above programs employ a process per element, row, or column of the result matrix. Suppose that there are fewer than `n` processors, which will usually be the case, especially if `n` is large. There is still a natural way to make full use of all the processors: Divide the result matrix into strips—of rows or columns—and use one *worker* process per strip. In particular, each worker computes the results for the elements in its strip. For example, suppose there are `P` processors and that `n` is a multiple of `P` (namely, `P` evenly divides `n`). Then if we use strips of rows, the worker processes can be programmed as follows:

```
process worker[w = 1 to P] {    # strips in parallel
  int first = (w-1) * n/P;      # first row of strip
  int last = first + n/P - 1;   # last row of strip
  for [i = first to last] {
    for [j = 0 to n-1] {
      c[i,j] = 0.0;
      for [k = 0 to n-1]
        c[i,j] = c[i,j] + a[i,k]*b[k,j];
    }
  }
}
```

The difference between this program and the previous one is that the `i` rows have been divided into `P` strips of `n/P` rows each. Hence, the extra lines in the above program are the bookkeeping needed to determine the first and last rows of each strip and a loop (on `i`) to compute the inner products for those rows.

To summarize: the essential requirement for being able to parallelize a program is to have independent computations—namely, computations that have disjoint write sets. For matrix multiplication, the inner products are independent computations, because each writes (and reads) a different element $c[i,j]$ of the result matrix. We can thus compute all inner products in parallel, all rows in parallel, all columns in parallel, or strips of rows in parallel. Finally, the parallel programs can be written using co statements or **process** declarations.

1.5 Recursive Parallelism: Adaptive Quadrature

A recursive program is one that contains procedures that call themselves—either directly or indirectly. Recursion is the dual of iteration, in the sense that iterative programs can be converted to recursive programs and vice versa. However, each programming style has its place, as some problems are naturally iterative and some are naturally recursive.

Many recursive procedures call themselves more than once in the body of a procedure. For example, *quicksort* is a common sorting algorithm. Quicksort partitions an array into two parts and then calls itself twice: first to sort the left partition and then to sort the right partition. Many algorithms on trees or graphs have a similar structure.

A recursive program can be implemented using concurrency whenever it has multiple, independent recursive calls. Two calls of a procedure (or function) are independent if the write sets are disjoint. This will be the case if (1) the procedure does not reference global variables or only reads them, and (2) reference and result arguments, if any, are distinct variables. For example, if a procedure does not reference global variables and has only value parameters, then every call of the procedure will be independent. (It is fine for a procedure to read and write local variables, because each instance of the procedure will have its own private copy of local variables.) The quicksort algorithm can be programmed to meet these requirements. Another interesting example follows.

The *quadrature problem* addresses the issue of approximating the integral of a continuous function. Suppose f(x) is such a function. As illustrated in Figure 1.4, the integral of f(x) from a to b is the area between f(x) and the x axis from x equals a to x equals b.

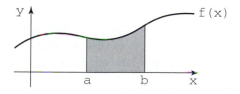

Figure 1.4   The quadrature problem.

There are two basic ways to approximate the value of an integral. One is to divide the interval from a to b into a fixed number of subintervals, and then to approximate the area of each subinterval by using something like the trapezoidal rule or Simpson's rule.

```
double fleft = f(a), fright, area = 0.0;
double width = (b-a) / INTERVALS;
for [x = (a + width) to b by width] {
  fright = f(x);
  area = area + (fleft + fright) * width / 2;
  fleft = fright;
}
```

Each iteration uses the trapezoidal rule to compute a small area and adds it to the total area. Variable width is the width of each trapezoid. The intervals move from left to right, so on each iteration the right-hand value becomes the new left-hand value.

The second way to approximate an integral is to use the divide-and-conquer paradigm and a variable number of subintervals. In particular, first compute the midpoint m between a and b. Then approximate the area of three regions under the curve defined by function f(): the one from a to m, the one from m to b, and the one from a to b. If the sum of the two smaller areas is within some acceptable tolerance EPSILON of the larger area, then the approximation is considered good enough. If not, the larger problem—from a to b—is divided into two subproblems—from a to m and from m to b—and the process is repeated. This approach is called *adaptive quadrature*, because the algorithm adapts to the shape of the curve. It can be programmed as follows:

```
double quad(double left,right,fleft,fright,lrarea) {
  double mid = (left + right) / 2;
  double fmid = f(mid);
  double larea = (fleft+fmid) * (mid-left) / 2;
  double rarea = (fmid+fright) * (right-mid) / 2;
  if (abs((larea+rarea) - lrarea) > EPSILON) {
    # recurse to integrate both halves
    larea = quad(left, mid, fleft, fmid, larea);
    rarea = quad(mid, right, fmid, fright, rarea);
  }
  return (larea + rarea);
}
```

The integral of `f(x)` from `a` to `b` is approximated by calling

```
area = quad(a, b, f(a), f(b), (f(a)+f(b))*(b-a)/2);
```

The function again uses the trapezoidal rule. The values of `f()` at the endpoints of an interval and the approximate area of that interval are passed to each call of `quad` to avoid computing them more than once.

The iterative program cannot be parallelized because the loop body both reads and writes the value of **area**. However, the recursive program has independent calls of `quad`, assuming that function `f()` has no side effects. In particular, the arguments to `quad` are passed by value and the body does not assign to any global variables. Thus, we can use a `co` statement as follows to specify that the recursive calls should be executed in parallel:

```
co larea = quad(left, mid, fleft, fmid, larea);
// rarea = quad(mid, right, fmid, fright, rarea);
oc
```

This is the only change we need to make to the recursive program. Because a `co` statement does not terminate until both calls have completed, the values of **larea** and **rarea** will have been computed before `quad` returns their sum.

The `co` statements in the matrix multiplication programs contain lists of statements that are executed for each value of the quantifier variable (`i` or `j`). The above `co` statement contains two function calls; these are separated by `//`. The first form of `co` is used to express iterative parallelism; the second form is used to express recursive parallelism.

To summarize, a program with multiple recursive calls can readily be turned into a parallel recursive program whenever the calls are independent. However, there is a practical problem: there may be too much concurrency. Each `co` statement above creates two processes, one for each function call. If the depth of recursion is large, this will lead to a large number of processes, perhaps too many to be executed in parallel. A solution to this problem is to *prune* the recursion tree when there are enough processes—namely, to switch from using concurrent recursive calls to sequential recursive calls. This topic is explored in the exercises and later in this book.

1.6 Producers and Consumers: Unix Pipes

A producer process computes and outputs a stream of results. A consumer process inputs and analyzes a stream of values. Many programs are producers and/or consumers of one form or another. The combination becomes especially interesting when producers and consumers are connected by a *pipeline*—a sequence of processes in which each consumes the output of its predecessor and produces output for its successor. A classic example is Unix pipelines, which we examine here. Other examples are given in later chapters.

A Unix application process typically reads from what is called its standard input file, `stdin`, and writes to what is called its standard output file, `stdout`. Usually, `stdin` is the keyboard of the terminal from which an application is invoked and `stdout` is the display of that terminal. However, one of the powerful features introduced by Unix was the fact that the standard input and output "devices" can also be bound to different kinds of files. In particular, `stdin` and/or `stdout` can be bound to a data file or to a special kind of "file" called a pipe.

A *pipe* is a buffer (FIFO queue) between a producer and consumer process. It contains a bounded sequence of characters. New values are appended when a producer process writes to the pipe. Values are removed when a consumer process reads from the pipe.

A Unix application program merely reads from `stdin`, without concern for where the input is actually from. If `stdin` is bound to a keyboard, input is the characters typed at the keyboard. If `stdin` is bound to a file, input is the sequence of characters in the file. If `stdin` is bound to a pipe, input is the sequence of characters written to that pipe. Similarly, an application merely writes to `stdout`, without concern for where the output actually goes.

Pipelines in Unix are typically specified using one of the Unix command languages, such as `csh` (C shell). As a specific example, the printed pages for this book were produced by a `csh` command similar to the following:

```
sed -f Script $* | tbl | eqn | groff Macros -
```

This pipeline contains four commands: (1) `sed`, a stream editor; (2) `tbl`, a table processor; (3) `eqn`, an equation processor; and (4) `groff`, a program that produces Postscript output from `troff` source files. A vertical bar, the C shell character for a pipe, separates each pair of commands.

Figure 1.5 illustrates the structure of the above pipeline. Each of the commands is a *filter* process. The input to the `sed` filter is a file of editing commands (`Script`) and the command-line arguments (`$*`), which for this book are

Figure 1.5   A pipeline of processes.

the appropriate source files for the text. The output from `sed` is passed to `tbl`, which passes its output to `eqn`, which passes its output to `groff`. The `groff` filter reads a file of `Macros` for the book and then reads and processes its standard input. The `groff` filter sends its output to the printer in the author's office.

Each pipe in Figure 1.5 is implemented by a bounded buffer: a synchronized, FIFO queue of values. A producer process waits (if necessary) until there is room in the buffer, then appends a new line to the end of the buffer. A consumer process waits (if necessary) until the buffer contains a line, then removes the first one. In Part 1 we show how to implement bounded buffers using shared variables and various synchronization primitives (flags, semaphores, and monitors). In Part 2 we introduce communication channels and the message passing primitives `send` and `receive`. We then show how to program filters using them and how to implement channels and message passing using buffers.

1.7 Clients and Servers: File Systems

Between a producer and a consumer, there is a one-way flow of information. This kind of interprocess relationship often occurs in concurrent programs, but it has no analog in sequential programs. This is because there is a single thread of control in a sequential program, whereas producers and consumers are independent processes with their own threads of control and their own rates of progress.

The client/server relationship is another common pattern in concurrent programs; indeed, it is the most common pattern. A *client* process requests a service, then waits for the request to be handled. A *server* process repeatedly waits for a request, handles it, then sends a reply. As illustrated in Figure 1.6, there is a two-way flow of information: from the client to the server and then back. The relationship between a client and a server is the concurrent programming analog of the relationship between the caller of a subroutine and the subroutine itself. Moreover, like a subroutine that can be called from many places, a server typically has many clients. Each client request has to be handled as an independent

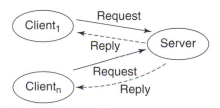

Figure 1.6   Clients and servers.

unit, but multiple requests might be handled concurrently, just as multiple calls of the same procedure might be active at the same time.

Client/server interactions occur within operating systems, object-oriented systems, networks, databases, and many other programs. A common example in all these applications is reading and writing a data file. In particular, assume there is a file server module that provides two operations on a file: **read** and **write**. When a client process wants to access the file, it calls the **read** or **write** operation in the appropriate file server module.

On a single-processor or other shared-memory system, a file server would typically be implemented by a collection of subroutines (for **read**, **write**, etc.) and data structures that represent files (e.g., file descriptors). Hence, the interaction between a client process and a file would typically be implemented by subroutine calls. However, if a file is shared, it is probably important that it be written to by at most one client process at a time. On the other hand, a shared file can safely be read concurrently by multiple clients. This kind of problem is an instance of what is called the readers/writers problem, a classic concurrent programming problem that is defined and solved in Chapter 4 and revisited in later chapters.

In a distributed system, clients and servers typically reside on different machines. For example, consider a query on the World Wide Web—for example, a query that arises when a user opens a new URL within a Web browser. The Web browser is a client process that executes on the user's machine. The URL indirectly specifies another machine on which the Web page resides. The Web page itself is accessed by a server process that executes on the other machine. This server process may already exist or it may be created; in either case it reads the Web page specified by the URL and returns it to the client's machine. In fact, as the URL is being translated, additional server processes could well be visited or created at intermediate machines along the way.

Clients and servers are programmed in one of two ways, depending on whether they execute on the same or on separate machines. In both cases clients are processes. On a shared-memory machine, a server is usually implemented by a collection of subroutines; these subroutines are programmed using mutual exclusion and condition synchronization to protect critical sections and to ensure that the subroutines are executed in appropriate orders. On a distributed-memory or network machine, a server is implemented by one or more processes that usually execute on a different machine than the clients. In both cases, a server is often a multithreaded program, with one thread per client.

Parts 1 and 2 present numerous applications of clients and server, including file systems, databases, memory allocators, disk scheduling, and two more classic problems—the dining philosophers and the sleeping barber. Part 1 shows how to

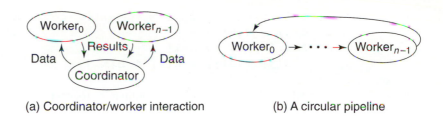

(a) Coordinator/worker interaction   (b) A circular pipeline

Figure 1.7   Matrix multiplication using message passing.

implement servers as subroutines, using semaphores or monitors for synchronization. Part 2 shows how to implement servers as processes that communicate with clients using message passing, remote procedure call, or rendezvous.

1.8 Peers: *Distributed Matrix Multiplication*

We earlier showed how to implement parallel matrix multiplication using processes that share variables. Here we present two ways to solve the problem using processes that communicate by means of message passing. (Chapter 9 presents additional, more sophisticated algorithms.) The first program employs a coordinator process and an array of independent worker processes. In the second program, the workers are peer processes that interact by means of a circular pipeline. Figure 1.7 illustrates the structure of these process interaction patterns. They occur frequently in distributed parallel computations, as we shall see in Part 2.

On a distributed-memory machine, each processor can access only its own local memory. This means that a program cannot use global variables; instead every variable has to be local to some process or procedure and can be accessed only by that process or procedure. Consequently, processes have to use message passing to communicate with each other.

Suppose as before that we want to compute the product of matrices **a** and **b**, storing the result in matrix **c**. Assume that **a**, **b**, and **c** are $n \times n$ matrices. Also assume for simplicity that there are **n** processors. We can then use an array of **n** worker processes, place one worker on each processor, and have each worker compute one row of the result matrix **c**. A program for the workers follows:

```
process worker[i = 0 to n-1] {
   double a[n];     # row i of matrix a
   double b[n,n];   # all of matrix b
   double c[n];     # row i of matrix c
   receive initial values for vector a and matrix b;
```

```
for [j = 0 to n-1] {
  c[j] = 0.0;
  for [k = 0 to n-1]
    c[j] = c[j] + a[k] * b[k,j];
}
send result vector c to the coordinator process;
}
```

Worker process i computes row i of result matrix c. To do so, it needs row i of source matrix a and all of source matrix b. Each worker first receives these values from a separate coordinator process. The worker then computes its row of results and sends them back to the coordinator. (Alternatively, the source matrices might be produced by a prior computation, and the result matrix might be input to a subsequent computation; this would be an example of a distributed pipeline.)

The coordinator process initiates the computation and gathers and prints the results. In particular, the coordinator first sends each worker the appropriate row of a and all of b. Then the coordinator waits to receive a row of c from every worker. An outline of the coordinator follows:

```
process coordinator {
  double a[n,n];  # source matrix a
  double b[n,n];  # source matrix b
  double c[n,n];  # result matrix c
  initialize a and b;
  for [i = 0 to n-1] {
    send row i of a to worker[i];
    send all of b to worker[i];
  }
  for [i = 0 to n-1]
    receive row i of c from worker[i];
  print the results, which are now in matrix c;
}
```

The **send** and **receive** statements used by the coordinator and workers are *message-passing primitives*. A send statement packages up a message and transmits it to another process; a receive statement waits for a message from another process, then stores it in local variables. We describe message passing in detail in Chapter 7 and use it to program numerous applications in Parts 2 and 3.

Suppose as above that each worker has one row of a and is to compute one row of c. However, now assume that each worker has only one column of b at a time instead of the entire matrix. Initially, worker i has column i of matrix b. With just this much of the source data, worker i can compute only the result for c[i,i]. In order for worker i to compute all of row i of matrix c, it has to acquire all columns of matrix b. It can do so if we use a circular pipeline—as illustrated in Figure 1.7 (b)—and circulate the columns among the worker processes. In particular, we have each worker execute a series of *rounds*; in each round it sends its column of b to the next worker and receives a different column of b from the previous worker. The program follows:

```
process worker[i = 0 to n-1] {
   double a[n];          # row i of matrix a
   double b[n];          # one column of matrix b
   double c[n];          # row i of matrix c
   double sum = 0.0;     # storage for inner products
   int nextCol = i;      # next column of results
   receive row i of matrix a and column i of matrix b;
   # compute c[i,i] = a[i,*] × b[*,i]
   for [k = 0 to n-1]
     sum = sum + a[k] * b[k];
   c[nextCol] = sum;
   # circulate columns and compute rest of c[i,*]
   for [j = 1 to n-1] {
     send my column of b to the next worker;
     receive a new column of b from the previous worker;
     sum = 0.0;
     for [k = 0 to n-1]
       sum = sum + a[k] * b[k];
     if (nextCol == 0)
       nextCol = n-1;
     else
       nextCol = nextCol-1;
     c[nextCol] = sum;
   }
   send result vector c to coordinator process;
}
```

Above the next worker is the one with the next higher index, and the previous worker is the one with the next lower index. (For worker n-1, the next worker is 0; for worker 0, the previous worker is n-1.) The columns of matrix b are passed circularly among the workers so that each worker eventually sees every column. Variable nextCol keeps track of where to place each inner product in vector c. As in the first computation, we assume that a coordinator process sends rows of a and columns of b to the workers and then receives rows of c from the workers.

The second program employs an interprocess relationship that we call *interacting peers*, or simply *peers*. Each worker executes the same algorithm and communicates with other workers in order to compute its part of the desired result. We will see further examples of interacting peers in Parts 2 and 3. In some cases, as here, each worker communicates with just two neighbors; in other cases each worker communicates with all the others.

In the first program above, the values in matrix b are *replicated*, with each worker process having its own copy. In the second program, each process has one row of a and one column of b at any point in time. This reduces the memory requirement per process, but the second program will take longer to execute than the first. This is because on each iteration of the second program, every worker process has to send a message to one neighbor and receive a message from another neighbor. The two programs illustrate the classic time/space tradeoff in computing. Section 9.3 presents additional algorithms for distributed matrix multiplication that illustrate additional time/space tradeoffs.

1.9 Summary of Programming Notation

The previous five sections presented examples of recurring patterns in concurrent programming: iterative parallelism, recursive parallelism, producers and consumers, clients and servers, and interacting peers. We will see numerous instances of these patterns in the rest of the book. The examples also introduced the programming notation that we will employ. This section summarizes the notation, although it should be pretty much self-evident from the examples.

Recall that a concurrent program contains one or more processes, and that each process is a sequential program. Our programming language thus contains mechanisms for sequential as well as concurrent programming. The sequential programming notation is based on the core aspects of C, C++, and Java. The concurrent programming notation uses the **co** statement and **process** declarations to specify parts of a program that are to execute concurrently. These were introduced earlier and are defined below. Later chapters will define mechanisms for synchronization and inter-process communication.

1.9.1 Declarations

A variable declaration specifies a data type and then lists the names of one or more variables of that type. A variable can be initialized when it is declared. Examples of declarations are

```
int i, j = 3;
double sum = 0.0;
```

An array is declared by appending the size of each dimension of the array to the name of the array. The default subscript range for each dimension is from 0 to one less than the size of the dimension. Alternatively, the lower and upper bounds of a range can be declared explicitly. Arrays can also be initialized when they are declared. Examples of array declarations are

```
int a[n];        # same as "int a[0:n-1];"
int b[1:n];      # array of n integers, b[1] ... b[n]
int c[1:n] = ([n] 0);   # vector of zeroes
double c[n,n] = ([n] ([n] 1.0));  # matrix of ones
```

Each declaration is followed by a descriptive comment, which begins with the sharp character (see Section 1.9.4). The last declaration says that c is a matrix of double precision numbers. The subscript ranges are 0 to n-1 for each dimension. The initial value of each element of c is 1.0.

1.9.2 Sequential Statements

An assignment statement has a target variable (left-hand side), an equal sign, and an expression (right-hand side). We will also use short-hand forms for increment, decrement, and similar assignments. Examples are

```
a[n] = a[n] + 1;    # same as "a[n]++;"
x = (y+z) * f(x);   # f(x) is a function call
```

The control statements we will use are if, while, and for. A simple if statement has the form

```
if (condition)
    statement;
```

where condition is a Boolean-valued expression (one that is true or false) and statement is some single statement. If more than one statement is to be executed conditionally, the statements are surrounded by braces, as in

```
if (condition) {
    statement1;
    ...
    statementN;
}
```

In subsequent chapters we will often use s to stand for such a list of statements. An if/then/else statement has the form

```
if (condition)
    statement1;
else
    statement2;
```

Again, the statements could be statement lists surrounded by braces.

A `while` statement has the general form

```
while (condition) {
    statement1;
    ...
    statementN;
}
```

If `condition` is true, the enclosed statements are executed, then the `while` statement repeats. The `while` statement terminates when `condition` is false. If there is only a single statement, we omit the braces.

The `if` and `while` statements are identical to those in C, C++, and Java. However, we will write `for` statements in a more compact way. The general form of our `for` statement is

```
for [quantifier1, ..., quantifierM] {
    statement1;
    ...
    statementN;
}
```

A *quantifier* introduces a *new* index variable, gives its initial value, and specifies the range of values of the index variable. Brackets are used around quantifiers to indicate that there is a range of values, as in an array declaration.

As a specific example, assume that `a[n]` is an array of integers. Then the following statement initializes each element `a[i]` to `i`:

```
for [i = 0 to n-1]
    a[i] = i;
```

Here, `i` is the new quantifier variable; it does not have to be declared earlier in the program. The scope of `i` is the body of the `for` statement. The initial value of `i` is `0` and it takes on all values, in order, from `0` to `n-1`.

Assume `m[n,n]` is an integer matrix. An example of a `for` statement with two quantifiers is

```
for [i = 0 to n-1, j = 0 to n-1]
    m[i,j] = 0;
```

An equivalent program using nested `for` statements is

```
for [i = 0 to n-1]
  for [j = 0 to n-1]
    m[i,j] = 0;
```

Both programs initialize the n^2 values of matrix `m` to `0`. Two more examples of quantifiers are

```
[i = 1 to n by 2]      # odd values from 1 to n
[i = 0 to n-1 st i!=x] # every value except i==x
```

The operator `st` in the second quantifier stands for "such that."

We write `for` statements using the above syntax for several reasons. First, it emphasizes that our `for` statements are different than those in C, C++, and Java. Second, the notation suggests that they are used with arrays—which have brackets, rather than parentheses, around subscripts. Third, our notation simplifies programs because we do not have to declare the index variable. (How many times have you forgotten to do so?) Fourth, it is often convenient to have more than one index variable and hence more than one quantifier. Finally, we use the same kinds of quantifiers in `co` statements and `process` declarations.

1.9.3 Concurrent Statements, Processes, and Procedures

By default, statements execute sequentially—one at a time, one after the other. The `co` (concurrent) statement specifies that two or more statements can execute in parallel. One form of `co` has two or more *arms*, as in

```
co statement1;
// ...
// statementN;
oc
```

Each arm contains a statement (or statement list). The arms are separated by the parallelism operator `//`. The above statement means the following: Start executing each of the statements in parallel, then wait for them to terminate. The `co` statement thus terminates after all the statements have been executed.

The second form of `co` statement uses one or more quantifiers as a shorthand way to express that a set of statements is to be executed in parallel for every combination of values of the quantifier variables. For example, the trivial `co` statement that follows initializes arrays `a[n]` and `b[n]` to zeros:

```
co [i = 0 to n-1] {
  a[i] = 0; b[i] = 0;
}
```

This creates n processes, one for each value of i. The scope of the quantifier variable is the process declaration, and each process has a different value of i. The two forms of co can also be mixed. For example, one arm might have a quantifier (within brackets) and another arm might not.

A process declaration is essentially an abbreviation for a co statement with one arm and/or one quantifier. It begins with the keyword **process** and an identifier to name the process; it ends with the keyword **end**. The body of a process contains declarations of local variables, if any, and a list of statements.

As a simple example, the following declares a process foo that sums the values from 1 to 10 then stores the result in global variable x:

```
process foo {
  int sum = 0;
  for [i = 1 to 10]
    sum += i;
  x = sum;
}
```

A **process** declaration occurs at the syntactic level of a **procedure** declaration; it is not a statement, whereas co is. Moreover, processes execute in the background, whereas the code that contains a co statement waits for the processes created by co to terminate before executing the next statement.

As a second simple example, the following process writes the values 1 to n to the standard output file:

```
process bar1 {
  for [i = 1 to n]
    write(i);   # same as "printf("%d\n, i);"
}
```

An array of processes is declared by appending a quantifier (in brackets) to the name of the process, as in

```
process bar2[i = 1 to n] {
  write(i);
}
```

Both **bar1** and **bar2** write the values 1 to n to standard output. However, the order in which **bar2** writes the values is *nondeterministic*. This is because **bar2** is an array of n distinct processes, and processes execute in an arbitrary order. In fact, there are n! different orders in which the array of processes could write the values (n factorial is the number of permutations of n values).

We will declare and call procedures and functions in essentially the same way as in C. Two simple examples are

```
int addOne(int v) {    # an integer function
  return (v + 1);
}

main() {    # a "void" procedure
  int n, sum;
  read(n);    # read an integer from stdin
  for [i = 1 to n]
    sum = sum + addOne(i);
  write("the final value is", sum);
}
```

If the input value n is 5, this program writes the line:

```
the final value is 20
```

1.9.4 Comments

We will write comments in one of two ways. One-line comments begin with the sharp character, #, and terminate with the end of the line. Multiple-line comments begin with /* and end with */. We use # to introduce one-line comments because the C++/Java one-line comment symbol, //, has long been used in concurrent programming as the separator between arms of concurrent statements.

An *assertion* is a predicate that specifies a condition that is assumed to be true at a certain point in a program. (Assertions are described in detail in Chapter 2.) Assertions can be thought of as very precise comments, so we will specify them by lines that begin with two sharp characters, as in

```
## x > 0
```

This comment asserts that x is positive.

Historical Notes

As noted in the text, concurrent programming originated in the 1960s after the introduction of independent device controllers (channels). Operating systems were the first software systems to be organized as multithreaded concurrent programs. The research and initial prototypes leading to modern operating systems occurred in the late 1960s and early 1970s. The first textbooks on operating systems appeared in the early 1970s.

The introduction of computer networks in the 1970s led to the development of distributed systems. The invention of the Ethernet in the late 1970s greatly accelerated the pace of activity. Almost immediately there was a plethora of new languages, algorithms, and applications. Subsequent hardware developments spurred further activity. For example, once workstations and local area networks became relatively cheap, people developed client/server computing; more recently the Internet has spawned Java, Web browsers, and a plethora of new applications.

Multiprocessors were invented in the 1970s, the most notable machines being the Illiac SIMD multiprocessors developed at the University of Illinois. Early machines were costly and specialized, however, so for many years high-performance scientific computing was done on vector processors. This started to change in the mid-1980s with the invention of hypercube machines at the California Institute of Technology and their commercial introduction by Intel. Then Thinking Machines introduced the massively parallel Connection Machine. Also, Cray Research and other makers of vector processors started to produce multiprocessor versions of their machines. For several years, numerous companies (and machines) came, and almost as quickly went. However, the set of players and machines is now fairly stable, and high-performance computing is pretty much synonymous with massively parallel processing.

The Historical Notes in subsequent chapters describe developments that are covered in the chapters themselves. Described below are several general references on hardware, operating systems, distributed systems, and parallel computing. These are the books the author has consulted most often while writing this text. (If there is a topic you wish to learn more about, you can also try a good Internet search engine.)

The now classic textbook on computer architecture is Hennessy and Patterson [1996]. If you want to learn how caches, interconnection networks, and multiprocessors work, start there. Hwang [1993] describes high-performance computer architectures. Almasi and Gottlieb [1994] give an overview of parallel computing applications, software, and architectures.

The most widely used textbooks on operating systems are Tanenbaum [1992] and Silberschatz, Peterson, and Galvin [1998]. Tanenbaum [1995] also gives an excellent overview of distributed operating systems. Mullender [1993] contains a superb collection of chapters on all aspects of distributed systems, including reliability and fault tolerance, transaction processing, file systems, real-time systems, and security. Two additional textbooks—Bacon [1998] and Bernstein and Lewis [1993]—cover multithreaded concurrent systems, including distributed database systems.

Dozens of books on parallel computing have been written in the last several years. Two competing books—Kumar et al. [1994] and Quinn [1994]—describe and analyze parallel algorithms for solving numerous numeric and combinatorial problems. Both books contain some coverage of hardware and software, but they emphasize the design and analysis of parallel algorithms.

Another four books emphasize software aspects of parallel computing. Brinch Hansen [1995] examines several interesting problems in computational science and shows how to solve them using a small number of recurring programming paradigms; the problem descriptions are notably clear. Foster [1995] examines concepts and tools for parallel programming, with an emphasis on distributed-memory machines; the book includes excellent descriptions of High Performance Fortran (HPF) and the Message Passing Interface (MPI), two of the most important current tools. Wilson [1995] describes four important programming models—data parallelism, shared variables, message passing, and generative communication—and shows how to use each to solve science and engineering problems; Appendix B of Wilson's book gives an excellent short history of major events in parallel computing. A recent book by Wilkinson and Allen [1999] describes dozens of applications and shows how to write parallel programs to solve them; the book emphasizes the use of message passing, but includes some coverage of shared-variable computing.

One additional book, edited by Foster and Kesselman [1999], presents a vision for a promising new approach to distributed, high-performance computing using what is called a computational grid. (We describe the approach in Chapter 12.) The book starts with a comprehensive introduction to computational grids and then covers applications, programming tools, services, and infrastructure. The chapters are written by the experts who are working on making computational grids a reality.

References

Almasi, G. S., and A. Gottlieb. 1994. *Highly Parallel Computing*, 2nd ed. Menlo Park, CA: Benjamin/Cummings.

Bacon, J. 1998. *Concurrent Systems: Operating Systems, Database and Distributed Systems: An Integrated Approach*, 2nd ed. Reading, MA: Addison-Wesley.

Bernstein, A. J., and P. M. Lewis. 1993. *Concurrency in Programming and Database Systems*. Boston, MA: Jones and Bartlett.

Brinch Hansen, P. 1995. *Studies in Computational Science*. Englewood Cliffs, NJ: Prentice-Hall.

Foster, I. 1995. *Designing and Building Parallel Programs.* Reading, MA: Addison-Wesley.

Foster, I., and C. Kesselman, eds. 1999. *The Grid: Blueprint for a New Computing Infrastructure.* San Francisco, CA: Morgan Kaufmann.

Hennessy, J. L., and D. A. Patterson. 1996. *Computer Architecture: A Quantitative Approach*, 2nd ed. San Francisco, CA: Morgan Kaufmann.

Hwang, K. 1993. *Advanced Computer Architecture: Parallelism, Scalability, Programmability.* New York, NY: McGraw-Hill.

Kumar, V., A. Grama, A. Gupta, and G. Karypis. 1994. *Introduction to Parallel Computing: Design and Analysis of Algorithms.* Menlo Park, CA: Benjamin/Cummings.

Mullender, S., ed. 1993. *Distributed Systems*, 2nd ed. Reading, MA: ACM Press and Addison-Wesley.

Quinn, M. J. 1994. *Parallel Computing: Theory and Practice.* New York, NY: McGraw-Hill.

Silberschatz, A., J. Peterson, and P. Galvin. 1998. *Operating System Concepts*, 5th ed. Reading, MA: Addison-Wesley.

Tanenbaum, A. S. 1992. *Modern Operating Systems.* Englewood Cliffs, NJ: Prentice-Hall.

Tanenbaum, A. S. 1995. *Distributed Operating Systems.* Englewood Cliffs, NJ: Prentice-Hall.

Wilkinson, B., and M. Allen. 1999. *Parallel Programming: Techniques and Applications Using Networked Workstations and Parallel Computers.* Englewood Cliffs, NJ: Prentice-Hall.

Wilson, G. V. 1995. *Practical Parallel Programming.* Cambridge, MA: MIT Press.

Exercises

1.1 Determine the characteristics of the multiple processor machines to which you have access. How many processors does each machine have and what are their clock speeds? How big are the caches and how are they organized? What is the size of the primary memory? What is the access time? What memory consistency protocol is used? How is the interconnection network organized? What is the remote memory access or message transfer time?

1.2   Many problems can be solved more efficiently using a concurrent program rather than a sequential program—assuming appropriate hardware. Consider the programs you have written in previous classes, and pick two that could be rewritten as concurrent programs. One program should be iterative and the other recursive. Then (a) write concise descriptions of the two problems, and (b) develop pseudocode for concurrent programs that solve the problems.

1.3   Consider the matrix multiplication problem described in Section 1.4.

(a) Write a sequential program to solve the problem. The size of the matrix n should be a command-line argument. Initialize each element of matrices a and b to 1.0. (Hence, the value of each element of the result matrix c will be n.)

(b) Write a parallel program to solve the problem. Compute strips of results in parallel using P worker processes. The matrix size n and the number of workers P should be command-line arguments. Again initialize each element of a and b to 1.0.

(c) Compare the performance of your programs. Experiment with different values for n and P. Prepare a graph of the results and explain what you observe.

(d) Modify your programs to multiply rectangular matrices. The size of matrix a should be $p \times q$, and the size of matrix b should be $q \times r$. Hence, the size of the result will be $p \times r$. Repeat part (c) for the new programs.

1.4   In the matrix multiplication programs, computing an inner product involves multiplying pairs of elements and adding the results. The multiplications could all be done in parallel. Pairs of products could also be added in parallel.

(a) Construct a binary expression tree to illustrate how this would work. Assume the vectors have length n, and for simplicity assume that n is a power of two. The leaves of the tree should be vector elements (a row of matrix a and a column of matrix b). The other nodes of the tree should be multiplication or addition operators.

(b) Many modern processors are what are called super-scalar processors. This means that they can issue (start executing) two or more instructions at the same time. Consider a machine that can issue two instructions at a time. Write assembly-level pseudocode to implement the binary expression tree you constructed in part (a). Assume there are instructions to load, add, and multiply registers, and there are as many registers as you need. Maximize the number of pairs of instructions that you can issue at the same time.

(c) Assume that a load takes 1 clock cycle, an add takes 1 clock cycle, and a multiply takes 8 clock cycles. What is the execution time of your program?

1.5   In the first parallel matrix multiplication program in Section 1.4, the first line has a `co` statement for rows, and the second line has a `for` statement for columns. Suppose the `co` is replaced by `for` and the `for` is replaced by `co`, but that otherwise the program is the same. In particular, the program computes rows sequentially but computes columns in parallel for each row.

(a) Will the program be correct? Namely, will it compute the same results?

(b) Will the program execute as efficiently? Explain your answer.

1.6   The points on a unit circle centered at the origin are defined by the function `f(x) = sqrt(1-x²)`. Recall that the area of a circle is πr^2, where `r` is the radius. Use the adaptive quadrature program in Section 1.5 to approximate the value of π by computing the area of the upper-right quadrant of a unit circle then multiplying the result by `4`. (Another function to try is the integral from `0.0` to `1.0` of `f(x) = 4/(1+x²)`.)

1.7   Consider the quadrature problem described in Section 1.5.

(a) Write four programs to solve the problem: a sequential iterative program that uses a fixed number of intervals, a sequential recursive program that uses adaptive quadrature, a parallel iterative program that uses a fixed number of intervals, and a recursive parallel program that uses adaptive quadrature. Integrate a function that has an interesting shape, such as `sin(x)*exp(x)`. Your programs should have command-line arguments for the range of values for `x`, the number of intervals (for fixed quadrature), and the value of `EPSILON` (for adaptive quadrature).

(b) Experiment with your programs for different values of the command-line arguments. What are their execution times? How accurate are the answers? How fast do the programs converge? Explain what you observe.

1.8   The parallel adaptive quadrature program in Section 1.5 will create a large number of processes, usually way more than the number of processors.

(a) Modify the program so that it creates approximately `T` processes, where `T` is a command-line argument that specifies a threshold. In particular, use a global variable to keep a count of the number of processes that you have created. (Assume for this problem that you can safely increment a global variable.) Within the body of `quad`, if over `T` processes have already been created, then use sequential recursion. Otherwise use parallel recursion and add two to the global counter.

(b) Implement and test the parallel program in the text and your answer to (a). Pick an interesting function to integrate, then experiment with different values of `T` and `EPSILON`. Compare the performance of the two programs.

1.9 Write a sequential recursive program to implement the quicksort algorithm for sorting an array of **n** values. Then modify your program to use recursive parallelism. Be careful to ensure that the parallel calls are independent. Implement both programs and compare their performance.

1.10 Gather information on Unix pipes. How are they implemented on your system? What is the maximum size of a pipe? How are **read** and **write** synchronized? See if you can construct an experiment that causes a **write** to a pipe to block because the pipe is full. See if you can construct a concurrent program that deadlocks (in other words, all the processes are waiting for each other).

1.11 Most computing facilities now employ server machines for electronic mail, Web pages, files, and so on. What kinds of server machines are used at your computing facility? Pick one of the servers (if there is one) and find out how the software is organized. What are the processes (threads) that it runs? How are they scheduled? What are the clients? Is there a thread per client request, or a fixed number of server threads, or what? What data do the server threads share? When and why do the threads synchronize with each other?

1.12 Consider the two programs for distributed matrix multiplication in Section 1.8.

(a) How many messages are sent (and received) by each program? What are the sizes of the messages? Don't forget that there is also a coordinator process in the second program.

(b) Modify the programs to use **P** worker processes, where **P** is a factor of **n**. In particular, each worker should compute **n/P** rows (or columns) of results rather than a single row of results.

(c) How many messages are sent by your program for part (b). What are the sizes of the messages?

1.13 The *transpose* of matrix **M** is a matrix **T** such that **T[i,j] = M[j,i]**, for all **i** and **j**.

(a) Write a parallel program using shared variables that computes the transpose of an **n** × **n** matrix **M**. Use **P** worker processes. For simplicity, assume that **n** is a multiple of **P**.

(b) Write a parallel program using message passing to compute the transpose of square matrix **M**. Again use **P** workers and assume **n** is a multiple of **P**. Figure out how to distribute the data and gather the results.

(c) Modify your programs to handle the case when **n** is not a multiple of **P**.

(d) Experiment with your programs for various values of **n** and **P**. What is their performance?

1.14 The `grep` family of Unix commands finds patterns in files. Write a simplified version of `grep` that has two arguments: a string and a filename. The program should print to `stdout` all lines in the file that contain the string.

(a) Modify your program so that it searches two files, one after the other. (Add a third argument to the program for the second filename.)

(b) Now change your program so that it searches the two files in parallel. Both processes should write to `stdout`.

(c) Experiment with your programs for (a) and (b). Their output should differ, at least some of the time. Moreover, the output of the concurrent program should not always be the same. See if you can observe these phenomena.

Part 1

Shared-Variable Programming

Sequential programs often employ shared variables as a matter of convenience—for global data structures, for example—but they can be written without them. In fact, many would argue that they *should* be written without them.

Concurrent programs, on the other hand, absolutely depend on the use of shared components. This is because the only way processes can work together to solve a problem is to communicate. And the only way they can communicate is if one process writes into *something* that the other process reads. That something can be a shared variable or it can be a shared communication channel. Thus, communication is programmed by writing and reading shared variables or by sending and receiving messages.

Communication gives rise to the need for synchronization. There are two basic kinds: mutual exclusion and condition synchronization. Mutual exclusion occurs whenever two processes need to take turns accessing shared objects, such as the records in an airline reservation system. Condition synchronization occurs whenever one process needs to wait for another—for example, when a consumer process needs to wait for data from a producer process.

Part 1 shows how to write concurrent programs in which processes communicate and synchronize by means of shared variables. We examine a variety of multithreaded and parallel applications. Shared-variable programs are most commonly executed on shared-memory machines, because every variable can be accessed directly by every processor. However, the shared-variable programming model can also be used on distributed-memory machines if it is supported by a software implementation of what is called a distributed shared memory; we examine how this is done in Chapter 10.

Chapter 2 introduces fundamental concepts of processes and synchronization by means of a series of small examples. The first half of the chapter describes ways to parallelize programs, illustrates the need for synchronization, defines atomic actions, and introduces the @await@ statement for programming synchronization. The second half of the chapter examines the semantics of concurrent programs and introduces several key concepts—such as interference, global invariants, safety properties, and fairness—that we will encounter over and over in later chapters.

Chapter 3 examines two basic kinds of synchronization—locks and barriers—and shows how to implement them using the kinds of instructions that are found on every processor. Locks are used to solved the classic critical section problem, which occurs in most concurrent programs. Barriers are a fundamental synchronization technique in parallel programs. The last two sections of the chapter examine and illustrate applications of two important models for parallel computing: data parallel and bag of tasks.

Chapter 4 describes semaphores, which simplify programming mutual exclusion and condition synchronization (signaling). The chapter introduces two more classic concurrent programming problems—the dining philosophers and readers/writers—as well as several others. At the end of the chapter we describe and illustrate the use of the POSIX threads (Pthreads) library, which supports threads and semaphores on shared-memory machines.

Chapter 5 describes monitors, a higher-level programming mechanism that was first proposed in the 1970s, then fell somewhat out of favor, but has once again become popular because it is supported by the Java programming language. Monitors are also used to organize and synchronize the code in operating systems and other multithreaded software systems. The chapter illustrates the use of monitors by means of several interesting examples, including communication buffers, readers/writers, timers, the sleeping barber (another classic problem), and disk scheduling. Section 5.4 describes Java's threads and synchronized methods and shows various ways to protect shared data in Java. Section 5.5 shows how to program monitors using the Pthreads library.

Chapter 6 shows how to implement processes, semaphores, and monitors on single processors and on shared-memory multiprocessors. The basis for the implementations is a *kernel* of data structures and primitive routines; these are the core for any implementation of a concurrent programming language or subroutine library. At the end of the chapter, we show how to implement monitors using semaphores.

2

Processes and Synchronization

Concurrent programs are inherently more complex than sequential programs. In many respects, they are to sequential programs what chess is to checkers or bridge is to pinochle: Each is interesting, but the former is more intellectually intriguing than the latter.

This chapter explores the "game" of concurrent programming, looking closely at its rules, playing pieces, and strategies. The rules are formal tools that help one to understand and develop correct programs; the playing pieces are language mechanisms for describing concurrent computations; the strategies are useful programming techniques.

The previous chapter introduced processes and synchronization and gave several examples of their use. This chapter examines processes and synchronization in detail. Section 2.1 takes a first look at the semantics (meaning) of concurrent programs and introduces five fundamental concepts: program state, atomic action, history, safety property, and liveness property. Sections 2.2 and 2.3 explore these concepts using two simple examples—finding a pattern in a file and finding the maximum value in an array; these sections also explore ways to parallelize programs and show the need for atomic actions and synchronization. Section 2.4 defines atomic actions and introduces the `await` statement as a means for expressing atomic actions and synchronization. Section 2.5 shows how to program the synchronization that arises in producer/consumer programs.

Section 2.6 presents a synopsis of the axiomatic semantics of sequential and concurrent programs. The fundamental new problem introduced by concurrency is the possibility of interference. Section 2.7 describes four methods for avoiding interference: disjoint variables, weakened assertions, global invariants, and synchronization. Finally, Section 2.8 shows how to prove safety properties and defines scheduling policies and fairness.

Many of the concepts introduced in this chapter are quite detailed, so they can be hard to grasp on first reading. But please persevere, study the examples, and refer back to this chapter as needed. The concepts are important because they provide the basis for developing and understanding concurrent programs. Using a disciplined approach is important for sequential programs; it is imperative for concurrent programs, because the order in which processes execute is nondeterministic. In any event, on with the game!

2.1 States, Actions, Histories, and Properties

The *state* of a concurrent program consists of the values of the program variables at a point in time. The variables include those explicitly declared by the programmer as well as implicit variables—such as the program counter for each process—that contain hidden state information. A concurrent program begins execution in some initial state. Each process in the program executes independently, and as it executes it examines and alters the program state.

A process executes a sequence of statements. A statement, in turn, is implemented by a sequence of one or more *atomic actions*, which are actions that *indivisibly* examine or change the program state. Examples of atomic actions are uninterruptible machine instructions that load and store memory words.

The execution of a concurrent program results in an *interleaving* of the sequences of atomic actions executed by each process. A particular execution of a concurrent program can be viewed as a *history*: $s_0 \rightarrow s_1 \rightarrow ... \rightarrow s_n$. In a history, s_0 is the initial state, the other s_n are subsequent states, and the transitions are made by atomic actions that alter the state. (A history is also called a *trace* of the sequence of states.) Even parallel execution can be modeled as a linear history, because the effect of executing a set of atomic actions in parallel is equivalent to executing them in some serial order. In particular, the state change caused by an atomic action is indivisible and hence cannot be affected by atomic actions executed at about the same time.

Each execution of a concurrent program produces a history. For all but the most trivial programs, the number of possible histories is enormous (see below for details). This is because the next atomic action in any one of the processes could be the next one in a history. Hence, there are many ways in which the actions can be interleaved, even if a program is always begun in the same initial state. In addition, each process will most likely contain conditional statements and hence will take different actions as the state changes.

The role of synchronization is to constrain the possible histories of a concurrent program to those histories that are desirable. Mutual exclusion is concerned with combining atomic actions that are implemented directly by hardware into sequences of actions called *critical sections* that appear to be atomic—i.e., that cannot be interleaved with actions in other processes that reference the same variables. Condition synchronization is concerned with delaying an action until the state satisfies a Boolean condition. Both forms of synchronization can cause processes to be delayed, and hence they restrict the set of atomic actions that can be executed next.

A *property* of a program is an attribute that is true of every possible history of that program and hence of all executions of the program. There are two kinds of properties: safety and liveness. A *safety property* is one in which the program never enters a bad state—i.e., a state in which some variables have undesirable values. A *liveness property* is one in which the program eventually enters a good state—i.e., a state in which variables have desirable values.

Partial correctness is an example of a safety property. A program is partially correct if the final state is correct, assuming that the program terminates. If a program fails to terminate, it may never produce the correct answer, but there is no history in which the program has terminated without producing the correct answer. *Termination* is an example of a liveness property. A program terminates if every loop and procedure call terminates—hence, if the length of every history is finite. *Total correctness* is a property that combines partial correctness and termination: A program is totally correct if it always terminates with a correct answer.

Mutual exclusion is an example of a safety property in a concurrent program. The bad state in this case would be one in which two processes are executing actions in different critical sections at the same time. Eventual entry to a critical section is an example of a liveness property in a concurrent program. The good state for each process is one in which it is executing within its critical section.

Given a program and a desired property, how might one go about demonstrating that the program satisfies the property? A common approach is *testing* or *debugging*, which can be characterized as "run the program and see what happens." This corresponds to enumerating some of the possible histories of a program and verifying that they are acceptable. The shortcoming of testing is that each test considers just one execution history, and a limited number of tests are unlikely to demonstrate the absence of bad histories.

A second approach is to use *operational reasoning*, which can be characterized as "exhaustive case analysis." In this approach, all possible execution histories of a program are enumerated by considering all the ways the atomic actions of each process might be interleaved. Unfortunately, the number of histories in a concurrent program is generally enormous (hence the approach is "exhaustive"). For example, suppose a concurrent program contains n processes and that each executes a sequence of m atomic actions. Then the number of different histories of the program is $(n \cdot m)! / (m!^n)$. In a program containing only three processes, each of which executes only two atomic actions, this is a total of 90 different histories! (The numerator in the formula is the number of permutations of the $n \cdot m$ actions. But each process executes a sequence of actions, so there is only one legal order of the m actions in each process; the denominator rules out all the illegal orders. The formula is the same as the number of ways to shuffle n decks of m cards each, assuming that the cards in each deck remain in the same order relative to each other.)

A third approach is to employ *assertional reasoning*, which can be characterized as "abstract analysis." In this approach, formulas of predicate logic called *assertions* are used to characterize sets of states—for example, all states in which $x > 0$. Atomic actions are then viewed as *predicate transformers*, because they change the state from satisfying one predicate to satisfying another predicate. The virtue of the assertional approach is that it leads to a compact representation of states and state transformations. More importantly, it leads to a way to develop and analyze programs in which the work involved is directly proportional to the number of atomic actions in the program.

We will use the assertional approach as a tool for constructing and understanding solutions to a variety of nontrivial problems. We will also use operational reasoning to guide the development of algorithms. Finally, many of the programs in the text have been tested since that helps increase confidence in the correctness of a program. One always has to be wary of testing alone, however, because it can reveal only the presence of errors, not their absence. Moreover, concurrent programs are extremely difficult to test and debug since (1) it is difficult to stop all processes at once in order to examine their state, and (2) each execution will in general produce a different history.

2.2 Parallelization: Finding Patterns in a File

Chapter 1 examined several kinds of applications and showed how they could be solved using concurrent programs. Here, we examine a single, simple problem and look in detail at ways to parallelize it.

Consider the problem of finding all instances of a **pattern** in **filename**. The **pattern** is a string; **filename** is the name of a file. This problem is readily solved in Unix by using one of the **grep**-style commands at the Unix command level, such as

```
grep pattern filename
```

Executing this command creates a single process. The process executes something similar to the following sequential program:

```
string line;
read a line of input from stdin into line;
while (!EOF) {    # EOF is end of file
  look for pattern in line;
  if (pattern is in line)
    write line;
  read next line of input;
}
```

We now want to consider two basic questions: Can the above program be parallelized? If so, how?

The fundamental requirement for being able to parallelize any program is that it contains *independent* parts, as described in Section 1.4. Two parts are dependent on each other if one produces results that the other needs; this can only happen if they read and write shared variables. Hence, two parts of a program are *independent* if they do not read and write the same variables. More precisely:

(2.1) **Independence of Parallel Processes.** Let the *read set* of a part of a program be the variables it reads but does not alter. Let the *write set* of a part be the variables it writes into (and possibly also reads). Two parts of a program are independent if the intersection of their write sets is empty.

A variable is any value that is read or written atomically. This includes simple variables—such as integers—that are stored in single words of storage as well as individual elements of arrays or structures (records).

From the above definition, two parts are independent if both only read shared variables, or if each part reads different variables than the ones written into by the other part. Occasionally, it is possible that two parts can safely execute in parallel even if they write into common variables. However, this is feasible only if the order in which the writes occur does not matter. For example, when two (or more) processes are periodically updating a graphics display, it may be fine for the updates to occur in any order.

Returning to the problem of finding a pattern in a file, what are the independent parts, and hence, what can be parallelized? The program starts by reading the first input line; this *has* to be done before anything else. Then the program enters a loop that looks for the pattern, outputs the line if the pattern is found, then reads a new line. We cannot output a line before looking for a pattern in that line, so the first two lines in the loop body cannot be executed in parallel with each other. However, we can read the next line of input while looking for a pattern in the previous line and possibly printing that line. Hence, consider the following, concurrent version of the above program:

```
string line;
read a line of input from stdin into line;
while (!EOF) {
  co look for pattern in line;
      if (pattern is in line)
          write line;
  // read next line of input into line;
  oc;
}
```

Note that the first arm of `co` is a sequence of statements. Are the two processes in this program independent? The answer is no, because the first process reads `line` and the second process writes into it. Thus, if the second process runs faster than the first, it will overwrite the line before it is examined by the first process.

As noted, parts of a program can be executed concurrently only if they read and write different variables. Suppose the second process reads into a different variable than the one that is examined by the first process. In particular, consider the following program:

```
string line1, line2;
read a line of input from stdin into line1;
while (!EOF) {
  co look for pattern in line1;
      if (pattern is in line1)
          write line1;
  // read next line of input into line2;
  oc;
}
```

Now, the two processes are working on different lines, which are stored in variables `line1` and `line2`. Hence, the processes can execute concurrently. But is the above program correct? Obviously not, because the first process continuously looks at `line1`, while the second process continuously reads into `line2`, which is never examined.

The solution is relatively straightforward: Swap the roles of the lines at the end of each loop iteration, so that the first process always examines the last line read and the second process always reads into a different variable from the one being examined. The following program accomplishes this:

```
string line1, line2;
read a line of input from stdin into line1;
while (! EOF) {
  co look for pattern in line1;
```

```
        if (pattern is in line1)
            write line1;
    //  read next line of input into line2;
    oc;
    line1 = line2;
}
```

In particular, at the end of each loop iteration—and after each process has finished—copy the contents of `line2` into `line1`. The processes within the `co` statement are now independent, but their actions are coupled because of the last statement in the loop, which copies `line2` into `line1`.

The above concurrent program is correct, but it is quite inefficient. First, the last line in the loop copies the contents of `line2` into `line1`. This is a sequential action not present in the first program, and it in general requires copying dozens of characters; thus, it is pure overhead. Second, the loop body contains a `co` statement, which means that on each iteration of the `while` loop, two processes will be created, executed, then destroyed. It is possible to do the "copying" much more efficiently by using an array of two lines, having each process index into a different line in the array, and then merely swapping array indices in the last line. However, process creation overhead would still dominate, because it takes much longer to create and destroy processes than to call procedures and much, much longer than to execute straight-line code (see Chapter 6 for details).

So, we come to our final question for this section. Is there another way to parallelize the program that avoids having a `co` statement inside the loop? As you no doubt guessed, the answer is yes. In particular, instead of having a `co` statement inside the `while` loop, we can put `while` loops inside each arm of the `co` statement. Figure 2.1 contains an outline of this approach. The program is in fact an instance of the producer/consumer pattern introduced in Section 1.6. Here, the first process is the producer and the second process is the consumer. They communicate by means of the shared `buffer`. Note that the declarations of `line1` and `line2` are now local to the processes because the lines are no longer shared.

We call the style of the program in Figure 2.1 "`while` inside `co`" as opposed to the "`co` inside `while`" style of the earlier programs in this section. The advantage of the "`while` inside `co`" style is that processes are created only once, rather than on each loop iteration. The down side is that we have to use two buffers, and we have to program the required synchronization. The statements that precede and follow access to the shared `buffer` indicate the kind of synchronization that is required. We will show how to program this synchronization in Section 2.5, but first we need to examine the topics of synchronization in general and atomic actions in particular.

```
      string buffer;  # contains one line of input
      bool done = false;  # used to signal termination

      co  # process 1:  find patterns
        string line1;
        while (true) {
           wait for buffer to be full or done to be true;
           if (done) break;
           line1 = buffer;
           signal that buffer is empty;
           look for pattern in line1;
           if (pattern is in line1)
             write line1;
        }
      //  # process 2:  read new lines
        string line2;
        while (true) {
           read next line of input into line2;
           if (EOF) {done = true; break; }
           wait for buffer to be empty;
           buffer = line2;
           signal that buffer is full;
        }
      oc;
```

Figure 2.1   Finding patterns in a file.

2.3 Synchronization: The Maximum of an Array

Now consider a different problem, one that requires synchronization between processes. The specific problem is to find the maximum element of array $a[n]$. We will assume that n is positive and that all elements of a are positive integers.

Finding the maximal element in array a is an example of an accumulation (or reduction) problem. In this case, we are accumulating the maximum seen so far, or equivalently reducing all values to their maximum. Let m be the variable that is to be assigned the maximal value. The goal of the program can then be expressed in predicate logic as

$$(\forall j: 1 <= j <= n: m >= a[j]) \wedge$$
$$(\exists j: 1 <= j <= n: m == a[j])$$

The first line says that when the program terminates, the value of m is to be at least as large as every value in array **a**. The second line says that **m** is to be equivalent to *some* value in array **a**.

To solve the problem, we can use the following sequential program:

```
int m = 0;
for [i = 0 to n-1] {
  if (a[i] > m)
    m = a[i];
}
```

This program iteratively looks at all values in array **a**; if one is found that is smaller than the current maximum, it is assigned to **m**. Since we assume that all values in **a** are positive, it is safe to initialize **m** to **0**.

Now consider ways to parallelize the above program. Suppose we fully parallelize the loop by examining every array element in parallel:

```
int m = 0;
co [i = 0 to n-1]
  if (a[i] > m)
    m = a[i];
```

This program is incorrect because the processes are not independent: each one both reads and writes variable **m**. In particular, suppose that each process executes at the same rate, and hence that each compares its **a[i]** to **m** at the same time. All processes will see that the comparison is true (because all elements of **a** are positive and the initial value of **m** is **0**). Hence, all processes will try to update **m**. The memory hardware will cause the updates to be done in some serial order—because writing into a memory word is atomic—and the final value of **m** will be the value of **a[i]** assigned by the last process that gets to update **m**.

In the above program, reading and writing **m** are separate actions. One way to deal with having too much parallelism is to use synchronization to combine separate actions into a single atomic action. The following program does so:

```
int m = 0;
co [i = 0 to n-1]
  ⟨if (a[i] > m)
    m = a[i];⟩
```

The angle brackets in the above code specify that each **if** statement is to be executed as an atomic action—namely, that each **if** statement both examines the current value of **m** and conditionally updates it as *a single, indivisible action*. (We describe the angle-bracket notation in detail in the next section.)

Unfortunately, the last program is almost the same as the sequential program. In the sequential program, the elements of **a** are examined in a fixed order—from `a[0]` to `a[n-1]`. In the last program the elements of `a` are examined in an arbitrary order—because processes execute in an arbitrary order—but they are still examined one at a time due to the synchronization.

The key issues in this application are to ensure that updates of `m` are atomic and that `m` is indeed the maximum. Suppose that we execute the comparisons in parallel but the updates one at a time, as in the following program:

```
int m = 0;
co [i = 0 to n-1]
  if (a[i] > m)
     ⟨m = a[i];⟩
```

Is this version correct? No, because this program is actually the same as the first concurrent program: Every process could compare its value of `a` to `m` and then update the value of `m`. Although this program specifies that updating `m` is atomic, the memory hardware of a machine will in fact ensure that.

So, what is the best way to solve this problem? The answer is to combine the last two programs. It is safe to do comparisons in parallel, because they are read-only actions. But it is necessary to ensure that when the program terminates, `m` is indeed the maximum. The following program accomplishes this:

```
int m = 0;
co [i = 0 to n-1]
  if (a[i] > m)          # check the value of m
     ⟨if (a[i] > m)      # recheck the value of m
       m = a[i];⟩
```

The idea is first to do the comparison, and then if it is true, to *double check* before doing the update. This may seem like a lot of wasted effort, but in fact often it is not. Once some process has updated `m`, it is probable that half the other processes will find their value of `a` to be less than the new value of `m`; hence, those processes will not execute the body of the `if` statement. After a further update, even fewer processes would find the first check to be true. Thus, if the checks themselves occur somewhat at random rather than concurrently, it is increasingly likely that processes will not have to do the second check.

This specific problem is not one that is going to benefit from being solved by a concurrent program, unless the program is executed on a SIMD machine, which is built to execute fine-grained programs efficiently. However, this section has made three key points. First, synchronization is required to get correct answers whenever processes both read and write shared variables. Second, angle brackets are used to specify actions that are to be atomic; we explore this topic in detail in the next section and later show how to implement atomic actions, which are in fact instances of critical sections. Third, the technique of double checking before updating a shared variable is quite useful—as we shall see in later examples—especially if it is possible that the first check is false and hence that the second check is not needed.

2.4 Atomic Actions and Await Statements

As mentioned earlier, we can view execution of a concurrent program as an interleaving of the atomic actions executed by individual processes. When processes interact, not all interleavings are likely to be acceptable. The role of synchronization is to prevent undesirable interleavings. This is done by combining fine-grained atomic actions into coarse-grained (composite) actions or by delaying process execution until the program state satisfies some predicate. The first form of synchronization is called *mutual exclusion*; the second, *condition synchronization*. This section examines aspects of atomic actions and presents a notation for specifying synchronization.

2.4.1 Fine-Grained Atomicity

Recall that an atomic action makes an indivisible state transformation. This means that any intermediate state that might exist in the implementation of the action must not be visible to other processes. A *fine-grained* atomic action is one that is implemented directly by the hardware on which a concurrent program executes.

In a sequential program, assignment statements appear to be atomic since no intermediate state is visible to the program (except possibly if there is a machine-detected fault). However, this is not generally the case in concurrent programs since an assignment statement might be implemented by a sequence of fine-grained machine instructions. For example, consider the following program, and assume that the fine-grained atomic actions are reading and writing the variables:

```
int y = 0, z = 0;
co x = y+z; // y = 1; z = 2; oc;
```

If x = y+z is implemented by loading a register with y and then adding z to it, the final value of x could be 0, 1, 2, or 3. This is because we could see the initial values for y and z, their final values, or some combination, depending on how far the second process has executed. A further peculiarity of the above program is that the final value of x could be 2, even though one could never stop the program and see a state in which y+z is 2.

We assume that machines have the following, realistic characteristics:

- Values of the basic types (e.g., `int`) are stored in memory elements (e.g., words) that are read and written as atomic actions.

- Values are manipulated by loading them into registers, operating on them there, then storing the results back into memory.

- Each process has its own set of registers. This is realized either by having distinct sets of registers or by saving and restoring register values whenever a different process is executed. (This is called a *context switch* since the registers constitute the execution context of a process.)

- Any intermediate results that occur when a complex expression is evaluated are stored in registers or in memory private to the executing process—e.g., on a private stack.

With this machine model, if an expression `e` in one process does not reference a variable altered by another process, expression evaluation will appear to be atomic, even if it requires executing several fine-grained atomic actions. This is because (1) none of the values on which `e` depends could possibly change while `e` is being evaluated, and (2) no other process can see any temporary values that might be created while the expression is being evaluated. Similarly, if an assignment `x = e` in one process does not reference any variable altered by another process—for example, it references only local variables—then execution of the assignment will appear to be atomic.

Unfortunately, most statements in concurrent programs that reference shared variables do not meet the above disjointness requirement. However, a weaker requirement is often met.

(2.2) **At-Most-Once Property.** A *critical reference* in an expression is a reference to a variable that is changed by another process. Assume that any critical reference is to a simple variable that is stored in a memory element that is read and written atomically. An assignment statement `x = e` satisfies the at-most-once property if either (1) `e` contains at most one critical reference and `x` is not read by another process, or (2) `e` contains no critical references, in which case `x` may be read by other processes.

This is called the At-Most-Once Property because there can be at most one shared variable, and it can be referenced at most one time. A similar definition applies to expressions that are not in assignment statements. Such an expression satisfies the At-Most-Once Property if it contains no more than one critical reference.

If an assignment statement meets the requirements of the At-Most-Once Property, then execution of the assignment statement will *appear* to be atomic. This is because the one shared variable in the statement will be read or written just once. For example, if **e** contains no critical references and **x** is a simple variable that is read by other processes, they will not be able to tell whether the expression is evaluated atomically. Similarly, if **e** contains just one critical reference, the process executing the assignment will not be able to tell how that variable is updated; it will just see some legitimate value.

A few examples will help clarify the definition. Both assignments in the following program satisfy the property

```
int x = 0, y = 0;
co x = x+1; // y = y+1; oc;
```

There are no critical references in either process, so the final values of **x** and **y** are both **1**.

Both assignments in the following program also satisfy the property:

```
int x = 0, y = 0;
co x = y+1; // y = y+1; oc;
```

The first process references **y** (one critical reference), but **x** is not read by the second process, and the second process has no critical references. The final value of **x** is either **1** or **2**, and the final value of **y** is **1**. The first process will see **y** either before or after it is incremented, but in a concurrent program it can never know which value it will see, because execution order is nondeterministic.

As a final example, neither assignment below satisfies the At-Most-Once Property:

```
int x = 0, y = 0;
co x = y+1; // y = x+1; oc;
```

The expression in each process contains a critical reference, and each process assigns to a variable read by the other. Indeed, the final values of **x** and **y** could be **1** and **2**, **2** and **1**, or even **1** and **1** (if the processes read **x** and **y** before either assigns to them). However, since each assignment refers only once to only one variable altered by another process, the final values will be those that actually existed in some state. This contrasts with the earlier example in which **y+z** referred to two variables altered by another process.

2.4.2 Specifying Synchronization: The Await Statement

If an expression or assignment statement does not satisfy the At-Most-Once Property, we often need to have it executed atomically. More generally, we often need to execute sequences of statements as a single atomic action. In both cases, we need to use a synchronization mechanism to construct a *coarse-grained* atomic action, which is a sequence of fine-grained atomic actions that appears to be indivisible.

As a concrete example, suppose a database contains two values x and y, and that at all times x and y are to be the same in the sense that no process examining the database is ever to see a state in which x and y differ. Then, if a process alters x, it must also alter y as part of the same atomic action.

As a second example, suppose one process inserts elements on a queue represented as a linked list. Another process removes elements from the list, assuming there are elements on the list. One variable points to the head of the list and another points to the tail of the list. Inserting and removing elements requires manipulating two values; e.g., to insert an element, we have to change the link of the previous element so it points to the new element, and we have to change the tail variable so it points to the new element. If the list contains just one element, simultaneous insertion and removal can conflict, leaving the list in an unstable state. Thus, insertion and removal must be atomic actions. Furthermore, if the list is empty, we need to delay execution of a remove operation until an element has been inserted.

We will specify atomic actions by means of angle brackets ⟨ and ⟩. For example, ⟨e⟩ indicates that expression e is to be evaluated atomically.

We will specify synchronization by means of the **await** statement:

(2.3)   ⟨**await** (B) S;⟩

Boolean expression B specifies a delay condition; S is a sequence of sequential statements that is guaranteed to terminate (e.g., a sequence of assignment statements). An **await** statement is enclosed in angle brackets to indicate that it is executed as an atomic action. In particular, B is guaranteed to be true when execution of S begins, and no internal state in S is visible to other processes. For example,

⟨**await** (s > 0) s = s-1;⟩

delays until s is positive, then decrements s. The value of s is guaranteed to be positive before s is decremented.

The **await** statement is a very powerful statement since it can be used to specify arbitrary, coarse-grained atomic actions. This makes it convenient for expressing synchronization—and we will therefore use `await` to develop initial solutions to synchronization problems. This expressive power also makes `await` very expensive to implement in its most general form. However, as we shall see in this and the next several chapters, there are many special cases of `await` that can be implemented efficiently. For example, the last `await` statement above is an example of the `P` operation on semaphore `s`, a topic in Chapter 4.

The general form of the `await` statement specifies both mutual exclusion and condition synchronization. To specify only mutual exclusion, we will abbreviate an `await` statement as follows:

    ⟨ `S;` ⟩

For example, the following increments `x` and `y` atomically:

    ⟨ `x = x+1; y = y+1;` ⟩

The internal state—in which `x` has been incremented but `y` has not—is, by definition, not visible to other processes that reference `x` or `y`. If `S` is a single assignment statement and meets the requirements of the At-Most-Once Property (2.2)—or if `S` is implemented by a single machine instruction—then `S` will be executed atomically; thus, ⟨ `S;` ⟩ has the same effect as `S`.

To specify only condition synchronization, we will abbreviate `await` as

    ⟨ `await (B);` ⟩

For example, the following delays the executing process until `count>0`:

    ⟨ `await (count > 0);` ⟩

If `B` meets the requirements of the At-Most-Once Property, as in this example, then ⟨ `await (B);` ⟩ can be implemented as

    `while (not B);`

This is an instance of what is called a *spin loop*. In particular, the `while` statement has an empty body, so it just spins until `B` becomes false.

An *unconditional* atomic action is one that does not contain a delay condition `B`. Such an action can execute immediately, subject of course to the requirement that it execute atomically. Hardware-implemented (fine-grained) actions, expressions in angle brackets, and `await` statements in which the guard is the constant true or is omitted are all unconditional atomic actions.

A *conditional* atomic action is an `await` statement with a guard `B`. Such an action cannot execute until `B` is true. If `B` is false, it can only become true as the result of actions taken by other processes. Thus a process waiting to execute a conditional atomic action could wait for an arbitrarily long time.

2.5 Producer/Consumer Synchronization

The last solution in Section 2.2 to the problem of finding patterns in a file employs a producer process and a consumer process. In particular, the producer repeatedly reads input lines, determines those that contained the desired pattern, and passes them on to the consumer process. The consumer then outputs the lines it receives from the producer. Communication between the producer and consumer is conducted by means of a shared `buffer`. We left unspecified how to synchronize access to the buffer. We are now in a position to explain how to do so.

Here we solve a somewhat simpler producer/consumer problem: copying all elements of an array from the producer to the consumer. We leave to the reader the task of adapting this solution to the specific problem at the end of Section 2.2 (see the exercises at the end of this chapter).

Two processes are given: `Producer` and `Consumer`. The `Producer` has a local array `a[n]` of integers; the `Consumer` has a local array `b[n]` of integers. We assume that array `a` has been initialized. The goal is to copy the contents of `a` into `b`. Because the arrays are not shared, the processes have to use shared variables to communicate with each other. Let `buf` be a single shared integer that will serve as a communication buffer.

The `Producer` and `Consumer` have to alternate access to `buf`. To begin, the `Producer` deposits the first element of `a` in `buf`, then `Consumer` fetches it, then `Producer` deposits the second element of `a`, and so on. Let shared variables `p` and `c` count the number of items that have been deposited and fetched, respectively. Initially, these values are both zero. The synchronization requirements between the `Producer` and `Consumer` can then be expressed by the following predicate:

$$PC: \quad c <= p <= c+1$$

In particular, the values of `c` and `p` can differ by at most one, meaning the `Producer` has deposited at most one more element than the `Consumer` has fetched. The actual code for the two processes is shown in Figure 2.2.

The `Producer` and `Consumer` use `p` and `c` as shown in Figure 2.2 to synchronize access to `buf`. In particular, they use `await` statements to wait until the buffer is empty or full. When `p == c` the buffer is empty (the previously deposited element has been fetched). When `p > c` the buffer is full.

```
int buf, p = 0, c = 0;
process Producer {
  int a[n];
  while (p < n) {
    ⟨await (p == c);⟩
    buf = a[p];
    p = p+1;
  }
}

process Consumer {
  int b[n];
  while (c < n) {
    ⟨await (p > c);⟩
    b[c] = buf;
    c = c+1;
  }
}
```

Figure 2.2   Copying an array from a producer to a consumer.

When synchronization is implemented in this way, a process is said to be *busy waiting* or *spinning*. This is because the process is busy checking the condition in its `await` statement, but all it does is spin in a loop until that condition is true. This kind of synchronization is common—indeed, necessary—at the lowest levels of software systems, such as operating systems and network protocols. Chapter 3 examines busy waiting in detail.

2.6 A Synopsis of Axiomatic Semantics

At the end of Section 2.1, we described how assertional reasoning can help us understand the properties of a concurrent program. More importantly, it can help us develop correct programs. Consequently, we will be using assertional reasoning frequently in the remainder of the text. In this and the next two sections, we introduce the formal basis for it. Later chapters will apply the concepts informally.

The basis for assertional reason is what is called a *programming logic*—a formal logical system that facilitates making precise statements about program execution. This section summarizes the topic and introduces key concepts. The Historical Notes at the end of this chapter describe sources of more detailed information, including many more examples.

2.6.1 Formal Logical Systems

Any formal logical system consists of rules defined in terms of

- a set of *symbols*,

- a set of *formulas* constructed from these symbols,

- a set of distinguished formulas called *axioms*, and

- a set of *inference rules*.

Formulas are well-formed sequences of symbols. The axioms are special formulas that are *a priori* assumed to be true. Inference rules specify how to derive additional true formulas from axioms and other true formulas. Inference rules have the form

$$\frac{H_1, H_2, \ldots, H_n}{C}$$

Each H_i is a *hypothesis*; C is a conclusion. The meaning of an inference rule is as follows: If all the hypotheses are true, then we can infer that the conclusion is also true. Both the hypotheses and conclusion are formulas or schematic representations of formulas.

A *proof* in a formal logical system is a sequence of lines, each of which is an axiom or can be derived from previous lines by application of an inference rule. A *theorem* is any line in a proof. Thus, theorems are either axioms or are obtained by applying an inference rule to other theorems.

By itself, a formal logical system is a mathematical abstraction—a collection of symbols and relations between them. A logical system becomes interesting when the formulas represent statements about some domain of discourse and the formulas that are theorems are true statements. This requires that we provide an interpretation of the formulas.

An *interpretation* of a logic maps each formula to true or false. A logic is *sound* with respect to an interpretation if all its axioms and inference rules are sound. An axiom is sound if it maps to true. An inference rule is sound if its conclusion maps to true, assuming all the hypotheses map to true. Thus, if a logic is sound, all theorems are true statements about the domain of discourse. In this case, the interpretation is called a *model* for the logic.

Completeness is the dual of soundness. A logic is *complete* with respect to an interpretation if formula that is mapped to true is a theorem—that is, every formula is provable in the logic. Thus, if *FACTS* is the set of true statements that are expressible as formulas in a logic and *THEOREMS* is the set of theorems of the logic, soundness means that *THEOREMS* $\subseteq$ *FACTS* and completeness means that $FACTS \subseteq THEOREMS$. A logic that is both sound and complete allows all true statements expressible in the logic to be proved.

Any logic that includes arithmetic cannot be complete, as shown by German mathematician Kurt Gödel in his famous incompleteness theorem. However, a logic that extends another one can be *relatively complete*, meaning that it does not introduce any incompleteness beyond that inherent in the logic it extends. Fortunately, relative completeness is good enough for the programming logic we present below since the arithmetic properties that we will employ are certainly true.

2.6.2 A Programming Logic

A *programming logic* is a formal logical system that allows one to state and prove properties of programs. This section summarizes a specific one that we call *PL* (Programming Logic).

As with any formal logical system, *PL* contains symbols, formulas, axioms, and inference rules. The symbols of *PL* are predicates, braces, and programming language statements. The formulas of *PL* are called *triples*. They have the following form:[1]

```
{P}  S  {Q}
```

Predicates P and Q specify relations between the values of program variables; S is a statement or statement list.

The purpose of a programming logic is to facilitate proving properties of program execution. Hence, the *interpretation* of a triple characterizes the relation between predicates P and Q and statement list S.

(2.4)   **Interpretation of a Triple**. The triple {P} S {Q} is true if, whenever execution of S is begun in a state satisfying P and execution of S terminates, the resulting state satisfies Q.

This interpretation is called *partial correctness*, which is a safety property as defined in Section 2.1. It says that, if the initial program state satisfies P, then the final state will satisfy Q, assuming S terminates. The related liveness property is *total correctness*, which is partial correctness plus termination—that is, all histories are finite.

---

[1] Predicates in triples are surrounded by braces, because that is the way they have traditionally been used in programming logics. However, braces are also used in our programming notation to enclose sequences of statements. To avoid possible confusion, we will use ## to specify a predicate in a program. Recall that the sharp character # is used to introduce a one-line comment. Think of a predicate as a very precise—hence very sharp—comment.

In a triple, predicates P and Q are often called *assertions* since they assert that the program state must satisfy the predicate in order for the interpretation of the triple to be true. Thus, an assertion characterizes an acceptable program state. Predicate P is called the *precondition* of S; it characterizes the condition that the state must satisfy before execution of S begins. Predicate Q is called the *postcondition* of S; it characterizes the state that results from executing S, assuming S terminates. Two special assertions are `true`, which characterizes all program states, and `false`, which characterizes no program state.

In order for interpretation (2.4) to be a model for our programming logic, the axioms and inference rules of *PL* must be sound with respect to (2.4). This will ensure that all theorems provable in *PL* are sound. For example, the following triple should be a theorem:

```
{x == 0} x = x+1; {x == 1}
```

However, the following should not be a theorem, because assigning a value to x cannot miraculously set y to 1:

```
{x == 0} x = x+1; {y == 1}
```

In addition to being sound, the logic should be (relatively) complete so that all triples that are true are in fact provable as theorems.

The most important axiom of a programming logic such as *PL* is the one relating to assignment:

Assignment Axiom: $\{P_{x \leftarrow e}\}$ `x = e` $\{P\}$

The notation $P_{x \leftarrow e}$ specifies textual substitution; it means "replace all free occurrences of variable x in predicate P by expression e." (A variable is free in a predicate if it is not captured by a bound variable of the same name in an existential or universal quantifier.) The Assignment Axiom thus says that if one wants an assignment to result in a state satisfying predicate P, then the prior state must satisfy P with variable x textually replaced by expression e.

As an example, the following triple is an instance of the axiom:

```
{1 == 1} x = 1; {x == 1}
```

The precondition simplifies to the predicate `true`, which characterizes all states. Thus, this triple says that no matter what the starting state, when we assign 1 to x we get a state that satisfies $x == 1$.

The more common way to view assignment is by "going forward." In particular, start with a predicate that characterizes what is true of the current state,

Composition Rule:

$$\frac{\{P\}\ S_1\ \{Q\},\ \{Q\}\ S_2\ \{R\}}{\{P\}\ S_1;\ S_2\ \{R\}}$$

If Statement Rule:

$$\frac{\{P \wedge B\}\ S\ \{Q\},\ (P \wedge \neg B)\ \Rightarrow\ Q}{\{P\}\ \text{if}\ (B)\ S;\ \{Q\}}$$

While Statement Rule:

$$\frac{\{I \wedge B\}\ S\ \{I\}}{\{I\}\ \text{while}(B)\ S;\ \{I\ \wedge\ \neg B\}}$$

Rule of Consequence:

$$\frac{P' \Rightarrow P,\ \{P\}\ S\ \{Q\},\ Q \Rightarrow Q'}{\{P'\}\ S\ \{Q'\}}$$

Figure 2.3   Inference rules in programming logic *PL*.

and then produce the predicate that is true of the state after the assignment takes place. For example, if we start in a state in which $x\ ==\ 0$ and add 1 to x, then x will be 1 in the resulting state. This is captured by the triple:

```
{x == 0} x = 1; {x == 1}
```

The Assignment Axiom describes how the state changes. The inference rules in a programming logic such as *PL* allow theorems resulting from instances of the Assignment Axiom to be combined. In particular, inference rules are used to characterize the effects of statement composition (statement lists) and of control statements such as `if` and `while`. They are also used to modify the predicates in triples.

Figure 2.3 gives four of the most important inference rules. The Composition Rule allows one to glue together the triples for two statements when the statements are executed one after the other. The first hypothesis in the If Statement Rule characterizes the effect of executing `s` when `B` is true; the second hypothesis characterizes what is true when `B` is false; the conclusion combines the two cases. As a simple example of the use of these two rules, the following program sets `m` to the maximum of `x` and `y`:

```
{true}
m = x;
{m == x}
if (y > m)
    m = y;
{(m == x ∧ m >= y) or (m == y) ∧ m > x)}
```

Whatever the initial state, the first assignment produces a state in which m == x. After the if statement has executed, m is equal to x and at least as large as y, or it is equal to y and greater than x.

The While Statement Rule requires a *loop invariant* I. This is a predicate that is true before and after each iteration of the loop. If I and loop condition B are true before the loop body S is executed, then execution of S must again make I true. Thus, when the loop terminates, I will still be true, but now B will be false. As an example, the following program searches array a for the first occurrence of the value of x. Assuming that x occurs in a, the loop terminates with variable i set to the index of the first occurrence.

```
i = 1;
{i == 1 ∧ (∀ j: 1 <= j < i: a[j] != x)}
while (a[i] != x)
    i = i+1;
{(∀ j: 1 <= j < i: a[j] != x) ∧ a[i] == x}
```

The loop invariant here is the quantified predicate. It is true before the loop because the range of the quantifier is empty. It is also true before and after each execution of the loop body. When the loop terminates, a[i] is equal to x and x does not occur earlier in a.

The Rule of Consequence allows preconditions to be strengthened and/or postconditions to be weakened. As an example, the following triple is true:

```
{x == 0} x = x+1; {x == 1}
```

Thus, from the Rule of Consequence, the following triple is also true:

```
{x == 0} x = x+1; {x > 0}
```

The postcondition in the second triple is *weaker* than the one in the first triple because it characterizes more states; even though x might indeed be exactly 1, it is also the case that it is nonnegative.

2.6.3 Semantics of Concurrent Execution

The concurrent statement co—or equivalently a process declaration—is a control statement. Hence, its effect is described by an inference rule that captures the effect of parallel execution. Processes are comprised of sequential statements and synchronization statements such as await.

With respect to partial correctness, the effect of an await statement

```
⟨await (B) S;⟩
```

is much like an `if` statement for which the guard B is true when execution of S begins. Hence, the inference rule for `await` is similar to the inference rule for `if`:

Await Statement Rule:
$$\frac{\{P \land B\} \ S \ \{Q\}}{\{P\} \ \langle await \ (B) \ S; \rangle \ \{Q\}}$$

The hypothesis says "if execution of S begins in a state in which both P and B are true, and S terminates, then Q will be true." The conclusion allows one to infer that it is then the case that the `await` statement yields state Q if begun in state P, assuming that the `await` statement terminates. (Inference rules say nothing about possible delays, as delays affect liveness properties, not safety properties.)

Now consider the effects of concurrent execution, such as that specified by the following statement:

```
co S₁; // S₂; // ... // Sₙ; oc;
```

Suppose that the following is true for every statement:

```
{Pᵢ} Sᵢ {Qᵢ}
```

According to the Interpretation of Triples (2.4), this means that, if S_i is begun in a state satisfying P_i and S_i terminates, then the state will satisfy Q_i. For this interpretation to hold when the processes are executed concurrently, the processes must be started in a state satisfying the conjunction of the P_i. If all the processes terminate, the final state will satisfy the conjunction of the Q_i. Thus, we get the following inference rule:

Co Statement Rule:
$$\frac{\{P_i\} \ S_i \ \{Q_i\} \ \text{are interference free}}{\begin{array}{c} \{P_1 \land \dots \land P_n\} \\ co \ S_1; \ // \ \dots \ // \ S_n; \ oc \\ \{Q_1 \land \dots \land Q_n\} \end{array}}$$

However, note the phrase in the hypothesis. For the conclusion to be true, the processes and their proofs must not interfere with each other.

One process *interferes* with another if it executes an assignment that invalidates an assertion in the other process. Assertions characterize what a process assumes to be true before and after each statement. Thus, if one process assigns to a shared variable and thereby invalidates an assumption of another process, the proof of the other process is not valid.

As an example, consider the following simple program:

```
{x == 0}
co ⟨x = x+1;⟩ // ⟨x = x+2;⟩ oc
{x == 3}
```

If the program is started in a state in which x is 0, then when the program terminates, x will be 3. But what is true about each process? Neither can assume that x is still 0 when it starts, because the order of execution is nondeterministic. In particular, if a process assumes that x is 0 when it begins, that assertion will be interfered with if the other process executes first. However, what is true is captured by the following:

```
{x == 0}
co {x == 0 ∨ x == 2}
   ⟨x = x+1;⟩
   {x == 1 ∨ x == 3}
// {x == 0 ∨ x == 1}
   ⟨x = x+2;⟩
   {x == 2 ∨ x == 3}
oc

{x == 3}
```

The assertions in each process account for the two possible execution orders. Note also that the conjunction of the preconditions is indeed x == 0 and that the conjunction of the postconditions is indeed x == 3.

The above display is an example of what is called a *proof outline*. There is an assertion before and after each statement, and all of the resulting triples are true. (There are three triples: one for each process and one for the co statement.) Hence, the proof outline captures all the key parts that would exist in a formal proof of the correctness of the above program.

The formal definition of noninterference follows. An *assignment action* is an assignment statement or an **await** statement that contains one or more assignments. A *critical assertion* is a precondition or postcondition that is not within an **await** statement.

(2.5) **Noninterference.** Let a be an assignment action in one process and let pre(a) be its precondition. Let c be a critical assertion in another process. If necessary, rename local variables in c so their names are different from the names of local variables in a and pre(a). Then a does not interfere with c if the following is a theorem in programming logic *PL*:

$$\{C \wedge \text{pre(a)}\} \ a \ \{C\}$$

In short, critical assertion c is invariant with respect to execution of assignment action a. The precondition of a is included in (2.5) because a can be executed only if the process is in a state satisfying pre(a).

As an example of the use of (2.5), consider the last program above. The precondition of the first process is a critical assertion. It is not interfered with by the assignment statement in the second process because the following triple is true:

```
{(x == 0 ∨ x == 2) ∧ (x == 0 ∨ x == 1)}
x = x+2;
{x == 0 ∨ x == 2}
```

The first predicate simplifies to x == 0, so after adding 2 to x, the value of x is either 0 or 2. What this triple expresses is the fact that if the second process executes before the first one, then the value of x will be 2 when the first process begins execution. There are three more critical assertions in the above program: the postcondition in the first process and the pre- and postconditions in the second process. The noninterference proofs are all similar to the one above.

2.7 Techniques for Avoiding Interference

The processes in a concurrent program work together to compute results. The key requirement for having a correct program is that the processes not interfere with each other. A collection of processes is interference-free if no assignment action in one process interferes with any critical assertion in another.

This section describes four basic techniques for avoiding interference, and hence four techniques that can be used to develop correct concurrent programs: (1) disjoint variables, (2) weakened assertions, (3) global invariants, and (4) synchronization. These techniques are employed extensively throughout the remainder of the book. All involve putting assertions and assignment actions in a form that ensures that noninterference formulas (2.5) are true.

2.7.1 Disjoint Variables

Recall that the *write set* of a process is the set of variables that it assigns to (and possibly also reads), and the *read set* of a process is the set of variables that it reads but does not alter. The *reference set* of a process is the set of variables that appear in the assertions in a proof of that process. The reference set of a process will often be the same as the union of the read and write sets, but it might not be. With respect to interference, the critical variables are those in assertions.

If the write set of one process is disjoint from the reference set of a second, and vice versa, then the two processes cannot interfere. Formally, this is because the Assignment Axiom employs textual substitution, which has no effect on a predicate that does not contain a reference to the target of the assignment. (Local variables in different processes are different variables, even if they happen to have the same name; thus they can be renamed before applying the Assignment Axiom.)

As an example, consider the following program:

```
co x = x+1; // y = y+1; oc
```

If x and y are initially 0, then from the Assignment Axiom, both of the following are theorems:

```
{x == 0} x = x+1; {x == 1}

{y == 0} y = y+1; {y == 1}
```

Each process contains one assignment statement and two assertions; hence there are four noninterference theorems to prove. Each one is trivially true because the two processes reference different variables, and hence the substitutions that result from the Assignment Axiom are vacuous.

Disjoint write/reference sets provide the basis for most parallel iterative algorithms, such as the matrix multiplication algorithm described in Section 1.4. As another example, different branches of the tree of possible moves in a game-playing program can be searched in parallel. Or, multiple transactions can examine a database in parallel or they can update different relations.

2.7.2 Weakened Assertions

Even when the write and reference sets of processes overlap, we can sometimes avoid interference by weakening assertions to take into account the effects of concurrent execution. A *weakened assertion* is one that admits more program states than another assertion that might be true of a process in isolation. We saw an example in Section 2.6 using the following program:

```
{x == 0}
co {x == 0 ∨ x == 2}
   ⟨x = x+1;⟩
   {x == 1 ∨ x == 3}

// {x == 0 ∨ x == 1}
   ⟨x = x+2;⟩
```

```
     {x == 2 ∨ x == 3}
oc
{x == 3}
```

Here, the preconditions and postconditions in each process are weaker than they could be in isolation. In particular, each process could assert in isolation that if **x** is initially **0**, then upon termination the value of **x** is **1** (first process) or **2** (second process). However, these stronger assertions would be interfered with.

Weakened assertions have more realistic applications than the simplistic problem above. For example, assume a process schedules operations on a moving-head disk. Other processes insert operations into a queue; when the disk is idle, the scheduler examines the queue, selects the best operation according to some criteria, and starts that operation. Although the scheduler may have selected the best operation at the time it examined the queue, it is not the case that at all times the disk is performing the best operation—or even that at the time an operation is started it is still the best one. This is because a process might have inserted another, better operation into the queue just after the selection was made—and even before the disk started to execute the selected operation. Thus, "best" in this case is a time-dependent property; however, it is sufficient for scheduling problems such as this.

As another example, many parallel algorithms for approximating solutions to partial differential equations have the following form. (See Chapter 11 for a specific example.) The problem space is approximated by a finite grid of points, say **grid[n,n]**. A process is assigned to each grid point—or more commonly, a block of grid points—as in the following program outline:

```
double grid[n,n];
process PDE[i = 0 to n-1, j = 0 to n-1] {
  while (not converged) {
     grid[i,j] = f(neighboring points);
  }
}
```

The function **f** computed on each iteration might, for example, be the average of the four neighboring points in the same row and column. For many problems, the value assigned to **grid[i,j]** on one iteration depends on the values of the neighbors from the previous iteration. Thus, the loop invariant would characterize this relation between old and new values for grid points.

In order to ensure that the loop invariant in each process is not interfered with, the processes must use two matrices and must synchronize after each iteration. In particular, on each iteration each **PDE** process reads values from one matrix, computes **f**, and then assigns the result to the second matrix. Each process then waits until all processes have computed the new value for their grid points. (The next chapter shows how to implement this kind of synchronization, which is called a *barrier*.) The roles of the matrices are then switched, and the processes execute another iteration.

A second way to synchronize the processes is to execute them in lockstep, with each process executing the same actions at the same time. Synchronous multiprocessors support this style of execution. This approach avoids interference since every process reads old values from `grid` before any process assigns a new value.

2.7.3 Global Invariants

Another, very powerful technique for avoiding interference is to employ a global invariant to capture the relations between shared variables. In fact, as we shall see starting in Chapter 3, one can use a global invariant to guide the development of a solution to *any* synchronization problem.

Suppose I is a predicate that references global variables. Then I is a *global invariant* with respect to a set of processes if: (1) I is true when the processes begin execution, and (2) I is preserved by every assignment action. Condition 1 is satisfied if I is true in the initial state of every process. Condition 2 is satisfied if, for every assignment action a, I is true after executing a assuming that I is true before executing a. In short, the two conditions are an instance of the use of mathematical induction.

Suppose predicate I is a global invariant. Further suppose that every critical assertion C in the proof of every process P_j has the form $I \wedge L$, where L is a predicate about local variables. In particular, each variable referenced in L is either local to process P_j or it is a global variable that only P_j assigns to. If all critical assertions can be put in this form $I \wedge L$, then the proofs of the processes will be interference-free. This is because (1) I is invariant with respect to every assignment action a, and (2) no assignment action in one process can interfere with a local predicate L in another process since the target (left-hand side) of a is different from the variables in L.

When all assertions use a global invariant and local predicate as above, Noninterference requirement (2.5) is met for every pair of assignment actions and critical assertions. Moreover, we have to check only the triples in each process to verify that each critical assertion has the above form and that I is a global invariant; we do not even have to consider assertions or statements in other processes. In fact, for an array of identical processes, we only have to check one of them. In any case, we only have to check a *linear* number of statements and assertions. Contrast this to having to check (or test) an *exponential* number of program histories, as described in Section 2.1.

We will employ the technique of global invariants extensively in the remainder of the text. We illustrate the usefulness and power of the technique at the end of this section after first introducing the fourth technique for avoiding interference: synchronization.

2.7.4 Synchronization

Sequences of assignment statements that are within `await` statements appear to other processes to be an indivisible unit. Hence we can ignore the effects of the individual statements when considering whether one process interferes with another. It is sufficient to consider only whether the *entire* sequence of statements might cause interference. For example, consider the following atomic action:

```
⟨x = x+1; y = y+1;⟩
```

Neither assignment by itself can cause interference, because no other process can see a state in which **x** has been incremented but **y** has not yet been incremented. Only the pair of assignments might cause interference.

Internal states of program segments within angle brackets are also invisible. Hence, no assertion about an internal state can be interfered with by another process. For example, the assertion in the middle of the atomic action below is not a critical assertion:

```
{x == 0 ∧ y == 0}
⟨x = x+1;   {x == 1 ∧ y == 0}   y = y+1;⟩
{x == 1 ∧ y == 1}
```

These two attributes of atomic actions lead to two ways to use synchronization to avoid interference: mutual exclusion and condition synchronization. Consider the following:

```
co P1: ... a; ...
// P2: ... S1; {C} S2; ...
oc
```

Here, **a** is an assignment statement in process **P1**, and **S1** and **S2** are statements in process **P2**. Critical assertion **C** is the precondition of **S2**.

Suppose that **a** interferes with **C**. One way to avoid interference is to use mutual exclusion to "hide" assertion **C** from **a**. This is done by combining statements **S1** and **S2** in the second process into a single atomic action:

```
⟨S1; S2;⟩
```

This executes S1 and S2 atomically and hence makes state C invisible to other processes.

Another way to avoid interference is to use condition synchronization to strengthen the precondition of a. In particular, we can replace a by the following conditional atomic action:

⟨await (!C or B) a;⟩

Here, B is a predicate characterizing a set of states such that executing a will make C true. Hence the above statement avoids interference by either waiting until C is false—and hence statement S2 could not possibly be about to execute—or by ensuring that executing a will make C true—and hence that it would then be fine to execute S2.

2.7.5 An Example: The Array Copy Problem Revisited

Most concurrent programs employ a combination of the above techniques. Here we illustrate *all* of them in a single, simple program: the array copy problem shown in Figure 2.2. Recall that the program uses a shared buffer buf to copy the contents of array a in the producer process to array b in the consumer process.

The Producer and Consumer processes in Figure 2.2 alternate access to buf. First Producer deposits the first element of a in buf, then Consumer fetches it, then Producer deposits the second element of a, and so on. Variables p and c count the number of items that have been deposited and fetched, respectively. The await statements are used to synchronize access to buf. When p == c the buffer is empty (the previously deposited element has been fetched); when p > c the buffer is full.

Suppose the initial contents of a[n] is some collection of values A[n]. (The A[i] are called logical variables; they are simply placeholders for whatever the values actually are.) The goal is to prove that, upon termination of the above program, the contents of b[n] are the same as A[n], the values in array a. This goal can be proved by using the following global invariant:

$$PC\text{: } c <= p <= c+1 \wedge a[0{:}n-1] == A[0{:}n-1] \wedge$$
$$(p == c+1) \Rightarrow (buf == A[p-1])$$

Since the processes alternate access to buf, at all times p is equal to c, or p is one more than c. Array a is not altered, so a[i] is always equal to A[i]. Finally, when the buffer is full (i.e., when p == c+1), it contains A[p-1].

Predicate *PC* is true initially, because both p and c are initially zero. It is maintained by every assignment statement, as illustrated by the proof outline in

Figure 2.4. In the figure, *IP* is an invariant for the loop in the `Producer` process, and *IC* is an invariant for the loop in the `Consumer` process. Predicates *IP* and *IC* are related to predicate *PC* as indicated.

Figure 2.4 is another example of a proof outline, because there is an assertion before and after every statement, and each triple in the proof outline is true. The triples in each process follow directly from the assignment statements in each process. Assuming each process continually gets a chance to execute, the

```
int buf, p = 0, c = 0;
{PC: c <= p <= c+1 ∧ a[0:n-1] == A[0:n-1] ∧
            (p == c+1) ⇒ (buf == A[p-1])}

process Producer {
   int a[n];      # assume a[i] is initialized to A[i]
   {IP: PC ∧ p <= n}
   while (p < n) {
      {PC ∧ p < n}
      ⟨await (p == c);⟩   # delay until buffer empty
      {PC ∧ p < n ∧ p == c}
      buf = a[p];
      {PC ∧ p < n ∧ p == c ∧ buf == A[p]}
      p = p+1;
      {IP}
   }
   {PC ∧ p == n}
}

process Consumer {
   int b[n];
   {IC: PC ∧ c <= n ∧ b[0:c-1] == A[0:c-1]}
   while (c < n) {
      {IC ∧ c < n}
      ⟨await (p > c);⟩    # delay until buffer full
      {IC ∧ c < n ∧ p > c}
      b[c] = buf;
      {IC ∧ c < n ∧ p > c ∧ b[c] == A[c]}
      c = c+1;
      {IC}
   }
   {IC ∧ c == n}
}
```

Figure 2.4　Proof outline for the array copy program.

await statements terminate since first one guard is true, then the other, and so on. Hence, each process terminates after n iterations. When the program terminates, the postconditions of both processes are true. Hence the final program state satisfies the predicate:

$$PC \land p \; == \; n \land IC \land c \; == \; n$$

Consequently, array b contains a copy of array a.

The assertions in the two processes do not interfere with each other. Most of them are a combination of the global invariant *PC* and a local predicate. Hence they meet the requirements for noninterference described at the start of the section on Global Invariants. The four exceptions are the assertions that specify relations between the values of shared variables p and c. These are not interfered with because of the await statements in the program.

The role of the await statements in the array copy program is to ensure that the producer and consumer processes alternate access to the buffer. This plays two roles with respect to avoiding interference. First, it ensures that the processes cannot access buf at the same time; this is an instance of mutual exclusion. Second, it ensures that the producer does not overwrite items (overflow) and that the consumer does not read an item twice (underflow); this is an instance of condition synchronization.

To summarize, this example—even though it is simple—illustrates all four techniques for avoiding interference. First, many of the statements and many parts of the assertions in each process are disjoint. Second, we use weakened assertions about the values of the shared variables; for example, we say that buf == A[p-1], but only if p == c+1. Third, we use the global invariant *PC* to express the relationship between the values of the shared variables; even though each variable changes as the program executes, this relationship does not change! Finally, we use synchronization—expressed using await statements— to ensure the mutual exclusion and condition synchronization required for this program.

2.8 Safety and Liveness Properties

Recall from Section 2.1 that a property of a program is an attribute that is true of every possible history of that program. Every interesting property can be formulated as safety or liveness. A safety property asserts that nothing bad happens during execution; a liveness property asserts that something good eventually happens. In sequential programs, the key safety property is that the final state is correct, and the key liveness property is termination. These properties are equally important for concurrent programs. In addition, there are other interesting safety and liveness properties that apply to concurrent programs.

Two important safety properties in concurrent programs are mutual exclusion and absence of deadlock. For mutual exclusion, the bad thing is having more than one process executing critical sections of statements at the same time. For deadlock, the bad thing is having all processes waiting for conditions that will never occur.

Examples of liveness properties of concurrent programs are that a process will eventually get to enter a critical section, that a request for service will eventually be honored, or that a message will eventually reach its destination. Liveness properties are affected by scheduling policies, which determine which eligible atomic actions are next to execute.

In this section we describe two methods for proving safety properties. Then we describe different kinds of processor scheduling policies and how they affect liveness properties.

2.8.1 Proving Safety Properties

Every action a program takes is based on its state. If a program fails to satisfy a safety property, there must be some "bad" state that fails to satisfy the property. For example, if the mutual exclusion property fails to hold, there must be some state in which two (or more) processes are simultaneously in their critical sections. Or if processes deadlock, there must be some state in which deadlock occurs.

These observations lead to a simple method for proving that a program satisfies a safety property. Let *BAD* be a predicate that characterizes a bad program state. Then a program satisfies the associated safety property if *BAD* is false in every state in every possible history of the program. Given program s, to show that *BAD* is not true in any state requires showing that it is not true in the initial state, the second state, and so on, where the state is changed as a result of executing atomic actions.

Alternatively, and more powerfully, if a program is never to be in a *BAD* state, then it must always be in a *GOOD* state, where *GOOD* is equivalent to *BAD*. Hence, an effective way to ensure a safety property is to specify *BAD*, then negate *BAD* to yield *GOOD*, then ensure that *GOOD* is a global invariant—a predicate that is true in every program state. Synchronization can be used—as we have seen and will see many more times in later chapters—to ensure that a predicate is a global invariant.

The above is a general method for proving safety properties. There is a related, but somewhat more specialized method that is also very useful. Consider the following program fragment:

```
co # process 1
   ...; {pre(S1)} S1; ...
// # process 2
   ...; {pre(S2)} S2; ...
oc
```

There are two statements, one per process, and two associated preconditions (predicates that are true before each statement is executed). Assume that the predicates are not interfered with. Now, suppose that the conjunctions of the preconditions is false:

```
pre(S1) ∧ pre(S2) == false
```

This means that the two processes cannot be at these statements at the same time! This is because a predicate that is false characterizes *no* program state (the empty set of states, if you will). This method is called *exclusion of configurations*, because it excludes the program configuration in which the first process is in state `pre(S1)` at the same time that the second process is in state `pre(S2)`.

As an example, consider the proof outline of the array copy program in Figure 2.4. The `await` statement in each process can cause delay. The processes would deadlock if they were both delayed and neither could proceed. The `Producer` process is delayed if it is at its `await` statement and the delay condition is false; in that state, the following predicate is true:

$$PC \wedge p < n \wedge p \mathrel{!=} c$$

Hence, `p > c` when the `Producer` is delayed. Similarly, the `Consumer` process is delayed if it is at its `await` statement and the delay condition is false; that state satisfies

$$IC \wedge c < n \wedge p \mathrel{<=} c$$

Because `p > c` and `p <= c` cannot be true at the same time, the processes cannot simultaneously be in these states. Hence, deadlock cannot occur.

2.8.2 Scheduling Policies and Fairness

Most liveness properties depend on *fairness*, which is concerned with guaranteeing that processes get the chance to proceed, regardless of what other processes do. Each process executes a sequence of atomic actions. An atomic action in a process is *eligible* if it is the next atomic action in the process that could be executed. When there are several processes, there are several eligible atomic actions. A *scheduling policy* determines which one will be executed next. This section defines three degrees of fairness that a scheduling policy might provide.

Recall that an unconditional atomic action is one that does not have a delay condition. Consider the following simple program, in which the processes execute unconditional atomic actions:

```
bool continue = true;

co while (continue);
// continue = false;
oc
```

Suppose a scheduling policy assigns a processor to a process until that process either terminates or delays. If there is only one processor, the above program will not terminate if the first process is executed first. However, the program will terminate if the second process eventually gets a chance to execute. This is captured by the following definition.

(2.6) **Unconditional Fairness.** A scheduling policy is unconditionally fair if every unconditional atomic action that is eligible is executed eventually.

For the above program, round-robin would be an unconditionally fair scheduling policy on a single processor, and parallel execution would be an unconditionally fair policy on a multiprocessor.

When a program contains conditional atomic actions—**await** statements with Boolean conditions **B**—we need to make stronger assumptions to guarantee that processes will make progress. This is because a conditional atomic action cannot be executed until **B** is true.

(2.7) **Weak Fairness.** A scheduling policy is weakly fair if (1) it is unconditionally fair, and (2) every conditional atomic action that is eligible is executed eventually, assuming that its condition becomes true and then remains true until it is seen by the process executing the conditional atomic action.

In short, if ⟨ **await (B) S;** ⟩ is eligible and **B** becomes true, then **B** remains true at least until after the conditional atomic action has been executed. Round-robin and time slicing are weakly fair scheduling policies if every process gets a chance to execute. This is because any delayed process will eventually see that its delay condition is true.

Weak fairness is not, however, sufficient to ensure that any eligible **await** statement eventually executes. This is because the condition might change value—from false to true and back to false—while a process is delayed. In this case, we need a stronger scheduling policy.

(2.8)   **Strong Fairness.** A scheduling policy is strongly fair if (1) it is unconditionally fair, and (2) every conditional atomic action that is eligible is
executed eventually, assuming that its condition is infinitely often true.

A condition is infinitely often true if it is true an infinite number of times in every
execution history of a (nonterminating) program. To be strongly fair, a scheduling policy cannot happen only to select an action when the condition is false; it
must sometime select the action when the condition is true.

   To see the difference between weak and strong fairness, consider

```
bool continue = true, try = false;

co while (continue) { try = true; try = false;}
// ⟨await (try) continue = false;⟩
oc
```

With a strongly fair policy, this program will eventually terminate, because `try`
is infinitely often true. However, with a weakly fair policy, the program might
not terminate, because `try` is also infinitely often false.

   Unfortunately, it is impossible to devise a processor scheduling policy that
is both practical and strongly fair. Consider the above program again. On a
single processor, a scheduler that alternates the actions of the two processes
would be strongly fair since the second process would see a state in which `try` is
true; however, such a scheduler is impractical to implement. Round-robin and
time slicing are practical, but they are not strongly fair in general because
processes execute in unpredictable orders. A multiprocessor scheduler that
executes the processes in parallel is also practical, but it too is not strongly fair.
This is because the second process might always examine `try` when it is false.
This is unlikely, of course, but it is theoretically possible.

   To further clarify the different kinds of scheduling policies, consider again
the array copy program in Figures 2.2 and 2.4. As noted earlier, that program is
deadlock-free. Thus, the program will terminate as long as each process continues to get a chance to make progress. Each process will make progress as long as
the scheduling policy is weakly fair. This is because, when one process makes
the delay condition of the other true, that condition remains true until the other
process continues and changes shared variables.

   Both `await` statements in the array copy program have the form ⟨`await`
`(B);`⟩, and `B` refers to only one variable altered by the other process. Consequently, both `await` statements can be implemented by busy-waiting loops. For
example, ⟨`await (p == c);`⟩ in the `Producer` can be implemented by

```
while (p != c);
```

The program will terminate if the scheduling policy is unconditionally fair, because now there are no conditional atomic actions and the processes alternate access to the shared buffer. It is not generally the case, however, that an unconditionally fair scheduling policy will ensure termination of a busy-waiting loop. This is because an unconditionally fair policy might always schedule the atomic action that examines the loop condition when the condition is true, as shown in the example program above.

If all busy waiting loops in a program spin forever, a program is said to suffer from *livelock*—the program is alive, but the processes are not going anywhere. Livelock is the busy-waiting analog of deadlock, and absence of livelock, like absence of deadlock, is a safety property; the bad state is one in which every process is spinning and none of the delay conditions is true. On the other hand, progress for any one of the processes is a liveness property; the good thing being that the spin loop of an individual process eventually terminates.

Historical Notes

One of the first, and most influential, papers on concurrent programming was by Edsger Dijkstra [1965]. That paper introduced the critical section problem and the `parbegin` statement, which later became called the `cobegin` statement. Our `co` statement is a generalization of the `cobegin` statement. Another Dijkstra paper [1968] introduced the producer/consumer and dining philosophers problems, as well as others that we examine in the next few chapters.

Art Bernstein [1966] was the first to specify the conditions that are sufficient to ensure that two processes are independent and hence can be executed in parallel. Bernstein's conditions, as they are still called, are expressed in terms of the input and output sets of each process; the input set contains variables read by a process, and the output set contains variables written by a process. Bernstein's three conditions for independence of two processes are that the intersections of the (input, output), (output, input), and (output, output) sets are all disjoint. Bernstein's conditions also provide the basis for the data dependency analysis done by parallelizing compilers, a topic we describe in Chapter 12. Our definition of independence (2.1) employs read and write sets for each process, and a variable is in exactly one set for each process. This leads to a simpler, but equivalent, condition.

Most operating systems texts show how implementing assignment statements using registers and fine-grained atomic actions leads to the critical section problem in concurrent programs. Modern hardware ensures that there is *some* base level of atomicity—usually a word—for reading and writing memory. Lamport [1977b] contains an interesting discussion of how to implement atomic reads and writes of "words" if only single bytes can be read and written atomically; his solution does not require using a locking mechanism for mutual exclusion. (See Peterson [1983] for more recent results.)

The angle bracket notation for specifying coarse-grained atomic actions was also invented by Leslie Lamport. However, it was popularized by Dijkstra [1977]. Owicki and Gries [1976a] used `await B then S end` to specify atomic actions. The specific notation used in this book combines angle brackets and a variant of `await`. The terms *unconditional* and *conditional atomic actions* are due to Fred Schneider [Schneider and Andrews 1986].

There is a wealth of material on logical systems for proving properties of sequential and concurrent programs. Schneider [1997] provides excellent coverage of all the topics summarized in Sections 2.6 through 2.8—as well as many more—and gives extensive historical notes and references. The actual content of these sections was condensed and revised from Chapters 1 and 2 of my prior book [Andrews 1991]. That material, in turn, was based on earlier work [Schneider and Andrews 1986]. A brief history of formal logical systems and its application to program verification is given below; for more information and references, consult Schneider [1997] or Andrews [1991].

Formal logic is concerned with the formalization and analysis of systematic reasoning methods. Its origins go back to the ancient Greeks, and for the next two millennia logic was of interest mostly to philosophers. However, the discovery of non-Euclidean geometries in the nineteenth century spurred renewed, widespread interest among mathematicians. This led to a systematic study of mathematics itself as a formal logical system and hence gave rise to the field of mathematical logic—which is also called metamathematics. Indeed, between 1910 and 1913, Alfred North Whitehead and Bertrand Russell published the voluminous *Principia Mathematica*, which presented what was claimed to be a system for deriving all of mathematics from logic. Shortly thereafter, David Hilbert set out to prove rigorously that the system presented in *Principia Mathematica* was both sound and complete. However, in 1931 Kurt Gödel demonstrated that there were valid statements that did not have a proof in that system or in *any* similar axiomatic system.

Gödel's incompleteness result placed limitations on formal logical systems, but it certainly did not stop interest in or work on logic. Quite the contrary. Proving properties of programs is just one of many applications. Formal logic is covered in all standard textbooks on mathematical logic or metamathematics. A lighthearted, entertaining introduction to the topic can be found in Douglas Hofstadter's Pulitzer Prize–winning book *Gödel, Escher, Bach: An Eternal Golden Braid* [Hofstadter 1979], which explains Gödel's result and also describes how logic is related to computability and artificial intelligence.

Robert Floyd [1967] is generally credited with being the first to propose a technique for proving that programs are correct. His method involves associating a predicate with each arc in a flowchart in such a way that, if the arc is traversed, the predicate is true. Inspired by Floyd's work, Hoare [1969] developed the first formal logic for proving partial correctness properties of sequential programs. Hoare introduced the concept of a triple, the interpretation for triples, and axioms and inference rules for sequential statements (in his case, a subset of Algol). Any logical system for sequential programming that is based on this style has since come to be called a "Hoare Logic." Programming logic *PL* is an example of a Hoare Logic.

The first work on proving properties of concurrent programs was also based on a flowchart representation [Ashcroft and Manna 1971]. At about the same time, Hoare [1972] extended his partial correctness logic for sequential programs to include inference rules for concurrency and synchronization, with synchronization specified by conditional critical regions (which are similar to `await` statements). However, that logic was incomplete since assertions in one process could not reference variables in another, and global invariants could not reference local variables.

Susan Owicki, in a dissertation supervised by David Gries, was the first to develop a complete logic for proving partial correctness properties of concurrent programs [Owicki 1975; Owicki and Gries 1976a, 1976b]. The logic covered `cobegin` statements and synchronization by means of shared variables, semaphores, or conditional critical regions. That work described the at-most-once property (2.2), introduced and formalized the concept of interference freedom, and illustrated several of the techniques for avoiding interference described in Section 2.7. On a personal note, the author had the good fortune to be at Cornell while this research was being done.

The Owicki-Gries work addresses only three safety properties: partial correctness, mutual exclusion, and absence of deadlock. Leslie Lamport [1977a] independently developed an idea similar to interference freedom—monotone assertions—as part of a general method for proving both safety and liveness properties. His paper also introduced the terms *safety* and *liveness*. The method in Section 2.8 for proving a safety property using a global invariant is based on Lamport's method. The method of exclusion of configurations is due to Schneider [Schneider and Andrews 1986]; it is in turn a generalization of the Owicki-Gries method.

Francez [1986] contains a thorough discussion of fairness and its relation to termination, synchronization, and guard evaluation. The terminology for unconditionally fair, weakly fair, and strongly fair scheduling policies comes from that book, which contains an extensive bibliography. These scheduling policies were first defined and formalized in Lehman et al. [1981], although with somewhat different terminology.

Programming logic (*PL*) is a logic for proving safety properties. One way to construct formal proofs of liveness properties is to extend *PL* with two temporal operators: henceforth and eventually. These enable one to make assertions about sequences of states and hence about the future. Such a *temporal logic* was first introduced in Pnueli [1977]. Owicki and Lamport [1982] show how to use temporal logic and invariants to prove liveness properties of concurrent programs. Again, see Schneider [1997] for an overview of temporal logic and how to use it to prove liveness properties.

References

Andrews, G. R. 1991. *Concurrent Programming: Principles and Practice.* Menlo Park, CA: Benjamin/Cummings.

Ashcroft, E., and Z. Manna. 1971. Formalization of properties of parallel programs. *Machine Intelligence* 6: 17–41.

Bernstein, A. J. 1966. Analysis of programs for parallel processing. *IEEE Trans. on Computers EC-15*, 5 (October): 757–62.

Dijkstra, E. W. 1965. Solution of a problem in concurrent programming control. *Comm. ACM* 8, 9 (September): 569.

Dijkstra, E. W. 1968. Cooperating sequential processes. In F. Genuys, ed. *Programming Languages.* New York: Academic Press, pp. 43–112.

Dijkstra, E. W. 1977. On two beautiful solutions designed by Martin Rem. EWD 629. Reprinted in E. W. Dijkstra. *Selected Writings on Computing: A Personal Perspective.* New York: Springer-Verlag, 1982, pp. 313–18.

Floyd, R. W. 1967. Assigning meanings to programs. *Proc Amer. Math. Society Symp. in Applied Mathematics* 19: 19–31.

Francez, N. 1986. *Fairness.* New York: Springer-Verlag.

Hoare, C. A. R. 1969. An axiomatic basis for computer programming. *Comm. ACM* 12, 10 (October): 576–80, 583.

Hoare, C. A. R. 1972. Towards a theory of parallel programming. In C. A. R. Hoare and R. H. Perrott, eds. *Operating Systems Techniques.* New York: Academic Press.

Hofstadter, D. J. 1979. *Gödel, Escher, Bach: An Eternal Golden Braid.* New York: Vintage Books.

Lamport, L. 1977a. Proving the correctness of multiprocess programs. *IEEE Trans. on Software Engr.* SE-3, 2 (March): 125–43.

Lamport, L. 1977b. Concurrent reading and writing. *Comm. ACM* 20, 11 (November): 806–11.

Lehman, D., A. Pnueli, and J. Stavii. 1981. Impartiality, justice, and fairness: The ethics of concurrent termination. *Proc. Eighth Colloq. on Automata, Langs., and Prog.*, Lecture Notes in Computer Science Vol. 115. New York: Springer-Verlag, 264–77.

Owicki, S. S. 1975. Axiomatic proof techniques for parallel programs. TR 75–251. Doctoral dissertation, Ithaca, NY: Cornell University.

Owicki, S. S., and D. Gries. 1976a. An axiomatic proof technique for parallel programs. *Acta Informatica* 6: 319–40.

Owicki, S. S., and D. Gries. 1976b. Verifying properties of parallel programs: An axiomatic approach. *Comm. ACM* 19, 5 (May): 279–85.

Owicki, S., and L. Lamport. 1982. Proving liveness properties of concurrent programs. *ACM Trans. on Prog. Languages and Systems* 4, 3 (July): 455–95.

Peterson, G. L. 1983. Concurrent reading while writing. *ACM. Trans. on Prog. Languages and Systems* 5, 1 (January): 46–55.

Pnueli, A. 1977. The temporal logic of programs. *Proc. 18th Symp. on the Foundations of Computer Science*, November, 46–57.

Schneider, F. B. 1997. *On Concurrent Programming.* New York: Springer.

Schneider, F. B., and G. R. Andrews. 1986. Concepts for concurrent programming. In *Current Trends in Concurrency*, Lecture Notes in Computer Science Vol. 224. New York: Springer-Verlag, 669–716.

Exercises

2.1 Consider the outline of the program in Figure 2.1 that prints all the lines in a file that contain `pattern`.

(a) Develop the missing code for synchronizing access to `buffer`. Use the `await` statement to program the synchronization code.

(b) Extend your program so that it reads two files and prints all the lines that contain `pattern`. Identify the independent activities and use a separate process for each. Show all synchronization code that is required.

2.2 Consider the solution to the array copy problem in Figure 2.2. Modify the code so that `p` is local to the producer process and `c` is local to the consumer. Hence, those variables cannot be used to synchronize access to `buf`. Instead, use two new Boolean-valued shared variables, `empty` and `full`, to synchronize the two processes. Initially, `empty` is `true` and `full` is `false`. Give the new code for the producer and consumer processes. Use `await` statements to program the synchronization.

2.3   The Unix `tee` command is invoked by executing:

```
tee filename
```

The command reads the standard input and writes it to both the standard output and to file `filename`. In short, it produces two copies of the input.

(a) Write a sequential program to implement this command.

(b) Parallelize your sequential program to use three processes: one to read from standard input, one to write to standard output, and one to write to file `file-name`. Use the "co inside `while`" style of program.

(c) Change your answer to (b) so that it uses the "`while` inside co" style. In particular, create the processes once. Use double buffering so that you can read and write in parallel. Use the `await` statement to synchronize access to the buffers.

2.4   Consider a simplified version of the Unix `diff` command for comparing two text files. The new command is invoked as

```
differ filename1 filename2
```

It examines the two files and prints out all lines in the two files that are different. In particular, for each pair of lines that differ, the command writes two lines to standard output:

```
lineNumber:   line from file 1
lineNumber:   line from file 2
```

If one file is longer than the other, the command also writes one line of output for each extra line in the longer file.

(a) Write a sequential program to implement `differ`.

(b) Parallelize your sequential program to use three processes: two to read the files, and one to write to standard output. Use the "co inside `while`" style of program.

(c) Change your answer to (b) so that it uses the "`while` inside co" style. In particular, create the processes once. Use double buffering for each file, so that you can read and write in parallel. Use the `await` statement to synchronize access to the buffers.

2.5 Given integer arrays `a[1:m]` and `b[1:n]`, assume that each array is sorted in ascending order, and that the values in each array are distinct.

(a) Develop a sequential program to compute the number of different values that appear in *both* `a` and `b`.

(b) Identify the independent operations in your sequential program and then modify the program to execute the independent operations in parallel. Store the answer in a shared variable. Use the `co` statement to specify concurrency and use the `await` statement to specify any synchronization that might be required.

2.6 Assume you have a tree that is represented using a linked structure. In particular, each node of the tree is a structure (record) that has three fields: a value and pointers to the left and right subtrees. Assume a null pointer is represented by the constant `null`.

Write a recursive parallel program to compute the sum of the values of all nodes in the tree. The total execution time of the computation should be on the order of the height of the tree.

2.7 Assume that the integer array `a[1:n]` has been initialized.

(a) Write an iterative parallel program to compute the sum of the elements of `a` using `PR` processes. Each process should work on a strip of the array. Assume that `PR` is a factor of `n`.

(b) Write a recursive parallel program to compute the sum of the elements of the array. Use a divide-and-conquer strategy to cut the size of the problem in half for each recursive step. Stop recursing when the problem size is less than or equal to some threshold `T`. Use the sequential iterative algorithm for the base case.

2.8 A queue is often represented using a linked list. Assume that two variables, `head` and `tail`, point to the first and last elements of the list. Each element contains a data field and a link to the next element. Assume that a null link is represented by the constant `null`.

(a) Write routines to (1) search the list for the first element (if any) that contains data value `d`, (2) insert a new element at the end of the list, and (3) delete the element from the front of the list. The search and delete routines should return `null` if they cannot succeed.

(b) Now assume that several processes access the linked list. Identify the read and write sets of each routine, as defined in (2.1). Which combinations of routines can be executed in parallel? Which combinations of routines must execute one at a time (i.e., atomically)?

(c) Add synchronization code to the three routines to enforce the synchronization you identified in your answer to (b). Make your atomic actions as small as possible, and do not delay a routine unnecessarily. Use the `await` statement to program the synchronization code.

2.9 Consider the code fragment in Section 2.6 that sets m to the maximum of x and y. The triple for the `if` statement in that code fragment uses the If Statement Rule from Figure 2.3. What are the predicates P, Q, and B in this application of the If Statement Rule?

2.10 Consider the following program:

```
int x = 0, y = 0;
co x = x + 1; x = x + 2;
// x = x + 2; y = y - x;
oc
```

(a) Suppose each assignment statement is implemented by a single machine instruction and hence is atomic. How many possible histories are there? What are the possible final values of x and y?

(b) Suppose each assignment statement is implemented by three atomic actions that load a register, add or subtract a value from that register, then store the result. How many possible histories are there now? What are the possible final values of x and y?

2.11 Consider the following program:

```
int u = 0, v = 1, w = 2, x;
co x = u + v + w;
// u = 3;
// v = 4;
// w = 5;
oc
```

Assume that the atomic actions are reading and writing individual variables.

(a) What are the possible final values of x, assuming that expression u + v + w is evaluated left to right?

(b) What are the possible final values of x if expression u + v + w can be evaluated in any order?

2.12 Consider the following program:

```
int x = 2, y = 3;
co ⟨x = x + y;⟩ // ⟨y = x * y;⟩
```

(a) What are the possible final values of x and y?

(b) Suppose the angle brackets are removed and each assignment statement is now implemented by three atomic actions: read a variable, add or multiply, and write to a variable. Now what are the possible final values of x and y?

2.13   Consider the following three statements:

```
S₁:   x = x + y;
S₂:   y = x - y;
S₃:   x = x - y;
```

Assume that x is initially 2 and that y is initially 5. For each of the following, what are the possible final values of x and y? Explain your answers.

(a) S₁; S₂; S₃;

(b) co ⟨S₁;⟩ // ⟨S₂;⟩ // ⟨S₃;⟩ oc

(c) co ⟨await (x > y) S₁; S₂;⟩ // ⟨S₃;⟩ oc

2.14   Consider the following program:

```
int x = 1, y = 1;
co ⟨x = x + y;⟩
// y = 0;
// x = x - y;
oc
```

(a) Does the program meet the requirements of the At-Most-Once Property (2.2)? Explain.

(b) What are the final values of x and y? Explain your answer.

2.15   Consider the following program:

```
int x = 0, y = 10;
co while (x != y)   x = x + 1;
// while (x != y)   y = y - 1;
oc
```

(a) Does the program meet the requirements of the At-Most-Once Property (2.2)? Explain.

(b) Will the program terminate? Always? Sometimes? Never? Explain your answer.

2.16 Consider the following program:

```
int x = 0;
co ⟨await (x != 0)   x = x - 2;⟩
// ⟨await (x != 0)   x = x - 3;⟩
// ⟨await (x == 0)   x = x + 5;⟩
oc
```

Develop a proof outline that demonstrates that the final value of **x** is **0**. Use the technique of weakened assertions. Identify which assertions are critical assertions, as defined in (2.5), and show that they are not interfered with.

2.17 Consider the following program:

```
co ⟨await (x >= 3)   x = x - 3; ⟩
// ⟨await (x >= 2)   x = x - 2; ⟩
// ⟨await (x == 1)   x = x + 5; ⟩
oc
```

For what initial values of **x** does the program terminate, assuming scheduling is weakly fair? What are the corresponding final values? Explain your answer.

2.18 Consider the following program:

```
co ⟨await (x > 0)   x = x - 1;⟩
// ⟨await (x < 0)   x = x + 2;⟩
// ⟨await (x == 0)   x = x - 1;⟩
oc
```

For what initial values of **x** does the program terminate, assuming scheduling is weakly fair? What are the corresponding final values? Explain your answer.

2.19 Consider the following program:

```
int x = 10, y = 0;
co  while (x != y) x = x - 1; y = y + 1;
//  ⟨await (x == y);⟩ x = 8; y = 2;
oc
```

Explain what it takes for the program to terminate. When the program does terminate, what are the final values for **x** and **y**?

2.20 Let **a[1:m]** and **b[1:n]** be integer arrays, **m > 0** and **n > 0**. Write predicates to express the following properties.

(a) All elements of **a** are less than all elements of **b**.

(b) Either **a** or **b** contains a single zero, but not both.

(c) It is not the case that both **a** and **b** contain zeros.

(d) The values in **b** are the same as the values in **a**, except they are in the reverse order. (Assume for this part that **m** == **n**.)

(e) Every element of **a** is an element of **b**.

(f) Some element of **a** is larger than some element of **b**, and vice versa.

2.21 The `if-then-else` statement has the form:

```
if (B)
  S1;
else
  S2;
```

If **B** is true, **S1** is executed; otherwise, **S2** is executed. Give an inference rule for this statement. Look at the If Statement Rule for ideas.

2.22 Consider the following `for` statement:

```
for [i = 1 to n]
  S;
```

Rewrite the statement using a `while` loop plus explicit assignment statements to the quantifier variable **i**. Then use the Assignment Axiom and While Statement Rule (Figure 2.3) to develop an inference rule for such a `for` statement.

2.23 The `repeat` statement

```
repeat
  S;
until (B);
```

repeatedly executes statement **S** until Boolean expression **B** is true at the end of some iteration.

(a) Develop an inference rule for `repeat`.

(b) Using your answer to (a), develop a proof outline that demonstrates that `repeat` is equivalent to

```
S; while (!B) S;
```

2.24 Consider the following precondition and assignment statement.

```
{x >= 4} ⟨x = x - 4;⟩
```

For each of the following triples, show whether the above statement interferes with the triple.

(a) `{x >= 0} <x = x + 5;> {x >= 5}`

(b) `{x >= 0} <x = x + 5;> {x >= 0}`

(c) `{x >= 10} <x = x + 5;> {x >= 11}`

(d) `{x >= 10} <x = x + 5;> {x >= 12}`

(e) `{x is odd} <x = x + 5;> {x is even}`

(f) `{x is odd} <y = x + 1> {y is even}`

(g) `{y is odd} <y = y + 1;> {y is even}`

(h) `{x is a multiple of 3} y = x; {y is a multiple of 3}`

2.25   Consider the following program:

```
int x = V1, y = V2;
x = x + y;
y = x - y;
x = x - y;
```

Add assertions before and after each statement to characterize the effects of this program. In particular, what are the final values of **x** and **y**?

2.26   Consider the following program:

```
int x, y;
co x = x - 1; x = x + 1;
// y = y + 1; y = y - 1;
oc
```

Show that `{x == y}` S `{x == y}` is a theorem, where S is the **co** statement. Show all noninterference proofs in detail.

2.27   Consider the following program:

```
int x = 0;
co <x = x+2;> // <x = x+3;> // <x = x+4;> oc
```

Prove that `{x == 0}` S `{x == 9}` is a theorem, where S is the **co** statement. Use the technique of weakened assertions.

2.28   (a) Write a parallel program that sets Boolean variable **allzero** to true if integer array **a[1:n]** contains all zeros; otherwise, the program should set **allzero** to false. Use a **co** statement to examine all array elements in parallel.

(b) Develop a proof outline that shows that your solution is correct. Show that the processes are interference-free.

2.29 (a) Develop a program to find the maximum value in integer array `a[1:n]` by searching even and odd subscripts of `a` in parallel.

(b) Develop a proof outline that shows that your solution is correct. Show that the processes are interference-free.

2.30 You are given three integer-valued functions: `f(i)`, `g(j)`, and `h(k)`. The domain of each function is the nonnegative integers. The range of each function is increasing; for example, `f(i) < f(i+1)` for all `i`. There is at least one value common to the range of the three functions. (This has been called the earliest common meeting time problem, with the ranges of the functions being the times at which three people can meet.)

(a) Write a concurrent program to set `i`, `j`, and `k` to the smallest integers such that `f(i) == g(j) == h(k)`. Use `co` to do comparisons in parallel. (This program uses fine-grained parallelism.)

(b) Develop a proof outline that shows that your solution is correct. Show that the processes are interference-free.

2.31 Assume that the triples $\{P_1\}$ `S`$_1$ $\{Q_1\}$ and $\{P_2\}$ `S`$_2$ $\{Q_2\}$ are both true and that they are interference-free. Assume that `S`$_1$ contains an `await` statement $\langle$`await (B) T`$\rangle$. Let `S`$_1$′ be `S`$_1$ with the `await` statement replaced by

```
while (!B);
T;
```

Answer the following as independent questions.

(a) Will $\{P_1\}$ `S`$_1$′ $\{Q_1\}$ still be true? Carefully explain your answer. Is it true always? Sometimes? Never?

(b) Will $\{P_1\}$ `S`$_1$′ $\{Q_1\}$ and $\{P_2\}$ `S`$_2$ $\{Q_2\}$ still be interference-free? Again, carefully explain your answer. Will they be interference-free always? Sometimes? Never?

2.32 Consider the following concurrent program:

```
int s = 1;
process foo[i = 1 to 2] {
  while (true) {
    〈await (s > 0) s = s-1;〉
    S_i;
    〈s = s+1;〉
  }
}
```

Assume s_i is a statement list that does not modify shared variable s.

(a) Develop proof outlines for the two processes. Demonstrate that the proofs of the processes are interference-free. Then use the proof outlines and the method of exclusion of configurations in Section 2.8 to show that s_1 and s_2 cannot execute at the same time and that the program is deadlock-free. (*Hint*: You will need to introduce auxiliary variables to the program and proof outlines. These variables should keep track of the location of each process.)

(b) What scheduling policy is required to ensure that a process delayed at its first await statement will eventually be able to proceed? Explain.

2.33 Consider the following program:

```
int x = 10, c = true;

co ⟨await x == 0⟩; c = false;
// while (c) ⟨x = x - 1⟩;
oc
```

(a) Will the program terminate if scheduling is weakly fair? Explain.

(b) Will the program terminate if scheduling is strongly fair? Explain.

(c) Add the following as a third arm of the co statement:

```
while (c) {if (x < 0) ⟨x = 10⟩;}
```

Repeat parts (a) and (b) for this three-process program.

2.34 The 8-queens problem is concerned with placing 8 queens on a chess board in such a way that no one queen can attack another. One can attack another if both are in the same row or column or are on the same diagonal.

Write a parallel recursive program to generate all 92 solutions to the 8-queens problem. (*Hint*: Use a recursive procedure to try queen placements and a second procedure to check whether a given placement is acceptable.)

2.35 The stable marriage problem is the following. Let Man[1:n] and Woman[1:n] be arrays of processes. Each man ranks the women from 1 to n, and each woman ranks the men from 1 to n. (A ranking is a permutation of the integers from 1 to n.) A *pairing* is a one-to-one correspondence of men and women. A pairing is *stable* if, for two men Man[i] and Man[j] and their paired women Woman[p] and Woman[q], both of the following conditions are satisfied:

1. Man[i] ranks Woman[p] higher than Woman[q], or Woman[q] ranks Man[j] higher than Man[i]; and

2.   `Man[j]` ranks `Woman[q]` higher than `Woman[p]`, or `Woman[p]` ranks `Man[i]` higher than `Man[j]`.

Put differently, a pairing is unstable if a man and woman would both prefer each other to their current pair. A solution to the stable marriage problem is a set of **n** pairings, all of which are stable.

(a) Give a predicate that specifies the goal for the stable marriage problem.

(b) Write a parallel program to solve the stable marriage problem. Be sure to explain your solution strategy. Also give pre- and postconditions for each process and invariants for each loop.

Locks and Barriers

Recall that concurrent programs employ two basic kinds of synchronization: mutual exclusion and condition synchronization. This chapter examines two important problems—critical sections and barriers—that illustrate how to program these kinds of synchronization. The critical section problem is concerned with implementing atomic actions in software; the problem arises in most concurrent programs. A barrier is a synchronization point that all processes must reach before any process is allowed to proceed; barriers are needed in many parallel programs.

Mutual exclusion is typically implemented by means of *locks* that protect critical sections of code. Section 3.1 defines the critical section problem and presents a coarse-grained solution that uses the `await` statement to implement a lock. Section 3.2 develops fine-grained solutions using what are called spin locks. Section 3.3 presents three fair solutions: the tie-breaker algorithm, the ticket algorithm, and the bakery algorithm. The various solutions illustrate different ways to approach the problem and have different performance and fairness attributes. The solutions to the critical section problem are also important, because they can be used to implement `await` statements and hence arbitrary atomic actions. We show how to do this at the end of Section 3.2.

The last half of the chapter introduces three techniques for parallel computing: barrier synchronization, data parallel algorithms, and what is called a bag of tasks. As noted earlier, many problems can be solved by parallel iterative algorithms in which several identical processes repeatedly manipulate a shared array. This kind of algorithm is called a *data parallel algorithm* since the shared data is manipulated in parallel. In such an algorithm, each iteration typically depends on the results of the previous iteration. Hence, at the end of an iteration, faster processes need to wait for the slower ones before beginning the next iteration. This kind of synchronization point is called a *barrier*. Section 3.4 describes various ways to implement barrier synchronization and discusses the performance trade-offs between them. Section 3.5 gives several examples of data parallel algorithms that use barriers and also briefly describes the design of synchronous multiprocessors (SIMD machines), which are especially suited to implementing data parallel algorithms. This is because SIMD machines execute instructions in lock step on every processor; hence, they provide barriers automatically after every machine instruction.

Section 3.6 presents another useful technique for parallel computing called a *bag of tasks* (or a work farm). This approach can be used to implement recursive parallelism and to implement iterative parallelism when there is a fixed number of independent tasks. An important attribute of the bag-of-tasks paradigm is that it facilitates load balancing—namely, ensuring that each processor does about the same amount of work. The bag-of-tasks paradigm employs locks to implement the bag and barrier-like synchronization to detect when a computation is done.

The programs in this chapter employ *busy waiting*, which is an implementation of synchronization in which a process repeatedly checks a condition until it becomes true. The virtue of busy waiting synchronization is that we can implement it using only the machine instructions available on modern processors. Although busy waiting is inefficient when processes share a processor (and hence their execution is interleaved), it is efficient when each process executes on its own processor. Large multiprocessors have been used for many years to support high-performance scientific computations. Small-scale (two to four CPU) multiprocessors are becoming common in workstations and even personal computers. The operating system kernels for multiprocessors employ busy waiting synchronization, as we shall see later in Section 6.2. Moreover, hardware itself employs busy waiting synchronization—for example, to synchronize data transfers on memory busses and local networks.

Software libraries for multiprocessor machines include routines for locks and sometimes for barriers. Those library routines are implemented using the techniques described in this chapter. Two examples of such libraries are Pthreads, described at the end of Chapter 4, and OpenMP, described in Chapter 12.

3.1 The Critical Section Problem

The *critical section problem* is one of the classic concurrent programming problems. It was the first problem to be studied extensively and remains of interest since most concurrent programs have critical sections of code. Moreover, a solution to the problem can be used to implement arbitrary `await` statements. This section defines the problem and develops a coarse-grained solution. The next two sections develop a series of fine-grained solutions that illustrate various ways to solve the problem and that use different kinds of machine instructions.

In the critical section problem, n processes repeatedly execute a critical then a noncritical section of code. The critical section is preceded by an entry protocol and followed by an exit protocol. Thus, we assume here that the processes have the following form:

(3.1)
```
process CS[i = 1 to n] {
    while (true) {
        entry protocol;
        critical section;
        exit protocol;
        noncritical section;
    }
}
```

Each critical section is a sequence of statements that access some shared object. Each noncritical section is another sequence of statements. We assume that a process that enters its critical section will eventually exit; thus, a process may terminate only outside its critical section. Our task is to design entry and exit protocols that satisfy the following four properties.

(3.2) **Mutual Exclusion.** At most one process at a time is executing its critical section.

(3.3) **Absence of Deadlock (Livelock).** If two or more processes are trying to enter their critical sections, at least one will succeed.

(3.4) **Absence of Unnecessary Delay.** If a process is trying to enter its critical section and the other processes are executing their noncritical sections or have terminated, the first process is not prevented from entering its critical section.

(3.5) **Eventual Entry.** A process that is attempting to enter its critical section will eventually succeed.

The first three are safety properties, the fourth is a liveness property. For mutual exclusion, the bad state is one in which two processes are in their critical section. For absence of deadlock, the bad state is one in which all the processes are waiting to enter, but none is able to do so. (This is called *absence* of *livelock* in a busy-waiting solution, because the processes are alive but looping forever.) For absence of unnecessary delay, the bad state is one in which the one process that wants to enter cannot do so, even though no other process is in the critical section. Eventual entry is a liveness property since it depends on the scheduling policy, as we shall see.

A trivial way to solve the critical section problem is to enclose each critical section in angle brackets—that is, to use unconditional **await** statements. Mutual exclusion follows immediately from the semantics of angle brackets. The other three properties would be satisfied if scheduling is unconditionally fair since that scheduling policy ensures that a process attempting to execute the atomic action corresponding to its critical section would eventually get to do so, no matter what the other processes did. However, this "solution" begs the issue of how to implement angle brackets.

While all four properties above are important, mutual exclusion is the most essential. Thus, we focus on it first and then consider how also to achieve the other properties. To specify the mutual exclusion property, we need a way to indicate whether a process is in its critical section. To simplify notation, we develop a solution for two processes, **CS1** and **CS2**; the solution generalizes readily to one for **n** processes.

Let **in1** and **in2** be Boolean variables that are initially false. When process **CS1** (**CS2**) is in its critical section, we will set **in1** (**in2**) true. The bad state we want to avoid is one in which both **in1** and **in2** are true. Thus, we want every state to satisfy the negation of the bad state:

MUTEX: ¬(**in1** ∧ **in2**)

Predicate *MUTEX* needs to be a global invariant, as defined in Section 2.7.

For *MUTEX* to be a global invariant, it has to be true in the initial state and after each assignment to **in1** or **in2**. In particular, before process **CS1** enters its critical section—and hence sets **in1** true—it needs to make sure that **in2** is false. This can be implemented by using a conditional atomic action:

⟨**await** (!**in2**) **in1** = **true**;⟩

The processes are symmetric, so we use the same kind of conditional atomic action for the entry protocol in process **CS2**. What then about the exit protocols? It is never necessary to delay when leaving a critical section, so we do not need to guard the assignments that set **in1** and **in2** false.

The solution is shown in Figure 3.1. By construction, the program satisfies the mutual exclusion property. Deadlock is avoided because if each process were blocked in its entry protocol, then both **in1** and **in2** would have to be true, but this contradicts the fact that both are false at this point in the code. Unnecessary delay is avoided because one process blocks only if the other one is not in its

```
bool in1 = false, in2 = false;
## MUTEX:  ¬(in1 ∧ in2) -- global invariant
process CS1 {
  while (true) {
    ⟨await (!in2) in1 = true;⟩   /* entry */
    critical section;
    in1 = false;                 /* exit  */
    noncritical section;
  }
}
process CS2 {
  while (true) {
    ⟨await (!in1) in2 = true;⟩   /* entry */
    critical section;
    in2 = false;                 /* exit  */
    noncritical section;
  }
}
```

Figure 3.1   Critical section problem: Coarse-grained solution.

critical section. (All three of these properties can be proven formally using the method of exclusion of configurations introduced in Section 2.8.)

Finally, consider the liveness property that a process trying to enter its critical section eventually is able to do so. If CS1 is trying to enter but cannot, then in2 is true, so CS2 is in its critical section. By the assumption that a process in its critical section eventually exits, in2 will eventually become false and hence CS1's entry guard will become true. If CS1 is still not allowed entry, it is either because the scheduler is unfair or because CS2 again gains entry to its critical section. In the latter situation, the above scenario repeats, so eventually in2 becomes false. Thus, in2 becomes false infinitely often—or CS2 halts, in which case in2 becomes and remains false. A strongly fair scheduling policy is required to ensure that CS1 eventually gains entry in either case. (The argument for CS2 is symmetric.) However, recall that a strongly fair scheduler is impractical. We will address this issue in Section 3.3.

3.2 Critical Sections: Spin Locks

The coarse-grained solution in Figure 3.1 employs two variables. To generalize the solution to n processes, we would have to use n variables. However, there

```
bool lock = false;
process CS1 {
  while (true) {
    ⟨await (!lock) lock = true;⟩   /* entry */
    critical section;
    lock = false;                  /* exit */
    noncritical section;
  }
}
process CS2 {
  while (true) {
    ⟨await (!lock) lock = true;⟩   /* entry */
    critical section;
    lock = false;                  /* exit */
    noncritical section;
  }
}
```

Figure 3.2   Critical sections using locks.

are only two interesting states: some process is in its critical section or no process is. One variable is sufficient to distinguish between these two states, independent of the number of processes.

Let `lock` be a Boolean variable that indicates when a process is in a critical section. That is, `lock` is true when either `in1` or `in2` is true, and it is false otherwise. Thus we have the following requirement:

```
lock == (in1 ∨ in2)
```

By using `lock` in place of `in1` and `in2`, the entry and exit protocols in Figure 3.1 can be implemented as shown in Figure 3.2.

A virtue of the entry and exit protocols in Figure 3.2 relative to those in Figure 3.1 is that they can be used to solve the critical section problem for any number of processes, not just two. In particular, any number of processes could share `lock` and execute the same protocols.

3.2.1 Test and Set

The significance of the above change of variables is that almost all machines, especially multiprocessors, have some special instruction that can be used to implement the conditional atomic actions in Figure 3.2. Here we use one called

Test and Set. We use another one, Fetch and Add, in the next section. Additional special instructions are described in the exercises.

The Test-and-Set (`TS`) instruction takes a shared `lock` variable as an argument and returns a Boolean result. As an atomic action, `TS` reads and saves the value of `lock`, sets `lock` to true, then returns the saved initial value of `lock`. The effect of the instruction is captured by the following function:

```
(3.6)  bool TS(bool lock) {
           ⟨ bool initial = lock;   /* save initial value */
             lock = true;           /* set lock */
             return initial; ⟩      /* return initial value */
       }
```

Using `TS`, we can implement the coarse-grained solution in Figure 3.2 by the algorithm in Figure 3.3. In particular, the conditional atomic actions in Figure 3.2 are replaced by loops that do not terminate until `lock` is false, and hence `TS` returns false. Since all processes execute the same protocols, the solution as shown works for any number of processes. When a lock variable is used as in Figure 3.3, it is typically called a *spin lock*. This is because the processes keep looping (spinning) while waiting for the lock to be cleared.

The program in Figure 3.3 has the following properties. Mutual exclusion (3.2) is ensured because, if two or more processes are trying to enter their critical section, only one can succeed in being the first to change the value of `lock` from false to true; hence, only one will terminate its entry protocol. Absence of deadlock (3.3) results from the fact that, if both processes are in their entry protocols, `lock` is false, and hence one of the processes will succeed in entering its critical section. Unnecessary delay (3.4) is avoided because, if both processes are outside their critical section, `lock` is false, and hence one can successfully enter if the other is executing its noncritical section or has terminated.

```
bool lock = false;              /* shared lock */

process CS[i = 1 to n] {
  while (true) {
    while (TS(lock)) skip;      /* entry protocol */
    critical section;
    lock = false;              /* exit protocol   */
    noncritical section;
  }
}
```

Figure 3.3   Critical sections using Test and Set.

On the other hand, eventual entry (3.5) is not necessarily guaranteed. If scheduling is strongly fair, a process trying to enter its critical section will eventually succeed, because `lock` will become false infinitely often. If scheduling is only weakly fair—which is most commonly the case—then a process could spin forever in its entry protocol. However, this can happen only if there are always other processes trying and succeeding to enter their critical sections, which should not be the case in practice. Hence, the solution in Figure 3.3 is likely to be fair.

A solution to the critical section problem similar to the one in Figure 3.3 can be employed on any machine that has some instruction that tests and alters a shared variable as a single atomic action. For example, some machines have an increment instruction that increments an integer value and also sets a condition code indicating whether the result is positive or nonnegative. Using this instruction, the entry protocol can be based on the transition from zero to one. The exercises consider several representative instructions. (This kind of question is a favorite of exam writers!)

The spin-lock solutions we have developed—and the ones you may have to construct—all have the following attribute, which is worth remembering:

(3.7)   **Exit Protocols in Spin-Lock Solutions.** In a spin-lock solution to the critical section problem, the exit protocol should simply reset the shared variables to their initial values.

In Figure 3.1, this is a state in which `in1` and `in2` are both false. In Figures 3.2 and 3.3, this is a state in which `lock` is false.

3.2.2 Test and Test and Set

Although the solution in Figure 3.3 is correct, experiments on multiprocessors have shown that it can lead to poor performance if several processes are competing for access to a critical section. This is because `lock` is a shared variable and every delayed process continuously references it. This "hot spot" causes *memory contention*, which degrades the performance of memory units and processor-memory interconnection networks.

In addition, the `TS` instruction writes into `lock` every time it is executed, even when the value of `lock` does not change. Since shared-memory multiprocessors employ caches to reduce traffic to primary memory, this makes `TS` significantly more expensive than an instruction that merely reads a shared variable. (When a variable is written by one processor, the caches on other processors need to be invalidated or altered if they contain a copy of the variable.)

```
bool lock = false;                  /* shared lock */

process CS[i = 1 to n] {
  while (true) {
    while (lock) skip;              /* entry protocol */
    while (TS(lock)) {
      while (lock) skip;
    }
    critical section;
    lock = false;                   /* exit protocol  */
    noncritical section;
  }
}
```

Figure 3.4   Critical sections using Test and Test and Set.

Memory contention and cache invalidation overhead can both be reduced by modifying the entry protocol. Instead of simply spinning until a `TS` instruction returns true, we can increase the likelihood that it returns true by using the following entry protocol:

```
while (lock) skip;        /* spin while lock set  */
while (TS(lock)) {        /* try to grab the lock */
  while (lock) skip;      /* spin again if fail   */
}
```

This is called a *Test-and-Test-and-Set protocol* because a process merely tests `lock` until there is the possibility that `TS` can succeed. In the two additional loops, `lock` is only examined, so its value can be read from a local cache without affecting other processors. Memory contention is thus reduced, but it does not disappear. In particular, when `lock` is cleared at least one and possibly all delayed processes will execute `TS`, even though only one can proceed. Below we describe ways to reduce memory contention further.

Figure 3.4 presents the full solution to the critical section problem using the Test-and-Test-and-Set entry protocol. The exit protocol merely clears `lock`, just as before.

3.2.3 Implementing Await Statements

Any solution to the critical section problem can be used to implement an unconditional atomic action ⟨ `s;` ⟩ by hiding internal control points from other processes. Let CSenter be a critical section entry protocol, and let CSexit be the corresponding exit protocol. Then $\langle$ `S;` $\rangle$ can be implemented by

```
CSenter;
S;
CSexit;
```

This assumes that all code sections in all processes that reference or alter variables altered by `S`—or that alter variables referenced by `S`—are also protected by similar entry and exit protocols. In essence, $\langle$ is replaced by CSenter, and $\rangle$ is replaced by CSexit.

The above code skeleton can also be used as a building block to implement $\langle$ `await (B) S;` $\rangle$. Recall that a conditional atomic action delays the executing process until `B` is true, then executes `S`. Also, `B` must be true when execution of `S` begins. To ensure that the entire action is atomic, we can use a critical section protocol to hide intermediate states in `S`. We can then use a loop to repeatedly test `B` until it is true:

```
CSenter;
while (!B) { ??? }
S;
CSexit;
```

Here we assume that critical sections in all processes that alter variables referenced in `B` or `S` or that reference variables altered in `S` are protected by similar entry and exit protocols.

The remaining concern is how to implement the above loop body. If the body is executed, `B` was false. Hence, the only way `B` will become true is if some other process alters a variable referenced in `B`. Since we assume that any statement in another process that alters a variable referenced in `B` must be in a critical section, we have to exit the critical section while waiting for `B` to become true. But to ensure atomicity of the evaluation of `B` and execution of `S`, we must reenter the critical section before reevaluating `B`. Hence a candidate refinement of the above protocol is

(3.8) ```
CSenter;
while (!B) { CSexit; CSenter; }
S;
CSexit;
```

This implementation preserves the semantics of conditional atomic actions, assuming the critical section protocols guarantee mutual exclusion. If scheduling is weakly fair, the process executing (3.8) will eventually terminate the loop,
```

assuming B eventually becomes true and remains true. If scheduling is strongly fair, the loop will terminate if B becomes true infinitely often.

Although (3.8) is correct, it is inefficient. This is because a process executing (3.8) is spinning in a "hard" loop—continuously exiting, then reentering its critical section—even though it cannot possibly proceed until at least some other process alters a variable referenced in B. This leads to memory contention since every delayed process continuously accesses the variables used in the critical section protocols and the variables in B.

To reduce memory contention, it is preferable for a process to delay for some period of time before reentering the critical section. Let Delay be some code that slows a process down. Then we can replace (3.8) by the following protocol for implementing a conditional atomic action:

(3.9)   CSenter;
```
        while (!B) { CSexit; Delay; CSenter; }
        S;
        CSexit;
```

The Delay code might, for example, be an empty loop that iterates a random number of times. (To avoid memory contention in this loop, the Delay code should access only local variables.) This kind of "back-off" protocol is also useful within the CSenter protocols themselves; e.g., it can be used in place of `skip` in the delay loop in the simple test-and-set entry protocol given in Figure 3.3.

If S is simply the `skip` statement, protocol (3.9) can of course be simplified by omitting S. If B also satisfies the requirements of the At-Most-Once Property (2.2), then ⟨ `await (B);` ⟩ can be implemented as

```
    while (!B) skip;
```

As mentioned at the start of the chapter, busy-waiting synchronization is often used within hardware. In fact, a protocol similar to (3.9) is used to synchronize access to an Ethernet—a common, local-area communication network. To transmit a message, an Ethernet controller first sends it on the Ethernet, then listens to see if the message collided with another message sent at about the same time by another controller. If no collision is detected, the transmission is assumed to have been successful. If a collision is detected, the controller delays a tad, then attempts to resend the message. To avoid a race condition in which two controllers repeatedly collide because they always delay about the same amount of time, the delay is randomly chosen from an interval that is doubled each time a collision occurs. Hence, this is called the *binary exponential back-off protocol*. Experiments have shown that this kind of back-off protocol is also useful in (3.9) and in critical section entry protocols.

3.3 Critical Sections: Fair Solutions

The spin-lock solutions to the critical section problem ensure mutual exclusion, are deadlock (livelock) free, and avoid unnecessary delay. However, they require a strongly fair scheduler to ensure eventual entry (3.5). As observed in Section 2.8, practical scheduling policies are only weakly fair. Although it is unlikely that a process trying to enter its critical section will never succeed, it could happen if two or more processes are always contending for entry. In particular, the spin-lock solutions do not control the order in which delayed processes enter their critical sections when two or more are trying to do so.

This section presents three fair solutions to the critical section problem: the tie-breaker algorithm, the ticket algorithm, and the bakery algorithm. They depend only on a weakly fair scheduler such as round-robin, which merely ensures that each process keeps getting a chance to execute and that delay conditions, once true, remain true. The tie-breaker algorithm is fairly simple for two processes and depends on no special machine instructions, but it is complex for **n** processes. The ticket algorithm is simple for any number of processes, but it requires a special machine instruction called Fetch-and-Add. The bakery algorithm is a variation on the ticket algorithm that requires no special machine instructions, but consequently it is more complex (although still simpler than the n-process tie-breaker algorithm).

3.3.1 The Tie-Breaker Algorithm

Consider the critical section solution for two processes shown in Figure 3.1. The shortcoming of this solution is that if each process is trying to enter its critical section, there is no control over which will succeed. In particular, one process could succeed, execute its critical section, race back around to the entry protocol, and then succeed again. To make the solution fair, the processes should take turns when both are trying to enter.

The *tie-breaker algorithm*—also called Peterson's algorithm—is a variation on the critical section protocol in Figure 3.1 that "breaks the tie" when both processes are trying to enter. It does so by using an additional variable to indicate which process was last to enter its critical section.

To motivate the tie-breaker algorithm, consider again the coarse-grained program in Figure 3.1. The goal now is to implement the conditional atomic actions in the entry protocols using only simple variables and sequential statements. As a starting point, consider implementing each `await` statement by first looping until the guard is false, then executing the assignment. Then the entry protocol for process `CS1` would be

```
while (in2) skip;
in1 = true;
```

Similarly, the entry protocol for `CS2` would be

```
while (in1) skip;
in2 = true;
```

The corresponding exit protocol for `CS1` would set `in1` to false, and that for `CS2` would set `in2` to false.

The problem with this "solution" is that the two actions in the entry protocols are not executed atomically. Consequently, mutual exclusion is not ensured. For example, the desired postcondition for the delay loop in `CS1` is that `in2` is false. Unfortunately this is interfered with by the assignment `in2 = true;`, because it is possible for both processes to evaluate their delay conditions at about the same time and to find that they are true.

Since each process wants to be sure that the other is not in its critical section when the `while` loop terminates, consider switching the order of the statements in the entry protocols. Namely, the entry protocol in `CS1` becomes

```
in1 = true;
while (in2) skip;
```

Similarly, the entry protocol in `CS2` becomes

```
in2 = true;
while (in1) skip;
```

This helps but still does not solve the problem. Mutual exclusion is ensured, but deadlock can now result: If `in1` and `in2` are both true, neither delay loop will terminate. However, there is a simple way to avoid deadlock: Use an additional variable to break the tie if both processes are delayed.

Let `last` be an integer variable that indicates which of `CS1` or `CS2` was last to start executing its entry protocol. Then if both `CS1` and `CS2` are trying to enter their critical sections—namely, when `in1` and `in2` are true—the last process to start its entry protocol delays. This yields the coarse-grained solution shown in Figure 3.5.

The algorithm in Figure 3.5 is very close to a fine-grained solution that does not require `await` statements. In particular, if each `await` statement satisfied the requirements of the At-Most-Once Property (2.4), then we could implement them by busy-waiting loops. Unfortunately, the `await` statements in Figure 3.5 reference two variables altered by the other process. However, in this case it is not necessary that the delay conditions be evaluated atomically. The reasoning follows.

```
bool in1 = false, in2 = false;
int last = 1;
process CS1 {
  while (true) {
     last = 1; in1 = true;      /* entry protocol */
     ⟨await (!in2 or last == 2);⟩
     critical section;
     in1 = false;                /* exit protocol */
     noncritical section;
  }
}
process CS2 {
  while (true) {
     last = 2; in2 = true;      /* entry protocol */
     ⟨await (!in1 or last == 1);⟩
     critical section;
     in2 = false;                /* exit protocol */
     noncritical section;
  }
}
```

Figure 3.5   Two-process tie-breaker algorithm: Coarse-grained solution.

Suppose process CS1 evaluates its delay condition and finds that it is true. If CS1 found in2 false, then in2 might now be true. However, in that case process CS2 has just set last to 2; hence the delay condition is still true even though in2 changed value. If CS1 found last == 2, then that condition will remain true, because last will not change until after CS1 executes its critical section. Thus, in either case, if CS1 thinks the delay condition is true, it is in fact true. (The argument for CS2 is symmetric).

Since the delay conditions need not be evaluated atomically, each await can be replaced by a while loop that iterates as long as the negation of the delay condition is false. This yields the fine-grained tie-breaker algorithm shown in Figure 3.6.

The program in Figure 3.6 solves the critical section problem for two processes. We can use the same basic idea to solve the problem for any number of processes. In particular, if there are n processes, the entry protocol in each process consists of a loop that iterates through n-1 stages. In each stage, we use instances of the two-process tie-breaker algorithm to determine which processes get to advance to the next stage. If we ensure that at most one process at a time is

```
bool in1 = false, in2 = false;
int last = 1;

process CS1 {
  while (true) {
    last = 1; in1 = true;      /* entry protocol */
    while (in2 and last == 1) skip;
    critical section;
    in1 = false;               /* exit protocol */
    noncritical section;
  }
}

process CS2 {
  while (true) {
    last = 2; in2 = true;      /* entry protocol */
    while (in1 and last == 2) skip;
    critical section;
    in2 = false;               /* exit protocol */
    noncritical section;
  }
}
```

Figure 3.6   Two-process tie-breaker algorithm: Fine-grained solution.

allowed to get through all n-1 stages, then at most one at a time can be in its critical section.

Let in[1:n] and last[1:n] be integer arrays. The value of in[i] indicates which stage CS[i] is executing; the value of last[j] indicates which process was the last to begin stage j. These variables are used as shown in Figure 3.7. The outer for loop executes n-1 times. The inner for loop in process CS[i] checks every other process. In particular, CS[i] waits if there is some other process in a higher or equal numbered stage and CS[i] was the last process to enter stage j. Once another process enters stage j or all processes "ahead" of CS[i] have exited their critical section, CS[i] can proceed to the next stage. Thus, at most n-1 processes can be past the first stage, n-2 past the second stage, and so on. This ensures that at most one process at a time can complete all n stages and hence be executing its critical section.

The n-process solution is livelock-free, avoids unnecessary delay, and ensures eventual entry. These properties follow from the fact that a process delays only if some other process is ahead of it in the entry protocol, and from the assumption that every process eventually exits its critical section.

```
        int in[1:n] = ([n] 0), last[1:n] = ([n] 0);
   process CS[i = 1 to n] {
     while (true) {
       for [j = 1 to n] {              /* entry protocol */
         /* remember process i is in stage j and is last */
         last[j] = i; in[i] = j;
         for [k = 1 to n st i != k] {
           /* wait if process k is in higher numbered stage
               and process i was the last to enter stage j */
           while (in[k] >= in[i] and last[j] == i) skip;
         }
       }
       critical section;
       in[i] = 0;                      /* exit protocol */
       noncritical section;
     }
   }
```

Figure 3.7   The n-process tie-breaker algorithm.

3.3.2 The Ticket Algorithm

The n-process tie-breaker algorithm is quite complex and consequently is hard to understand. This is in part because it was not obvious how to generalize the two-process algorithm to n processes. Here we develop an n-process solution to the critical section problem that is much easier to understand. The solution also illustrates how integer counters can be used to order processes. The algorithm is called a *ticket algorithm* since it is based on drawing tickets (numbers) and then waiting turns.

Some stores—such as ice cream stores and bakeries—employ the following method to ensure that customers are serviced in order of arrival. Upon entering the store, a customer draws a number that is one larger than the number held by any other customer. The customer then waits until all customers holding smaller numbers have been serviced. This algorithm is implemented by a number dispenser and by a display indicating which customer is being served. If the store has one employee behind the service counter, customers are served one at a time in their order of arrival. We can use this idea to implement a fair critical section protocol.

Let **number** and **next** be integers that are initially 1, and let **turn[1:n]** be an array of integers, each of which is initially 0. To enter its critical section, process **CS[i]** first sets **turn[i]** to the current value of **number** and then

```
int number = 1, next = 1, turn[1:n] = ([n] 0);
## predicate TICKET is a global invariant (see text)

process CS[i = 1 to n] {
  while (true) {
    ⟨turn[i] = number; number = number + 1;⟩
    ⟨await (turn[i] == next);⟩
    critical section;
    ⟨next = next + 1;⟩
    noncritical section;
  }
}
```

Figure 3.8   The ticket algorithm: Coarse-grained solution.

increments **number**. These are a single atomic action to ensure that customers draw unique numbers. Process **CS[i]** then waits until the value of **next** is equal to the number it drew. Upon completing its critical section, **CS[i]** increments **next**, again as an atomic action.

This protocol results in the algorithm shown in Figure 3.8. Since **number** is read and incremented as an atomic action and **next** is incremented as an atomic action, the following predicate is a global invariant:

> $TICKET$:   next > 0 ∧ (∀ i: 1 <= i <= n:
> (**CS[i]** in its critical section) ⇒ (turn[i] == next) ∧
> (turn[i] > 0) ⇒ (∀ j: 1 <= j <= n, j != i:
> turn[i] != turn[j]))

The last line says that nonzero values of **turn** are unique. Hence, at most one **turn[i]** is equal to **next**. Hence, at most one process can be in its critical section. Absence of deadlock and absence of unnecessary delay also follow from the fact that nonzero values in **turn** are unique. Finally, if scheduling is weakly fair, the algorithm ensures eventual entry, because once a delay condition becomes true, it remains true.

Unlike the tie-breaker algorithm, the ticket algorithm has a potential shortcoming that is common in algorithms that employ incrementing counters: the values of **number** and **next** are unbounded. If the ticket algorithm runs for a very long time, incrementing a counter will eventually cause arithmetic overflow. This is *extremely* likely to be a problem in practice, however.

The algorithm in Figure 3.8 contains three coarse-grained atomic actions. It is easy to implement the **await** statement using a busy-waiting loop since the Boolean expression references only one shared variable. The last atomic action, which increments **next**, can be implemented using regular load and store instructions, because at most one process at a time can execute the exit protocol. Unfortunately, it is hard in general to implement the first atomic action, which reads **number** and then increments it.

Some machines have instructions that return the old value of a variable and increment or decrement it as a single indivisible operation. This kind of instruction does exactly what is required for the ticket algorithm. As a specific example, Fetch-and-Add is an instruction with the following effect:

```
FA(var, incr):
    ⟨int tmp = var; var = var + incr; return(tmp);⟩
```

Figure 3.9 gives the ticket algorithm implemented using **FA**.

On machines that do not have Fetch-and-Add or a comparable instruction, we have to use another approach. The key requirement in the ticket algorithm is that every process draw a unique number. If a machine has an atomic increment instruction, we might consider implementing the first step in the entry protocol by

```
turn[i] = number; ⟨number = number + 1;⟩
```

This ensures that **number** is incremented correctly, but it does not ensure that processes draw unique numbers. In particular, every process could execute the first assignment above at about the same time and draw the same number! Thus it is essential that both assignments be executed as a single atomic action.

We have already seen two other ways to solve the critical section problem: spin locks and the tie-breaker algorithm. Either of these could be used within the

```
int number = 1, next = 1, turn[1:n] = ([n] 0);

process CS[i = 1 to n] {
  while (true) {
    turn[i] = FA(number,1);        /* entry protocol */
    while (turn[i] != next) skip;
    critical section;
    next = next + 1;               /* exit protocol  */
    noncritical section;
  }
}
```

Figure 3.9   The ticket algorithm: Fine-grained solution.

ticket algorithm to make number drawing atomic. In particular, suppose CSenter is a critical section entry protocol and CSexit is the corresponding exit protocol. Then we could replace the Fetch-and-Add statement in Figure 3.9 by

(3.10) CSenter; turn[i] = number; number = number+1; CSexit;

Although this might seem like a curious approach, in practice it would actually work quite well, especially if an instruction like Test-and-Set is available to implement CSenter and CSexit. With Test-and-Set, processes might not draw numbers in exactly the order they attempt to—and theoretically a process could spin forever—but with very high probability every process would draw a number, and most would be drawn in order. This is because the critical section within (3.10) is very short, and hence a process is not likely to delay in CSenter. The major source of delay in the ticket algorithm is waiting for turn[i] to be equal to next.

3.3.3 The Bakery Algorithm

The ticket algorithm can be implemented directly on machines that have an instruction like Fetch-and-Add. If such an instruction is not available, we can simulate the number drawing part of the ticket algorithm using (3.10). But that requires using another critical section protocol, and the solution might not be fair. Here we present a ticket-like algorithm—called the *bakery algorithm*—that is fair and that does not require any special machine instructions. The algorithm is consequently more complex than the ticket algorithm in Figure 3.9.

In the ticket algorithm, each customer draws a unique number and then waits for its number to be equal to next. The bakery algorithm takes a different approach. In particular, when customers enter the store, they first look around at all other customers and draw a number one larger than any other. All customers must then wait for their number to be called. As in the ticket algorithm, the customer with the smallest number is the one that gets serviced next. The difference is that customers check with each other rather than with a central next counter to decide on the order of service.

As in the ticket algorithm, let turn[1:n] be an array of integers, each of which is initially zero. To enter its critical section, process CS[i] first sets turn[i] to one more than the maximum of all the current values in turn. Then CS[i] waits until turn[i] is the smallest of the nonzero values of turn. Thus the bakery algorithm keeps the following predicate invariant:

$BAKERY:$ $(\forall$ i: 1 <= i <= n:
$\quad$(CS[i] in its critical section) $\Rightarrow$ (turn[i] > 0) $\wedge$
$\quad$(turn[i] > 0) $\Rightarrow$ ($\forall$ j: 1 <= j <= n, j != i:
$\qquad\qquad\qquad$ turn[j] == 0 $\vee$ turn[i] < turn[j]))

Upon completing its critical section, CS[i] resets turn[i] to zero.

Figure 3.10 contains a coarse-grained bakery algorithm meeting these specifications. The first atomic action guarantees that nonzero values of turn are unique. The for statement ensures that the consequent in predicate $BAKERY$ is true when P[i] is executing its critical section. The algorithm satisfies the mutual exclusion property because not all of turn[i] != 0, turn[j] != 0, and $BAKERY$ can be true at once. Deadlock cannot result since nonzero values of turn are unique, and as usual we assume that every process eventually exits its critical section. Processes are not delayed unnecessarily since turn[i] is zero when CS[i] is outside its critical section. Finally, the bakery algorithm ensures eventual entry if scheduling is weakly fair since once a delay condition becomes true, it remains true. (The values of turn in the bakery algorithm can get arbitrarily large. However, the turn[i] continue to get larger only if there is *always* at least one process trying to get into its critical section. This is not likely to be a practical problem.)

The bakery algorithm in Figure 3.10 cannot be implemented directly on contemporary machines. The assignment to turn[i] requires computing the maximum of n values, and the await statement references a shared variable (turn[j]) twice. These actions could be implemented atomically by using another critical section protocol such as the tie-breaker algorithm, but that would be quite inefficient. Fortunately, there is a simpler approach.

```
int turn[1:n] = ([n] 0);
## predicate BAKERY is a global invariant -- see text
process CS[i = 1 to n] {
  while (true) {
    ⟨turn[i] = max(turn[1:n]) + 1;⟩
    for [j = 1 to n st j != i]
      ⟨await (turn[j] == 0 or turn[i] < turn[j]);⟩
    critical section;
    turn[i] = 0;
    noncritical section;
  }
}
```

Figure 3.10   The bakery algorithm: Coarse-grained solution.

When **n** processes need to synchronize, it is often useful first to develop a two-process solution and then to generalize that solution. This was the case earlier for the tie-breaker algorithm and is again useful here since it helps illustrate the problems that have to be solved. Thus, consider the following entry protocol for process **CS1**:

```
turn1 = turn2 + 1;
while (turn2 != 0 and turn1 > turn2) skip;
```

The corresponding entry protocol for process **CS2** is

```
turn2 = turn1 + 1;
while (turn1 != 0 and turn2 > turn1) skip;
```

Each process above sets its value of **turn** by an optimized version of (3.10), and the **await** statements are tentatively implemented by a busy-waiting loop.

The problem with the above "solution" is that neither the assignment statements nor the **while** loop guards will be evaluated atomically. Consequently, the processes could start their entry protocols at about the same time, and both could set **turn1** and **turn2** to **1**. If this happens, both processes could be in their critical section at the same time.

The two-process tie-breaker algorithm in Figure 3.6 suggests a partial solution to the above problem: If both **turn1** and **turn2** are **1**, let one of the processes proceed and have the other delay. For example, let the lower-numbered process proceed by strengthening the second conjunct in the delay loop in **CS2** to **turn2 >= turn1**.

Unfortunately, it is still possible for both processes to enter their critical section. For example, suppose **CS1** reads **turn2** and gets back **0**. Then suppose **CS2** starts its entry protocol, sees that **turn1** is still **0**, sets **turn2** to **1**, and then enters its critical section. At this point, **CS1** can continue its entry protocol, set **turn1** to **1**, and then proceed into its critical section since both **turn1** and **turn2** are **1** and **CS1** takes precedence in this case. This kind of situation is called a *race condition* since **CS2** "raced by" **CS1** and hence **CS1** missed seeing that **CS2** was changing **turn2**.

To avoid this race condition, we can have each process set its value of **turn** to **1** (or any nonzero value) at the start of the entry protocol. Then it examines the other's value of **turn** and resets its own. In particular, the entry protocol for process **CS1** is

```
turn1 = 1; turn1 = turn2 + 1;
while (turn2 != 0 and turn1 > turn2) skip;
```

Similarly, the entry protocol for process **CS2** is

```
turn2 = 1; turn2 = turn1 + 1;
while (turn1 != 0 and turn2 >= turn1) skip;
```

One process cannot now exit its `while` loop until the other has finished setting its value of `turn` if it is in the midst of doing so. The solution gives `CS1` precedence over `CS2` in case both processes have the same (nonzero) value for `turn`.

The entry protocols above are not quite symmetric, because the delay conditions in the second loop are slightly different. However, we can rewrite them in a symmetric form as follows. Let `(a,b)` and `(c,d)` be pairs of integers, and define the greater than relation between such pairs as follows:

```
(a,b) > (c,d) == true    if a > c or if a == c and b > d
              == false   otherwise
```

Then we can rewrite `turn1 > turn2` in `CS1` as `(turn1,1) > (turn2,2)` and `turn2 >= turn1` in `CS2` as `(turn2,2) > (turn1,1)`.

The virtue of a symmetric specification is that it is now easy to generalize the two-process bakery algorithm to an n-process algorithm, as shown in Figure 3.11. Each process first indicates that it wants to enter by setting its value of `turn` to `1`. Then it computes the maximum of all the `turn[i]` and adds one to the result. Finally, the process employs a `for` loop as in the coarse-grained solution so that it delays until it has precedence over all other processes. Note that the maximum is approximated by reading each element of `turn` and selecting the largest. It is *not* computed atomically and hence is not necessarily accurate. However, if two or more processes compute the same value, they are ordered as described above.

```
int turn[1:n] = ([n] 0);

process CS[i = 1 to n] {
  while (true) {
    turn[i] = 1; turn[i] = max(turn[1:n]) + 1;
    for [j = 1 to n st j != i]
      while (turn[j] != 0 and
             (turn[i],i) > (turn[j],j)) skip;
    critical section;
    turn[i] = 0;
    noncritical section;
  }
}
```

Figure 3.11   Bakery algorithm: Fine-grained solution.

3.4 Barrier Synchronization

Many problems can be solved using iterative algorithms that successively compute better approximations to an answer, terminating when either the final answer has been computed or—in the case of many numerical algorithms—when the final answer has converged. Such an algorithm typically manipulates an array of values, and each iteration performs the same computation on all array elements. Hence, we can often use multiple processes to compute disjoint parts of the solution in parallel. We have already seen a few examples and will see many more in the next section and in later chapters.

A key attribute of most parallel iterative algorithms is that each iteration typically depends on the results of the previous iteration. One way to structure such an algorithm is to implement the body of each iteration using one or more co statements. Ignoring termination, and assuming there are n parallel tasks on each iteration, this approach has the general form

```
while (true) {
  co [i = 1 to n]
     code to implement task i;
  oc
}
```

Unfortunately, the above approach is quite inefficient since co spawns n processes on each iteration. It is much more costly to create and destroy processes than to implement process synchronization. Thus an alternative structure will result in a more efficient algorithm. In particular, create the processes once at the beginning of the computation, then have them synchronize at the end of each iteration:

```
process Worker[i = 1 to n] {
  while (true) {
     code to implement task i;
  wait for all n tasks to complete;
  }
}
```

This is called *barrier synchronization*, because the delay point at the end of each iteration represents a barrier that all processes have to arrive at before any are allowed to pass. Barriers can be needed both at the ends of loops, as above, and at intermediate stages, as we shall see.

Below we develop several implementations of barrier synchronization. Each employs a different process interaction technique. We also describe when each kind of barrier is appropriate to use.

3.4.1 Shared Counter

The simplest way to specify the requirements for a barrier is to employ a shared integer, count, which is initially zero. Assume there are n worker processes that need to meet at a barrier. When a process arrives at the barrier, it increments count; when count is n, all processes can proceed. This specification leads to the following code outline:

(3.11)
```
int count = 0;

process Worker[i = 1 to n] {
    while (true) {
        code to implement task i;
        ⟨count = count + 1;⟩
        ⟨await (count == n);⟩
    }
}
```

We can implement the await statement by a busy-waiting loop. If we also have an indivisible increment instruction, such as the Fetch-and-Add instruction defined in Section 3.3, we can implement the above barrier by

```
FA(count,1);
while (count != n) skip;
```

The above code is not fully adequate, however. The difficulty is that count must be 0 at the start of each iteration, which means that count needs to be reset to 0 each time all processes have passed the barrier. Moreover, count has to be reset before any process again tries to increment count.

It is possible to solve this reset problem by employing two counters, one that counts up to n and another that counts down to 0, with the roles of the counters being switched after each stage. However, there are additional, pragmatic problems with using shared counters. First, they have to be incremented and/or decremented as atomic actions. Second, when a process is delayed in (3.11), it is continuously examining count. In the worst case, n-1 processes might be delayed waiting for the last process to arrive at the barrier. This could lead to severe memory contention, except on multiprocessors with coherent caches. But even then, the value of count is continuously changing, so every cache needs to be updated. Thus it is appropriate to implement a barrier using counters only if the target machine has atomic increment instructions, coherent caches, and efficient cache update. Moreover, n should be relatively small.

3.4.2 Flags and Coordinators

One way to avoid the memory contention problem is to distribute the implementation of `count` by using n variables that sum to the same value. In particular, let `arrive[1:n]` be an array of integers initialized to zeros. Then replace the increment of `count` in (3.11) by `arrive[i] = 1`. With this change, the following predicate is a global invariant:

$$\texttt{count == (arrive[1] + ... + arrive[n])}$$

Memory contention would be avoided as long as elements of `arrive` are stored in different cache lines (to avoid contention when they are written by the processes).

With the above change, the remaining problems are implementing the `await` statement in (3.11) and resetting the elements of `arrive` at the end of each iteration. Using the above relation, the `await` statement could obviously be implemented as

$$\langle\, \texttt{await ((arrive[1] + ... + arrive[n]) == n);} \,\rangle$$

However, this reintroduces memory contention, and, moreover, it is inefficient since the sum of the `arrive[i]` is continually being computed by every waiting `Worker`.

We can solve both the memory contention and reset problems by using an additional set of shared values and by employing an additional process, `Coordinator`. Instead of having each `Worker` sum and test the values of `arrive`, let each worker wait for a single value to become true. In particular, let `continue[1:n]` be another array of integers, initialized to zeros. After setting `arrive[i]` to 1, `Worker[i]` delays by waiting for `continue[i]` to be set to 1:

(3.12) `arrive[i] = 1;`
        `⟨await (continue[i] == 1);⟩`

The `Coordinator` process waits for all elements of `arrive` to become 1, then sets all elements of `continue` to 1:

(3.13) `for [i = 1 to n] ⟨await (arrive[i] == 1);⟩`
        `for [i = 1 to n] continue[i] = 1;`

The `await` statements in (3.12) and (3.13) can be implemented by `while` loops since each references a single shared variable. The `Coordinator` can use a `for` statement to wait for each element of `arrive` to be set; moreover, because all `arrive` flags must be set before any `Worker` is allowed to continue, the `Coordinator` can test the `arrive[i]` in any order. Finally, memory contention is not a problem since the processes wait for different variables to be set and these variables could be stored in different cache lines.

Variables `arrive` and `continue` in (3.12) and (3.13) are examples of what is called a *flag variable*—a variable that is raised by one process to signal that a synchronization condition is true. The remaining problem is augmenting (3.12) and (3.13) with code to clear the flags by resetting them to `0` in preparation for the next iteration. Here two general principles apply.

(3.14)   **Flag Synchronization Principles.** (a) The process that waits for a synchronization flag to be set is the one that should clear that flag. (b) A flag should not be set until it is known that it is clear.

The first principle ensures that a flag is not cleared before it has been seen to be set. Thus in (3.12) `Worker[i]` should clear `continue[i]` and in (3.13) `Coordinator` should clear all elements of `arrive`. The second principle ensures that another process does not again set the same flag before it is cleared, which could lead to deadlock if the first process later waits for the flag to be set again. In (3.13) this means `Coordinator` should clear `arrive[i]` before setting `continue[i]`. The `Coordinator` can do this by executing another `for` statement after the first one in (3.13). Alternatively, `Coordinator` can clear `arrive[i]` immediately after it has waited for it to be set. Adding flag-clearing code, we get the coordinator barrier shown in Figure 3.12.

Although Figure 3.12 implements barrier synchronization in a way that avoids memory contention, the solution has two undesirable attributes. First, it requires an extra process. Busy-waiting synchronization is inefficient unless each process executes on its own processor, so the `Coordinator` should execute on its own processor. However, it would probably be better to use that processor for another worker process.

The second shortcoming of using a coordinator is that the execution time of each iteration of `Coordinator`—and hence each instance of barrier synchronization—is proportional to the number of `Worker` processes. In iterative algorithms, each `Worker` often executes identical code. Hence, each is likely to arrive at the barrier at about the same time, assuming every `Worker` is executed on its own processor. Thus, all `arrive` flags will get set at about the same time. However, `Coordinator` cycles through the flags, waiting for each one to be set in turn.

We can overcome both problems by combining the actions of the coordinator and workers so that each worker is also a coordinator. In particular, we can organize the workers into a tree, as shown in Figure 3.13. Workers can then send arrival signals up the tree and continue signals back down the tree. In particular, a worker node first waits for its children to arrive, then tells its parent node that it too has arrived. When the root node learns that its children have arrived,

```
int arrive[1:n] = ([n] 0),   continue[1:n] = ([n] 0);

process Worker[i = 1 to n] {
  while (true) {
    code to implement task i;
    arrive[i] = 1;
    ⟨await (continue[i] == 1);⟩
    continue[i] = 0;
  }
}

process Coordinator {
  while (true) {
    for [i = 1 to n] {
      ⟨await (arrive[i] == 1);⟩
      arrive[i] = 0;
    }
    for [i = 1 to n] continue[i] = 1;
  }
}
```

Figure 3.12   Barrier synchronization using a coordinator process.

it knows that all other workers have also arrived. Hence the root can tell its children to continue; they in turn can tell their children to continue, and so on. The specific actions of each kind of worker process are listed in Figure 3.14. The `await` statements can, of course, be implemented by spin loops.

The implementation in Figure 3.14 is called a *combining tree barrier*. This is because each process combines the results of its children, then passes them on to its parent. This barrier uses the same number of variables as the centralized

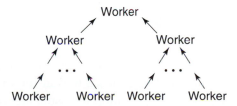

Figure 3.13   Tree-structured barrier.

```
leaf node L:    arrive[L] = 1;
                ⟨await (continue[L] == 1);⟩
                continue[L] = 0;

interior node I:  ⟨await (arrive[left] == 1);⟩
                  arrive[left] = 0;
                  ⟨await (arrive[right] == 1);⟩
                  arrive[right] = 0;
                  arrive[I] = 1;
                  ⟨await (continue[I] == 1);⟩
                  continue[I] = 0;
                  continue[left] = 1; continue[right] = 1;

root node R:    ⟨await (arrive[left] == 1);⟩
                arrive[left] = 0;
                ⟨await (arrive[right] == 1);⟩
                arrive[right] = 0;
                continue[left] = 1; continue[right] = 1;
```

Figure 3.14   Barrier synchronization using a combining tree.

coordinator, but it is much more efficient for large n, because the height of the tree is proportional to $\log_2 n$.

We can make the combining tree barrier even more efficient by having the root node broadcast a single message that tells all other nodes to continue. In particular, the root sets one **continue** flag, and all other nodes wait for it to be set. This **continue** flag can later be cleared in either of two ways. One is to use double buffering—that is, use two continue flags and alternate between them. The other way is to alternate the sense of the continue flag—that is, on odd-numbered rounds to wait for it to be set to 1, and on even-numbered rounds to wait for it to be set to 0.

3.4.3 Symmetric Barriers

In the combining-tree barrier, processes play different roles. In particular, those at interior nodes in the tree execute more actions than those at the leaves or root. Moreover, the root node needs to wait for arrival signals to propagate up the tree. If every process is executing the same algorithm and every process is executing on a different processor, then all processes should arrive at the barrier at about the same time. Thus if all processes take the exact same sequence of actions when they reach a barrier, then all might be able to proceed through the barrier at the same rate. This section presents two *symmetric barriers*. These are especially suitable for shared-memory multiprocessors with nonuniform memory access time.

A symmetric n-process barrier is constructed from pairs of simple, two-process barriers. To construct a two-process barrier, we could use the coordinator/worker technique. However, the actions of the two processes would then be different. Instead, we can construct a fully symmetric barrier as follows. Let each process have a flag that it sets when it arrives at the barrier. It then waits for the other process to set its flag and finally clears the other's flag. If `W[i]` is one process and `W[j]` is the other, the symmetric two-process barrier is then implemented as follows:

```
(3.15)   /* barrier code for worker process W[i] */
         ⟨await (arrive[i] == 0);⟩   /* key line -- see text */
         arrive[i] = 1;
         ⟨await (arrive[j] == 1);⟩
         arrive[j] = 0;


         /* barrier code for worker process W[j] */
         ⟨await (arrive[j] == 0);⟩   /* key line -- see text */
         arrive[j] = 1;
         ⟨await (arrive[i] == 1);⟩
         arrive[i] = 0;
```

The last three lines in each process serve the roles described above. The existence of the first line in each process may at first seem odd, as it just waits for a process's own flag to be cleared. However, it is needed to guard against the possible situation in which a process races back to the barrier and sets its own flag before the other process *from the previous use of the barrier* cleared the flag. In short, all four lines are needed in order to follow the Flag Synchronization Principles (3.14).

The question now is how to combine instances of two-process barriers to construct an n-process barrier. In particular, we need to devise an interconnection scheme so that each process eventually learns that all others have arrived. The best we can do is to use some sort of binary interconnection, which will have a size proportional to $\log_2 n$.

Let `Worker[1:n]` be the array of processes. If n is a power of 2, we could combine them as shown in Figure 3.15. This kind of barrier is called a *butterfly barrier* due to the shape of the interconnection pattern, which is similar to the butterfly interconnection pattern for the Fourier transform. As shown, a butterfly barrier has $\log_2 n$ stages. Each worker synchronizes with a different

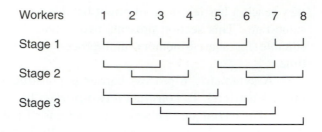

Figure 3.15   Butterfly barrier for eight processes.

other worker at each stage. In particular, in stage **s** a worker synchronizes with a worker at distance 2^{s-1} away. When every worker has passed through all the stages, all workers must have arrived at the barrier and hence all can proceed. This is because every worker has directly or indirectly synchronized with every other one. (When **n** is not a power of 2, a butterfly barrier can be constructed by using the next power of 2 greater than **n** and having existing worker processes substitute for the missing ones at each stage. This is not very efficient, however.)

A different interconnection pattern is shown in Figure 3.16. This pattern is better because it can be used for any value of **n**, not just those that are powers of 2. Again there are several stages, and in stage **s** a worker synchronizes with one at distance 2^{s-1} away. However, in each two-process barrier a process sets the arrival flag of a worker to its right (modulo **n**) and waits for, then clears, its own arrival flag. This structure is called a *dissemination barrier*, because it is based on a technique for disseminating information to **n** processes in $\lceil \log_2 n \rceil$ rounds. Here, each worker disseminates notice of its arrival at the barrier.

A critical aspect of correctly implementing an **n** process barrier—independent of which interconnection pattern is used—is to avoid race conditions that can result from using multiple instances of the basic two-process barrier.

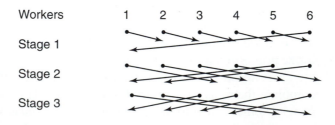

Figure 3.16   Dissemination barrier for six processes.

Consider the butterfly barrier pattern in Figure 3.15. Assume there is only one array of flag variables and that they are used as shown in (3.15). Suppose that process 1 arrives at its first stage and sets its flag `arrive[1]`. Further suppose process 2 is slow, so has not yet arrived. Now suppose processes 3 and 4 arrive at the first stage of the barrier, set and wait for each other's flags, clear them, and proceed to the second stage. In the second stage, process 3 wants to synchronize with process 1, so it waits for `arrive[1]` to be 1. *It already is*, so process 3 clears `arrive[1]` and merrily proceeds to stage 3, even though process 1 had set `arrive[1]` for process 2. The net effects are that some processes will exit the barrier before they should and that some processes will wait forever to get to the next stage. The same problem can occur with the dissemination barrier in Figure 3.16.

The above synchronization anomaly results from using only one set of flags per process. One way to solve the problem is to use a different set of flags for each stage of an n-process barrier. A better way is to have the flags take on more values.

If the flags are integers—as above—they can be used as incrementing counters that record the number of barrier stages each process has executed. The initial value of each flag is 0. Any time worker i arrives at a new barrier stage—whether it is the first stage of a new barrier or an intermediate stage of a barrier—it increments `arrive[i]`. Then worker i determines the appropriate partner j for the current stage and waits for the value of `arrive[j]` to be *at least* `arrive[i]`. The actual code follows:

```
# barrier code for worker process i
for [s = 1 to num_stages] {
   arrive[i] = arrive[i] + 1;
   # determine neighbor j for stage s
   while (arrive[j] < arrive[i]) skip;
}
```

In this way, worker i is assured that worker j has also proceeded at least as far.

This approach of using incrementing counters and stages removes the above race condition, removes the need for a process to wait for its own flag to be reset—the first line in (3.15)—and removes the need for a process to reset another's flag—the last line in (3.15). Thus every stage of every barrier is just three lines of code. The only downside is that the counters always increase, so they could theoretically overflow. However, this is *extremely* unlikely to occur.

To summarize the topic of barriers, there are many possible choices. A counter barrier is the simplest and is reasonable for a small number of processes when there is an atomic Fetch-and-Add instruction. A symmetric barrier provides the most general and efficient choice for a shared-memory machine, because each process will execute the same code, ideally at about the same rate. (On a distributed-memory machine, a tree-structured barrier is often more efficient because it results in fewer interprocess communications.) Whatever the structure of the barrier, however, the critical coding problem is to avoid race conditions. This is achieved either by using multiple flags—one per stage for each pair of processes—or by using incrementing counters as above.

3.5 Data Parallel Algorithms

In *data parallel algorithms* several processes execute the same code and work on different parts of shared data. Barriers are used to synchronize the execution phases of the processes. This kind of algorithm is most closely associated with synchronous multiprocessors—i.e., single instruction stream, multiple data stream (SIMD) machines that support fine-grained computations and barrier synchronization in hardware. However, data parallel algorithms are also extremely useful on asynchronous multiprocessors as long as the granularity of the processes is large enough to more than compensate for barrier synchronization overhead.

This section develops data parallel solutions for three problems: partial sums of an array, finding the end of a linked list, and Jacobi iteration for approximating the solution to a partial differential equation. These illustrate the basic techniques that arise in data parallel algorithms and illustrate uses of barrier synchronization. At the end of the section, we describe SIMD multiprocessors and show how they remove many sources of interference and hence remove the need for programming barriers. An entire chapter later in the text (Chapter 11), shows how to implement data parallel algorithms efficiently on shared-memory multiprocessors and distributed machines.

3.5.1 Parallel Prefix Computations

It is frequently useful to apply an operation to all elements of an array. For example, to compute the average of an array of values a[n], we first need to sum all the elements, then divide by n. Or we might want to know the averages for all prefixes a[0:i] of the array, which requires computing the sums of all prefixes. Because of the importance of this kind of computation, the APL language provides special operators called *reduce* and *scan*. Massively parallel SIMD machines, such as the Connection Machine, provide reduction operators in hardware for combining values in messages.

In this section, we show how to compute in parallel the sums of all prefixes of an array. This is thus called a *parallel prefix computation*. The basic algorithm can be used for any associative binary operator, such as addition, multiplication, logic operators, or maximum. Consequently, parallel prefix computations are useful in many applications, including image processing, matrix computations, and parsing a regular language. (See the exercises at the end of this chapter.)

Suppose we are given array `a[n]` and are to compute `sum[n]`, where `sum[i]` is to be the sum of the first `i` elements of `a`. The obvious way to solve this problem sequentially is to iterate across the two arrays:

```
sum[0] = a[0];
for [i = 1 to n-1]
  sum[i] = sum[i-1] + a[i];
```

In particular, each iteration adds `a[i]` to the already computed sum of the previous `i-1` elements.

Now consider how we might parallelize this approach. If our task were merely to find the sum of all elements, we could proceed as follows. First, add pairs of elements in parallel—for example, add `a[0]` and `a[1]` in parallel with adding other pairs. Second, combine the results of the first step, again in parallel—for example, add the sum of `a[0]` and `a[1]` to the sum of `a[2]` and `a[3]` in parallel with computing other partial sums. If we continue this process, in each step we would double the number of elements that have been summed. Thus in $\lceil \log_2 n \rceil$ steps we would have computed the sum of all elements. This is the best we can do if we have to combine all elements two at a time.

To compute the sums of all prefixes in parallel, we can adapt this technique of doubling the number of elements that have been added. First, set all the `sum[i]` to `a[i]`. Then, in parallel add `sum[i-1]` to `sum[i]`, for all `i>=1`. In particular, add elements that are distance 1 away. Now double the distance and add `sum[i-2]` to `sum[i]`, in this case for all `i >= 2`. If you continue to double the distance, then after $\lceil \log_2 n \rceil$ rounds you will have computed all partial sums. As a specific example, the following table illustrates the steps of the algorithm for a six-element array:

initial values of **a**	1	2	3	4	5	6
sum after distance 1	1	3	5	7	9	11
sum after distance 2	1	3	6	10	14	18
sum after distance 4	1	3	6	10	15	21

Figure 3.17 gives an implementation of this algorithm. Each process first initializes one element of `sum`. Then it repeatedly computes partial sums. In the

```
int a[n], sum[n], old[n];

process Sum[i = 0 to n-1] {
  int d = 1;
  sum[i] = a[i];    /* initialize elements of sum */
  barrier(i);
  ## SUM:  sum[i] = (a[i-d+1] + ... + a[i])
  while (d < n) {
    old[i] = sum[i];   /* save old value */
    barrier(i);
    if ((i-d) >= 0)
      sum[i] = old[i-d] + sum[i];
    barrier(i);
    d = d+d;    /* double the distance */
  }
}
```

Figure 3.17   Computing all partial sums of an array.

algorithm, `barrier(i)` is a call to a procedure that implements a barrier synchronization point; argument `i` is the identity of the calling process. The procedure call returns after all `n` processes have called `barrier`. The body of the procedure would use one of the algorithms in the previous section. (For this problem, the barriers can be optimized since only pairs of processes need to synchronize in each step.)

The barrier points in Figure 3.17 are needed to avoid interference. For example, all elements of `sum` need to be initialized before any process examines them. Also, each process needs to make a copy of the old value in `sum[i]` before it updates that value. Loop invariant *SUM* specifies how much of the prefix of `a` each process has summed on each iteration.

As mentioned, we can modify this algorithm to use any associative binary operator. All that we need to change is the operator in the statement that modifies `sum`. Since we have written the expression in the combining step as `old[i-d] + sum[i]`, the binary operator need not be commutative. We can also adapt the algorithm in Figure 3.17 to use fewer than `n` processes. In this case, each process would be responsible for computing the partial sums of a slice of the array.

3.5.2 *Operations on Linked Lists*

When working with linked data structures such as trees, programmers often use balanced structures such as binary trees in order to be able to search for and insert items in logarithmic time. When data parallel algorithms are used, however, even with linear lists many operations can be implemented in logarithmic time. Here we show how to find the end of a serially linked list. The same kind of algorithm can be used for other operations on serially linked lists—for example, computing all partial sums of data values, inserting an element in a priority list, or matching up elements of two lists.

Suppose we have a linked list of up to **n** elements. The links are stored in array **link[n]**, and the data values are stored in array **data[n]**. The head of the list is pointed to by another variable, **head**. If element **i** is part of the list, then either **head == i** or **link[j] == i** for some **j** between 0 and n-1. The **link** field of the last element on the list is a null pointer, which we will represent by **null**. We also assume that the **link** fields of elements not on the list are null pointers and that the list is already initialized. The following is a sample list:

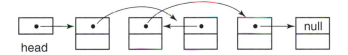

The problem is to find the end of the list. The standard sequential algorithm starts at list element **head** and follows links until finding a null link; the last element visited is the end of the list. The execution time of the sequential algorithm is thus proportional to the length of the list. However, we can find the end of the list in time proportional to the logarithm of the length of the list by using a data parallel algorithm and the technique of doubling that was introduced in the previous section.

We assign a process **Find** to each list element. Let **end[n]** be a shared array of integers. If element **i** is a part of the list, the goal of **Find[i]** is to set **end[i]** to the index of the end of the last element on the list; otherwise **Find[i]** should set **end[i]** to **null**. To avoid special cases, we will assume that the list contains at least two elements.

Initially each process sets **end[i]** to **link[i]**—that is, to the index of the next element on the list (if any). Thus **end** initially reproduces the pattern of links in the list. Then the processes execute a series of rounds. In each round, a process looks at **end[end[i]]**. If both it and **end[i]** are not null pointers, then the process sets **end[i]** to **end[end[i]]**. Thus after the first round **end[i]** will point to a list element two links away (if there is one). After two

```
int link[n], end[n];
process Find[i = 0 to n-1] {
  int new, d = 1;
  end[i] = link[i];    /* initialize elements of end */
  barrier(i);
  ## FIND:  end[i] == index of end of the list
  ##          at most 2^(d-1) links away from node i
  while (d < n) {
    new = null;    /* see if end[i] should be updated */
    if (end[i] != null and end[end[i]] != null)
      new = end[end[i]];
    barrier(i);
    if (new != null)      /* update end[i] */
      end[i] = new;
    barrier(i);
    d = d + d;                /* double the distance */
  }
}
```

Figure 3.18   Finding the end of a serially linked list.

rounds, **end[i]** will point to a list element four links away (again, if there is one). After $\lceil \log_2 n \rceil$ rounds, every process will have found the end of the list.

Figure 3.18 gives an implementation of this algorithm. Since the programming technique is the same as in the parallel prefix computation, the structure of the algorithm is also the same. Again, **barrier(i)** indicates a call to a procedure that implements barrier synchronization for process **i**. Loop invariant *FIND* specifies what **end[i]** points to before and after each iteration. If the end of the list is fewer than 2^{d-1} links away from element **i**, then **end[i]** will not change on further iterations.

To illustrate the execution of this algorithm, consider a six-element list linked together as follows:

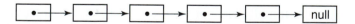

At the start of the **while** loop in **Find**, the **end** pointers contain these links. After the first iteration of the loop, **end** will contain the following links:

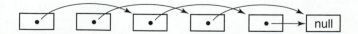

Notice that the `end` links for the last two elements have not changed since they are already correct. After the second round, the `end` links will be as follows:

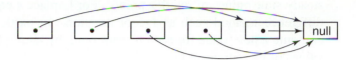

After the third and final round, the `end` links will have their final values:

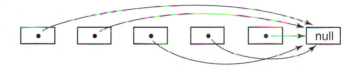

As with the parallel prefix computation, we can adapt this algorithm to use fewer than **n** processes. In particular, each would then be responsible for computing the values for a subset of the `end` links.

3.5.3 Grid Computations: Jacobi Iteration

Many problems in image processing or scientific modeling can be solved using what are called *grid* or *mesh computations*. The basic idea is to employ a matrix of points that superimposes a grid or mesh on a spatial region. In an image processing problem, the matrix is initialized to pixel values, and the goal is to do something like find sets of neighboring pixels having the same intensity. Scientific modeling often involves approximating solutions to partial differential equations, in which case the edges of the matrix are initialized to boundary conditions, and the goal is to compute an approximation for the value of each interior point. (This corresponds to finding a steady state solution to an equation.) In either case, the basic outline of a grid computation is

```
initialize the matrix;
while (not yet terminated)  {
    compute a new value for each point;
    check for termination;
}
```

On each iteration, the new values of points can typically be computed in parallel.

As a specific example, here we present a simple solution to Laplace's equation in two dimensions: $\Delta^2 = 0$. (This is a partial differential equation; see Section 11.1 for details.) Let `grid[n+1,n+1]` be a matrix of points. The edges of grid—the left and right columns, and the top and bottom rows—represent the boundary of a two-dimensional region. The $n \times n$ interior elements of grid correspond to a mesh that is superimposed on the region. The goal is to compute the steady state values of interior points. For Laplace's equation, we can use a finite difference method such as Jacobi iteration. In particular, on each iteration we compute a new value for each interior point by taking the average of the previous values of its four closest neighbors.

Figure 3.19 presents a grid computation that solves Laplace's equation using Jacobi iteration. Once again we use barriers to synchronize steps of the computation. In this case, there are two main steps per iteration: update newgrid and check for convergence, then move the contents of newgrid into grid. Two matrices are used so that new values for grid points depend only on old values. We can terminate the computation either after a fixed number of iterations or when values in newgrid are all within some tolerance EPSILON of those in grid. If differences are used, they can be checked in parallel, but the results need to be combined. This can be done using a parallel prefix computation; we leave the details to the reader (see the exercises at the end of this chapter).

The algorithm in Figure 3.19 is correct, but it is simplistic in several respects. First, it copies newgrid back into grid on each iteration. It would be far more efficient to "unroll" the loop once and have each iteration first update points going from grid to newgrid and then back from newgrid to grid. Second, it would be better still to use an algorithm that converges faster, such as red-black successive over relaxation (SOR). Third, the algorithm in Figure 3.19 is too fine grain for asynchronous multiprocessors. For those, it would be far

```
real grid[n+1,n+1], newgrid[n+1,n+1];
bool converged = false;

process Grid[i = 1 to n, j = 1 to n] {
  while (not converged) {
    newgrid[i,j] = (grid[i-1,j] + grid[i+1,j] +
                    grid[i,j-1] + grid[i,j+1]) / 4;
    check for convergence as described in the text;
    barrier(i);
    grid[i,j] = newgrid[i,j];
    barrier(i);
  }
}
```

Figure 3.19   Grid computation for solving Laplace's equation.

better to partition the grid into blocks and to assign one process (and processor) to each block. All these points are considered in detail in Chapter 11, where we show how to solve grid computations efficiently on both shared-memory multiprocessors and distributed machines.

3.5.4 Synchronous Multiprocessors

On an asynchronous multiprocessor, each processor executes a separate process, and the processes execute at potentially different rates. Such multiprocessors are called MIMD machines, because they have multiple instruction streams and multiple data streams—that is, they have multiple independent processors. This is the execution model we have assumed.

Although MIMD machines are the most widely used and flexible multiprocessors, synchronous multiprocessors (SIMD machines) have recently been available, e.g., the Connection Machine in the early 1990s and Maspar machines in the mid to late 1990s. An SIMD machine has multiple data streams but only a single instruction steam. In particular, every processor executes exactly the same sequence of instructions, and they do so *in lock step*. This makes SIMD machines especially suited to executing data parallel algorithms. For example, on an SIMD machine the algorithm in Figure 3.17 for computing all partial sums of an array simplifies to

```
int a[n], sum[n];

process Sum[i = 0 to n-1] {
  sum[i] = a[i];    /* initialize elements of sum */
  while (d < n) {
    if ((i-d) >= 0)    /* update sum */
      sum[i] = sum[i-d] + sum[i];
    d = d + d;    /* double the distance */
  }
}
```

We do not need to program barriers since every process executes the same instructions at the same time; hence every instruction and indeed every memory reference is followed by an implicit barrier. In addition, we do not need to use extra variables to hold old values. In the assignment to `sum[i]`, *every* process(or) fetches the old values from `sum` before any assigns new values. Hence, parallel assignment statements appear to be atomic on an SIMD machine, which reduces some sources of interference.

It is technologically much easier to construct an SIMD machine with a massive number of processors than it is to construct a massively parallel MIMD machine. This makes SIMD machines attractive for large problems that can be solved using data parallel algorithms. On the other hand, SIMD machines are special purpose in the sense that the entire machine executes one program at a time. (This is the main reason they have fallen out of favor.) Moreover, it is a challenge for the programmer to keep the processors busy doing useful work. In the above algorithm, for example, fewer and fewer processors update `sum[i]` on each iteration, yet each has to evaluate the condition in the `if` statement and then, if the condition is false, has to delay until all other processes have updated `sum`. In general, the execution time of an `if` statement is the *total* of the execution time for *every* branch, even if the branch is not taken. For example, the time to execute an `if/then/else` statement on each processor is the sum of the times to evaluate the condition, execute the `then` part, and execute the `else` part.

3.6 Parallel Computing with a Bag of Tasks

Many iterative problems can be solved using a data parallel programming style, as shown in the previous section. Recursive problems that arise from the divide and conquer paradigm can be parallelized by executing recursive calls in parallel rather than sequentially, as was shown in Section 1.5.

This section presents a different way to implement parallel computations using what is called a *bag of tasks*. A task is an independent unit of work. Tasks are placed in a bag that is shared by two or more worker processes. Each worker executes the following basic code:

```
while (true) {
    get a task from the bag;
    if  (no more tasks)
       break;      # exit the while loop
    execute the task, possibly generating new ones;
}
```

This approach can be used to implement recursive parallelism, in which case the tasks are the recursive calls. It can also be used to solve iterative problems having a fixed number of independent tasks.

The bag-of-tasks paradigm has several useful attributes. First, it is quite easy to use. One has only to define the representation for a task, implement the bag, program the code to execute a task, and figure out how to detect termination. Second, programs that use a bag of tasks are *scalable*, meaning that one can use any number of processors merely by varying the number of workers. (However, the performance of the program might not scale.) Finally, the paradigm makes it easy to implement *load balancing*. If tasks take different amounts of time to execute, some workers will probably execute more than others. However, as long as there are enough more tasks than workers (e.g., two or three times as many), the total amount of computation executed by each worker should be approximately the same.

Below we show how to use a bag of tasks to implement matrix multiplication and adaptive quadrature. In matrix multiplication there is a fixed number of tasks. With adaptive quadrature, tasks are created dynamically. Both examples use critical sections to protect access to the bag and use barrier-like synchronization to detect termination.

3.6.1 Matrix Multiplication

Consider again the problem of multiplying two $n \times n$ matrices a and b. This requires computing n^2 inner products, one for each combination of a row of a and a column of b. Each inner product is an independent computation, so each could be executed in parallel. However, suppose we are going to execute the program on a machine with PR processors. Then we would like to employ PR worker processes, one per processor. To balance the computational load, each should compute about the same number of inner products. In Section 1.4 we statically assigned parts of the computation to each worker. Here, we will use a bag of tasks, and have each worker grab a task whenever it is needed.

If PR is much smaller than n, a good size for a task would be one or a few rows of the result matrix c. (This leads to reasonable data locality for matrices a and c, assuming matrices are stored in row-major order.) For simplicity, we will use single rows. Initially, the bag contains n tasks, one per row. Since these can be ordered in any way we wish, we can represent the bag by simply counting rows:

```
int nextRow = 0;
```

A worker gets a task out of the bag by executing the atomic action:

```
⟨ row = nextRow; nextRow++; ⟩
```

where row is a local variable. The bag is empty if row is at least n. The atomic action above is another instance of drawing a ticket. It can be implemented using a Fetch-and-Add instruction, if one is available, or by using locks to protect the critical section.

Figure 3.20 contains an outline of the full program. We assume that the matrices have been initialized. Workers compute inner products in the usual way. The program terminates when each worker has broken out of its `while` loop. If

```
int nextRow = 0;  # the bag of tasks
double a[n,n], b[n,n], c[n,n];

process Worker[w = 1 to P] {
  int row;
  double sum;   # for inner products
  while (true) {
    # get a task
    ⟨ row = nextRow; nextRow++; ⟩
    if (row >= n)
      break;
    compute inner products for c[row,*];
  }
}
```

Figure 3.20   Matrix multiplication using a bag of tasks.

we want to detect this, we could employ a shared counter, **done**, that is initially
zero and that is incremented atomically before a worker executes **break**. Then if
we want to have the last worker print the results, we could add the following code
to the end of each worker:

```
if (done == n)
  print matrix c;
```

This uses **done** like a counter barrier.

3.6.2 Adaptive Quadrature

Recall that the quadrature problem is to approximate the integral of a function
f(x) from **a** to **b**. With adaptive quadrature, one first computes the midpoint **m**
between **a** and **b**. Then one approximates three areas: from **a** to **m**, from **m** to **b**,
and from **a** to **b**. If the sum of the two smaller areas is within some acceptable
tolerance of the larger area, then the approximation is considered good enough.
If not, the larger problem is divided into two subproblems and the process is
repeated.

We can use the bag-of-tasks paradigm as follows to implement adaptive
quadrature. Here, a task is an interval to examine; it is defined by the end points
of the interval, the value of the function at those endpoints, and the approximation of the area for that interval. Initially there is just one task, for the entire
interval **a** to **b**.

A worker repeatedly takes a task from the bag and executes it. In contrast to the matrix multiplication program, however, the bag may (temporarily) be empty and a worker might thus have to delay before getting a task. Moreover, executing one task will usually lead to producing two smaller tasks, which a worker needs to put back into the bag. Finally, it is more difficult to determine when all the work has been done because it is not sufficient simply to wait until the bag is empty. (Indeed, the bag will *be* empty the minute the first task is taken.) Rather, all the work is done only when both (1) the bag is empty and (2) each worker is waiting to get another task.

Figure 3.21 contains a program for adaptive quadrature using a bag of tasks. The bag is represented by a queue and a counter. Another counter keeps track of the number of idle workers. All the work has been finished when `size` is 0 and `idle` is `n`. Note that the program contains several atomic actions. These are needed to protect the critical sections that access the shared variables. All but one of the atomic actions are unconditional, so they can be protected using locks. However, the one `await` statement has to be implemented using the more elaborate protocol in Section 3.2 or using a more powerful synchronization mechanism such as semaphores or monitors.

The program in Figure 3.21 makes excessive use of the bag of tasks. In particular, when a worker decides to generate two tasks, it puts both of them in the bag, then loops around and takes a new task out of the bag (perhaps even one that it just put in). Instead, we could have a worker put one task in the bag and keep the other. Once the bag contains enough work to lead to a balanced computational load, a further optimization would be to have a worker execute a task fully, using sequential recursion, rather than putting more tasks into the bag.

Historical Notes

The critical section problem was first described by Edsger Dijkstra [1965]. Because the problem is fundamental, it has been studied by scores of people who have published literally hundreds of papers on the topic. This chapter has presented four of the most important solutions. (Raynal [1986] has written an entire book on mutual exclusion algorithms.) Although devising busy-waiting solutions was early on mostly an academic exercise—since busy waiting is inefficient on a single processor—the advent of multiprocessors has spurred renewed interest in such solutions. Indeed, all multiprocessors now provide instructions that support at least one busy-waiting solution. The exercises at the end of this chapter describe most of these instructions.

Dijkstra's paper [1965] presented the first `n`-process software solution. It is an extension of the first two-process solution designed by Dutch mathematician T. Dekker (see the exercises). However, Dijkstra's original formulation of the

```
type task = (double left, right, fleft, fright, lrarea);
queue bag(task);        # the bag of tasks
int size;               # number of tasks in bag
int idle = 0;           # number of idle workers
double total = 0.0;     # the total area
```

compute approximate area from a to b;
insert task (a, b, f(a), f(b), area) in the bag;
count = 1;

```
process Worker[w = 1 to PR] {
  double left, right, fleft, fright, lrarea;
  double mid, fmid, larea, rarea;
  while (true) {
    # check for termination
    ⟨ idle++;
      if (idle == n && size == 0) break; ⟩
    # get a task from the bag
    ⟨ await (size > 0)
      remove a task from the bag;
      size--; idle--; ⟩
    mid = (left+right) / 2;
    fmid = f(mid);
    larea = (fleft+fmid) * (mid-left) / 2;
    rarea = (fmid+fright) * (right-mid) / 2;
    if (abs((larea+rarea) - lrarea) > EPSILON) {
      ⟨ put (left, mid, fleft, fmid, larea) in the bag;
        put (mid, right, fmid, fright, rarea) in the bag;
        size = size + 2; ⟩
    } else
      ⟨ total = total + lrarea; ⟩
  }
  if (w == 1)   # worker 1 prints the result
    printf("the total is %f\n", total);
}
```

Figure 3.21   Adaptive quadrature using a bag of tasks.

problem did not require the eventual entry property (3.5). Donald Knuth [1966] was the first to publish a solution that also ensures eventual entry.

The tie-breaker algorithm was discovered by Gary Peterson [1981]; it is often called Peterson's algorithm as a result. This algorithm is particularly simple for two processes, unlike the earlier solutions of Dekker, Dijkstra, and others.

Peterson's algorithm also generalizes readily to an n-process solution, as shown in Figure 3.7. That solution requires that a process go through all n-1 stages, even if no other process is trying to enter its critical section. Block and Woo [1990] present a variation that requires only m stages if just m processes are contending for entry (see the exercises).

The bakery algorithm was devised by Leslie Lamport [1974]. (Figure 3.11 contains an improved version that appeared in Lamport [1979].) In addition to being more intuitive than earlier critical section solutions, the bakery algorithm allows processes to enter in essentially FIFO order. It also has the interesting property that it is tolerant of some hardware failures. First, if one process reads `turn[i]` while another process is setting it in the entry protocol, the read can return any value between 1 and the value being written. Second, a process `CS[i]` may fail at any time, assuming it immediately sets `turn[i]` to 0. However, the value of `turn[i]` can become unbounded in Lamport's solution if there is always at least one process in its critical section.

The ticket algorithm is the simplest of the n-process solutions to the critical section problem; it also allows processes to enter in the order in which they draw numbers. The ticket algorithm can in fact be viewed as an optimization of the bakery algorithm. However, it requires a Fetch-and-Add instruction, something that few machines provide (see Almasi and Gottlieb [1994] for machines that do).

Harry Jordan [1978] was one of the first to recognize the importance of barrier synchronization in parallel iterative algorithms; he is credited with coining the term barrier. Although barriers are not nearly as commonplace as critical sections, they too have been studied by dozens of people who have developed several different implementations. The combining tree barrier in Figures 3.13 and 3.14 is similar to one devised by Yew, Tzeng, and Lawrie [1987]. The butterfly barrier was devised by Brooks [1986]. Hensgen, Finkel, and Manber [1988] developed the dissemination barrier; their paper also describes a tournament barrier, which is similar in structure to a combining tree. Gupta [1989] describes a "fuzzy barrier," which includes a region of statements a process can execute while it waits for a barrier; his paper also describes a hardware implementation of fuzzy barriers.

As described in several places in the chapter, busy-waiting implementations of locks and barriers can lead to memory and interconnection-network contention. Thus it is important for delayed processes to spin on the contents of local memory, e.g., cached copies of variables. Chapter 8 of Hennessy and Patterson's architecture book [1996] discusses synchronization issues in multiprocessors, includes an interesting historical perspective, and provides an extensive set of references.

An excellent paper by Mellor-Crummy and Scott [1991] analyzes the performance of several lock and barrier protocols, including most of those described in the text. That paper also presents a new, list-based lock protocol and a scalable, tree-based barrier with only local spinning. A recent paper [McKenney 1996] describes different kinds of locking patterns in parallel programs and gives guidelines for selecting which locking primitives to use. Another recent paper [Savage et al. 1997] describes a tool called Eraser that can detect data races due to synchronization mistakes in lock-based multithreaded programs.

On multiprogrammed (time-sliced) systems, performance can suffer greatly if a process is preempted while holding a lock. One way to overcome this problem is to use *nonblocking*—or *lock free*—algorithms instead of using mutual exclusion locks. An implementation of a data structure is nonblocking if some process will complete an operation in a finite number of steps, regardless of the execution speed of other processes. Herlihy and Wing [1990] introduces this concept and presents a nonblocking implementation of concurrent queues. In Herlihy and Wing's implementation, the insert operation is also *wait free*—i.e., every insert operation will complete in a finite number of steps, again regardless of execution speeds. Herlihy [1990] presents a general methodology for implementing highly concurrent data structures, and Herlihy [1991] contains a comprehensive discussion of wait-free synchronization. A recent paper by Michael and Scott [1998] evaluates the performance of nonblocking implementations of several data structures; they also consider the alternative of lock-based implementations that are modified to be preemption safe. They conclude that nonblocking implementations are superior for those data structures for which they exist (e.g., queues), and that preemption-safe locks outperform normal locks on multiprogrammed systems.

Data parallel algorithms are most closely associated with massively parallel machines since those machines permit thousands of data elements to be operated on in parallel. Many of the earliest examples of data parallel algorithms were designed for the NYU Ultracomputer [Schwartz 1980]; all have the characteristic attribute that execution time is logarithmic in the size of the data. The Ultracomputer is a MIMD machine, and its designers realized the importance of efficient critical section and barrier synchronization protocols. Consequently, they implemented a Replace-and-Add operation in an early hardware prototype [Gottlieb et al. 1983]; this instruction adds a value to a memory word and then returns the result. However, more recent versions of the Ultracomputer provide a Fetch-and-Add operation instead [Almasi & Gottlieb 1994], which returns the value of a memory word before adding to it. This change was made because Fetch-and-Add, unlike Replace-and-Add, generalizes to any binary combining operator—for example, Fetch-and-Max or Fetch-and-And. This general kind of instruction is called a Fetch-and-Φ operation.

The introduction of the Connection Machine in the mid-1980s spurred renewed interest in data parallel algorithms. That machine was designed by

Daniel Hillis [1985] as part of his doctoral dissertation at MIT. (Precious few dissertations have been as influential!) The Connection Machine was a SIMD machine, so barrier synchronization was automatically provided after every machine instruction. The Connection Machine also had thousands of processing elements; this enables a data parallel algorithm to have a very fine granularity—for example, a processor can be assigned to every element of an array. Hillis and Steele [1986] give an overview of the original Connection Machine and describe several interesting data parallel algorithms.

The bag-of-tasks paradigm for parallel computing was introduced by Carriero, Gelernter, and Leichter [1986]. That paper shows how to implement the task bag in the Linda programming notation, which we describe in Chapter 7. They called the associated programming model *replicated workers*, because any number of workers can share the bag. Some now call this the *work farm model*, because the tasks in the bag are farmed out to the workers. We prefer the phrase "bag of tasks" because it characterizes the essence of the approach: a shared bag of tasks.

References

Almasi, G. S., and A. Gottlieb. 1994. *Highly Parallel Computing*, 2nd ed. Menlo Park, CA: Benjamin/Cummings.

Block, K., and T.-K. Woo. 1990. A more efficient generalization of Peterson's mutual exclusion algorithm. *Information Processing Letters* 35 (August): 219–22.

Brooks, E. D., III. 1986. The butterfly barrier. *Int. Journal of Parallel Prog.* 15, 4 (August): 295–307.

Carriero, N., D. Gelernter, and J. Leichter. 1986. Distributed data structures in Linda. *Thirteenth ACM Symp. on Principles of Prog. Langs.*, January, pp. 236–42.

Dijkstra, E. W. 1965. Solution of a problem in concurrent programming control. *Comm. ACM* 8, 9 (September): 569.

Gottlieb, A., B. D. Lubachevsky, and L. Rudolph. 1983. Basic techniques for the efficient coordination of very large numbers of cooperating sequential processors. *ACM Trans. on Prog. Languages and Systems* 5, 2 (April): 164–89.

Gupta, R. 1989. The fuzzy barrier: a mechanism for high speed synchronization of processors. *Third Int. Conf. on Architectural Support for Prog. Languages and Operating Systems*, April, pp. 54–63.

Hennessy, J. L., and D. A. Patterson. 1996. *Computer Architecture: A Quantitative Approach*, 2nd ed. San Francisco: Morgan Kaufmann.

Hensgen, D., R. Finkel, and U. Manber. 1988. Two algorithms for barrier synchronization. *Int. Journal of Parallel Prog.* 17, 1 (January): 1–17.

Herlihy, M. P. 1990. A methodology for implementing highly concurrent data structures. *Proc. Second ACM Symp. on Principles & Practice of Parallel Prog.*, March, pp. 197–206.

Herlihy, M. P. 1991. Wait-free synchronization. *ACM Trans. on Prog. Languages and Systems* 11, 1 (January): 124–49.

Herlihy, M. P., and J. M. Wing. 1990. Linearizability: a correctness condition for concurrent objects. *ACM Trans. on Prog. Languages and Systems* 12, 3 (July): 463–92.

Hillis, W. D. 1985. *The Connection Machine*. Cambridge, MA: MIT Press.

Hillis, W. D., and G. L. Steele., Jr. 1986. Data parallel algorithms. *Comm. ACM* 29, 12 (December): 1170–83.

Jordan, H. F. 1978. A special purpose architecture for finite element analysis. *Proc. 1978 Int. Conf. on Parallel Processing*, pp. 263–6.

Knuth, D. E. 1966. Additional comments on a problem in concurrent programming control. *Comm. ACM* 9, 5 (May): 321–2.

Lamport, L. 1974. A new solution of Dijkstra's concurrent programming problem. *Comm. ACM* 17, 8 (August): 453–5.

Lamport, L. 1979. A new approach to proving the correctness of multiprocess programs. *ACM Trans. on Prog. Languages and Systems* 1, 1 (July): 84–97.

Lamport, L. 1987. A fast mutual exclusion algorithm. *ACM Trans. on Computer Systems* 5, 1 (February): 1–11.

McKenney, P. E. 1996. Selecting locking primitives for parallel programming. *Comm. ACM* 39, 10 (October): 75–82.

Mellor-Crummey, J. M., and M. L. Scott. 1991. Algorithms for scalable synchronization on shared-memory multiprocessors. *ACM Trans. on Computer Systems* 9, 1 (February): 21–65.

Michael, M. M., and M. L. Scott. 1998. Nonblocking algorithms and preemption-safe locking on multiprogrammed shared memory multiprocessors. *Journal of Parallel and Distributed Computer* 51, 1–26.

Peterson, G. L. 1981. Myths about the mutual exclusion problem. *Information Processing Letters* 12, 3 (June): 115–6.

Raynal, M. 1986. *Algorithms for Mutual Exclusion.* Cambridge, MA: MIT Press.

Savage, S., M. Burrows, G. Nelson, P. Sobalvarro, and T. Anderson. 1997. Eraser: a dynamic data race detector for multithreaded programs. *ACM. Trans. on Computer Systems* 15, 4 (November): 391–411.

Schwartz, J. T. 1980. Ultracomputers. *ACM Trans. on Prog. Languages and Systems* 2, 4 (October): 484–521.

Yew, P.-C., N.-F. Tzeng, and D. H. Lawrie. 1987. Distributing hot-spot addressing in large-scale multiprocessors. *IEEE Trans. on Computers* C-36, 4 (April): 388–95.

Exercises

3.1 Following is Dekker's algorithm, the first solution to the critical section problem for two processes:

```
bool enter1 = false, enter2 = false;
int turn = 1;

process P1 {
  while (true) {
    enter1 = true;
    while (enter2)
      if (turn == 2) {
        enter1 = false;
        while (turn == 2) skip;
        enter1 = true;
      }
    critical section;
    enter1 = false; turn = 2;
    noncritical section;
  }
}

process P2 {
  while (true) {
    enter2 = true;
    while (enter1)
      if (turn == 1) {
        enter2 = false;
        while (turn == 1) skip;
        enter2 = true;
      }
```

```
        critical section;
        enter2 = false; turn = 1;
        noncritical section;
    }
}
```

Explain clearly how the program ensures mutual exclusion, avoids deadlock, avoids unnecessary delay, and ensures eventual entry. For the eventual entry property, how many times can one process that wants to enter its critical section be bypassed by the other before the first gets in? Explain.

3.2   Suppose a computer has atomic decrement DEC and increment INC instructions that also return the value of the sign bit of the result. In particular, the decrement instruction has the following effect:

```
DEC(var, sign):
  ⟨ var = var - 1;
    if (var >= 0) sign = 0; else sign = 1; ⟩
```

INC is similar, the only difference being that it adds 1 to variable.

Using DEC and/or INC, develop a solution to the critical section problem for n processes. Do not worry about the eventual entry property. Describe clearly how your solution works and why it is correct.

3.3   Suppose a computer has an atomic swap instruction, defined as follows:

```
Swap(var1, var2):
  ⟨ tmp = var1; var1 = var2; var2 = tmp; ⟩
```

In the above, tmp is an internal register.

(a) Using Swap, develop a solution to the critical section problem for n processes. Do not worry about the eventual entry property. Describe clearly how your solution works and why it is correct.

(b) Modify your answer to (a) so that it will perform well on a multiprocessor system with caches. Explain what changes you make (if any) and why.

(c) Using Swap, develop a fair solution to the critical section problem—namely, one that also ensures eventual entry to each waiting process. The key is to order the processes, where first-come, first-served is the most obvious ordering. Note that you cannot just use your answer to (a) to implement the atomic action in the ticket algorithm, because you cannot get a fair solution using unfair components. You may assume that each process has a unique identity, say, the integers from 1 to n. Explain your solution, and give convincing arguments why it is correct and fair.

3.4   Suppose a computer has an atomic Compare-and-Swap instruction, which has the following effect:

```
CSW(a, b, c):
   〈 if (a == c)
        { c = b; return (0); }
      else
        { a = c; return (1); } 〉
```

Parameters a, b, and c are simple variables, such as integers. Using CSW, develop a solution to the critical section problem for n processes. Do not worry about the eventual entry property. Describe clearly how your solution works and why it is correct.

3.5   Some RISC (reduced instruction set computer) machines provide the following two instructions:

```
LL(register, variable)  # load locked
   〈 register = variable; location = &variable; 〉

SC(variable, value)     # store conditional
   〈 if (location == &variable)
        { variable = value; return (1); }
      else
           return (0); 〉
```

The (LL) (load locked) instruction atomically loads variable into register and saves the address of the variable in a special register. The location register is shared by all processors, and it is changed *only* as a result of executing LL instructions. The SC (store conditional) instruction atomically checks to see if the address of variable is the same as the address currently stored in location. If it is, SC stores value in variable and returns a 1; otherwise SC returns a 0.

(a) Using these instructions, develop a solution to the critical section problem. Do not worry about the eventual entry property.

(b) Are these instructions powerful enough to develop a fair solution to the critical section problem? If so, give one. If not, explain why not.

3.6   Consider the load locked (LL) and store conditional (SC) instructions defined in the previous exercise. These instructions can be used to implement an atomic Fetch-and-Add (FA) instruction. Show how to do so. (*Hint*: You will need to use a spin loop.)

3.7   Consider the following critical section protocol [Lamport 1987]:

```
int lock = 0;
process CS[i = 1 to n] {
  while (true) {
    ⟨await (lock == 0)⟩; lock = i; Delay;
    while (lock != i) {
      ⟨await (lock == 0)⟩; lock = i; Delay;
    }
    critical section;
    lock = 0;
    noncritical section;
  }
}
```

(a) Suppose the Delay code is deleted. Does the protocol ensure mutual exclusion? Does it avoid deadlock? Does the protocol avoid unnecessary delay? Does it ensure eventual entry? Carefully explain each of your answers.

(b) Suppose the processes execute with true concurrency on a multiprocessor. Suppose the Delay code spins for long enough to ensure that every process i that waits for `lock` to be `0` has time to execute the assignment statement that sets `lock` to i. Does the protocol now ensure mutual exclusion, avoid deadlock, avoid unnecessary delay, and ensure eventual entry? Again, carefully explain each of your answers.

3.8   Suppose your machine has the following atomic instruction:

```
flip(lock)
  ⟨ lock = (lock + 1 ) % 2;   # flip the lock
    return (lock); ⟩          # return the new value
```

Someone suggests the following solution to the critical section problem for *two* processes:

```
int lock = 0;   # shared variable
process CS[i = 1 to 2] {
  while (true) {
    while (flip(lock) != 1)
      while (lock != 0) skip;
    critical section;
    lock = 0;
    noncritical section;
  }
}
```

(a) Explain why this solution will *not* work—in other words, give an execution order that results in both processes being in their critical sections at the same time.

(b) Suppose that the first line in the body of `flip` is changed to do addition module 3 rather than modulo 2. Will the solution now work for two processes? Explain your answer.

3.9 Consider the following variation on the n-process tie-breaker algorithm [Block and Woo 1990]:

```
int in = 0, last[1:n];   # shared variables
process CS[i = 1 to n] {
  int stage;
  while (true) {
    ⟨in = in + 1;⟩; stage = 1; last[stage] = i;
    ⟨await (last[stage] != i or in <= stage);⟩
    while (last[stage] != i) {   # go to next stage
       stage = stage + 1; last[stage] = i;
       ⟨await (last[stage] != i or in <= stage);⟩
    }
    critical section;
    ⟨in = in - 1;⟩
    noncritical section;
  }
}
```

(a) Explain clearly how this program ensures mutual exclusion, avoids deadlock, and ensures eventual entry.

(b) Compare the performance of this algorithm to that of the tie-breaker algorithm in Figure 3.7. In particular, which is faster if only one process is trying to enter the critical section? How much faster? Which is faster if all n processes are trying to enter the critical section? How much faster?

(c) Convert the coarse-grained solution above to a fine-grained solution in which the only atomic actions are reading and writing variables. Do not assume increment and decrement are atomic. (*Hint*: Change `in` to an array.)

3.10 (a) Modify the coarse-grained ticket algorithm in Figure 3.8 so `next` and `number` do not overflow. (*Hint*: Pick a constant `MAX` greater than `n`, and use modular arithmetic.)

(b) Using your answer to (a), modify the fine-grained ticket algorithm in Figure 3.9 so `next` and `number` do not overflow. Assume the Fetch-and-Add instruction is available.

3.11   In the bakery algorithm (Figure 3.11), the values of `turn` are unbounded if there is always at least one process in its critical section. Assume reads and writes are atomic. Is it possible to modify the algorithm so that values of `turn` are always bounded? If so, give a modified algorithm. If not, explain why not.

3.12   In the critical section protocols in the text, every process executes the same algorithm. It is also possible to solve the problem using a coordinator process. In particular, when a regular process `CS[i]` wants to enter its critical section, it tells the coordinator, then waits for the coordinator to grant permission.

(a)   Develop protocols for the regular processes and the coordinator. Do not worry about the eventual entry property. (*Hint*: See the coordinator barrier in Figure 3.12 for ideas).

(b)   Modify your answer to (a) so that it also ensures eventual entry.

3.13   Display (3.11) shows how to use a shared counter for barrier synchronization, but that solution does not solve the problem of resetting the counter to zero. Develop a complete solution by using two counters. First develop a coarse-grained solution using `await` statements. Then develop a fine-grained solution; assume the Fetch-and-Add instruction is available. Be careful about a process coming back around to the barrier before all others have left it. (*Hint*: The "increment" in Fetch-and-Add can be negative.)

3.14   A *tournament barrier* has the same kind of tree structure as in Figure 3.13, but the worker processes interact differently than in the combining-tree barrier of Figure 3.14. In particular, each worker is a leaf node. Pairs of adjacent workers wait for each other to arrive. One "wins" and proceeds to the next level up the tree; the other waits. The winner of the "tournament" at the top of the tree announces that all workers have reached the barrier—i.e., it tells all of them that they can continue.

(a)   Write programs for the workers, showing all details of how they synchronize. Assume that the number of workers, `n`, is a power of 2. Either use two sets of variables or reset their values so that the worker processes can use the tournament barrier again on their next loop iteration.

(b)   Compare your answer to (a) with the combining-tree barrier in Figure 3.14. How many variables are required for each kind of barrier? If each assignment and `await` statement takes one unit of time, what is the total time required for barrier synchronization in each algorithm? What is the total time for the combining-tree barrier if it is modified so that the root broadcasts a single `continue` message, as described in the text?

3.15 (a) Give complete details for a butterfly barrier for eight processes. Show all variables that are needed, and give the code that each process would execute. The barrier should be reusable.

(b) Repeat (a) for a dissemination barrier for eight processes.

(c) Compare your answers to (a) and (b). How many variables are required for each kind of barrier? If each assignment and `await` statement takes one unit of time, what is the total time required for barrier synchronization in each algorithm?

(d) Repeat (a), (b), and (c) for a six-process barrier.

(e) Repeat (a), (b), and (c) for a 14-process barrier.

3.16 Consider the following implementation of a single n-process barrier:

```
int arrive[1:n] = ([n] 0);   # shared array
code executed by Worker[1]:
   arrive[1] = 1;
   ⟨await (arrive[n] == 1);⟩
code executed by Worker[i = 2 to n]:
   ⟨await (arrive[i-1] == 1);⟩
   arrive[i] = 1;
   ⟨await (arrive[n] == 1);⟩
```

(a) Explain how this barrier works.

(b) What is the time complexity of the barrier?

(c) Extend the above code so that the barrier is reusable.

3.17 Assume there are n worker processes, numbered from 1 to n. Also assume that your machine has an atomic increment instruction. Consider the following code for an n-process barrier that is supposed to be reusable:

```
int count = 0; go = 0;   # shared variables
code executed by Worker[1]:
   ⟨await (count == n-1);⟩
   count = 0;
   go = 1;
code executed by Worker[2:n]:
   ⟨count++;⟩
   ⟨await (go == 1);⟩
```

(a) Explain what is wrong with the above code?

(b) Fix the code so that it works. Do not use any more shared variables, but you may introduce local variables.

(c) Suppose the above code were correct. Assume all processes arrive at the barrier at the same time. How long does it take before every process can leave the barrier? Count each assignment statement as 1 time unit, and count each `await` statement as 1 time unit once the condition becomes true.

3.18 In the parallel prefix algorithm in Figure 3.17, there are three barrier synchronization points. Some of these can be optimized since it is not always necessary for all processes to arrive at a barrier before any can proceed. Identify the barriers that can be optimized, and give the details of the optimization. Use the smallest possible number of two-process barriers.

3.19 Modify each of the following algorithms to use only k processes instead of n processes. Assume that n is a multiple of k.

(a) The parallel prefix computation in Figure 3.17.

(b) The linked-list computation in Figure 3.18.

(c) The grid computation in Figure 3.19.

3.20 One way to to sort n integers is to use an odd/even exchange sort (also called an odd/even transposition sort). Assume there are n processes `P[1:n]` and that n is even. In this kind of sorting method, each process executes a series of rounds. On odd-numbered rounds, odd-numbered processes `P[odd]` exchange values with `P[odd+1]` if the values are out of order. On even-numbered rounds, even-numbered processes `P[even]` exchange values with `P[even+1]`, again if the values are out of order. (`P[1]` and `P[n]` do nothing on even numbered rounds.)

(a) Determine how many rounds have to be executed in the worst case to sort n numbers. Then write a data parallel algorithm to sort integer array `a[1:n]` into ascending order.

(b) Modify your answer to (a) to terminate as soon as the array has been sorted (e.g., it might initially be in ascending order).

(c) Modify your answer to (a) to use k processes; assume n is a multiple of k.

3.21 Assume there are n processes `P[1:n]` and that `P[1]` has some local value v that it wants to broadcast to all the others. In particular, the goal is to store v in every entry of array `a[1:n]`. The obvious sequential algorithm requires linear time. Write a data parallel algorithm to store v in `a` in logarithmic time.

3.22 Assume `P[1:n]` is an array of processes and `b[1:n]` is a shared Boolean array.

(a) Write a data parallel algorithm to count the number of `b[i]` that are true.

(b) Suppose the answer to (a) is `count`, which will be between `0` and `n`. Write a data parallel algorithm that assigns a unique integer index between `1` and `count` to each `P[i]` for which `b[i]` is true.

3.23   Suppose you are given two serially linked lists. Write a data parallel algorithm that matches corresponding elements. In particular, when the algorithm terminates, the ith elements on each list should point to each other. (If one list is longer that the other, extra elements on the longer list should have null pointers.) Define the data structures you need. Do not modify the original lists; instead store the answers in additional arrays.

3.24   Suppose that you are given a serially linked list and that the elements are linked together in ascending order of their data fields. The standard sequential algorithm for inserting a new element in the proper place takes linear time (on average, half the list has to be searched). Write a data parallel algorithm to insert a new element into the list in logarithmic time.

3.25   Consider a simple language for expression evaluation with the following syntax:

> *expression ::= operand | expression operator operand*
> *operand ::= identifier | number*
> *operator ::= + | ***

An identifier is as usual a sequence of letters or digits, beginning with a letter. A number is a sequence of digits. The operators are + and *.

An array of characters `ch[1:n]` has been given. Each character is a letter, a digit, a blank, +, or *. The sequence of characters from `ch[1]` to `ch[n]` represents a sentence in the above expression language.

Write a data parallel algorithm that determines for each character in `ch[1:n]` the token (nonterminal) to which it belongs. Assume you have `n` processes, one per character. The result for each character should be one of `ID`, `NUMBER`, `PLUS`, `TIMES`, or `BLANK`. (*Hints*: A regular language can be parsed by a finite-state automaton, which can be represented by a transition matrix. The rows of the matrix are indexed by states, the columns by characters; the value of an entry is the new state the automaton would enter, given the current state and next character. The composition of state transition functions is associative, which makes it amenable to a parallel prefix computation.)

3.26   The following region-labeling problem arises in image processing. Given is integer array `image[1:n,1:n]`. The value of each entry is the intensity of a pixel. The neighbors of a pixel are the four pixels to the left, right, above, and below it. Two pixels belong to the same region if they are neighbors and they have the same value. Thus, a region is a maximal set of pixels that are connected and that all have the same value.

The problem is to find all regions and assign every pixel in each region a unique label. In particular, let `label[1:n,1:n]` be a second matrix, and assume that the initial value of `label[i,j]` is `n*i + j`. The final value of `label[i,j]` is to be the largest of the initial labels in the region to which pixel `[i,j]` belongs.

Write a data parallel grid computation to compute the final values of `label`. The computation should terminate when no `label` changes value.

3.27   Using a grid computation to solve the region-labeling problem of the previous exercise requires worst-case execution time of $O(n^2)$. This can happen if there is a region that "snakes" around the image. Even for simple images, the grid computation requires $O(n)$ execution time.

The region-labeling problem can be solved as follows in time $O(\log n)$. First, for each pixel, determine whether it is on the boundary of a region and, if so, which of its neighbors are also on the boundary. Second, have each boundary pixel create pointers to its neighbors that are on the boundary; this produces doubly linked lists connecting all pixels that are on the boundary of a region. Third, using the lists, propagate the largest label of any of the boundary pixels to the others that are on the boundary. (The pixel with the largest label for any region will be on its boundary.) Finally, use a parallel prefix computation to propagate the label for each region to pixels in the interior of the region.

Write a data parallel program that implements this algorithm. Analyze its execution time, which should be $O(\log n)$.

3.28   Consider the problem of generating all prime numbers up to some limit `L` using the bag-of-tasks paradigm. One way to solve this problem is to mimic the sieve of Eratosthenes in which you have an array of `L` integers and repeatedly cross out multiples of primes: `2`, `3`, `5`, and so on. In this case the bag would contain the next prime to use. This approach is easy to program, but it uses lots of storage because you need to have an array of `L` integers.

A second way to solve the problem is to check all odd numbers, one after the other. In this case, the bag would contain all odd numbers. (They do not have to be stored, because you can generate the next odd number from the current one.) For each candidate, see whether it is prime; if it is, add it to a growing list of known primes. The list of primes is used to check future candidates. This second approach requires far less space than the first approach, but it has a tricky synchronization problem.

Write parallel programs that implement each of these approaches. Use `w` worker processes. At the end of each program, print the last `10` primes that you have found and the execution time for the computational part of the program.

Compare the time and space requirements of these two programs for various values of L and W.

3.29 Consider the problem of determining the number of words in a dictionary that contain unique letters—namely, the number of words in which no letter appears more than once. Treat upper and lower case versions of a letter as the same letter. (Most Unix systems contain one or more online dictionaries, for example in /usr/dict/words.)

Write a parallel program to solve this problem. Use the bag-of-tasks paradigm and W worker processes. At the end of the program, print the number of words that contain unique letters, and also print all those that are the longest. You may read the dictionary file into shared variables before starting the parallel computation.

3.30 A concurrent queue is a queue in which insert and delete operations can execute in parallel. Assume the queue is stored in array queue[1:n]. Two variables front and rear point to the first full element and the next empty slot, respectively. The delete operation delays until there is an element in queue[front], then removes it and increments front (modulo n). The insert operation delays until there is an empty slot, then puts a new element in queue[rear] and increments rear (modulo n).

Design algorithms for queue insertion and deletion that maximize parallelism. In particular, except at critical points where they access shared variables, inserts and deletes ought to be able to proceed in parallel with each other and with themselves. You will need additional variables. You may also assume the Fetch-and-Add instruction is available.

4

Semaphores

As we saw in the last chapter, most busy-waiting protocols are quite complex. Also, there is no clear distinction between variables that are used for synchronization and those that are used for computing results. Consequently, one has to be very careful when designing or using busy-waiting protocols.

A further deficiency of busy waiting is that it is inefficient in most multi-threaded programs. Except in parallel programs in which the number of processes matches the number of processors, there are usually more processes than processors. Hence, a processor executing a spinning process can usually be more productively employed executing another process.

Because synchronization is fundamental to concurrent programs, it is desirable to have special tools that aid in the design of correct synchronization protocols and that can be used to block processes that must be delayed. *Semaphores* were the first and remain one of the most important synchronization tools. They make it easy to protect critical sections and can be used in a disciplined way to implement signaling and scheduling. Consequently, they are included in all threads and parallel programming libraries of which the author is aware. Moreover, semaphores can be implemented in more than one way—using busy-waiting techniques from the previous chapter or using a kernel, as described in Chapter 6.

The concept of a semaphore—and indeed the very term—is motivated by one of the ways in which railroad traffic is synchronized to avoid train collisions. A railroad semaphore is a signal flag that indicates whether the track ahead is clear or is occupied by another train. As a train proceeds, semaphores are set and cleared; they remain set long enough to allow another train time to stop if necessary. Thus railroad semaphores can be viewed as mechanisms that signal conditions in order to ensure mutually exclusive occupancy of critical sections of track.

Semaphores in concurrent programs are similar: They provide a basic signaling mechanism and are used to implement mutual exclusion and condition synchronization.

This chapter defines the syntax and semantics of semaphores and then illustrates how to use them to solve synchronization problems. For comparison purposes, we reexamine some of the problems considered in previous chapters, including critical sections, producers and consumers, and barriers. In addition, we introduce several interesting new problems: bounded buffers, dining philosophers, readers and writers, and shortest-job-next resource allocation. Along the way, we introduce three useful programming techniques: (1) changing variables, (2) split binary semaphores, and (3) passing the baton, a general technique that can be used to control the order in which processes execute.

4.1 Syntax and Semantics

A semaphore is a special kind of shared variable that is manipulated only by two *atomic* operations, P and V. Think of a semaphore as an instance of a semaphore class and of P and V as the two methods of the class, with the additional attribute that the methods are atomic.

The value of a semaphore is a *nonnegative integer*. The V operation is used to signal the occurrence of an event, so it increments the value of a semaphore. The P operation is used to delay a process until an event has occurred, so it waits until the value of a semaphore is positive then decrements the value.[1] The power of semaphores results from the fact that P operations might have to delay.

A semaphore is declared as follows:

```
sem s;
```

The default initial value is zero. Alternatively, a semaphore can be initialized to any nonnegative value, as in

```
sem lock = 1;
```

Arrays of semaphores can also be declared—and optionally initialized—in the usual fashion, as in

```
sem forks[5] = ([5] 1);
```

---

[1] The letters P and V are mnemonic for Dutch words, as described in the historical notes at the end of the chapter. Think of P as standing for "pass", and think of the upward shape of V as signifying increment. Some authors use wait and signal instead of P and V, but we will reserve the use of the terms wait and signal for the next chapter on monitors.

If there were no initialization clause in the above declaration, each semaphore in the array `forks` would be initialized to zero.

After a semaphore has been declared and initialized, it can be manipulated *only* by using the `P` and `V` operations. Each is an atomic operation with one argument. Let `s` be a semaphore. Then the definitions of `P(s)` and `V(s)` are

```
P(s):  ⟨await (s > 0) s = s - 1;⟩
V(s):  ⟨s = s + 1;⟩
```

The `V` operation atomically increments the value of `s`. The `P` operation decrements the value of `s`, but to ensure that `s` is never negative, the `P` operation waits until `s` is positive.

The delay and decrement in the `P` operation are a *single* atomic action. Suppose `s` is a semaphore with current value `1`. If two processes try at the same time to execute `P(s)` operations, only one process will succeed. However, if one process tries to execute `P(s)` at the same time that another process tries to execute `V(s)`, the two operations will both succeed—in an unpredictable order—and the final value of `s` will again be `1`.

A *general semaphore* is one that can take on any nonnegative value. A *binary semaphore* is one whose value is always either `0` or `1`. In particular, a `V` operation on a binary semaphore is executed only when the semaphore has value `0`. (One could define the `V` operation on a binary semaphore to be one that waits until the value of the semaphore is less than `1`, then does the increment.)

Since the semaphore operations are defined in terms of **await** statements, their formal semantics follow directly from applications of the Await Statement Rule given in Section 2.6. In particular, inference rules for `P` and `V` result directly from specializing the Await Statement Rule by the actual **await** statements used above.

Fairness attributes of semaphore operations also follow from the fact that they are defined in terms of **await** statements. Using the terminology of Section 2.8, if `s > 0` becomes and then remains true, execution of `P(s)` will terminate if the underlying scheduling policy is weakly fair. If `s > 0` is infinitely often true, execution of `P(s)` will terminate if the underlying scheduling policy is strongly fair. Since the `V` operation on a general semaphore is an unconditional atomic action, `V` will terminate if the underlying scheduling policy is unconditionally fair.

As will be shown in Chapter 6, implementations of semaphores usually ensure that when processes are delayed while executing `P` operations, they are awakened in the order they were delayed. Consequently, as long as other processes execute an adequate number of `V` operations, a process waiting at a `P` operation will eventually be able to proceed.

4.2 Basic Problems and Techniques

Semaphores directly support the implementation of mutual exclusion, as in the critical section problem. They also directly support simple forms of condition synchronization in which semaphores are used to signal the occurrence of events. These two uses of semaphores can also be combined to solve more complex synchronization problems.

This section illustrates the use of semaphores for mutual exclusion and condition synchronization by presenting solutions to four problems: (1) critical sections, (2) barriers, (3) producers/consumers, and (4) bounded buffers. The solutions to the last two problems also illustrate the important programming technique of *split binary semaphores*. Later sections show how to use the techniques introduced here to construct solutions to more complex synchronization problems.

4.2.1 Critical Sections: Mutual Exclusion

Recall that in the critical section problem, each of n processes repeatedly executes a critical section of code, in which it requires exclusive access to some shared resource, and then executes a noncritical section, in which it computes using only local objects. In particular, in its critical section each process requires mutually exclusive access to the shared resource.

Semaphores were conceived in part to make the critical section problem easy to solve. Figure 3.2 presented a solution using lock variables in which variable `lock` is true when no process is in its critical section and `lock` is false otherwise. Let true be represented by `1` and let false be represented by `0`. Then, a process enters its critical section by first waiting for `lock` to be `1` and then setting `lock` to `0`. A process leaves its critical section by resetting `lock` to `1`.

These are *exactly* the operations supported by semaphores. Hence, let `mutex` be a semaphore that has initial value 1. Execution of `P(mutex)` is the same as waiting for `lock` to be `1` then setting `lock` to `0`. Similarly, execution of `V(mutex)` is the same as setting `lock` to `1` (assuming `lock` is set to `1` only when it is known to be `0`). These observations lead to the solution to the critical section problem shown in Figure 4.1.

4.2.2 Barriers: Signaling Events

We introduced barrier synchronization in Section 3.4 as a means to synchronize stages of parallel iterative algorithms, such as the data parallel algorithms in Section 3.5. The busy-waiting implementations of barriers used flag variables that

```
sem mutex = 1;

process CS[i = 1 to n] {
  while (true) {
    P(mutex);
    critical section;
    V(mutex);
    noncritical section;
  }
}
```

Figure 4.1   Semaphore solution to the critical section problem.

processes set and cleared as they arrived at and left a barrier. As was the case with the critical section problem, semaphores make it relatively easy to implement barrier synchronization. The basic idea is to use one semaphore for each synchronization flag. A process sets a flag by executing a V operation; a process waits for a flag to be set and then clears it by executing a P operation. (If each process in a parallel program executes on its own processor, then delays at barriers should be implemented using spin loops, not by blocking processes. Thus, we would want to use a busy-waiting implementation of semaphores.)

Consider first the problem of implementing a two-process barrier. Recall that two properties are required. First, neither process can get past the barrier until both have arrived. Second, the barrier must be reusable since in general the same processes will need to synchronize after each stage of the computation. For the critical section problem, we need to use only one semaphore as a lock, because the only concern is whether a process is inside or outside its critical section. However, barrier synchronization requires using two semaphores as signals, because we need to know each time a process arrives at or departs from the barrier.

A *signaling semaphore* s is one that is (usually) initialized to 0. A process signals an event by executing V(s); other processes wait for that event by executing P(s). For a two-process barrier, the two significant events are the processes arriving at the barrier. Hence, we can solve the problem using two signaling semaphores, arrive1 and arrive2. Each process signals its arrival by executing a V operation on its own semaphore, then waits for the other process to arrive by executing a P operation on the other process's semaphore. The solution is shown in Figure 4.2. Because barrier synchronization is symmetric, each process takes the same actions—each just signals and waits on different semaphores. When semaphores are used in this way, they are much like flag variables, and their use follows the Flag Synchronization Principles (3.14).

```
        sem arrive1 = 0, arrive2 = 0;

        process Worker1 {
          ...
          V(arrive1);     /* signal arrival          */
          P(arrive2);     /* wait for other process  */
          ...
        }

        process Worker2 {
          ...
          V(arrive2);     /* signal arrival          */
          P(arrive1);     /* wait for other process  */
          ...
        }
```

Figure 4.2   Barrier synchronization using semaphores.

We can use the two-process barrier as shown in Figure 4.2 to implement an n-process butterfly barrier having the structure shown in Figure 3.15. Or we can use the same idea to implement an n-process dissemination barrier having the structure shown in Figure 3.16. In both cases, we would employ an array of **arrive** semaphores. At each stage, a process i first signals its arrival by executing **V(arrive[i])**, then waits for another process by executing **P** on that process's instance of **arrive**. Unlike the situation with flag variables, only one array of **arrive** semaphores is required. This is because **V** operations are "remembered", whereas the value of a flag variable might be overwritten.

Alternatively, we can use semaphores as signal flags to implement n-process barrier synchronization using a central coordinator process (Figure 3.12) or a combining tree (Figure 3.14). Again, because **V** operations are remembered, we would need to use fewer semaphores than flag variables; for example, only one semaphore would be needed for the **Coordinator** in Figure 3.12.

4.2.3 Producers and Consumers: Split Binary Semaphores

This section reexamines the producers/consumers problem introduced in Section 1.6 and revisited in Section 2.5. There we assumed that there was one producer and one consumer; here we consider the general situation in which there are multiple producers and consumers. The solution illustrates another use of semaphores as signaling flags. It also introduces the important concept of a split binary semaphore, which provides another way to protect critical sections of code.

In the producers/consumers problem, producers send messages that are received by consumers. The processes communicate using a single shared buffer, which is manipulated by two operations: `deposit` and `fetch`. Producers insert messages into the buffer by calling `deposit`; consumers receive messages by calling `fetch`. To ensure that messages are not overwritten and that they are received only once, execution of `deposit` and `fetch` must alternate, with `deposit` executed first.

The way to program the required alternation property is again to use signaling semaphores. Such semaphores can be used either to indicate when processes reach critical execution points or to indicate changes to the status of shared variables. Here, the critical execution points are starting and ending `deposit` and `fetch` operations. The corresponding changes to the shared buffer are its becoming empty or full. Because there might be multiple producers or consumers, it is simpler to associate a semaphore with each of the two states of the buffer rather than the execution points of the processes.

Let `empty` and `full` be two semaphores indicating whether the buffer is empty or full. Initially, the buffer is empty so the initial value of `empty` is `1` (i.e., the "make the buffer empty" event has already occurred). The initial value of `full` is `0`. When a producer wants to execute `deposit`, it must first wait for the buffer to be empty; after a producer deposits an item, the buffer becomes full. Similarly, when a consumer wants to execute `fetch`, it must first wait for the buffer to be full, and then it makes the buffer empty. A process waits for an event by executing `P` on the appropriate semaphore and signals an event by executing `V`, so we get the solution shown in Figure 4.3.

In Figure 4.3, `empty` and `full` are both binary semaphores. Together they form what is called a *split binary semaphore*, because at most one of `empty` or `full` is `1` at a time. The term split binary semaphore comes from the fact that `empty` and `full` can be viewed as a single binary semaphore that has been split into two binary semaphores. In general, a split binary semaphore can be formed from any number of binary semaphores.

Split binary semaphores are important because they can be used as follows to implement mutual exclusion. Suppose that one of the binary semaphores has an initial value of `1` (hence the others are initially `0`). Further suppose that, in the processes that use the semaphores, *every* execution path starts with a `P` operation on one of the semaphores, and ends with a `V` operation on one of the semaphores. Then all statements between any `P` and the next `V` execute with mutual exclusion. In particular, whenever any process is between a `P` and a `V`, the semaphores are all `0`, and hence no other process can complete a `P` until the first process executes a `V`.

The solution to the producers/consumers problem in Figure 4.3 illustrates this use of split binary semaphores. Each `Producer` alternately executes

```
typeT buf;       /* a buffer of some type T */
sem empty = 1, full = 0;

process Producer[i = 1 to M] {
  while (true) {
    ...
    /* produce data, then deposit it in the buffer */
    P(empty);
    buf = data;
    V(full);
  }
}

process Consumer[j = 1 to N] {
  while (true) {
    /* fetch result, then consume it */
    P(full);
    result = buf;
    V(empty);
    ...
  }
}
```

Figure 4.3   Producers and consumers using semaphores.

P(empty) then V(full), and each Consumer alternately executes P(full) then V(empty). In Section 4.4, we will use this property of split binary semaphores to construct a general method for implementing await statements.

4.2.4 Bounded Buffers: Resource Counting

The last example showed how to synchronize access to a single communication buffer. If data are produced at approximately the same rate at which they are consumed, a process would not generally have to wait very long to access the single buffer. Commonly however, producer and consumer execution is bursty. For example, a producer might produce several items in quick succession, then do more computation before producing another set of items. In such cases, a buffer capacity larger than one can significantly increase performance by reducing the number of times processes block. (This is an example of the classic time/space tradeoff in computing.)

Here we develop a solution to what is called the *bounded buffer problem*. In particular, a bounded buffer is a multislot communication buffer. The solution builds upon the solution in the previous section. It also illustrates the use of general semaphores as resource counters.

Assume for now that there is just one producer and one consumer. The producer deposits messages in a shared buffer; the consumer fetches them. The buffer contains a queue of messages that have been deposited but not yet fetched. This queue can be represented by a linked list or by an array. We will use the array representation here, because it is simpler to program. In particular, let the buffer be represented by `buf[n]`, where n is greater than 1. Let `front` be the index of the message at the front of the queue, and let `rear` be the index of the first empty slot past the message at the rear of the queue. Initially, `front` and `rear` are set to the same value, say 0.

With this representation for the buffer, the producer deposits a message with value `data` by executing

```
buf[rear] = data; rear = (rear+1) % n;
```

Similarly, the consumer fetches a message into its local variable `result` by executing

```
result = buf[front]; front = (front+1) % n;
```

The modulo operator (`%`) is used to ensure that the values of `front` and `rear` are always between 0 and n-1. The queue of buffered messages is thus stored in slots from `buf[front]` up to but not including `buf[rear]`, with `buf` treated as a circular array in which `buf[0]` follows `buf[n-1]`. As an example, one possible configuration of *buf* is shown below:

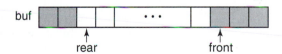

The shaded slots are full; the blank ones are empty.

When there is a single buffer—as in the producers/consumers problem—execution of **deposit** and **fetch** must alternate. When there are multiple buffers, **deposit** can execute whenever there is an empty slot, and **fetch** can execute whenever there is a stored message. In fact, **deposit** and **fetch** can execute concurrently if there is both an empty slot and a stored message, because **deposit** and **fetch** will then access different slots, and hence they will not interfere with each other. However, the synchronization requirements are *identical* for both a single-slot and a bounded buffer. In particular, the

```
typeT buf[n];          /* an array of some type T */
int front = 0, rear = 0;
sem empty = n, full = 0;     /* n-2 <= empty+full <= n */
process Producer {
  while (true) {
    ...
    produce message data and deposit it in the buffer;
    P(empty);
    buf[rear] = data; rear = (rear+1) % n;
    V(full);
  }
}

process Consumer {
  while (true) {
    fetch message result and consume it;
    P(full);
    result = buf[front]; front = (front+1) % n;
    V(empty);
    ...
  }
}
```

Figure 4.4   Bounded buffer using semaphores.

use of the P and V operations is the same. The only difference is that semaphore
empty is initialized to n rather than 1, as there are initially n empty slots. The
solution is shown in Figure 4.4.

In Figure 4.4, the semaphores serve as *resource counters*: each counts the
number of units of a resource. In this case, empty counts the number of empty
buffer slots, and full counts the number of full slots. When neither process is
executing deposit or fetch, the sum of the values of the two semaphores is n,
the total number of buffer slots. Resource-counting semaphores are useful whenever processes compete for access to multiple-unit resources such as buffer slots
or memory blocks.

We have assumed that there is only one producer and only one consumer in
Figure 4.4; this ensures that deposit and fetch execute as atomic actions.
Suppose, however, that there are two (or more) producers. Then each could
be executing deposit at the same time, assuming there are at least two empty
slots. In that case, both producers could try to deposit their message into the
same slot! (This would happen if both assign to buf[rear] before either

increments `rear`.) Similarly, if there are two (or more) consumers, both could execute `fetch` at the same time and retrieve the same message. In short, `deposit` and `fetch` become critical sections. Both operations must be executed with mutual exclusion—but they can execute concurrently with each other because `empty` and `full` are used in such a way that producers and consumers access different buffer slots. We can implement the required exclusion using the solution to the critical section problem shown in Figure 4.1, with separate semaphores being used to protect each critical section. The complete solution is shown in Figure 4.5.

We solved the two problems above separately—first the synchronization between one producer and one consumer, then the synchronization between

```
typeT buf[n];        /* an array of some type T */
int front = 0, rear = 0;
sem empty = n, full = 0;      /* n-2 <= empty+full <= n */
sem mutexD = 1, mutexF = 1;   /* for mutual exclusion   */
process Producer[i = 1 to M] {
   while (true) {
      ...
      produce message data and deposit it in the buffer;
      P(empty);
      P(mutexD);
      buf[rear] = data; rear = (rear+1) % n;
      V(mutexD);
      V(full);
   }
}

process Consumer[j = 1 to N] {
   while (true) {
      fetch message result and consume it;
      P(full);
      P(mutexF);
      result = buf[front]; front = (front+1) % n;
      V(mutexF);
      V(empty);
      ...
   }
}
```

Figure 4.5   Multiple producers and consumers using semaphores.

multiple producers and multiple consumers. This made it easy to combine the solutions to the two subproblems to get a solution to the full problem. We will use the same idea in solving the readers/writers problem in Section 4.3. In general, whenever there are multiple kinds of synchronization, it is useful to implement them separately and then to combine the solutions.

4.3 The Dining Philosophers

The last section showed how to use semaphores to solve the critical section problem. This section and the next build upon that solution to implement selective forms of mutual exclusion in two classic synchronization problems: the dining philosophers and readers and writers. The solution to the dining philosophers illustrates how to implement mutual exclusion between processes that compete for access to overlapping sets of shared variables. The solution to the readers/writers problem illustrates how to implement a combination of concurrent and exclusive access to shared variables. The exercises contain additional examples of selective mutual exclusion problems.

Although the dining philosophers problem is more whimsical than practical, it is similar to realistic problems in which a process requires simultaneous access to more than one resource. Consequently, the problem is often used to illustrate and compare different synchronization mechanisms.

(4.1) **Dining Philosophers Problem**. Five philosophers sit around a circular table. Each philosopher spends his life alternately thinking and eating. In the center of the table is a large platter of spaghetti. Because the spaghetti is long and tangled—and the philosophers are not mechanically adept—a philosopher must use two forks to eat a helping. Unfortunately, the philosophers can afford only five forks. One fork is placed between each pair of philosophers, and they agree that each will use only the forks to the immediate left and right. The problem is to write a program to simulate the behavior of the philosophers. The program must avoid the unfortunate (and eventually fatal) situation in which all philosophers are hungry but none is able to acquire both forks—for example, each holds one fork and refuses to give it up.

The setting for this problem is depicted in Figure 4.6. Clearly, two neighboring philosophers cannot eat at the same time. Also, with only five forks, at most two philosophers at a time can be eating.

We will simulate the actions of the philosophers as shown below. We assume that the lengths of the thinking and eating periods vary; this could, for example, be simulated in a program by using random delays.

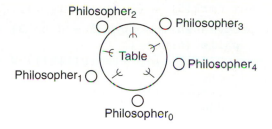

Figure 4.6   The dining philosophers.

```
process Philosopher[i = 0 to 4] {
  while (true) {
    think;
    acquire forks;
    eat;
    release forks;
  }
}
```

Solving the problem requires programming the actions "acquire forks" and "release forks." Because the forks are the shared resource, we will focus upon acquiring and releasing them. (Alternatively, we could solve the problem by considering whether or not philosophers are eating; see the exercises at the end of this chapter.)

Each fork is like a critical section lock: it can be held by at most one philosopher at a time. Hence, we can represent the forks by an array of semaphores initialized to ones. Picking up a fork is then simulated by executing a P operation on the appropriate semaphore, and putting down a fork is simulated by executing a V operation on the semaphore.

The processes are essentially identical, so it is natural to think of having them execute identical actions. For example, we could have each process first pick up its left fork and then its right fork. However, this could lead to deadlock. In particular, suppose all philosophers have picked up their left fork; then all would wait forever trying to pick up their right fork.

A necessary condition for deadlock is that there is circular waiting—i.e., one process is waiting for a resource held by a second, which is waiting for a resource held by a third, and so on up to some process that is waiting for a resource held by the first process. Thus, to avoid deadlock it is sufficient to

```
        sem fork[5] = {1, 1, 1, 1, 1};
    process Philosopher[i = 0 to 3] {
      while (true) {
        P(fork[i]); P(fork[i+1]); # get left fork then right
        eat;
        V(fork[i]); V(fork[i+1]);
        think;
      }
    }
    process Philosopher[4] {
      while (true) {
        P(fork[0]); P(fork[4]);    # get right fork then left
        eat;
        V(fork[0]); V(fork[4]);
        think;
      }
    }
```

Figure 4.7   Dining philosophers solution using semaphores.

ensure that circular waiting cannot occur. For this problem, we can have one of
the processes—say the last one, **Philosopher[4]**—pick up its right fork first.
Figure 4.7 gives this solution. Alternatively, we could have odd-numbered
philosophers pick up forks in one order and even-numbered philosophers pick
them up in the other order.

4.4 Readers and Writers

The readers and writers is another classic synchronization problem. Like the
dining philosophers, it is often used to compare and contrast synchronization
mechanisms. It is also an eminently practical problem.

(4.2)   **Readers/Writers Problem.** Two kinds of processes—readers and writers—share a database. Readers execute transactions that examine
database records; writers execute transactions that both examine and
update the database. The database is assumed initially to be in a consistent
state (i.e., one in which relations between data are meaningful). Each
transaction, if executed in isolation, transforms the database from one consistent state to another. To preclude interference between transactions, a

writer process must have exclusive access to the database. Assuming no writer is accessing the database, any number of readers may concurrently execute transactions.

The above definition implies a shared database, but this could also be a shared file, linked list, table, and so on.

The readers/writers problem is another example of selective mutual exclusion. In the dining philosophers problem, pairs of processes compete for access to forks. Here, classes of processes compete for access to the database. In particular, reader processes compete with writers, and individual writer processes compete with each other. Readers and writers is also an example of a general condition synchronization problem: Reader processes must wait until no writers are accessing the database; writer processes must wait until no readers or other writers are accessing the database.

This section develops two distinct solutions to the readers/writers problem. The first approaches it as a mutual exclusion problem. This solution is short and quite straightforward to develop. However, it gives preference to readers over writers—as explained fully below—and it cannot easily be modified—for example, to be fair. The second solution approaches readers/writers as a condition synchronization problem. This solution is longer and appears to be more complex, but it too is quite easy to develop. Moreover, the second solution can readily be modified to implement different scheduling policies between readers and writers. Most importantly, the second solution introduces a powerful programming technique we call *passing the baton*, which can be used to solve *any* condition synchronization problem.

4.4.1 *Readers/Writers as an Exclusion Problem*

Writer processes need mutually exclusive access to the database. Reader processes—as a group—also need exclusive access with respect to any writer process. A useful way to approach any selective mutual exclusion problem is first to overconstrain the solution—implementing more exclusion than is required—and then to relax the constraints. In particular, start by treating the problem as an instance of the critical section problem. Here, the obvious overconstraint is to ensure that each reader and writer process have exclusive access to the database. Let `rw` be a mutual exclusion semaphore—and hence let it be initialized to 1. The result is the overconstrained solution shown in Figure 4.8.

Now consider how to relax the solution in Figure 4.8 so that reader processes can execute concurrently. Readers—as a group—need to lock out writers, but only the *first* reader needs to grab the mutual exclusion lock by executing

```
sem rw = 1;
process Reader[i = 1 to M] {
  while (true) {
    ...
    P(rw);      # grab exclusive access lock
    read the database;
    V(rw);      # release the lock
  }
}
process Writer[j = 1 to N] {
  while (true) {
    ...
    P(rw);      # grab exclusive access lock
    write the database;
    V(rw);      # release the lock
  }
}
```

Figure 4.8   An overconstrained readers/writers solution.

P(rw). Subsequent readers can directly access the database. Similarly, when a reader finishes, it should release the lock only if it is the last active reader. This leads to the solution outline shown in Figure 4.9.

In Figure 4.9 variable nr counts the number of active readers. The entry protocol for reader processes first increments nr and then tests whether the value of nr is 1. The increment and test have to be executed as a critical section to avoid interference with other reader processes; hence, we have used angle brackets to specify the atomic action in the entry protocol for readers. Similarly, the decrement and test of nr in the reader's exit protocol have to be executed atomically, so the exit protocol is also enclosed by angle brackets.

To refine the solution outline in Figure 4.9 into a complete solution using semaphores, we merely have to implement the atomic actions using semaphores. Each is just a critical section, and we saw how to implement critical sections in Figure 4.1. Here, let mutexR be a semaphore used to provide mutual exclusion between reader processes. It is used as shown in Figure 4.10, which provides a complete solution to the readers/writers problem. Note that mutexR is initialized to 1, that the start of each atomic action is implemented by P(mutexR), and that the end of each atomic action is implemented by V(mutexR).

The algorithm in Figure 4.10 implements what is called a *readers' preference* solution to the readers/writers problem. In particular, if some reader is

```
int nr = 0;        # number of active readers
sem rw = 1;        # lock for reader/writer exclusion

process Reader[i = 1 to M] {
  while (true) {
    ...
    〈 nr = nr+1;
      if (nr == 1) P(rw);   # if first, get lock
    〉
    read the database;
    〈 nr = nr-1;
      if (nr == 0) V(rw);   # if last, release lock
    〉
  }
}

process Writer[j = 1 to N] {
  while (true) {
    ...
    P(rw);
    write the database;
    V(rw);
  }
}
```

Figure 4.9   Outline of readers and writers solution.

accessing the database and both another reader and a writer arrive at their entry protocols, then the new reader gets preference over the writer. Hence, this solution is not fair, because a continual stream of readers can permanently prevent writers from accessing the database. It is quite difficult to modify the solution in Figure 4.10 to make it fair (see the Historical Notes), but below we develop a different solution that can readily be changed into one that is fair.

4.4.2 Readers/Writers Using Condition Synchronization

We approached the above readers/writers problem as an exercise in mutual exclusion. The focus was on ensuring that writers excluded each other, and that readers as a class excluded writers. The resulting solution (Figure 4.10) thus consisted of overlapping solutions to two critical section problems: one between readers and writers—for access to the database—and one between readers—for access to variable **nr**.

```
int nr = 0;        # number of active readers
sem rw = 1;        # lock for access to the database
sem mutexR = 1;    # lock for reader access to nr

process Reader[i = 1 to m] {
  while (true) {
    ...
    P(mutexR);
      nr = nr+1;
      if (nr == 1) P(rw);   # if first, get lock
    V(mutexR);
    read the database;
    P(mutexR);
      nr = nr-1;
      if (nr == 0) V(rw);   # if last, release lock
    V(mutexR);
  }
}

process Writer[j = 1 to n] {
  while (true) {
    ...
    P(rw);
    write the database;
    V(rw);
  }
}
```

Figure 4.10   Readers and writers exclusion using semaphores.

We now develop a different solution to the problem by starting from a different—and simpler—specification of the required synchronization. The new solution introduces a general programming technique called *passing the baton*, which employs split binary semaphores both to provide exclusion and to signal delayed processes. The technique of passing the baton can be used to implement arbitrary `await` statements and thus to implement arbitrary condition synchronization. The technique can also be used to control precisely the order in which delayed processes are awakened.

As defined in (4.2), readers examine a shared database, and writers both examine and alter it. To preserve database consistency, a writer requires exclusive access, but any number of readers may execute concurrently. A simple way to specify this synchronization is to count the number of each kind of process trying to access the database, then to constrain the values of the counters. In particular, let **nr** and **nw** be nonnegative integers that respectively record the number of readers and writers accessing the database. The bad states to be avoided are ones in which both **nr** and **nw** are positive or in which **nw** is greater than one:

$$BAD: \quad (\text{nr} > 0 \land \text{nw} > 0) \lor \text{nw} > 1$$

The complementary set of good states is thus characterized by the negation of the above predicate, which simplifies to

$$RW: \quad (\text{nr} == 0 \lor \text{nw} == 0) \land \text{nw} <= 1$$

The first term says readers and writers cannot access the database at the same time; the second says there is at most one active writer. With this specification of the problem, an outline of the key part of reader processes is

```
⟨nr = nr+1;⟩
read the database;
⟨nr = nr-1;⟩
```

The corresponding outline for writer processes is

```
⟨nw = nw+1;⟩
write the database;
⟨nw = nw-1;⟩
```

To refine this outline into a coarse-grained solution, we need to guard the assignments to the shared variables to ensure that predicate *RW* is a global invariant. In reader processes, this means guarding the increment of **nr** by (**nw** == 0), because if **nr** is going to be incremented, then **nw** had better be zero. In writer processes, the required guard is (**nr** == 0 and **nw** == 0), because if **nw** is going to be incremented, both **nr** and **nw** had better be zero. We do not, however, need to guard either decrement, because it is never necessary to delay a process that is giving up use of a resource. Inserting the required guards yields the coarse-grained solution in Figure 4.11.

4.4.3 The Technique of Passing the Baton

Sometimes, **await** statements can be implemented directly using semaphores or other primitive operations. However, in general they cannot. Consider the two guards in the **await** statements in Figure 4.11. They overlap in that the guard in the entry protocol for writer processes requires that both **nw** and **nr** be zero, whereas the guard in the entry protocol in reader processes requires only that **nw** be zero. No one semaphore could discriminate between these conditions, so we

```
int nr = 0, nw = 0;
## RW:    (nr == 0 ∨ nw == 0) ∧ nw <= 1
process Reader[i = 1 to m] {
  while (true) {
    ...
    ⟨await (nw == 0) nr = nr+1;⟩
    read the database;
    ⟨nr = nr-1;⟩
  }
}
process Writer[j = 1 to n] {
  while (true) {
    ...
    ⟨await (nr == 0 and nw == 0) nw = nw+1;⟩
    write the database;
    ⟨nw = nw-1;⟩
  }
}
```

Figure 4.11   A coarse-grained readers/writers solution.

require a general technique for implementing `await` statements such as these. The one introduced here is called *passing the baton*, for reasons explained below. As we shall see, this technique is powerful enough to implement any `await` statement.

There are four atomic statements in Figure 4.11. The first ones in each of the reader and writer processes have the form

```
⟨await (B) S;⟩
```

where, as usual, `B` stands for a Boolean expression and `S` stands for a statement list. The last atomic statements in the processes have the form

```
⟨S;⟩
```

As observed in Section 2.4, *all* condition synchronization can be represented by the first form, and the second is merely an abbreviation for a special case of the first in which the guard `B` is the constant true. Hence, if we know how to implement `await` statements using semaphores, we can solve *any* condition synchronization problem.

Split binary semaphores can be used as follows to implement the `await` statements in Figure 4.11. First, let `e` be a binary semaphore whose initial value is one. It will be used to control entry into each of the atomic statements, hence the e for "entry."

Second, associate one semaphore and one counter with each different guard B; each of these semaphores and counters is initialized to zero. The semaphore will be used to delay processes that have to wait for the guard to become true; the counter will record the number of delayed processes. Above, we have two different guards—in the entry protocols for each of the readers and writers—so we need two semaphores and two counters. Let r be the semaphore associated with the guard in reader processes, and let dr be the associated number of delayed readers. Similarly, let w be the semaphore associated with the guard in writer processes, and let dw be the number of delayed writers. Initially, no readers or writers are waiting for entry, so all of r, dr, w, and dw are zero.

The three semaphores—e, r, and w—and the two delay counters—dr and dw—are then used as shown in Figure 4.12. The comments in the code indicate how the coarse-grained atomic statements from Figure 4.11 get implemented. The code labeled *SIGNAL* is used to exit each of the atomic statements. It is an abbreviation for the following:

```
if (nw == 0 and dr > 0) {
   dr = dr-1; V(r);   # awaken a reader, or
   }
elseif (nr == 0 and nw == 0 and dw > 0) {
   dw = dw-1; V(w);   # awaken a writer, or
   }
else
   V(e);                    # release the entry lock
```

The role of the *SIGNAL* code is to signal exactly *one* of the three semaphores. In particular, if there are no active writers and there is a delayed reader, then a reader can be awakened by executing V(r). If there are no active readers or writers, and there is a delayed writer, then a writer can be awakened by executing V(w). Otherwise—i.e., if there is no delayed process that can safely proceed—signal the entry semaphore by executing V(e).

The three semaphores in Figure 4.12 form a split binary semaphore, because at most one of the semaphores at a time is 1, and every execution path starts with a P and ends with a V. Hence, the statements between every P and V execute with mutual exclusion. The synchronization invariant *RW* is true initially and just before each V operation, so it is true whenever one of the semaphores is 1. Moreover, each guard B is guaranteed to be true whenever the statement it guards is executed. This is because either the process checked B and found it to be true, or the process delayed on a semaphore that is signaled only when B is true. Finally, this code transformation does not introduce deadlock since a delay

```
      int nr = 0,    ## RW: (nr == 0 or nw == 0) and nw <= 1
          nw = 0;
      sem e = 1,     # controls entry to critical sections
          r = 0,     # used to delay readers
          w = 0;     # used to delay writers
                     # at all times 0 <= (e+r+w) <= 1
      int dr = 0,    # number of delayed readers
          dw = 0;    # number of delayed writers

      process Reader[i = 1 to M] {
        while (true) {
          # ⟨await (nw == 0) nr = nr+1;⟩
            P(e);
            if (nw > 0) { dr = dr+1; V(e); P(r); }
            nr = nr+1;
            SIGNAL;        # see text for details
          read the database;
          # ⟨nr = nr-1;⟩
            P(e);
            nr = nr-1;
            SIGNAL;
        }
      }


      process Writer[j = 1 to N] {
        while (true) {
          # ⟨await (nr == 0 and nw == 0) nw = nw+1;⟩
            P(e);
            if (nr > 0 or nw > 0) { dw = dw+1; V(e); P(w); }
            nw = nw+1;
            SIGNAL;
          write the database;
          # ⟨nw = nw-1;⟩
            P(e);
            nw = nw-1;
            SIGNAL;
        }
      }
```

Figure 4.12   Outline of readers and writers with passing the baton.

semaphore is signaled only if some process is waiting on, or is about to be waiting on, the semaphore. (A process could have incremented a delay counter and executed `V(e)` but might not yet have executed the `P` operation on the delay semaphore.)

This programming technique is called *passing the baton* because of the way in which semaphores are signaled. When a process is executing within a critical section, think of it as holding a baton that signifies permission to execute. When that process reaches a *SIGNAL* code fragment, it passes the baton to one other process. If some process is waiting for a condition that is now true, the baton is passed to one such process, which in turn executes its critical section and passes the baton to another process. When no process is waiting for a condition that is true, the baton is passed to the next process that tries to enter the critical section for the first time—i.e., the next process that executes `P(e)`.

In Figure 4.12—and in general—many of the instances of the *SIGNAL* code can be simplified or eliminated. For example, in reader processes, `nr` is positive and `nw` is zero before execution of the first instance of *SIGNAL*—i.e., the instance at the end of the entry protocol in readers. Hence, that signal fragment can be simplified to

```
if (dr > 0) { dr = dr-1; V(r); }
else V(e);
```

Before the second instance of *SIGNAL* in readers, both `nw` and `dr` are zero. In writer processes, `nr` is zero and `nw` is positive before the *SIGNAL* code at the end of the writer entry protocol. Finally, both `nr` and `nw` are zero before the final instance of *SIGNAL* in writer processes. Using these facts to simplify the signal protocols, we get the final passing-the-baton solution shown in Figure 4.13.

In that figure, when a writer finishes, if there is more than one delayed reader and one is awakened, the others are awakened in cascading fashion. In particular, the first reader increments `nr`, then awakens the second delayed reader, which increments `nr` and awakens the third, and so on. The baton keeps getting passed from one delayed reader to another until all are awakened— namely, until `dr` is zero. Also in Figure 4.13, the last `if` statement in writers first checks for delayed readers, then it checks for delayed writers. The order of these checks could safely be switched, because if both kinds of processes are delayed, either could be signaled when a writer finishes its exit protocol.

4.4.4 Alternative Scheduling Policies

The readers/writers solution in Figure 4.13 is certainly longer than the one in Figure 4.9. However, it is based on repeated application of a simple principle—

```
            int nr = 0,    ## RW: (nr==0 or nw==0) and nw<=1
                nw = 0;
            sem e = 1,     # controls entry to critical sections
                r = 0,     # used to delay readers
                w = 0;     # used to delay writers
                           # at all times 0 <= (e+r+w) <= 1
            int dr = 0,    # number of delayed readers
                dw = 0;    # number of delayed writers

            process Reader[i = 1 to M] {
              while (true) {
                # <await (nw == 0) nr = nr+1;>
                  P(e);
                  if (nw > 0) { dr = dr+1; V(e); P(r); }
                  nr = nr+1;
                  if (dr > 0) { dr = dr-1; V(r); }
                  else V(e);
                read the database;
                # <nr = nr-1;>
                  P(e);
                  nr = nr-1;
                  if (nr == 0 and dw > 0) { dw = dw-1; V(w); }
                  else V(e);
              }
            }

            process Writer[j = 1 to N] {
              while (true) {
                # <await (nr == 0 and nw == 0) nw = nw+1;>
                  P(e);
                  if (nr > 0 or nw > 0) { dw = dw+1; V(e); P(w); }
                  nw = nw+1;
                  V(e);
                write the database;
                # <nw = nw-1;>
                  P(e);
                  nw = nw-1;
                  if (dr > 0) { dr = dr-1; V(r); }
                  elseif (dw > 0) { dw = dw-1; V(w); }
                  else V(e);
              }
            }
```

Figure 4.13   A readers/writers solution using passing the baton.

always pass the mutual exclusion baton to one process at a time. Like the solution in Figure 4.9, the one in Figure 4.13 also gives readers preference over writers. But because we can control how the baton is passed, we can readily modify the solution in Figure 4.13 to schedule processes in other ways. For example, to give writers preference, it is necessary to ensure that

- new readers are delayed if a writer is waiting, and

- a delayed reader is awakened only if no writer is currently waiting.

We can meet the first requirement by strengthening the delay condition in the first `if` statement in readers:

```
if (nw > 0 or dw > 0) { dr = dr+1; V(e); P(r); }
```

We can meet the second requirement by switching the order of the first two arms of the `if` statement in writers:

```
if (dw > 0) { dw = dw-1; V(w); }
elseif (dr > 0) { dr = dr-1; V(r); }
else V(e);
```

This awakens a reader only when no writers are known to be waiting; that reader can in turn awaken another reader and so on. (A new writer could arrive, but until it gets past the entry semaphore, no other process can know that it has arrived.)

Neither of the above changes alters the structure of the solution. This is a virtue of the passing-the-baton technique: Guards can be manipulated to alter the order in which processes are awakened without affecting the basic correctness of the solution.

We can also alter the solution in Figure 4.13 to ensure fair access to the database, assuming the semaphore operations are themselves fair. For example, we could force readers and writers to alternate turns when both are waiting. To implement this solution, we need to

- delay a new reader when a writer is waiting;

- delay a new writer when a reader is waiting;

- awaken one waiting writer (if any) when a reader finishes;

- awaken all waiting readers (if any) when a writer finishes; otherwise awaken one waiting writer (if any).

We can delay new readers as shown above; we can delay new writers in a similar way. The program in Figure 4.13 already meets the last two requirements. Again the structure of the solution is unchanged.

This technique of passing the baton can also be used to provide finer-grained control over the order in which processes use resources. The next section illustrates this. The only thing we cannot control is the order in which processes delayed on the entry semaphore are awakened. This depends on the underlying implementation of semaphores.

4.5 Resource Allocation and Scheduling

Resource allocation is the problem of deciding when a process can be given access to a resource. In concurrent programs, a resource is anything that a process might be delayed waiting to acquire. This includes entry to a critical section, access to a database, a slot in a bounded buffer, a region of memory, use of a printer, and so on. We have already examined several specific resource allocation problems. In most, the simplest possible allocation policy was employed: If some process is waiting and the resource is available, allocate it. For example, the solution to the critical section problem in Section 4.2 ensured that *some* waiting process was given permission to enter; it did not attempt to control *which* process was given permission if there was a choice. Similarly, the solution to the bounded buffer problem in Section 4.2 made no attempt to control which producer or which consumer next got access to the buffer. The only more complex allocation policy considered so far was in the readers/writers problem. However, our concern there was giving preference to classes of processes, not to individual processes.

This section shows how to implement general resource allocation policies and in particular shows how to control explicitly which process gets a resource when more than one is waiting. First we describe the general solution pattern. Then we implement one specific allocation policy—shortest job next. The solution employs the technique of passing the baton. It also introduces the concept of private semaphores, which provide the basis for solving other resource allocation problems.

4.5.1 Problem Definition and General Solution Pattern

In any resource allocation problem, processes compete for use of units of a shared resource. A process requests one or more units by executing the `request` operation, which is often implemented by a procedure. Parameters to `request` indicate how many units are required, identify any special characteristics such as the size of a memory block, and give the identity of the requesting process. Each unit of the shared resource is either free or in use. A request can be satisfied when all the required units are free. Hence **request** delays until enough units are free, then returns the requested number of units. After using allocated resources, a process returns them to the free pool by executing the **release** operation. Parameters to **release** indicate the identities of the units being returned. A process can return resources in different amounts and different orders than it acquires them.

Ignoring the representation of resource units, the **request** and **release** operations have the following general outline:

```
request (parameters):
    ⟨await (request can be satisfied)  take units;⟩
release (parameters):
    ⟨return units;⟩
```

The operations need to be atomic since both need to access the representation of resource units. As long as this representation uses variables different from others in the program, the operations will appear to be atomic with respect to other actions and hence can execute concurrently with other actions.

This general solution pattern can be implemented using the passing-the-baton technique introduced in Section 4.4. In particular, **request** has the form of a general **await** statement, so it is implemented by the program fragment

```
request (parameters):
    P(e);
    if (request cannot be satisfied)  DELAY;
    take units;
    SIGNAL;
```

Similarly, **release** has the form of a simple atomic action, so it can be implemented by the program fragment

```
release (parameters):
    P(e);
    return units;
    SIGNAL;
```

As before, **e** is a semaphore that controls entry to the critical sections, and *SIGNAL* is a code fragment that either awakens a delayed process—if some pending request can be satisfied—or unlocks the entry semaphore by executing **v(e)**. The *DELAY* code in **request** is a program fragment like that at the start of the entry protocols for readers and writers (see Figures 4.12 and 4.13). In particular, it records that there is a new request that is about to be delayed, unlocks the entry semaphore by executing **v(e)**, then blocks the requesting process on a delay semaphore.

The exact details of how *SIGNAL* is implemented for a specific resource-allocation problem depend on what the different delay conditions are and how they are represented. In any event, the *DELAY* code needs to save the parameters describing a delayed request so that they can be examined in the *SIGNAL* code. Also, there needs to be one condition semaphore for each different delay condition.

The next section develops a solution to one specific resource allocation problem then describes how to solve any such problem. Several additional allocation problems are given in the exercises.

4.5.2 Shortest-Job-Next Allocation

Shortest job next (SJN) is an allocation policy that occurs in many guises and is used for many different kinds of resources. For now, assume the shared resource has a single unit (the general case of multiple units is considered at the end of this section). Then the SJN policy is defined as follows.

(4.3) **Shortest-Job-Next (SJN) Allocation**. Several processes compete for use of a single shared resource. A process requests use of the resource by executing `request(time,id)`, where `time` is an integer that specifies how long the process will use the resource and `id` is an integer that identifies the requesting process. When a process executes `request`, if the resource is free it is immediately allocated to the process; if not, the process delays. After using the resource, a process makes it free by executing `release`. When the resource is freed, it is allocated to the delayed process (if any) that has the minimum value for `time`. If two or more processes have the same value for `time`, the resource is allocated to the one that has waited the longest.

For example, the SJN policy can be used for processor allocation (using `time` as execution time), for spooling files to a printer (using `time` as printing time), or for remote file transfer (ftp) service (using `time` as the estimated file-transfer time).

The SJN policy is attractive because it minimizes average job completion time. However, it is inherently unfair: a process can be delayed forever if there is a continual stream of requests specifying shorter usage times. (Such unfairness is extremely unlikely in practice unless a resource is totally overloaded.) If unfairness is of concern, the SJN policy can be modified slightly so that a process that has been delayed a long time is given preference. This technique is called *aging*.

If a process makes a request and the resource is free, the request can be satisfied immediately since there are no other pending requests. Thus, the SJN aspect of the allocation policy comes into play only if there is more than one pending request. Since there is a single resource, it is sufficient to use a single variable to record whether the resource is available. Let **free** be a Boolean variable that is true when the resource is available and false when it is in use. To implement the SJN policy, pending requests need to be remembered and ordered. Let **pairs** be a set of records (**time**, **id**), ordered by the values of **time** fields. If two records have the same value for **time**, let them occur in **pairs** in the order in which they were inserted. With this specification, the following predicate is to be a global invariant:

SJN: **pairs** is an ordered set $\wedge$ **free** $\Rightarrow$ (**pairs** $==$ $\emptyset$)

In words, **pairs** is ordered, and if the resource is free, **pairs** is the empty set. Initially, **free** is true and **pairs** is empty, so predicate *SJN* is true.

Ignoring the SJN policy for the moment, a request can be satisfied exactly when the resource is available. This results in the coarse-grained solution:

```
bool free = true;     # shared variable
request(time,id):  ⟨await (free) free = false;⟩
release():  ⟨free = true;⟩
```

With the SJN policy, however, a process executing **request** needs to delay until the resource is free *and* the process's request is the next one to be honored according to the SJN policy. From the second conjunct of *SJN*, if **free** is true at the time a process executes **request**, then set **pairs** is empty. Hence the above delay condition is sufficient to determine whether a request can be satisfied immediately. The **time** parameter comes into play only if a request must be delayed—i.e., if **free** is false. Based on these observations, we can implement **request** as

```
request(time,id):
  P(e);
  if (!free) DELAY;
  free = false;
  SIGNAL;
```

And we can implement **release** as

```
release():
  P(e);
  free = true;
  SIGNAL;
```

In `request`, we assume that `P` operations on the entry semaphore `e` complete in the order in which they are attempted—i.e., `P(e)` is FCFS. If this is not the case, requests will not necessarily be serviced in SJN order.

The remaining concern is to implement the SJN aspect of the allocation policy. This involves using set `pairs` and semaphores to implement *DELAY* and *SIGNAL*. When a request cannot be satisfied, it needs to be saved so it can be examined later when the resource is released. Thus, in *DELAY* a process needs to

- insert its parameters in `pairs`,

- release control of the critical section by executing `V(e)`, then

- delay on a semaphore until the request can be satisfied.

When the resource is freed, if set `pairs` is not empty, the resource needs to be allocated to exactly one process in accordance with the SJN policy. In short, if there is a delayed process that can now proceed, it needs to be signaled by executing a `V` operation on a delay semaphore.

In earlier examples, there were just a few different delay conditions, so just a few condition semaphores were needed; for example, there were only two delay conditions in the readers/writers solution at the end of the previous section. Here, however, each process has a different delay condition, depending on its position in set `pairs`: the first process in `pairs` needs to be awakened before the second, and so on. Thus each process needs to wait on a different delay semaphore.

Assume there are `n` processes that use the resource. Let `b[n]` be an array of semaphores, each element of which is initially `0`. Also assume the values of process `ids` are unique and are in the range from `0` to `n-1`. Then process `id` delays on semaphore `b[id]`. Augmenting the `request` and `release` operations above with uses of `pairs` and `b` as specified, we get the solution to the SJN allocation problem shown in Figure 4.14.

In Figure 4.14, the insert operation in `request` is assumed to place the pair in the proper place in `pairs` in order to maintain the first conjunct in *SJN*. Hence, *SJN* is indeed invariant outside `request` and `release`; i.e., *SJN* is true just after each `P(e)` and just before each `V(e)`. The `if` statement in the signal code in `release` awakens exactly one process if there is a pending request, and hence `pairs` is not empty. The "baton" is passed to that process, which sets `free` to false. This ensures that the second conjunct in *SJN* is true when `pairs` is not empty. Since there is only a single resource, no further requests could be satisfied, so the signal code in `request` is simply `V(e)`.

The elements of the array of semaphores `b` in Figure 4.14 are examples of what are called private semaphores.

(4.4) **Private Semaphore.** Semaphore `s` is called a private semaphore if exactly one process executes `P` operations on `s`.

```
bool free = true;
sem e = 1, b[n] = ([n] 0);   # for entry and delay
typedef Pairs = set of (int, int);
Pairs pairs = ∅;
## SJN:   pairs is an ordered set ∧ free ⇒ (pairs == ∅)

request(time,id):
  P(e);
  if (!free) {
     insert (time,id) in pairs;
     V(e);                 # release entry lock
     P(b[id]);            # wait to be awakened
  }
  free = false;
  V(e);      # optimized since free is false here

release():
  P(e);
  free = true;
  if (P != ∅) {
     remove first pair (time,id) from pairs;
     V(b[id]);   # pass baton to process id
  }
  else V(e);
```

Figure 4.14   *Shortest-job-next allocation using semaphores.*

In particular, when a process has to delay, it executes `P(b[id])` to block on its own element of array `b`.

Private semaphores are useful in any situation in which it is necessary to be able to signal individual processes. For some allocation problems, however, there may be fewer different delay conditions than there are processes that compete for a resource. In that case, it can be more efficient to use one semaphore for each different condition than to use private semaphores for each process. For example, if memory blocks are allocated in a few sizes only—and it does not matter what order blocks are allocated to processes competing for the same size—then it would be sufficient to have one delay semaphore for each different block size.

We can readily generalize the solution in Figure 4.14 to resources having more than one unit. In this case, each unit would either be free or allocated, and `request` and `release` would have a parameter, `amount`, to indicate how many units a process requires or is returning. We would then modify the solution in Figure 4.14 as follows:

- Replace Boolean variable `free` by an integer `avail` that records the number of available units.

- In `request`, test whether `amount <= avail`. If so, allocate `amount` units. If not, record how many units are required before delaying.

- In `release`, increase `avail` by `amount`, then determine whether the oldest delayed process that has the minimum value for `time` can have its request satisfied. If so, awaken it. If not, execute `V(e)`.

The other modification is that it might now be possible to satisfy more than one pending request when units are released. For example, there could be two delayed processes that together require no more units than were released. In this case, the first one that is awakened needs to signal the second after taking the units it requires. In short, the signaling protocol at the end of `request` needs to be the same as the one at the end of `release`.

4.6 Case Study: Pthreads

Recall that a *thread* is a lightweight process—namely, a process that has its own program counter and execution stack but none of the "heavy weight" context (such as page tables) associated with an application process. Some operating systems have provided mechanisms that allow programmers to write multithreaded applications. However, the mechanisms differed, so applications were not portable to different operating systems, or even to variants of the same operating system. To rectify this situation, a large group of people in the mid-1990s defined a standard set of C library routines for multithreaded programming. The group was working under the auspices of an organization called POSIX— portable operating systems interface—so the library is called Pthreads, for POSIX threads. The library is now widely available on various flavors of the UNIX operating system, as well as some others.

The Pthreads library contains dozens of functions for thread management and synchronization. Here we describe a basic set that is sufficient to fork and later join with new threads and to synchronize their execution using semaphores. (Section 5.5 describes functions for locks and condition variables.) We also present a simple, yet complete example of a producer/consumer application. It can serve as a basic template for other applications that use the Pthreads library.

4.6.1 Thread Creation

Using Pthreads with a C program involves four steps. First, include the standard header for the Pthreads library:

```
# include <pthread.h>
```

Second, declare variables for one thread attributes descriptor and one or more thread descriptors, as in

```
pthread_attr_t tattr;   /* thread attributes */
pthread_t tid;          /* thread descriptor */
```

Third, initialize the attributes by executing

```
pthread_attr_init(&tattr);
pthread_attr_setscope(&tattr, PTHREAD_SCOPE_SYSTEM);
```

Finally, create the threads, as described below.

The initial attributes of a thread are set before the thread is created; many can later be altered by means of thread-management functions. Thread attributes include the size of the thread's stack, its scheduling priority, and its scheduling scope (local or global). The default attribute values are often sufficient, with the exception of scheduling scope. A programmer usually wants a thread to be scheduled globally rather than locally, meaning that it competes with all threads for processor time rather than just with other threads created by the same parent thread (and hence same parent process). The call of `pthread_attr_ setscope` illustrated above accomplishes this.[2]

A new thread is created by calling the `pthread_create` function, as in

```
pthread_create(&tid, &tattr, start_func, arg);
```

The first argument is the address of a thread descriptor that is filled in if creation is successful. The second is the address of a previously initialized thread attributes descriptor. The new thread begins execution by calling `start_func` with a single argument, `arg`. If thread creation is successful, `pthread_ create` returns a zero; a nonzero return value indicates an error.

A thread terminates its owns execution by calling

```
pthread_exit(value);
```

---

[2] The Pthreads programs in the text have been tested using the Solaris implementation. You may need to use different settings for some of the attributes on other systems. For example, on an IRIX implementation the scheduling scope should be `PTHREAD_SCOPE_PROCESS`, which is the default.

The `value` is a single return value (or `NULL`). The `exit` routine is called implicitly if the thread returns from the function that it started executing.

A parent thread can wait for a child to terminate by executing

```
pthread_join(tid, value_ptr);
```

where `tid` is a child's descriptor and `value_ptr` is the address of a location for the return value. The return value is filled in when the child calls `exit`.

4.6.2 Semaphores

Threads communicate with each other using variables declared global to the functions executed by the threads. Threads can synchronize with each other using busy waiting, locks, semaphores, or condition variables. We describe semaphores here; locks and monitors are described in Section 5.5.

The headers file `semaphore.h` contains definitions and operation prototypes for semaphores. Semaphore descriptors are declared global to threads that will use them, as in

```
sem_t mutex;
```

A descriptor is initialized by calling the `sem_init` function. For example, the following initializes `mutex` to 1:

```
sem_init(&mutex, SHARED, 1);
```

If `SHARED` is nonzero, the semaphore can be shared between processes; otherwise it can only be shared between threads in the same process. The Pthreads equivalent of the `P` operation is `sem_wait` and the equivalent of the `V` operation is `sem_post`. Thus, one way to protect a critical section of code is to use semaphore `mutex` as follows:

```
sem_wait(&mutex);       /* P(mutex); */
critical section;
sem_post(&mutex);       /* V(mutex); */
```

The Pthreads library also contains functions to conditionally wait on a semaphore, retrieve its current value, and destroy it.

4.6.3 Example: A Simple Producer and Consumer

Figure 4.15 contains a complete example of a simple producer/consumer program, which is similar to the program shown earlier in Figure 4.3. The

```c
# include <pthread.h>        /* standard lines */
# include <semaphore.h>
# define SHARED 1
# include <stdio.h>

void *Producer(void *);   /* the two threads */
void *Consumer(void *);

sem_t empty, full;        /* global semaphores */
int data;                 /* shared buffer      */
int numIters;

/* main() -- read command line and create threads */
int main(int argc, char *argv[]) {
  pthread_t pid, cid;         /* thread and attributes */
  pthread_attr_t attr;     /* descriptors            */
  pthread_attr_init(&attr);
  pthread_attr_setscope(&attr, PTHREAD_SCOPE_SYSTEM);

  sem_init(&empty, SHARED, 1);  /* sem empty = 1 */
  sem_init(&full, SHARED, 0);   /* sem full = 0  */

  numIters = atoi(argv[1]);
  pthread_create(&pid, &attr, Producer, NULL);
  pthread_create(&cid, &attr, Consumer, NULL);
  pthread_join(pid, NULL);
  pthread_join(cid, NULL);
}

/* deposit 1, ..., numIters into the data buffer */
void *Producer(void *arg) {
  int produced;
  for (produced = 1; produced <= numIters; produced++) {
    sem_wait(&empty);
    data = produced;
    sem_post(&full);
  }
}

/* fetch numIters items from the buffer and sum them */
void *Consumer(void *arg) {
  int total = 0, consumed;
  for (consumed = 1; consumed <= numIters; consumed++) {
    sem_wait(&full);
    total = total + data;
    sem_post(&empty);
  }
  printf("the total is %d\n", total);
}
```

Figure 4.15   Simple producer/consumer using Pthreads.

`Producer` and `Consumer` functions are executed as independent threads. They share access to a single buffer, `data`. The `Producer` deposits a sequence of integers from `1` to `numIters` into the buffer. The `Consumer` fetches these values and adds them. Two semaphores, `empty` and `full` are used to ensure that the producer and consumer alternate access to the buffer.

The `main` function initializes the descriptors and semaphores, creates the two threads, and then waits for them to terminate. The threads implicitly call `pthread_exit` when they complete. Neither thread in this program is passed an argument (hence the `NULL` pointer value in `pthread_create`). Section 5.5 contains an example in which threads are passed arguments.

Historical Notes

In the mid-1960s, Edsger Dijkstra and five colleagues developed one of the first multiprogrammed operating systems at the Technological University of Eindhoven in the Netherlands. (The designers humbly named it "THE" multiprogramming system, after the Dutch initials of the institution!) The system has an elegant structure, which consists of a kernel and layers of virtual machines implemented by processes [Dijkstra 1968a]. It also introduced semaphores, which Dijkstra invented in order to have a useful tool for implementing mutual exclusion and for signaling the occurrence of events such as interrupts. Dijkstra also invented the term *private semaphore*.

Because Dijkstra is Dutch, `P` and `V` stand for Dutch words. In particular, `P` is the first letter of the Dutch word *passeren*, which means "to pass"; `V` is the first letter of *vrijgeven*, which means "to release." (Note the analogy to railroad semaphores.) Dijkstra and his group later observed that `P` might better stand for *prolagen*—formed from the Dutch words *proberen* ("to try") and *verlagen* ("to decrease")—and that `V` might better stand for *verhogen* ("to increase").

At about the same time, Dijkstra [1968b] wrote an important paper on cooperating sequential processes. His paper showed how to use semaphores to solve a variety of synchronization problems and introduced the problems of the dining philosophers and the sleeping barber (see Section 5.2).

In his seminal paper on monitors (discussed in Chapter 5), Tony Hoare [1974] introduced the concept of a split binary semaphore and showed how to use it to implement monitors. However, Dijkstra was the one who later named the technique and illustrated its general utility. In particular, Dijkstra [1979] showed how to use split binary semaphores to solve the readers/writers problem; Dijkstra [1980] showed how to implement general semaphores using only split binary semaphores.

The author of this book developed the technique of passing the baton [Andrews 1989]. It was inspired by Dijkstra's papers on split binary semaphores.

In fact, passing the baton is basically an optimization of Dijkstra's algorithms [1979, 1980].

The solution to the dining philosophers problem in Figure 4.7 is deterministic—i.e., every process takes a predictable set of actions. Lehman and Rabin [1981] show that any deterministic solution has to use asymmetry or an outside agent if it is to be deadlock free and starvation free. They also present an interesting probabilistic algorithm that is perfectly symmetric (see Exercise 4.19). The basic idea is that philosophers use coin flips to determine the order in which to try to pick up forks—which introduces asymmetry—and the philosopher who has most recently used a fork defers to a neighbor if they both want to use the same fork.

Courtois, Heymans, and Parnas [1971] introduced the readers/writers problem and presented two solutions using semaphores. The first is the readers' preference solution developed in Section 4.4 (see Figure 4.10). The second solution gives writers preference; it is much more complex than their readers' preference solution and uses five semaphores and two counters (see Exercise 4.20). Their writers' preference solution is also quite difficult to understand. In contrast, as shown at the end of Section 4.4 and in Andrews [1989], by using the technique of passing the baton we can readily modify a readers' preference solution to give writers preference or to get a fair solution.

Scheduling properties of algorithms often depend on the semaphore operations being strongly fair—namely, that a process delayed at a P operation eventually proceeds if enough V operations are executed. The kernel implementation in Chapter 6 provides strongly fair semaphores since blocked lists are maintained in FIFO order. However, if blocked processes were queued in some other order—e.g., by their execution priority—then the P operation might be only weakly fair. Morris [1979] shows how to implement a starvation-free solution to the critical section problem using weakly fair binary semaphores. Martin and Burch [1985] present a somewhat simpler solution to the same problem. Udding [1986] solves the same problem in a systematic way that makes clearer why his solution is correct. All three papers use split binary semaphores and a technique quite similar to passing the baton.

Many people have proposed variations on semaphores. For example, Patil [1971] proposed a `PMultiple` primitive, which waits until a set of semaphores are all nonnegative and then decrements them (see Exercise 4.28). Reed and Kanodia [1979] present mechanisms called eventcounts and sequencers, which can be used to construct semaphores but can also be used directly to solve additional synchronization problems (see Exercise 4.38). More recently, Faulk and Parnas [1988] have examined the kinds of synchronization that arise in hard-real-time systems, which have critical timing deadlines. They argue that in real-time systems, the P operation on semaphores should be replaced by two more primitive operations: `pass`, which waits until the semaphore is nonnegative; and `down`, which decrements it.

Semaphores are often used for synchronization within operating systems. Many operating systems also provide system calls that make them available to application programmers. As noted in Section 4.6, the Pthreads library was developed as a portable standard for threads and low-level synchronization mechanisms, including semaphores. (However, Pthreads does not include routines for barrier synchronization.) Several books describe threads programming in general and Pthreads programming in particular; Lewis and Berg [1998] is one example. The Website for this book (see the Preface) contains links to information on Pthreads.

References

Andrews, G. R. 1989. A method for solving synchronization problems. *Science of Computer Prog.* 13, 4 (December): 1–21.

Courtois, P. J., F. Heymans, and D. L. Parnas. 1971. Concurrent control with "readers" and "writers." *Comm. ACM* 14, 10 (October): 667–68.

Dijkstra, E. W. 1968a. The structure of the "THE" multiprogramming system. *Comm. ACM* 11, 5 (May): 341–46.

Dijkstra, E. W. 1968b. Cooperating sequential processes. In F. Genuys, ed., *Programming Languages*. New York: Academic Press, pp. 43–112.

Dijkstra, E. W. 1979. A tutorial on the split binary semaphore. EWD 703, Neunen, Netherlands, March.

Dijkstra, E. W. 1980. The superfluity of the general semaphore. EWD 734, Neunen, Netherlands, April.

Faulk, S. R., and D. L. Parnas. 1988. On synchronization in hard-real-time systems. *Comm. ACM* 31, 3 (March): 274–87.

Herman, J. S. 1989. A comparison of synchronization mechanisms for concurrent programming. Master's thesis, CSE-89-26, University of California at Davis.

Hoare, C. A. R. 1974. Monitors: An operating system structuring concept. *Comm. ACM* 17, 10 (October): 549–57.

Lehmann, D., and M. O. Rabin. 1981. A symmetric and fully distributed solution to the dining philosophers problem. *Proc. Eighth ACM Symp. on Principles of Programming Languages*, January, pp. 133–38.

Lewis, B., and D. Berg. 1998. *Multithreaded Programming with Pthreads.* Mountain View, CA: Sun Microsystems Press.

Martin, A. J., and A. J. Burch. 1985. Fair mutual exclusion with unfair P and V operations. *Information Processing Letters* 21, 2 (August): 97–100.

Morris, J. M. 1979. A starvation-free solution to the mutual exclusion problem. *Information Processing Letters* 8, 2 (February): 76–80.

Parnas, D. L. 1975. On a solution to the cigarette smoker's problem (without conditional statements). *Comm. ACM* 18, 3 (March): 181–83.

Patil, S. S. 1971. Limitations and capabilities of Dijkstra's semaphore primitives for coordination among processes. MIT Project MAC Memo 57, February.

Reed, D. P., and R. K. Kanodia. 1979. Synchronization with eventcounts and sequencers. *Comm. ACM* 22, 2 (February): 115–23.

Udding, J. 1986. Absence of individual starvation using weak semaphores. *Information Processing Letters* 23, 3 (October): 159–62.

Exercises

4.1   Develop a simulation of general semaphores using only binary semaphores. Specify a global invariant, then develop a coarse-grained solution, and finally a fine-grained solution. (*Hint:* Use the technique of passing the baton.)

4.2   The semaphore operations are defined in Section 4.1 using `await` statements. Consequently, inference rules for `P` and `V` can be derived by applying the Await Statement Rule given in Section 2.6.

(a) Develop inference rules for `P` and `V`.

(b) Using your rules, prove that the critical section program in Figure 4.1 is correct. In particular, use the method of exclusion of configurations described in Section 2.8 to prove that two process cannot be in their critical sections at the same time.

4.3   Recall that Fetch-and-Add, `FA(var, increment)`, is an atomic function that returns the old value of `var` and adds `increment` to it. Using `FA`, develop a simulation of the `P` and `V` operations on general semaphore `s`. Assume that memory reads and writes are atomic but that `FA` is the only more powerful atomic operation.

4.4   A precedence graph is a directed, acyclic graph. Nodes represent tasks, and arcs indicate the order in which tasks are to be accomplished. In particular, a task can execute as soon as all its predecessors have been completed. Assume that the tasks are processes and that each process has the following outline:

```
process T {
    wait for predecessors, if any;
    body of the task;
    signal successors, if any;
}
```

(a) Using semaphores, show how to synchronize five processes whose permissible execution order is specified by the following precedence graph:

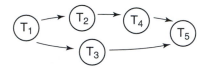

Minimize the number of semaphores that you use, and do not impose constraints not specified in the graph. For example, **T2** and **T3** can execute concurrently after **T1** completes.

(b) Describe how to synchronize processes, given an arbitrary precedence graph. In particular, devise a general method for assigning semaphores to edges or processes and for using them. Do not try to use the absolute minimum number of semaphores since determining that is an NP-hard problem for an arbitrary precedence graph!

4.5 Suppose a machine has atomic increment and decrement instructions, **INC(var)** and **DEC(var)**. These respectively add **1** to or subtract **1** from **var**. Assume that memory reads and writes are atomic but that **INC** and **DEC** are the only more powerful atomic operations.

(a) Is it possible to simulate the **P** and **V** operations on a general semaphore **s**? If so, give a simulation and explain how it works. If not, explain carefully why it is not possible to simulate **P** and **V**.

(b) Suppose **INC** and **DEC** also return the sign bit of the final value of **var**. In particular, if the final value of **var** is negative, they return **1**; otherwise, they return **0**. Is it now possible to simulate the **P** and **V** operations on a general semaphore **s**? If so, give a simulation and explain how it works. If not, explain carefully why it is still not possible to simulate **P** and **V**.

4.6 The UNIX kernel provides two primitives similar to the following:

```
sleep():    block the executing process
wakeup():   awaken all blocked processes
```

Each of these is an atomic operation. A call of **sleep** always blocks the calling process. A call of **wakeup** awakens every process that is blocked at the time **wakeup** is called.

Develop an implementation of these primitives using semaphores for synchronization. (*Hint:* Use the method of passing the baton.)

4.7 Consider the **sleep** and **wakeup** primitives defined in the previous exercise. Process **P1** is to execute statements **S1** and **S2**; process **P2** is to execute statements **S3** and **S4**. Statement **S4** must be executed after **S1**. A colleague gives you the following program:

```
process P1 {                process P2 {
   S1; wakeup(); S2;           S3; sleep(); S4;
}                            }
```

Is the solution correct? If so, explain why. If not, explain how it can fail, then describe how to change the primitives so that it is correct.

4.8 Give all possible final values of variable **x** in the following program. Explain how you got your answer.

```
int x = 0; sem s1 = 1, s2 = 0;
co P(s2); P(s1); x = x*2; V(s1);
// P(s1); x = x*x; V(s1);
// P(s1); x = x+3; V(s2); V(s1);
oc
```

4.9 Consider the combining tree barrier in Figures 3.13 and 3.14.

(a) Using semaphores for synchronization, give the actions of the leaf nodes, interior nodes, and root node. Make sure the barrier can be reused by the same set of processes.

(b) If there are **n** processes, what is the total execution time for one complete barrier synchronization as a function of **n**? Assume each semaphore operation takes one time unit. Illustrate your answer by showing the structure of the combining tree and giving the execution time for a few values of **n**.

4.10 Consider the butterfly and dissemination barriers in Figures 3.15 and 3.16.

(a) Using semaphores for synchronization, give complete details for a butterfly barrier for eight processes. Show the code that each process would execute. The barrier should be reusable.

(b) Repeat (a) for a dissemination barrier for eight processes.

(c) Compare your answers to (a) and (b). How many variables are required for each kind of barrier? If each semaphore operation takes one unit of time, what is the total time required for barrier synchronization in each algorithm?

(d) Repeat (a), (b), and (c) for a seven-process barrier.

(e) Repeat (a), (b), and (c) for a 12-process barrier.

4.11 It is possible to implement a reusable n-process barrier with two semaphores and one counter. These are declared as follows:

```
int count = 0;
sem arrive = 1, go = 0;
```

Develop a solution. (*Hint:* Use the idea of passing the baton.)

4.12 It is possible to construct a simple $O(n)$ execution time barrier for n worker processes using an array of n semaphores. Show how to do so. The workers should synchronize with each other; do not use any other processes. Be sure to show the initial values for the semaphores.

4.13 Consider the following proposal for implementing await statements using semaphores:

```
sem e = 1, d = 0;   # entry and delay semaphores
int nd = 0;          # delay counter

# implementation of ⟨await (B) S;⟩
P(e);
while (!B)
   { nd = nd+1; V(e); P(d); P(e); }
S;
while (nd > 0)
   { nd = nd-1; V(d); }
V(e);
```

Does this code ensure that the await statement is executed atomically? Does it avoid deadlock? Does it guarantee that B is true before S is executed? For each of these questions, either give a convincing argument why the answer is yes, or give an execution sequence that illustrates why the answer is no.

4.14 Develop a concurrent implementation of a bounded buffer with multiple producers and multiple consumers. In particular, modify the solution in Figure 4.4 so that multiple deposits and multiple fetches can execute at the same time. Each deposit must place a message into a different empty slot. Fetches must retrieve messages from different full slots.

4.15 Another way to solve the bounded buffer problem is as follows. Let `count` be an integer between 0 and n. Then `deposit` and `fetch` can be programmed as follows:

```
deposit:
   〈 await (count < n)
         buf[rear] = data;
         rear = (rear+1) % n; count = count+1; 〉
fetch:
   〈 await (count > 0)
         result = buf[front];
         front = (front+1) % n; count = count-1; 〉
```

Implement these `await` statements using semaphores. (*Hint:* Use a variation of passing the baton.)

4.16 *Atomic Broadcast.* Assume one producer process and n consumer processes share a buffer. The producer deposits messages into the buffer, consumers fetch them. Every message deposited by the producer has to be fetched by all n consumers before the producer can deposit another message into the buffer.

(a) Develop a solution for this problem using semaphores for synchronization.

(b) Now assume the buffer has b slots. The producer can deposit messages only into empty slots and every message has to be received by all n consumers before the slot can be reused. Furthermore, each consumer is to receive the messages in the order they were deposited. However, different consumers can receive messages at different times. For example, one consumer could receive up to b more messages than another if the second consumer is slow. Extend your answer to (a) to solve this more general problem.

4.17 Solve the dining philosophers problem by focusing on the state of the philosophers rather than the forks. In particular, let `eating[5]` be a Boolean array; `eating[i]` is true if `Philosopher[i]` is eating, and is false otherwise.

(a) Specify a global invariant, then develop a coarse-grained solution, and finally develop a fine-grained solution that uses semaphores for synchronization. Your solution should be deadlock-free, but an individual philosopher might starve. (*Hint:* Use the technique of passing the baton.)

(b) Modify your answer to (a) to avoid starvation. In particular, if a philosopher wants to eat, eventually he gets to.

4.18 Solve the dining philosophers problem using a centralized coordinator process. In particular, when a philosopher wants to eat, he informs the coordinator and then waits for permission (i.e., the philosopher waits to be given both forks).

Use semaphores for synchronization. Your solution should avoid deadlock and starvation.

4.19 In the dining philosophers problem, assume that a philosopher flips a perfect coin to determine which fork to pick up first.

(a) Develop a fully symmetric solution to this problem. In particular, every philosopher should execute the same algorithm. Use busy waiting, semaphores, or both for synchronization. Your solution should be deadlock-free, but an individual philosopher might starve (with low probability). (*Hint:* Have a philosopher put his first fork back down and flip the coin again if the second fork is unavailable.)

(b) Extend your answer to (a) to guarantee absence of starvation. Clearly explain your solution. (*Hint:* Use extra variables to preclude one philosopher from eating again if a neighbor wants to eat.)

4.20 Consider the following writers' preference solution to the readers/writers problem [Courtois et al. 1971]:

```
int nr = 0, nw = 0;
sem m1 = 1, m2 = 1, m3 = 1; # mutex semaphores
sem read = 1, write = 1;    # read/write semaphores
```

Reader processes:
```
P(m3);
  P(read);
  P(m1);
    nr = nr+1;
    if (nr == 1) P(write);
  V(m1);
  V(read);
V(m3);
read the database;
P(m1);
  nr = nr-1;
  if (nr == 0) V(write);
V(m1);
```

Writer processes:
```
P(m2);
  nw = nw+1;
  if (nw == 1) P(read);
V(m2);
P(write);
write the database;
V(write);
P(m2);
  nw = nw-1;
  if (nw == 0) V(read);
V(m2);
```

The code executed by reader processes is similar to that in Figure 4.10, but the code for writer processes is much more complex.

Explain the role of each semaphore. Develop assertions that indicate what is true at critical points. In particular, show that the solution ensures that writers have exclusive access to the database and a writer excludes readers. Give a convincing argument that the solution gives writers preference over readers.

4.21 Consider the following solution to the readers/writers problem. It employs the same counters and semaphores as in Figure 4.13, but uses them differently.

```
int nr = 0, nw = 0;    # numbers of readers and writers
sem e = 1;             # mutual exclusion semaphore
sem r = 0, w = 0;      # delay semaphores
int dr = 0, dw = 0;    # delay counters

process Reader[i = 1 to M] {
  while (true) {
    P(e);
      if (nw == 0) { nr = nr+1; V(r); }
      else  dr = dr+1;
    V(e);
    P(r);    # wait for permission to read
    read the database;
    P(e);
      nr = nr-1;
      if (nr == 0 and dw > 0)
        { dw = dw-1; nw = nw+1; V(w); }
    V(e);
  }
}

process Writer[j = 1 to N] {
  while (true) {
    P(e);
      if (nr == 0 and nw == 0) { nw = nw+1; V(w); }
      else  dw = dw+1;
    V(e);
    P(w);
    write the database;
    P(e);
      nw = nw-1;
      if (dw > 0) { dw = dw-1; nw = nw+1; V(w); }
      else
        while (dr > 0) { dr = dr-1; nr = nr+1; V(r); }
    V(e);
  }
}
```

(a) Carefully explain how this solution works. What is the role of each semaphore? Show that the solution ensures that writers have exclusive access to the database and a writer excludes readers.

(b) What kind of preference does the above solution have? Readers preference? Writers preference? Alternating preference?

(c) Compare this solution to the one in Figure 4.13. How many P and V operations are executed by each process in each solution in the best case? In the worst case? Which program do you find easier to understand, and why?

4.22   Consider the readers/writers program in Figure 4.13.

(a) Alter the program to give writers preference over readers. The text describes the basic idea; you are to fill in the details.

(b) Compare your answer to (a) with the program in the previous exercise. How many semaphore operations are executed by readers and by writers in each solution in the best case? In the worst case?

4.23   Modify the readers/writers solution in Figure 4.13 so that the exit protocol in **Writer** processes awakens all waiting readers, if there are any. (*Hint:* You will also need to modify the entry protocol in **Reader** processes.)

4.24   Assume there are **n** reader processes in the readers/writers problem. Let **rw** be a semaphore with initial value **n**. Suppose the reader's protocol is

```
P(rw);
read the database;
V(rw);
```

Develop a protocol for writer processes that ensures the required exclusion, is deadlock-free, and avoids starvation (assuming the P operation is strongly fair).

4.25   *The Water Molecule Problem.* Suppose hydrogen and oxygen atoms are bouncing around in space trying to group together into water molecules. This requires that two hydrogen atoms and one oxygen atom synchronize with each other. Let the hydrogen (H) and oxygen (O) atoms be simulated by processes (threads). Each H atom calls a procedure **Hready** when it wants to combine into a water molecule. Each O atom calls another procedure **Oready** when it wants to combine.

Your job is to write the two procedures, using semaphores for synchronization. An H atom has to delay in **Hready** until another H atom has also called **Hready** *and* one O atom has called **Oready**. Then *one* of the processes (say the O atom) should call a procedure **makeWater**. After **makeWater** returns, *all three* processes should return from their calls of **Hready** and **Oready**. Your solution should not use busy waiting and it must avoid deadlock and starvation. This is a tricky problem, so be careful. (*Hint:* Consider starting with a global invariant and using passing the baton.)

4.26   Suppose the P and V operations on semaphores are replaced by the following:

```
PChunk(s, amt):   ⟨await (s >= amt) s = s - amt;⟩
VChunk(s, amt):   ⟨s = s + amt;⟩
```

The value of amt is a positive integer. These primitives generalize P and V by allowing amt to be other than 1.

(a) Use PChunk and VChunk to construct a simple reader's preference solution to the readers/writers problem. First give a global invariant, then develop a coarse-grained solution, and finally develop a fine-grained solution.

(b) Identify other problems that could benefit from the use of these two primitives and explain why. (*Hint:* Consider other problems in the text and in these exercises.)

4.27   *Cigarette Smokers Problem* [Patil 1971; Parnas 1975]. Suppose there are three smoker processes and one agent process. Each smoker continuously makes a cigarette and smokes it. Making a cigarette requires three ingredients: tobacco, paper, and a match. One smoker process has tobacco, the second paper, and the third matches. Each has an infinite supply of these ingredients. The agent places a random two ingredients on the table. The smoker who has the third ingredient picks up the other two, makes a cigarette, then smokes it. The agent waits for the smoker to finish. The cycle then repeats.

Develop a solution to this problem using semaphores for synchronization. You may also need to use other variables.

4.28   Suppose the P and V operations on semaphores are replaced by the following:

```
PMultiple(s1, ..., sN):
  ⟨ await (s1 > 0 and ... and sN > 0)
          s1 = s1-1; ...; sN = sN-1; ⟩
VMultiple(s1, ..., sN):
  ⟨ s1 = s1+1; ...; sN = sN+1; ⟩
```

The arguments are one or more semaphores. These primitives generalize P and V by allowing a process to simultaneously do a P or V operation on multiple semaphores.

(a) Use PMultiple and VMultiple to construct a simple solution to the cigarette smokers problem defined in the previous exercise.

(b) Consider other problems in Chapter 4 and these exercises. Which ones could benefit from the use of these two primitives and why?

4.29 Consider a function `exchange(value)` that is called by two processes to exchange the values of their arguments. The first process to call `exchange` has to delay. When a second process calls `exchange`, the two values are swapped and returned to the processes. The same scenario is repeated for the third and fourth calls to `exchange`, the fifth and sixth calls, and so on.

Develop code to implement the body of `exchange`. Use semaphores for synchronization. Be sure to declare and initialize every variable and semaphore you need, and to place shared variables global to the procedure.

4.30 *The Unisex Bathroom.* Suppose there is one bathroom in your department. It can be used by both men and women, but not at the same time.

(a) Develop a solution to this problem. First specify a global invariant, then develop a solution using semaphores for synchronization. Allow any number of men or women to be in the bathroom at the same time. Your solution should ensure the required exclusion and avoid deadlock, but it need not be fair.

(b) Modify your answer to (a) so that at most four people are in the bathroom at the same time.

(c) Modify your answer to (a) to ensure fairness. You might want to solve the problem differently. (*Hint:* Use the technique of passing the baton.)

4.31 *The One-Lane Bridge.* Cars coming from the north and the south arrive at a one-lane bridge. Cars heading in the same direction can cross the bridge at the same time, but cars heading in opposite directions cannot.

(a) Develop a solution to this problem. First specify a global invariant, then develop a solution using semaphores for synchronization. Do not worry about fairness.

(b) Modify your answer to (b) to ensure that any car that is waiting to cross the bridge eventually gets to do so. You may want to solve the problem differently. (*Hint:* Use the technique of passing the baton.)

4.32 *Search/Insert/Delete.* Three kinds of processes share access to a singly linked list: searchers, inserters, and deleters. Searchers merely examine the list; hence they can execute concurrently with each other. Inserters add new items to the end of the list; insertions must be mutually exclusive to preclude two inserters from inserting new items at about the same time. However, one insert can proceed in parallel with any number of searches. Finally, deleters remove items from anywhere in the list. At most one deleter process can access the list at a time, and deletion must also be mutually exclusive with searches and insertions.

(a) This problem is an example of selective mutual exclusion. Develop a solution using semaphores that is similar in style to the readers/writers solution in Figure 4.10.

(b) This is also an example of a condition synchronization problem. Derive a solution that is similar in style to the readers/writers solution in Figure 4.13. First specify the synchronization property as a global invariant. Use three counters: `ns`, the number of active searchers; `ni`, the number of active inserters; and `nd`, the number of active deleters. Then develop a coarse-grained solution. Finally, develop a fine-grained solution using the technique of passing the baton.

4.33 Consider the following memory allocation problem. Suppose there are two operations: `request(amount)` and `release(amount)`, where `amount` is an integer. When a process calls `request`, it delays until at least `amount` free pages of memory are available, then takes `amount` pages. A process returns `amount` pages to the free pool by calling `release`. (Pages may be released in different quantities than they are acquired.)

(a) Develop implementations of `request` and `release` that use the shortest-job-next (SJN) allocation policy. In particular, smaller requests take precedence over larger ones. Your solution should have the style of the program in Figure 4.14.

(b) Develop implementations of `request` and `release` that use a first-come, first-served (FCFS) allocation policy. This means that a pending request might have to delay, even if there is enough memory available.

4.34 Suppose n processes `U[1:n]` share two printers. Before using a printer, `U[i]` calls `request(printer)`. This operation waits until one of the printers is available, then returns the identity of a free printer. After using that printer, `U[i]` returns it by calling `release(printer)`. Both `request` and `release` are atomic operations.

(a) Develop implementations of `request` and `release` using semaphores for synchronization.

(b) Assume each process has a priority stored in global array `priority[1:n]`. Modify `request` and `release` so that a printer is allocated to the highest priority waiting process. You may assume that each process has a unique priority.

4.35 *The Hungry Birds.* Given are n baby birds and one parent bird. The baby birds eat out of a common dish that initially contains F portions of food. Each baby repeatedly eats one portion of food at a time, sleeps for a while, and then comes back to eat. When the dish becomes empty, the baby bird who empties the dish awakens the parent bird. The parent refills the dish with F portions, then waits for the dish to become empty again. This pattern repeats forever.

Represent the birds as processes and develop code that simulates their actions. Use semaphores for synchronization.

4.36 *The Bear and the Honeybees.* Given are n honeybees and a hungry bear. They share a pot of honey. The pot is initially empty; its capacity is H portions of honey. The bear sleeps until the pot is full, then eats all the honey and goes back to sleep. Each bee repeatedly gathers one portion of honey and puts it in the pot; the bee who fills the pot awakens the bear.

Represent the bear and honeybees as processes and develop code that simulates their actions. Use semaphores for synchronization.

4.37 *The Roller Coaster Problem* [Herman 1989]. Suppose there are n passenger processes and one car process. The passengers repeatedly wait to take rides in the car, which can hold c passengers, c < n. However, the car can go around the tracks only when it is full.

(a) Develop code for the actions of the passenger and car processes. Use semaphores for synchronization.

(b) Generalize your answer to (a) to employ m car processes, m > 1. Since there is only one track, cars cannot pass each other; i.e., they must finish going around the track in the order in which they started. Again, a car can go around the tracks only when it is full.

4.38 An eventcount is used to record the number of times an event has occurred. It is represented by an integer initialized to zero and is manipulated by three primitives:

```
advance(ec):  ⟨ec = ec+1;⟩
read(ec):  ⟨return(ec);⟩
wait(ec, value):  ⟨await (ec >= value);⟩
```

A sequencer dispenses unique values. It is also represented by an integer initialized to zero and is manipulated by the following atomic function:

```
ticket(seq):  ⟨temp = seq; seq = seq+1; return(temp);⟩
```

A sequencer is often used in the second argument to the wait primitive.

(a) Using these primitives, develop a solution to the bounded buffer problem. Assume there is one producer and one consumer and that the communication buffer contains n slots (see Figure 4.4).

(b) Extend your answer to (b) to permit multiple producers and consumers.

(c) Using these primitives, develop implementations of the P and V operations on a general semaphore.

5

Monitors

Semaphores are a fundamental synchronization mechanism. As shown in Chapter 4, they make it easy to program mutual exclusion and signaling. Moreover, they can be used in a systematic way to solve any synchronization problem. However, semaphores are also a low-level mechanism. This means it is easy to make errors when using them. For example, a programmer must be careful not to omit a P or V accidentally, to execute one too many P or V operations, to employ the wrong semaphore, or to fail to protect all critical sections. Semaphores are also global to all processes. Thus, to see how a semaphore—or any other shared variable—is being used, one must examine the entire program. Finally, with semaphores both mutual exclusion and condition synchronization are programmed using the same pair of primitives. This makes it difficult to identify the purpose of a given P or V without looking at other operations on the same semaphore. Since mutual exclusion and condition synchronization are distinct concepts, they should ideally be programmed in different ways.

Monitors are program modules that provide more structure than semaphores yet can be implemented as efficiently. First and foremost, monitors are a data abstraction mechanism. A monitor encapsulates the representation of an abstract object and provides a set of operations that are the *only* means by which that representation is manipulated. In particular, a monitor contains variables that store the object's state and procedures that implement operations on the object. A process can access the variables in a monitor only by calling one of the monitor's procedures. Mutual exclusion is provided implicitly by ensuring that procedures in the same monitor are not executed concurrently. This is similar to the implicit mutual exclusion provided by **await** statements. Condition synchronization in monitors is provided explicitly by means of *condition variables*. These are similar to semaphores, but as we shall see there are important differences in how condition variables are defined and hence in how they are used for signaling.

When a concurrent program uses monitors for communication and synchronization, it contains two kinds of modules: active processes and passive monitors. Assuming all shared variables are within monitors, two processes interact only by calling procedures in the same monitor. The resulting modularization has two important benefits. First, a process that calls a monitor procedure can ignore how the procedure is implemented; all that matters are the visible effects of calling the procedure. Second, the programmer of a monitor can ignore how or where the monitor's procedures are used and can change the way in which the monitor is implemented, so long as the visible procedures and their effects are not changed. These benefits make it possible to design each process and monitor relatively independently. This makes a concurrent program easier to develop and also easier to understand.

This chapter describes monitors in detail and illustrates their use with numerous examples, some that we have seen before and many that are new. Section 5.1 defines the syntax and semantics of monitors. Section 5.2 describes a variety of useful programming techniques, using a sequence of examples: bounded buffers, readers/writers, shortest-job-next scheduling, an interval timer, and a classic problem called the sleeping barber. In Section 5.3 we take a different tack, focusing more on the *structure* of solutions to concurrent programming problems. We use another interesting problem—scheduling access to a moving-head disk—as the motivating example and show several ways to solve the problem.

Because of their utility and efficiency, monitors have been employed in several concurrent programming languages, most recently (and notably) in Java, which we describe in Section 5.4. The underlying synchronization mechanisms of monitors—implicit exclusion and condition variables for signaling—are also employed in the Unix operating system. Finally, condition variables are supported by several concurrent programming libraries. Section 5.5 describes the routines provided by the POSIX threads (Pthreads) library.

5.1 Syntax and Semantics

A monitor is used to group together the representation and implementation of a shared resource (class). It has an interface and a body. The interface specifies the operations (methods) provided by the resource. The body contains variables that represent the state of the resource and procedures that implement the operations in the interface.

Monitors are declared and created in different ways in different languages. For simplicity, we will assume here that each monitor is a static object and that the interface and body are declared together as follows:

```
monitor mname {
  declarations of permanent variables
  initialization statements
  procedures
}
```

The procedures implement the visible operations. The permanent variables are shared by all the procedures within the body of the monitor; they are called permanent variables because they exist and retain their values as long as the monitor exists. The procedures may also, as usual, have their own local variables; each procedure call gets its own copy of these.

A monitor has three properties that are a consequence of its being an instance of an abstract data type. First, only the procedure names are visible outside the monitor—they provide the only gates through the "wall" defined by a monitor declaration. Thus, to alter the resource state represented by the permanent variables, a process must call one of the monitor procedures. Calls of monitor procedures have the form:

```
call mname.opname(arguments)
```

where **mname** is the name of a monitor, **opname** is one of the operations (procedures) of the monitor, and arguments are a set of arguments to that operation. If **opname** is unique in the scope of the calling process, then the "**mname.**" part may be omitted from the call statement.

The second property of a monitor is that statements within the monitor—i.e., initialization statements and statements within procedures—may not access variables declared outside the monitor.

The third property is that permanent variables are initialized before any procedure is called. This is implemented by executing the initialization statements when the monitor is created, and hence before any procedure is called.

One of the attractive attributes of a monitor—or any abstract data type—is that it can be developed in relative isolation. However, this means that the programmer of a monitor cannot know *a priori* the order in which the monitor's procedures might be called. Whenever execution order is indeterminate, it is useful to define a predicate that is true independent of the execution order. In particular, a *monitor invariant* is a predicate that specifies the "reasonable" states of the permanent variables when no process is accessing them. The initialization code in a monitor must establish the invariant; each procedure must maintain it. (A monitor invariant is like a global invariant, but just for the variables within a single monitor.) We include a monitor invariant—in comments starting with ##—in each example in the chapter.

What distinguishes a monitor from a data abstraction mechanism in a sequential programming language is that a monitor is shared by concurrently executing processes. Thus processes executing in monitors may require mutual exclusion—to avoid interference—and may require condition synchronization—to delay until the monitor state is conducive to continued execution. We now consider how processes synchronize within monitors.

5.1.1 Mutual Exclusion

Synchronization is easiest to understand and hence to program if mutual exclusion and condition synchronization are provided in different ways. It is best if mutual exclusion is implicit, because this automatically precludes interference. It also makes programs easier to read, because there are no explicit critical section entry and exit protocols.

In contrast, condition synchronization must be programmed explicitly, because different programs require different synchronization conditions. Although it is often easiest to synchronize by means of Boolean conditions as in `await` statements, lower-level mechanisms can be implemented much more efficiently. They also provide the programmer with finer control over execution order, which aids in solving allocation and scheduling problems.

Based on these considerations, mutual exclusion in monitors is provided implicitly and condition synchronization is programmed using what are called condition variables.

A monitor procedure is called by an external process. A procedure is *active* if some process is executing a statement in the procedure. At most one instance of one monitor procedure may be active at a time. For example, two calls of different procedures may not be active at the same time, nor can two calls of the same procedure.

Monitor procedures *by definition* execute with mutual exclusion. In particular, it is up to the implementation of a language, library, or operating system to provide mutual exclusion. It is *not* up to the programmer who uses monitors. In practice, languages and libraries implement mutual exclusion by using locks or semaphores; single-processor operating systems implement mutual exclusion by inhibiting external interrupts; and multiprocessor operating systems implement mutual exclusion by using locks (between processors) and by inhibiting interrupts (on a processor). Chapter 6 discusses implementation issues and techniques in detail.

5.1.2 Condition Variables

A *condition variable* is used to delay a process that cannot safely continue executing until the monitor's state satisfies some Boolean condition. It is also used to awaken a delayed process when the condition becomes true. The declaration of a condition variable has the form

```
cond cv;
```

Hence, `cond` is a new data type. An array of condition variables is declared in the usual way by appending range information to the variable's name. Condition variables may be declared, and hence used, only within monitors.

The value of a condition variable `cv` is a queue of delayed processes. Initially, this queue is empty. The value of `cv` is not, however, directly visible to the programmer. Instead it is accessed indirectly by several special operations, as described below.

A process can query the state of a condition variable by calling

```
empty(cv)
```

This function returns true if `cv`'s queue is empty; otherwise it returns false.

A process blocks on a condition variable by executing

```
wait(cv);
```

Execution of `wait` causes the executing process to delay at the rear of `cv`'s queue. So that some other process can eventually enter the monitor to awaken the delayed process, execution of `wait` also causes the process to relinquish exclusive access to the monitor.

Processes that are blocked on condition variables get awakened by means of `signal` statements. Execution of

```
signal(cv);
```

examines `cv`'s delay queue. If it is empty, `signal` has no effect. However, if there is some delayed process, then `signal` awakens the process *at the front of the queue*. Thus, `wait` and `signal` provide a FIFO signaling discipline: processes are delayed in the order they call `wait` and they are awakened in the order that `signal` is called. We will later see how to add scheduling priorities to the delay queue, but the default is that the queue is FIFO.

5.1.3 Signaling Disciplines

When a process executes `signal`, it is executing within a monitor, and hence it has control of the lock implicitly associated with the monitor. This leads to a dilemma. If `signal` awakens another process, there are now two processes that could execute: the one that executed `signal` and the one that was just awakened. At most one process can execute next (even on a multiprocessor), because at most one can have exclusive access to the monitor. Thus, there are two possibilities:

- *Signal and Continue:* The signaler continues and the signaled process executes at some later time.

- *Signal and Wait:* The signaler waits until some later time and the signaled process executes now.

Signal and Continue (SC) is *nonpreemptive*: The process executing `signal` retains exclusive control of the monitor and the awakened process executes at some later time when it can have exclusive access to the monitor. In essence, a `signal` is merely a hint that the awakened process might continue, so it goes back onto the queue of processes waiting for the monitor lock.

On the other hand, Signal and Wait (SW) is *preemptive*: The process executing `signal` passes control of the monitor lock to the process awakened by the `signal`, and hence the awakened process preempts the signaler. In this case, the signaler goes back onto the queue of processes waiting for the monitor lock. (A variation is to put the signaler at the front of the queue of processes waiting for the monitor lock; this is called Signal and Urgent Wait.)

The state diagram in Figure 5.1 illustrates how monitor synchronization works. When a process calls a monitor procedure, the caller goes onto the entry queue if another process is executing in the monitor; otherwise the caller passes through the entry queue and immediately starts executing in the monitor. When the monitor becomes free—due to a return or `wait`—one process can move from the entry queue to executing in the monitor. When a process executes `wait(cv)` it moves from executing in the monitor to the queue associated with the condition variable. When a process executes `signal(cv)`, with Signal and Continue (the arc labeled SC) the process at the front of the condition variable queue moves to the entry queue; with Signal and Wait (the two arcs labeled SW), the process executing in the monitor moves to the entry queue and the process at the front of the condition variable queue moves to executing in the monitor.

Figure 5.2 contains a monitor that implements a semaphore. It illustrates all the components of a monitor and will further clarify the differences between the SC and SW signaling disciplines. (Although one would most likely not ever use monitors to implement semaphores, the example illustrates that monitors can do

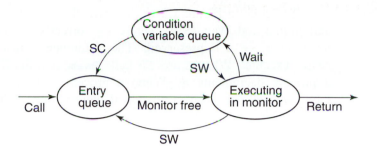

Figure 5.1   State diagram for synchronization in monitors.

so. In Chapter 6 we will show how to implement monitors using semaphores. Monitors and semaphores are thus duals in the sense that each can implement the other and hence can be used to solve the same synchronization problems. However, monitors are a higher-level mechanism than semaphores for the reasons described at the start of the chapter.)

In Figure 5.2 integer **s** represents the value of the semaphore. When a process calls the **Psem** operation, it delays until **s** is positive, then decrements the value of **s**. In this case, the delay is programmed by using a **while** loop that causes the process to wait on condition variable **pos** if **s** is 0. The **Vsem** operation increments the value of **s**, then signals **pos**. If there is at least one delayed process, the oldest one is awakened.

```
monitor Semaphore {
  int s = 0;   ## s >= 0
  cond pos;    #  signaled when s > 0

  procedure Psem() {
    while (s == 0) wait(pos);
    s = s-1;
  }

  procedure Vsem() {
    s = s+1;
    signal(pos);
  }
}
```

Figure 5.2   Monitor implementation of a semaphore.

The code in Figure 5.2 works correctly for both Signal and Continue (SC) and Signal and Wait (SW), where by correctly we mean that the semaphore invariant `s >= 0` is preserved. The difference is just the order in which processes execute. When a process calls `Psem`, it waits if `s` is `0`; after awakening, a process decrements `s`. When a process calls `Vsem`, it first increments `s` then awakens one delayed process if there is one. With the SW discipline, the awakened process executes *now* and decrements `s`. With the SC discipline, the awakened process executes some time *after* the signaler. The awakened process needs to recheck the value of `s` to ensure that it is still positive; this is because there could be some other process waiting on the entry queue and that process could execute `Psem` first and decrement `s`. Hence, the code in Figure 5.2 implements a FIFO semaphore for the SW discipline but *not* for the SC discipline.

Figure 5.2 illustrates another difference between the SC and SW signaling disciplines. In particular, with the SW discipline the `while` loop in the `Psem` operation can be replaced by a simple `if` statement:

```
if (s == 0) wait(pos);
```

Again this is because the signaled process executes immediately, so it is guaranteed that `s` is positive when that process decrements `s`.

The monitor in Figure 5.2 can be changed so that it (1) works correctly for both Signal and Continue and Signal and Wait, (2) does not use a `while` loop, and (3) implements a FIFO semaphore. To understand how, reconsider the program in Figure 5.2. When a process first calls the `Psem` operation, it needs to delay if `s` is `0`. When a process calls the `Vsem` operation, it wants to awaken a delayed process, if there is one. The difference between SC and SW signaling is that if the signaler continues, the value of `s` has already been incremented and could be seen to be positive by some process other than the one that is awakened. The way to avoid this problem is to have a process executing `Vsem` make a decision: If there is delayed process, then signal `pos` *but* do not increment `s`; otherwise, increment `s`. A process executing `Psem` then takes corresponding actions: if it has to wait, then it does not later decrement `s`, because the signaler will not have incremented `s`.

Figure 5.3 gives a monitor that uses the above approach. We call this technique *passing the condition*, because in essence the signaler implicitly passes the condition that `s` is positive to the process that it awakens. By not making the condition visible, no process other than the one awakened by `signal` can see that the condition is true and fail to wait.

The technique of passing the condition can be used whenever procedures that use `wait` and `signal` contain complementary actions. In Figure 5.3, the

```
monitor FIFOsemaphore {
  int s = 0;   ## s >= 0
  cond pos;    #  signaled when s > 0

  procedure Psem() {
    if (s == 0)
      wait(pos);
    else
      s = s-1;
  }

  procedure Vsem() {
    if (empty(pos))
      s = s+1;
    else
      signal(pos);
  }
}
```

Figure 5.3   FIFO semaphore using passing the condition.

complementary actions are decrementing s in procedure Psem and incrementing s in procedure Vsem. In Sections 5.2 and 5.3 we will see additional examples that use this same technique to solve scheduling problems.

Figures 5.2 and 5.3 illustrate that condition variables are similar to the P and V operations on semaphores. The wait operation, like P, delays a process, and the signal operation, like V, awakens a process. However, there are two important differences. First, wait *always* delays a process until a later signal is executed, whereas a P operation causes a process to delay only if the semaphore's value is currently 0. Second, signal has no effect if no process is delayed on the condition variable, whereas a V operation either awakens a delayed process or increments the value of the semaphore; in short, the fact that signal has been executed is not remembered. These differences cause condition synchronization to be programmed differently than with semaphores.

In the remainder of this chapter, we will assume that monitors use the Signal and Continue discipline. Although Signal and Wait was the first discipline proposed for monitors, SC is the signaling discipline used within the Unix operating system, the Java programming language, and the Pthreads library. The reasons for preferring Signal and Continue are that: (1) it is compatible with priority-based process scheduling, and (2) it has simpler formal semantics. (The Historical Notes section discusses these issues.)

5.1.4 *Additional Operations on Condition Variables*

Above we used the `empty`, `wait`, and `signal` operations on condition variables. Three additional operations are also useful: priority `wait`, `minrank`, and `signal_all`. All have simple semantics and can be implemented efficiently, because they merely provide additional operations on the queue associated with a condition variable. For reference, Table 5.1 summarizes all six operations.

With `wait` and `signal`, delayed processes are awakened in the order in which they delayed; i.e., the delay queue is a first-in, first-out (FIFO) queue. The *priority* `wait` statement allows the programmer to exert more control over the order in which delayed processes are queued and hence awakened. This statement has the form

```
wait(cv, rank)
```

Here, `cv` is a condition variable and `rank` is an integer-valued expression. Processes are delayed on `cv` in ascending order of `rank`, and hence they get awakened in this order; the process delayed the longest is awakened in the case of a tie. To avoid potential confusion resulting from using both regular and priority `wait` on the same condition variable, the programmer should always use one kind of `wait` or the other.

For scheduling problems that use priority `wait`, it is often useful to be able to determine the rank of the process at the front of a delay queue. A call of the integer-valued function

```
minrank(cv)
```

returns the delay rank of the process at the front of `cv`'s delay queue, assuming that the delay queue is not empty and that the process at the front used the priority `wait` statement; otherwise, `minrank` returns some arbitrary integer value.

`wait(cv)`	Wait at end of queue
`wait(cv, rank)`	Wait in order of increasing value of rank
`signal(cv)`	Awaken process at front of queue then continue
`signal_all(cv)`	Awaken all processes on queue then continue
`empty(cv)`	True if wait queue is empty; false otherwise
`minrank(cv)`	Value of rank of process at front of wait queue

Table 5.1   Operations on condition variables.

Broadcast `signal` is the final operation on condition variables. It is used if more than one delayed process could possibly proceed or if the signaler does not know which delayed processes might be able to proceed (because they themselves need to recheck delay conditions). This operation has the form

```
signal_all(cv)
```

Execution of `signal_all` awakens *all* processes delayed on `cv`. For the Signal and Continue discipline, its effect is the same as executing:

```
while (!empty(cv)) signal(cv);
```

Each awakened process resumes execution in the monitor at some time in the future, subject to the usual mutual exclusion constraint. Like `signal`, `signal_all` has no effect if no process is delayed on `cv`. Also, the signaling process continues execution in the monitor.

The `signal_all` operation is well-defined when monitors use the Signal and Continue discipline, because the signaler always continues executing next in the monitor. However, it is not a well-defined operation with the Signal and Wait discipline, because it is not possible to transfer control to more than one other process *and* to give each mutually exclusive access to the monitor. This is another reason why Unix, Java, Pthreads, and this book use the Signal and Continue discipline.

5.2 Synchronization Techniques

This section develops monitor-based solutions to five problems: (1) bounded buffers, (2) readers/writers, (3) shortest-job-next scheduling, (4) interval timers, (5) and the sleeping barber. Each is an interesting problem in its own right and also illustrates a programming technique that is useful with monitors, as indicated by the subtitles in the section headings.

5.2.1 Bounded Buffers: Basic Condition Synchronization

Consider again the bounded buffer problem introduced in Section 4.2. A producer process and a consumer process communicate by sharing a buffer having n slots. The buffer contains a queue of messages. The producer sends a message to the consumer by depositing the message at the end of the queue. The consumer receives a message by fetching the one at the front of the queue. Synchronization is required so that a message is not deposited if the queue is full and a message is not fetched if the queue is empty.

```
monitor Bounded_Buffer {
    typeT buf[n];      # an array of some type T
    int front = 0,     # index of first full slot
        rear = 0;      # index of first empty slot
        count = 0;     # number of full slots
    ## rear == (front + count) % n
    cond not_full,     # signaled when count < n
        not_empty;     # signaled when count > 0
    procedure deposit(typeT data) {
      while (count == n) wait(not_full);
      buf[rear] = data; rear = (rear+1) % n; count++;
      signal(not_empty);
    }
    procedure fetch(typeT &result) {
      while (count == 0) wait(not_empty);
      result = buf[front]; front = (front+1) % n; count--;
      signal(not_full);
    }
}
```

Figure 5.4   Monitor implementation of a bounded buffer.

Figure 5.4 contains a monitor that implements a bounded buffer. We again represent the message queue using an array **buf** and two integer variables **front** and **rear**; these point to the first full slot and the first empty slot, respectively. Integer variable **count** keeps track of the number of messages in the buffer. The two operations on the buffer are **deposit** and **fetch**, so these are the monitor procedures. Mutual exclusion is implicit, so semaphores are not needed to protect critical sections. Condition synchronization is implemented using two condition variables, as shown.

In Figure 5.4, both **wait** statements are enclosed in loops. This is always a safe way to ensure that the desired condition is true before the permanent variables are accessed. It is also necessary if there are multiple producers and consumers. (Recall that we are using Signal and Continue.)

When a process executes **signal**, it merely gives a hint that the signaled condition is now true. Because the signaler and possibly other processes may execute in the monitor before the process awakened by **signal**, the awaited condition may no longer be true when the awakened process resumes execution. For example, a producer could be delayed waiting for an empty slot, then a consumer could fetch a message and awaken the delayed producer. However, before the producer gets a turn to execute, another producer could enter `deposit` and fill the empty slot. An analogous situation could occur with consumers. Thus, in general, it is necessary to recheck the delay condition.

The `signal` statements in `deposit` and `fetch` are executed unconditionally since in both cases the signaled condition is true at the point of the `signal`. In fact, as long as `wait` statements are enclosed in loops that recheck the awaited condition, `signal` statements can be executed *at any time* since they merely give hints to delayed processes. A program will execute more efficiently, however, if `signal` is executed only if it is certain—or at least likely—that some delayed process could proceed.

5.2.2 Readers and Writers: Broadcast Signal

The readers/writers problem was introduced in Section 4.4. Recall that reader processes query a database and writer processes examine and alter it. Readers may access the database concurrently, but writers require exclusive access. Although the database is shared, we cannot encapsulate it by a monitor, because readers could not then access it concurrently since all code within a monitor executes with mutual exclusion. Instead, we use a monitor merely to arbitrate access to the database. The database itself is global to the readers and writers— for example, it could be stored in a shared memory table or an external file. As we shall see, this same basic structure is often employed in monitor-based programs.

For the readers/writers problem, the arbitration monitor grants permission to access the database. To do so, it requires that processes inform it when they want access and when they have finished. There are two kinds of processes and two actions per process, so the monitor has four procedures: (1) `request_read`, (2) `release_read`, (3) `request_write`, and (4) `release_write`. These procedures are used in the obvious ways. For example, a reader calls `request_read` before reading the database and calls `release_read` after reading the database.

To synchronize access to the database, we need to record how many processes are reading and how many are writing. As before let `nr` be the number of readers, and let `nw` be the number of writers. These are the permanent variables of the monitor; for proper synchronization, they must satisfy the monitor invariant:

$$RW: \quad (\text{nr} \texttt{ == } 0 \lor \text{nw} \texttt{ == } 0) \land \text{nw} \texttt{ <= } 1$$

Initially, `nr` and `nw` are `0`. Each variable is incremented in the appropriate request procedure and decremented in the appropriate release procedure.

```
monitor RW_Controller {
  int nr = 0, nw = 0;   ## (nr == 0 ∨ nw == 0) ∧ nw <= 1
  cond oktoread;     #  signaled when nw == 0
  cond oktowrite;    #  signaled when nr == 0 and nw == 0

  procedure request_read() {
    while (nw > 0) wait(oktoread);
    nr = nr + 1;
  }

  procedure release_read() {
  nr = nr - 1;
  if (nr == 0) signal(oktowrite);   # awaken one writer
  }

  procedure request_write() {
    while (nr > 0 || nw > 0) wait(oktowrite);
    nw = nw + 1;
  }

  procedure release_write() {
    nw = nw - 1;
    signal(oktowrite);        # awaken one writer and
    signal_all(oktoread);     # all readers
  }

}
```

Figure 5.5   Readers/writers solution using monitors.

Figure 5.5 contains a monitor that meets this specification. While loops and **wait** statements are used to ensure that *RW* is invariant. At the start of **request_read**, a reader needs to delay until **nw** is zero; **oktoread** is the condition variable on which readers delay. Similarly, writers need to delay at the start of **request_write** until both **nr** and **nw** are zero; **oktowrite** is the condition variable on which they delay. In **release_read** a writer is signaled when **nr** is zero. Since writers recheck their delay condition, the solution would still be correct if writers were always signaled. However, the solution would then be less efficient since a signaled writer would have to go right back to sleep if **nr** were zero. On the other hand, at the end of **release_write**, we know that both **nr** and **nw** are zero. Hence any delayed process could proceed. The solution in Figure 5.5 does not arbitrate between readers and writers. Instead it awakens *all* delayed processes and lets the underlying process scheduling policy determine which executes first and hence which gets to access the database. If a writer goes first, the awakened readers go back to sleep; if a reader goes first, the awakened writer goes back to sleep.

5.2.3 Shortest-Job-Next Allocation: Priority Wait

A condition variable is by default a FIFO queue, so when a process executes `wait` it delays at the end of the queue. The priority wait statement `wait(cv, rank)` delays processes in ascending order of rank. It is used to implement non-FIFO scheduling policies. Here we revisit the Shortest-Job-Next allocation problem, which was introduced in Section 4.5.

A shortest-job-next allocator has two operations: `request` and `release`. When a process calls `request`, it delays until the resource is free or is allocated to it. After acquiring and using the resource, a process calls `release`. The resource is then allocated to the requesting process that will use it the shortest length of time; if there are no pending requests, the resource is freed.

Figure 5.6 gives a monitor that implements an SJN allocator. The permanent variables are a Boolean variable `free` that indicates whether the resource is

```
monitor Shortest_Job_Next {

    bool free = true;   ## Invariant SJN:  see text
    cond turn;          #  signaled when resource available

    procedure request(int time) {
      if (free)
        free = false;
      else
        wait(turn, time);
    }

    procedure release() {
      if (empty(turn))
        free = true
      else
        signal(turn);
    }

}
```

Figure 5.6   Shortest-job-next allocation with monitors.

free, and a condition variable `turn` that is used to delay processes. Together these satisfy the monitor invariant:

SJN: `turn` ordered by time $\wedge$ (`free` $\Rightarrow$ `turn` is empty)

The procedures in Figure 5.6 again use the technique of passing the condition. Priority `wait` is used to order delayed processes by the amount of time they will use the resource; `empty` is used to determine if there are delayed processes. When the resource is released, if there are delayed processes, the one with minimal rank is awakened; otherwise, the resource is marked as being free. The resource is not marked as free if a process is signaled to ensure that no other process can take the resource first.

5.2.4 Interval Timer: Covering Conditions

We now turn to a new problem: the design of an interval timer that makes it possible for processes to sleep for a specified number of time units. Such a facility is often provided by operating systems to enable users to do such things as periodically execute utility commands. We will develop two solutions that illustrate two generally useful techniques. The first solution employs what is called a covering condition; the second uses priority `wait` to provide a compact, efficient delay mechanism.

A monitor that implements an interval timer is another example of a resource controller. In this case, the resource is a logical clock. The clock has two operations: `delay(interval)`, which delays the calling process for `interval` ticks of the clock, and `tick`, which increments the value of the logical clock. Other operations might also be provided—for example, to return the value of the clock or to delay a process until the clock has reached a specific value.

Application processes call `delay(interval)`, where `interval` is nonnegative. The `tick` operation is called by a process that is periodically awakened by a hardware timer. This process typically has a high execution priority so that the value of the logical clock remains fairly accurate.

To represent the value of the logical clock, we use integer variable `tod` (time of day). Initially, `tod` is `0`; it satisfies the simple invariant

CLOCK: `tod >= 0` $\wedge$ `tod` increases monotonically by `1`

When a process calls `delay`, it must not return until the clock has "ticked" at least `interval` times. We do not insist on exact equality since a delayed process might not execute before the high-priority process that calls `tick` has done so again.

A process that calls `delay` first needs to compute the desired wakeup time. This is accomplished in the obvious way by executing

```
wake_time = tod + interval;
```

Here, `wake_time` is a variable local to the body of `delay`; hence each process that calls `delay` computes its own private wake-up time. Next the process needs to wait until `tick` has been called often enough. This is accomplished by using a `while` loop that causes the process to wait until `wake_time` is at least as large as `tod`. The body of the `tick` procedure is even simpler: it merely increments `tod` and then awakens delayed processes.

The remaining step is to implement the synchronization between delayed processes and the process that calls `tick`. One approach is to employ one condition variable for each different delay condition. Here, each delayed process could be waiting for a different time, so each process would need a private condition variable. Before delaying, a process would record in permanent variables the time it wishes to be awakened. When `tick` is called, the permanent variables would be consulted, and, if some processes were due to be awakened, their private condition variables would be signaled. Although certainly feasible, and for some problems necessary, this approach is more cumbersome and inefficient than required for the `Timer` monitor.

A much simpler way to implement the required synchronization is to employ a single condition variable and to use a technique called a *covering condition*. Such a condition variable is one for which the associated Boolean condition "covers" the actual conditions for which different processes are waiting. When any of the covered conditions could be true, all processes delayed on the covering condition variable are awakened. Each such process rechecks its specific condition and either continues or waits again.

In the `Timer` monitor, we can employ one covering condition variable, `check`, with associated condition "`tod` has increased." Processes wait on `check` in the body of `delay`; every waiting process is awakened each time `tick` is called. In particular, we get the `Timer` monitor shown in Figure 5.7. In `tick` a broadcast signal, `signal_all`, is used to awaken all delayed processes.

Although the solution in Figure 5.7 is compact and simple, it is not very efficient for this problem. Using a covering condition is appropriate only if the expected cost of false alarms—i.e., awakening a process that finds that its delay condition is false so immediately goes back to sleep—is lower than the cost of maintaining a record of the conditions of all waiting processes and only awakening a process when its condition is true. Often this is the case (see the exercises at the end of this chapter), but here it is likely that processes delay for relatively long intervals and hence would be needlessly awakened numerous times.

```
monitor Timer {
    int tod = 0;     ## invariant CLOCK -- see text
    cond check;      #  signaled when tod has increased
    procedure delay(int interval) {
        int wake_time;
        wake_time = tod + interval;
        while (wake_time > tod) wait(check);
    }
    procedure tick() {
        tod = tod + 1;
        signal_all(check);
    }
}
```

Figure 5.7   Interval timer with a covering condition.

By using priority **wait**, we can transform the solution in Figure 5.7 into one that is equally simple, yet highly efficient. In particular, priority **wait** can be used whenever there is a static order between the conditions for which different processes are waiting. Here, waiting processes can be ordered by their wake-up times. When **tick** is called, it uses **minrank** to determine if it is time to awaken the first process delayed on **check**; if so, that process is signaled. Incorporating these refinements, we have the second version of the **Timer** monitor shown in Figure 5.8. A **while** loop is no longer needed in **delay** since **tick** ensures that a process is awakened only when its delay condition is true. However, the **signal** in **tick** has to be embedded in a loop, because there may be more than one process waiting for the same wake-up time.

To summarize, there are three basic ways to implement condition synchronization when the delay conditions depend on variables local to the waiting process. The preferred choice—because it leads to compact, efficient solutions—is to use priority **wait**, as in Figure 5.8 and earlier in Figure 5.6. This approach can be used whenever there is a static order between delay conditions.

The second best choice, because it also leads to compact solutions, is to use a covering condition variable. This approach can be used whenever it is possible for waiting processes to recheck their own conditions; however, it cannot be used when waiting conditions depend on a function of the states of other waiting processes. Use of covering condition variables is appropriate as long as the cost of false alarms is less than the cost of maintaining in permanent variables exact records of waiting conditions.

```
monitor Timer {
   int tod = 0;     ## invariant CLOCK -- see text
   cond check;      #  signaled when minrank(check) <= tod

   procedure delay(int interval) {
     int wake_time;
     wake_time = tod + interval;
     if (wake_time > tod) wait(check, wake_time);
   }

   procedure tick() {
     tod = tod+1;
     while (!empty(check) && minrank(check) <= tod)
       signal(check);
   }
}
```

Figure 5.8   Interval timer with priority wait.

The third choice is to record in permanent variables the waiting conditions of delayed processes and to employ private condition variables to awaken such processes when appropriate. This approach produces more complex solutions, but it is required if neither of the other choices can be employed or if the second choice is not efficient enough. The exercises contain problems that explore the tradeoffs between these three choices.

5.2.5 The Sleeping Barber: Rendezvous

As a final basic example, we consider another classic synchronization problem: the sleeping barber. Like the dining philosophers problem, this one has a colorful definition. Moreover, the sleeping barber is representative of practical problems, such as the disk head scheduler described in the next section. The problem illustrates the important client/server relationship that often exists between processes. It also requires an important type of synchronization called a rendezvous. Finally, the problem serves as an excellent illustration of the need to use a systematic approach when solving synchronization problems. *Ad hoc* techniques are far too error-prone for solving complex problems such as this one.

Sleeping Barber Problem. An easygoing town contains a small barbershop having two doors and a few chairs. Customers enter through one door and leave through the other. Because the shop is small, at most one customer or the barber can move around in it at a time. The barber spends his life serving customers. When none are in the shop, the barber sleeps in the barber's chair. When a customer arrives and finds the barber sleeping, the customer awakens the barber, sits in the barber's chair, and sleeps while the barber cuts his hair. If the barber is busy when a customer arrives, the customer goes to sleep in one of the other chairs. After giving a haircut, the barber opens the exit door for the customer and closes it when the customer leaves. If there are waiting customers, the barber then awakens one and waits for the customer to sit in the barber's chair. Otherwise, the barber goes back to sleep until a new customer arrives.

The customers and barber are processes, and the barber's shop is a monitor within which the processes interact, as shown in Figure 5.9. Customers are *clients* that request a service from the barber, in this case, haircuts. The barber is a *server* who repeatedly provides the service. This type of interaction is an example of a *client/server* relationship.

To implement these interactions, we can model the barbershop by a monitor that has three procedures: `get_haircut`, `get_next_customer`, and `finished_cut`. Customers call `get_haircut`; the procedure returns after a customer has received a haircut. The barber repeatedly calls `get_next_customer` to wait for a customer to sit in the barber's chair, then gives the customer a haircut, and finally calls `finished_cut` to allow the customer to leave the shop. Permanent variables are used to record the status of the processes and to represent the various chairs in which processes sleep.

Within the sleeping barber monitor, we need to synchronize the actions of the barber and customers. First, a barber and a customer need to *rendezvous*— i.e., the barber has to wait for a customer to arrive and a customer has to wait for the barber to be available. A rendezvous is similar to a two-process barrier since

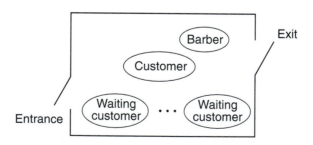

Figure 5.9   The sleeping barber problem.

both parties must arrive before either can proceed. It differs from a two-process barrier, however, since the barber can rendezvous with any customer.

Second, the customer needs to wait until the barber has finished giving him a haircut, which is indicated by the barber's opening the exit door. Finally, before closing the exit door, the barber needs to wait until the customer has left the shop. In short, both the barber and customer proceed through a series of synchronized stages, starting with a rendezvous.

The most straightforward way to specify synchronization stages such as these is to employ incrementing counters that record the number of processes that have reached each stage. Customers have two important stages: sitting in the barber's chair and leaving the barber shop. Let `cinchair` and `cleave` be counters for these stages. The barber repeatedly goes through three stages: becoming available, giving a haircut, and finishing a haircut. Let `bavail`, `bbusy`, and `bdone` be the counters for these stages. All counters are initially zero. Since the processes pass sequentially through these stages, the counters must satisfy the invariant

$C1$:   `cinchair >= cleave` $\wedge$ `bavail >= bbusy >= bdone`

To ensure that the barber and a customer rendezvous before the barber starts cutting the customer's hair, a customer cannot sit in the barber's chair more times than the barber has become available. In addition, the barber cannot become busy more times than customers have sat in the barber's chair. Thus we also require the invariance of

$C2$:   `cinchair <= bavail` $\wedge$ `bbusy <= cinchair`

Finally, customers cannot leave the shop more times than the barber has finished giving haircuts, which is expressed by the invariant

$C3$:   `cleave <= bdone`

The monitor invariant for the barbershop is then the conjunction of three predicates:

BARBER: $C1 \wedge C2 \wedge C3$

Although incrementing counters are useful for recording stages through which processes pass, their values can increase without bound. However, we can avoid this problem by changing variables. We can do this whenever synchronization depends only on the differences between counter values. Because there are three key differences here, let `barber`, `chair`, and `open` be three new variables, as follows:

```
barber == bavail - cinchair
chair == cinchair - bbusy
open == bdone - cleave
```

These variables are initially 0 and each always has value 0 or 1. In particular, the value of **barber** is 1 when the barber is waiting for a customer to sit in the barber's chair, **chair** is 1 when the customer has sat in the chair but the barber has not yet become busy, and **open** is 1 when the exit door has been opened but the customer has not yet left.

The remaining task is to use condition variables to implement the required synchronization between the barber and the customers. There are four different synchronization conditions: customers need to wait for the barber to be available, customers need to wait for the barber to open the door, the barber needs to wait for a customer to arrive, and the barber needs to wait for a customer to leave. Thus, we use four condition variables, one for each of the four conditions. The processes wait for the conditions by using **wait** statements embedded in loops. Finally, processes execute **signal** statements at points where conditions are made true.

The full solution is given in Figure 5.10. The problem is much more complex than the ones considered earlier, so the solution is naturally longer and more complex. However, by proceeding systematically when developing the solution, we were able to break the synchronization into small pieces, solve each, then "glue" the solutions together.

The monitor in Figure 5.10 is also the first monitor we have seen that has a procedure, **get_haircut**, containing more than one **wait** statement. This is because a customer proceeds through two stages: first waiting for the barber to be available, then waiting for the barber to finish giving a haircut.

5.3 Disk Scheduling: Program Structures

The previous examples examined several small problems and presented a variety of useful synchronization techniques. In this section, we examine various ways in which processes and monitors might be organized to solve a single, larger problem. In doing so, we consider issues of "programming in the large"—namely, issues that occur when considering different ways to structure a program. This change in emphasis pervades the rest of the book.

As a specific example, we examine the problem of scheduling access to a moving head disk, which is used to store data files. We will show how the techniques described in the previous section can be applied to develop a solution. As importantly, we will examine three different ways in which the solution can be

```
monitor Barber_Shop {
    int barber = 0, chair = 0, open = 0;
    cond barber_available;    # signaled when barber > 0
    cond chair_occupied;      # signaled when chair > 0
    cond door_open;           # signaled when open > 0
    cond customer_left;       # signaled when open == 0

    procedure get_haircut() {
        while (barber == 0) wait(barber_available);
        barber = barber - 1;
        chair = chair + 1; signal(chair_occupied);
        while (open == 0) wait(door_open);
        open = open - 1; signal(customer_left);
    }
    procedure get_next_customer() {
        barber = barber + 1; signal(barber_available);
        while (chair == 0) wait(chair_occupied);
        chair = chair - 1;
    }
    procedure finished_cut() {
        open = open + 1; signal(door_open);
        while (open > 0) wait(customer_left);
    }

}
```

Figure 5.10   Sleeping barber monitor.

structured. The disk-scheduling problem is representative of numerous scheduling problems. Also, each of the solution structures is applicable in numerous other situations. We begin by summarizing the relevant characteristics of moving-head disks.

Figure 5.11 shows the structure of a moving-head disk. The disk contains several platters that are connected to a central spindle and that rotate at constant speed. Data is stored on the surfaces of the platters. Each platter is like a phonograph record, except that the recording tracks form separate, concentric circles rather than being connected in a spiral. The tracks in the same relative position on different platters form a cylinder. Data is accessed by positioning a read/write head over the appropriate track, then waiting for the platter to rotate until the desired data passes by the head. Normally there is one read/write head per platter. These heads are connected to a single arm, which can move in and out so that read/write heads can be placed at any cylinder and hence over any track.

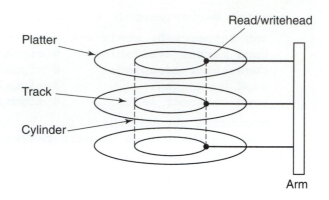

Figure 5.11   A moving-head disk.

The physical address of any piece of data stored on a disk consists of a cylinder, a track number, which specifies the platter, and an offset, which specifies the distance from a fixed clock point that is the same on every track. To access the disk, a program executes a machine-specific input/output instruction. The parameters to the instruction are a physical disk address, a count of the number of bytes to transfer, an indication of the kind of transfer to perform (read or write), and the address of a data buffer.

Disk access time depends on three quantities: (1) *seek time* to move a read/write head to the appropriate cylinder, (2) *rotational delay*, and (3) *data transmission time*. Transmission time depends totally on the number of bytes to be transferred, but the other two quantities depend on the state of the disk. In the best case, a read/write head is already at the requested cylinder, and the requested track area is just beginning to pass under the read/write head. In the worst case, read/write heads have to be moved clear across the disk, and the requested track has to make a full revolution. A characteristic of moving-head disks is that the time required to move the read/write heads from one cylinder to another is an increasing function of the distance between the two cylinders. Also, the time it takes to move a read/write head even one cylinder is much greater than platter rotation time. Thus the most effective way to reduce the average disk access time is to minimize head motion and hence to reduce seek time. (It also helps to reduce rotational delay, but this is harder to accomplish since rotational delays are typically quite short.)

We assume there are several clients that use a disk. For example, in a multiprogrammed operating system, these could be processes executing user commands or system processes implementing virtual memory management. Whenever only one client at a time wants to access the disk, nothing can be gained by not allowing the disk to be accessed immediately since we cannot in general know when another client may also want to access the disk. Thus disk scheduling is applied only if two or more clients want to access the disk at about the same time.

An attractive scheduling strategy is always to select the pending request that wants to access the cylinder closest to the one at which the read/write heads are currently positioned. This is called the *shortest-seek-time* (SST) strategy since it minimizes seek time. However, SST is an unfair strategy since a steady stream of requests for cylinders close to the current position could starve requests farther away. Although such starvation is extremely unlikely, there is no bound on how long a request might be delayed. SST is the strategy used within the UNIX operating system; a whimsical interpretation of the rationale is that if fairness is an issue, the best thing to do is to buy more disks!

An alternative, fair scheduling strategy is to move the disk heads in only one direction until all requests in that direction have been serviced. In particular, select the client request closest to the current head position in the direction the disk heads last moved. If there is no pending request in the current search direction, reverse directions. This strategy is variously called SCAN, LOOK, or—more colorfully—the *elevator algorithm* since it is analogous to the way in which an elevator visits floors, picking up and unloading customers. The only problem with this strategy is that a pending request just behind the current head position will not be serviced until the head moves away and then back. This leads to a large variance in the expected waiting time before a request is serviced.

A third strategy is similar to the second but greatly reduces the variance in expected waiting time. In this strategy, which is called CSCAN or CLOOK (C for circular), requests are serviced in only one direction—for example, from the outermost to the innermost cylinder. In particular, there is only one search direction, and the request closest to the current head position in that direction is selected. When there are no further requests ahead of the current head position, searching starts over from the outermost cylinder. This is analogous to an elevator that only takes passengers up. (They presumably either walk down or jump!) CSCAN is nearly as efficient as the elevator algorithm with respect to reducing seek time, because for most disks it takes only approximately twice as long to move the heads across all cylinders as it does to move them from one cylinder to the next. Moreover, the CSCAN strategy is fair as long as a continual stream of requests for the current head position is not allowed to starve other pending requests.

In the remainder of this section, we develop three structurally different solutions to the disk-scheduling problem. In the first, the scheduler is implemented by a distinct monitor, as in the solution to the readers/writers problem (Figure 5.5). In the second, the scheduler is implemented by a monitor that acts as an

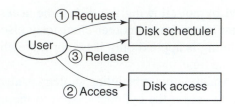

Figure 5.12   Disk scheduler as separate monitor.

intermediary between users of the disk and a process that performs actual disk access; this structure is similar to that of the solution to the sleeping barber problem (Figure 5.10). The third solution uses nested monitors, with the first performing scheduling and the second performing disk access.

All three scheduling monitors implement the CSCAN strategy, but they can easily be modified to implement any of the various scheduling strategies. For example, we show how to implement the SST strategy in Chapter 7.

5.3.1 *Using a Separate Monitor*

One way to organize a solution to the disk-scheduling problem is to have the scheduler be a monitor that is separate from the resource being controlled, in this case a disk. This structure is depicted in Figure 5.12. The solution has three kinds of components: (1) user processes, (2) the scheduler, and (3) the procedures or process that performs disk transfers. The scheduler is implemented by a monitor so that scheduling data is accessed by only one user process at a time. The monitor provides two operations: `request` and `release`.

A user process wishing to access cylinder `cyl` first calls `request(cyl)`; the process returns from `request` when the scheduler has selected its request. The user process then accesses the disk—for example, by calling a procedure or by communicating with a disk driver process. After accessing the disk, the user calls `release` so that another request can be selected. The user interface to the scheduler is thus

```
Disk_Scheduler.request(cyl)
access the disk
Disk_Scheduler.release()
```

`Disk_Scheduler` has the dual roles of scheduling requests and ensuring that at most one process at a time uses the disk. Thus, all users *must* follow the above protocol.

We assume that disk cylinders are numbered from 0 to **MAXCYL** and that scheduling is to employ the CSCAN strategy with a search direction from 0 to **MAXCYL**. As usual, the critical step in deriving a correct solution is to state precisely the properties the solution is to have. Here, at most one process at a time can be allowed to use the disk, and pending requests are to be serviced in CSCAN order.

Let **position** indicate the current head position—i.e., the cylinder being accessed by the process using the disk. When the disk is not being accessed, we will set **position** to **-1**. (Any invalid cylinder number would do, or we could use an additional variable.)

To implement CSCAN scheduling, we need to distinguish between pending requests to be serviced on the current scan across the disk and those to be serviced on the next scan across the disk. Let **C** and **N** be disjoint sets that contain these requests. Both sets are ordered by increasing value of **cyl**; requests for the same cylinder are ordered by set-insertion time. In particular, set **C** contains requests for cylinders greater than or equal to the current head position, and set **N** contains requests for cylinders less than or equal to the current head position. This is expressed by the following predicate, which will be our monitor invariant:

> *DISK*: **C** and **N** are ordered sets $\wedge$
> all elements of set **C** are **>= position** $\wedge$
> all elements of set **N** are **<= position** $\wedge$
> (**position == -1**) $\Rightarrow$ (**C** $== \emptyset \wedge$ **N** $== \emptyset$)

A pending request for which **cyl** is equal to **position** might be in either set, but it is placed in set **N** when the request is first issued, as described in the next paragraph.

When a process calls **request**, it takes one of three actions. If **position** is **-1**, the disk is free; thus, the process sets **position** to **cyl** and proceeds to access the disk. If the disk is not free and if **cylinder > position**, the process inserts **cyl** in set **C**; otherwise, it inserts **cyl** in set **N**. We use **N** rather than **C** when **cyl** equals **position** to avoid potential unfairness; in this case, the request waits until the next scan across the disk. After recording **cyl** in the appropriate set, the process delays until it is granted access to the disk—i.e., until **position** equals **cyl**.

When a process calls **release**, it updates the permanent variables so as to maintain *DISK*. If **C** is not empty, there are pending requests for the current scan. In this case, the releasing process removes the first element of **C** and sets **position** to its value. If **C** is empty but **N** is not, we need to start the next scan—i.e., it needs to become the current scan. The releasing process accomplishes this by swapping sets **C** and **N** (which sets **N** to the null set), then removing the first element of `C` and setting `position` to its value. Finally, if both `C` and `N` are empty, the releasing process sets `position` to `-1` to indicate that the disk is free.

The final step in developing a solution is to implement the synchronization between `request` and `release`. We have here a situation like that in the interval timer problem: There is a static order between waiting conditions, and thus it is possible to use priority `wait` to implement ordered sets. In particular, requests in sets `C` and `N` are both serviced in ascending order of `cyl`. We also have a situation like that in the FIFO semaphore: When the disk is released, permission to access the disk is transferred to one specific waiting process. In particular, we need to set `position` to the value of the pending request that is to be serviced next. Because of these two attributes, we can implement synchronization efficiently by combining aspects of the `Timer` monitor in Figure 5.8 and the `FIFOsemaphore` monitor in Figure 5.3.

To represent sets `C` and `N`, let `scan[2]` be an array of condition variables indexed by integers `c` and `n`. When a requesting process needs to insert its parameter `cyl` in set `C` and then wait for `position` to be equal to `cyl`, it simply executes `wait(scan[c],cyl)`. Similarly, a process inserts its request in set `N` and then delays by executing `wait(scan[n],cyl)`. In addition, we use `empty` to test whether a set is empty, use `minrank` to determine its smallest value, and use `signal` to remove the first element and at the same time awaken the appropriate requesting process. Also, we swap the sets `C` and `N` when needed simply by swapping the values of `c` and `n`. (This is why `scan` is an array.)

Incorporating these changes, we have the final solution shown in Figure 5.13. At the end of `release`, `c` is the index of the current scan, so it is sufficient to include just one `signal` statement. If in fact `position` is `-1` at this point, `scan[c]` will be empty, and thus `signal` will have no effect.

Scheduling problems such as this are among the most difficult to solve correctly, whatever synchronization mechanism is employed. The key is specifying exactly the order in which processes are to be served. When the service order is static—as it is here—we can use priority `wait` statements. However, as noted earlier, when the service order is dynamic we have to use either private condition variables to awaken individual processes or covering conditions to let delayed processes schedule themselves.

5.3.2 Using an Intermediary

Implementing `Disk_Scheduler`, or any resource controller, as a separate monitor is a viable way to structure a solution to a scheduling/allocation problem. Because the scheduler is separate, it can be designed independently of the other components. However, this very separation introduces two potential problems:

```
monitor Disk_Scheduler {  ## Invariant DISK
  int position = -1, c = 0, n = 1;
  cond scan[2];   # scan[c] signaled when disk released
  procedure request(int cyl) {
    if (position == -1)   # disk is free, so return
      position = cyl;
    elseif (position != -1 && cyl > position)
      wait(scan[c],cyl);
    else
      wait(scan[n],cyl);
  }
  procedure release() {
    int temp;
    if (!empty(scan[c]))
      position = minrank(scan[c]);
    elseif (empty(scan[c]) && !empty(scan[n])) {
      temp = c; c = n; n = temp;         # swap c and n
      position = minrank(scan[c]);
    }
    else
      position = -1;
    signal(scan[c]);
  }
}
```

Figure 5.13   Separate disk scheduler monitor.

- The presence of the scheduler is visible to the processes that use the disk; if the scheduler is deleted, user processes change.

- All user processes must follow the required protocol of requesting the disk, then using it, then releasing it. If any process fails to follow this protocol, scheduling is defeated.

Both problems can be alleviated if the disk-use protocol is embedded in a procedure and user processes do not directly access either the disk or the disk scheduler. However, this introduces another layer of procedures and some attendant inefficiency.

There is a third problem if the disk is accessed by a disk driver process rather than by procedures that are called directly by user processes. In particular, after being granted access to the disk, a user process must communicate with the driver to pass arguments and to receive results (see again Figure 5.12). These communication paths could be implemented by two instances of the bounded buffer monitor of Figure 5.4. But the user interface would then consist of three monitors—the scheduler and two bounded buffers—and the user would have to make a total of four monitor calls every time it uses the device. Since the disk users and disk driver have a client/server relationship, we could implement the communication interface using a variant of the solution to the sleeping barber problem. But we would still have two monitors—one for scheduling and one for interaction between user processes and the disk driver.

When a disk is controlled by a driver process, the best possible approach is to combine the scheduler and communication interface into a single monitor. Essentially, the scheduler becomes an intermediary between the user processes and the disk driver, as shown in Figure 5.14. The monitor forwards user requests to the driver in the desired order of preference. This approach provides three benefits. First, the disk interface employs only one monitor, and the user must make only one monitor call per disk access. Second, the presence or absence of scheduling is transparent. Third, there is no multistep protocol the user can fail to follow. Thus, this approach overcomes all three difficulties caused by the scheduler being a separate monitor.

In the remainder of this section, we show how to transform the solution to the sleeping barber problem (Figure 5.10) into a disk driver interface that both provides communication between clients and the disk driver and implements CSCAN scheduling. We need to make several changes to the sleeping barber solution. First, we need to rename the processes, monitor, and monitor procedures as described below and shown in Figure 5.15. Second, we need to parameterize the monitor procedures to transfer requests from users (customers) to the disk driver (barber) and to transfer results back; in essence, we need to turn the "barber's chair" and "exit door" into communication buffers. Finally, we need to add scheduling to the user/disk-driver rendezvous so that the driver services the preferred user request. These changes yield a disk interface with the outline shown in Figure 5.15.

To refine this outline into an actual solution, we employ the same basic synchronization as in the sleeping barber solution (Figure 5.10). However, we add

Figure 5.14   Disk scheduler as an intermediary.

```
monitor Disk_Interface  {
```
permanent variables for status, scheduling, and data transfer
```
    procedure use_disk(int cyl, transfer and result parameters) {
```
wait for turn to use driver
store transfer parameters in permanent variables
wait for transfer to be completed
retrieve results from permanent variables
```
    }
    procedure get_next_request(someType &results) {
```
select next request
wait for transfer parameters to be stored
set **results** to transfer parameters
```
    }
    procedure finished_transfer(someType results) {
```
store results in permanent variables
wait for **results** to be retrieved by client
```
    }
}
```

Figure 5.15   Outline of disk interface monitor.

scheduling as in the **Disk_Scheduler** monitor (Figure 5.13) and add parameter passing as in a bounded buffer (Figure 5.4). Essentially, the monitor invariant for **Disk_Interface** becomes the conjunction of barbershop invariant *BARBER*, disk scheduler invariant *DISK*, and bounded buffer invariant *BB* (simplified to the case of a single-slot buffer).

A user process waits its turn to access the disk by executing the same actions as in the **request** procedure of the **Disk_Scheduler** monitor in Figure 5.13. Similarly, the driver process indicates it is available by executing the same actions as in the **release** procedure of the **Disk_Scheduler** monitor. Initially, however, we will set **position** to **-2** to indicate that the disk is neither available nor in use until after the driver makes its first call to **get_next_request**; hence, users need to wait for the first scan to start.

When it becomes a user's turn to access the disk, the user process deposits its transfer arguments in permanent variables, then waits to fetch results. After selecting the next user request, the driver process waits to fetch the user's transfer arguments. The driver then performs the requested disk transfer. When it is done, the driver deposits the results, then waits for them to be fetched. The deposits and fetches are implemented as for a single-slot buffer. These refinements lead to the monitor shown in Figure 5.16.

```
monitor Disk_Interface {
  int position = -2, c = 0, n = 1, args = 0, results = 0;
  cond scan[2];
  cond args_stored, results_stored, results_retrieved;
  argType arg_area; resultType result_area;

  procedure use_disk(int cyl; argType transfer_params;
                     resultType &result_params) {
    if (position == -1)
      position = cyl;
    elseif (position != -1 and cyl > position)
      wait(scan[c],cyl);
    else
      wait(scan[n],cyl);
    arg_area = transfer_params;
    args = args+1; signal(args_stored);
    while (results == 0) wait(results_stored);
    result_params = result_area;
    results = results-1; signal(results_retrieved);
  }

  procedure get_next_request(argType &transfer_params) {
    int temp;
    if (!empty(scan[c]))
      position = minrank(scan[c]);
    elseif (empty(scan[c]) && !empty(scan[n])) {
      temp = c; c = n; n = temp;        # swap c and n
      position = minrank(scan[c]);
      }
    else
      position = -1;
    signal(scan[c]);
    while (args == 0) wait(args_stored);
    transfer_params = arg_area; args = args-1;
  }

  procedure finished_transfer(resultType result_vals) {
    result_area := result_vals; results = results+1;
    signal(results_stored);
    while (results > 0) wait(results_retrieved);
  }
}
```

Figure 5.16   Disk interface monitor.

Although this user/disk-driver interface is quite efficient, it can be made even more efficient by two relatively simple changes. First, the disk driver can begin servicing the next user request sooner if `finished_transfer` is modified so that the driver does not wait for results from the previous transfer to be retrieved. One must be careful, however, to ensure that the results area is not overwritten in the event the driver completes another transfer before the results from the previous one have been retrieved. The second change is to combine the two procedures called by the disk driver. This eliminates one monitor call per disk access. Implementing this change requires modifying the initialization of `results`. We leave incorporating both of these changes to the reader.

5.3.3 Using a Nested Monitor

When the disk scheduler is a separate monitor, user processes have to follow the protocol of requesting the disk, accessing it, then releasing it. The disk itself is controlled by a process or by a monitor. When the disk scheduler is an intermediary, the user interface is simplified—a user has to make only a single request—but the monitor is much more complex, as can be seen by comparing the monitors in Figure 5.13 and 5.16. Moreover, the solution in Figure 5.16 assumes that the disk is controlled by a driver process.

A third approach is to combine the two styles by using *two* monitors: one for scheduling, and one for access to the disk. This structure is shown in Figure 5.17. However, in order to utilize this structure, it is imperative that the calls from the scheduling monitor release exclusion in that monitor. Below we explore this issue of nested monitor calls, and then outline a third solution to the disk scheduling problem.

The permanent variables of a monitor can be accessed by at most one process at a time, because processes execute with mutual exclusion within monitor procedures. However, what happens if a process executing a procedure in one monitor calls a procedure in another and hence temporarily leaves the first monitor? If monitor exclusion is retained when such a nested call is made, the call is termed a *closed call*. The alternative is to release monitor exclusion when a

Figure 5.17   Disk access using nested monitors.

nested call is made and to reacquire exclusion when the call returns; this kind of nested call is termed an *open call*.

Permanent monitor variables are clearly protected from concurrent access on a closed call since no other process can enter the monitor while the nested call is being executed. Permanent variables are also protected from concurrent access on an open call, as long as such variables are not passed by reference as arguments on the call. However, since an open call releases exclusion, the monitor invariant must be true before the call. Thus open calls have slightly more complex semantics than closed calls. On the other hand, a closed call is more prone to deadlock. In particular, if a process is delayed at a **wait** statement after making a nested call, it cannot be awakened by another process that has to make the same set of nested calls.

The disk-scheduling problem provides a concrete example of these issues. As noted we can restructure a solution to the problem as shown in Figure 5.17. In essence, the **Disk_Scheduler** of Figure 5.13 is replaced by two monitors. User processes make *one* call to the **doIO** operation of the **Disk_Access** monitor. That monitor schedules access as in Figure 5.13. When it is a process's turn to access the disk, it makes a second call to the **read** or **write** operation of a second monitor, **Disk_Transfer**. This second call happens from *within* the **Disk_Access** monitor. In particular, the **Disk_Access** monitor has the following structure:

```
monitor Disk_Access {
    permanent variables as in Disk_Scheduler;
    procedure doIO(int cyl; transfer and result arguments)  {
        actions of Disk_Scheduler.request;
        call Disk_Transfer.read or Disk_Transfer.write;
        actions of Disk_Scheduler.release;
    }
}
```

The calls to **Disk_Transfer** are nested calls. In order for disk scheduling to take place, they must be open calls. Otherwise, at most one process at a time could ever be within **doIO**, making the **request** and **release** actions superfluous. Open calls can be used here since only local variables (parameters to **doIO**) are passed as arguments to **Disk_Transfer**, and the disk scheduler invariant, *DISK*, will be true before **read** or **write** is called.

Independent of the semantics of nested calls, there is the issue of mutual exclusion within a monitor. By having monitor procedures execute one at a time, permanent variables cannot be accessed concurrently. However, this is not always necessary to avoid interference. If a procedure reads but does not alter permanent variables, different calls of the procedure could execute concurrently. Or, if a procedure merely returns the value of some permanent variable and this value can be read atomically (e.g., it is a simple variable), then the procedure can be allowed to execute concurrently with any monitor procedure. By the time the calling process examines the returned value, it might not be the same as the permanent variable's current value, but this is always the case in a concurrent program. As a concrete example, we could add a procedure `read_clock` to the `Timer` monitor in Figures 5.7 or 5.8. Whether or not `read_clock` executes with mutual exclusion, a process that calls `read_clock` could only know that the return value is no greater than the current value of `tod`.

Even in situations where different monitor procedures alter permanent variables, they can sometimes safely execute in parallel. For example, we have seen in previous chapters that a producer and a consumer can concurrently access different slots of a bounded buffer (e.g., see Figure 4.5). If monitor procedures must execute with mutual exclusion, it is awkward to program such a buffer. Either each buffer slot has to be encapsulated by a separate monitor, or the buffer has to be global to processes, which then synchronize using monitors that implement semaphores. Fortunately, such situations are rare.

We have raised two new issues in this section. First, when using monitors the programmer needs to know whether nested calls—ones from within one monitor to a second—are open or closed. Second, the programmer needs to know whether there is a way to relax the implicit exclusion of a monitor in cases where it is safe to have some procedures execute in parallel. In the next section we explore these issues further in the context of the Java programming language.

5.4 Case Study: Java

Java is the latest craze to hit computing. It was motivated by the desire to provide a way to write portable programs for the World Wide Web. Like most innovations in computer science, Java borrows heavily from its predecessors, in this case interpreted languages, object-oriented languages, and concurrent languages. Java recombines old features and adds several new ones to produce an interesting combination. It also provides extensive libraries for graphics, distributed programming, and other applications.

Java is an example of an object-oriented language. Although the details of object-oriented languages are beyond the scope of this book, the essential idea is that a program consists of a collection of interacting objects. Each object is an instance of a class. A class has two kinds of members: data fields and methods. Data fields represent the state of instances of the class (objects) or of the class itself. The methods are procedures that are used to manipulate data fields, most commonly in individual objects.

For our purposes, the most interesting aspects of Java are that it supports threads, monitors as defined in this chapter, and distributed programming as covered in Part 3. This section describes Java's mechanisms for processes (threads) and monitors (synchronized methods), and then illustrates the use of these features to solve variations on the readers/writers problem. (Sections 7.9 and 8.5 describe Java's mechanisms for message passing and remote method invocation.) The Historical Notes give pointers to more information on Java in general and concurrent programming in Java in particular.

5.4.1 The Threads Class

A Java thread is a lightweight process; it has its own stack and execution context but it also has direct access to all variables in its scope. Threads are programmed by extending the `Thread` class or by implementing a `Runnable` interface. Both the `Thread` class and the `Runnable` interface are part of the standard Java libraries, in particular the `java.lang` package.

A thread is created by creating an instance of the `Thread` class:

```
Thread foo = new Thread();
```

This constructs a new thread `foo`. To actually start the thread, one executes

```
foo.start()
```

The `start` operation is one of the methods defined by the `Thread` class; there are numerous others such as `stop` and `sleep`.

The above example will not in fact do anything, because by default the body of a thread is empty. More precisely, the `start` method in `Thread` invokes the `run` method in `Thread`, and the default definition of `run` does nothing. Thus to create a useful thread, one needs to define a new class that extends the `Thread` class (or that uses the `Runnable` interface) and that provides a new definition of the `run` method. For example, consider the following `class` definition:

```
class Simple extends Thread {
  public void run() {
    System.out.println("this is a thread");
  }
}
```

We can create an instance of the class and start the new thread by executing

```
Simple s = new Simple();
s.start();      // calls the run() method in object s
```

The thread will print a single line of output then terminate. If we do not need to keep a reference to the thread, we can simplify the last two lines to

```
new Simple().start();
```

An alternative way to program the previous example is to use the `Runnable` interface. First change `Simple` as follows:

```
class Simple implements Runnable {
  public void run() {
    System.out.println("this is a thread");
  }
}
```

Then create an instance of the class, pass that instance to the `Thread` constructor, and start the thread:

```
Runnable s = new Simple();
new Thread(s).start();
```

The advantage of using the `Runnable` interface is that then class `Simple` could also extend some system or user-defined class. This is not allowed with the first approach, because Java does not allow a class to extend more than one other class.

To summarize, there are four steps in creating and starting threads in Java: (1) define a new class that extends the Java `Thread` class or that implements the `Runnable` interface; (2) define a `run` method in the new class; it will contain the body of the thread; (3) create an instance of the new class using the `new` statement; and (4) start the thread using the `start` method.

5.4.2 Synchronized Methods

Threads in Java execute concurrently—at least conceptually. Hence they could simultaneously access shared variables. Consider the following class:

```
class Interfere {
  private int data = 0;
  public void update() {
    data++;
  }
}
```

This class contains a private field `data` that is accessible only within the class, and it exports a public method `update` that, when called, increments the value of `data`. If `update` is called simultaneously by two threads, obviously they will interfere with each other.

Java supports mutual exclusion by means of the `synchronized` keyword, which can be used with an entire method or with a sequence of statements. For example, to make the `update` method atomic, one could reprogram the above code as

```
class Interfere {
  private int data = 0;
  public synchronized void update() {
    data++;
  }
}
```

This is a simple example of how a monitor is programmed in Java: the monitor's permanent variables are private data in a class, and the monitor procedures are implemented using synchronized methods. There is exactly one lock per object in Java; when a `synchronized` method is invoked, it waits to obtain that lock, then executes the body of the method, then releases the lock.

An alternative way to program the above example is to use a `synchronized` statement within a method, as in

```
class Interfere {
  private int data = 0;
  public void update() {
    synchronized (this) {  // lock this object
      data++;
    }
  }
}
```

The keyword `this` refers to the object on which the `update` method was invoked, and hence to the lock on that object. A `synchronized` statement is thus like an `await` statement whereas a `synchronized` method is like a monitor procedure.

Java supports condition synchronization by means of `wait` and `notify`. These are very similar to the monitor `wait` and `signal` statements as used earlier in this chapter. However, `wait` and `notify` in Java are in fact methods of the class `Object`, which is the parent of all classes in Java. Both `wait` and `notify` must be executed within `synchronized` portions of code, and hence when an object is locked.

The `wait` method releases the lock on an object and delays the executing thread. There is a *single* delay queue per object. It is usually a FIFO queue but not necessarily. Java does not provide condition variables, but one can think of there being exactly one (implicitly declared) condition variable per synchronized object.

The `notify` method awakens the thread at the front of the delay queue, if there is one. The thread that invokes `notify` continues to hold the object's lock, so the awakened thread will execute at some future time when it can reacquire the lock. Hence, `notify` has Signal and Continue semantics. Java also supports a broadcast signal by means of the `notifyAll` method, which is analogous to `signal_all`. Since there is only one (implicit) condition variable per object, the `wait`, `notify`, or `notifyAll` methods have empty parameter lists.

If a synchronized method (or statement) in one object contains a call to a method in another object, the lock on the first object is retained while the call is executed. Thus, nested calls from synchronized methods are closed calls in Java. This precludes using the structure shown in Figure 5.17 for solving the disk scheduling problem using nested monitors. It can also lead to deadlock if a synchronized method in one object calls a synchronized method in another object and vice versa.

5.4.3 Parallel Readers/Writers

This and the next two subsections present a series of examples that illustrate the concurrency and synchronization aspects of Java, as well as Java's use of classes, declarations, and statements. All three programs are self-contained: they can be compiled by the Java compiler `javac` and then executed by the Java interpreter `java`. (Consult your local installation for details on how to use Java; see also the Website for this book for source code for the programs.)

First consider a parallel version of readers and writers—namely, a program in which readers and writers can access a database in parallel. Although this program can lead to interference, it serves to illustrate the structure of Java programs and the use of threads.

The starting point for the program is a class that encapsulates a database. Here, we will use a very simple database—namely, a single integer. The class exports two operations (methods), `read` and `write`. It is defined as follows.

```
// basic read or write; no exclusion
class RWbasic {
  protected int data = 0;  // the "database"
```

```
    public void read() {
      System.out.println("read:   " + data);
    }
    public void write() {
      data++;
      System.out.println("wrote:   " + data);
    }
  }
```

The members of the class are one field, **data**, and two methods, **read** and **write**. The **data** field is declared as **protected**, which means that it is acces-sible only within the class or within subclasses that inherit the class (or within other classes declared in the same package). The **read** and **write** methods are declared as **public**, which means they are accessible anywhere the class is accessible. Each method, when invoked, prints a single line of output that indi-cates the current value of **data**; the **write** method also increments the value of **data**.

The next parts of our example are two classes—**Reader** and **Writer**—that contain the code for reader and writer processes. Each of these classes extends the **Thread** class. Each also contains an initialization method with the same name as the class; this method is invoked when new instances of the class are cre-ated. Finally, each class contains a **run** method that gives the code for a thread. The **Reader** class is declared as follows:

```
class Reader extends Thread {
  int rounds;
  RWbasic RW;   // a reference to an RWbasic object
  public Reader(int rounds, RWbasic RW) {
    this.rounds = rounds;
    this.RW = RW;
  }
  public void run() {
    for (int i = 0; i < rounds; i++) {
      RW.read();
    }
  }
}
```

The **Writer** class is declared similarly:

```
class Writer extends Thread {
  int rounds;
  RWbasic RW;
```

```
    public Writer(int rounds, RWbasic RW) {
      this.rounds = rounds;
      this.RW = RW;
    }
    public void run() {
      for (int i = 0; i < rounds; i++) {
        RW.write();
      }
    }
  }
```

When an instance of either class is created, the new object is passed two parameters: the number of `rounds` to execute and an instance of the `RWbasic` class. The initialization methods store the parameters in permanent variables `rounds` and `RW`. Within the initialization methods, these variables are prefixed by the keyword `this` to differentiate between the permanent variable and the parameter of the same name.

The above three classes—`RWbasic`, `Reader`, and `Writer`—are the building blocks for a readers/writers program in which readers and writers can access the same instance of `RWbasic` in parallel. To complete the program, we need a main class that creates one instance of each of the above classes and then starts the `Reader` and `Writer` threads:

```
  class Main {
    static RWbasic RW = new RWbasic();
    public static void main(String[] args) {
      int rounds = Integer.parseInt(args[0],10);
      new Reader(rounds, RW).start();
      new Writer(rounds, RW).start();
    }
  }
```

The program starts execution in the `main` method, which has a parameter `args` that contains the command-line arguments. In this case, there is a single argument for the number of rounds each thread should execute. The output of the program is a sequence of lines that list the data values that are read and written. A total of `2*rounds` lines are printed, because there are two threads and each executes a loop that executes for `rounds` iterations.

5.4.4 Exclusive Readers/Writers

The above program allows each thread to access the `data` field concurrently. We can modify the code as follows to provide mutually exclusive access to

data. First, define a new class `RWexclusive` that extends `RWbasic` to use synchronized `read` and `write` methods:

```
// mutually exclusive read and write methods
class RWexclusive extends RWbasic {
  public synchronized void read() {
    System.out.println("read:   " + data);
  }
  public synchronized void write() {
    data++;
    System.out.println("wrote:   " + data);
  }
}
```

Because `RWexclusive` extends `RWbasic`, it inherits the `data` field. However, the `read` and `write` methods have been redefined so that they will now execute with mutual exclusion.

Second, modify the `Reader` and `Writer` classes so that their local `RW` variables are instances of `RWexclusive` rather than `RWbasic`. For example, the `Reader` becomes

```
class Reader extends Thread {
  int rounds;
  RWexclusive RW;
  public Reader(int rounds, RWexclusive RW) {
    this.rounds = rounds;
    this.RW = RW;
  }
  public void run() {
    for (int i = 0; i < rounds; i++) {
      RW.read();
    }
  }
}
```

The `Writer` class is changed similarly.

Finally, modify the `Main` class so that it creates instances of `RWexclusive` rather than `RWbasic`. In particular, change the first line of `Main` above to

```
static RWexclusive RW = new RWexclusive();
```

With these changes, the threads in the new program access variable `data` in `RWbasic` indirectly by calling the `synchronized` methods in `RWexclusive`.

5.4.5 *True Readers/Writers*

The first readers/writers example allows concurrent access to `data`, and the second makes access to `data` mutually exclusive. The true readers/writers problem allows either concurrent reads or a single write. We can implement this change by reprogramming the `RWexclusive` class as follows:

```
// concurrent read or exclusive write
class ReadersWriters extends RWbasic {
  private int nr = 0;
  private synchronized void startRead() {
    nr++;
  }
  private synchronized void endRead() {
    nr--;
    if (nr == 0) notify(); // awaken waiting Writers
  }
  public void read() {
    startRead();
    System.out.println("read:  " + data);
    endRead();
  }
  public synchronized void write() {
    while (nr > 0)    // delay if any active Readers
      try { wait(); }
        catch (InterruptedException ex) {return;}
    data++;
    System.out.println("wrote:  " + data);
    notify();      // awaken another waiting Writer
  }
}
```

We also need to change the `Reader`, `Writer`, and `Main` classes to use this new class rather than `RWexclusive`. *However, nothing else has to change.* (This is one of the virtues of object-oriented programming languages.)

The `ReadersWriters` class adds two local (`private`) methods: `startRead` and `startWrite`. These are called by the `read` method before and after it accesses the database. The `startRead` method increments a private variable, `nr`, that counts the number of active reader threads. The `endRead` method decrements `nr`; if it is now zero, `notify` is called to awaken one waiting writer, if any.

The `startRead`, `endRead`, and `write` methods are synchronized, so at most one can execute at a time. Hence, a writer thread cannot execute while either `startRead` or `endRead` is active. However, the `read` method is not synchronized, which means it can be called concurrently by multiple threads. If a writer thread calls `write` while a reader thread is actually reading, then the value of `nr` will be positive so the writer needs to wait. A writer is awakened when `nr` is zero; after accessing `data`, a writer uses `notify` to awaken another writer if one is waiting. Because `notify` has Signal and Continue semantics, that writer might not execute before another reader increments `nr`, so the writer rechecks the value of `nr`.

In the `write` method above, the call of `wait` is within what is called a `try` statement. This is Java's exception handling mechanism, which is how Java lets the programmer deal with abnormal situations. Because a waiting thread might be stopped or might have terminated abnormally, Java *requires* that every use of `wait` be within a `try` statement that catches the `InterruptedException`. The code above has the `write` method simply return if an exception occurs while a thread is waiting.

A virtue of the above readers/writers solution relative to the one given earlier in Figure 5.5 is that the interface for writer threads is a single procedure, `write`, rather than two procedures `request_write()` and `release_write()`. However, both solutions give readers preference over writers. We leave it to the reader to figure out how to modify the Java solution to give writers preference or to make it fair (see the exercises at the end of this chapter).

5.5 Case Study: Pthreads

The Pthreads library was introduced in Section 4.6. We saw there how to create threads and how to synchronize their execution using semaphores. The library also supports locks and condition variables. Locks can be used on their own to protect critical sections, or they can be used in combination with condition variables to simulate monitors. Below we describe the Pthreads functions for locks and condition variables and then illustrate how they can be used to program a monitor that implements a counter barrier. The headers for the data types and functions described here are located in file `pthread.h`.

5.5.1 Locks and Condition Variables

Locks in Pthreads are called mutex locks—or simply mutexes—because they are used to implement mutual exclusion. The basic code pattern for declaring and initializing a mutex is similar to that for a thread. First, declare global variables for a mutex descriptor and a mutex attributes descriptor. Second, initialize the descriptors. Finally, use the mutex primitives.

If a mutex lock is going to be used by threads in the same (heavyweight) process but not by threads in different processes, the first two steps can be simplified to

```
pthread_mutex_t mutex;
   ...
pthread_mutex_init(&mutex, NULL);
```

This initializes `mutex` with the default attributes. A critical section of code then uses `mutex` as follows:

```
pthread_mutex_lock(&mutex);
critical section;
pthread_mutex_unlock(&mutex);
```

A mutex can be unlocked *only* by the thread that holds the lock. There is also a nonblocking version of `lock`.

Condition variables in Pthreads are very similar to those we have been using. Like mutex locks, they have descriptors and attributes. A condition variable is declared and initialized with the default attributes as follows:

```
pthread_cond_t cond;
   ...
pthread_cond_init(&cond, NULL);
```

The main operations on condition variables are wait, signal, and broadcast (which is identical to `signal_all`). These must be executed while holding a mutex lock. In particular, a monitor procedure is simulated using Pthreads by locking a mutex at the start of the procedure and unlocking the mutex at the end.

The parameters to `pthread_cond_wait` are a condition variable and a mutex lock. A thread that wants to wait must first hold the lock. For example, suppose a thread has already executed

```
pthread_mutex_lock(&mutex);
```

and then later executes

```
pthread_cond_wait(&cond, &mutex);
```

This causes the thread to release `mutex` and wait on `cond`. When the process resumes execution after a signal or broadcast, the thread will again own `mutex` and it will be locked. When another thread executes

```
pthread_cond_signal(&cond);
```

it awakens one thread (if one is blocked), but the signaler continues execution and continues to hold onto `mutex`.

5.5.2 Example: *Summing the Elements of a Matrix*

Figure 5.18 contains a complete program that uses locks and condition variables. The program uses `numWorkers` threads to sum the elements of a shared `matrix` with `size` rows and columns. Although the program is not particularly useful, its structure and components are typical of those found in parallel iterative computations.

```c
# include <pthread.h>
# include <stdio.h>
# define SHARED 1
# define MAXSIZE 2000    /* maximum matrix size */
# define MAXWORKERS 4    /* maximum number of workers */

pthread_mutex_t barrier;   /* lock for the barrier */
pthread_cond_t go;         /* condition variable */
int numWorkers;            /* number of worker threads */
int numArrived = 0;        /* number who have arrived */

/* a reusable counter barrier */
void Barrier() {
  pthread_mutex_lock(&barrier);
  numArrived++;
  if (numArrived < numWorkers)
    pthread_cond_wait(&go, &barrier);
  else {
    numArrived = 0;   /* last worker awakens others */
    pthread_cond_broadcast(&go);
  }
  pthread_mutex_unlock(&barrier);
}

void *Worker(void *);
int size, stripSize;    /* size == stripSize*numWorkers */
int sums[MAXWORKERS];   /* sums computed by each worker */
int matrix[MAXSIZE][MAXSIZE];

/* read command line, initialize, and create threads */
int main(int argc, char *argv[]) {
  int i, j;
  pthread_attr_t attr;
  pthread_t workerid[MAXWORKERS];

  /* set global thread attributes */
  pthread_attr_init(&attr);
  pthread_attr_setscope(&attr, PTHREAD_SCOPE_SYSTEM);
```

```
    /* initialize mutex and condition variable */
    pthread_mutex_init(&barrier, NULL);
    pthread_cond_init(&go, NULL);

    /* read command line */
    size = atoi(argv[1]);
    numWorkers = atoi(argv[2]);
    stripSize = size/numWorkers;

    /* initialize the matrix */
    for (i = 0; i < size; i++)
      for (j = 0; j < size; j++)
        matrix[i][j] = 1;

    /* create the workers, then exit main thread */
    for (i = 0; i < numWorkers; i++)
      pthread_create(&workerid[i], &attr,
                     Worker, (void *) i);
    pthread_exit(NULL);
}

/* Each worker sums the values in one strip.
   After a barrier, worker(0) prints the total */
void *Worker(void *arg) {
  int myid = (int) arg;
  int total, i, j, first, last;

  /* determine first and last rows of my strip */
  first = myid*stripSize;
  last = first + stripSize - 1;

  /* sum values in my strip */
  total = 0;
  for (i = first; i <= last; i++)
    for (j = 0; j < size; j++)
      total += matrix[i][j];
  sums[myid] = total;
  Barrier();
  if (myid == 0) {   /* worker 0 computes the total */
    total = 0;
    for (i = 0; i < numWorkers; i++)
      total += sums[i];
    printf("the total is %d\n", total);
  }
}
```

Figure 5.18   Parallel matrix summation using Pthreads.

The integer variables and `Barrier` function at the top of the figure implement a reusable counter barrier. They are not encapsulated within a `monitor` declaration, but they behave as if they were. The body of `Barrier` starts by locking `mutex` and ends by unlocking `mutex`. Within the function, the first workers to arrive at the barrier wait on condition variable `go` (and release the lock). The last worker to arrive at the barrier reinitializes `numArrived` then uses the broadcast primitive to awaken all the other workers. Those workers will resume execution one at a time, holding `mutex`; each unlocks `mutex` then returns from `Barrier`.

The `main` function initializes the shared variables and then creates the threads. The last argument of `pthread_create` is used to pass each worker thread a unique identity. The last action of `main` is to call `pthread_exit`. This causes the main thread to terminate while the other threads continue executing. If instead the main thread were to return—because the call to `pthread_exit` were deleted—then the entire program would terminate.

Each worker thread computes the sum of all values in its strip of the matrix and stores the result in its element of global array `sums`. We use an array for `sums` rather than a single variable in order to avoid critical sections. After all workers have reached the barrier synchronization point, worker `0` computes and prints the final total.

Historical Notes

The concept of data encapsulation originated with the `class` construct of Simula-67. Edsger Dijkstra [1971] is generally credited with being the first to advocate using data encapsulation to control access to shared variables in a concurrent program. He called such a unit a "secretary" but did not propose any syntactic mechanism for programming secretaries. Per Brinch Hansen [1972] advocates the same idea, a specific language proposal called a `shared class` is found in Brinch Hansen [1973].

Monitors were named and popularized by Hoare [1974] in an excellent and influential paper that contains numerous interesting examples, including a bounded buffer, interval timer, and disk head scheduler (using the elevator algorithm). Condition synchronization in Hoare's proposal employs the Signal and Urgent Wait (SU) signaling discipline. The reader might find it instructive to compare Hoare's solutions, which use SU signaling, with those in this chapter, which use SC signaling. Hoare [1974] also introduced the concept of a split binary semaphore and showed how to use it to implement monitors.

Concurrent Pascal [Brinch Hansen 1975] was the first concurrent programming language to include monitors. Its three structuring components are processes, monitors, and classes. Classes are like monitors, except they cannot be shared by processes and hence have no need for mutual exclusion or condition synchronization. Concurrent Pascal has been used to write several operating systems [Brinch Hansen 1977]. In Concurrent Pascal, I/O devices and the like are treated as special monitors that are implemented by the language's run-time system, which thus hides the notion of an interrupt.

Several additional languages have also included monitors. Modula was developed by Nicklaus Wirth—the designer of Pascal—as a systems language for programming dedicated computer systems, including process control applications [Wirth 1977]. (The original Modula is quite different than its successors, Modula-2 and Modula-3.) Mesa was developed at Xerox PARC [Mitchell et al. 1979]. Lampson and Redell [1980] give an excellent description of experiences with processes and monitors in Mesa; they also discuss the technique of using a *covering condition* to awaken delayed processes, which we described in Section 5.2. Pascal Plus [Welsh & Bustard 1979] introduced the `minrank` primitive, which the designers called the `PRIORITY` function. Two books, Welsh and McKeag [1980] and Bustard et al. [1988], give several large examples of systems programs written in Pascal Plus.

Per Brinch Hansen [1993] has written an interesting personal history of the development of the monitor concept and its realization in Concurrent Pascal. Gehani and McGettrick [1988] contains reprints of many of the most important papers on concurrent programming, including three cited above—Hoare [1974], Brinch Hansen [1975], and Lampson & Redell [1980]—as well as others that examine the use of monitors.

Ric Holt and his colleagues at the University of Toronto have designed a series of monitor-based languages. The first, CSP/k [Holt et al. 1978], is a superset of SP/k, which is in turn a structured subset of PL/I. Concurrent Euclid [Holt 1983] extends Euclid; it has been used to implement a UNIX-compatible nucleus called Tunis. Holt [1983] contains an excellent overview of concurrent programming as well as very readable descriptions of Concurrent Euclid, UNIX, and operating system and kernel design. Holt's most recent language is Turing Plus, an extension of the Turing language [Holt & Cordy 1988]. All of CSP/k, Concurrent Euclid, and Turing Plus employ the Signal and Wait (SW) discipline. Turing Plus also supports the Signal and Continue (SC) discipline and requires its use within device monitors so that interrupt handlers are not preempted.

Emerald is a different kind of language than the above [Raj et al. 1991]. In particular, Emerald is an object-oriented distributed programming language. It is not based on monitors but rather includes them as a synchronization mechanism. As in other object-oriented languages, an object has a representation and is manipulated by invoking operations. However, objects in Emerald can execute concurrently, and within an object invocations can execute concurrently. When mutual exclusion and condition synchronization are required, variables and the operations that access them can be defined within a monitor. Objects in Emerald can also be mobile—i.e., they can move during program execution. Thus, Emerald was in a way a precursor of Java.

Two modern and widely used languages—Java and Ada 95—also provide mechanisms that can be used to program monitors. We gave an overview of Java's mechanisms in Section 5.4. General information on Java can be found in the many books on the language; a wealth of information is also online at www.javasoft.com. Two books specifically cover concurrent programming in Java. Doug Lea [1997] describes design principles and patterns. Stephen Hartley [1998] covers many of the same topics as this text (semaphores, monitors, etc.) and includes dozens of example programs. A new book by Jeff Magee and Jeff Kramer [1999] provides more general coverage of concurrency, including modeling concurrent behavior, and uses Java to illustrate the concepts.

The first version of the Ada programming language, Ada 83, supported concurrent programming by means of tasks (processes) and rendezvous (see Section 8.2). The latest version of the language, Ada 95, added protected types, which are similar to monitors. Ada's concurrent programming mechanisms are described in Section 8.6. In particular, Figure 8.17 shows how to implement a counter barrier in Ada using a protected type. A general Web resource for Ada information, including books and online tutorials, is located at adahome.com.

Dijkstra [1968] introduced the sleeping barber problem in his important paper on using semaphores. Teory and Pinkerton [1972] and Geist and Daniel [1987] discuss and analyze a variety of different disk scheduling algorithms. Section 5.3 uses the circular scan algorithm. Later we will show how to implement shortest seek time (Section 7.3). Hoare [1974] illustrates the elevator algorithm.

Lister [1977] first raised the problem of what to do about nested monitor calls. This led to a flurry of follow-up papers and letters in *Operating Systems Review*, the quarterly newsletter of the ACM Special Interest Group on Operating Systems (SIGOPS). These papers discussed several possibilities, including the following: prohibit nested calls; use open calls; use closed calls and release exclusion only in the last monitor; use closed calls and release all locks when a process blocks, then reacquire them before the process continues; and finally, let the programmer specify whether a specific call is open or closed.

In reaction to Lister's paper, David Parnas [1978] argued that the fundamental issue is data integrity, which does not necessarily require mutual exclusion. In particular, concurrent execution of monitor procedures is fine as long as processes in a monitor do not interfere with each other. At about the same time, Andrews and McGraw [1977] defined a monitor-like construct that permits the programmer to specify which procedures can execute in parallel. Another approach is to use *path expressions* [Campbell & Kolstad 1980], a high-level mechanism that allows one to specify the order in which procedures execute and obviates the need for condition variables (see Exercise 5.26). The Mesa language provides mechanisms that give the programmer control over the granularity of exclusion. More recently, as shown in Section 5.4, Java has taken this approach of allowing the programmer to decide which methods are synchronized and which can execute concurrently.

References

Andrews, G. R., and J. R. McGraw. 1977. Language features for process inter-action. *Proc. ACM Conference on Language Design for Reliable Software*, *SIGPLAN Notices* 12, 3 (March): 114–27.

Brinch Hansen, P. 1972. Structured multiprogramming. *Comm. ACM* 15, 7 (July), 574–78.

Brinch Hansen, P. 1973. *Operating System Principles*. Englewood Cliffs, NJ: Prentice-Hall.

Brinch Hansen, P. 1975. The programming language Concurrent Pascal. *IEEE Trans. on Software Engr. SE-1*, 2 (June): 199–206.

Brinch Hansen, P. 1977. *The Architecture of Concurrent Programs*. Englewood Cliffs, NJ: Prentice-Hall.

Brinch Hansen, P. 1993. Monitors and Concurrent Pascal: A personal history. History of Programming Languages Conference (HOPL-II), *ACM Sigplan Notices* 28, 3 (March): 1–70.

Bustard, D., J. Elder, and J. Welsh. 1988. *Concurrent Program Structures*. New York: Prentice-Hall International.

Campbell, R. H., and R. B. Kolstad. 1980. An overview of Path Pascal's design and Path Pascal user manual. *SIGPLAN Notices* 15, 9 (September): 13–24.

Dijkstra, E. W. 1968. Cooperating sequential processes. In F. Genuys, ed., *Programming Languages*. New York: Academic Press, pp. 43–112.

Dijkstra, E. W. 1971. Hierarchical ordering of sequential processes. *Acta Informatica* 1, 115–38.

Gehani, N. H., and A. D. McGettrick. 1988. *Concurrent Programming*. Reading, MA: Addison-Wesley.

Geist, R., and S. Daniel. 1987. A continuum of disk scheduling algorithms. *ACM Trans. on Computer Systems* 5, 1 (February): 77–92.

Habermann, A. N. 1972. Synchronization of communicating processes. *Comm. ACM* 15, 3 (March): 171–76.

Hartley, S. J. 1998. *Concurrent Programming: The Java Programming Language.* New York: Oxford University Press.

Hoare, C.A.R. 1974. Monitors: An operating system structuring concept. *Comm. ACM* 17, 10 (October): 549–57.

Holt, R. C. 1983. *Concurrent Euclid, The UNIX System, and Tunis.* Reading, MA: Addison-Wesley.

Holt, R. C., and J. R. Cordy. 1988. The Turing programming language. *Comm. ACM* 31, 12 (December): 1410–23.

Holt, R. C., G. S. Graham, E. D. Lazowska, and M. A. Scott. 1978. *Structured Concurrent Programming with Operating System Applications.* Reading, MA: Addison-Wesley.

Lampson, B. W., and D. D. Redell. 1980. Experience with processes and monitors in Mesa. *Comm. ACM* 23, 2 (February): 105–17.

Lea, D. L. 1997. *Concurrent Programming in Java: Design Principles and Patterns.* Reading, MA: Addison-Wesley.

Lister, A. 1977. The problem of nested monitor calls. *Operating Systems Review* 11, 3 (July): 5–7.

Magee, J., and J. Kramer. 1999. *Concurrency: State Models and Java Programs.* New York: Wiley.

Mitchell, J. G., W. Maybury, and R. Sweet. 1979. Mesa language manual, version 5.0. Xerox Palo Alto Research Center Report CSL-79-3, April.

Parnas, D. L. 1978. The non-problem of nested monitor calls. *Operating Systems Review* 12, 1 (January): 12–14.

Raj, R. K., E. Tempero, H. M. Levy, A. P. Black, N. C. Hutchinson, and E. Jul, 1991. Emerald: A general purpose programming language. *Software—Practice and Experience* 21, 1 (January): 91–118.

Teorey, T. J., and T. B. Pinkerton. 1972. A comparative analysis of disk scheduling policies. *Comm. ACM* 15, 3 (March): 177–84.

Welsh, J., and D. W. Bustard. 1979. Pascal-Plus—another language for modular multiprogramming. *Software—Practice and Experience* 9, 947–57.

Welsh, J., and M. McKeag. 1980. *Structured System Programming.* New York: Prentice-Hall International.

Wirth, N. 1977. Modula: A language for modular multiprogramming. *Software—Practice and Experience* 7, 3–35.

Exercises

5.1   Suppose that the `empty` primitive is not available, but that you want to be able to tell whether any process is waiting on a condition variable queue. Develop a way to simulate `empty`. In particular, show the code you would need to add before and after each `wait(cv)` and `signal(cv)` statement. (Do not worry about `signal_all`.) Your solution should work for both the Signal and Continue and Signal and Wait disciplines.

5.2   Consider the `Shortest_Job_Next` monitor in Figure 5.6. Is the monitor correct if the Signal and Wait discipline is used? If so, explain why. If not, change the monitor so it is correct.

5.3   Consider the following proposed solution to the shortest-job-next allocation problem in Section 5.2:

```
monitor SJN {
   bool free = true;
   cond turn;
   procedure request(int time) {
     if (!free)
        wait(turn, time);
     free = false;
   }
   procedure release() {
      free = true;
      signal(turn);
   }
}
```

Does this solution work correctly for the Signal and Continue discipline? Does it work correctly for Signal and Wait? Clearly explain your answers.

5.4   The following problems deal with the readers/writers monitor in Figure 5.5. Assume Signal and Continue semantics for all four problems.

(a) Suppose there is no `signal_all` primitive. Modify the solution so that it uses only `signal`.

(b) Modify the solution to give writers preference instead of readers.

(c) Modify the solution so that readers and writers alternate if both are trying to access the database.

(d) Modify the solution so that readers and writers are given permission to access the database in FCFS order. Allow readers concurrent access when that does not violate the FCFS order of granting permission.

5.5   Consider the following definition of semaphores [Habermann 1972]. Let **na** be the number of times a process has attempted a **P** operation, let **np** be the number of completed **P** operations, and let **nv** be the number of completed **V** operations. The semaphore invariant for this representation is

```
np == min(na, nv)
```

This invariant specifies that a process delayed in a **P** operation should be awakened and allowed to continue as soon as enough **V** operations have been executed.

(a) Develop a monitor that implements semaphores using this representation and invariant. Use the Signal and Continue discipline.

(b) Develop a monitor that implements semaphores using this representation and invariant. Use the preemptive Signal and Wait discipline.

5.6   Consider the dining philosophers problem defined in Section 4.3.

(a) Develop a monitor to implement the required synchronization. The monitor should have two operations: **getforks(id)** and **relforks(id)**, where **id** is the identity of the calling philosopher. First specify a monitor invariant, then develop the body of the monitor. Your solution need not be fair. Use the Signal and Continue discipline.

(b) Modify your answer to (a) so that it is fair—i.e., so that a philosopher who wants to eat eventually gets to.

5.7   *The One-Lane Bridge.* Cars coming from the north and the south arrive at a one-lane bridge. Cars heading in the same direction can cross the bridge at the same time, but cars heading in opposite directions cannot.

(a) Develop a solution to this problem. Model the cars as processes, and use a monitor for synchronization. First specify the monitor invariant, then develop the body of the monitor. Do not worry about fairness, and do not give preference to any one kind of car. Use the Signal and Continue discipline.

(b) Modify your answer to (a) to ensure fairness. (*Hint:* Have cars take turns.)

5.8   *The Savings Account Problem.* A savings account is shared by several people (processes). Each person may deposit or withdraw funds from the account. The current balance in the account is the sum of all deposits to date minus the sum of all withdrawals to date. The balance must never become negative. A deposit never has to delay (except for mutual exclusion), but a withdrawal has to wait until there are sufficient funds.

(a) Develop a monitor to solve this problem. The monitor should have two procedures: **deposit(amount)** and **withdraw(amount)**. First specify a monitor invariant. Assume the arguments to `deposit` and `withdraw` are positive. Use the Signal and Continue discipline.

(b) Modify your answer to (a) so that withdrawals are serviced FCFS. For example, suppose the current balance is $200, and one customer is waiting to withdraw $300. If another customer arrives, he must wait, even if he wants to withdraw at most $200. Assume there is a magic function `amount(cv)` that returns the value of the amount parameter of the first process delayed on `cv`.

(c) Suppose a magic `amount` function does not exist. Modify your answer to (b) to simulate it in your solution.

5.9   *The Water Molecule Problem.* Suppose hydrogen and oxygen atoms are bouncing around in space trying to group together into water molecules. This requires that two hydrogen atoms and one oxygen atom synchronize with each other. Let the hydrogen (H) and oxygen (O) atoms be simulated by processes (threads). Each H atom calls a procedure `Hready` when it wants to combine into a water molecule. Each O atom calls another procedure `Oready` when it wants to combine.

Your job is to write a monitor that implements `Hready` and `Oready`. An H atom has to delay in `Hready` until another H atom has also called `Hready` *and* one O atom has called `Oready`. Then *one* of the processes (say the O atom) should call a procedure `makeWater`. After `makeWater` returns, *all three* processes should return from their calls of `Hready` and `Oready`. Your solution must avoid deadlock and starvation. This is a tricky problem, so be careful.

5.10   *Atomic Broadcast.* Assume one producer process and n consumer processes share a bounded buffer having b slots. The producer deposits messages in the buffer; consumers fetch them. Every message deposited by the producer is to be received by all n consumers. Furthermore, each consumer is to receive the messages in the order they were deposited. However, consumers can receive messages at different times. For example, one consumer could receive up to b more messages than another if the second consumer is slow.

Develop a monitor that implements this kind of communication. Use the Signal and Continue discipline.

5.11   Develop a monitor that allows pairs of processes to exchange values. The monitor has one operation: `exchange(int *value)`. After two processes have called `exchange`, the monitor swaps the values of the arguments and returns them to the processes. The monitor should be reusable in the sense that it exchanges the parameters of the first pair of callers, then the second pair of callers, and so on. You may use either the Signal and Continue or Signal and Wait discipline, *but state which one you are using.*

5.12 *The Dining Savages.* A tribe of savages eats communal dinners from a large pot that can hold M servings of stewed missionary. When a savage wants to eat, he helps himself from the pot, unless it is empty. If the pot is empty, the savage wakes up the cook and then waits until the cook has refilled the pot. The behavior of the savages and cook is specified by the following processes:

```
process Savage[1:n] {
   while (true) { get serving from pot; eat; }
}
process Cook {
   while (true) { sleep; put M servings in pot; }
}
```

Develop code for the actions of the savages and cook. Use a monitor for synchronization. Your solution should avoid deadlock and awaken the cook only when the pot is empty. Use the Signal and Continue discipline.

5.13 *Search/Insert/Delete.* Three kinds of processes share access to a singly linked list: searchers, inserters, and deleters. Searchers merely examine the list; hence they can execute concurrently with each other. Inserters add new items to the end of the list; insertions must be mutually exclusive to preclude inserting two items at about the same time. However, one insert can proceed in parallel with any number of searches. Finally, deleters remove items from anywhere in the list. At most one deleter process can access the list at a time, and deletion must also be mutually exclusive with searches and insertions.

Develop a monitor to implement this kind of synchronization. First specify a monitor invariant. Use the Signal and Continue discipline.

5.14 *Memory Allocation.* Suppose there are two operations: `request(amount)` and `release(amount)`, where `amount` is a positive integer. When a process calls `request`, it delays until at least `amount` free pages of memory are available. A process returns `amount` pages to the free pool by calling `release`. Pages may be released in different quantities than they are acquired.

(a) Develop a monitor that implements `request` and `release`. First specify a global invariant. Do not worry about the order in which requests are serviced. Use the Signal and Continue discipline. (*Hint:* Use a covering condition.)

(b) Modify your answer to (a) to use the shortest-job-next (SJN) allocation policy. In particular, smaller requests take precedence over larger ones.

(c) Modify your answer to (a) to use a first-come, first-served (FCFS) allocation policy. This means that a pending request might have to delay, even if there is enough memory available.

(d) Suppose `request` and `release` acquire and return contiguous pages of memory; i.e., if a process requests two pages, it delays until two adjacent pages are available. Develop a monitor that implements these versions of `request` and `release`. First choose a representation for the status of memory pages and specify a monitor invariant.

5.15   Suppose `n` processes `P[1:n]` share two printers. Before using a printer, `P[i]` calls `request(printer)`. This operation returns the identity of a free printer. After using that printer, `P[i]` returns it by calling `release(printer)`.

(a) Develop a monitor that implements `request` and `release`. First specify a monitor invariant. Use the Signal and Continue discipline.

(b) Assume each process has a priority that it passes to the monitor as an additional argument to `request`. Modify `request` and `release` so that a printer is allocated to the highest priority waiting process. If two processes have the same priority, their requests should be granted in FCFS order.

5.16   Suppose a computer center has two printers, `A` and `B`, that are similar but not identical. Three kinds of processes use the printers: those that must use `A`, those that must use `B`, and those that can use either `A` or `B`.

Develop a monitor to allocate the printers, and show the code that the processes execute to request and release a printer. Your solution should be fair, assuming that printers are eventually released. Use the Signal and Continue discipline.

5.17   *The Roller Coaster Problem.* Suppose there are `n` passenger processes and one car process. The passengers repeatedly wait to take rides in the car, which can hold `c` passengers, `c < n`. However, the car can go around the tracks only when it is full.

(a) Develop code for the actions of the passenger and car processes, and develop a monitor to synchronize them. The monitor should have three operations: `takeRide`, which is called by passengers, and `load` and `unload`, which are called by the car process. Specify an invariant for your monitor. Use the Signal and Continue discipline.

(b) Generalize your answer to (a) to employ `m` car processes, `m > 1`. Since there is only one track, cars cannot pass each other; i.e., they must finish going around the track in the order in which they started. Again, a car can go around the tracks only when it is full.

5.18   *File Buffer Allocation.* Many operating systems, such as UNIX, maintain a cache of file access buffers. Each buffer is the size of a disk block. When a user process wants to read a disk block, the file system first looks in the cache. If the block is there, the file system returns the data to the user. Otherwise, the file system selects the least recently used buffer, reads the disk block into it, then returns the data to the user.

Similarly, if a user process wants to write a disk block that is in the cache, the file system simply updates the block. Otherwise, the file system selects the least recently used buffer and writes into that one. The file system keeps track of which buffers contain new data—i.e., which have been modified—and writes them to disk before letting them be used for a different disk block. (This is called a *write-back cache policy*.)

Develop a monitor to implement a buffer cache having the above specifications. First define the procedures you need and their parameters, then develop the body of the monitor. Use the Signal and Continue discipline. Explain any additional mechanisms you need—for example, a clock and a disk-access process.

5.19 The following problems deal with the sleeping barber monitor in Figure 5.10.

(a) Some of the `while` loops can be replaced by `if` statements. Determine which ones, and modify the monitor appropriately. Assume the Signal and Continue discipline.

(b) Is the monitor, as given, correct for the Signal and Wait discipline? If so, give a convincing argument. If not, modify the monitor so that it is correct.

(c) Is the monitor, as given, correct for the Signal and Urgent Wait discipline? If so, give a convincing argument. If not, modify the monitor so that it is correct.

5.20 In the sleeping barber problem (Section 5.2), suppose there are several barbers rather than just one. Develop a monitor to synchronize the actions of the customers and barbers. First specify a monitor invariant. The monitor should have the same procedures as in Figure 5.10. Be careful to ensure that `finished_cut` awakens the same customer that a barber rendezvoused with in `get_next_customer`. Use the Signal and Continue discipline.

5.21 The following problems deal with the separate disk scheduler monitor in Figure 5.13.

(a) Modify the monitor to employ the elevator algorithm. First specify a monitor invariant, then develop a solution.

(b) Modify the monitor to employ the shortest-seek-time algorithm. First specify a monitor invariant, then develop a solution.

5.22 The following problems deal with the disk interface monitor in Figure 5.16.

(a) Give the details of the monitor invariant.

(b) Modify `finished_transfer` so that the disk driver process does not wait for a user process to fetch its results. However, be careful that the disk driver does not overwrite the results area.

(c) Combine the procedures `get_next_request` and `finished_transfer` that are called by the disk driver. Be careful about the initialization of the monitor's variables.

5.23 Figure 5.17 illustrates the use of a `Disk_Access` monitor, and the text outlines its implementation. Develop a complete implementation of `Disk_Access`. Use the SCAN (elevator) disk-scheduling strategy. First specify an appropriate monitor invariant, and then develop the body of procedure `doIO`. Do not worry about implementing the `Disk_Transfer` monitor; just show the calls to it at appropriate points from within `Disk_Access` (and assume they are open calls).

5.24 The main difference between the various monitor signaling disciplines is the order in which processes execute. However, it is possible to simulate the semantics of one monitor signaling discipline using a different signaling discipline. In particular, it is possible to transform a monitor that uses one signaling discipline into a monitor that has the same behavior but uses a different signaling discipline. This requires changing the code and adding extra variables.

(a) Show how to simulate Signal and Continue using Signal and Wait. Illustrate your simulation using one of the monitors earlier in the chapter.

(b) Show how to simulate Signal and Wait using Signal and Continue. Develop an example that illustrates your simulation.

(c) Show how to simulate Signal and Wait using Signal and Urgent Wait, and vice versa. Develop an example that illustrates your simulation.

5.25 Suppose input and output on a terminal are supported by two procedures:

```
getline(string &str, int &count)
putline(string str)
```

An application process calls `getline` to receive the next line of input; it calls `putline` to send a line to the display. A call of `getline` returns when there is another line of input; result argument `str` is set to the contents of the line, and `count` is set to its actual length. A line contains at most `MAXLINE` characters; it is terminated by a `NEWLINE` character, which is not part of the line itself.

Assume both input and output are buffered—i.e., up to `n` input lines can be stored waiting to be retrieved by `getline` and up to `n` output lines can be stored waiting to be printed. Also assume that input lines are echoed to the display—i.e., each complete input line is also sent to the display. Finally, assume that input lines are "cooked"—i.e., backspace and line-kill characters are processed by `getline` and do not get returned to the application process.

Develop a monitor that implements `getline` and `putline`. Assume there are two device driver processes. One reads characters from the keyboard; the other writes lines to the display. Your monitor will need to have additional procedures that these processes call.

5.26 Path expressions are a high-level mechanism for specifying synchronization between procedures in a module [Campbell & Kolstad 1980]. They can be used to specify which procedures execute with mutual exclusion and which can execute in parallel, and they obviate the need for condition variables and explicit `wait` and `signal` statements. The syntax of an open path expression is defined by the following BNF grammar:

path_declaration	::=	"path" list "end"
list	::=	sequence { "," sequence }
sequence	::=	item { ";" item }
item	::=	bound ":" "(" list ")" | "[" list "]" |
		"(" list ")" | identifier

Braces denote zero or more occurrences of the enclosed items, and quotes enclose literal items (nonterminals). In the choices for item, bound is a positive integer, and identifier is the name of a procedure.

The comma operator in a list imposes no synchronization constraints. The semi-colon operator in a sequence imposes the constraint that one execution of the first item must complete before each execution of the second item, which must complete before each execution of the third item, and so on. The bound operator limits the number of elements of the enclosed list that can be active at a time. The bracket operator [...] allows any number of elements of the enclosed list to be active at once. For example, the following specifies that any number of calls of procedures **a** or **b** can proceed in parallel but that **a** and **b** are mutually exclusive with respect to each other:

```
path 1: ([a], [b]) end
```

(a) Give a path expression to express the synchronization for a bounded buffer with n slots (Figure 5.4). The operations on the buffer are `deposit` and `fetch`. They are to execute with mutual exclusion.

(b) Give a path expression to express the synchronization for a bounded buffer with n slots. Allow maximal parallelism; i.e., instances of `deposit` and `fetch` can execute in parallel, as long as they are accessing different slots.

(c) Give a path expression to express the synchronization for the dining philosophers problem (Section 4.3). Explain your answer.

(d) Give a path expression to express the synchronization for the readers-writers problem (Figure 5.5). Explain your answer.

(e) Give a path expression to express the synchronization for the sleeping barber problem (Figure 5.10). Explain your answer.

(f) Show how to implement path expressions using semaphores. In particular, suppose you are given a path expression that specifies the synchronization for a set of procedures. Show what code you would insert at the start and end of each procedure to enforce the specified synchronization. Start with some simple examples, and then generalize your solution.

5.27 The following problems refer to the Java programs in Section 5.4. The source for the programs can be downloaded from the Website for this book (see the Preface).

(a) Write a simple program that has two classes. One defines a thread and has a `run` method that prints a line; the second is the main class that creates a thread. In the main class, create and start the thread as described in the text. Then try calling the `run` method directly rather than indirectly via `start`. (Namely, use `s.run()` if `s` is the thread.) What happens? Why?

(b) Develop more realistic simulations of the readers/writers programs. Use multiple readers and writers and modify them so that you can observe that they synchronize correctly. Perhaps modify the database to make it somewhat more realistic, or at least to have `read` and `write` take longer. Also have each thread sleep for a small random amount of time before (or after) every access to the database. Java provides several methods—such as `nap`, `age`, `random`, and `seed`—that you can use to construct your simulations. Write a brief report summarizing what you observe.

(c) Modify the `ReadersWriters` class to give writers preference. Repeat your simulations from part (b), and summarize what you observe.

(d) Modify the `ReadersWriters` class to make it fair. Repeat your simulations from part (b), and summarize what you observe.

5.28 Develop a Java program to simulate the dining philosophers problem (Section 4.3). Your program should have **5** philosopher threads and a class that implements a monitor to synchronize the philosophers. The monitor should have two methods: `getforks(id)` and `relforks(id)`, where `id` is an integer between **1** and **5**. Have the philosophers eat and sleep for random amounts of time. Add print statements to your program to generate a trace of the activity of the program. Write a brief report summarizing what you observe.

6

Implementations

The previous chapters defined mechanisms for concurrent programming with shared variables and showed how to use them. At a minimum, modern multiprocessors provide machine instructions that the systems programmer can use to implement locks and barriers, as described in Chapter 3. Some multiprocessors provide hardware support for processes, context switching, locks, barriers, and sometimes even the spinning aspect of semaphores. However, in general concurrent programming mechanisms are implemented in software.

This chapter describes software implementations of processes, semaphores, and monitors. The basis for the implementations is what is called a *kernel*: a small set of data structures and subroutines that are at the core of any concurrent program. (A kernel is sometimes called a *nucleus*; both terms indicate that the software is common to every software module.) The role of a kernel is to provide a virtual processor to each process so that the process has the illusion that it is executing on its own processor. The data structures represent the states of processes, semaphores, and condition variables. The subroutines implement operations on the data structures; each is called a *primitive* operation because it is implemented so that it executes atomically.

Section 6.1 describes a kernel that implements processes on a single processor. Section 6.2 extends that kernel to one for a multiprocessor. Sections 6.3 and 6.4 add kernel primitives to support semaphores and monitors, respectively. Finally, Section 6.5 describes how to implement monitors using semaphores. Our focus is on implementing processes and synchronization, so we do not cover many additional issues, such as dynamic storage allocation and priority scheduling, that arise in practice.

6.1 A Single-Processor Kernel

We have used the `co` statement and **process** declarations in previous chapters to specify concurrent activity. Processes are merely special cases of `co` statements, so we focus on how to implement `co` statements. Consider the following program fragment:

```
S0;
co   P1: S1; // ... // Pn: Sn; oc
Sn+1;
```

The `Pi` are process names. The `Si` are statement lists and optional declarations of variables local to process `Pi`.

Three mechanisms are needed to implement the above program fragment:

- one to create processes and start them executing,

- one to stop (and destroy) a process, and

- one to determine when the `co` statement has completed.

A *primitive* is a routine that is implemented by a kernel in such a way that it executes as an atomic action. Processes are created and destroyed by means of two kernel primitives: `fork` and `quit`.

When one process invokes `fork`, another process is created and made eligible for execution. The arguments to `fork` give the address of the first instruction to be executed by the new process, and any other data needed to specify its initial state—for example, its parameters. The new process is called a *child*; the process that executes `fork` is called its *parent*. When a process invokes `quit`, it ceases to exist. The `quit` primitive has no arguments.

A third kernel primitive, `join`, is used to wait for processes to complete execution, and hence to determine that a `co` statement has completed. In particular, when a parent process executes `join`, it waits for a child process that it previously forked to execute `quit`. The argument to the `join` primitive is the name of a child process. (Alternatively, `join` could have no arguments, in which case `join` waits for *any* child to terminate and perhaps returns the identity of the child.)

These three kernel primitives—`fork`, `join`, and `quit`—can be used as shown here to implement the above program fragment. Each child processes `Pi` executes the following code:

```
Si; quit();
```

The main process executes the following code:

```
S0;
for [i = 1 to n]    # create the child processes
  fork(Pi);
for [i = 1 to n]    # wait for each one to terminate
  join(Pi);
Sn+1;
```

We assume that the main process is created implicitly and automatically begins execution. We also assume that the code and data for all the processes are already stored in memory when the main process begins.

The second `for` loop above waits for child **1** to quit, then child **2**, and so on. Alternatively, one could use a no-argument version of `join` and wait for the n children to quit in any order. If the children are declared using `process` declarations—and hence are to be executed in the background—the main process would fork them in the same way but would not wait for them to quit.

We now present a single-processor kernel that implements `fork`, `join`, and `quit`. We also describe how to schedule processes so that each gets a periodic chance to execute—namely, a scheduler that is weakly fair in the sense defined in Section 2.8.

Any kernel contains data structures that represent processes and three basic kinds of routines: interrupt handlers, the primitives themselves, and a dispatcher. The kernel may also contain other data structures and functionality—for example, file descriptors and file access routines. We focus here just on the parts of a kernel that implement processes.

There are two basic ways to organize a kernel:

- as a monolithic unit in which each kernel primitive executes as an atomic action; or

- as a concurrent program in which more than one user process may be executing a kernel primitive at the same time.

We use the first approach here since that is the simplest for a small, single-processor kernel. We use the second approach in the multiprocessor kernel in the next section.

Each process is represented in the kernel by a *process descriptor*. When a process is idle, its descriptor contains its *state* or *context*—namely, all the information needed to execute the process. The state (context) includes the address of the next instruction the process will execute and the contents of processor registers.

The kernel starts executing when an interrupt occurs. Interrupts can be divided into two broad categories: external interrupts from peripheral devices and internal interrupts or traps triggered by the executing process. When an interrupt occurs, the processor automatically saves enough state information so that the interrupted process can be resumed. Then the processor enters an *interrupt handler;* there is typically one handler for each kind of interrupt.

To invoke a kernel primitive, a process causes an internal interrupt by executing a machine instruction variously named a supervisor call (SVC) or trap. The process passes an argument with the SVC instruction to indicate what primitive is to be executed and passes other arguments in registers. The SVC interrupt handler first saves the state of the executing process. Then it calls the appropriate primitive, which is implemented within the kernel by a procedure. When the primitive completes, it calls the **dispatcher** routine (processor scheduler). The **dispatcher** selects a process for execution and then loads its state. Because the state of a process is called its context, the last action of the **dispatcher** is called *context switching.*

To ensure that the primitives are executed atomically, the first action of an interrupt handler is to inhibit further interrupts, and the last action of the **dispatcher** is to enable interrupts. Further interrupts are inhibited automatically by the hardware when an interrupt occurs; the kernel re-enables interrupts as a side-effect of loading a process state. (Some machines have multiple interrupt classes or levels. In this case, each interrupt handler need inhibit only those interrupts that could interfere with the one being processed.)

Figure 6.1 illustrates the kernel components and shows the flow of control through the kernel. Control flows in one direction: from interrupt handlers through the primitives to the **dispatcher** and then back out to one active process. Hence, the calls within the kernel do not return. This is because the kernel will often start executing another process rather than return to the one that was executing when the kernel was entered.

We will represent the process descriptors by an array:

```
processType processDescriptor[maxProcs];
```

The **processType** is a structure (record) describing the fields in a process descriptor. A parent process asks the kernel to create a child process by calling

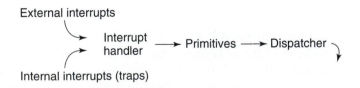

Figure 6.1   Kernel components and flow of control.

the `fork` primitive, which allocates and initializes an empty descriptor. When the kernel's `dispatcher` schedules a process, it needs to find the descriptor of a process that is eligible to execute. Both `fork` and the `dispatcher` could be implemented by searching through the array of process descriptors, assuming each record contains a field indicating whether the entry is free or in use. More commonly, however, two lists are used: a *free list* of empty descriptors and a *ready list* of descriptors of processes that are waiting a turn to execute. We use the list representation below. We also use an additional *waiting* list for parents that are waiting for children to quit. Finally, the kernel contains a variable, `executing`, whose value is the index of the descriptor of the process that is currently executing.

We assume that when the kernel is initialized—which happens as a result of "booting" the processor—one process is created and `executing` is set to point to its descriptor. All other descriptors are placed on the free list. The ready and waiting lists are thus initially empty.

With this representation for the kernel data structures, the `fork` primitive takes a descriptor off the free list, initializes it, and inserts it on the end of the ready list. The `join` primitive checks to see if a child process has previously quit; if not, it blocks the executing (parent) process. The `quit` primitive records that the process has quit, puts the descriptor of the executing process on the free list, awakens the parent process if that process is waiting, and sets `executing` to zero to indicate to the `dispatcher` that the process no longer wants to execute.

When the `dispatcher` is called at the end of a primitive, it checks the value of `executing`. If it is not zero, the currently executing process is to continue executing. Otherwise, the `dispatcher` removes the first descriptor from the ready list and sets `executing` to point to it. The `dispatcher` then loads the state of that process. We assume here that the ready list is a first-in, first-out (FIFO) queue.

Our remaining concern is to ensure fairness of process execution. If the executing processes were always to terminate in finite time, the above implementation of the kernel would ensure fairness since we assume the ready list is a FIFO queue. However, if any process waits for a condition that is not yet true, it will spin forever unless it is forced to relinquish the processor. (A process will also spin forever if it erroneously contains a nonterminating loop.) We can use an interval timer to ensure that processes periodically release control of the processor, assuming of course that such a timer is provided by the hardware. This, plus the fact that the ready list is a FIFO queue, will guarantee each process periodic chances to execute. Hence, scheduling will be weakly fair.

An *interval timer* is a hardware device that is initialized with a positive integer value and then decrements the value at a fixed rate and triggers a timer interrupt when the value becomes zero. The kernel uses such a timer as follows. First, before loading the state of the process that is to execute next, the `dispatcher` initializes the timer. Then, if the timer interrupt occurs, the timer interrupt handler places the descriptor of the process referenced by `executing` at the end of the ready list, sets `executing` to `0`, and then calls the `dispatcher`. This causes processes to take turns executing in round-robin fashion.

Putting all these pieces together, we have the outline for a single-processor kernel shown in Figure 6.2. We assume that a side-effect of starting the interval timer in `dispatcher` is to disable any interrupt that might have been pending as a consequence of the timer reaching zero while the kernel is executing. With this reasonable assumption, the process that is selected for execution will not immediately get interrupted and lose control of the processor.

The kernel in Figure 6.2 ignores exceptions that might occur, such as the free list being empty when `fork` is called. This implementation also assumes that there is always at least one ready process. In practice, a kernel would always have one "do nothing" process that is dispatched when there is no useful work to be done; the next section shows how to do so. We have also ignored several other issues that have to be addressed in practice—for example, I/O interrupt handling, device control, file access, and memory management.

6.2 A Multiprocessor Kernel

A shared-memory multiprocessor has two or more processors and memory that is accessible to every processor. It is relatively straightforward to extend the single-processor kernel to a multiprocessor kernel. The main changes we need to make are as follows:

- Store kernel procedures and data structures in shared memory.

- Access the data structures with mutual exclusion when that is needed to avoid interference.

- Change the `dispatcher` routine to exploit the multiple processors.

There are some subtleties, however, as discussed below. These result from the characteristics of multiprocessors.

We assume that internal interrupts (traps) are serviced by the processor that was executing the process that caused the trap and assume that every processor has an interval timer. For now, we also assume that each kernel operation and process can be executed by any processor. (At the end of the section, we describe how to deal with binding processes to processors and how to deal with effects of caches and nonuniform memory access time.)

```
processType processDescriptor[maxProcs];
int executing = 0;      # index of the executing process
declarations of variables for the free, ready, and waiting lists;

SVC_Handler: {    # entered with interrupts inhibited
  save state of executing;
  determine which primitive was invoked, then call it;
}

Timer_Handler: {    # entered with interrupts inhibited
  insert descriptor of executing at end of ready list;
  executing = 0;
  dispatcher();
}

procedure fork(initial process state) {
  remove a descriptor from the free list and initialize it;
  insert the descriptor on the end of the ready list;
  dispatcher();
}

procedure quit() {
  record that executing has quit;
  insert descriptor of executing at end of free list;
  executing = 0;
  if (parent process is waiting for this child) {
    remove parent from the waiting list; put parent on the ready list; }
  dispatcher();
}

procedure join(name of child process) {
  if (child has not yet quit) {
    put the descriptor of executing on the waiting list;
    executing = 0;
  }
  dispatcher();
}

procedure dispatcher() {
  if (executing == 0) { # current process blocked or quit
    remove descriptor from front of ready list;
    set executing to point to it;
  }
  start the interval timer;
  load state of executing;      # with interrupts enabled
}
```

Figure 6.2   Outline of a single-processor kernel.

When a processor is interrupted, it enters the kernel and inhibits further interrupts *on that processor*. This makes execution in the kernel indivisible on that processor, but it does not prevent other processors from simultaneously executing in the kernel.

To preclude interference between the processors, we could make the entire kernel a critical section. However, this is a poor choice for two reasons. First, it unnecessarily precludes some safe concurrent execution because only access to shared data structures such as the free and ready lists is critical. Second, making the entire kernel into a critical section results in unnecessarily long critical sections. This decreases performance because it delays processors trying to enter the kernel, and it increases memory contention for the variables that implement the kernel critical section protocol. The following principle elucidates a much better choice.

(6.1) **Multiprocessor Locking Principle.** Make critical sections short by individually protecting each critical data structure. Use separate critical sections—with separate variables for the entry and exit protocols—for each critical data structure.

In our kernel, the critical data are the free, ready, and waiting lists. To protect access to these, we can use any of the critical section protocols given earlier in this chapter. On a particular multiprocessor, the choice of which to use will be affected by which special instructions are available. For example, if there is a Fetch-and-Add instruction, we can use the simple and fair ticket algorithm in Figure 3.9.

Because we assume that traps are handled by the processor on which the trap occurs and that each processor has its own interval timer, the trap and timer interrupt handlers are essentially the same as those found in the single-processor kernel. There are only two differences: `executing` needs now to be an array, with one entry per processor, and `Timer_Handler` needs to lock and unlock the ready list.

The code for the three kernel primitives is also essentially the same. Again, the differences are that `executing` is an array and that the free, ready, and waiting lists need to be accessed in critical sections.

The greatest changes are to the code for `dispatcher`. Before, we had one processor and assumed it always had a process to execute. Now there could be fewer processes than processors, and hence some processors could be idle. When a new process is forked (or awakened after an I/O interrupt), it needs to be assigned to an idle processor, if there is one. This functionality can be provided in one of three ways:

- Have each processor, when idle, execute a special process that periodically examines the ready list until it finds a ready process.

- Have a processor executing `fork` search for an idle processor and assign the new process to it.

- Use a separate dispatcher process that executes on its own processor and continuously attempts to assign ready processes to idle processors.

The first approach is the most efficient, in part because idle processors have nothing else to do until they find some process to execute.

When the dispatcher finds that the ready list is empty, it sets `executing[i]` to point to the descriptor of an idle process and then loads the state of that process. The code for the idle process is shown in Figure 6.3. In essence, `Idle` is a self-dispatcher. It first spins until the ready list is not empty, then it removes a process descriptor and begins executing that process. To avoid memory contention, `Idle` should not continuously examine the ready list or continuously lock and unlock it. Thus we use a Test-and-Test-and-Set protocol similar in structure to the one in Figure 3.4. Since the ready list might be empty again before `Idle` acquires the lock for the ready list, it needs to retest whether the list is empty.

Our remaining concern is to ensure fairness. Again, we will employ timers to ensure that processes executing outside the kernel are forced to relinquish processors. We assume each processor has its own timer, which it uses as in the single-processor kernel. However, timers alone are not sufficient since processes can now be delayed within the kernel waiting to acquire access to the shared

```
process Idle {
  while (executing[i] == the Idle process) {
    while (ready list empty) Delay;
    lock ready list;
    if (ready list not empty) {
      remove descriptor from front of ready list;
      set executing[i] to point to it;
    }
    unlock ready list;
  }
  start the interval timer on processor i;
  load state of executing[i];    # with interrupts enabled
```

Figure 6.3   Code for the idle process.

kernel data structures. Thus we need to use a fair solution to the critical section problem such as the Tie-Breaker, Ticket, or Bakery algorithms given in Chapter 3. If instead we use the Test-and-Set protocol, there is the possibility that processes might starve. This is not very likely, however, since the critical sections in the kernel are very short.

Figure 6.4 outlines a multiprocessor kernel that incorporates all these assumptions and decisions. Variable i is the index of the processor executing the routines, and `lock` and `unlock` are critical section entry and exit protocols. Again, we have ignored possible exceptions and have not included code for I/O interrupt handlers, memory management, and so on.

The multiprocessor kernel in Figure 6.4 employs a single ready list that is assumed to be a FIFO queue. If processes have different priorities, the ready list needs to be a priority queue. However, this will cause a processor to take longer when accessing the ready list, at least when doing an insertion, because it has to search for the appropriate place in the queue and then insert the new process at that location. Thus the ready list might become a bottleneck. If there are a fixed number of priority levels, an efficient solution is to have one queue per priority level and one lock per queue. With this representation, inserting a process on the ready list requires only inserting it at the end of the appropriate queue. If the number of priority levels is dynamic, however, the most commonly used scheme is to employ a single ready list.

The kernel in Figure 6.4 also assumes that a process can execute on any processor. In particular, the dispatcher always selects the first ready process. On some multiprocessors, processes such as device drivers or file servers might have to execute on a specific processor because a peripheral device is attached only to that processor. In this case, each such processor should have its own ready list and perhaps its own dispatcher. (The situation gets more complicated if a special processor can also execute regular processes since it then needs to be able to schedule them, too.)

```
processType processDescriptor[maxProcs];
int executing[maxProcs];   # one entry per processor
declarations of free, ready, and waiting lists and their locks;

SVC_Handler: {
   # entered with interrupts inhibited on processor i
   save state of executing[i];
   determine which primitive was invoked, then call it;
}

Timer_Handler: {
   # entered with interrupts inhibited on processor i
```

```
      lock ready list; insert executing[i] at end; unlock ready list;
      executing[i] = 0;
      dispatcher();
}

procedure fork(initial process state) {
      lock free list; remove a descriptor; unlock free list;
      initialize the descriptor;
      lock ready list; insert descriptor at end; unlock ready list;
      dispatcher();
}

procedure quit() {
      lock free list; insert executing[i] at end; unlock free list;
      record that executing[i] has quit; executing[i] = 0;
      if (parent process is waiting) {
         lock waiting list; remove parent from that list; unlock waiting list;
         lock ready list; put parent on ready list; unlock ready list;
      }
      dispatcher();
}

procedure join(name of child process) {
      if (child has already quit)
         return;
      lock waiting list; put executing[i] on that list; unlock waiting list;
      dispatcher();
}

procedure dispatcher() {
      if (executing[i] == 0) {
         lock ready list;
         if (ready list not empty) {
            remove descriptor from ready list;
            set executing[i] to point to it;
         }
         else     # ready list is empty
            set executing[i] to point to Idle process;
         unlock ready list;
      }
      if (executing[i] is not the Idle process)
         start timer on processor i;
      load state of executing[i];     # with interrupts enabled
}
```

Figure 6.4   Outline of a kernel for a shared-memory multiprocessor.

Even if a process can execute on any processor, it may be very inefficient to schedule it on an arbitrary processor. On a nonuniform memory access machine, for example, processors can access local memory more rapidly than remote memory. Hence, a process should ideally execute on the processor whose local memory contains its code. This suggests having a separate ready list per processor and assigning processes to processors depending on where their code is stored. Having separate ready lists, however, raises the issue of *load balancing*—i.e., having each processor handle about the same amount of computational load. It is not sufficient to assign the same number of processes to each processor; different processes in general generate different loads, and this can vary dynamically.

Regardless of whether memory access time is uniform or not, it is common for processors to have cache memories or virtual memory translation buffers. In this case, a process should be rescheduled on the processor where it last executed, assuming part of its state is in the cache or translation buffers. Moreover, if two processes share data and that data is in a cache, they might execute most efficiently if they are multiplexed on the same processor rather than executed on different processors; this is called *co-scheduling*. Again this suggests having a separate ready list per processor, which in turn raises the issue of load balancing. The references and exercises at the end of this chapter contain further information on these issues.

6.3 Implementing Semaphores in a Kernel

Since the semaphore operations are special cases of `await` statements, we can implement them using busy waiting and the techniques of Chapter 3. However, the only reason one might want to do so is to be able to write parallel programs using semaphores rather than lower-level spin locks and flags. Consequently, we will just show how to add semaphores to the kernel described in the previous sections. This involves augmenting the kernel with semaphore descriptors and three additional primitives: `createSem`, `Psem`, and `Vsem`. (A library such as Pthreads is implemented in a similar way; however, a library runs on top of an operating system, so it is entered by means of normal procedure calls and contains software signal handlers rather than hardware interrupt handlers.)

A semaphore descriptor contains the value of one semaphore; it is initialized by invoking `createSem`. The `Psem` and `Vsem` primitives implement the `P` and `V` operations. We assume here that all semaphores are general semaphores. We first show how to add semaphores to the single-processor kernel of Section 6.1 and then show how to change the resulting kernel to support multiple processors, as in Section 6.2.

Recall that in a single-processor kernel, one process at a time is executing, and all others were ready to execute or are waiting for their children to quit. As before, the index of the descriptor of the executing process is stored in variable **executing**, and the descriptors for all ready processes are stored on the ready list.

When semaphores are added to the kernel, there is a fourth possible process state: blocked on a semaphore. In particular, a process is blocked if it is waiting to complete a **P** operation. To keep track of blocked processes, each semaphore descriptor contains a linked list of the descriptors of processes blocked on that semaphore. On a single processor, exactly one process is executing, and its descriptor is on no list; all other process descriptors are on the ready list, the waiting list, or a blocked list of some semaphore.

For each semaphore declaration in a concurrent program, one call to the **createSem** primitive is generated; the semaphore's initial value is passed as an argument. The **createSem** primitive finds an empty semaphore descriptor, initializes the semaphore's value and blocked list, and returns a "name" for the descriptor. This name is typically either the descriptor's address or an index into a table that contains the address.

After a semaphore is created, it is used by invoking the **Psem** and **Vsem** primitives, which are the kernel routines for the **P** and **V** programming primitives. Both have a single argument that is the name of a semaphore descriptor. The **Psem** primitive checks the value in the descriptor. If the value is positive, it is decremented; otherwise, the descriptor of the executing process is inserted on the semaphore's blocked list. Similarly, **Vsem** checks the semaphore descriptor's blocked list. If it is empty, the semaphore's value is incremented; otherwise one process descriptor is removed from the blocked list and inserted on the ready list. It is common for each blocked list to be implemented as a FIFO queue since this ensures that the semaphore operations are fair.

Figure 6.5 gives outlines of these primitives. They are added to the routines in the single processor kernel given earlier in Figure 6.2. Again, the **dispatcher** procedure is called at the end of each primitive; its actions are the same as before.

For simplicity, the implementation of the semaphore primitives in Figure 6.5 does not reuse semaphore descriptors. This would be sufficient if all semaphores are created once, but in general this is not the case. Thus it is usually necessary to reuse semaphore descriptors as well as process descriptors. One approach is for the kernel to provide an additional **destroySem** primitive; this would then be invoked by a process when it no longer needs a semaphore. An alternative is to record in the descriptor of each process the names of all semaphores that the process created, and when the process invokes **quit**, to

```
procedure createSem(initial value, int *name) {
    get an empty semaphore descriptor;
    initialize the descriptor;
    set name to the name (index) of the descriptor;
    dispatcher();
}
procedure Psem(name) {
    find semaphore descriptor of name;
    if (value > 0)
        value = value - 1;
    else {
        insert descriptor of executing at end of blocked list;
        executing = 0;      # indicate executing is blocked
    }
    dispatcher();
}
procedure Vsem(name) {
    find semaphore descriptor of name;
    if (blocked list empty)
        value = value + 1;
    else {
        remove process descriptor from front of blocked list;
        insert the descriptor at end of ready list;
    }
    dispatcher();
}
```

Figure 6.5   Semaphore primitives for a single-processor kernel.

destroy the semaphores it created. With either approach, it is imperative that a semaphore not be used after it has been destroyed. Detecting misuse requires that each descriptor have a unique name that is validated each time `Psem` or `Vsem` is called. This can be implemented by letting the name of a descriptor be a combination of an index—which is used to locate the descriptor—and a unique sequence number.

We can extend the single-processor implementation of the semaphore primitives in Figure 6.5 into one for a multiprocessor in the same way as described in Section 6.2 and shown in Figure 6.4. Again, the critical requirement is to lock shared data structures, but only for as long as absolutely required. Hence, there should be a separate lock for each semaphore descriptor. A semaphore descriptor is locked in `Psem` and `Vsem` just before it is accessed; the lock is released as soon as the descriptor is no longer needed. Locks are again acquired and released by means of a busy-waiting solution to the critical section problem.

The issues that were discussed at the end of Section 6.2 also arise in a multiprocessor kernel that implements semaphores. In particular, a process might need to execute on a specific processor, it may be important to execute a process on the same processor that it last executed on, or it may be important to co-schedule processes on the same processor. To support this functionality—or to avoid contention for a shared ready list—each processor might well have its own ready list. In this case, when a process is awakened in the `Vsem` primitive, the process needs to be put on the appropriate ready list. Thus either the `Vsem` primitive needs to lock a possibly remote ready list, or it needs to inform another processor and let that processor put the unblocked process on its ready list. The first approach requires remote locking; the second requires using something like interprocessor interrupts to send a message from one processor to another.

6.4 *Implementing Monitors in a Kernel*

Monitors can also be readily implemented in a kernel; this section shows how to do so. They can also be simulated using semaphores; we show how to do that in the next section. The locks and condition variables in a library such as Pthreads or a language such as Java are also implemented in a manner similar to the kernel described here.

We assume the monitor semantics defined in Chapter 5. In particular, procedures execute with mutual exclusion, and condition synchronization uses the Signal and Continue discipline. We also assume that a monitor's permanent variables are stored in memory accessible to all processes that call the monitor's procedures. Code that implements the procedures can be stored in shared memory, or copies of the code can be stored in local memory on each processor that executes processes that use the monitor. Finally, we assume the permanent variables are initialized before the procedures are called. This can be accomplished by, for example, allocating and initializing permanent variables before creating any processes that will access them. (Alternatively, initialization code could be executed on the first call of a monitor procedure. However, this is less efficient since every call would have to check to see if it were the first.)

To implement monitors, we need to add primitives to our kernel for monitor entry, monitor exit, and each of the operations on condition variables. Primitives are also needed to create descriptors for each monitor and each condition variable (unless these are created when the kernel itself is initialized); these are not shown here, because they are analogous to the `createSem` primitive in Figure 6.5.

Each monitor descriptor `mName` contains a lock `mLock` and an entry queue of descriptors of processes waiting to enter (or reenter) the monitor. The lock is used to ensure mutual exclusion. When the lock is set, exactly one process is executing in the monitor; otherwise, no process is executing in the monitor.

The descriptor for a condition variable contains the head of a queue of descriptors of processes waiting on that condition variable. Thus every process descriptor—except perhaps those of executing processes—is linked to either the ready list, a monitor entry queue, or a condition variable queue. Condition variable descriptors are commonly stored adjacent to the descriptor of the monitor in which the condition variables are declared. This is done to avoid excessive fragmentation of kernel storage and to allow the run-time identity of a condition variable simply to be an offset from the start of the appropriate monitor descriptor.

The monitor entry primitive `enter(mName)` finds the descriptor for monitor `mName`, then either sets the monitor lock and allows the executing process to proceed or blocks the process on the monitor entry queue. To enable the descriptor to be found quickly, the run-time identity of `mName` is typically the address of the monitor descriptor. The monitor exit primitive `exit(mName)` either moves one process from the entry queue to the ready list or clears the monitor lock.

The `wait(cv)` statement is implemented by invoking the kernel primitive `wait(mName,cName)`, and the `signal(cv)` statement is implemented by invoking the kernel primitive `signal(mName,cName)`. In both primitives, `mName` is the "name" of the monitor within which the primitive is invoked—this could either be the index or address of the monitor's descriptor—and `cName` is the index or address of the descriptor of the appropriate condition variable. Execution of `wait` delays the executing process on the specified condition variable queue and then either awakens some process on the monitor entry queue or clears the monitor lock. Execution of `signal` checks the condition variable queue. If it is empty, the primitive simply returns; otherwise, the descriptor at the front of the condition variable queue is moved to the end of the monitor entry queue.

Figure 6.6 gives code outlines for these primitives. As in previous kernels, the primitives are entered as a result of a supervisor call, `executing` points to the descriptor of the executing process, and `executing` is set to `0` when the executing process blocks. Since a process that calls `wait` exits the monitor, the `wait` primitive simply calls the `exit` primitive after blocking the executing process. The last action of the `enter`, `exit`, and `signal` primitives is to call the dispatcher.

It is straightforward to implement the other operations on condition variables. For example, implementing `empty(cv)` merely involves testing whether `cv`'s delay queue is empty. In fact, if the delay queue is directly accessible to processes, it is not necessary to use a kernel primitive to implement `empty`. This is because the executing process already has the monitor locked, so the contents

```
procedure enter(int mName) {
   find descriptor for monitor mName;
   if (mLock == 1) {
      insert descriptor of executing at end of entry queue;
      executing = 0;
   }
   else
      mLock = 1;      # acquire exclusive access to mName
   dispatcher();
}

procedure exit(int mName) {
   find descriptor for monitor mName;
   if (entry queue not empty)
      move process from front of entry queue to rear of ready list;
   else
      mLock = 0;      # clear the lock
   dispatcher();
}

procedure wait(int mName; int cName) {
   find descriptor for condition variable cName;
   insert descriptor of executing at end of delay queue of cName;
   executing = 0;
   exit(mName);
}

procedure signal(int mName; int cName) {
   find descriptor for monitor mName;
   find descriptor for condition variable cName;
   if (delay queue not empty)
      move process from front of delay queue to rear of entry queue;
   dispatcher();
}
```

Figure 6.6   Monitor kernel primitives.

of the condition queue cannot be changed by another process. By implementing **empty** without locking, we would avoid the overhead of a supervisor call and return.

We can also make the implementation of **signal** more efficient than is shown in Figure 6.6. In particular, we could modify **signal** so that it *always* moves a descriptor from the front of the appropriate delay queue to the end of the appropriate entry queue. Then, **signal** in a program would be translated into code that tests the delay queue and invokes `mSignal` in the kernel only if the delay queue is empty. By making these changes, the overhead of kernel entry and exit is avoided when `signal` has no effect. Independent of how `signal` is implemented, `signal_all` is implemented by a kernel primitive that moves all descriptors from the specified delay queue to the end of the ready list.

Priority `wait` is implemented analogously to nonpriority `wait`. The only difference is that the descriptor of the executing process needs to be inserted at the appropriate place on the delay queue. To keep that queue ordered, the rank of each waiting process needs to be recorded; the logical place to store the rank is in process descriptors. This also makes implementation of `minrank` trivial. In fact, `minrank`—like `empty`—can be implemented without entering the kernel, as long as the minimum rank can be read directly by the executing process.

This kernel can be extended to one for a multiprocessor using the techniques described in Section 6.2. Again, the key requirement is to protect kernel data structures from being accessed simultaneously by processes executing on different processors. And again, one has to worry about avoiding memory contention, exploiting caches, co-scheduling processes, and balancing processor load.

On a single processor, monitors can in some cases be implemented even more efficiently without using a kernel. If there are no nested monitor calls—or if nested calls are all open calls—and all monitor procedures are short and guaranteed to terminate, it is both possible and reasonable to implement mutual exclusion by inhibiting interrupts. This is done as follows. On entry to a monitor, the executing process inhibits all interrupts. When it returns from a monitor procedure, it enables interrupts. If the process has to wait within a monitor, it blocks on a condition variable queue, and the fact that the process was executing with interrupts inhibited is recorded. (This is often encoded in a processor status register that is saved when a process blocks.) When a waiting process is awakened as a result of `signal`, it is moved from the condition variable queue to the ready list; the signaling process continues to execute. Finally, whenever a ready process is dispatched, it resumes execution with interrupts inhibited or enabled, depending on whether interrupts were inhibited or enabled at the time the process blocked. (Newly created processes begin execution with interrupts enabled.)

This implementation does away with kernel primitives—they become either in-line code or regular subroutines—and it does away with monitor descriptors. Since interrupts are inhibited while a process is executing in a monitor, it cannot be forced to relinquish the processor. Thus the process has exclusive access to the monitor until it waits or returns. Assuming monitor procedures terminate, eventually the process will wait or return. If the process waits, when it is awakened and resumes execution, interrupts are again inhibited. Consequently, the process again has exclusive control of the monitor in which it waited. Nested monitor calls cannot be allowed, however. If they were, another process might start executing in the monitor from which the nested call was made while a process is waiting in a second monitor.

Monitors are implemented in essentially this way in the UNIX operating system. In fact, on entry to a monitor procedure in UNIX, interrupts are inhibited only from those devices that could cause some other process to call the same monitor before the interrupted process waits or returns from the monitor. In general, however, a kernel implementation is needed since not all monitor-based programs meet the requirements for this specialized implementation. In particular, only in a "trusted" program such as an operating system is it likely that all monitor procedures can be guaranteed to terminate. Also, the specialized implementation only works on a single processor. On a multiprocessor, locks of some form are still required to ensure mutual exclusion of processes executing on different processors.

6.5 *Implementing Monitors Using Semaphores*

The previous section showed how to implement monitors using a kernel. Here we show how to implement them using semaphores. The reasons for doing so are that (1) a software library might support semaphores but not monitors, or (2) a language might provide semaphores but not monitors. In any event, the solution illustrates another example of the use of semaphores.

Again we assume the monitor semantics defined in Section 5.1. Hence, our concerns are implementing mutual exclusion of monitor procedures and condition synchronization between monitor procedures. In particular, we need to develop (1) entry code that is executed after a process calls a monitor procedure but before the process begins executing the procedure body, (2) exit code that is executed just before a process returns from a procedure body, and (3) code that implements `wait`, `signal` and the other operations on condition variables. For simplicity, we assume there is only one condition variable; the code we develop below can readily be generalized to having more condition variables by using arrays of delay queues and counters.

To implement monitor exclusion, we use one entry semaphore for each monitor. Let `e` be the semaphore associated with monitor `M`. Since `e` is to be used for mutual exclusion, its initial value is `1`, and its value is always `0` or `1`. The purpose of the entry protocol of each procedure in `M` is to acquire exclusive access to `M`; as usual with semaphores, this is implemented by `P(e)`. Similarly, the exit protocol of each procedure releases exclusive access, so it is implemented by `V(e)`.

Execution of `wait(cv)` releases monitor exclusion and delays the executing process on condition variable `cv`. The process resumes execution in the monitor after it has been signaled and after it can regain exclusive control of the monitor. Because a condition variable is essentially a queue of delayed processes, we can assume there is a `queue` data type that implements a FIFO queue of processes and we can use an array `delayQ` of this type. We can also use an integer counter, `nc`, to count the number of delayed processes. Initially `delayQ` is empty and `nc` is zero, because there are no waiting processes.

When a process executes `wait(cv)`, it increments `nc` then adds its descriptor to `delayQ`. The process next releases the monitor lock by executing `V(e)` and then blocks itself on a *private* semaphore, one that only it waits on. After the process is awakened, it waits to reenter the monitor by executing `P(e)`.

When a process executes `signal(cv)`, it first checks `nc` to see if there are any waiting processes. If not, the `signal` has no effect. If there are waiting processes, the signaler decrements `nc`, removes the oldest waiting process from the front of `delayQ`, then signals its private semaphore.[1]

Figure 6.7 contains the code for implementing monitor synchronization using semaphores. Mutual exclusion is ensured since semaphore `e` is initially `1` and every execution path executes alternate `P(e)` and `V(e)` operations. Also, `nc` is positive when at least one process is delayed or is about to delay.

Given the above representation for condition variables, it is straightforward to implement the `empty` primitive. In particular, `empty` returns true if `nc` is zero, and it returns false if `nc` is positive. It is also straightforward to implement `signal_all`: Remove each waiting process from `delayQ` and signal its private semaphore, then set `nc` to zero. To implement priority wait, it is sufficient to make `delayQ` a priority queue ordered by delay ranks. This requires adding a field for the delay rank to each queue element. With this addition, it is trivial to implement `minrank`: just return the delay rank of the process at the front of `delayQ`.

Historical Notes

The `fork`, `join`, and `quit` primitives were introduced by Dennis and Van Horn [1966]. Variants of `fork`, `join`, and `quit` are provided by most operating systems; for example, UNIX [Ritchie & Thompson 1974] provides similar

---

[1] One might think that it would be sufficient to use a semaphore for the delay queue, because a semaphore is essentially a queue of blocked processes. This would obviate the need for an explicit delay queue and an array of private semaphores. However, there is a subtle problem: Although `P` and `V` operations are atomic, sequences of them are not. In particular, a process could be preempted in `wait` after executing `V(e)` and before blocking. Exercise 6.12 explores this problem.

```
shared variables:   sem e = 1;        # one copy per monitor
                    int nc = 0;       # one copy per condition
                    queue delayQ;     #   variable cv
                    sem private[N];   # one entry per process

monitor entry:  P(e);

wait(cv):    nc = nc+1; insert myid on delayQ; V(e);
             P(private[myid]); P(e);

signal(cv):  if (nc > 0) {
                nc = nc-1;
                remove otherid from delayQ;
                V(private[otherid]);
             }

monitor exit:   V(e);
```

Figure 6.7   Implementing monitors using semaphores.

system calls named `fork`, `wait`, and `exit`. Similar primitives have also been included in several programming languages, such as PL/I, Mesa, and Modula-3.

Many operating system texts describe implementations of single-processor kernels. Bic and Shaw [1988] and Holt [1983] contain particularly good descriptions. Those books also describe the other functions an operating system must support—such as a file system and memory management—and how they relate to the kernel. Thompson [1978] describes the implementation of the UNIX kernel; Holt [1983] describes a UNIX-compatible system called Tunis.

Unfortunately, operating systems texts do not describe multiprocessor kernels in any detail. However, an excellent report on experience with some of the early multiprocessors developed at Carnegie-Mellon University appears in a survey paper by Jones and Schwarz [1980]; the Multiprocessor Locking Principle (6.1) comes from that paper. A few multiprocessor operating systems are discussed in Hwang [1993] and Almasi and Gottlieb [1994]. Tucker and Gupta [1989] describe process control and scheduling issues for shared-memory multiprocessors with uniform memory access time. Scott et al. [1990] discuss kernel issues for nonuniform memory access (NUMA) multiprocessors, including the use of multiple ready lists. In general, the proceedings of the following three conferences are excellent sources for much of the best recent work on language and software issues related to multiprocessors: Architectural Support for Programming Languages and Operating Systems (ASPLOS), Symposium on

Operating Systems Principles (SOSP), and Principles and Practice of Parallel Programming (PPoPP).

Several papers and books describe kernel implementations of monitors. Wirth [1977] describes the Modula kernel. Holt et al. [1978] describe both single and multiple processor kernels for CSP/k. Holt [1983] describes kernels for Concurrent Euclid. Joseph et al. [1984] present the design and implementation of a complete operating system for a shared-memory multiprocessor; they use monitors within the operating system and show how to implement them using a kernel. Thompson [1978] and Holt [1983] describe the implementation of UNIX.

The UNIX kernel implements mutual exclusion by performing context switches only when user processes block or exit the kernel and by inhibiting external interrupts at critical points. The UNIX equivalent of a condition variable is called an event—an arbitrary integer that is typically the address of a descriptor such as a process or file descriptor. Within the kernel, a process blocks by executing `sleep(e)`. It is awakened when another process executes `wakeup(e)`. The `wakeup` primitive has Signal and Continue semantics. It is also a broadcast primitive; namely, `wakeup(e)` awakens all processes blocked on event `e`. UNIX has no equivalent of the `signal` primitive to awaken just one process. Thus, if more than one process could be waiting for an event, each has to check if the condition it was waiting for is still true and go back to sleep if it is not.

Hoare's classic paper on monitors [1974] describes how to implement them using semaphores. However, he assumed the Signal and Urgent Wait discipline rather than Signal and Continue or Signal and Wait.

References

Almasi, G. S., and A. Gottlieb. 1994. *Highly Parallel Computing*, 2nd ed. Menlo Park, CA: Benjamin/Cummings.

Bic, L., and A. C. Shaw. 1988. *The Logical Design of Operating Systems*, 2nd ed. Englewood Cliffs, NJ: Prentice-Hall.

Dennis, J. B., and E. C. Van Horn. 1966. Programming semantics for multi-programmed computations. *Comm. ACM* 9, 3 (March): 143–55.

Hoare, C.A.R. 1974. Monitors: An operating system structuring concept. *Comm. ACM* 17, 10 (October): 549–57.

Holt, R. C. 1983. *Concurrent Euclid, The UNIX System, and Tunis*. Reading, MA: Addison-Wesley.

Holt, R. C., G. S. Graham, E. D. Lazowska, and M. A. Scott. 1978. *Structured Concurrent Programming with Operating System Applications*. Reading, MA: Addison-Wesley.

Hwang, K. 1993. *Advanced Computer Architecture: Parallelism, Scalability, Programmability*. New York: McGraw-Hill.

Jones, A. K., and P. Schwarz. 1980. Experience using multiprocessor systems— a status report. *ACM Computing Surveys* 12, 2 (June): 121–65.

Joseph, M., V. R. Prasad, and N. Natarajan. 1984. *A Multiprocessor Operating System*. New York: Prentice-Hall International.

Ritchie, D. M., and K. Thompson. 1974. The UNIX timesharing system. *Comm. ACM* 17, 7 (July): 365–75.

Scott, M. L., T. J. LeBlanc, and B. D. Marsh. 1990. Multi-model parallel programming in Psyche. *Proc. Second ACM Symp. on Principles & Practice of Parallel Prog.*, March, pp. 70–78.

Thompson, K. 1978. UNIX implementation. *The Bell System Technical Journal* 57, 6, part 2 (July-August): 1931–46.

Tucker, A., and A. Gupta. 1989. Process control and scheduling issues for multiprogrammed shared-memory multiprocessors. *Proc. Twelfth ACM Symp. on Operating Systems Principles*, December, pp. 159–66.

Wirth, N. 1977. Design and implementation of Modula. *Software—Practice and Experience* 7, 67–84.

Exercises

6.1 In the multiprocessor kernel described in Section 6.2, a processor executes the `Idle` process when it finds the ready list empty (Figure 6.3). On some machines, there is a bit in the processor status word that, if set, causes a processor to do nothing until it is interrupted. Such machines also provide interprocessor interrupts—i.e., one processor can interrupt a second, which causes the second processor to enter a kernel CPU interrupt handler.

Modify the multiprocessor kernel in Figure 6.4 so that a processor sets its idle bit if it finds the ready list empty. Hence another processor will need to awaken it when there is a process for it to execute.

6.2 Suppose process dispatching is handled by one master processor. In particular, all the master does is execute a dispatcher process. Other processors execute regular processes and kernel routines.

Design the dispatcher process, and modify the multiprocessor kernel in Figure 6.4 as appropriate. Define any data structures you need. Remember that an idle processor must not block inside the kernel since that prevents other processors from entering the kernel.

6.3   In a multiprocessor system, assume each processor has its own ready list and that it executes only those processes on its ready list. As discussed in the text, this raises the issue of load balancing since a new process has to be assigned to some processor.

There are numerous load-balancing schemes—e.g., assign to a random processor, assign to a "neighbor," or keep ready lists roughly equal in length. Pick some scheme, justify your choice, and modify the multiprocessor kernel in Figure 6.4 to use multiple ready lists and the load-balancing scheme you choose. Also show how to handle idle processors. Try to minimize overhead due to extra code or lock contention. (For example, if each processor is the only one that accesses its own ready list, ready lists do not need to be locked.)

6.4   Modify the multiprocessor kernel in Figure 6.4 so that a process is generally executed by the same processor that executed it last. However, your solution should avoid starving processes; i.e., every process should periodically get a chance to execute. Also consider what to do about idle processors. Define any data structures you need. Explain the rationale for your solution.

6.5   Add an additional primitive, `multifork(initialState[*])`, to the multiprocessor kernel (Figure 6.4). The argument is an array of initial process states. Execution of `multifork` creates one process for each argument and specifies that all of the newly created processes are to be co-scheduled on the same processor—for example, because the processes share cached data.

Modify the other parts of the kernel as needed to implement co-scheduling. Your solution should avoid starving processes—i.e., every process should periodically get a chance to execute. Also consider what to do about idle processors.

6.6   The semaphore primitives in Figure 6.5 and the monitor primitives in Figure 6.6 are assumed to be part of the single processor kernel in Figure 6.2. Modify the primitives so that they can be added to the multiprocessor kernel in Figure 6.4. Identify what needs to change and then make the changes.

6.7   Suppose input and output on a terminal are supported by two procedures:

```
char getc()
putc(char ch)
```

An application process calls `getc` to receive the next input character; it calls `putc` to send a character to the display. Assume both input and output are buffered—i.e., up to **n** input characters can be stored waiting to be retrieved by `getc`, and up to **n** output characters can be stored waiting to be printed.

(a) Develop implementations of `getc` and `putc`, assuming that they are procedures that execute outside of the kernel. These procedures should use semaphores for synchronization. Define any additional processes you need, and show the actions the kernel should take when an input or output interrupt occurs. Use a `startread` primitive to initiate reading from the keyboard, and use `startwrite` to initiate writing to the display.

(b) Develop implementations of `getc` and `putc`, assuming that they are kernel primitives. Again, specify the actions the kernel should take when an input or output interrupt occurs, use `startread` to initiate reading from the keyboard, and use `startwrite` to initiate writing to the display.

(c) Analyze and compare the efficiency of your answers to (a) and (b). Consider factors such as the number of statements that get executed in each case, the number of context switches, and the length of time the kernel is locked.

(d) Extend your answer to (a) to support echoing of input characters. In particular, each character that is input from the keyboard should automatically be written to the display.

(e) Extend your answer to (b) to support echoing of input characters.

6.8 Suppose input and output on a terminal are supported by two procedures:

```
int getline(string *str)
putline(string *str)
```

An application process calls `getline` to read input lines; `getline` delays until there is another line of input, stores the line in `str`, and returns the number of characters in the line. An application process calls `putline` to print the line in `str` on the display. A line contains at most MAXLINE characters, and it is terminated by a newline character, which is not part of the line itself.

Assume both input and output are buffered—i.e., up to **n** input lines can be stored waiting to be retrieved by `getline`, and up to **n** output lines can be stored waiting to be printed. Also assume that input lines are echoed to the display—i.e., each complete input line is also sent to the display. Finally, assume that input lines are "cooked"—i.e., backspace and line-kill characters are processed by `getline` and do not get returned to the application process.

(a) Develop implementations of `getline` and `putline`, assuming that they are procedures that execute outside of the kernel. These procedures should use semaphores for synchronization. Define any additional processes you need, and show the actions the kernel should take when an input or output interrupt occurs. Use a `startread` primitive to initiate reading from the keyboard, and use `startwrite` to initiate writing to the display.

(b) Develop implementations of `getline` and `putline`, assuming that they are kernel primitives. Again, specify the actions the kernel should take when an input or output interrupt occurs, use `startread` to initiate reading from the keyboard, and use `startwrite` to initiate writing to the display.

6.9   Some machines provide instructions that implement the `P` and `V` operations on semaphores. These instructions manipulate the value of the semaphore, then trap into the kernel if a process needs to be blocked or awakened. Design implementations for these machine instructions, and give the kernel code for the associated interrupt handlers. (*Hint:* Let the value of the semaphore become negative; if a semaphore is negative, its absolute value indicates the number of blocked processes.)

6.10 Figure 6.6 gives kernel primitives that implement monitor entry, monitor exit, `wait`, and `signal` for the Signal and Continue discipline.

(a) Modify the primitives to use the Signal and Wait discipline.

(b) Modify the primitives to use the Signal and Urgent Wait discipline.

6.11 Figure 6.7 shows how to use semaphores to implement monitor entry, monitor exit, `wait`, and `signal` for the Signal and Continue discipline.

(a) Modify the implementation for the Signal and Wait discipline.

(b) Modify the implementation for the Signal and Urgent Wait discipline.

6.12 Figure 6.7 shows how to use semaphores to implement monitor entry, monitor exit, `wait`, and `signal` for the Signal and Continue discipline. One would think that we could simplify the implementation by using a semaphore `c` for the delay queue, as follows:

```
shared variables:   sem e = 1, c = 0; int nc = 0;
monitor entry:   P(e);
wait(cv):    nc = nc+1; V(e); P(c); P(e);
signal(cv):   if (nc > 0) { nc = nc-1; V(c); }
monitor exit:   V(e);
```

Unfortunately, this simpler implementation is incorrect. The problem occurs if a process is preempted in `wait(cv)` after `V(e)` and before `P(c)`. Explain clearly what can go wrong and construct an example to illustrate the problem. (*Hint:* It is possible for one process to miss a signal and for another to incorrectly see two signals; this can lead to a deadlock that should not occur.)

Part 2

Distributed Programming

The synchronization constructs we have examined so far are based on reading and writing shared variables. Consequently, they are most commonly used in concurrent programs that execute on hardware in which processors share memory.

Distributed-memory architectures are now common. These include distributed-memory multicomputers as well as networks of machines, as described in Section 1.2. In addition, hybrid combinations of shared-memory and network architectures are sometimes employed, such as a network containing workstations and multiprocessors. In a distributed architecture, processors have their own private memory and they interact using a communication network rather than a shared memory. Hence, processes cannot communicate directly by sharing variables. Instead, they have to exchange *messages* with each other.

To write programs for a distributed-memory architecture, it is first necessary to define the interfaces with the communication network. These could simply be read and write operations analogous to read and write operations on shared variables. However, this would mean that programs would have to employ busy-waiting synchronization. A better approach is to define special network operations that include synchronization, much as semaphore operations are special operations on shared variables. Such network operations are called *message-passing primitives*. In fact, message passing can be viewed as extending semaphores to convey data as well as to provide synchronization. With message passing, processes share *channels*. Each channel provides a communication path between processes and hence is an abstraction of a communication network that provides a physical path between processors.

Concurrent programs that employ message passing are called *distributed programs*, because the processes may be distributed across the processors of a distributed-memory architecture. A distributed program can, however, be executed on a shared-memory multiprocessor, just as any concurrent program can be executed on a single, multiplexed processor. In this case, channels are implemented using shared memory instead of a communication network.

In a distributed program, channels are typically the only objects processes share. Thus each variable is local to one process, its *caretaker*. This implies that variables are never subject to concurrent access and therefore that no special mechanism for mutual exclusion is required. This also implies that processes must communicate in order to interact. Hence our main concern in Part 2 is synchronizing interprocess communication. How this is done depends on the pattern of process interaction: producers and consumers, clients and servers, or interacting peers (see Section 1.3).

Several different mechanisms for distributed programming have been proposed. These vary in the way channels are named and used and the way communication is synchronized. For example, channels can provide one-way or two-way information flow, and communication can be asynchronous (nonblocking) or synchronous (blocking). In Part 2, we describe the four combinations: asynchronous message passing, synchronous message passing, remote procedure call (RPC), and rendezvous. All four mechanisms are equivalent in the sense that a program written using one set of primitives can be rewritten using any of the others. However, as we shall see, message passing is best for programming producers and consumers and interacting peers, whereas RPC and rendezvous are best for programming clients and servers.

The figure below illustrates how the four distributed programming mechanisms are related to each other as well as to the mechanisms using shared variables described in Part 1. In particular, semaphores are an outgrowth of busy waiting; monitors combine implicit exclusion with the explicit signaling of semaphores; message passing extends semaphores with data; and RPC and rendezvous combine the procedural interface of monitors with implicit message passing.

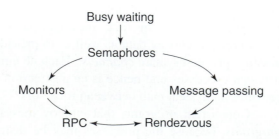

Chapter 7 examines *message passing*, in which communication channels provide a one-way path from a sending to a receiving process. Channels are FIFO queues of pending messages. They are accessed by means of two primitives: `send` and `receive`. To initiate a communication, a process sends a message to a channel; another process acquires the message by receiving from the channel. Sending a message can be asynchronous (nonblocking) or synchronous (blocking); receiving a message is invariably blocking, as that makes programming easier and more efficient. In Chapter 7, we first define asynchronous message passing primitives and then present a number of examples that show how to use them. We also describe the duality between monitors and message passing: They are equivalent and each can directly be converted to the other. Section 7.5 explains synchronous message passing. The last four sections give case studies of the CSP programming notation, the Linda primitives, the MPI library, and the Java network package.

Chapter 8 examines *remote operations* and the two ways in which they can be realized: remote procedure call (RPC) and rendezvous. Remote operations combine aspects of monitors and synchronous message passing. As with monitors, a module or process exports operations, and the operations are invoked by a `call` statement. As with synchronous message passing, execution of `call` is synchronous—the calling process delays until the invocation has been serviced and any results have been returned. An operation is thus a two-way communication channel, from the caller to the process that services the invocation and then back to the caller. An invocation is serviced in one of two ways. One approach is to create a new process. This is called *remote procedure call* (*RPC*) since the servicing process is declared as a procedure and it might execute on a different processor than the calling process. The second approach is to *rendezvous* with an existing process. A rendezvous is serviced by means of an input (or accept) statement that waits for an invocation, processes it, then returns results. Three case studies illustrate these mechanisms: Java's remote method invocation package (RPC), the Ada programming language (rendezvous), and the SR programming language (multiple primitives, including RPC and rendezvous).

Chapter 9 describes several paradigms for process interaction in distributed programs. Each is an instance of a communication pattern that arises in numerous applications. The first three paradigms are commonly used to implement parallel computations on distributed-memory machines: managers/workers (distributed bag of tasks), heartbeat, and pipeline. The other four paradigms are used to coordinate the activities of a distributed collection of processes: probe/echo, broadcast, token passing, and decentralized servers.

Chapter 10 describes implementations of message-passing primitives. First, we show how to implement channels and message passing, then we show how to implement RPC and rendezvous. When writing a program for a shared-memory machine, we usually employ the techniques described in Part 1 of this book. When writing a program for a distributed-memory machine, we usually employ message passing, RPC, or rendezvous. However, it is also possible to mix and match: shared variables can be used on distributed-memory machines, and message passing can be used on shared-memory machines. Section 10.4 describes how to implement a *distributed share memory* (DSM), which provides a shared-memory programming model on a distributed-memory machine.

7

Message Passing

As noted, message passing can be asynchronous or synchronous. Asynchronous message passing—the more commonly used mechanism—will be the focus of this chapter. With asynchronous message passing, channels are like semaphores that carry data, and the `send` and `receive` primitives are like the `V` and `P` operations, respectively. In fact, if a channel contains only null messages—messages without any data—then `send` and `receive` are exactly like `V` and `P`, with the number of queued "messages" being the value of the semaphore.

Section 7.1 defines the asynchronous message-passing primitives, and Section 7.2 shows how to use them to program filters. Section 7.3 considers a variety of client/server applications, including resource allocation, disk scheduling, and file servers. These applications show the duality between monitors and message passing; they also illustrate how to program what is called *conversational continuity*, in which a client continues to interact with a server (as in a Web application). Section 7.4 gives an example of interacting peers and illustrates three common communication patterns: centralized, symmetric, and ring. Section 7.5 describes synchronous message passing and the tradeoffs between it and asynchronous message passing.

The last four sections of the chapter give case studies of three languages and a subroutine library: (1) CSP (Communicating Sequential Processes), which introduces synchronous message passing and what is called guarded communication; (2) Linda, which provides a unique combination of a shared, associative memory (tuple space) and six message-like primitives; (3) MPI, a commonly used library that provides a variety of process-to-process and global communication primitives; and (4) Java's network package, which shows how to use sockets to program a simple file server.

7.1 Asynchronous Message Passing

Many different notations have been proposed for asynchronous message passing. Here, we employ one that is representative and also simple.

With asynchronous message passing, a channel is a queue of messages that have been sent but not yet received. A channel declaration has the form

```
chan ch(type₁ id₁, ..., typeₙ idₙ);
```

Identifier `ch` is the channel's name. The $type_i$ and id_i are the types and names of the data fields in messages transmitted via the channel. The types are required, but the field names are optional; we will use them when it is helpful to document what each field represents. As examples, the following declares two channels:

```
chan input(char);
chan disk_access(int cylinder, int block,
                 int count, char* buffer;)
```

The first channel, `input`, is used to transmit single-character messages. The second channel, `disk_access`, contains messages having four fields, with the field names indicating their roles. In many examples we will employ arrays of channels, as in

```
chan result[n](int);
```

The indices range from `0` to `n-1` unless we declare another range.

A process sends a message to channel `ch` by executing

```
send ch(expr₁, ..., exprₙ);
```

The $expr_i$ are expressions whose types must be the same as those of the corresponding fields in the declaration of `ch`. The effect of executing `send` is to evaluate the expressions, then to append a message containing these values to the end of the queue associated with channel `ch`. Because this queue is unbounded (at least conceptually), execution of `send` never causes delay; hence `send` is a *nonblocking* primitive.

A process receives a message from channel `ch` by executing

```
receive ch(var₁, ..., varₙ);
```

The var_i are variables whose types must be the same as those of the corresponding fields in the declaration of `ch`. The effect of executing `receive` is to delay the receiver until there is at least one message on the channel's queue. Then the message at the front of the queue is removed, and its fields are assigned to the

var_i. Thus, `receive` is a *blocking* primitive since it might cause delay. The `receive` primitive has blocking semantics so the receiving process does not have to use busy-waiting to poll the channel if it has nothing else to do until a message arrives.

We assume that access to the contents of each channel is atomic and that message delivery is reliable and error-free. Thus, every message that is sent to a channel is eventually delivered, and messages are not corrupted. Because each channel is also a first-in/first-out queue, messages will be received in the order in which they were appended to a channel. Hence, if a process sends a message to a channel and later sends a second message to the same channel, the two messages will be received in the order in which they were sent.

As a simple example, Figure 7.1 contains a filter process that receives a stream of characters from channel `input`, assembles the characters into lines, and sends the resulting lines to channel `output`. The carriage-return character `CR` indicates the end of a line; a line contains at most `MAXLINE` characters; a special value `EOL` is appended to the output to indicate the end of the line. (`CR`, `MAXLINE`, and `EOL` are symbolic constants.)

Channels will be declared global to processes, as in Figure 7.1, since they are shared by processes. Any process may send to or receive from any channel. When channels are used in this way they are sometimes called *mailboxes*. However, in many examples we will consider, each channel will have exactly one

```
chan input(char), output(char [MAXLINE]);

process Char_to_Line {
  char line[MAXLINE]; int i = 0;
  while (true) {
    receive input(line[i]);
    while (line[i] != CR and i < MAXLINE) {
      # line[0:i-1] contains the last i input characters
      i = i+1;
      receive input(line[i]);
    }
    line[i] = EOL;
    send output(line);
    i = 0;
  }
}
```

Figure 7.1   Filter process to assemble lines of characters.

receiver, although it may have many senders. In this case, a channel is often called an *input port* since it provides a window (porthole) into the receiving process. If a channel has just one sender and one receiver, it is often called a *link* since it provides a direct path from the sending to the receiving process.

Usually a process will want to delay when it executes `receive`, but not always. For example, the process might have other useful work to do if a message is not yet available for receipt. Or, a process such as a scheduler may need to examine all queued messages in order to select the best one to service next (e.g., the disk scheduler in Section 7.3). To determine whether a channel's queue is currently empty, a process can call the Boolean-valued function

```
empty(ch)
```

This function is true if channel `ch` contains no messages; otherwise, it is false. Unlike what happens with the corresponding primitive on monitor condition variables, if a process calls `empty` and gets back true, there may in fact be queued messages by the time the process continues execution. Moreover, if a process calls `empty` and gets back false, there may not be any queued messages when the process tries to receive one. (This second situation cannot happen if the process is the only one to receive from the channel.) Although `empty` is a useful primitive, one needs to be careful when using it.

7.2 Filters: A Sorting Network

A *filter* is a process that receives messages from one or more input channels and sends messages to one or more output channels. The output of a filter is a function of its input and its initial state. Hence, an appropriate specification for a filter is a predicate that relates the value of messages sent on output channels to the values of messages received on input channels. The actions the filter takes in response to receiving input must ensure this relation every time the filter sends output.

To illustrate how filters are developed and programmed, consider the problem of sorting a list of **n** numbers into ascending order. The most direct way to solve the problem is to write a single filter process, `Sort`, that receives the input from one channel, employs one of the standard sorting algorithms, then writes the result to another channel. Let `input` be the input channel, and let `output` be the output channel. Assume that the **n** values to be sorted are sent to `input` by some unspecified process. Then the goal of the sorting process is to ensure that the values sent to `output` are ordered and are a permutation of the values received from `input`. Let `sent[i]` indicate the `i`'th value sent to `output`. Thus the goal can be specified by the following predicate:

> *SORT*: $(\forall$ `i: 1 <= i < n: sent[i] <= sent[i+1])` $\wedge$
> values sent to `output` are a permutation of values from `input`

An outline of the `Sort` process is

```
process Sort {
    receive all numbers from channel input;
    sort the numbers;
    send the sorted numbers to channel output;
}
```

Since `receive` is a blocking primitive, a practical concern is for `Sort` to determine when it has received all the numbers. One solution is for `Sort` to know the value of `n` in advance. A more general solution is for `n` to be the first input value and for the numbers themselves to be the next `n` input values. An even more general solution is to end the input stream with a *sentinel* value, which is a special value that indicates that all numbers have been received. The latter solution is the most general since the process producing the input does not itself need to know in advance how many values it will produce.

If processes are "heavyweight" objects, as they are in most operating systems, then the approach used above in `Sort` would be the most efficient way to solve the sorting problem. However, a different approach—which is amenable to direct implementation in hardware—is to employ a network of small processes that execute in parallel and interact to solve the problem. (A hybrid approach would be to employ a network of medium-sized processes.) There are many kinds of sorting networks, just as there are many different internal sorting algorithms. Here we present a *merge network*.

The idea behind a merge network is repeatedly—and in parallel—to merge two sorted lists into a longer sorted list. The network is constructed out of `Merge` filters. Each `Merge` filter receives values from two ordered input streams `in1` and `in2` and produces one ordered output stream `out`. Assume that the ends of the input streams are marked by a sentinel `EOS` as discussed above. Also assume that `Merge` appends `EOS` to the end of the output stream. If there are `n` input values, not counting the sentinels, then the following should be true when `Merge` terminates:

> *MERGE*: `in1` and `in2` are empty $\wedge$ `sent[n+1]` `==` `EOS` $\wedge$
> $(\forall$ `i: 1 <= i < n: sent[i] <= sent[i+1])` $\wedge$
> values sent to `out` are a permutation of values from `in1` and `in2`

The first line of *MERGE* says all input has been consumed and `EOS` has been appended to the end of `out`; the second line says the output is ordered; the last two lines say that the output is a permutation of the input.

One way to implement `Merge` is to receive all input values, merge them, then send the merged list to `out`. However, this requires storing all input values. Since the input streams are ordered, a better way to implement `Merge` is repeatedly to compare the next two values received from `in1` and `in2` and to send the smaller to `out`. Let `v1` and `v2` be these values. This leads to the filter process shown in Figure 7.2.

To form a sorting network, we can employ a collection of `Merge` processes and arrays of input and output channels. Assuming that the number of input values `n` is a power of 2, the processes and channels are connected so that the

```
chan in1(int), in2(int), out(int);

process Merge {
  int v1, v2;
  receive in1(v1);  # get first two input values
  receive in2(v2);
  # send smaller value to output channel and repeat
  while (v1 != EOS and v2 != EOS) {
    if (v1 <= v2)
      { send out(v1); receive in1(v1); }
    else    # (v2 < v1)
      { send out(v2); receive in2(v2); }
  }
  # consume the rest of the non-empty input channel
  if (v1 == EOS)
    while (v2 != EOS)
      { send out(v2); receive in2(v2); }
  else    # (v2 == EOS)
    while (v1 != EOS)
      { send out(v1); receive in1(v1); }
  # append a sentinel to the output channel
  send out(EOS);
}
```

Figure 7.2   A filter process that merges two input streams.

resulting communication pattern forms a tree, as depicted in Figure 7.3. Information in the sorting network flows from left to right. Each node at the left is given two input values, which it merges to form a stream of two sorted values. The next nodes form streams of four sorted values, and so on. The rightmost node produces the final sorted stream. The sorting network contains **n-1** processes; the width of the network is log_2 **n**.

To realize the sorting network in Figure 7.3, the input and output channels need to be shared. In particular, the output channel used by one instance of **Merge** needs to be the same as one of the input channels used by the next instance of **Merge** in the graph. This can be programmed in one of two ways. The first approach is to use *static naming*: declare all channels to be a global array, and have each instance of **Merge** receive from two elements of the array and send to one other element. This requires embedding the tree in an array so that the channels accessed by **Merge**$_i$ are a function of **i**. The second approach is to use *dynamic naming*: declare all channels to be global as above, parameterize the processes, and give each process three channels when it is created. This makes the programming of the **Merge** processes easier since each is textually identical. However, it requires having a main process that dynamically creates the channels and then passes them as parameters to the various **Merge** processes.

A key attribute of filters like **Merge** is that we can interconnect them in different ways. All that is required is that the output produced by one filter meet the input assumptions of another filter. An important consequence of this attribute is that as long as the externally observable input and output behaviors are the same, we can replace one filter process—or a network of filters—by a different process or network. For example, we can replace the single **Sort** process described

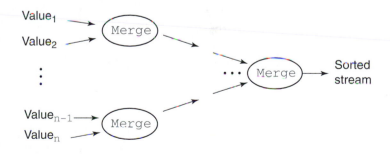

Figure 7.3 A sorting network of **Merge** processes.

earlier by a network of **Merge** processes plus a process (or network) that distributes the input values to the merge network.

Networks of filters can be used to solve a variety of parallel programming problems. For example, Section 7.6 examines prime number generation, and Section 9.3 examines distributed matrix multiplication. The exercises describe additional applications.

7.3 Clients and Servers

Recall that a server is a process that repeatedly handles requests from client processes. This section shows how to use asynchronous message passing to program servers and their clients. The first examples show how to turn monitors into servers and how to implement resource managers. These examples also point out the *duality* between monitors and message passing: each can directly simulate the other.

We then show how to implement a self-scheduling disk driver and a file server. The self-scheduling disk driver illustrates a third way to structure a solution to the disk-scheduling problem introduced in Section 5.3. The file server illustrates an important programming technique called *conversational continuity*. Both examples also illustrate program structures that are directly supported by message passing, in the sense that they yield solutions that are more compact than is possible using any of the synchronization mechanisms based on shared variables.

7.3.1 Active Monitors

A monitor is a resource manager. It encapsulates permanent variables that record the state of the resource, and it provides a set of procedures that are called to access the resource. Moreover, the procedures execute with mutual exclusion and use condition variables for condition synchronization. Here we show how to simulate these attributes using server processes and message passing. In short, we show how to program monitors as active processes rather than as passive collections of procedures.

Assume for now that a monitor has just one operation **op** and that it does not employ condition variables. The structure of the monitor is thus

```
monitor Mname {
    declarations of permanent variables;
    initialization code;
```

```
procedure op(formals) {
    body of op;
  }
}
```

Assume that *MI* is the monitor invariant—namely, a predicate that specifies the state of the permanent variables when no call is active.

To simulate `Mname` using message passing, we employ one server process `Server`. The permanent variables of `Mname` become `Server`'s local variables; `Server` is thus the caretaker for those variables. The server first initializes the variables, then executes a permanent loop in which it repeatedly services "calls" of `op`. A call is simulated by having a client process send a message to a request channel, then receive the result from a reply channel. Thus, the server repeatedly receives from the request channel and sends results to reply channels. The formal parameters in `Mname` become additional variables local to `Server`. To avoid having one client see the result intended for another, each client needs its own private result channel. If the result channels are declared as a global array, a client thus needs to pass the index of its private element of the result array to the server as part of the request message. (Some message-passing primitives allow a receiving process to determine the identity of the sender.)

Figure 7.4 gives outlines for the server and its clients. Monitor invariant *MI* becomes the loop invariant of the `Server` process. It is true after the initialization code is executed and before and after each request is serviced. In particular, *MI* is true at all points at which `Server` communicates with client processes. As shown in Figure 7.4, a client immediately waits for a reply after sending a request. However, the client could execute other actions before waiting if it has other work it could productively do. This is not often the case, but it is possible since a call is simulated by two distinct statements: `send` and then `receive`.

The program in Figure 7.4 employs static naming since channels are global to the processes and hence can be referenced directly. Consequently, each process must be coded carefully so that it uses the correct channels. For example, `Client[i]` must not use the reply channel of some other `Client[j]`. Alternatively, we could employ dynamic naming by having each client create a private reply channel, which it then passes to `Server` as the first field of `request` in place of the integer index. This would ensure that clients could not access each other's reply channels. It would also permit the number of clients to vary dynamically. (In Figure 7.4, there is a fixed number `n` of clients.)

In general, a monitor has multiple procedures. To extend Figure 7.4 to handle this case, a client needs to indicate which operation it is calling. This is done by including an additional argument in request messages; the type of this

```
chan request(int clientID, types of input values);
chan reply[n](types of results);

process Server {
    int clientID;
    declarations of other permanent variables;
    initialization code;
    while (true) {    ## loop invariant MI
        receive request(clientID, input values);
        code from body of operation op;
        send reply[clientID](results);
    }
process Client[i = 0 to n-1] {
    send request(i, value arguments);      # "call" op
    receive reply[i](result arguments);    # wait for reply
}
```

Figure 7.4   Clients and server with one operation.

argument is an enumeration type with one enumeration literal for each kind of operation. Since different operations will no doubt have different value and result formals, we also need to distinguish between them. This can be programmed using a variant record or a union type. (Alternatively, we could make the argument parts of request and reply messages strings of bytes, and let clients and the server encode and decode these.)

Figure 7.5 gives outlines for clients and a server with multiple operations. The **if** statement in the server is like a case statement, with one branch for each different kind of operation. The body of each operation retrieves arguments from **args** and places result values in **results**. After the **if** statement terminates, **Server** sends these results to the appropriate client.

So far we have assumed that **Mname** does not employ condition variables. Hence, **Server** never needs to delay while servicing a request since the body of each operation will be a sequence of sequential statements. We now show how to handle the general case of a monitor that has multiple operations and that uses condition synchronization. (The clients do not change since they still just "call" an operation by sending a request and later receiving a reply; the fact that a request might not be serviced immediately is transparent.)

To see how to translate a monitor with condition variables into a server process, we begin by considering a specific example and then describe how to generalize the example. In particular, consider the problem of managing a multiple

```
type op_kind = enum(op₁, ..., opₙ);
type arg_type = union(arg₁, ..., argₙ);
type result_type = union(res₁, ..., resₙ);

chan request(int clientID, op_kind, arg_type);
chan reply[n](res_type);

process Server {
  int clientID; op_kind kind; arg_type args;
  res_type results;  declarations of other variables;
  initialization code;
  while (true) {      ## loop invariant MI
    receive request(clientID, kind, args);
    if (kind == op₁)
      { body of op₁; }
    ...
    else if (kind == opₙ)
      { body of opₙ; }
    send reply[clientID](results);
  }
}

process Client[i = 0 to n-1] {
  arg_type myargs; result_type myresults;
  place value arguments in myargs;
  send request(i, opⱼ, myargs);    # "call" opⱼ
  receive reply[i](myresults);      # wait for reply
}
```

Figure 7.5   Clients and server with multiple operations.

unit resource—such as memory or file blocks. Clients acquire units of the resource, use them, and later release them back to the manager. For simplicity, clients acquire and release units one at a time. Figure 7.6 gives a monitor implementation of this resource allocator. We use the method of passing the condition—as described in Section 5.1—since that program structure is most readily translated into a server process. The free units are stored in a set, which is accessed by insert and remove operations.

The resource allocation monitor has two operations, so the equivalent server process will have the general structure shown in Figure 7.5. One key difference is that when no units are available, the server process cannot wait when servicing a request. It must save the request and defer sending a reply. Later, when a unit

```
monitor Resource_Allocator {
  int avail = MAXUNITS;
  set units = initial values;
  cond free;   # signaled when a process wants a unit
  procedure acquire(int &id) {
    if (avail == 0)
      wait(free);
    else
      avail = avail-1;
    remove(units, id);
  }
  procedure release(int id) {
    insert(units, id);
    if (empty(free))
      avail = avail+1;
    else
      signal(free);
  }
}
```

Figure 7.6   Resource allocation monitor.

is released, the server needs to honor one saved request, if there is one, by sending the released unit to the requester.

Figure 7.7 gives an outline for the resource allocation server and its clients.
The server now has nested **if** statements. The outer ones have branches for each
kind of operation, and the inner ones correspond to the **if** statements in the
monitor procedures. After sending a request message, a client waits to receive a
unit. However, after sending a release message, the client does not wait for the
message to be processed since there is no need to.

This example illustrates how to simulate a specific monitor by a server
process. We can use the same basic pattern to simulate any monitor that is programmed using the technique of passing the condition. However, many of the
monitors in Chapter 5 had **wait** statements embedded in loops, or they had
unconditionally executed **signal** statements. To simulate such **wait** statements,
the server would need to save the pending request as in Figure 7.7 and would also
need to record what actions should be taken when the request can be serviced.
To simulate an unconditional **signal** statement, the server needs to check the
queue of pending requests. If it is empty, the server does nothing; if

```
type op_kind = enum(ACQUIRE, RELEASE);
chan request(int clientID, op_kind kind, int unitid);
chan reply[n](int unitID);

process Allocator {
  int avail = MAXUNITS; set units = initial values;
  queue pending;  # initially empty
  int clientID, unitID; op_kind kind;
  declarations of other local variables;
  while (true) {
    receive request(clientID, kind, unitID);
    if (kind == ACQUIRE) {
      if (avail > 0) {  # honor request now
        avail--; remove(units, unitID);
        send reply[clientID](unitID);
      } else    # remember request
        insert(pending, clientID);
    } else {    # kind == RELEASE
      if empty(pending) {  # return unitID to units
        avail++; insert(units, unitid);
      } else {  # allocate unitID to a waiting client
        remove(pending, clientID);
        send reply[clientID](unitID);
      }
    }
  }
}

process Client[i = 0 to n-1] {
  int unitID;
  send request(i, ACQUIRE, 0)     # "call" request
  receive reply[i](unitID);
  # use resource unitID, then release it
  send request(i, RELEASE, unitID);
  ...
}
```

Figure 7.7   Resource allocator and clients.

Monitor-Based Programs	Message-Based Programs
Permanent variables	Local server variables
Procedure identifiers	`request` channel and operation kinds
Procedure call	`send request(); receive reply`
Monitor entry	`receive request()`
Procedure return	`send reply()`
`wait` statement	Save pending request
`signal` statement	Retrieve and process pending request
Procedure bodies	Arms of case statement on operation kind

Table 7.1   Duality between monitors and message passing.

there is a pending request, the server removes one from the queue and processes it *after* processing the operation containing the `signal`. The exact details depend on the monitor being simulated; several exercises explore specific examples.

The `Resource_Allocator` monitor in Figure 7.6 and the `Allocator` server in Figure 7.7 point out the *duality* between monitors and message passing. In particular, there is a direct correspondence between the various mechanisms used in monitor-based programs and those used in message passing programs. Table 7.1 lists the correspondences.

Since the bodies of monitor procedures have direct duals in the arms of the server case statement, the relative performance of monitor-based versus message-based programs depends only on the relative efficiency of the implementation of the different mechanisms. On shared-memory machines, procedure calls and actions on condition variables are more efficient than message-passing primitives. For this reason, most operating systems for such machines are based on a monitor-style implementation. On the other hand, most distributed systems are based on message passing since that is both efficient and the appropriate abstraction. It is also possible to combine aspects of both styles and implementations, as we will see in Chapter 8 when we discuss remote procedure call and rendezvous. In fact, this makes the duality between monitors and message passing even stronger.

7.3.2 A Self-Scheduling Disk Server

In Section 5.3 we considered the problem of scheduling access to a moving head disk. In that section we considered two main solution structures. In the first

(Figure 5.12), the disk scheduler was a monitor separate from the disk. Thus clients first called the scheduler to request access, then used the disk, and finally called the scheduler to release access. In the second structure (Figure 5.14), the scheduler was an intermediary between clients and a disk server process. Thus clients had to call only a single monitor operation. (We also considered a third structure using nested monitors; when reprogrammed to use message passing, that structure is essentially equivalent to using an intermediary.)

We can readily mimic these structures in a message-based program by implementing each monitor as a server process using the techniques from the previous section. However, with message passing an even simpler structure is possible. In particular, we can combine the intermediary and disk driver of Figure 5.14 into a single, self-scheduling server process. (We cannot do this with monitors since we have to use a monitor to implement the communication path between clients and the disk driver.)

Figure 7.8 illustrates these structures for solving the disk-scheduling problem. In all cases, we assume the disk is controlled by a server process that performs all disk accesses. The principal differences between the three structures are the client interface—as described above—and the number of messages that must be exchanged per disk access—as described below.

When the scheduler is separate from the disk server, five messages must be exchanged per disk access: two to request scheduling and get a reply, two to request disk access and get a reply, and one to release the disk. A client is

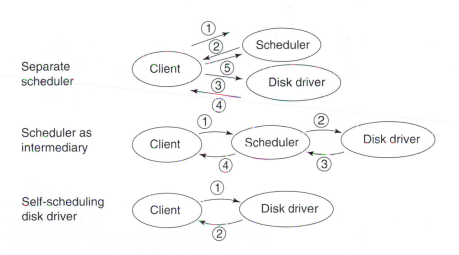

Figure 7.8   Disk-scheduling structures with message passing.

involved in all five communications. When the scheduler is an intermediary, four kinds of messages have to be exchanged: The client has to send a request and wait to receive a reply, and the disk driver has to ask the scheduler for the next request and get the reply. (The driver process can return the results of one disk access request when it asks for the next one.) As can be seen in Figure 7.8, a self-scheduling disk driver has the most attractive structure. In particular, only two messages need to be exchanged. The remainder of this section shows how to program the self-scheduling driver process.

If the disk driver process did no scheduling—i.e., if disk access were first come, first served—then it would have the structure of server `Server` in Figure 7.4. In order to do scheduling, the driver must examine all pending requests, which means it must receive all messages that are waiting on the `request` channel. It does this by executing a loop that terminates when the `request` channel is empty and there is at least one saved request. The driver then selects the best request, accesses the disk, and finally sends a reply to the client who sent the request. The driver can use any of the disk-scheduling policies described in Section 5.3.

Figure 7.9 outlines a disk driver that employs the shortest-seek-time (SST) scheduling policy. The driver stores pending requests in one of two ordered queues, `left` or `right`, depending on whether the request is to the left or right of the current position of the disk head. Requests in `left` are ordered by decreasing cylinder value; those in `right` are ordered by increasing cylinder value. Variable `headpos` indicates the current head position; `nsaved` is a count of the number of saved requests. The invariant for the outer loop of the driver is

> *SST*: `left` is an ordered queue from largest to smallest `cyl` $\wedge$
> all values of `cyl` in `left` are `<= headpos` $\wedge$
> `right` is an ordered queue from smallest to largest `cyl` $\wedge$
> all values of `cyl` in `right` are `>= headpos` $\wedge$
> (`nsaved == 0`) $\Rightarrow$ both `left` and `right` are empty

In Figure 7.9, the `empty` primitive is used in the condition of the inner `while` loop to determine whether there are more messages queued on the `request` channel. This is an example of the programming technique called *polling*. In this case, the disk driver process repeatedly polls the `request` channel to determine if there are pending requests. If there are, the driver receives another one, so it has more requests to choose from. If not, the driver services the best saved request. Polling is also useful in other situations and is often employed within hardware—for example, to arbitrate access to a communication bus.

```
chan request(int clientID, int cyl, types of other arguments);
chan reply[n](types of results);

process Disk_Driver {
  queue left, right;  # ordered queues of saved requests
  int clientID, cyl, headpos = 1, nsaved = 0;
  variables to hold other arguments in a request;
  while (true) {        ## loop invariant SST
    while (!empty(request) or nsaved == 0) {
      # wait for first request or receive another one
      receive request(clientID, cyl, ...);
      if (cyl <= headpos)
        insert(left, clientID, cyl, ...);
      else
        insert(right, clientID, cyl, ...);
      nsaved++;
    }
    # select best saved request from left or right
    if (size(left) == 0)
      remove(right, clientID, cyl, args);
    else if (size(right) == 0)
      remove(left, clientID, cyl, args);
    else
      remove request closest to headpos from left or right;
    headpos = cyl; nsaved--;
    access the disk;
    send reply[clientID](results);
  }
}
```

Figure 7.9   Self-scheduling disk driver.

7.3.3 File Servers: Conversational Continuity

As a final example of client/server interaction, we present one way to implement
file servers, which are processes that provide access to external files stored on
disk. To access a disk file, a client first opens the file. If the file can be opened—
the file exists and the client has permission to access it—then the client makes a
series of read and write requests. Eventually the client closes the file.

Suppose that up to n files may be open at once. Further suppose that access
to each open file is provided by a separate file server process; hence, there are up

to **n** active file servers. When a client wants to open a file, it first needs to acquire a free file server. If all file servers are identical, any free one will do.

We could allocate file servers to clients by using a separate allocator process. However, since all are identical and communication channels are shared, there is a much simpler approach. In particular, let **open** be a global channel. To acquire a file server, a client sends a request to **open**. Each file server, when idle, tries to receive from **open**. A specific **open** request from a client will thus be received by one of the idle file servers. That server sends a reply to the client, then proceeds to wait for access requests. A client sends these to a different channel, **access[i]**, where **i** is the index of the file server that replied to the client's request to open a file. Thus, **access** is an array of **n** channels. Eventually the client closes the file, at which time the file server becomes idle and again waits for an open request.

Figure 7.10 gives outlines for the file servers and their clients. A client sends **READ** and **WRITE** requests to the same server channel. This is necessary since the file server cannot in general know the order in which these requests will be made and hence cannot use different channels for each. For the same reason, when a client wants to close a channel, it sends a **CLOSE** request to the same access channel.

The interaction between a client and a server in Figure 7.10 is an example of *conversational continuity*. A client starts a conversation with a file server when that server receives the client's **open** request. The client then continues to converse with the same server. This is programmed by having the file server first receive from **open**, then repeatedly receive from its element of **access**.

The program in Figure 7.10 illustrates one possible way to implement file servers. It assumes that **open** is a shared channel from which any file server can receive a message. If each channel can have only one receiver, then a separate file allocator process would be needed. That process would receive open requests and allocate a free server to a client; file servers would thus need to tell the allocator when they are free.

The solution in Figure 7.10 also employs a fixed number **n** of file servers. In a language that supports dynamic process and channel creation, a better approach would be to create file servers and access channels dynamically as needed. This is better since at any point in time there would only be as many servers as are actually being used; more importantly, there would not be a fixed upper bound on the number of file servers. At the other extreme, there could simply be one file server per disk. In this case, however, either the file server or the client interface will be much more complex than shown in Figure 7.10. This is because either the file server has to keep track of the information associated with

```
type kind = enum(READ, WRITE, CLOSE);
chan open(string fname; int clientID);
chan access[n](int kind,  types of other arguments);
chan open_reply[m](int serverID);  # server id or error
chan access_reply[m](types of results);  # data, error, ...

process File_Server[i = 0 to n-1] {
  string fname; int clientID;
  kind k;  variables for other arguments;
  bool more = false;
  variables for local buffer, cache, etc.;
  while (true) {
    receive open(fname, clientID);
    open file fname;  if successful then:
    send open_reply[clientID](i); more = true;
    while (more) {
      receive access[i](k,  other arguments);
      if (k == READ)
        process read request;
      else if (k == WRITE)
        process write request;
      else    # k == CLOSE
        { close the file; more = false; }
      send access_reply[clientID](results);
    }
  }
}

process Client[j = 0 to m-1] {
  int serverID;   declarations of other variables;
  send open("foo", j);      # open file "foo"
  receive open_reply[j](serverID);  # get back server id
  # use file then close it by executing the following
  send access[serverID](access arguments);
  receive access_reply[j](results);
    ...
}
```

Figure 7.10   File servers and clients.

all clients who have files open or clients have to pass file state information with every request.

Yet another approach, which is used in the Sun Network File System (NFS), is to implement file access solely by means of remote procedures. Then, "opening" a file consists of acquiring a descriptor (called a file handle in NFS) and a set of file attributes. These are subsequently passed on each call to a file access procedure. Unlike the `File_Server` processes in Figure 7.10, the access procedures in NFS are themselves stateless—all information needed to access a file is passed as arguments on each call to a file access procedure. This increases the cost of passing arguments but greatly simplifies the handling of both client and server crashes. In particular, if a file server crashes, the client simply resends the request until a response is received. If a client crashes, the server need do nothing since it has no state information.

7.4 Interacting Peers: Exchanging Values

The previous examples in this chapter showed how message passing is used to program filters, clients, and servers. Here we examine a simple example of interacting peers. Our main purposes are to illustrate three useful communication patterns—centralized, symmetric, and ring—and to describe the tradeoffs between them. Chapters 9 and 11 give numerous, larger examples of the use of these communication patterns. They occur frequently in distributed parallel computations and in decentralized distributed systems.

Suppose there are **n** processes and that each process has a local integer value **v**. The goal is for every process to learn the smallest and largest of the **n** local values. One way to solve this problem is to have one process, say `P[0]`, gather all **n** values, compute the minimum and maximum of them, and then send the results to the other processes. Figure 7.11 presents a centralized solution using this approach. It employs a total of `2(n-1)` messages. (If there is a `broadcast` primitive, which transmits copies of a message to every other process, that could be used by `P[0]` to send the results; in this case, the total number of messages would be **n**.)

In Figure 7.11, one process does all the "work" of computing the smallest and largest values; the other processes merely send their values then wait to get back the global result. A second way to solve the problem is to use a symmetric approach in which each process executes the same algorithm. In particular, each process first sends its local value to all the others; then each process, in parallel, computes for itself the minimum and maximum of the set of **n** values. Figure 7.12 gives the solution. It is an example of a single-program, multiple data

```
chan values(int), results[n](int smallest, int largest);
process P[0] {   # coordinator process
  int v;   # assume v has been initialized
  int new, smallest = v, largest = v;  # initial state
  # gather values and save the smallest and largest
  for [i = 1 to n-1] {
    receive values(new);
    if (new < smallest)
      smallest = new;
    if (new > largest)
      largest = new;
  }
  # send the results to the other processes
  for [i = 1 to n-1]
    send results[i](smallest, largest)
}
process P[i = 1 to n-1] {
  int v;   # assume v has been initialized
  int smallest, largest;
  send values(v);
  receive results[i](smallest, largest);
}
```

Figure 7.11   Exchanging values: Centralized solution.

```
chan values[n](int);
process P[i = 0 to n-1] {
  int v;   # assume v has been initialized
  int new, smallest = v, largest = v;  # initial state
  # send my value to the other processes
  for [j = 0 to n-1 st j != i]
    send values[j](v);
  # gather values and save the smallest and largest
  for [j = 1 to n-1] {
    receive values[i](new);
    if (new < smallest)
      smallest = new;
    if (new > largest)
      largest = new;
  }
}
```

Figure 7.12   Exchanging values: Symmetric solution.

(SPMD) solution; in particular, each process executes the same program, but works on different data. However, it employs a total of `n(n-1)` messages. (Again, if there is a **broadcast** primitive, that could be used, resulting in a total of **n** distinct messages.)

A third way to solve this problem is to organize the processes into a logical ring, in which each process `P[i]` receives messages from its predecessor and sends messages to its successor. In particular, `P[0]` sends to `P[1]`, which sends to `P[2]`, and so on, with `P[n-1]` sending messages to `P[0]`. Each process executes two stages. In the first it receives two values, determines the minimum and maximum of those two values plus its own value, and sends the results to its successor. In the second stage, each process receives the global minimum and maximum and passes them on to its successor. One process, say `P[0]`, acts as the initiator of the computation. Figure 7.13 presents the solution. It is almost symmetric (only `P[0]` is slightly different), and it employs only `2(n-1)` messages.

Figure 7.14 illustrates the communication structures of these programs for the case of **6** processes. The processes are nodes in a graph, and the edges are pairs of communication channels. As can be seen, the centralized solution has a star-shaped graph, with the coordinator process in the center. The symmetric solution has the structure of a complete graph in which each node is connected to every other node. The ring solution naturally has the structure of a circular ring—or a pipeline that is closed back on itself.

The symmetric solution is the shortest, and it is easy to program because every process does exactly the same thing. On the other hand, it uses the largest number of messages (unless **broadcast** is available). These are sent and received at about the same time, so they could be transmitted in parallel if the underlying communications network supports concurrent transmissions. In general, however, the larger the number of messages sent by a program, the slower the program will run. Stated differently, communication overhead greatly diminishes performance improvements (speedup) that might be gained from parallel execution. (These topics are discussed in detail in the introduction to Part 3.)

The centralized and ring solutions both employ a linear number of messages, but they have different communication patterns that lead to different performance characteristics. In the centralized solution, the messages sent to the coordinator are all sent at about the same time; hence only the first **receive** statement executed by the coordinator is likely to delay for very long. Similarly, the results are sent one after the other from the coordinator to the other processes, so the other processes should be able to awaken rapidly.

In the ring solution, all processes are both producers and consumers, and they are connected in a circular pipeline. Thus, the last process in the pipeline

```
chan values[n](int smallest, int largest);
process P[0] {   # initiates the exchanges
    int v;    # assume v has been initialized
    int smallest = v, largest = v;   # initial state
    # send v to next process, P[1]
    send values[1](smallest, largest);
    # get global smallest and largest from P[n-1] and
    #    pass them on to P[1]
    receive values[0](smallest, largest);
    send values[1](smallest, largest);
}

process P[i = 1 to n-1] {
    int v;    # assume v has been initialized
    int smallest, largest;
    # receive smallest and largest so far, then update
    #    them by comparing their values to v
    receive values[i](smallest, largest)
    if (v < smallest)
        smallest = v;
    if (v > largest)
        largest = v;
    # send the result to the next processes, then wait
    # to get the global result
    send values[(i+1) mod n](smallest, largest);
    receive values[i](smallest, largest);
}
```

Figure 7.13   Exchanging values using a circular ring.

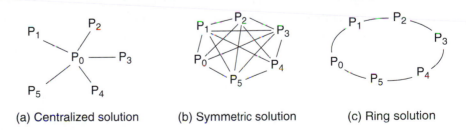

(a) Centralized solution   (b) Symmetric solution   (c) Ring solution

Figure 7.14   Communication structures of the three programs.

(`P[n-1]`) has to wait until every other process has—one at a time—received a message, done a small amount of computation, and sent its result to the next process in the pipeline. Messages have to circulate around the pipeline two full times before every process has learned the global result. In short, the solution is inherently linear, with no possibility of overlapping message transmissions or of getting rid of delays in `receive` statements. Hence, the ring-based solution will perform poorly for this simple problem. On the other hand, this communication structure is very effective if received messages can quickly be forwarded, and if each process then has to do a reasonably large amount of computation before receiving the next message. We will see examples where this is the case in Chapters 9 and 11.

7.5 Synchronous Message Passing

The `send` primitive is nonblocking, so a process that sends a message can proceed asynchronously with respect to the process that will eventually receive the message. With synchronous message passing, sending a message causes the sender to block until the message is received. We will distinguish a blocking send by using a different primitive: `synch_send`. The arguments of the two primitive are the same—the name of a channel and the message to be sent—but the semantics are different.

The advantage of synchronous message passing is that there is a bound on the size of communication channels, and hence on buffer space. This is because a process can have at most one message at a time queued up on any channel. Not until that message is received can the sending process continue and send another message. In fact, an implementation of synchronous message passing can leave a message in the address space of the sending process until the receiver is ready for it, then the implementation can copy the message directly into the receiver's address space. With this kind of implementation, the content of a channel is merely a queue of addresses of messages that are waiting to be sent.

However, synchronous message passing has two disadvantages relative to asynchronous message passing. First, concurrency is reduced. When two processes communicate, at least one of them will have to block—depending on whether the sender or receiver tries to communicate first. Consider the following producer/consumer example:

```
channel values(int);

process Producer {
  int data[n];
```

```
      for [i = 0 to n-1] {
        do some computation;
        synch_send values(data[i]);
      }
    }

    process Consumer {
      int results[n];
      for [i = 0 to n-1] {
        receive values(results[i]);
        do some computation;
      }
    }
```

Suppose the computational parts are such that `Producer` is at times faster than `Consumer` and at times slower; hence, the processes will arrive at communication statements at different times. This will cause each pair of send/receive statements to delay, and the total execution time will be increased by the sum of all the delay times. In contrast, with asynchronous message passing there might be no delay time—when the `Producer` is faster, its messages will get queued on the channel, and when `Consumer` is faster, there might be enough messages queued up so that `receive` never blocks. To achieve the same effects with synchronous message passing requires interposing a buffer process between `Producer` and `Consumer`. (We show how to do so in the next section.)

Concurrency is also reduced in some client/server interactions. When a client is releasing a resource—as in Figure 7.7—there is usually no reason it needs to delay until the server has received the release message. However, with synchronous message passing, it has to delay. A second example occurs when a client process wants to write to a graphics display, a file, or some other output device managed by a server process. Often the client wants to continue immediately after issuing a write request; it does not care whether the write is acted upon now or in the near future, as long as it is done eventually. With synchronous message passing, however, the client *has* to wait until a write request is actually received by the server.

The second disadvantage of synchronous message passing is that programs that use it are more prone to deadlock. In particular, the programmer has to be careful that all send and receive statements match up in the sense that whenever a process could be at a send (receive) statement, eventually some other process will be at a receive (send) statement that uses the same channel. This is typically the case in producer/consumer interactions, because a producer sends to and the consumer receives from the channel that connects them. It is also typically the case in client/server interactions: A client "calls" a server by executing a send statement followed by a receive statement; the server executes a receive statement to get a request followed by a send statement to give a reply.

One has to be careful when programming interacting peers, however. Consider the following attempt, for example, in which two processes exchange values:

```
channel in1(int), in2(int);

process P1 {
  int value1 = 1, value2;
  synch_send in2(value1);
  receive in1(value2);
}

process P2 {
  int value1, value2 = 2;
  synch_send in1(value2);
  receive in2(value1);
}
```

This program will deadlock because both processes will block at their `synch_send` statements. One or the other of the processes—but not both—has to be changed so that it executes `receive` first. In contrast, with asynchronous message passing, it is perfectly fine to use the symmetric approach above. Moreover, the symmetric approach is much easier to scale to more than two processes.

To summarize, `send` and `synch_send` are often interchangeable. In fact, all but one example in earlier sections of this chapter will work correctly if `send` is replaced by `synch_send`. The one exception is the program in Figure 7.12, which uses a symmetric approach to exchanging values. Thus the main difference between asynchronous and synchronous message passing is the tradeoff between having possibly more concurrency and having bounded communication buffers. Since memory is plentiful and asynchronous send is less prone to deadlock, most programmers prefer it.

7.6 Case Study: CSP

Communicating Sequential Processes (CSP) is one of the most influential developments in the history of concurrent programming. CSP was first described in a 1978 paper by Tony Hoare. That paper introduced both synchronous message passing and what has come to be called *guarded communication*. CSP directly influenced the design of the Occam programming language and also influenced several other languages, including Ada and SR (which are described in Chapter 8). Moreover, CSP spawned a plethora of research and papers on formal models and the semantics of message passing.

This section describes Communicating Sequential Processes. The examples include producers and consumers, clients and servers, and an interesting program for generating prime numbers using a pipeline. We use a syntax that is similar to the one used in Hoare's paper and in other programs in this text. At the end of the section we briefly describe Occam and the latest version of CSP, which is now a formal language for modeling and analyzing the behavior of concurrent communicating systems.

7.6.1 *Communication Statements*

Suppose process **A** wishes to communicate the value of expression **e** to process **B**. This is accomplished in CSP by the following program fragments:

```
process A { ... B!e; ... }
process B { ... A?x; ... }
```

B!e is called an *output statement*. It names a destination process **B** and specifies an expression **e** whose value is to be sent to that process. **A?x** is called an *input statement*. It names a source process **A** and specifies the variable **x** into which an input message from the source is to be stored. These are called output and input statements rather than send and receive statements, because they are used for external communication as well as interprocesses communication. (The output operator **!** is pronounced "shriek" or "bang;" the input operator **?** is pronounced "query.")

Assuming the types of **e** and **x** are the same, the two statements above are said to *match*. An input or output statement delays the executing process until another process reaches a matching statement. The two statements are then executed simultaneously. The effect is to assign the value of the expression in the output statement to the variable in the input statement. Execution of matching communication statements can thus be viewed as a *distributed assignment* that transfers a value from one process to a variable in another. The two processes are synchronized while communication takes place, then each proceeds independently.

The above example employs the simplest forms of output and input statements. The general forms of these statements are

```
Destination!port(e₁, ..., eₙ);
Source?port(x₁, ..., xₙ);
```

`Destination` and `Source` name a single process, as in the first example, or an element of an array of processes. The CSP paper employed this kind of *direct naming* of communication channels because it is simple. However, it is easier to construct modular programs if channels have names and are global to processes (as in Section 7.1). The Occam language described later uses this approach.

The `Source` can also name *any* element of an array of processes, which is indicated as `Source[*]`. The `port` names a communication channel in the destination process. The expressions e_i in an output statement are sent to the named port of the destination process. An input statement receives a message on the designated port from the source process and assigns the values to local variables x_i. Ports are used to distinguish between different kinds of messages that a process might receive. If there is only one kind of message, the port is omitted. Also, if there is only one e_i or x_i, the parentheses may be omitted. Both abbreviations were employed in the first example.

As a simple example, the following filter process repeatedly inputs a character from process `West`, then outputs that character to process `East`:

```
process Copy {
  char c;
  do true ->
    West?c;   # input a character from West
    East!c;   # output the character to East
  od
}
```

The input statement waits until `West` is ready to send a character; the output statement waits until `East` is ready to take it.

The `do` and `if` statements in CSP use Dijkstra's *guarded commands* notation. A guarded command has the form `B -> S`, where `B` is a Boolean expression (the guard) and `S` is a statement list (the command). The above `do` statement loops forever. We will explain other uses of guarded commands as they arise.

As a second example, the following server process uses Euclid's algorithm to compute the greatest common divisor of two positive integers `x` and `y`:

```
process GCD {
  int id, x, y;
  do true ->
    Client[*]?args(id, x, y);   # input a "call"
    # repeat the following until x == y
    do x > y -> x = x - y;
    [] x < y -> y = y - x;
    od
```

```
        Client[id]!result(x);  # return the result
    od
}
```

GCD waits to receive input on its `args` port from any one of an array of client process. The client that succeeds in matching with the input statement also sends its identity. GCD then computes the answer and sends it back to the client's `result` port. In the inner `do` loop, if `x > y` then `y` is subtracted from `x`; if `x < y` then `x` is subtracted from `y`. The loop terminates when neither of these conditions is true—namely, when `x == y`.

A client `Client[i]` communicates with GCD by executing

```
... GCD!args(i,v1,v2); GCD?result(r); ...
```

Here the port names are not actually needed; however, they help indicate the role of each channel.

7.6.2 Guarded Communication

Input and output statements enable processes to communicate. By themselves, however, they are somewhat limited, because both are blocking statements. Often a process wishes to communicate with more than one other process— perhaps over different ports—yet does not know the order in which the other processes might wish to communicate with it. For example, consider extending the `Copy` process above so that up to, say, `10` characters are buffered. If more than `1` but fewer than `10` characters are buffered, `Copy` can either input another character from `West` or output another character to `East`. However, `Copy` cannot know which of `West` or `East` will next reach a matching statement.

Guarded communication statements support nondeterministic communication. These combine aspects of conditional and communication statements and have the form

```
    B; C -> S;
```

Here `B` is a Boolean expression, `C` is a communication statement, and `S` is a statement list. The Boolean expression can be omitted, in which case it has the implicit value `true`.

Together, `B` and `C` comprise what is called the *guard*. A guard *succeeds* if `B` is true and executing `C` would not cause a delay—i.e., some other process is waiting at a matching communication statement. A guard *fails* if `B` is false. A guard *blocks* if `B` is true but `C` cannot yet be executed.

Guarded communication statements appear within `if` and `do` statements. For example, consider

```
if  B₁;  C₁ -> S₁;
[]  B₂;  C₂ -> S₂;
fi
```

This statement has two arms—each of which is a guarded communication statement. You can execute it as follows. First, evaluate the Boolean expressions in the guards. If both guards fail, then the `if` statement terminates with no effect; if at least one guard succeeds, then choose one of them (nondeterministically); if both guards block, then wait until one of the guards succeeds. Second, after choosing a guard that succeeds, execute the communication statement `c` in the chosen guard. Third, execute the corresponding statement `s`. At this point the `if` statement terminates.

A `do` statement is executed in a similar way. The difference is that the above selection process is repeated until all guards fail. The examples below will (hopefully) make all this clear.

As a simple illustration of guarded communication, we can reprogram the previous version of the `Copy` process as follows:

```
process Copy {
  char c;
  do West?c -> East!c;  od
}
```

Here we have moved the input statement into the guard of the `do` statement. Since the guard does not contain a Boolean expression, it will never fail, and hence the `do` statement will loop forever.

As a second example, we can extend the above process so that it buffers up to two characters instead of just one. Initially, `Copy` has to input one character from `West`. But once it holds one character, it could either output that character to `East` or input another character from `West`. It has no way of knowing which choice to make, so it can use guarded communication as follows:

```
process Copy {
  char c1, c2;
  West?c1;
  do West?c2 -> East!c1; c1 = c2;
  [] East!c1 -> West?c1;
  od
}
```

At the start of every iteration of do, one character is buffered in c1. The first arm of do waits for a second character from West, outputs the first character to East, then assigns c2 to c1, thus getting the process back to the starting state for the loop. The second arm of do outputs the first character to East, then inputs another character from West. If both guards of do succeed—i.e., if West is ready to send another character and East is ready to accept one—either one can be chosen. Since neither guard ever fails, the do loop never terminates.

We can readily generalize the above program to a bounded buffer by implementing a queue inside the Copy process. For example, the following buffers up to 10 characters:

```
process Copy {
  char buffer[10];
  int front = 0, rear = 0, count = 0;
  do count < 10; West?buffer[rear] ->
        count = count+1; rear = (rear+1) mod 10;
  [] count > 0; East!buffer[front] ->
        count = count-1; front = (front+1) mod 10;
  od
}
```

This version of Copy again employs a do statement with two arms, but now the guards contain Boolean expressions as well as communication statements. The guard in the first arm succeeds if there is room in the buffer and West is ready to output a character; the guard in the second arm succeeds if the buffer contains a character and East is ready to input it. Again the do loop never terminates, in this case because at least one of the Boolean conditions is always true.

Another example will illustrate the use of multiple ports in a server process. In particular, consider the resource allocator programmed in Figure 7.7 using asynchronous message passing. The Allocator process can be programmed in CSP as follows:

```
process Allocator {
  int avail = MAXUNITS;
  set units = initial values;
  int index, unitid;
  do avail > 0; Client[*]?acquire(index) ->
        avail--; remove(units, unitid);
        Client[index]!reply(unitid);
  [] Client[*]?release(index, unitid) ->
        avail++; insert(units,unitid);
  od
}
```

This process is *much* more concise than the `Allocator` in Figure 7.7. In particular, we do not need to merge `acquire` and `release` messages on the same channel; instead we use different ports and a `do` statement with one arm for each port. Moreover, we can delay receiving an `acquire` message until there are available units; this does away with the need to save pending requests. However, these differences are due to the use of guarded communication; they are *not* due to the differences between asynchronous and synchronous message passing. In fact, it is possible to use guarded communication with asynchronous message passing, as we shall see in Section 8.3.

As a final example, suppose we have two processes that want to exchange the values of two local variables—the problem we examined at the end of Section 7.5. There we had to use an asymmetric solution to avoid deadlock. By using guarded communication statements, we can program a symmetric exchange as follows:

```
process P1 {
  int value1 = 1, value2;
  if P2!value1 -> P2?value2;
  [] P2?value2 -> P2!value1;
  fi
}
process P2 {
  int value1, value2 = 2;
  if P1!value2 -> P1?value1;
  [] P1?value1 -> P1!value2;
  fi
}
```

This employs the nondeterministic choice that occurs when there is more than one pair of matching guards. The communication statement in the first guard in `P1` matches the communication statement in the second guard in `P2`, and the other pair of communication statements also match. Hence, either pair can be chosen. The solution is symmetric, but it is still not nearly as simple as a symmetric solution using asynchronous message passing.

7.6.3 Example: The Sieve of Eratosthenes

One of the examples in Hoare's 1978 paper on CSP was an interesting parallel program for generating primes. We develop the solution here both as a complete example of a CSP program and as another example of the use of a pipeline of processes to parallelize a sequential algorithm.

The sieve of Eratosthenes—named after the Greek mathematician who developed it—is a classic algorithm for determining which numbers in a given range are prime. Suppose we want to generate the primes between **2** and **n**. First, write down a list with all the numbers:

2   3   4   5   6   7   ...   n

Starting with the first uncrossed-out number in the list, **2**, go through the list and cross out multiples of that number. If **n** is odd, this yields the list:

2   3   4̸   5   6̸   7   ...   n

At this point, crossed-out numbers are not prime; the other numbers are still candidates for being prime. Now move to the next uncrossed-out number in the list, **3**, and repeat the above process by crossing out multiples of **3**. If we continue this process until every number has been considered, the uncrossed-out numbers in the final list will be all the primes between **2** and **n**. In essence, the sieve catches the primes and lets multiples of the primes fall through.

Now consider how we might parallelize this algorithm. One possibility is to assign a different process to each number in the list and hence to have each in parallel cross out multiples of its number. However, this approach has two problems. First, since processes can communicate only by exchanging messages, we would have to give each process a private copy of all the numbers, and we would have to use another process to combine the results. Second, we would use way too many processes. We only need as many processes as there are primes, but we do not know in advance which numbers are prime!

We can overcome both problems by parallelizing the sieve of Eratosthenes using a pipeline of filter processes. Each filter receives a stream of numbers from its predecessor and sends a stream of numbers to its successor. The first number that a filter receives is the next largest prime; it passes on to its successor all numbers that are not multiples of the first.

The actual program is shown in Figure 7.15. The first process, `Sieve[1]`, sends all the odd numbers to `Sieve[2]`. Every other process receives a stream of numbers from its predecessor. The first number p that process `Sieve[i]` receives is the *i*th prime. Each `Sieve[i]` subsequently passes on all other numbers it receives that are not multiples of its prime **p**. The total number **L** of *Sieve* processes must be large enough to guarantee that all primes up to **n** are generated. For example, there are **25** primes less than **100**; the percentage decreases for increasing values of **n**.

Process `Sieve[1]` terminates when it runs out of odd numbers to send to `Sieve[2]`. Every other process eventually blocks waiting for more input from

```
process Sieve[1] {
  int p = 2;
  for [i = 3 to n by 2]
    Sieve[2]!i;    # pass odd numbers to Sieve[2]
}

process Sieve[i = 2 to L] {
  int p, next;
  Sieve[i-1]?p;                  # p is a prime
  do Sieve[i-1]?next ->          # receive next candidate
    if (next mod p) != 0 ->      # if it might be prime,
      Sieve[i+1]!next;           #    pass it on
    fi
  od
}
```

Figure 7.15   Sieve of Eratosthenes in CSP.

its predecessor. When the program stops, the values of **p** in the processes are the primes. We could easily modify the program to terminate normally and to print the primes in ascending order by using a sentinel to mark the end of the list of numbers. When a process sees the sentinel (a zero for example), it prints its value of **p**, sends the sentinel to its successor, and then quits.

7.6.4 Occam and Modern CSP

The Communicating Sequential Processes notation described above has been widely used in papers but CSP itself has never been implemented. However, several languages based on CSP have been implemented and used. Occam is the best known of these. It extends the CSP notation to use global channels rather than direct naming, provides procedures and functions, and allows nested parallelism.

Hoare and others went on to develop a formal language that is used to describe and reason about concurrent communicating systems. The formal language was influenced by ideas in the original CSP notation—and it too is named CSP—but it is not a language that is used to write application programs. Rather it is used to model their behavior.

Below we summarize the attributes of Occam and modern CSP and give a few examples to illustrate the flavor of each. The Historical Notes at the end of this chapter describe sources of detailed information, including a library of Java packages that support the Occam/CSP programming model.

Occam

Occam contains a very small number of mechanisms (hence the name, which comes from Occam's razor) and has a unique syntax. The first version of Occam was designed in the mid-1980s; Occam 2 appeared in 1987; a proposal is now underway for an Occam 3. Although Occam is a language in its own right, it was developed in concert with the *transputer*, an early multicomputer, and was essentially the machine language of the transputer.

The basic units of an Occam program are declarations and three primitive "processes": assignment, input, and output. An assignment process is simply an assignment statement. The input and output processes are similar to the input and output commands of CSP. However, channels have names and are global to processes; moreover, each channel must have exactly one sender and one receiver.

Primitive processes are combined into conventional processes using what Occam calls constructors. These include sequential constructors, a parallel constructor similar to the `co` statement, and a guarded communication statement. In Occam's distinctive syntax, each primitive process, constructor, and declaration occupies a line by itself; declarations have a trailing colon; and the language imposes an indentation convention.

An Occam program contains a static number of processes and static communication paths. Procedures and functions provide the only form of modularization. They are essentially parameterized processes and can share only channels and constants. Occam does not support recursion or any form of dynamic creation or naming. This makes many algorithms harder to program. However, it ensures that an Occam compiler can determine exactly how many processes a program contains and how they communicate with each other. This, and the fact that different constructors cannot share variables, makes it possible for a compiler to assign processes and data to processors on a distributed-memory machine such as a transputer.

In most languages, the default is to execute statements sequentially; the programmer has to say explicitly to execute statements concurrently. Occam takes a different approach: There is no default! Instead, Occam contains two basic constructors: `SEQ` for sequential execution and `PAR` for parallel execution. For example, the following program increments `x` then `y`:

```
INT x, y :
SEQ
  x := x + 1
  y := y + 1
```

Since the two statements access different variables, they can, of course, be executed concurrently. This is expressed by changing **SEQ** to **PAR** in the above program. Occam contains a variety of other constructors, such as **IF**, **CASE**, **WHILE**, and **ALT**, which is used for guarded communication. Occam also contains an interesting mechanism called a replicator. It is similar to a quantifier and is used in similar ways.

Processes are created by using **PAR** constructors. They communicate using channels, which are accessed by the primitive input **?** and output **!** processes. The following is a simple sequential program that echoes keyboard characters to a display:

```
WHILE TRUE
  BYTE ch :
  SEQ
    keyboard ? ch
    screen ! ch
```

Here **keyboard** and **screen** are channels that are assumed to be connected to peripheral devices. (Occam provides mechanisms for binding I/O channels to devices.)

The above program uses a single character buffer, **ch**. It can be turned into a concurrent program that uses double buffering by employing two processes, one to read from the keyboard and one to write to the screen. The processes communicate using an additional channel **comm**; each has a local character **ch**.

```
CHAN OF BYTE comm :
PAR
  WHILE TRUE      -- keyboard input process
    BYTE ch :
    SEQ
      keyboard ? ch
      comm ! ch
  WHILE TRUE      -- screen output process
    BYTE ch :
    SEQ
      comm ? ch
      display ! ch
```

This program clearly indicates Occam's unique syntax. The requirement that every item be on a separate line leads to long programs, but the required indentation avoids the need for closing keywords.

The `ALT` constructor supports guarded communication. A guard consists of an input process, or a Boolean expression and an input process, or a Boolean expression and a `SKIP`. As a simple example, the following defines a process that can buffer up to two characters of data:

```
PROC Copy(CHAN OF BYTE West, Ask, East)
  BYTE c1, c2, dummy :
  SEQ
    West ? c1
    WHILE TRUE
      ALT
        West ? c2      -- West has a byte
          SEQ
            East ! c1
            c1 := c2
        Ask ? dummy   -- East wants a byte
          SEQ
            East ! c1
            West ? c1
```

We have declared `Copy` as a procedure to illustrate that aspect of Occam. A `Copy` process would be created by calling the procedure in a `PAR` constructor and passing it three channels.

Occam does not allow output commands in guards of `ALT` constructors. This makes processes such as the above harder to program, because the process that inputs from channel `East` first has to use channel `Ask` to say it wants a byte. However, this restriction greatly simplifies the implementation, which was especially important on the transputer. Because Occam also does not allow null messages (signals), a value has to be sent across the `Ask` channel above even though that value is not used.

Modern CSP

As noted, CSP has evolved from a programming notation into a formal language for modeling concurrent systems in which processes interact by means of communication. In addition, CSP is a collection of formal models and tools that help one understand and analyze the behavior of systems described using CSP.

The modern version of CSP was first described in 1985 in a book by Tony Hoare. The main purpose of the book was to present a theory of communicating processes; in doing so, Hoare modified his original notation to one that is more abstract and amenable to formal analysis. The underlying concept of CSP remained the same—processes that interact by means of synchronous message passing—but CSP became a calculus for studying systems of communicating processes rather than a language for writing application programs. The focus of the early work with the new CSP was developing several semantic theories: operational, denotational, trace, and algebraic. Now there are several automated proof tools that make it practical to use CSP and its theories to model practical applications (see the Historical Notes). For example, CSP has been used to model communications protocols, real-time control systems, security protocols, and fault tolerant systems, among others.

In modern CSP, a process is characterized by the way it communicates with its environment—which could be other processes or the external environment. All interaction occurs as a result of communication events. A collection of communicating processes is modeled by specifying the communication pattern of each process. The new CSP notation is functional rather than imperative. The fundamental operators are prefixing (sequencing), recursion (repetition), and guarded alternatives (nondeterministic choice). There is a mathematical version of CSP that is used in books and papers as well as a machine-readable version that is used by the analysis tools. The following simple examples will give a flavor of modern CSP; they are written in machine-readable notation.

The prefixing operator `->` is used to specify a sequential ordering of communication events. If `red` and `green` are two communication events, then a traffic signal that turns `green` then `red` *just once* can be specified as

```
green -> red -> STOP
```

The last element above is the simplest CSP process, `STOP`, which halts without communicating.

Recursion is used to specify repetition. For example, the following specifies a traffic light that repeatedly turns `green` then `red`:

```
LIGHT = green -> red -> LIGHT
```

This says that process `LIGHT` first communicates `green`, then communicates `red`, then repeats. The behavior of this process can be specified in several other ways—for example, by using two mutually recursive processes, one that communicates `green` and one that communicates `red`. The key point is that behavior—traces of communication events—is what matters, not how the process is "programmed."

The two communication events above are sent to the external environment. More commonly, one wants to have processes communicate with each other. CSP uses channels for this, as in the following example of a single character buffer process:

```
COPY1 = West?c:char -> East!c -> COPY1
```

The greatest-common-divisor program given earlier in Section 7.6 could be programmed in the new CSP as

```
GCD = Input?id.x.y -> GCD(id, x, y)

GCD(id, x, y) = if (x = y) then
                    Output!id.x -> GCD
                else if (x > y) then
                    GCD(id, x-y, y)
                else
                    GCD(id, x, y-x)
```

This uses two mutually recursive processes. The first waits for an input event and then invokes the second process. The second recurses until $x = y$, then outputs the result and invokes the first process to wait for another input event.

As a final example, the following specifies the behavior of a system that buffers up to two characters of data:

```
COPY = West?c1:char -> COPY2(c1)

COPY2(c1) =   West?c2:char -> East!c1 -> COPY2(c2)
              []
                East!c1 -> West?c1:char -> COPY2(c1)
```

The second process uses the guarded alternative operator `[]`. The guard in the first alternative waits for input from channel `West`; the guard in the second waits to send output to channel `East`. The choice is nondeterministic if both communications can occur. The communication behavior is thus the same as that of the two-character `Copy` process given earlier in the section on guarded communication. Modern CSP also provides an elegant way to specify an **n**-element buffer process using what is called a *linked parallel operator* to chain together **n** instances of a parameterized version of **COPY1** above.

7.7 Case Study: Linda

Linda embodies a distinctive approach to concurrent programming that synthe-sizes and generalizes aspects of shared variables and asynchronous message passing. Not itself a language, Linda is rather a collection of six primitives that are used to access what is called *tuple space* (TS), a shared, associative memory consisting of a collection of tagged data records called tuples. Any sequential programming language can be augmented with the Linda primitives to yield a concurrent programming variant of that language.

Tuple space is like a single shared communication channel, except that tuples are unordered. The operation to deposit a tuple, OUT, is like a **send** state-ment; the operation to extract a tuple, IN, is like a **receive** statement; and the operation to examine a tuple, RD, is like a **receive** that leaves the message stored on the channel. A fourth operation, EVAL, provides process creation. The final two operations, INP and RDP, provide nonblocking input and reading.

Although TS is logically shared by processes, it can be implemented by dis-tributing parts among processors in a multicomputer or network. Thus TS can be used to store distributed data structures, and different processes can concurrently access different elements of the data structure. As a later example will show, this directly supports the bag-of-tasks paradigm for process interaction. TS can also be made persistent—retaining its contents after a program terminates—and can thus be used to implement files or database systems.

Linda was first conceived in the early 1980s. (The name has a colorful ori-gin; see the Historical Notes.) The initial proposal had three primitives; the others were added later. Several languages have been augmented with the Linda primitives, including C and Fortran.

7.7.1 Tuple Space and Process Interaction

Tuple space consists of an unordered collection of passive data tuples and active process tuples. Data tuples are tagged records that contain the shared state of a computation. Process tuples are routines that execute asynchronously. They interact by reading, writing, and generating data tuples. When a process tuple terminates, it turns into a data tuple, as described below.

Each data tuple in TS has the form

```
("tag", value_1, ..., value_n)
```

The tag is a string that is used to distinguish between tuples representing different data structures. The values are zero or more data values—for example, integers, reals, or arrays.

Linda defines three basic primitives for manipulating data tuples: OUT, IN, and RD. All three are atomic (indivisible) operations. A process deposits a tuple in TS by executing

```
OUT("tag", expr₁, ..., exprₙ);
```

Execution of OUT terminates once the expressions have been evaluated and the resulting data tuple has been deposited in TS. The OUT operation is thus similar to a **send** statement, except that the tuple is deposited in TS rather than appended to a specific channel.

A process extracts a data tuple from TS by executing

```
IN("tag", field₁, ..., fieldₙ);
```

Each field$_i$ is either an expression or a formal parameter of the form **?var** where **var** is a variable in the executing process. The arguments to IN are called a template. The process executing IN delays until TS contains at least one tuple that matches the template, then removes one from TS.

A template **t** matches a data tuple **d** if (1) the tags are identical; (2) **t** and **d** have the same number of fields, and corresponding fields have the same type; and (3) the value of each expression in **t** is equal to the corresponding value in **d**. After a matching tuple is removed from TS, formal parameters in the template are assigned the corresponding values from the tuple. Thus IN is like a **receive** statement, with the tag and values in the template serving to identify the channel.

Two simple examples will help clarify these concepts. Let **sem** be the symbolic name of a semaphore. Then the **V** operation is simply OUT("sem"), and the **P** operation is simply IN("sem"). The value of the semaphore is the number of **sem** tuples in TS. To simulate an array of semaphores, we would use an additional field to represent the array index, for example:

```
IN("forks", i);     # P(forks[i])
 ...
OUT("forks", i);    # V(forks[i])
```

The template in the IN statement matches any tuple having the same tag **forks** and the same value **i**.

The third basic primitive is RD, which is used to examine tuples. If **t** is a template, execution of RD(t) delays the process until TS contains a matching data tuple. As with IN, variables in **t** are then assigned values from the corresponding fields of the data tuple. However, the tuple remains in TS.

There are also nonblocking variants of IN and RD. Operations INP and RDP are predicates that return true if there is a matching tuple in TS, and return false otherwise. If they return true, they have the same effect as IN and RD, respectively.

Using the three basic primitives, we can modify and examine a "global" variable. For example, we can implement a single-use counter barrier for n processes as follows. First, some process initializes the barrier by depositing a counter in TS:

```
OUT("barrier", 0);
```

When a process reaches a barrier synchronization point, it first increments the counter by executing

```
IN("barrier", ?counter);    # get barrier tuple
OUT("barrier", counter+1);  # put back new value
```

Then the process waits until all n processes have arrived by executing

```
RD("barrier", n);
```

The sixth and final Linda primitive is EVAL, which creates process tuples. This operation has the same form as OUT and also produces a new tuple:

```
EVAL("tag", expr_1, ..., expr_n);
```

At least one of the expressions is typically a procedure or function call. Logically, all fields of the tuple are evaluated concurrently by separate processes. Moreover, the process that executes EVAL does not wait. In practice, Linda implementations fork new processes only to evaluate fields that consist of a single function call; other fields are evaluated sequentially. In any event, after all expressions have been evaluated—hence, after any forked processes have terminated—the results are combined and the tuple becomes a passive data tuple. The tag of this tuple is the same as the tag in the EVAL, and the value of each field is the value of the corresponding expression.

The EVAL primitive provides the means by which concurrency is introduced into a Linda program. (Recall that the Linda primitives are added to a standard sequential language.) As a simple example, consider the following concurrent statement:

```
co [i = 1 to n]
   a[i] = f(i);
```

This statement evaluates **n** calls of **f** in parallel and assigns the results to shared array **a**. The corresponding C-Linda code is

```
for (i = 1; i <= n; i++)
    EVAL("a", i, f(i));
```

This forks **n** process tuples; each evaluates one call of **f(i)**. When a process tuple terminates, it turns into a data tuple containing the array name, an index, and the value of that element of **a**.

TS can also be used to implement conventional message passing. For example, a process can send a message to a channel **ch** by executing

```
OUT("ch", expressions);
```

Again, the name of a shared object is turned into a tag on a tuple. Another process can receive the message by executing

```
IN("ch", variables);
```

However, this statement extracts any matching tuple. If it is important that messages be received in the order they are sent, the programmer has to impose an ordering. This can be done by using counters to put sequence numbers on messages, and then reading them in sequence-number order.

7.7.2 Example: Prime Numbers with a Bag of Tasks

In Section 7.6, we showed how to generate prime numbers using the Sieve of Eratosthenes. In that approach, candidate numbers pass through a pipeline of filter processes. Each filter holds one prime factor and checks whether that prime divides each candidate; if not, the candidate might be prime so it is passed to the next filter process in the pipeline.

We can also generate primes using the bag-of-tasks paradigm (which was introduced in Section 3.6). As usual, the workers share a bag of tasks. In this case, the bag contains the candidate numbers; it is stored in tuple space. A manager process deposits candidates into the bag and gathers results.

Each worker repeatedly removes a candidate from the bag and determines whether it is prime by dividing it by smaller primes. But how can a worker acquire all the primes it needs? The answer is to check candidates in strictly increasing order. In this way, the prime factors needed to check a new candidate will already have been generated before they are needed. A worker might have to delay—waiting for another worker to generate a smaller prime—but workers will not deadlock since all smaller primes will eventually be generated.

Figure 7.16 contains a C-Linda program that generates the first `limit` primes using a bag of tasks stored in tuple space. The structure of a C-Linda program is essentially that of a C program. However, the main routine is named `real_main` rather than `main`.

```
# include "linda.h"
# define LIMIT 1000       /* upper bound for limit */

void worker() {
  int primes[LIMIT] = {2,3};   /* table of primes */
  int numPrimes = 1, i, candidate, isprime;

  /* repeatedly get candidates and check them */
  while(true) {
    if (RDP("stop"))  /* check for termination */
      return;
    IN("candidate", ?candidate);    /* get candidate */
    OUT("candidate", candidate+2);  /* output next one */
    i = 0; isprime = 1;
    while (primes[i]*primes[i] <= candidate) {
      if (candidate%primes[i] == 0) { /* not prime */
        isprime = 0; break;
      }
      i++;
      if (i > numPrimes) {  /* need another prime */
        numPrimes++;
        RD("prime", numPrimes, ?primes[numPrimes]);
      }
    }
    /* tell manager the result */
    OUT("result", candidate, isprime);
  }
}

real_main(int argc, char *argv[]) {
  int primes[LIMIT] = {2,3};   /* my table of primes */
  int limit, numWorkers, i, isprime;
  int numPrimes = 2, value = 5;
  limit = atoi(argv[1]);  /* read command line */
  numWorkers = atoi(argv[2]);
```

```
      /* create workers and put first candidate in bag */
      for (i = 1; i <= numWorkers; i++)
        EVAL("worker", worker());
      OUT("candidate", value);

      /* get results from workers in increasing order */
      while (numPrimes < limit) {
        IN("result", value, ?isprime);
        if (isprime) {    /* put value in table and TS */
          primes[numPrimes] = value;
          OUT("prime", numPrimes, value);
          numPrimes++;
        }
        value = value + 2;
      }
      /* tell workers to quit, then print the primes */
      OUT("stop");
      for (i = 0; i < limit; i++)
        printf("%d\n", primes[i]);
    }
```

Figure 7.16   Prime number generation in C-Linda.

The main routine executes first as a single process. It begins by reading command-line arguments to determine how many primes to generate and how many workers to use. It then uses EVAL to fork the worker processes and uses OUT to deposit the first candidate, 5, in TS.

The main routine then assumes the role of a manager process. In particular, it uses IN to receive the results from workers; these are received in order so that primes can be counted. When real_main receives a prime, it puts the prime and its count into TS and updates its local table. For example, 5 is the third prime, 7 is the fourth, and so on.

The program terminates when real_main has received limit primes. The manager tells the workers to stop by depositing a stop token in TS, then it prints the primes stored in its local table.

Each worker process repeatedly gets a candidate number from TS, checks its primality, and sends the result to the manager by depositing the result in TS. After a worker extracts a candidate number using IN, it deposits the next odd candidate into TS. Thus, there is at most one candidate number in TS at a time, and the candidates are increasing odd integers.

Each worker keeps a local table of prime factors. It extends this table when it needs another prime factor to check a candidate number. It gets the prime by reading it from TS. To avoid deadlock, workers read primes in strictly increasing order.

On each iteration, a worker uses the conditional read primitive, `RDP`, to see if it should stop. This primitive returns true if there is a `stop` tuple in TS; otherwise it returns false. Since the workers will not see the `stop` tuple until after the manager has acquired `limit` primes, more candidates than necessary will be checked. This is hard to avoid without having the processes exchange many more messages.

The program in Figure 7.16 is not the most efficient one we could devise. This is because each candidate is deposited and extracted twice—once in a `candidate` tuple and then in a `result` tuple. Accessing TS is much less efficient than accessing local variables. To increase the use of local variables, we could have the manager deposit ranges of candidates—say 10 or 20 numbers at a time. We could then have the workers compute all primes in a given range and send the collective result to the manager. We could also seed the tables of primes in the manager and workers with more of the small primes.

7.8 Case Study: MPI

The Message Passing Interface (MPI) is a library of message-passing routines. When MPI is used, the processes in a distributed program are written in a sequential language such as C or Fortran; they communicate and synchronize by calling functions in the MPI library.

The MPI application programmer's interface (API) was defined in the mid-1990s by a large group of people from academia, government, and industry. The interface reflects people's experiences with earlier message-passing libraries, such as PVM. The goal of the group was to develop a single library that could be implemented efficiently on the variety of multiple processor machines. MPI has now become the de facto standard, and several implementations exist.

MPI programs have what is called an SPMD style—single program, multiple data. In particular, every processor executes a copy of the same program. (In an application written in C, the `main` routine in the program is started on every processor.) Each instance of the program can determine its own identity and hence take different actions. The instances interact by calling MPI library functions. The MPI functions support process-to-process communication, group communication, setting up and managing communication groups, and interacting with the environment.

Below we present a simple but complete program that illustrates process-to-process message passing. We then describe the MPI functions for group communication. (See Figure 12.2 for a larger example of an MPI program.)

7.8.1 Basic Functions

Recall the problem introduced in Section 7.4 that involved two processes exchanging values with each other. Figure 7.17 contains a complete C program that uses the MPI library to solve the problem.

The first line includes the MPI header file, which contains types, constants, and function prototypes. The program is compiled and linked with the MPI library. It is then executed by means of a command (e.g., `mpirun`) that is

```
# include <mpi.h>

main(int argc, char *argv[]) {
  int myid, otherid, size;
  int length = 1, tag = 1;
  int myvalue, othervalue;
  MPI_Status status;

  /* initialize MPI and get own id (rank) */
  MPI_Init(&argc, &argv);
  MPI_Comm_size(MPI_COMM_WORLD, &size);
  MPI_Comm_rank(MPI_COMM_WORLD, &myid);

  if (myid == 0) {
    otherid = 1; myvalue = 14;
  } else {
    otherid = 0; myvalue = 25;
  }
  MPI_Send(&myvalue, length, MPI_INT, otherid,
           tag, MPI_COMM_WORLD);
  MPI_Recv(&othervalue, length, MPI_INT, MPI_ANY_SOURCE,
           tag, MPI_COMM_WORLD, &status);
  printf("process %d received a %d\n", myid, othervalue);

  MPI_Finalize();
}
```

Figure 7.17   MPI program to exchange values between two processes.

provided by the specific implementation of MPI that is being used. That command will create some specified number of processes, and each will start executing the `main` routine.

The program uses six basic MPI routines; these are used in almost all MPI programs.

> `MPI_Init`. Initialize the MPI library and get back a copy of the command-line arguments that were passed to the program. Every instance of the program gets a copy. One effect of this call is to initialize the variable `MPI_COMM_WORLD`, which is the collection of processes that were started.
>
> `MPI_Comm_size`. Determine the number of processes that were started (`size`). There should be two for this program.
>
> `MPI_Comm_rank`. Determine your rank (identity). Ranks range from `0` to `size-1`.
>
> `MPI_Send`. Send a message to another process. The arguments are: the buffer containing the message, the number of elements to send, the type of data in the message, the identity (rank) of the destination process, a programmer specified tag that can be used to distinguish types of messages, and the ubiquitous `MPI_COMM_WORLD`.
>
> `MPI_Receive`. Receive a message from another process. The arguments are: the buffer into which to put the message, the number of elements in the message, the type of data in the message, the identity of the sending process or "don't care" (`MPI_ANY_SOURCE`), a message tag, the communication group, and a return status.
>
> `MPI_Finalize`. Clean up the MPI library and terminate this process.

In the program, process `0` sends the value `14` to process `1`, which sends the value `25` to process `0`. The exchange is coded symmetrically, as a send followed by a receive. If more than two copies of the program are started, then all of processes `1` to `size-1` will send `25` to process `0`. Process `0` will receive one copy of `25` from one of the other processes, but it sends its value only to process `1`.

The `MPI_Send` routine delays until the message is buffered or until it is received by the specified destination process (`otherid`). Thus the combination of `MPI_Send` and `MPI_Receive` provides asynchronous message passing, although technically an implementation of MPI is not obligated to buffer messages. (This can cause problems when writing MPI programs, because it can lead to deadlock.) MPI also supports other modes of sending and receiving messages. For example, the programmer can provide buffer space and thus guarantee that a send will not block. Other functions include synchronous send and polling (nonblocking) receive.

7.8.2 Global Communication and Synchronization

MPI also includes a variety of functions for global communication and synchronization. These allow each member of a group of processes to interact directly with all the members. The most interesting—and commonly used—global functions are as follows:

> `MPI_Barrier`. Signal arrival at a barrier point; this returns when all other processes in the group have also called the function. (The default group is `MPI_COMM_WORLD`.)
>
> `MPI_Bcast`. Broadcast a copy of a message to all group members (including the sender).
>
> `MPI_Scatter`. Scatter an array `a` of `size` elements by sending a message containing `a[i]` to every process `i` in the group.
>
> `MPI_Gather`. Gather messages from every process in the group and store them in an array of `size` elements; the message from process `i` is stored in array element `i`.
>
> `MPI_Reduce`. Gather values from every process and reduce them into one value; the reduction operators include `MPI_SUM`, `MPI_MAX`, and other associative and commutative binary operators.
>
> `MPI_Allreduce`. Same as `MPI_Reduce` except that *every* process gets a copy of the reduced value.

The functionality provided by these routines can be programmed explicitly using process-to-process messages. For example, a broadcast send can be programmed by a loop that sends a message to each process. However, by using these routines it is much easier to write many applications.

For example, consider the programs in Figures 7.11 and 7.12. The coordinator process `P[0]` in Figure 7.11 could use `MPI_Gather` to collect a message from every other process and could use `MPI_Bcast` to send out the results. The symmetric processes in Figure 7.12 could be reprogrammed to use just two calls of `MPI_Allreduce`! The first call would be used to reduce all the local values to the smallest; the second would be used to reduce all local values to the largest. As another example, Figure 12.2 illustrates the use of `MPI_Reduce`.

A further benefit of the global communication routines is that the MPI system can implement them more efficiently than the programmer. One payoff is that there will be far less context switching, because an application process issues one function call, then blocks until it can complete. A second payoff is that buffer space can be reduced. Finally, the MPI system will have more opportunities to overlap message transfers with internal processing and to exploit parallelism that might be available in the communications network.

7.9 Case Study: Java

The Java language supports concurrent programming by means of threads, shared variables, and synchronized methods, as we saw in Section 5.4. Java can also be used to write distributed programs. It does not contain built-in primitives for message passing, but it does contain a standard package `java.net`. Classes in this package support low-level communication using datagrams, higher-level communication using sockets, and Internet communication using URLs (Uniform Resource Locators). Below we give a brief introduction to networks and sockets, then we present a complete example of a remote file reader and its client.

7.9.1 Networks and Sockets

A network consists of a collection of hosts connected by a communication medium. For example, a local area network might consist of a collection of workstations and servers connected by an Ethernet. The Internet is an example of a global, long-haul network, containing millions of hosts and thousands of interconnected communication networks. Each host has a unique name so other hosts can communicate with it. In fact, each host on the Internet has two unique names: a symbolic Internet domain name and a numeric Internet Protocol (IP) address. For example, this book was written on host `paloverde.cs.arizona.edu`, IP address `192.12.69.16`.

Programs executing on different hosts use *communication protocols* to interact with each other. Dozens of such protocols exist. They support different types of data—from text and graphics to movies—different levels of abstraction—such as file transfers or data packets—and different tradeoffs—for example, speed versus reliability. Two protocols that are commonly used by system programmers are TCP (Transmission Control Protocol) and UDP (Unreliable Datagram Protocol). These are usually implemented on top of IP, which is in turn implemented on top of hardware-level protocols, such as an Ethernet driver.

At the other extreme, the file transfer protocol (FTP) and the Web's hypertext transfer protocol (HTTP) are high-level protocols that are implemented on top of TCP.

TCP communication is based on connections and streams. A connection is a link between two hosts that is established before communication occurs and that persists until it is closed. Think of a connection as a "soft wire" between hosts. A communication stream is a sequence of messages that is sent over a connection. A stream provides reliable and ordered communication, meaning that messages are not lost and that they are delivered in the order they were sent. Thus a stream has the same semantics as a channel (Section 7.1).

The UDP protocol is based on datagrams. A datagram contains a destination address and a small "packet" of data, which is simply an array of bytes. Connections are not needed, because each datagram contains a destination address. However, UDP communication is unreliable: datagrams can be lost or arrive out of order. On the other hand, datagram communication is much quicker than stream-based communication. The main tradeoff between TCP and UDP is reliability versus speed.

The `java.net` package contains a number of classes that support both stream-based and datagram-based communication. Below we illustrate the use of two classes, `Socket` and `ServerSocket`, which are commonly used in client/server applications.

7.9.2 Example: A Remote File Reader

Many computing facilities contain workstations that are used by individuals and shared servers for file storage, Internet access, and so on. Suppose client applications execute on workstations that are connected to a file-server machine. The file server provides access to a file system stored on its local disks. (We will assume that the server machine runs Unix and hence that it has a Unix file system.) When a client wants to read a file stored on the file server, it communicates with a server process that executes on the server machine. In particular, the client sends the server the name of the file it wishes to read. Assuming the file can be opened, the server reads the lines in the file and sends them to the client.

Figure 7.18 contains Java code for the server process. The server first creates a server socket and listens for a connection on port `9999`. (A port is a number, hopefully unique, that is used by clients and servers to distinguish a specific connection.) The server then waits for a client to connect. Next the server creates input and output streams that use the socket. After the server reads a file name from the client, it opens the file. If the file does not exist, the server sends

```java
// Read a file and send it back to a client
import java.io.*; import java.net.*;

public class FileReaderServer {
 public static void main(String args[]) {
   try {
     // create server socket and
     // listen for connection on port 9999
     ServerSocket listen = new ServerSocket(9999);

     while (true) {
       System.out.println("waiting for connection");
       Socket socket = listen.accept();  // wait for client
       // create input and output streams to talk to client
       BufferedReader from_client =
         new BufferedReader(new InputStreamReader
           (socket.getInputStream()));
       PrintWriter to_client = new PrintWriter
           (socket.getOutputStream());

       // get filename from client and check if it exists
       String filename = from_client.readLine();
       File inputFile = new File(filename);
       if (!inputFile.ex ists()) {
         to_client.println("cannot open " + filename);
         to_client.close(); from_client.close();
         socket.close();
         continue;
       }

       // read lines from filename and send to the client
       System.out.println("reading from file " + filename);
       BufferedReader input =
         new BufferedReader(new FileReader(inputFile));
       String line;
       while ((line = input.readLine()) != null)
         to_client.println(line);
       to_client.close(); from_client.close();
       socket.close();
   }}
   catch (Exception e) // report any exceptions
     { System.err.println(e); }
}}
```

Figure 7.18   A file reader server in Java.

an error message to the client, closes the streams and socket, and waits for another client connection. If the file exists, the server reads each line and sends it to the client (using a `println` method). When the end of file is reached, the server closes the streams and socket and then waits for another client connection. If an exception occurs, the server prints an error message and terminates.

Figure 7.19 contains Java code for a client. After reading host and file names from the command line, the client tries to open a socket connection to

```java
// Get file from RemoteFileServer and print on stdout
import java.io.*; import java.net.*;
public class Client {
 public static void main(String[] args) {
  try {
   // read command-line arguments
   if (args.length != 2) {
     System.out.println("need 2 arguments");
     System.ex it(1);
   }
   String host = args[0];
   String filename = args[1];

   // open socket, then input and output streams to it
   Socket socket = new Socket(host,9999);
   BufferedReader from_server =
     new BufferedReader(new InputStreamReader
       (socket.getInputStream()));
   PrintWriter to_server = new PrintWriter
       (socket.getOutputStream());

   // send filename to server, then read and print lines
   // until the server closes the connection
   to_server.println(filename); to_server.flush();
   String line;
   while ((line = from_server.readLine()) != null) {
     System.out.println(line);
   }
  }
  catch (Exception e)     // report any exceptions
    { System.err.println(e); }
}}
```

Figure 7.19   A file reader client in Java.

`host` on port `9999`—the agreed upon number of the server's port. If the server can accept the connection, the client sends `filename` to the server, gets back the lines in the file, and prints them on the local display. Again, if an exception occurs, the client prints an error message and terminates.

These two programs are executed as follows. First, each is compiled on its host machine using a Java compiler such as `javac`. Second, the server is started by executing

```
java FileReaderServer
```

Third, a client is started on a different (or the same) host by executing

```
java Client hostname filename
```

where `hostname` is the name of the host on which the server is executing and `filename` is the name of the file the client wishes to read. The server will continue executing until it is killed or catches an exception, so additional clients can later be started. The reader is encouraged to experiment with these programs to see how they behave. For example, what happens if the client is started before the server? What happens if two clients try to connect to the server at about the same time?

Historical Notes

The concept of message passing originated in the late 1960s. Even though general-purpose multiprocessors and computer networks did not exist at that time, some operating system designers realized that it would be attractive to organize an operating system as a collection of communicating processes. This is because every process has a specific function, and one process cannot interfere with another since they do not share variables.

The multiprogramming nucleus developed by Per Brinch Hansen [1970] for the Danish RC 4000 computer was, in this author's opinion, the most elegant early message-passing proposal. Brinch Hansen's original nucleus provided four primitives that support client/server communication using a shared pool of fixed-length buffers. He later added two primitives to allow a process to examine its message queue and answer buffers and to receive specific messages or answers; this allows a process to engage in more than one conversation at a time. The textbook on operating systems by Bic and Shaw [1988, pp. 24–26] describes Brinch Hansen's original primitives.

Because it is more efficient for processes to communicate using shared variables than message passing, most operating systems for single processors and shared-memory multiprocessors use shared variables for process interaction within the operating system. However, these operating systems provide message-passing primitives so that processes can communicate with other machines on a network. For example, UNIX provides sockets and a variety of system calls for sending and receiving messages. Of necessity, operating systems for distributed memory multiprocessors provide and use message-passing primitives. Almasi and Gottlieb [1994] and Hwang [1993] give overviews of multicomputer hardware and software.

Many programming languages have been based on message passing or have included message-passing facilities. In the text we describe CSP and Occam (Section 7.6), Linda (Section 7.7), Java (Section 7.9), and SR (Section 8.7). An excellent survey paper by Bal, Steiner, and Tanenbaum [1989] categorizes and explains dozens of programming languages for distributed computing. These include several based on asynchronous and on synchronous message passing.

The duality between monitors and message passing was noticed and analyzed by Hugh Lauer and Roger Needham [1978]. Bjarne Stroustrup [1982]—who later created the C++ language—investigated the two styles and found that performance is about the same for client/server applications on shared-memory machines, although message passing is occasionally slower. On the other hand, monitors and message passing are typically used quite differently; the examples in Chapters 5 and 7 illustrate this. Moreover, monitors do not directly support filters or interacting peers; for these all they provide is a mechanism for implementing communication buffers.

Synchronous communication was introduced by Hoare [1978] in his now classic paper on Communicating Sequential Processes (CSP). That paper, like Hoare's earlier paper on monitors [1974], is a model of clarity. The mechanisms described in Section 7.6 are essentially the same as those introduced in Hoare's paper. The major difference is that we allow output statements in guards. However, Hoare recognized the utility of this—and discusses the issue in Section 7.8 of his paper. In a later book on the semantics of CSP, Hoare [1985] permits output statements in guards.

Occam is the best-known language based on synchronous message passing. It was developed in the early 1980s by David May and colleagues at INMOS, a British computer firm; that company also developed the transputer machine. (Tony Hoare, the creator of CSP, was a consultant to May's group.) May [1983] gives an overview of what is now called Occam 1. Occam 2 was released in 1987. Alan Burns [1988] gives a thorough overview of Occam 2 and the transputer machine and compares Occam to Ada. An excellent source for information and tools on Occam is the Internet Parallel Computing Archive at `www.hensa.ac.uk/parallel`.

The modern version of CSP was introduced in Hoare [1985], a book that focuses on the semantics of communicating sequential processes. Hoare and several colleagues have continued to develop the theory and notation. In addition, people have developed (and continue to refine) automated proof tools for CSP, as well as simulators and animators that let one experiment with CSP specifications. Roscoe [1998] describes the latest version of CSP and its underlying theory, practical applications, and tools. The home pages for Roscoe's book, which contains extensive information, and for the main CSP archive are found at

```
www.comlab.ox.ac.uk/oucl/publications/books/concurrency/
www.comlab.ox.ac.uk/archive/csp.html
```

Groups have also developed Java class libraries that support the CSP model. Links to these can be found at the Internet Parallel Computing Archive listed above or in the CSP archive.

Linda was developed in 1983 by David Gelernter in his doctoral dissertation at the State University of New York Stony Brook. The name is the result of Gelernter's wry graduate student humor. The Ada language was being developed at that time, and it was named after Ada Augusta Lovelace, who is regarded as the first programmer. So Gelernter whimsically decided to name his language after another Lovelace who was in the news at the time—as an actress in X-rated movies. The name stuck.

Gelernter [1985] introduces the Linda primitives. Carriero, Gelernter, and Leichter [1986] describe how Linda can be used to implement distributed data structures and the bag-of-tasks programming paradigm. Carriero and Gelernter [1986] give a detailed description of an implementation of Linda. Carriero and Gelernter [1989a] compare Linda with message passing, concurrent objects, concurrent logic programming, and functional programming; the bibliography in that paper includes several papers that describe specific applications of Linda. Finally, Carriero and Gelernter [1989b] describe three methods for parallel programming—result parallelism, agenda parallelism, and specialist parallelism—and show how each method can be implemented in Linda. The Linda prime number program in Figure 7.16 is adapted from that paper.

The Linda primitives have been added to several sequential languages, and Linda implementations exist for several workstations, multiprocessors, and multicomputers. Linda is distributed by Scientific Computing Associates, `www.sca.com`.

As noted in the text, the MPI interface was defined in the mid-1990s by Snir et al. [1996]. There are now several free implementations. The two the author has used are LAM and MPICH; the home pages for these are found at

```
www.mpi.nd.edu/lam/
www-unix.mcs.anl.gov/mpi/mpich/
```

Each site contains extensive documentation, links to other sites, and source code for the implementation.

Parallel Virtual Machine (PVM) is another message-passing library that is often used [Geist et al. 1994]. Experience with PVM heavily influenced the design of MPI, which followed later. The kinds of message-passing primitives in the two libraries are similar. The main differences between PVM and MPI are that PVM supports a networked collection of heterogeneous machines and that it has features to support fault tolerance. To do so, PVM employs daemon processes that run in the background on each host; the daemons manage the hosts and coordinate interactions between application processes. The PVM home page is located at

```
www.epm.ornl.gov/pvm/pvm_home.html
```

That site contains a wealth of information and software.

The sources I consulted for information on Java's `java.net` package were two books by David Flanagan [1997a, 1997b]. The source code for the examples in Flanagan [1997b] is available on the Web at `www.ora.com/cata-log/jenut/`. That site also contains information on several other sources on Java, including books on threads, network programming, and distributed computing.

A different approach to distributed programming in Java is taken in Hartley [1998] and Magee and Kramer [1999]. Both books describe how to implement channels and asynchronous and synchronous message passing—pretty much as we have defined them—as Java classes. Hartley in particular shows how to program in Java many of the algorithms in this book. The home page for Hartley's book is at

```
www.mcs.drexel.edu/~shartley/ConcProgJava/
```

The site contains the source for his Java programs.

References

Almasi, G. S., and A. Gottlieb. 1994. *Highly Parallel Computing*, 2nd ed. Menlo Park, CA: Benjamin/Cummings.

Bal, H. E., J. G. Steiner, and A. S. Tanenbaum. 1989. Programming languages for distributed computing systems. *ACM Computing Surveys* 21, 3 (September): 261–322.

Bic, L., and A. C. Shaw. 1988. *The Logical Design of Operating Systems*, 2nd ed. Englewood Cliffs, NJ: Prentice-Hall.

Brinch Hansen, P. 1970. The nucleus of a multiprogramming system. *Comm. ACM* 13, 4 (April): 238–41.

Burns, A. 1988. *Programming in occam 2*. Reading, MA: Addison-Wesley.

Carriero, N., and D. Gelernter. 1986. The S/Net's Linda kernel. *ACM Trans. Computer Systems* 4, 2 (May): 110–29.

Carriero, N., and D. Gelernter. 1989a. Linda in Context. *Comm. ACM* 32, 4 (April): 444–58.

Carriero, N., and D. Gelernter. 1989b. How to write parallel programs: A guide to the perplexed. *ACM Computing Surveys* 21, 3 (September): 323–58.

Carriero, N., D. Gelernter, and J. Leichter. 1986. Distributed data structures in Linda. *Thirteenth ACM Symp. on Principles of Prog. Langs.*, January, 236–42.

Flanagan, D. 1997a. *Java in a Nutshell: A Desktop Quick Reference*, 2nd ed. Sebastopol, CA: O'Reilly & Associates.

Flanagan, D. 1997b. *Java Examples in a Nutshell: A Tutorial Companion to Java in a Nutshell.* Sebastopol, CA: O'Reilly & Associates.

Geist, A., A. Beguelin, J. Dongarra, W. Wiang, R. Manchek, and V. Sunderam. 1994. *PVM: Parallel Virtual Machine, A User's Guide and Tutorial for Networked Parallel Computing.* Cambridge, MA: MIT Press.

Gelernter, D. 1985. Generative communication in Linda. *ACM Trans. on Prog. Languages and Systems* 7, 1 (January): 80–112.

Hartley, S. J. 1998. *Concurrent Programming: The Java Programming Language.* New York: Oxford University Press.

Hoare, C. A. R. 1974. Monitors: An operating system structuring concept. *Comm. ACM* 17, 10 (October): 549–57.

Hoare, C. A. R. 1978. Communicating sequential processes. *Comm. ACM* 21, 8 (August): 666–77.

Hoare, C. A. R. 1985. *Communicating Sequential Processes*. Englewood Cliffs, NJ: Prentice-Hall International.

Hwang, K. 1993. *Advanced Computer Architecture: Parallelism, Scalability, Programmability.* New York: McGraw-Hill.

Lauer, H. C., and R. M. Needham. 1978. On the duality of operating system structures. *Proc. Second Int. Symp. on Operating Systems*, October; reprinted in *Operating Systems Review* 13, 2 (April 1979): 3–19.

Magee, J, and J. Kramer. 1999. *Concurrency: State Models and Java Programs.* New York: Wiley.

May, D. 1983. OCCAM. *SIGPLAN Notices* 18, 4 (April): 69–79.

Roscoe, A. W. 1998. *The Theory and Practice of Concurrency.* Englewood Cliffs, NJ: Prentice-Hall International.

Snir, M., S. Otto, S. Huss-Lederman, D. Walker, and J. Dongarra. 1996. *MPI: The Complete Reference.* Cambridge, MA: MIT Press.

Stroustrup, B. 1982. An experiment with the interchangeability of processes and monitors. *Software—Practice and Experience* 12, 1011–25.

Exercises

7.1 For the sorting network shown in Figure 7.3, suppose the merge processes are declared as an array `Merge[1:n]`. Give the declarations of the channels, and give the body of the array of `Merge` processes. Since the processes are to be identical, you will have to figure out how to embed the merge tree in an array.

7.2 Consider a filter process `Partition` having the following specifications. `Partition` receives unsorted values from one input channel `in` and sends the values it receives to one of two output channels, `out1` or `out2`. `Partition` uses the first value `v` it receives to partition the input values into two sets. It sends all values less than or equal to `v` to `out1`; it sends all values greater than `v` to `out2`. Finally, `Partition` sends `v` to `out1` and sends a sentinel `EOS` to both `out1` and `out2`. The end of the input stream is marked by a sentinel `EOS`.

(a) Develop an implementation of `Partition`. First give predicates specifying the contents of the channels, then develop the body of `Partition`.

(b) Show how to construct a sorting network out of `Partition` processes. Assume that there are `n` input values and that `n` is a power of `2`. In the worst case, how big does the network have to be? (This is not a good way to do sorting; this is just an exercise!)

7.3 It is possible to sort an array of `n` values using a pipeline of `n` filter processes. The first process inputs all the values one at a time, keeps the minimum, and passes the others on to the next process. Each filter does the same thing: it receives a stream of values from the previous process, keeps the smallest, and passes the others to the next process. Assume each process has local storage for only two values—the next input value and the minimum it has seen so far.

(a) Develop code for the filter processes. Declare the channels and use asynchronous message passing.

(b) Compare the performance of your answer to (a) to the sorting network of **Merge** processes in Figure 7.3. How many messages are sent by each program to sort **n** values? Consider which messages can be sent in parallel (assuming appropriate hardware) and which are sent sequentially. What is the total execution time of each program expressed as the length of the longest chain of sequentially-ordered messages?

7.4   Consider the program in Figure 7.7. Answer the following as independent exercises.

(a) Modify the program to allow clients to request and release more than one unit at a time.

(b) The program shows how to simulate the specific monitor in Figure 7.6 using a server process. Develop a simulation of an arbitrary monitor. In particular, show how you would simulate every monitor mechanism in Section 5.1, including **signal_all**, priority **wait**, and **empty**. Show the actions of the client processes as well as the server.

7.5   Consider the dining philosophers problem defined in Section 4.3. Develop a server process to synchronize the actions of the philosophers. Show the client (philosopher) interface to the server. The processes should interact using asynchronous message passing.

7.6   Consider the readers/writers problem defined in Section 4.4. Develop a server process to implement the database. Show the reader and writer interfaces to the server. The processes should interact using asynchronous message passing.

7.7   Develop an implementation of a time-server process. The server provides two operations that can be called by client processes: one to get the time of day and one to delay for a specified interval. In addition, the time server receives periodic "tick" messages from a clock interrupt handler. Also show the client interface to the time server for the time of day and delay operations.

7.8   *The Savings Account Problem.* A savings account is shared by several people. Each person may deposit or withdraw funds from the account. The current balance in the account is the sum of all deposits to date minus the sum of all withdrawals to date. The balance must never become negative.

Develop a server to solve this problem, and show the client interface to the server. Clients make two kinds of requests: one to deposit `amount` dollars and one to withdraw `amount` dollars. The withdraw operation must delay until there are sufficient funds. Assume that `amount` is positive.

7.9   Two kinds of processes, `A`'s and `B`'s, enter a room. An `A` process cannot leave until it meets two `B` processes, and a `B` process cannot leave until it meets one `A` process. Each kind of process leaves the room—without meeting any other processes—once it has met the required number of other processes.

(a) Develop a server process to implement this synchronization. Show the interface of `A` and `B` processes to the server.

(b) Modify your answer to (a) so that the first of the two `B` processes that meets an `A` process does not leave the room until after the `A` process meets a second `B` process.

7.10 Suppose a computer center has two printers, A and B, that are similar but not identical. Three kinds of client processes use the printers: those that must use A, those that must use B, and those that can use either A or B.

Develop code that each kind of client executes to request and release a printer, and develop a server process to allocate the printers. Your solution should be fair assuming that a client using a printer eventually releases it.

7.11 *The One-Lane Bridge.* Cars coming from the north and south arrive at a one-lane bridge. Cares heading in the same direction can cross the bridge at the same time, but cars heading in opposite directions cannot.

(a) Develop a server process to manage use of the bridge. Assume the cars are client processes. Use asynchronous message passing for process interaction, and show how the clients interact with the server.

(b) Develop a simulation of your answer to part (a). Use C and the MPI library or Java and the sockets package. Have cars repeatedly try to cross the bridge. They should spend a random amount of time on the bridge and should delay for a random amount of time before crossing again. Print a trace of the key events in your simulation.

7.12 *The Roller Coaster Problem.* Suppose there are `n` passenger processes and one car process. The passengers repeatedly wait to take rides in the car, which can hold `c` passengers, `c` < `n`. However, the car can go around the tracks only when it is full.

(a) Develop code for the actions of the passenger and car processes. Use message passing for communication.

(b) Generalize your answer to (a) to employ m car processes, m > 1. Since there is only one track, cars cannot pass each other—i.e., they must finish going around the track in the order in which they started. Again, a car can go around the tracks only when it is full.

(c) Develop a simulation of your answer to part (a). Use C and the MPI library or Java and the sockets package. Have passengers repeatedly take some number R of rides. Have the car take a fixed amount of time to go around the track, and have passengers delay for a random amount of time before taking another ride. Print a trace of the key events in your simulation.

7.13   Consider the self-scheduling disk driver process in Figure 7.9.

(a) Modify the process to use the CSCAN scheduling strategy that was employed in the monitor in Figure 5.13.

(b) Modify the self-scheduling disk driver in Figure 7.9 to use the SCAN (elevator) scheduling strategy described at the start of Section 5.3.

7.14   The following exercises deal with the file server program in Figure 7.10.

(a) In the program, the file servers share channel open; in particular, all of them receive from it. In many implementations of message passing, each channel can have only one receiver (but usually many senders). Modify the file server program so that it meets this restriction.

(b) In the program, each client process uses a different file server. Suppose there is only one file server. Modify the file server program so that all clients use the same server. Your solution should permit every client to have a file open at the same time.

(c) In the program, each client process uses a different file server. Suppose that clients that want to access the same file use the same file server. In particular, if a file is already open, the client should converse with the server that is managing that file; otherwise the client should start a conversation with a free file server. Modify the file server program to meet these requirements.

7.15   *Stable Marriage Problem.* Let Man and Woman each be arrays of n processes. Each man ranks the women from 1 to n and each woman ranks the men from 1 to n. A *pairing* is a one-to-one correspondence of men and women. A pairing is *stable* if, for two men m_1 and m_2 and their paired women w_1 and w_2, both of the following conditions are satisfied:

- m_1 ranks w_1 higher than w_2 or w_2 ranks m_2 higher than m_1; and

- m_2 ranks w_2 higher than w_1 or w_1 ranks m_1 higher than m_2.

Expressed differently, a pairing is unstable if a man and woman would both prefer each other to their current pair. A solution to the stable marriage problem is a set of n pairings, all of which are stable.

(a) Write a program to solve the stable marriage problem. The processes should communicate using asynchronous message passing. The men should propose and the women should listen. A woman has to accept the first proposal she gets, because a better one might not come along; however, she can dump the first man if she later gets a better proposal.

(b) Develop a simulation of your answer to (a). Use C with the MPI library or Java and the sockets package. Print a trace of key events as they happen, or animate your program so that you can watch the action in real time. (In an animation, you will need to have the processes nap some so that they execute slowly enough for you to observe their actions.)

7.16 You are given three processes F, G, and H, each having a local array of integers. All three arrays are sorted in nondecreasing order. At least one value is in all three arrays. Develop a program in which the three processes interact until each has determined the smallest common value. Give key assertions in each process. Messages should contain only one value at a time.

7.17 *Distributed Pairing.* You are given n processes, each corresponding to a node in a connected graph. Each node can communicate only with its neighbors. The problem is for each process to pair itself with one of its neighbors. When the processes finish pairing up, each process should be paired or single, and no two neighboring processes should be single.

Solve this problem using asynchronous message passing for communication. Every process is to execute the same algorithm. When the program terminates, every process should have stored in local variable `pair` the index of the neighbor it is paired with; the final value of `pair` should be i if process i is single. Your solution need not be optimal, in the sense of minimizing the number of single processes (that makes the problem *very* hard).

7.18 Figure 7.15 contains a CSP program for generating prime numbers using the sieve of Eratosthenes. Modify the program to use the asynchronous message-passing primitives defined in Section 7.1. Also add a coordinator process to gather the results and print them.

7.19 Figures 7.15 and 7.16 present two different algorithms for generating prime numbers.

(a) Implement the algorithms using C together with the MPI library.

(b) Compare the performance of your two programs for different limits on the number of primes to generate. What is the total execution time? What is the total number of messages?

7.20   Consider the three programs in Section 7.4 for exchanging values.

(a) Implement each algorithm using C together with the MPI library. Use global communication primitives where appropriate. Each program should execute a sequence of R rounds of exchanges.

(b) Compare the performance of your programs. What is the total execution time of each program as a function of the number of processes and number of rounds?

(c) Exchanging values would typically just be a small part of a larger computation, such as a grid computation (see Section 12.1). In particular, every round each process would compute for a while and then exchange values. Add code to your programs for (a) to simulate computation; use a loop that does something simple like incrementing a counter for C iterations. If possible, place the computation loop so that it can be overlapped with communication (namely, after sends but before receives). At this point what is the total execution time of each program as a function of the number of processes, number of rounds, and value of C?

7.21   Linda's tuple space could be implemented by a server process. Application processes would then interact with the server whenever they wanted to execute a Linda primitive such as OUT, IN, or EVAL. Develop code for the server process showing how it could implement tuple space and the six Linda primitives. Also show the code that an application process would execute for each primitive. The application and server processes should interact using asynchronous message passing.

7.22   Table 7.1 illustrates the duality between monitors and message passing. The Historical Notes mention experiments that showed that the performance of programs in the two styles was close to identical on shared-memory multiprocessors. Construct a set of experiments to confirm (or refute) these results. Take a set of applications—such as the dining philosophers, readers/writers, and disk scheduler—and program them in both styles. For example, use Pthreads to implement the monitor programs and use MPI to implement the message passing programs. Then measure the performance of each program. As a control measure, you should also implement message passing directly in Pthreads so you can see how much overhead, if any, MPI has relative to Pthreads.

7.23   Consider the Java remote file reader in Figures 7.18 and 7.19.

(a) Get the program to work at your site, then answer the two questions at the end of Section 7.9 as well as any similar questions that occur to you.

(b) Modify the program to so that it writes remote files instead of reading them. In particular, the client should read lines from standard input and send them to a remote file writer.

(b) Combine the programs for (a) and (b) to support both reading and writing remote files. You will need to add a command-line option to indicate whether the client wishes to read or write a remote file. Experiment with your new program and report the results that you observe. You may want to make the client program interactive to facilitate experimentation.

7.24   Consider the prime number generation program written in C-Linda (Figure 7.16). Implement the program in Java. Since there is no shared tuple space, have the manager implement the bag of tasks. Use sockets for communication between the workers and manager.

7.25   Develop a simulation of the dining philosophers using either C and the MPI library or Java and the sockets package. Your program should have five philosopher processes and one server process that manages the table. Simulate eating and thinking by having a philosopher sleep for a random amount of time. Your program should print a trace of the interesting events as they happen.

7.26   Design, implement, and document a parallel or distributed program that makes creative use of several processes. Use a programming language or subroutine library that is available on your local installation.

The following is a list of possible projects. Either pick one of these or design your own project having a comparable level of difficulty. Provide your instructor with a brief description of your project before you begin, and demonstrate your program when the project is completed.

(a) Take some problem that could be parallelized or distributed in different ways—e.g, sorting, prime number generation, traveling sales rep, matrix multiplication. Develop different algorithms to solve the problem, and perform a series of experiments to determine which approach works best under different assumptions. Ideally, perform experiments on both a shared-memory multiprocessor and a distributed-memory machine.

(b) Construct an automated teller system having several customer "terminals" and several banks. Each ATM is connected to one bank, and the banks are connected to each other. Each account is stored at one bank, but a customer should be able to use any ATM to access his or her account. Your program should implement several kinds of user transactions, such as deposits, withdrawals, and balance inquiries. Ideally, construct a user interface that looks like a teller machine.

(c) Construct an airline reservation system that allows users to ask about flights and to reserve and cancel seats. Support multiple reservation agents. This project is similar to implementing an automated teller system.

(d) Develop a program that plays some game and employs several displays, either to show the results for different players or to enable several players to play against each other and perhaps "the machine." If you choose this project, keep the game relatively simple so that you do not get bogged down just getting the game itself programmed. For example, implement a simple card game such as (basic) blackjack or concentration, or a simple video game.

(e) Implement a "talk" or "chat" command that allows users on different terminals to converse with each other. Support both private conversations and conference calls. Allow a person to join a conversation that is already in progress.

(f) Develop a discrete-event simulation of some physical system. For example, simulate traffic moving through an intersection, planes arriving and departing at an airport, or customers riding elevators in a building. Implement the various entities in the simulation as processes that generate events and react to them. You may want to have the processes interact directly with each other as events occur, or you may want to use a scheduler process to keep track of an event list and update a simulation clock. Animate your program so that users can see the simulation execute and possibly interact with it.

8

RPC and Rendezvous

Message passing is ideally suited to programming filters and interacting peers, because these kinds of processes send information in one direction through communication channels. As we have seen, message passing can also be used to program clients and servers. However, the two-way information flow between clients and servers has to be programmed with two explicit message exchanges using two different message channels. Moreover, each client needs a different reply channel; this leads to a large number of channels.

This chapter examines two additional programming notations—remote procedure call (RPC) and rendezvous—that are ideally suited to programming client/server interactions. Both combine aspects of monitors and synchronous message passing. As with monitors, a module or process exports operations, and the operations are invoked by a `call` statement. As with a synchronous send statement, execution of `call` delays the caller. The novelty of RPC and rendezvous is that an operation is a two-way communication channel from the caller to the process that services the call and then back to the caller. In particular, the caller delays until the called operation has been executed and any results have been returned.

The difference between RPC and rendezvous is the way in which invocations of operations are serviced. One approach is to declare a procedure for each operation and to create a new process (at least conceptually) to handle each call. This is called *remote procedure call* since the caller and procedure body may be on different machines. The second approach is to *rendezvous* with an existing process. A rendezvous is serviced by means of an input (or accept) statement that waits for an invocation, processes it, then returns results. (This is sometimes called an extended rendezvous to contrast it with the simple rendezvous between send and receive statements in synchronous message passing.)

Sections 8.1 and 8.2 describe representative programming notations for RPC and rendezvous and illustrates their use. As mentioned, each facilitates programming client/server interactions. Each can also be used to program filters and interacting peers, but we will see that this is cumbersome since neither RPC nor rendezvous directly supports asynchronous communication. Fortunately, we can overcome this problem by combining RPC, rendezvous, and asynchronous message passing into a powerful yet quite simple language, which we introduce in Section 8.3.

We illustrate the use of these notations and the tradeoffs between them by means of several examples. Some examine problems we have solved previously and thus facilitate comparison of the various forms of message passing. Some problems are new and demonstrate the utility of RPC or rendezvous for programming client/server interactions. For example, Section 8.4 shows how to implement an encapsulated database and replicated files. Sections 8.5 to 8.7 summarize the distributed programming mechanisms of three languages: Java (RPC), Ada (rendezvous), and SR (multiple primitives).

8.1 Remote Procedure Call

In Chapter 5, we used two kinds of components in programs: processes and monitors. Monitors encapsulate shared variables; processes communicate and synchronize by calling monitor procedures. Also, the processes and monitors in a program are all assumed to be in the same shared address space.

With RPC, we will use one program component—the module—that contains both processes and procedures. Also, we will allow modules to reside in different address spaces—for example, on different nodes in a network.[1] Processes within a module can share variables and call procedures declared in that module. However, a process in one module can communicate with processes in a second module only by calling procedures exported by the second module.

To distinguish between procedures that are local to a module and those that provide communication channels, a module has two parts. The specification part contains headers of operations that can be called from other modules. The body contains procedures that implement these operations; it can also contain local

---

[1] Processes in the same address space are often called *lightweight threads*. The term *thread* indicates that each has a distinct thread of execution. The term *lightweight* comes from the fact that relatively little information needs to be saved on a context switch. This is in contrast to heavyweight processes—such as those in UNIX—that have their own address space. Switching context between heavyweight processes requires saving and loading memory management tables as well as registers.

variables, initialization code, and local procedures and processes. The form of a module is

```
module mname
    headers of exported operations;
body
    variable declarations;
    initialization code;
    procedures for exported operations;
    local procedures and processes;
end mname
```

Local processes are called *background processes* to distinguish them from processes that result from calls of exported operations (see below).

The header of an operation `opname` is specified by an `op` declaration:

```
op opname(formals)  [returns result]
```

The formals and `returns` part specify the types and optionally the names of the formal parameters and return value; the `returns` part is optional. With RPC, an operation is implemented by a `proc`:

```
proc opname(formal identifiers)  returns result identifier
    declarations of local variables;
    statements
end
```

A `proc` is thus like a procedure, except the types of the parameters and result do not need to be repeated, because they were specified in the `op` declaration. (Another way to look at it is that a procedure is simply an abbreviation for an `op` declaration and a `proc`.)

As with monitors, a process (or procedure) in one module calls a procedure in another module by executing

```
call mname.opname(arguments)
```

The `call` keyword is optional for procedure calls; it is not used for function calls. For a local call, the module name may also be omitted.

The implementation of an intermodule call is different than for a local call, however, since the two modules might be in different address spaces. In particular, a *new process* services the call and arguments are passed as messages between the caller and this server process. The calling process delays while the server process executes the body of the procedure that implements `opname`. When the server returns from `opname`, it sends result arguments and any return value to the calling process, then the server terminates. After receiving results, the calling process continues. The sending and receiving of results are implicit, however, rather than explicitly programmed.

If the calling process and procedure are in the same address space, it is often possible to avoid creating a new process to service a remote call—because the calling process can temporarily become the server and execute the procedure body (see Chapter 10 for details). But in general, a call will be remote, so a server process must be created or allocated from a preexisting pool of available servers.

To help clarify the interaction between the calling process and the server process, the following diagram depicts their execution:

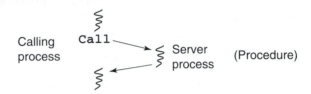

Time moves down the figure, and the squiggly lines indicate when a process is executing. When the calling process reaches a `call` statement, it delays while the server process executes the body of the called procedure. After the server returns results, the calling process continues.

8.1.1 *Synchronization in Modules*

By itself, RPC is simply a communication mechanism. Although a calling process is synchronized with its server, the server's only role is to act on the caller's behalf. Conceptually, it is as if the calling process itself were executing the call, and thus the synchronization between the caller and server is implicit.

We also need some way for the processes in a module to have mutually exclusive access to shared variables and to synchronize with each other. The processes include server processes that are executing remote calls as well as background processes declared in the module.

There are two approaches to providing synchronization in modules. The first is to assume that all processes in the same module execute with mutual exclusion—i.e., at most one at a time is active. This is similar to the implicit exclusion defined for monitors and guarantees that shared variables are protected against concurrent access. However, the processes need some way to program condition synchronization. For this we could use condition variables, as with monitors, or we could use semaphores.

The second approach is to assume that processes execute concurrently, and thus explicitly to program both mutual exclusion and condition synchronization. In this case, each module is itself a concurrent program, so we could use any of the methods described earlier in the book. For example, we could use semaphores, or we could use local monitors. In fact, as we will see later in this chapter, we could use rendezvous. (We could even use message passing.)

A program containing modules is executed by first executing the initialization code in every module. The initialization code in different modules can be executed concurrently, assuming this code does not make remote calls. Then the background processes are started. If exclusion is implicit, one background process per module can execute at a time; when it delays or terminates, another can execute. If processes in modules execute concurrently, then all background processes can begin execution at once.

There are two benefits when exclusion is implicit. First, modules are somewhat simpler to program, because shared variables are automatically protected from interference due to concurrent access. Second, the implementation can be more efficient for any module that executes on a single processor. This is because context switching will occur only at entry, exit, or delay points in procedures or processes, not at arbitrary points where intermediate results of a computation might be in registers.

On the other hand, it is more general to assume that processes can execute concurrently. For one, concurrent execution is the natural model for programs that execute on shared-memory multiprocessors, which are increasingly common. In addition, with the concurrent execution model we can implement time slicing to divide execution time among processes and to gain control over runaway processes (i.e., processes in permanent loops). This is not possible with the exclusive execution model unless processes are certain to relinquish the processor in a reasonable amount of time, since one may switch context only when the executing process reaches an exit or delay point.

Because it is more general, we will assume that processes within a module execute concurrently, and hence that both mutual exclusion and condition synchronization have to be programmed. The next two sections show how to program a time server and a distributed file system cache. For now, we use semaphores to program synchronization within modules.

8.1.2 A Time Server

Consider the problem of implementing a time server—i.e., a module that provides timing services to client processes in other modules. Suppose the time

```
module TimeServer
  op get_time() returns int;  # retrieve time of day
  op delay(int interval);     # delay interval ticks
body
  int tod = 0;             # the time of day
  sem m = 1;               # mutual exclusion semaphore
  sem d[n] = ([n] 0);  # private delay semaphores
  queue of (int waketime, int process_id) napQ;
  ## when m == 1, tod < waketime for delayed processes

  proc get_time() returns time {
    time = tod;
  }

  proc delay(interval) {     # assume interval > 0
    int waketime = tod + interval;
    P(m);
    insert (waketime, myid) at appropriate place on napQ;
    V(m);
    P(d[myid]);     # wait to be awakened
  }

  process Clock {
    start hardware timer;
    while (true) {
      wait for interrupt, then restart hardware timer;
      tod = tod+1;
      P(m);
      while (tod >= smallest waketime on napQ) {
        remove (waketime, id) from napQ;
        V(d[id]);  # awaken process id
      }
      V(m);
    }
  }
end TimeServer
```

Figure 8.1 A time-server module.

server defines two visible operations: `get_time` and `delay`. A client process gets the time of day by calling `get_time`. A client calls `delay` to block for `interval` time units. The time server also contains an internal process that continuously starts a hardware timer, then increments the time of day when the timer interrupt occurs.

Figure 8.1 contains the program for the time-server module. The time of day is stored in variable `tod`. Multiple clients can call `get_time` and `delay` at the same time, and hence several processes can be servicing these calls concurrently. It is safe for processes servicing calls of `get_time` to execute concurrently, because they merely read the value of `tod`. However, `delay` and `tick` need to execute with mutual exclusion when they are manipulating `napQ`, the queue of "napping" client processes. (In `delay`, the assignment to `wake_time` need not be in a critical section since `tod` is the only shared variable and it is merely read. In addition, the increment of `tod` in the `Clock` process need not be in a critical section because `Clock` is the only process that assigns to `tod`.)

The value of `myid` in `delay` is assumed to be a unique integer between `0` and `n-1`; it is used to indicate the private semaphore on which a client is waiting. After a clock interrupt, the `Clock` process executes a loop to check the `napQ`; it signals the appropriate delay semaphore when a delay interval has transpired. A loop is used since more than one process may be waiting for the same wake-up time.

8.1.3 Caches in a Distributed File System

Now consider a simplified version of a problem that arises in distributed file and database systems. Suppose application processes are executing on a workstation and that data files are stored on a file server. We will ignore how files are opened and closed and just focus on reading and writing them. When an application process wants to access a file, it calls a `read` or `write` procedure in a local module `FileCache`. We assume that applications read and write arrays of characters (bytes). At times an application will read or write just a few characters; at other times it might read or write thousands.

Files are stored on the file server's disk in fixed-size blocks (e.g., of 1024 bytes). The `FileServer` module manages access to disk blocks. It provides two operations, `readblk` and `writeblk`, for reading and writing entire blocks.

The `FileCache` module maintains a cache of recently read data blocks. When an application asks to read a part of a file, `FileCache` first checks to see if the needed bytes are in its cache. If so, it can quickly satisfy the client's

```
module FileCache    # located on each diskless workstation
  op read(int count; result char buffer[*]);
  op write(int count; char buffer[]);
body
  cache of file blocks;
  variables to record file descriptor information;
  semaphores for synchronization of cache access (if needed);

  proc read(count,buffer) {
    if (needed data is not in cache) {
      select cache block to use;
      if (need to write out the cache block)
        FileServer.writeblk(...);
      FileServer.readblk(...);
    }
    buffer = appropriate count bytes from cache block;
  }

  proc write(count,buffer) {
    if (appropriate block not in cache) {
      select cache block to use;
      if (need to write out the cache block)
        FileServer.writeblk(...);
    }
    cache block = count bytes from buffer;
  }
end FileCache
```

Figure 8.2 (a)   Distributed file system: File cache.

request. If not, it has to call the **readblk** procedure of the **FileServer** module to get the disk block(s) containing the data. (**FileCache** might also perform read-ahead if it detects that a file is being accessed sequentially, which is often the case.)

Write requests are handled in a similar manner. When an application calls **write**, the data is stored in a block in the local cache. When a block is full or is needed to satisfy another request, **FileCache** calls the **writeblk** operation in **FileServer** to store the block on disk. (Or **FileCache** may use a write-through strategy, in which case it will call **writeblk** after every write request. Using write-through guarantees that the data is stored on disk when a **write** operation completes, but it slows down the operation.)

```
module FileServer    # located on a file server
  op readblk(int fileid, offset; result char blk[1024]);
  op writeblk(int fileid, offset; char blk[1024]);
body
    cache of disk blocks;
    queue of pending disk access requests;
    semaphores to synchronize access to the cache and queue;
    # N.B. synchronization code not shown below

    proc readblk(fileid, offset, blk) {
      if (needed block not in the cache) {
        store read request in disk queue;
        wait for read operation to be processed;
      }
      blk = appropriate disk block;
    }

    proc writeblk(fileid, offset, blk) {
      select block from cache;
      if (need to write out the selected block) {
        store write request in disk queue;
        wait for block to be written to disk;
      }
      cache block = blk;
    }

    process DiskDriver {
      while (true) {
        wait for a disk access request;
        start a disk operation; wait for interrupt;
        awaken process waiting for this request to complete;
      }
    }
end FileServer
```

Figure 8.2 (b)   Distributed file system: File server.

Figure 8.2 contains outlines of these modules. Each executes on a different machine. Application calls to `FileCache` are in fact local calls, but calls from within `FileCache` to operations in `FileServer` are remote calls. The `File-Cache` is a server for application processes; the `FileServer` is a server for multiple `FileCache` clients, one per workstation.

Assuming that there is one `FileCache` module per application process, `FileCache` does not need internal synchronization since at most one `read` or `write` call could be executing at a time. However, if application processes use the same `FileCache` module—or if the module contains a process that implements read-ahead—then `FileCache` will need to use semaphores to ensure mutually exclusive access to the shared cache.

The `FileServer` module requires internal synchronization since it is shared by several `FileCache` modules and since it contains an internal `DiskDriver` process. In particular, processes handling calls to `readblk` and `writeblk` and the `DiskDriver` process need to synchronize with each other to protect access to the cache of disk blocks and to schedule disk access operations. Figure 8.2 does not contain the synchronization code, but it is straightforward to program using the techniques in Chapter 4.

8.1.4 A Sorting Network of Merge Filters

Although RPC makes it easy to program client/server interactions, RPC is awkward for programming filters or interacting peers. This section reexamines the problem of implementing a sorting network using merge filters, which was introduced in Section 7.2. It also introduces a way to support dynamic communication paths by means of capabilities, which are pointers to operations in other modules.

Recall that a merge filter consumes two input streams and produces one output stream. Each input stream is assumed to be sorted; the task of the filter is to merge the values in the input streams to produce a sorted output stream. As in Section 7.2, we will assume that the end of an input stream is marked by a sentinel `EOS`.

One problem with using RPC to program a merge filter is that RPC does not support direct process-to-process communication. Instead, we need to implement interprocess communication explicitly in our program; it is not provided as a primitive as it is with message passing.

Another problem we have to address is how to link instances of merge filters to each other. In particular, each filter needs to direct its output stream to one of the input streams of another filter. However, operation names—which provide the communication channels—are distinct identifiers. Thus, each input stream needs to be implemented by a distinct procedure. This makes it difficult to use static naming since a merge filter needs to know the literal name of the operation to call to give an output value to the next filter. A much better approach is to employ dynamic naming, in which each filter is passed a link to the operation to use for output. A dynamic link is represented by a *capability*, which can be thought of as a pointer to an operation.

Figure 8.3 contains a module that implements an array of `Merge` filters. The first line is a global declaration that says that `stream` is a type of operation that has a single integer as a parameter. Each module exports two operations, `in1` and `in2`, that provide input streams; other modules call these operations to produce the input values. Each module also exports a third operation, `initialize`, that a main module (not shown) would call to pass the module a capability for the output stream it is to use. For example, the main routine could give `Merge[i]` a capability for operation `in2` of `Merge[j]` by executing

```
call Merge[i].initialize(Merge[j].in2)
```

We assume that each module is initialized before any of them starts producing output.

The rest of the module is similar to the `Merge` process shown in Figure 7.2. Variables `v1` and `v2` correspond to the variables of the same name in Figure 7.2, and process `M` mimics the actions of the `Merge` process. However, `M` uses `call` rather than `send` to deposit the next value on the output channel `out`. Also, process `M` uses semaphore operations to receive the next value from the appropriate input stream. Within the module, the implicit server processes that handle calls of `in` and `in2` are producers; process `M` is a consumer. These processes synchronize in the same way as the producer and consumer processes in Figure 4.3.

Comparing Figures 8.3 and 7.2, we can clearly see the disadvantages of RPC relative to message passing when it comes to programming filters. Although the processes in the two figures are similar, all the other parts of Figure 8.3 are extra, yet necessary. The resulting program will execute approximately as efficiently, but the programmer has to write a lot more when using RPC.

8.1.5 Interacting Peers: Exchanging Values

RPC can also be used to program the information exchanges that arise when peer processes interact, but as with filters, RPC leads to awkward programs relative to the use of message passing. As a concrete example, suppose two processes in different modules wish to exchange values with each other. To communicate with the other module, each process has to use RPC, which means that each module has to export a procedure that the other module calls.

Figure 8.4 shows one way to program an exchange. The `deposit` operation is used to send a value from one module to the other module. An exchange

```
optype stream = (int);  # type of data stream operations

module Merge[i = 1 to n]
  op in1 stream, in2 stream;  # input streams
  op initialize(cap stream);  # link to output stream
body
  int v1, v2;     # input values from streams 1 and 2
  cap stream out;  # capability for output stream
  sem empty1 = 1, full1 = 0, empty2 = 1, full2 = 0;

  proc initialize(output) {  # provide output stream
    out = output;
  }

  proc in1(value1) {  # produce next value for stream 1
    P(empty1); v1 = value1; V(full1);
  }

  proc in2(value2) {  # produce next value for stream 2
    P(empty2); v2 = value2; V(full2);
  }

  process M {
    P(full1); P(full2);  # wait for two input values
    while (v1 != EOS and v2 != EOS)
      if (v1 <= v2)
          { call out(v1); V(empty1); P(full1); }
      else # v2 < v1
          { call out(v2); V(empty2); P(full2); }
    # consume the rest of the non-empty input stream
    if (v1 == EOS)
      while (v2 != EOS)
          { call out(v2); V(empty2); P(full2); }
    else  # v2 == EOS
      while (v1 != EOS)
          { call out(v1); V(empty1); P(full1); }
    call out(EOS);  # append sentinel
  }
end Merge
```

Figure 8.3   Merge-sort filters using RPC.

```
module Exchange[i = 1 to 2]
  op deposit(int);
body
  int othervalue;
  sem ready = 0;    # used for signaling

  proc deposit(other) {    # called by other module
    othervalue = other;    # save other's value
    V(ready);              # let Worker pick it up
  }
  process Worker {
    int myvalue;
    call Exchange[3-i].deposit(myvalue);  # send to other
    P(ready);             # wait to receive other's value
    ...
  }
end Exchange
```

Figure 8.4   Exchanging values using RPC.

is realized by having each worker process execute two steps: deposit `myvalue` in the other module, then wait until the other worker has deposited its value locally. (The expression `3-i` is used by each module to compute the index of the other module; for example, in module `1`, the value of `3-i` is `2`.) A semaphore `ready` is used within each module to ensure that the worker process does not access `othervalue` until it has been assigned to from within the `deposit` operation.

8.2 Rendezvous

RPC by itself provides only an intermodule communication mechanism. Within a module, we still need to program synchronization. Also, we sometimes need to write extra processes simply to manipulate the data communicated by means of RPC. This was shown in the `Merge` module in Figure 8.3.

Rendezvous combines communication and synchronization. As with RPC, a client process invokes an operation by means of a `call` statement. However, an operation is serviced by an existing process rather than by a newly created process. In particular, a server process uses an *input statement* to wait for and then act upon a single call. Hence, operations are serviced one at a time rather than concurrently.

As in the previous section, the specification part of a module contains declarations of the headers of operations exported by the module. However, in this section the body of a module consists of a single process that services the operations. (We will generalize this in the next section.) We will also employ arrays of operations, which are declared by appending a range to the name of an operation.

8.2.1 Input Statements

Suppose a module exports the following operation:

    op opname (types of formals);

The server process in the module performs a rendezvous with a caller of `opname` by executing an input statement. The simplest form of this statement is

    in opname (formal identifiers) -> S; ni

The parts between `in` and `ni` are called a *guarded operation.* The guard names an operation and provides identifiers for the formal parameters, if any; `S` is a statement list that services an invocation of the operation. The scope of the formals is the entire guarded operation, so `S` can read value formals and write to result formals.

An input statement delays the server process until there is at least one pending call of `opname`. The process then selects the oldest pending call, copies the value arguments into the value formals, executes statement list `S`, and finally returns the result parameters to the caller. At that point, *both* the server process executing `in` and the client process that called `opname` can continue execution.

The diagram below depicts the relation between the calling and server processes. Again, time moves down the figure and the squiggly lines indicate when a process is executing.

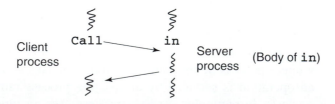

As with RPC, the calling process delays when it reaches a `call` statement; it continues after the server process executes the called operation. However, with rendezvous the server is an active process that executes both before and after servicing a remote invocation. As indicated above, the server will also delay if it reaches the **in** statement and there are no pending invocations. The reader might find it useful to compare this diagram with the corresponding one for RPC.

The input statement above services a single operation. As we saw in Section 7.6, guarded communication is useful since it allows a process to wait for one of several alternatives. We can combine guarded communication with rendezvous by using the general form of the following input statement:

```
in  op₁(formals₁) and B₁ by e₁ -> S₁;
[]  ...
[]  opₙ(formalsₙ) and Bₙ by eₙ -> Sₙ;
ni
```

Each arm of **in** is a guarded operation. The part before `->` is called the *guard*; each S_i is a statement list. Each guard contains the name of an operation and its formals, an optional *synchronization expression*, **and** B_i, and an optional *scheduling expression*, **by** e_i. Both the synchronization and scheduling expressions may reference the formal parameters in the operation.

The Ada language (Section 8.6) supports rendezvous by means of the **accept** statement and supports guarded communication by means of the **select** statement. An **accept** is nearly identical to the simple form of **in**; **select** is similar to the general form of **in**. However, a **select** statement is less powerful than the general form of **in** because **select** cannot reference arguments to operations or contain scheduling expressions. The ramifications of these differences are discussed in Section 8.6.

A guard in an input statement *succeeds* when (1) the operation has been called, and (2) the corresponding synchronization expression is true (or omitted). The scope of the formal parameters is the entire guarded operation, so the synchronization expression can depend on the values of the formals and hence on the values of the arguments in a call. Thus one call of an operation might make the guard succeed, but another call of the same operation might not.

Execution of **in** delays until some guard succeeds. If more than one guard succeeds (and there are no scheduling expressions), the **in** statement services the oldest invocation that makes some guard succeed. In particular, the arguments of that call are copied into the formal parameters, and then the corresponding statement list is executed. When the statement list terminates, result formals and the return value (if any) are sent back to the process that called the operation. At that point, both the **call** and **in** statements terminate.

A scheduling expression is used to alter the default, oldest-invocation-first order of servicing invocations. In particular, if there is more than one invocation that makes a particular guard succeed, then the oldest invocation that also minimizes the value of the scheduling expression is serviced first. As with a synchronization expression, a scheduling expression can reference the formals in the operation and hence its value can depend on the arguments in a call. In fact, if a scheduling expression refers only to local variables, its value will be the same for all invocations, and hence it will have no effect on the order in which invocations are serviced.

As we shall see, synchronization and scheduling expressions are both very useful. They are not fundamentally tied to the use of rendezvous, however; they could also be used with asynchronous and synchronous message passing. For example, we could have allowed **receive** statements to look at their parameters. Indeed, message-passing libraries often provide some means to control which message is received. For example, MPI allows the receiver of a message to specify the sender and/or the type of message.

8.2.2 Client/Server Examples

This section presents a series of small examples that illustrate the use of input statements. Let's consider again the problem of implementing a bounded buffer. In particular, we want a process that has a local buffer of up to **n** data items and that services two operations: **deposit** and **fetch**. A producer process deposits an item into the buffer by calling the **deposit** operation; a consumer process retrieves an item by calling the **fetch** operation. As usual, **deposit** must delay if there are already **n** items in the buffer, and **fetch** must delay until there is at least one item in the buffer.

Figure 8.5 contains a module that implements a bounded buffer. The **Buffer** process declares local variables to represent the buffer, then repeatedly executes an input statement. On each iteration, **Buffer** waits for a call of **deposit** or **fetch**. The synchronization expressions in the guards ensure that calls of **deposit** and **fetch** delay as necessary.

The reader might find it instructive to compare the **Buffer** process with the monitor in Figure 5.4. The interface to client processes is the same—and the effects of calling **deposit** and **fetch** are the same—but the implementation is quite different. In particular, the procedure bodies in the monitor implementation become the statement lists in an input statement. Also, condition synchronization is expressed using Boolean synchronization expressions rather than condition variables.

As a second example, Figure 8.6 contains a module that implements a centralized solution to the dining philosophers problem. The structure of the

```
module BoundedBuffer
  op deposit(typeT), fetch(result typeT);
body
  process Buffer {
    typeT buf[n];
    int front = 0, rear = 0, count = 0;
    while (true)
      in deposit(item) and count < n ->
            buf[rear] = item;
            rear = (rear+1) mod n; count = count+1;
      [] fetch(item) and count > 0 ->
            item = buf[front];
            front = (front+1) mod n; count = count-1;
      ni
  }
end BoundedBuffer
```

Figure 8.5   Rendezvous implementation of a bounded buffer.

```
module Table
  op getforks(int), relforks(int);
body
  process Waiter {
    bool eating[5] = ([5] false);
    while (true)
      in getforks(i) and not (eating[left(i)] and
            not eating[right(i)] -> eating[i] = true;
      [] relforks(i) ->
            eating[i] = false;
      ni
  }
end Table

process Philosopher[i = 0 to 4] {
  while (true) {
    call getforks(i);
    eat;
    call relforks(i);
    think;
  }
}
```

Figure 8.6   Centralized dining philosophers using rendezvous.

`Waiter` process is identical to that of `Buffer`. In this case, a call of `getforks` can be serviced when neither neighbor is eating; a call of `relforks` can always be serviced. A philosopher passes its index `i` to the `Waiter`, which uses this in the synchronization expression in the guard for `getforks`. In that guard, the function calls `left(i)` and `right(i)` are assumed to return the indices of the left and right neighbors of `Philosopher[i]`.

Figure 8.7 contains a time server module similar in functionality to the module in Figure 8.1. The process exports `get_time` and `delay` operations for clients; it also exports a `tick` operation that is assumed to be called by the clock interrupt handler. In Figure 8.7, the argument to `delay` is the actual time that a client process wants to be awakened. This is a slightly different client interface than that shown in Figure 8.1. We have the clients pass wake-up times so that we can use a synchronization expression to control the order in which calls of `delay` get serviced. With rendezvous, the `Timer` process does not need to maintain a queue of napping processes; instead, the napping processes are simply the ones whose wake-up times have not yet been reached. (Their calls remain queued on the `delay` channel.)

The final example uses a scheduling expression as well as a synchronization expression. Figure 8.8 contains a shortest-job-next allocator module. The client interface in this case is the same as that in the monitor in Figure 5.6, but the implementation of `request` and `release` is quite different. The `SJN` process, like the `Timer` process, does not need to maintain internal queues. Instead it

```
module TimeServer
  op get_time() returns int;
  op delay(int);
  op tick();        # called by clock interrupt handler
body TimeServer
  process Timer {
    int tod = 0;  # time of day
    while (true)
      in get_time() returns time -> time = tod;
      [] delay(waketime) and waketime <= tod -> skip;
      [] tick() -> { tod = tod+1;  restart timer;  }
      ni
  }
end TimeServer
```

Figure 8.7   A time server using rendezvous.

```
module SJN_Allocator
  op request(int time), release();
body
  process SJN {
    bool free = true;
    while (true)
      in request(time) and free by time -> free = false;
      [] release() -> free = true;
      ni
  }
end SJN_Allocator
```

Figure 8.8   Shortest-job-next allocator using rendezvous.

merely delays accepting calls of **request** until the resource is free, and then it accepts the call with the smallest argument for **time**.

8.2.3 A Sorting Network of Merge Filters

Consider again the problem of implementing a sorting network using merge filters. Here we want to solve the problem using rendezvous. There are two approaches we could take. First, we could employ two kinds of processes: one to implement the merge filters and one to implement the communication buffers. In particular, place a buffer process—implemented as in Figure 8.5—between each pair of filters. Each filter process would fetch new values from the buffers between it and the previous filters in a network, merge them, and deposit its output in the buffer between it and the next filter in the network.

Networks of filters are implemented in essentially the same way in UNIX, with buffers being provided by what UNIX calls pipes. A filter receives input by reading from an input pipe (or file); it sends results by writing to an output pipe (or file). Pipes are not actually implemented by processes—they are more like monitors—but filter processes use them in the same way.

We can also program filters using a second approach, in which a filter uses input statements to fetch input and **call** statements to deposit output. With the second approach, filters communicate directly with each other. Figure 8.9 contains an array of filters for merge sorting, programmed using the second approach. As in Figure 8.3, each filter receives values from two input streams and sends results to an output stream. Also, we have again used dynamic naming to give each process, through operation **initialize**, a capability for the

```
optype stream = (int);  # type of data streams

module Merge[i = 1 to n]
  op in1 stream, in2 stream;  # input streams
  op initialize(cap stream);  # link to output stream
body
  process Filter {
    int v1, v2;       # values from input streams
    cap stream out;  # capability for output stream
    in initialize(c) -> out = c ni
    # get first values from input streams
    in in1(v) -> v1 = v; ni
    in in2(v) -> v2 = v; ni
    while (v1 != EOS and v2 != EOS)
      if (v1 <= v2)
          { call out(v1); in in1(v) -> v1 = v; ni }
      else    # v2 < v1
          { call out(v2); in in2(v) -> v2 = v; ni }
    # consume the rest of the non-empty input stream
    if (v1 == EOS)
      while (v2 != EOS)
          { call out(v2); in in2(v) -> v2 = v; ni }
    else  # v2 == EOS
      while (v1 != EOS)
          { call out(v1); in in1(v) -> v1 = v; ni }
    call out(EOS);
  }
end Merge
```

Figure 8.9   Merge sort filters using rendezvous.

output stream it should use; that stream is bound to an input stream in another element of the array of **Merge** modules. Other than these similarities, however, the programs in Figures 8.3 and 8.8 are quite different. This is because rendezvous supports direct process-to-process communication, whereas RPC does not. This makes rendezvous easier to use for programming filter processes.

The process in Figure 8.9 is quite similar to the process in Figure 7.2, which was programmed using asynchronous message passing. The communication statements are programmed differently, but they are in exactly the same places. However, because **call** is a blocking statement, process execution is much more tightly coupled with rendezvous than with asynchronous message passing. In particular, the various `Filter` processes will execute at about the same rate because each stream will contain at most one value at a time. (A filter process cannot output a second value until another filter has received the first output value.)

8.2.4 Interacting Peers: Exchanging Values

Consider again the problem of having processes in two different modules exchange values with each other. We saw in Figure 8.4 that this is awkward to program using RPC. We can do better using rendezvous, although still not as well as we can using message passing.

With rendezvous, processes can communicate directly with each other. However, if both processes issue calls at the same time, they will deadlock. Similarly, they cannot both execute `in` statements at the same time. Thus, the solution must be made asymmetric, by having one process execute `call` then `in` while the other process executes `in` then `call`. Figure 8.10 contains the solution. The requirement for asymmetry leads to the `if` statement in each `Worker`. (We could write a symmetric solution by mimicking the RPC solution in Figure 8.4, but this is even more awkward.)

```
module Exchange[i = 1 to 2]
  op deposit(int);
body
  process Worker {
    int myvalue, othervalue;
    if (i == 1) {    # one process calls
      call Exchange[2].deposit(myvalue);
      in deposit(othervalue) -> skip; ni
    } else {         # the other process receives
      in deposit(othervalue) -> skip; ni
      call Exchange[1].deposit(myvalue);
    }
    ...
  }
end Exchange
```

Figure 8.10   Exchanging values using rendezvous.

8.3 A Multiple Primitives Notation

With both RPC and rendezvous, a process initiates communication by executing a `call` statement, and execution of `call` blocks the caller until the call has been serviced and results have been returned. This is ideal for programming client/server interactions, but it makes it difficult to program filters and interacting peers, as we saw in the last two sections. On the other hand, the one-way flows of information between filters and peers are easy to program using asynchronous message passing.

This section describes a programming notation that combines RPC, rendezvous, and asynchronous message passing into one coherent package. This multiple primitives notation combines the advantages of the three component notations and provides additional power as well.

8.3.1 Invoking and Servicing Operations

We will again structure a program as a collection of modules. A visible operation is declared in the specification part of a module. It can be invoked by processes in other modules; it is serviced by a process or procedure in the declaring module. We will now also employ *local* operations, which are declared, invoked, and serviced within the body of a single module.

In the multiple primitives notation, an operation may be invoked by either a synchronous `call` or an asynchronous `send`. These have the forms

```
call  Mname.opname(arguments);
send  Mname.opname(arguments);
```

A `call` statement terminates when the operation has been serviced and result arguments have been returned. A `send` statement terminates as soon as the arguments have been evaluated. If an operation returns results, it can be invoked within an expression; in this case the `call` keyword is omitted. (If an operation has result parameters and is invoked by `send`, or if a function is invoked by `send`, or if a function is not in an expression, then return values are ignored.)

In the multiple primitives notation, an operation may be serviced either by a procedure (`proc`) or by rendezvous (`in` statements). The choice is up to the programmer of the module that declares the operation. It depends upon whether the programmer wants each invocation to be serviced by a new process or whether it is more appropriate to rendezvous with an existing process. Later examples will discuss this tradeoff.

When an operation is serviced by a `proc`, a new process services the invocation. If the operation was called, the effect is the same as with RPC. If the operation was invoked by **send**, the effect is the same as forking a new process, because the invoker proceeds asynchronously with the process that services the invocation. In either case, an invocation is serviced immediately; thus, there is never a queue of pending invocations.

The other way to service operations is by using input statements, which have the form given in Section 8.2. In this case, there is a queue of pending invocations associated with each operation and access to the queue is atomic. An operation is selected for service according to the semantics of input statements. If such an operation is called, the effect is a rendezvous since the caller delays. If such an operation is invoked by **send**, the effect is similar to asynchronous message passing since the sender continues.

In summary, there are two ways to invoke an operation—**call** and **send**—and two ways to service an invocation—**proc** and **in**. These four combinations have the following effects:

invocation	*service*	*effect*
call	proc	procedure call
call	in	rendezvous
send	proc	dynamic process creation
send	in	asynchronous message passing

A procedure call will be local if the caller and **proc** are in the same module; otherwise it will be remote. An operation cannot be serviced by both **proc** and **in** since the meaning would be unclear. (Is the operation serviced immediately or is it queued?) However, an operation can be serviced by more than one input statement, and these can be in more than one process in the module that declares the operation. In this case, the processes share the queue of pending invocations, but they access it atomically.

With monitors and asynchronous message passing, we defined an **empty** primitive to determine whether a condition variable or message channel was empty. In this chapter we will use a similar but slightly different primitive. In particular, if **opname** is an operation, then **?opname** is a function that returns the number of pending invocations of **opname**. This is often useful in input statements. For example, the following gives priority to **op1** over **op2**:

```
in op1(...) -> S1;
[] op2(...) and ?op1 == 0 -> S2;
ni
```

The synchronization expression in the second guard allows **op2** to be selected only if there are no invocations of **op1** at the time **?op1** is evaluated.

8.3.2 Examples

Three small, closely related examples will illustrate various ways operations can be invoked and serviced. First consider the implementation of a queue shown in Figure 8.11. When `deposit` is invoked, a new item is stored in `buf`. If `deposit` is called, the invoker waits; if `deposit` is invoked by `send`, the invoker continues before the item is actually stored (in which case the invoker had better be sure overflow will not occur). When `fetch` is invoked, an item is removed from `buf`; in this case, `fetch` needs to be invoked by a `call` statement, or the invoker will not get back the result.

The `Queue` module is suitable for use by a single process in another module. It cannot be shared by more than one process because it does not use critical sections to protect the module variables. In particular, interference could result if the operations are invoked concurrently.

If we need a synchronized queue, we can change the `Queue` module into one that implements a bounded buffer. Figure 8.5 given earlier contains just such

```
module Queue
  op deposit(typeT), fetch(result typeT);
body
  typeT buf[n];
  int front = 1, rear = 1, count = 0;

  proc deposit(item) {
    if (count < n) {
      buf[rear] = item;
      rear = (rear+1) mod n; count = count+1;
    } else
      take actions appropriate for overflow;
  }

  proc fetch(item) {
    if (count > 0) {
      item = buf[front];
      front = (front+1) mod n; count = count-1;
    } else
      take actions appropriate for underflow;
  }
end Queue
```

Figure 8.11   A sequential queue.

a module. The visible operations are the same as those in `Queue`. However, the operations are serviced by an input statement in a single process; thus invocations are serviced one at a time. Although `fetch` should be invoked by a `call` statement, it is perfectly fine to invoke `deposit` by a `send` statement.

The modules in Figures 8.5 and 8.11 illustrate two different ways to implement the same interface. The choice is up to the programmer and depends on how the queue will be used. In fact, there is also another way to implement a bounded buffer that illustrates yet another combination of the various ways to invoke and service operations in the multiple primitives notation.

Consider the following input statement, which waits for `op` to be invoked, then assigns the parameters to permanent variables:

```
in op(f1, ..., fn) -> v1 = f1; ...; vn = fn; ni
```

The effect is *identical* to a `receive` statement:

```
receive op(v1, ..., vn);
```

Since `receive` is just an abbreviation for a special case of `in`, we will use `receive` when that is how we want to service an invocation.

Now consider an operation that has no arguments and that is invoked by `send` and serviced by `receive` (or the equivalent `in` statement). In this case, *the operation is equivalent to a semaphore*, with `send` being a `V`, and `receive` being a `P`. The initial value of the semaphore is zero; its current value is the number of "null" messages that have been sent to the operation, minus the number that has been received.

Figure 8.12 gives a different implementation of `BoundedBuffer` that uses semaphores for synchronization. The `deposit` and `fetch` operations are serviced by procedures as in Figure 8.11. Hence, there could be more than one instance of these procedures active at a time. However, here we use semaphore operations to implement mutual exclusion and condition synchronization as in Figure 4.5. The structure of this module is like that of a monitor (see Figure 5.4), but synchronization is implemented by means of semaphores rather than by monitor exclusion and condition variables.

The two implementations of a bounded buffer (Figures 8.5 and 8.11) illustrate important relationships between synchronization expressions in input statements and explicit synchronization in procedures. First, they are often used for the same purposes. Second, since synchronization expressions in input statements can depend on arguments of pending invocations, the two synchronization techniques are equally powerful. However, unless one needs the concurrency provided by multiple invocations of procedures, it is more efficient to have clients rendezvous with a single process.

```
module BoundedBuffer
  op deposit(typeT), fetch(result typeT);
body
  typeT buf[n];
  int front = 1, rear = 1;
  # local operations used to simulate semaphores
  op empty(), full(), mutexD(), mutexF();
  send mutexD(); send mutexF();
  for [i = 1 to n]  # initialize empty "semaphore"
    send empty();

  proc deposit(item) {
    receive empty(); receive mutexD();
    buf[rear] = item; rear = (rear+1) mod n;
    send mutexD(); send full();
  }

  proc fetch(item) {
    receive full(); receive mutexF();
    item = buf[front]; front = (front+1) mod n;
    send mutexF(); send empty();
  }
end BoundedBuffer
```

Figure 8.12   A bounded buffer using semaphore operations.

8.4 Readers/Writers Revisited

With the multiple primitives notation, we can program filters and interacting peers as in Chapter 7. Since the notation includes both RPC and rendezvous, we can also program clients and servers as in Sections 8.1 and 8.2. Multiple primitives also provide additional flexibility, which we now illustrate. First, we develop another solution to the readers/writers problem, which was introduced in Section 4.4. Unlike previous solutions, this one encapsulates access to the database. Then we extend the solution to a distributed implementation of replicated files or databases. We also discuss how the solutions could be programmed using just RPC and local synchronization or using just rendezvous.

8.4.1 Encapsulated Access

Recall that in the readers/writers problem, reader processes examine the database and may do so concurrently; writer processes modify the database, so they need exclusive access. In earlier solutions—using semaphores in Figures 4.10 and 4.13 or monitors in Figure 5.5—the database was global to the reader and writer processes, so that readers could access it concurrently. However, the processes had to be trusted to request permission before accessing the database, then to release control when finished. It is far better to encapsulate the database within a module to hide the request/release protocols and to ensure that they are used. Java supports this approach, as shown at the end of Section 5.4, because the programmer can choose whether methods (exported operations) execute concurrently or one at a time. With the multiple primitives notation, we can structure a solution in a similar way and have the added advantages that the solution is shorter and the synchronization is clearer.

Figure 8.13 contains a single module that encapsulates access to the database. Client processes simply call the `read` or `write` operation; the module hides how these calls are synchronized. The implementation of the module employs both RPC and rendezvous. The `read` operation is implemented by a `proc`, so multiple readers can execute concurrently. On the other hand, the `write` operation is implemented by rendezvous with the `Writer` process; this ensures that writes are serviced one at a time. The module also contains two local operations, `startread` and `endread`, which are used to ensure that reads and writes are mutually exclusive. The `Writer` process also services these, so it can keep track of the number of active readers and delay `write` as necessary. By using rendezvous, the `Writer` process can express synchronization constraints directly using Boolean conditions rather than indirectly using condition variables or semaphores. Notice that the local `endread` operation is invoked by means of `send`, not `call`, because a reader does not need to delay until `endread` is serviced.

In a language that provides RPC but not rendezvous, the module would have to be programmed differently. In particular, `read` and `write` would both be implemented by exported procedures, and they in turn would have to call local procedures to request permission to access the database and then to release permission. Internal synchronization would be programmed using semaphores or monitors.

The situation is worse in a language that provides only rendezvous. This is because operations are serviced by existing processes, and each process can service only one operation at a time. Thus, the only way to support concurrent reading of the database would be to export an array of read operations, one per client,

```
module ReadersWriters
  op read(result result types);   # uses RPC
  op write(value types);      # uses rendezvous
body
  op startread(), endread();   # local operations
  storage for the database or file transfer buffers;

  proc read(results) {
    call startread();      # get read permission
    read the database;
    send endread();        # release read permission
  }

  process Writer {
    int nr = 0;
    while (true) {
      in startread() -> nr = nr+1;
      [] endread() -> nr = nr-1;
      [] write(values) and nr == 0 ->
            write the database;
      ni
    }
  }
end ReadersWriters
```

Figure 8.13   Readers and writers with an encapsulated database.

and to use a separate process to service each one. This is clumsy and inefficient, to say the least.

The solution in Figure 8.13 gives priority to readers. We can give priority to writers by changing the input statement to use the ? function as follows to delay invocations of **startread** whenever there are pending invocations of **write**:

```
in startread() and ?write == 0 -> nr = nr+1;
[] endread() -> nr = nr-1;
[] write(values) and nr == 0 -> write the database;
ni
```

We leave developing a fair solution to the reader.

The module in Figure 8.13 locks the entire database for readers or for a writer. This is usually satisfactory for small data files. However, database transactions typically need to lock individual records as they proceed. This is because a transaction does not know in advance what records it will access; for example, it has to examine some records before it knows which ones to examine next. To implement this kind of dynamic locking, we could employ multiple modules, one per database record. However, this would not encapsulate access to the database. Alternatively, we could employ a more elaborate and finer-grained locking scheme within the `ReadersWriters` module. For example, each `read` and `write` could acquire the locks it needs. Database management systems typically use the latter approach.

8.4.2 Replicated Files

A simple way to increase the likelihood that a critical data file is always accessible is to keep a back-up copy of the file on another disk, usually one that is attached to a different machine. The user can do this manually by periodically making a backup copy of a file. Alternatively, the file system can automatically maintain the backup copy. In either case, however, users wishing to access the file will have to know whether the primary copy was available and, if not, access the backup copy instead. (A related problem is bringing the primary copy back up to date when it becomes accessible again.)

A third approach is for the file system to provide transparent replication. In particular, suppose there are **n** copies of a data file and **n** server modules. Each server provides access to one copy of the file. A client interacts with any one of the server modules, e.g., one executing on the same processor as the client. The servers interact with each other to present clients with the illusion that there is a single copy of the file. Figure 8.14 shows the structure of this interaction pattern.

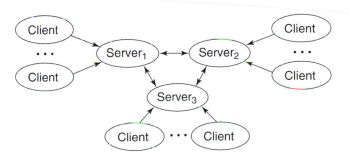

Figure 8.14   Replicated file server interaction pattern.

Each server module exports four operations: `open`, `close`, `read`, and `write`. When a client wants to access the file, it calls the `open` operation of its server, indicating whether the file will be read or written. The client then converses with the same server by calling the `read` and `write` operations. If the file was opened for reading, only `read` may be used; otherwise both `read` and `write` may be used. Eventually, the client ends the conversation by calling `close`. (This interaction pattern is the same as the one seen at the end of Section 7.3.)

The file servers interact with each other to ensure that copies of the file are kept consistent and that at most one client at a time is permitted to write into the file. Each file server has a local lock manager process that implements a solution to the readers/writers problem. When a client opens a file for reading, the `open` operation calls the `startread` operation of the local lock manager. However, when a client opens a file for writing, the `open` operation calls the `startwrite` operation of all `n` lock managers.

Figure 8.15 contains the `FileServer` module. For simplicity, we have used an array and static naming; in practice the different servers would be created dynamically and placed on different processors. In any event, there are several interesting aspects of the implementation of the module.

```
module FileServer[myid = 1 to n]
  type mode = (READ, WRITE);
  op open(mode), close(),         # client operations
     read(result result types), write(value types);
  op startwrite(), endwrite(),  # server operations
     remote_write(value types);
body
  op startread(), endread();   # local operations
  mode use;  declarations for file buffers;

  proc open(m) {
    if (m == READ) {
      call startread();     # get local read lock
      use = READ;
    } else {     # mode assumed to be WRITE
      # get write locks for all copies
      for [i = 1 to n]
        call FileServer[i].startwrite();
      use = WRITE;
    }
  }
```

```
proc close() {
  if (use == READ)    # release local read lock
    send endread();
  else    # use == WRITE, so release all write locks
    for [i = 1 to n]
      send FileServer.endwrite()
}

proc read(results) {
  read from local copy of file and return results;
}

proc write(values) {
  if (use == READ)
    return with error: file was not opened for writing;
  write values into local copy of file;
  # concurrently update all remote copies
  co [i = 1 to n st i != myid]
    call FileServer[i].remote_write(values);
}

proc remote_write(values) { # called by other servers
  write values into local copy of file;
}

process Lock {
  int nr = 0, nw = 0;
  while (true) {
    ## RW: (nr == 0 ∨ nw == 0) ∧ nw <= 1
    in startread() and nw == 0 -> nr = nr+1;
    [] endread() -> nr = nr-1;
    [] startwrite() and nr == 0 and nw == 0 ->
          nw = nw+1;
    [] endwrite() -> nw = nw-1;
    ni
  }
}
end FileServer
```

Figure 8.15   Replicated files using one lock per copy.

- Each `FileServer` exports two sets of operations: those called by its clients and those called by other file servers. The `open`, `close`, `read` and `write` operations are implemented by procedures; however, `read` is the only one that has to be implemented by a procedure in order to permit concurrent reading. The locking operations are implemented by rendezvous with the lock manager.

- Each module keeps track of the current access mode—i.e., the last way in which the file was opened. It uses this to ensure that the file is not written if it was opened for reading and to determine what actions to take when the file is closed. However, a module does not protect itself from a client that accesses a file without first opening it. This can be solved by using dynamic naming or by adding checks to the other operations.

- Within the `write` procedure, a module first updates its local copy of the file and then concurrently updates every remote copy. This is analogous to using a write-through cache update policy. An alternative approach would be to use a write-back policy in which `write` updates only the local copy; remote copies would then be updated when the file is closed.

- In `open`, a client acquires write locks, one at a time, from every lock process. Each client acquires write locks in the same order to avoid the deadlock that could result if two clients acquired them in different orders. In `close`, a client releases write locks using `send` rather than `call` since there is no need to delay when releasing the locks.

- The lock manager process implements the classic readers' preference solution to the readers/writers problem. It is an active monitor, so its loop invariant is the same as the monitor invariant in Figure 5.5.

In the program in Figure 8.15, a reader has to get only one read lock in order to be able to read the file. However, a writer has to get all **n** write locks, one from each instance of `FileServer`. A generalization of this scheme is to use what is called *weighted voting*.

Let `readWeight` be the number of locks required to read the file, and let `writeWeight` be the number of locks required to write the file. In our example, `readWeight` is 1 and `writeWeight` is n. A different choice would be to use a `readWeight` of 2 and a `writeWeight` of n-2. This would mean that a reader would have to get 2 read locks, but only n-2 write locks. Any assignment of weights can be used as long as the following two conditions are met:

```
writeWeight > n/2   and
(readWeight + writeWeight) > n
```

With weighted voting, when a writer closes the file, only the copies that have been locked for writing need to be updated. However, every copy has to have a timestamp indicating the time at which it was last written. The first requirement above ensures that at least half of the copies will have the latest data and latest timestamp. (We describe how to implement a global clock and time-stamps in Section 9.4.)

When a reader opens the file and obtains read locks, it also needs to read the timestamps on each copy and then to use a copy that has the largest timestamp. The second requirement above ensures that there will be at least one copy with the largest timestamp and hence the most recent data. Our program in Figure 8.15 did not need to worry about timestamps, because we made sure every copy was updated when the file was closed.

8.5 Case Study: Java

Section 5.4 introduced Java and presented programs for reading and writing a simple, shared database. Section 7.9 showed how to construct a client/server application using message passing with sockets and the `java.net` package. Java also supports the use of RPC in distributed programs. Since operations on Java objects are called methods rather than procedures, RPC in Java is called *remote method invocation* (RMI). It is supported by two packages: `java.rmi` and `java.rmi.server`.

Below we give an overview of remote method invocation and then illustrate how to use it to implement a simple remote database. The database has the same interface as the earlier Java examples in Chapter 5, but its implementation employs a client and a server, both of which can execute on different machines.

8.5.1 Remote Method Invocation

An application that uses remote method invocation has three components: an interface that declares headers for remote methods, a server class that implements the interface, and one or more clients that call the remote methods. It is pro-grammed as follows:

- Write a Java interface that extends `Remote` (which is defined in the `java.rmi` package). The methods in the interface each need to declare that they throw remote exceptions.

- Write a server class that extends `UnicastRemoteObject` and that imple-ments the methods in the interface. (The server can, of course, also contain protected data and methods.) Also write code that creates an instance of the server and registers its name with what is called a *registry service* (see below). This code can be within a main method in the server class or within another class.

• Write a client class that interacts with the server. The client should first set the standard RMI security manager to protect itself from erroneous stub code (see below) that might be loaded over the network. The client then calls **Naming.lookup** to get a server object from the registry service. Now the client can call the server's remote methods.

These components are compiled and executed as described below. See the next section for a concrete example.

The client program invokes the server's methods as if they were local (in the same Java virtual machine). However, when methods are remote, the interaction between a client and server is actually managed by what are called a server *stub* and a server *skeleton*. These are created—after the program is compiled—by executing the **rmic** command. The stub and skeleton are pieces of code that are included automatically in your program. They sit between the actual client and server code in the Java source program. In particular, when a client invokes a remote method, it actually invokes a method in the stub. The stub *marshals* the arguments of the remote call—gathers them together into a single message—and sends them over the network to the skeleton. The skeleton receives a message with the arguments, generates a local method invocation to the server, waits for the result, then sends it back to the stub. Finally, the stub returns the result to the client code. The stub and skeleton thus hide the details of network communication.

Another consequence of using remote methods is that the client and server are separate programs that execute on separate hosts. Hence, they need a way to name each other; moreover, server names need to be unique, because there may be other servers running at the same time. By convention, remote server names employ a variation on the URL naming scheme. They have the form **rmi://hostname:port/pathname**. The **hostname** is the Internet domain name of the host on which the server will execute, **port** is a user-chosen port number, and **pathname** is a user-chosen path name on the server.

A registry service is a special program that maintains a list of registered server names on a host. It is started in the background on the server machine by executing "**rmiregistry port &**." (A server program can also provide its own registry service using the **java.rmi.registry** package.) The interface to the registry service is provided by a `Naming` object; two key methods of that object are `bind` to register a name and server and `lookup` to retrieve the server bound to a name.

The final step in executing a client/remote server program is to start the server and client(s) using the `java` interpreter. The server is started first on machine `hostname`. A client is started on any host connected to the server. Two cautions, however: The user needs permission to read Java's `.class` files on both machines, and the server machine has to permit remote invocations from the client machine.

8.5.2 Example: A Remote Database

Figure 8.16 contains a complete program for a simple but interesting example of the use of remote method invocation. The interface, `RemoteDatabase`, defines the `read` and `write` methods that the server implements. Because these will be executed remotely from the client, each is declared to throw the `RemoteException` condition.

The class `Client` defines the client. It consists of a `main` method that can be started on any machine. A client first sets the standard RMI security manager to protect itself against an erroneous server stub. The client next looks up the server's name and gets back a reference to the server. The remaining client code invokes the `read` and `write` methods in the server for the number of `rounds` specified as a command line argument when the client is started.

The server class, `RemoteDatabaseServer`, implements the interface. The "database" itself is simply a protected integer. The `main` method in the server creates an instance of the server, registers its name, and prints a line on the server's host to indicate that it is running. The server remains running until it is killed. The server machine and port used in this program are `paloverde:9999` (the author's workstation).

Both parts of this program need to be stored in a single file named `RemoteDatabase.java`, because that is the name of the interface. Executing the following commands on host `paloverde` will compile the program, create the stubs, start the registry service, and start the server:

```
javac RemoteDatabase.java
rmic RemoteDatabaseServer
rmiregistry 9999 &
java RemoteDatabaseServer
```

```java
import java.rmi.*;
import java.rmi.server.*;

public interface RemoteDatabase extends Remote {
 public int read() throws RemoteException;
 public void write(int value) throws RemoteException;
}

class Client {
 public static void main(String[] args) {
  try {
   // set the standard RMI security manager
   System.setSecurityManager(new RMISecurityManager());

   // get remote database object
   String name =
       "rmi://paloverde:9999/database";
   RemoteDatabase db =
       (RemoteDatabase) Naming.lookup(name);

   // read command-line argument and access database
   int value, rounds = Integer.parseInt(args[0]);
   for (int i = 0; i < rounds; i++) {
     value = db.read();
     System.out.println("read: " + value);
     db.write(value+1);
   }
  }
  catch (Exception e) {
    System.err.println(e);
  }
 }
}


class RemoteDatabaseServer extends UnicastRemoteObject
          implements RemoteDatabase {
 protected int data = 0;   // the "database"

 public int read() throws RemoteException {
   return data;
 }

 public void write(int value) throws RemoteException {
   data = value;
   System.out.println("new value is: " + data);
 }
```

```
    // constructor required because of throws clause
    public RemoteDatabaseServer() throws RemoteException {
      super();
    }

    public static void main(String[] args) {
      try {
        // create a remote database server object
        RemoteDatabaseServer server =
            new RemoteDatabaseServer();
        // register name and start serving!
        String name =
            "rmi://paloverde:9999/database";
        Naming.bind(name, server);
        System.out.println(name + " is running");
      }
      catch (Exception e) {
        System.err.println(e);
      }
    }
  }
```

Figure 8.16   Remote database interface, client, and server.

A client is started on `paloverde` or a machine on the same network by executing

```
    java Client rounds
```

The reader is encouraged to experiment with this program to see how it behaves. For example, what happens if there is more than one client? What happens if a client is started before the server?

8.6 Case Study: Ada

Ada was developed under the sponsorship of the U.S. Department of Defense to be the standard language for programming defense applications ranging from real-time embedded systems to large information systems. The concurrency features of Ada are an important part of the language—and are critical for its intended uses. Ada also contains a rich set of mechanisms for sequential programming.

Ada resulted from an extensive international design competition in the late 1970s and was first standardized in 1983. Ada 83 introduced the rendezvous mechanism for interprocess communication; indeed, the term *rendezvous* was chosen in part because the leader of the design team is French. A second version of Ada was standardized in 1995. Ada 95 is upward compatible—so Ada 83 programs remain valid—but also adds several features. The two most interesting new features for concurrent programming are protected types, which are similar to monitors, and a `requeue` statement to give the programmer more control over synchronization and scheduling.

In this section we first summarize the main concurrency mechanisms of Ada: tasks, rendezvous, and protected types. Then we show how to program a barrier as a protected type and how to program the dining philosophers as tasks that interact using rendezvous. The examples also illustrate several of the sequential programming features of Ada.

8.6.1 Tasks

An Ada program is comprised of subprograms, packages, and tasks. A subprogram is a procedure or function, a package is a set of declarations, and a task is an independent process. Each component has a specification part and a body. The specification declares visible objects; the body contains local declarations and statements. Subprograms and packages can also be generic—i.e., they can be parameterized by data types.

The basic form of a task specification is

```
task Name is
  entry declarations;
end;
```

Entry declarations are similar to `op` declarations in modules. They define operations serviced by the task and have the form

```
entry Identifier(formals);
```

Parameters are passed by copy-in (the default), copy-out, or copy-in/copy-out. Ada supports arrays of entries, which are called entry families.

The basic form of a task body is

```
task body Name is
  local declarations;
begin
  statements;
end Name;
```

A task must be declared within a subprogram or package. The simplest concurrent program in Ada is thus a single procedure that contains task specifications and bodies. The declarations in any component are *elaborated* one at a time, in the order in which they appear. Elaborating a task declaration creates an instance of the task. After all declarations are elaborated, the sequential statements in the subprogram begin execution as an anonymous task.

A task specification/body pair defines a single task. Ada also supports arrays of tasks, but in a way that is different than in most other concurrent programming languages. In particular, the programmer first declares a task type and then declares an array of instances of that type. The programmer can also use task types in conjunction with pointers—which Ada calls access types—to create tasks dynamically.

8.6.2 Rendezvous

In Ada 83 rendezvous was the primary communication mechanism and the sole synchronization mechanism. (Tasks on the same machine could also read and write shared variables.) Everything else had to be programmed using rendezvous. Ada 95 also supports protected types for synchronized access to shared objects, as described in the next section.

Suppose task T declares entry E. Other tasks in the scope of the specification of T can invoke E as follows:

```
call T.E(actuals);
```

As usual, execution of `call` delays the caller until entry E has terminated (or aborted or raised an exception).

Task T services calls of entry E by means of the `accept` statement. This has the form

```
accept E(formals) do
  statement list;
end;
```

Execution of `accept` delays the task until there is an invocation of E, copies input arguments into input formals, then executes the statement list. When the statement list terminates, output formals are copied to output arguments. At that point, both the caller and the executing process continue. An `accept` statement is thus like an input statement (Section 9.2) with one guard, no synchronization expression, and no scheduling expression.

To support nondeterministic task interaction, Ada provides three kinds of `select` statements: selective wait, conditional entry call, and timed entry call. The selective wait statement supports guarded communication. The most common form of this statement is

```
select when B₁ => accept statement; additional statements;
or ...
or      when Bₙ => accept statement; additional statements;
end select;
```

Each line is called an *alternative*. Each B_i is a Boolean expression; the `when` clauses are optional. An alternative is said to be *open* if B_i is true or the `when` clause is omitted.

This form of selective wait delays the executing process until the `accept` statement in some open alternative can be executed—i.e., there is a pending invocation of the entry named in the `accept` statement. Since each guard B_i precedes an `accept` statement, the guard *cannot* reference the parameters of an entry call. Also, Ada does not provide scheduling expressions. As we discussed in Section 8.2 and will see in the examples in the next two sections, this complicates solving many synchronization and scheduling problems.

A selective wait statement can contain an optional `else` alternative, which is selected if no other alternative can be. In place of an `accept` statement, the programmer can also use a `delay` statement or a `terminate` alternative. An open alternative with a `delay` statement is selected if the delay interval has transpired; this provides a timeout mechanism. The `terminate` alternative is selected if all the tasks that rendezvous with this one have terminated or are themselves waiting at a `terminate` alternative (see the example in Figure 8.19).

A conditional entry call is used if one task wants to poll another. It has the form

```
select entry call; additional statements;
else    statements;
end select;
```

The entry call is selected if it can be executed immediately; otherwise, the `else` alternative is selected.

A timed entry call is used if a calling task wants to wait at most a certain interval of time. Its form is similar to that of a conditional entry call:

```
select entry call; additional statements;
or      delay statement; additional statements;
end select;
```

In this case, the entry call is selected if it can be executed before the delay interval expires.

Ada 83—and hence Ada 95—provides a few additional mechanisms for concurrent programming. Tasks can share variables; however, they cannot assume that these variables are updated except at synchronization points (e.g., rendezvous statements). The **abort** statement allows one task to terminate another. There is a mechanism for setting the priority of a task. Finally, there are so-called attributes that enable one to determine whether a task is callable or has terminated or to determine the number of pending invocations of an entry.

8.6.3 Protected Types

Ada 95 enhances the concurrent programming mechanisms of Ada 83 in several ways. The two most significant are protected types, which support synchronized access to shared data, and the **requeue** statement, which supports scheduling and synchronization that depends on the arguments of calls.

A protected type encapsulates shared data and synchronizes access to it. Each instance of a protected type is similar to a monitor. The specification part of a protected type has the form

```
protected type Name is
  function, procedure, or entry declarations;
private
  variable declarations;
end Name;
```

The body has the form

```
protected body Name is
  function, procedure, or entry bodies;
end Name;
```

Protected functions provide read-only access to the private variables; hence, such a function can be called simultaneously by multiple tasks. Protected procedures provide exclusive read/write access to the private variables. Protected entries are like protected procedures except that they also have a **when** clause that specifies a Boolean synchronization condition. At most one task at a time can be executing a protected procedure or entry. A call of a protected entry delays until the synchronization condition is true *and* the caller can have exclusive access to the private variables; the synchronization condition cannot, however, depend on the parameters of a call.

Calls of protected procedures and entries are serviced in FIFO order, subject to synchronization conditions on entries. The `requeue` statement can be used within the body of a protected procedure or entry to defer completion of the call that is being serviced. (It can also be used within the body of an `accept` statement.) This statement has the form

```
requeue Opname;
```

where `Opname` is the name of an entry or protected procedure that either has no parameters or has the same parameters as the operation being serviced. The effect of `requeue` is to place the call being serviced on the queue for `Opname`, just as if the calling task had directly called `Opname`.

As an example of the use of a protected type and `requeue`, Figure 8.17 contains Ada code for an `N`-task counter barrier. We assume that `N` is a global constant. An instance of the barrier is declared and used as follows:

```
protected type Barrier is
  procedure Arrive;
private
  entry Go;                    -- used to delay early arrivals
  count : Integer := 0; -- number who have arrived
  time_to_leave : Boolean := False;
end Barrier;

protected body Barrier is
  procedure Arrive is begin
    count := count+1;
    if count < N then
      requeue Go;    -- wait for others to arrive
    else
      count := count-1; time_to_leave := True;
    end if;
  end;

  entry Go when time_to_leave is begin
    count := count-1;
    if count = 0 then time_to_leave := False; end if;
  end;
end Barrier;
```

Figure 8.17   Barrier synchronization in Ada.

```
B : Barrier;    -- declaration of a barrier
...
B.Arrive;       -- or "call B.Arrive;"
```

The first `N-1` tasks to arrive at the barrier increment `count` and then delay by being requeued on private entry `Go`. The last task to arrive at the barrier sets `time_to_leave` to `True`; this allows the requeued calls that are waiting on `Go` to awaken—one at a time. Each task decrements `count` before returning from the barrier; the last one resets `time_to_leave` so the barrier can be used again. (The semantics of protected types ensure that every task delayed on `Go` will execute before any further call of `Arrive` is serviced.) The reader might find it instructive to compare this barrier to the one in Figure 5.18, which is programmed using the Pthreads library.

8.6.4 Example: The Dining Philosophers

This section presents a complete Ada program for the dining philosophers problem (Section 4.3). The program illustrates the use of tasks and rendezvous as well as several general features of Ada. For convenience in the program, we assume the existence of two functions, `left(i)` and `right(i)` that return the indices of the left and right neighbor of philosopher `i`.

Figure 8.18 contains the main procedure `Dining_Philosophers`. Before the procedure are `with` and `use` clauses. The `with` clause says this procedure depends on the objects in package `Ada.Text_IO`. The `use` clause makes the names of the objects exported by that package directly visible (i.e., so they do not have to be qualified by the package name).

The main procedure first declares `ID` to be an integer between `1` and `5`. The specification of the `Waiter` task declares two entries—`Pickup` and `Putdown` that are called by a philosopher when it wants to pick up or put down its forks. The body of `Waiter` is separately compiled; it is given in Figure 8.19.

`Philosopher` has been specified as a task type so that we can declare an array `DP` of `5` such tasks. The instances of the five philosophers are created when the declaration of array `DP` is elaborated. Each philosopher first waits to accept a call of its initialization entry `init`, then it executes `rounds` iterations. Variable `rounds` is declared global to the bodies of the philosophers so each can read it. The body of the main procedure at the end of Figure 8.18 initializes `rounds` by reading an input value. Then it passes each philosopher its index by calling `DP(j).init(j)`.

Figure 8.19 contains the body of the `Waiter` task. It is more complicated than the `Waiter` process in Figure 8.6, because the `when` conditions in the Ada

```
with Ada.Text_IO; use Ada.Text_IO;
procedure Dining_Philosophers is
  subtype ID is Integer range 1..5;

  task Waiter is             -- Waiter spec
    entry Pickup(I : in ID);
    entry Putdown(I : in ID);
  end
  task body Waiter is separate;

  task type Philosopher is   -- Philosopher spec
    entry init(who : ID);
  end;

  DP : array(ID) of Philosopher;  -- the philosophers
  rounds : Integer;               -- number of rounds

  task body Philosopher is   -- Philosopher body
    myid : ID;
  begin
    accept init(who); myid := who; end;
    for j in 1..rounds loop
      -- "think"
      Waiter.Pickup(myid);   -- pick forks up
      -- "eat"
      Waiter.Putdown(myid); -- put forks down
    end loop;
  end Philosopher;

begin  -- read in rounds, then start the philosophers
  Get(rounds);
  for j in ID loop
    DP(j).init(j);
  end loop;
end Dining_Philosophers;
```

Figure 8.18   Dining philosophers in Ada: Main program.

`select` statement cannot reference entry parameters. Each waiter repeatedly accepts calls of `Pickup` and `Putdown`. When `Pickup` is accepted, the waiter checks to see if either of the calling philosopher's neighbors is eating. If not, then philosopher i can eat now. However, if a neighbor is eating, the call of `Pickup` has to be requeued so that the philosopher does not get reawakened too

```
separate (Dining_Philosophers)
task body Waiter is
  entry Wait(ID);      -- used to requeue philosophers
  eating : array (ID) of Boolean; -- who is eating
  want : array (ID) of Boolean;   -- who wants to eat
  go : array(ID) of Boolean;      -- who can go now
begin
  for j in ID loop            -- initialize the arrays
    eating(j) := False; want(j) := False;
  end loop;
  loop                -- basic server loop
   select
     accept Pickup(i : in ID) do  -- DP(i) needs forks
       if not(eating(left(i)) or eating(right(i))) then
         eating(i) := True;
       else
         want(i) := True; requeue Wait(i);
       end if;
     end;
   or
     accept Putdown(i : in ID) do  -- DP(i) is done
       eating(i) := False;
     end;
     -- check neighbors to see if they can eat now
     if want(left(i)) and not eating(left(left(i))) then
       accept Wait(left(i));
       eating(left(i)) := True; want(left(i)) := False;
     end if;
     if want(right(i)) and not eating(right(right(i)))
       then  accept Wait(right(i));
       eating(right(i)) := True; want(right(i)) := False;
     end if;
   or
     terminate;  -- quit when philosophers have quit
   end select;
  end loop;
end Waiter;
```

Figure 8.19   Dining philosophers in Ada: Waiter task.

early. A local array of five entries, `Wait(ID)`, is used to delay philosophers who have to wait; each philosopher is requeued on a distinct element of the array.

After eating, a philosopher calls `Putdown`. When a waiter accepts this call, it checks if either neighbor wants to eat and whether that neighbor may do so. If so, the waiter accepts a delayed call of `Wait` to awaken a philosopher whose call of `Pickup` had been requeued. The `accept` statement that services `Putdown` could surround the entire select alternative—i.e., the end of `accept` could be after the two `if` statements. We have placed it earlier, however, because there is no need to delay the philosopher who called `Putdown`.

8.7 Case Study: SR

Synchronizing Resources (SR) was developed in the 1980s. The first version of the language introduced the rendezvous mechanisms described in Section 8.2. The language evolved to provide the multiple primitives described in Section 8.3. SR supports both shared-variable and distributed programming, and it can be used to implement directly almost all the programs in this book. SR programs can execute on shared-memory multiprocessors and networks of workstations, as well as on single-processor machines.

Although SR contains a variety of mechanisms, they are based on a small number of orthogonal concepts. Also, the sequential and concurrent mechanisms are integrated so that similar things are done in similar ways. Sections 8.2 and 8.3 introduced and illustrated many aspects of SR—without actually saying so. This section summarizes additional aspects: program structure, dynamic creation and placement, and additional statements. As an example, we present a program that simulates the execution of processes entering and exiting critical sections.

8.7.1 Resources and Globals

An SR program is comprised of resources and globals. A *resource declaration* specifies a pattern for a module and has a structure quite similar to that of a `module`:

```
resource name     # specification part
   import clauses
   operation and type declarations
body name(formals)  # body
   variable and other local declarations
```

```
            initialization code
            procedures and processes
            finalization code
      end name
```

A resource contains import clauses if it makes use of the declarations exported from other resources or from globals. Declarations and initialization code in the body can be intermixed; this supports dynamic arrays and permits the programmer to control the order in which variables are initialized and processes are created. If there is no specification part, it can be omitted. The specification and body can also be compiled separately.

Resource instances are created dynamically by means of the **create** statement. For example, executing

```
      rcap := create name(actuals)
```

passes the actuals (by value) to an new instance of resource **name** and then executes that resource's initialization code. When the initialization code terminates, a *resource capability* is returned and assigned to variable **rcap**. This variable can subsequently be used to invoke operations exported by the resource or to destroy the instance. Resources can be destroyed dynamically be means of the **destroy** statement. Execution of **destroy** stops any activity in the named resource, executes the finalization code (if any), and then frees storage allocated to the resource.

By default, components of an SR program reside in one address space. The **create** statement can also be used to create additional address spaces, which are called virtual machines:

```
      vmcap := create vm() on machine
```

This statement creates the virtual machine on the indicated host machine, then returns a capability for it. Subsequent resource creation statements can use "**on vmcap**" to place a new resource in that address space. Thus SR, unlike Ada, gives the programmer complete control over how resources are mapped to machines and this mapping can depend on input to the program.

A *global component* is used to declare types, variables, operations, and procedures that are shared by resources. It is essentially a single instance of a resource. One copy of a global is stored on every virtual machine that needs it. In particular, when a resource is created, any globals that it imports are created implicitly if they have not yet been created.

An SR program contains one distinguished main resource. Execution of a program begins with implicit creation of one instance of this resource. The initialization code in the main resource is then executed; it often creates instances of other resources.

An SR program terminates when every process has terminated or is blocked, or when a `stop` statement is executed. At that point, the run-time system executes the finalization code (if any) in the main resource and then the finalization code (if any) in globals. This provides a way for the programmer to regain control to print results or timing information.

As a simple example, the following SR program writes two lines of output:

```
resource silly()
  write("Hello world.")
  final
    write("Goodbye world.")
  end
end
```

The resource is created automatically. It writes a line, then terminates. Now the finalization code is executed; it writes a second line. The effect is the same as if `final` and the first `end` were deleted from the program.

8.7.2 Communication and Synchronization

The distinguishing attribute of SR is its variety of communication and synchronization mechanisms. Processes in the same resource can share variables, as can resources in the same address space (through the use of globals). Processes can also communicate and synchronize using all the primitives described in Section 8.3: semaphores, asynchronous message passing, RPC, and rendezvous. Thus SR can be used to implement concurrent programs for shared memory multiprocessors as well as for distributed systems.

Operations are declared in `op` declarations, which have the form given earlier in this chapter. Such declarations can appear in resource specifications, in resource bodies, and even within processes. An operation declared within a process is called a *local operation*. The declaring process can pass a capability for a local operation to another process, which can then invoke the operation. This supports conversational continuity (Section 7.3).

An operation is invoked using synchronous `call` or asynchronous `send`. To specify which operation to invoke, an invocation statement uses an operation capability or a field of a resource capability. Within the resource that declares it, the name of an operation is in fact a capability, so an invocation statement can use it directly. Resource and operation capabilities can be passed between resources, so communication paths can vary dynamically.

An operation is serviced either by a procedure (`proc`) or by input statements (`in`). A new process is created to service each remote call of a `proc`; calls from within the same address space are optimized so that the caller itself executes the procedure body. All processes in a resource execute concurrently, at least conceptually.

The input statement supports rendezvous. It has the form shown in Section 8.2 and can have both synchronization and scheduling expressions that depend on parameters. The input statement can also contain an optional `else` clause, which is selected if no other guard succeeds.

SR also contains several mechanisms that are abbreviations for common uses of operations. A `process` declaration is an abbreviation for an `op` declaration and a `proc` to service invocations of the operation. One instance of the process is created by an implicit `send` when the resource is created. (The programmer can also declare arrays of processes.) A `procedure` declaration is an abbreviation for an `op` declaration and a `proc` to service invocations of the operation.

Two additional abbreviations are the `receive` statement and semaphores. A `receive` abbreviates an input statement that services one operation and that merely stores the arguments in local variables. A semaphore declaration (`sem`) abbreviates the declaration of a parameterless operation. The `P` statement is a special case of `receive`, and the `V` statement is a special case of `send`.

SR provides a few additional statements that have proven to be useful. The `reply` statement is a variation of the `return` statement; it returns values, but the replying process continues execution. The `forward` statement can be used to pass an invocation on to another process for further service; it is similar to the `requeue` statement of Ada. Finally, SR contains a `co` statement that can be used to invoke operations in parallel.

8.7.3 Example: Critical Section Simulation

Figure 8.20 contains a complete program that employs several of the message-passing mechanisms available in SR. The program also illustrates how to construct a simple simulation, in this case of a solution to the critical section problem.

The global, `CS`, exports two operations: `CSenter` and `CSexit`. The body of `CS` contains an `arbitrator` process that implements these operations. It first uses an input statement to wait for an invocation of `CSenter`:

```
global CS
  op CSenter(id: int) {call}     # must be called
  op CSexit()    # may be invoked by call or send
body CS
  process arbitrator
    do true ->
      in CSenter(id) by id ->
          write("user", id, "in its CS at", age())
      ni
      receive CSexit()
    od
  end
end

resource main()
  import CS
  var numusers, rounds: int
  getarg(1, numusers); getarg(2, rounds)

  process user(i := 1 to numusers)
    fa j := 1 to rounds ->
      call CSenter(i)            # enter critical section
      nap(int(random(100)))     # delay up to 100 msec
      send CSexit()             # exit critical section
      nap(int(random(1000)))    # delay up to 1 second
    af
  end
end
```

Figure 8.20   An SR program to simulate critical sections.

```
in CSenter(id) by id ->
    write("user", id, "in its CS at", age())
ni
```

This is SR's rendezvous mechanism. If there is more than one invocation of
CSenter, the one that has the smallest value for parameter **id** is selected, and a
message is then printed. Next the **arbitrator** uses a **receive** statement to
wait for an invocation of **CSexit**. In this program we could have put the
arbitrator process and its operations within the **main** resource. However, by
placing them in a global component, they could also be used by other resources
in a larger program.

The `main` resource reads two command-line arguments, then it creates `numusers` instances of the `user` process. Each process executes a for-all loop (`fa`) in which it calls the `CSenter` operation to get permission to enter its critical section, passing its index `i` as an argument. We simulate the duration of critical and noncritical sections of code by having each `user` process "nap" for a random number of milliseconds. After napping the process invokes the `CSexit` operation. The `CSenter` operation must be invoked by a synchronous `call` statement because the `user` process has to wait to get permission. This is enforced by means of the operation restriction `{call}` in the declaration of the `CSenter` operation. However, since a `user` process does not need to delay when leaving its critical section, it invokes the `CSexit` operation by means of the asynchronous `send` statement.

The program employs several of SR's predefined functions. The `write` statement prints a line of output, and `getarg` reads a command-line argument. The `age` function in the `write` statement returns the number of milliseconds the program has been executing. The `nap` function causes a process to "nap" for the number of milliseconds specified by its argument. The `random` function returns a pseudo-random real number between `0` and its argument. We also use the `int` type-conversion function to convert the result from `random` to an integer, as required by `nap`.

Historical Notes

Both remote procedure call (RPC) and rendezvous originated in the late 1970s. Early research on the semantics, use, and implementation of RPC occurred in the operating systems community and continues to be an interest of that group. Bruce Nelson did many of the early experiments at Xerox's Palo Alto Research Center (PARC) and wrote an excellent dissertation on the topic [Nelson 1981]. While pursuing his Ph.D., Nelson also collaborated with Andrew Birrell to produce what is now viewed as a classic on how to implement RPC efficiently in an operating system kernel [Birrell and Nelson 1984]. Down the road from PARC at Stanford University, Alfred Spector [1982] wrote a dissertation on the semantics and implementation of RPC.

Per Brinch Hansen [1978] conceived the basic idea of RPC (although he did not call it that) and designed the first programming language based on the concept. His language is called Distributed Processes (DP). Processes in DP can export procedures. When a procedure is called by another process, it is executed by a new thread of control. A process can also have one "background" thread, which is executed first and may continue to loop. Threads in a process execute with mutual exclusion. They synchronize using shared variables and the `when` statement, which is similar to an `await` statement (Chapter 2).

RPC has been included in several other languages, such as Cedar, Eden, Emerald, and Lynx. Additional languages based on RPC include Argus, Aeolus, and Avalon. The latter three languages combine RPC with what are called *atomic transactions*. A transaction is a group of operations (procedures calls). It is atomic if it is both indivisible and recoverable. If a transaction *commits*, all the operations appear to have been executed exactly once each and as an indivisible unit. If a transaction *aborts*, it has no visible effect. Atomic transactions originated in the database community; they are used to program fault-tolerant distributed applications.

Stamos and Gifford [1990] present an interesting generalization of RPC called remote evaluation (REV). With RPC, a server module provides a fixed set of predefined services. With REV, a client can include a program as an argument in a remote call; when the server receives the call, it executes the program and then returns results. This allows a server to provide an unlimited set of services. Stamos and Gifford's paper describes how REV can simplify the design of many distributed systems and describes the developers' experience with a prototype implementation. Java applets provide a similar kind of functionality, although most commonly on the client side; in particular, an applet is usually returned by a server and executed on the client's machine.

Rendezvous was developed simultaneously and independently in 1978 by Jean-Raymond Abrial of the Ada design team and by this book's author when developing SR. The term *rendezvous* was coined by the Ada designers, many of whom are French. Concurrent C is another language based on rendezvous [Gehani & Roome 1986, 1989]. It extends C with processes, rendezvous using an `accept` statement, and guarded communication using a `select` statement. The `select` statement is like that in Ada, but the `accept` statement is more powerful. In particular, Concurrent C borrows two ideas from SR: synchronization expressions can reference parameters and an `accept` statement can contain a scheduling expression (`by` clause). Concurrent C also allows operations to be invoked by `call` or `send`, as in SR. Later, Gehani and Roome [1988] developed Concurrent C++, which combines Concurrent C with C++.

Several languages include multiple primitives. SR is the best known (see below for references). StarMod is an extension of Modula that supports asynchronous message passing, RPC, rendezvous, and dynamic process creation. Lynx supports RPC and rendezvous. A novel aspect of Lynx is that it supports dynamic program reconfiguration and protection with what are called *links*.

The extensive survey paper by Bal, Steiner, and Tanenbaum [1989] contains information on and references to all the languages mentioned above. The anthology by Gehani and McGettrick [1988] contains reprints of key papers on several of the languages (Ada, Argus, Concurrent C, DP, and SR), comparative surveys, and assessments of Ada.

Most distributed operating systems implement file caches on client workstations. The file system outlined in Figure 8.2 is essentially identical to that in Amoeba. Tanenbaum et al. [1990] give an overview of Amoeba and describe experience with the system. Amoeba uses RPC as its basic communication system. Within a module, threads execute concurrently; they synchronize using locks and semaphores.

Section 8.4 described ways to implement replicated files. The technique of weighted voting is examined in detail in Gifford [1979]. The main reason for using replication is to make a file system fault tolerant. We discuss fault tolerance and additional ways to implement replicated files in the Historical Notes at the end of Chapter 9.

Remote method invocation (RMI) was added to Java starting with version 1.1 of the language. Explanations of RMI and examples of its use can be found in Flanagan [1997] and Hartley [1998]. (See the end of the Historical Notes in Chapter 7 for information on these books and their Web sites.) Further information on RMI can also be found at the main Java Web site `www.javasoft.com`.

In response to the growing development and maintenance costs of software, the U.S. Department of Defense (DoD) began the "common higher order language" program in 1974. The early stages of the program produced a series of requirements documents that culminated in what were called the Steelman specifications. Four industrial/university design teams submitted language proposals in the spring of 1978. Two—code named Red and Green—were selected for the final round and given several months to respond to comments and to refine their proposals. The Red design team was led by Intermetrics, the Green team by Cii Honeywell Bull; both teams were assisted by numerous outside experts. The Green design was selected in the spring of 1979. (Interestingly, the initial Green proposal was based on synchronous message passing similar to that in CSP; the design team changed to rendezvous in the summer and fall of 1978.)

The DoD named the new language Ada, in honor of Augusta Ada Lovelace, daughter of the poet Lord Byron and assistant to Charles Babbage, the inventor of the Analytical Engine. Based on further comments and early experience, the initial version of Ada was refined further and then standardized in 1983. The new language met with both praise and criticism—praise for the major improvement over languages then in use by the DoD; criticism for the size and complexity of the language. With hindsight, the language no longer seems overly complex. In any event, some of the criticisms of Ada 83 and another decade's experience using it led to the refinements embodied in Ada 95, which includes new concurrent programming mechanisms as described in Section 8.6.

Several companies market Ada implementations and programming environments for a variety of machines. In addition, there are numerous books that describe the language. Gehani [1983] emphasizes the advanced features of Ada 83; the dining philosophers algorithm in Figures 8.18 and 8.19 was adapted from that book. Burns and Wellings [1995] describe the concurrent programming mechanisms of Ada 95 and show how to use Ada to program real-time and distributed systems. A comprehensive Web source for information on Ada is `www.adahome.com`.

The basic ideas in SR—resources, operations, input statements, and asynchronous and synchronous invocation—were conceived by the author of this book in 1978; they are described in [Andrews 1981]. A full language was defined in the early 1980s and implemented by several graduate students. Andrews and Ron Olsson designed a new version in the mid 1980s; it added RPC, semaphores, early reply, and several additional mechanisms [Andrews et al. 1988]. Further experience, plus the desire to provide better support for parallel programming, led to the design of version 2.0. Andrews and Olsson [1992] describe SR 2.0, give numerous examples, and provide an overview of the implementation. A book by Stephen Hartley [1995] describes concurrent programming in SR and is intended as a lab book for operating systems or concurrent programming classes. The home page for the SR project and implementation is `www.cs.arizona.edu/sr`.

The focus of this book is on how to write multithreaded, parallel, and/or distributed programs. A related, but higher-level topic is how to glue together existing or future application programs so they can work together in a distributed, Web-based environment. Software systems that provide this glue have come to be called *middleware*. CORBA, Active-X, and DCOM are three of the best known examples. They and most other middleware systems are based on object-oriented technologies. Common Object Request Broker Architecture (COBRA) is a collection of specifications and tools to solve problems of interoperability in distributed systems. Active-X is a technology for combining Web applications such as browsers and Java applets with desktop services such as document processors and spreadsheets. Distributed Component Object Model (DCOM) serves as a basis for remote communications—for example, between Active-X components. A book by Amjad Umar [1997] describes these technologies as well as many others. A useful Web site for CORBA is `www.omg.org`; one for Active-X and DCOM is `www.activex.org`.

References

Andrews, G. R. 1981. Synchronizing resources. *ACM Trans. on Prog. Languages and Systems* 3, 4 (October): 405–30.

Andrews, G. R., and R. A. Olsson. 1992. *Concurrent Programming in SR.* Menlo Park, CA: Benjamin/Cummings.

Andrews, G. R., R. A. Olsson, M. Coffin, I. Elshoff, K. Nilsen, T. Purdin, and G. Townsend. 1988. An overview of the SR language and implementation. *ACM Trans. on Prog. Languages and Systems* 10, 1 (January): 51–86.

Bal, H. E., J. G. Steiner, and A. S. Tanenbaum. 1989. Programming languages for distributed computing systems. *ACM Computing Surveys* 21, 3 (September): 261–322.

Birrell, A. D., and B. J. Nelson. 1984. Implementing remote procedure calls. *ACM Trans. on Computer Systems* 2, 1 (February): 39–59.

Brinch Hansen, P. 1978. Distributed processes: A concurrent programming concept. *Comm. ACM* 21, 11 (November): 934–41.

Burns, A., and A. Wellings. 1995. *Concurrency in Ada.* Cambridge, England: Cambridge University Press.

Flanagan, D. 1997. *Java Examples in a Nutshell: A Tutorial Companion to Java in a Nutshell.* Sebastopol, CA: O'Reilly & Associates.

Gehani, N. 1983. *Ada: An Advanced Introduction.* Englewood Cliffs, NJ: Prentice-Hall.

Gehani, N. H., and A. D. McGettrick. 1988. *Concurrent Programming.* Reading, MA: Addison-Wesley.

Gehani, N. H., and W. D. Roome. 1986. Concurrent C. *Software—Practice and Experience* 16, 9 (September): 821–44.

Gehani, N. H., and W. D. Roome. 1988. Concurrent C++: Concurrent programming with class(es). *Software—Practice and Experience* 18, 12 (December): 1157–77.

Gehani, N. H., and W. D. Roome. 1989. *The Concurrent C Programming Language.* Summit, NJ: Silicon Press.

Gifford, D. K. 1979. Weighted voting for replicated data. *Proc. Seventh Symp. on Operating Systems Principles* (December): 150–62.

Hartley, S. J. 1995. *Operating Systems Programming: The SR Programming Language.* New York: Oxford University Press.

Hartley, S. J. 1998. *Concurrent Programming: The Java Programming Language.* New York: Oxford University Press.

Nelson, B. J. 1981. Remote procedure call. Doctoral dissertation, CMU-CS-81-119, Carnegie-Mellon University, May.

Spector, A. Z. 1982. Performing remote operations efficiently on a local computer network. *Comm. ACM* 25, 4 (April): 246–60.

Stamos, J. W, and D. K Gifford. 1990. Remote evaluation. *ACM Trans. on Prog. Languages and Systems* 12, 4 (October): 537–65.

Tanenbaum, A. S, R. van Renesse, H. van Staveren, G. J. Sharp, S. J. Mullender, J. Jansen, and G. van Rossum. 1990. Experiences with the Amoeba distributed operating system. *Comm. ACM* 33, 12 (December): 46–63.

Umar, A. 1997. *Object-Oriented Client/Server Internet Environments.* Englewood Cliffs, NJ: Prentice-Hall.

Exercises

8.1 Modify the time server module in Figure 8.1 so that the clock process does not get awakened on every tick of the clock. Instead, the clock process should set the hardware timer to go off at the next interesting event. Assume that the time of day is maintained in milliseconds and that the timer can be set to any number of milliseconds. Also assume that processes can read how much time is left before the hardware timer will go off. Finally, assume that the timer can be reset at any time.

8.2 Consider the distributed file system in Figure 8.2.

(a) Develop complete programs for the file cache and file server modules. Develop implementations of the caches, add synchronization code, and so on.

(b) The distributed file system modules are programmed using RPC. Reprogram the file system using the rendezvous primitives defined in Section 8.2. Give a level of detail comparable to that in Figure 8.2.

8.3 Assume modules have the form shown in Section 8.1 and that processes in different modules communicate using RPC. In addition, suppose that processes servicing remote calls execute with mutual exclusion (as in monitors). Condition synchronization is programmed using the statement **when B**. This delays the executing process until Boolean expression **B** is true; **B** can reference any variables in the scope of the statement.

(a) Reprogram the time server module in Figure 8.1 to use these mechanisms.

(b) Reprogram the merge filter module in Figure 8.3 to use these mechanisms.

8.4 The `Merge` module in Figure 8.3 has three procedures and a local process. Change the implementation to get rid of process `M`. In particular, let the processes servicing calls to `in1` and `in2` take on the role of `M`.

8.5 Rewrite the `TimeServer` process in Figure 8.7 so that the `delay` operation specifies an interval as in Figure 8.1 rather than an actual wake-up time. Use only the rendezvous primitives defined in Section 8.2. (*Hint:* You will need one or more additional operations, and the client will not be able simply to call `delay`.)

8.6 Consider a self-scheduling disk driver process as in Figure 7.9. Suppose the process exports one operation: `request(cylinder, ...)`. Show how to use rendezvous and an `in` statement to implement each of the following disk-scheduling algorithms: shortest seek time, circular scan, and elevator. (*Hint:* Use scheduling expressions.)

8.7 Ada provides rendezvous primitives similar to those defined in Section 8.2 (see Section 8.6 for details). However, in the Ada equivalent of the `in` statement, synchronization expressions cannot reference formal parameters of operations. Moreover, Ada does not provide scheduling expressions.

Using either the rendezvous primitives of Section 8.2 and this restricted form of `in` or the actual Ada primitives (`select` and `accept`), reprogram the following algorithms.

(a) The centralized dining philosophers in Figure 8.6.

(b) The time server in Figure 8.7.

(c) The shortest-job-next allocator in Figure 8.8.

8.8 Consider the following specification for a program to find the minimum of a set of integers. Given is an array of processes `Min[1:n]`. Initially, each process has one integer value. The processes repeatedly interact, with each one trying to give another the minimum of the set of values it has seen. If a process gives away its minimum value, it terminates. Eventually, one process will be left, and it will know the minimum of the original set.

(a) Develop a program to solve this problem using only the RPC primitives defined in Section 8.1.

(b) Develop a program to solve this problem using only the rendezvous primitives defined in Section 8.2.

(c) Develop a program to solve this problem using the multiple primitives defined in Section 8.3. Your program should be as simple as you can make it.

8.9 The readers/writers algorithm in Figure 8.13 gives readers preference.

(a) Change the input statement in **Writer** to give writers preference.

(b) Change the input statement in **Writer** so that readers and writers alternate turns when both want to access the database.

8.10 The **FileServer** module in Figure 8.15 uses **call** to update remote copies. Suppose the **call** of **remote_write** is replaced by asynchronous **send**. Will the solution still work? If so, explain why. If not, explain what can go wrong.

8.11 Suppose processes communicate using only the RPC mechanisms defined in Section 8.1. Processes within a module synchronize using semaphores. Reprogram each of the following algorithms.

(a) The **BoundedBuffer** module in Figure 8.5.

(b) The **Table** module in Figure 8.6.

(c) The **SJN_Allocator** module in Figure 8.8.

(d) The **ReadersWriters** module in Figure 8.13.

(e) The **FileServer** module in Figure 8.15.

8.12 Develop a server process that implements a reusable barrier for **n** worker processes. The server has one operation, **arrive()**. A worker calls **arrive()** when it arrives at a barrier; the call terminates when all **n** processes have arrived. Use the rendezvous primitives of Section 8.2 to program the server and workers. Assume the existence of a function **?opname**—as defined in Section 8.3—that returns the number of pending calls of **opname**.

8.13 Figure 7.15 presented an algorithm for checking primality using a sieve of filter processes; it was programmed using CSP's synchronous message passing. Figure 7.16 presented a second algorithm using a manager and a bag of tasks; it was programmed using Linda's tuple space.

(a) Reprogram the algorithm in Figure 7.15 using the multiple primitives defined in Section 8.3.

(b) Reprogram the algorithm in Figure 7.16 using the multiple primitives defined in Section 8.3.

(c) Compare the performance of your answers to (a) and (b). How many messages get sent to check the primality of all odd numbers from **3** to **n**? Count a send/receive pair as one message. Count a call as two messages, even if no value is returned.

8.14 *The Savings Account Problem.* A savings account is shared by several people. Each person may deposit or withdraw funds from the account. The current balance in the account is the sum of all deposits to date minus the sum of all withdrawals to date. The balance must never become negative.

Using the multiple primitives notation, develop a server to solve this problem and show the client interface to the server. The server exports two operations: deposit(amount) and withdraw(amount). Assume that amount is positive and that withdraw must delay until there are sufficient funds.

8.15 Two kinds of processes, A's and B's, enter a room. An A process cannot leave until it meets two B processes, and a B process cannot leave until it meets one A process. Each kind of process leaves the room—without meeting any other processes—once it has met the required number of other processes.

(a) Develop a server process to implement this synchronization. Show the interface of the A and B processes to the server. Use the multiple primitives notation defined in Section 8.3.

(b) Modify your answer to (a) so that the first of the two B processes that meets an A process does not leave the room until after the A process meets a second B process.

8.16 Suppose a computer center has two printers, A and B, that are similar but not identical. Three kinds of client processes use the printers: those that must use A, those that must use B, and those that can use either A or B.

Using the multiple primitives notation, develop code that each kind of client executes to request and release a printer, and develop a server process to allocate the printers. Your solution should be fair, assuming a client using a printer eventually releases it.

8.17 *The Roller Coaster Problem.* Suppose there are n passenger processes and one car process. The passengers repeatedly wait to take rides in the car, which can hold C passengers, C < n. However, the car can go around the tracks only when it is full.

(a) Develop code for the actions of the passenger and car processes. Use the multiple primitives notation.

(b) Generalize your answer to (a) to employ m car processes, m > 1. Since there is only one track, cars cannot pass each other—i.e., they must finish going around the track in the order in which they started. Again, a car can go around the tracks only when it is full.

8.18 *Stable Marriage Problem.* Let `Man` and `Woman` each be arrays of n processes. Each man ranks the women from 1 to n, and each woman ranks the men from 1 to n. A *pairing* is a one-to-one correspondence of men and women. A pairing is *stable* if, for two men m_1 and m_2 and their paired women w_1 and w_2, both of the following conditions are satisfied:

- m_1 ranks w_1 higher than w_2 or w_2 ranks m_2 higher than m_1; and

- m_2 ranks w_2 higher than w_1 or w_1 ranks m_1 higher than m_2.

Expressed differently, a pairing is unstable if a man and woman would both prefer each other to their current pairing. A solution to the stable marriage problem is a set of n pairings, all of which are stable.

(a) Using the multiple primitives notation, write a program to solve the stable marriage problem.

(b) The stable roommates problem is a generalization of the stable marriage problem. In particular, there are 2 n people. Each person has a ranked list of preferences for a roommate. A solution to the roommates problem is a set of n pairings, all of which are stable in the same sense as for the marriage problem. Using the multiple primitives notation, write a program to solve the stable roommates problem.

8.19 The `FileServer` module in Figure 8.15 uses one lock per copy of the file. Modify the program to use weighted voting, as defined at the end of Section 8.4.

8.20 Figure 8.15 shows how to implement replicated files using the multiple primitives notation defined in Section 8.3.

(a) Write a Java program to solve the same problem. Use RMI and synchronized methods. Experiment with your program, placing different file servers on different machines in a network. Write a short report describing your program and experiments and what you have learned.

(b) Write an Ada program to solve the same problem. You will have to do research to figure out how to distribute the file servers onto different machines. Experiment with your program. Write a short report describing your program and experiments and what you have learned.

(c) Write an SR program to solve the same problem. Experiment with your program, placing different file servers on different machines in a network. Write a short report describing your program and experiments and what you have learned.

8.21   Experiment with the Java program for a remote database in Figure 8.16. Try running the program and seeing what happens. Modify the program to have multiple clients. Modify the program to have a more realistic database (at least with operations that take longer). Write a brief report describing what you have tried and what you have learned.

8.22   Figure 8.16 contains a Java program that implements a simple remote database. Rewrite the program in Ada or in SR, then experiment with your program. For example, add multiple clients and make the database more realistic (at least with operations that take longer). Write a brief report describing how you implemented the program in Ada or SR, what experiments you tried, and what you learned.

8.23   Figures 8.18 and 8.19 contain an Ada program that implements a simulation of the dining philosophers problem.

(a) Get the program to run, then experiment with it. For example, have the philosophers sleep for random periods when they are thinking and eating, and try different numbers of rounds. Write a brief report describing what you tried and what you learned.

(b) Rewrite the program in Java or in SR, then experiment with your program. For example, have the philosophers sleep for random periods when they are thinking and eating, and try different numbers of rounds. Write a brief report describing how you implemented the program in Java or SR, what experiments you tried, and what you learned.

8.24   Figure 8.20 contains an SR program that simulates a solution to the critical section problem.

(a) Get the program to run, then experiment with it. For example, modify the two delay intervals or change the scheduling priority. Write a brief report describing what you tried and what you learned.

(b) Rewrite the program in Java or Ada, then experiment with your program. For example, modify the two delay intervals or change the scheduling priority. Write a brief report describing how you implemented the program in Java or Ada, what experiments you tried, and what you learned.

8.25   Exercise 7.26 describes several parallel and distributed programming projects. Pick one of those or something similar, then design and implement a solution using Java, Ada, SR, or a subroutine library that supports RPC or rendezvous. When you have finished, write a report describing your problem and solution and demonstrate how your program works.

9

Paradigms for Process Interaction

As we have seen several times, there are three basic process-interaction patterns: producer/consumer, client/server, and interacting peers. Chapter 7 showed how to program these patterns using message passing; Chapter 8 showed how to program them using RPC and rendezvous.

The three basic patterns can also be combined in numerous ways. This chapter describes several of these larger process-interaction patterns and illustrates their use. Each pattern is a *paradigm* (model) for process interaction. In particular, each paradigm has a unique structure that can be used to solve many different problems. The paradigms we describe are as follows:

- manager/workers, which represent a distributed implementation of a bag of tasks;

- heartbeat algorithms, in which processes periodically exchange information using a send then receive interaction;

- pipeline algorithms, in which information flows from one process to another using a receive then send interaction;

- probes (sends) and echoes (receives), which disseminate and gather information in trees and graphs;

- broadcast algorithms, which are used for decentralized decision making;

- token-passing algorithms, which are another approach to decentralized decision making; and

- replicated server processes, which manage multiple instances of resources such as files.

The first three paradigms are commonly used in parallel computations; the other four arise in distributed systems. We illustrate how the paradigms can be used to solve a variety of problems, including sparse matrix multiplication, image processing, distributed matrix multiplication, computing the topology of a network, distributed mutual exclusion, distributed termination detection, and decentralized dining philosophers. We later use the three parallel computing paradigms to solve the scientific computing problems in Chapter 11. Additional applications are described in the exercises, including sorting and the traveling salesman.

9.1 Manager/Workers (Distributed Bag of Tasks)

We introduced the bag-of-tasks paradigm in Section 3.6 and showed how to implement it using shared variables for communication and synchronization. Recall the basic idea: Several worker processes share a bag that contains independent tasks. Each worker repeatedly removes a task from the bag, executes it, and possibly generates one or more new tasks that it puts into the bag. The benefits of this approach to implementing a parallel computation are that it is easy to vary the number of workers and it is relatively easy to ensure that each does about the same amount of work.

Here we show how to implement the bag-of-tasks paradigm using message passing rather than shared variables. This is done by employing a manager process to implement the bag, hand out tasks, collect results, and detect termination. The workers get tasks and deposit results by communicating with the manager. Thus the manager is essentially a server process and the workers are clients.

The first example below shows how to multiply sparse matrices (matrices for which most entries are zero). The second example revisits the quadrature problem and uses a combination of static and adaptive integration intervals. In both examples, the total number of tasks is fixed, but the amount of work per task is variable.

9.1.1 Sparse Matrix Multiplication

Assume that A and B are $n \times n$ matrices. The goal, as before, is to compute the matrix product $A \times B = C$. This requires computing n^2 inner products. Each inner product is the sum (plus reduction) of the pairwise products of two vectors of length n.

A matrix is said to be *dense* if most entries are nonzero and it is *sparse* if most entries are zero. If A and B are dense matrices, then C will also be dense (unless there is considerable cancellation in the inner products). On the other hand, if either A or B is sparse, then C will also be sparse. This is because each zero in A or B will lead to a zero in n vector products and hence will not contribute to the result of n of the inner products. For example, if some row of A contains all zeros, then the corresponding row of C will also contain all zeros.

Sparse matrices arise in many contexts, such as numerical approximations to partial differential equations and large systems of linear equations. A tridiagonal matrix is an example of a sparse matrix; it has zeros everywhere except on the main diagonal and the two diagonals immediately above and below the main diagonal. When we know that matrices are sparse, we can save space by storing only the nonzero entries, and we can save time when multiplying matrices by ignoring entries that are zero.

We will represent sparse matrix A as follows by storing information about the rows of A:

```
int lengthA[n];
pair *elementsA[n];
```

The value of lengthA[i] is the number of nonzero entries in row i of A. Variable elementsA[i] points to a list of the nonzero entries in row i. Each entry is represented by a pair (record): an integer column index and a double precision data value. Thus if lengthA[i] is 3, then there are three pairs in the list elementsA[i]. These will be ordered by increasing values of the column indexes. As a concrete example, consider the following:

```
lengthA   elementsA

   1        (3, 2.5)
   0
   0
   2        (1, -1.5)   (4, 0.6)
   0
   1        (0, 3.4)
```

This represents a six by six matrix containing four nonzero elements: one in row 0 column 3, one in row 3 column 1, one in row 3 column 4, and one in row 5, column 0.

We will represent matrix C in the same way as A. However, to facilitate matrix multiplication, we will represent matrix B by columns rather than rows. In particular, lengthB indicates the number of nonzero elements in each column of B, and elementsB contains pairs of row index and data value.

Computing the matrix product of A and B requires as usual examining the n^2 pairs of rows and columns. With sparse matrices, the most natural size for a

```
module Manager
  type pair = (int index, double value);
  op getTask(result int row, len; result pair [*]elems);
  op putResult(int row, len; pair [*]elems);
body Manager
  int lengthA[n], lengthC[n];
  pair *elementsA[n], *elementsC[n];
  # matrix A is assumed to be initialized
  int nextRow = 0, tasksDone = 0;

  process manager {
    while (nextRow < n or tasksDone < n) {
      # more tasks to do or more results needed
      in getTask(row, len, elems) ->
          row = nextRow;
          len = lengthA[i];
          copy pairs in *elementsA[i] to elems;
          nextRow++;
      [] putResult(row, len, elems) ->
          lengthC[row] = len;
          copy pairs in elems to *elementsC[row];
          tasksDone++;
      ni
    }
  }
end Manager
```

Figure 9.1 (a) Sparse matrix multiplication: Manager process.

task is one row of the result matrix C, because an entire row is represented by a single vector of (column, value) pairs. Thus there are as many tasks as there are rows of A. (An obvious optimization would be to skip over rows of A that are entirely zeros—namely, those for which lengthA[i] is 0, because the corresponding rows of C would also be all zeros. This is not likely in realistic applications, however.)

Figure 9.1 contains code to implement sparse matrix multiplication using a manager and several worker processes. We assume that matrix A is already initialized in the manager and that each worker contains an initialized copy of matrix B. The processes interact using the rendezvous primitives of Chapter 8, because that leads to the simplest program. To use asynchronous message passing, the manager would be programmed in the style of an active monitor (Section 7.3) and the call in the workers would be replaced by send then receive.

```
process worker[w = 1 to numWorkers] {
  int lengthB[n];
  pair *elementsB[n];  # assumed to be initialized
  int row, lengthA, lengthC;
  pair *elementsA, *elementsC;
  int r, c, na, nb;  # used in computing
  double sum;         #   inner products
  while (true) {
    # get a row of A, then compute a row of C
    call getTask(row, lengthA, elementsA);
    lengthC = 0;
    for [i = 0 to n-1]
      INNER_PRODUCT(i);  # see body of text
    send putResult(row, lengthC, elementsC);
  }
}
```

Figure 9.1 (b)   Sparse matrix multiplication: Worker processes.

The manager process in Figure 9.1 (a) implements the bag and accumulates results. It services two operations: `getTask` and `putResult`. Integer `nextRow` identifies the next task—namely, the next row. Integer `tasksDone` counts the number of results that have been returned. When a task is handed out, `nextRow` is incremented; when a result is returned, `tasksDone` is incremented. When both values are equal to n, all tasks have been completed.

The code for the worker processes is shown in Figure 9.1 (b). Each worker repeatedly gets a new task, performs it, then sends the result to the manager. A task consists of computing a row of the result matrix `C`, so a worker executes a `for` loop to compute n inner products, one for every column of `B`. However, the code for computing an inner product of two sparse vectors differs significantly from the loop for computing an inner product of two dense vectors. In particular, the meaning of `INNER_PRODUCT(i)` in the worker code is

```
sum = 0.0; na = 1; nb = 1;
c = elementsA[na]->index;      # column in row of A
r = elementsB[i][nb]->index;  # row in column of B
while (na <= lengthA and nb <= lengthB) {
  if (r == c) {
    sum += elementsA[na]->value *
             elementsB[i][nb]->value;
    na++; nb++;
```

```
        c = elementsA[na]->index;
        r = elementsB[i][nb]->index;
   } else if (r < c) {
      nb++; r = elementsB[i][nb]->index;
   } else { # r > c
      na++; c = elementsA[na]->index;
   }
  }
  if (sum != 0.0) {   # extend row of C
    elementsC[lengthC] = pair(i, sum);
    lengthC++;
  }
```

The basic idea is to scan through the sparse representations for the row of A and column i of B. (The above code assumes that the row and column each contain at least one nonzero element.) The inner product will be nonzero only if there are pairs of values that have the *same* column index c in A and row index r in B. The while loop above finds all these pairs and adds up their products. If the sum is nonzero when the loop terminates, then a new pair is added to the vector representing the row of C. (We assume that space for the elements has already been allocated.) After all n inner products have been computed, a worker sends the row of C to the manager, then calls the manager to get another task.

9.1.2 Adaptive Quadrature Revisited

The quadrature problem was introduced in Section 1.5, where we presented static (iterative) and dynamic (recursive) algorithms for approximating the integral of function f(x) from a to b. Section 3.6 showed how to implement adaptive quadrature using a shared bag of tasks.

Here we use a manager to implement a distributed bag of tasks. However, we use a combination of the static and dynamic algorithms rather than the "pure" adaptive quadrature algorithm used in Figure 3.21. In particular, we divide the interval from a to b into a fixed number of subintervals and then use the adaptive quadrature algorithm within each subinterval. This combines the simplicity of an iterative algorithm with the greater accuracy of an adaptive algorithm. In particular, by using a static number of tasks, the manager and workers are simpler and there are far fewer interactions between them.

Figure 9.2 contains the code for the manager and workers. Because the manager is essentially a server process, we again use rendezvous for interaction

```
module Manager
  op getTask(result double left, right);
  op putResult(double area);
body Manager
  process manager {
    double a, b;            # interval to integrate
    int numIntervals;       # number of intervals to use
    double width = (b-a)/numIntervals;
    double x = a, totalArea = 0.0;
    int tasksDone = 0;
    while (tasksDone < numIntervals) {
      in getTask(left, right) st x < b ->
          left = x; x += width; right = x;
      [] putResult(area) ->
          totalArea += area;
          tasksDone++;
      ni
    }
  print the result totalArea;
  }
end Manager

double f() { ... }          # function to integrate
double quad(...) { ... }    # adaptive quad function

process worker[w = 1 to numWorkers] {
  double left, right, area = 0.0;
  double fleft, fright, lrarea;
  while (true) {
    call getTask(left, right);
    fleft = f(left); fright = f(right);
    lrarea = (fleft + fright) * (right - left) / 2;
    # calculate area recursively as shown in Section 1.5
    area = quad(left, right, fleft, fright, lrarea);
    send putResult(area);
  }
}
```

Figure 9.2   Adaptive quadrature using manager/workers paradigm.

between the manager and workers. Thus the manager has the same structure as that shown in Figure 9.1 (a) and again exports two operations, `getTask` and `putResult`. However, the operations have different parameters, because now a task is defined by the endpoints of an interval, `left` and `right`, and a result consists of the area under `f(x)` over that interval. We assume the values of `a`, `b`, and `numIntervals` are given, perhaps as command-line arguments. From these values, the manager computes the width of each interval. The manager then loops, accepting calls of `getTask` and `putResult`, until it has received one result for each interval (and hence task). Notice the use of a synchronization expression "`st x< b`" in the arm for `getTask` in the input statement; this prevents `getTask` from handing out another task when the bag is empty.

The worker processes in Figure 9.2 share or have their own copies of the code for functions `f` and `quad`, where `quad` is the recursive function given in Section 1.5. Each worker repeatedly gets a task from the manager, calculates the arguments needed by `quad`, calls `quad` to approximate the area under `f(left)` to `f(right)`, then sends the result to the manager.

When the program in Figure 9.2 terminates, every worker will be blocked at its call of `getTask`. This is often harmless, as here, but at times it can indicate deadlock. We leave to the reader modifying the program so that the workers terminate normally. (*Hint:* Make `getTask` a function that returns `true` or `false`.)

In this program the amount of work per task varies, depending on how rapidly the function `f` varies. Thus, if there are only about as many tasks as workers, the computational load will almost certainly be unbalanced. On the other hand, if there are too many tasks, then there will be unnecessary interactions between the manager and workers, and hence unnecessary overhead. The ideal is to have just enough tasks so that, on average, each worker will be responsible for about the same total amount of work. A reasonable heuristic is to have from two to three times as many tasks as workers, which here means that `numIntervals` should be two to three times larger than `numWorkers`.

9.2 Heartbeat Algorithms

The bag-of-tasks paradigm is useful for solving problems that have a fixed number of independent tasks or that result from use of the divide-and-conquer paradigm. The *heartbeat paradigm* is useful for many data parallel iterative applications. In particular, it can be used when the data is divided among workers, each is responsible for updating a particular part, and new data values depend on values held by workers or their immediate neighbors. Applications include grid computations, which arise in image processing or solving partial differential equations, and cellular automata, which arise in simulations of phenomena such as forest fires or biological growth.

Suppose we have an array of data. Each worker is responsible for a part of the data and has the following code outline:

```
process Worker[i = 1 to numWorkers] {
    declarations of local variables;
    initialize local variables;
    while (not done) {
        send  values to neighbors;
        receive  values from neighbors;
        update local values;
    }
}
```

We call this type of process interaction a *heartbeat algorithm* because the actions of each worker are like the beating of a heart: expand, sending information out; contract, gathering new information; then process the information and repeat.

If the data is a two-dimensional grid, it could be divided into strips or blocks. With strips there would be a vector of workers, and each would have two neighbors (except perhaps for the workers at the ends). With blocks there would be a matrix of workers, and each would have from two to eight neighbors, depending on whether the block is on the corner, edge, or interior of the array of data, and depending on how many neighboring values are needed to update local values. Three-dimensional arrays of data could be divided similarly into planes, rectangular prisms, or cubes.

The **send/receive** interaction pattern in a heartbeat algorithm produces a "fuzzy" barrier among the workers. Recall that a barrier is a synchronization point that all workers must reach before any can proceed. In an iterative computation, a barrier ensures that every worker finishes one iteration before starting the next. Above, the message exchange ensures that a worker does not begin a new update phase until its neighbors have completed the previous update phase. Workers that are not neighbors can get more than one iteration apart, but neighbors cannot. A true barrier is not required because workers share data only with their neighbors.

Below we develop heartbeat algorithms for two problems: region labeling, an example of image processing, and the Game of Life, an example of cellular automata. Chapter 11 and the exercises describe additional applications.

9.2.1 Image Processing: Region Labeling

An *image* is a representation of a picture; it typically consists of a matrix of numbers. Each element of an image is called a *pixel* (picture element), and has a value that is its light intensity or color.

There are dozens of image-processing operations, and each can benefit from parallelization. Moreover, the same operation is often applied to a stream of images. Image-processing operations range from point operations on individual pixels, such as contrast stretching, to local operations on groups of pixels, such as smoothing or noise reduction, to global operations on all the pixels, such as encoding or decoding.

Here we examine a local operation called *region labeling*. Let an image be represented by a matrix `image[m,n]` of integers, and for simplicity assume that each pixel has value `1` (lit) or `0` (unlit). Assume that the neighbors of a pixel are the four pixels above and below and to the left and right of it. (Pixels on the corners of the image have two neighbors; those on the edges have three.)

The region labeling problem is to find regions of lit pixels and to assign a unique label to each. Two lit pixels belong to the same region if they are neighbors. For example, consider the image below, in which lit pixels are displayed as dots and unlit pixels as blanks.

The image contains *three* regions. The "curve" in the lower-right corner does not form a region because the dots are connected by diagonals, not horizontal or vertical lines.

The label of each pixel is stored in a second matrix `label[m,n]`. Initially, each point is given a unique label, such as the linear function `m*i+j` of its coordinates. The final value of `label[i,j]` is to be the largest of the initial labels in the region to which the pixel belongs.

The natural way to solve this problem is by means of an iterative algorithm. On each iteration, we examine every pixel and its neighbors. If a pixel and a neighbor are both lit, then we set the label of the pixel to the maximum of its current label and that of its neighbor. We can do this in parallel for every pixel, because the values of labels never decrease.

The algorithm terminates if no label changes during an iteration. Typically regions are fairly compact, in which case the algorithm will terminate after about

$O(\text{m})$ iterations. However, in the worst case, $O(\text{m n})$ iterations will be required since there could be a region that "snakes" around the image.

For this problem pixels are independent, so we can employ `m*n` parallel tasks. This would be appropriate on a massively parallel SIMD machine, but each task is too small to be efficient on an MIMD machine. Suppose we have an MIMD machine with `P` processors, and suppose that `m` is a multiple of `P`. A good way to solve the region-labeling problem is to partition the image into `P` strips or blocks of pixels and to assign one worker process to each strip or block. We will use strips, because that is simpler to program. Using strips also results in fewer messages than using blocks, because each worker has fewer neighbors. (On machines organized as a grid or a cube, it would be efficient to use blocks of points, because the interconnection network would undoubtedly support simultaneous message transmissions.)

Each worker computes the labels for the pixels in its strip. To do so, it needs its own strip of `image` and `label` as well as the edges of the strips above and below it. Since regions can span block boundaries, each process needs to interact with its neighbors. In particular, on each iteration a process exchanges the labels of pixels on the edges of its strip with its two neighbors, then it computes new labels.

Figure 9.3 (a) contains an outline of the worker processes. After initializing local variables, each worker exchanges the edges of its portion of `image` with its neighbors. First it sends an edge to the neighbor above it, then its sends an edge to the neighbor below, then it receives from the worker below, then it sends to the worker above. Two arrays of channels, `first` and `second`, are used for the exchange. As shown, workers `1` and `P` are special cases because they have only one neighbor.

At the start of each iteration of the `while` loop, neighboring workers exchange edges of `label`, using the same message-passing pattern as before. Then each worker updates the labels of the pixels in its strip. The update code could examine each pixel just once, or it could iterate until no label changes in the local strip. The latter approach will result in fewer exchanges of labels between workers, and hence will improve performance by increasing the ratio of computation to communication.

In this application, a worker cannot determine by itself when to terminate. Even if there is no local change on an iteration, some label in another strip could have changed, and that pixel could belong to a region that spans more than one strip. The computation is done only when no label in the entire image changes. (Actually, it is done one iteration earlier, but there is no way to detect this.)

We use a coordinator process to detect termination, as shown in Figure 9.3 (b). (One of the workers could play the role of the coordinator; we have used

```
chan first[1:P](int edge[n]);      # for exchanging edges
chan second[1:P](int edge[n]);
chan answer[1:P](bool);            # for termination check

process Worker[w = 1 to P] {
  int stripSize = m/W;
  int image[stripSize+2,n];      # local values plus edges
  int label[stripSize+2,n];      #    from neighbors
  int change = true;
  initialize image[1:stripSize,*] and label[1:stripSize,*];

  # exchange edges of image with neighbors
  if (w != 1)
    send first[w-1](image[1,*]);         # to worker above
  if (w != P)
    send second[w+1](image[stripSize,*]);   # to below
  if (w != P)
    receive first[w](image[stripSize+1,*]); # from below
  if (w != 1)
    receive second[w](image[0,*]);    # from worker above

  while (change) {
    exchange edges of label with neighbors, as above;
    update label[1:stripSize,*] and set change to true if
      the value of the label changes;
    send result(change);           # tell coordinator
    receive answer[w](change);   # and get back answer
  }
}
```

Figure 9.3 (a) Region labeling: Worker processes.

a separate process to simplify the code.) At the end of each iteration, every worker sends a message to the coordinator indicating whether that worker changed any label. The coordinator combines these messages and sends the answer to every worker. Channels `result` and `answer[n]` are used for these communications.

Using a central coordinator to check for termination requires `2*P` messages per iteration of the algorithm. If the answer could be broadcast, this would reduce to `P+1` messages. However, the execution time for the coordinator is $O(P)$ because it receives the results one at a time. By using a tree of coordinators, we

```
chan result(bool);   # for results from workers

process Coordinator {
  bool chg, change = true;
  while (change) {
    change = false;
    # see if there has been a change in any strip
    for [i = 1 to P] {
      receive result(chg);
      change = change or chg;
    }
    # broadcast answer to every worker
    for [i = 1 to P]
      send answer[i](change);
  }
}
```

Figure 9.3 (b)   Region labeling: Coordinator process.

could reduce the execution time to $O(\log_2 P)$. Better yet, we could use a global reduction operation, such as the `MPI_Allreduce` operation in the MPI library. This would definitely simplify the code, but whether it would improve performance depends on how the MPI library is implemented on a given machine.

9.2.2 Cellular Automata: The Game of Life

Many biological or physical systems can be modeled as a collection of bodies that repeatedly interact and evolve over time. Some systems, especially simple ones, can be modeled using what are called cellular automata. (We examine a more complex system, gravitational interaction, in Chapter 11.) The idea is to divide the biological or physical problem space into a collection of cells. Each cell is a finite state machine. After the cells are initialized, all make one state transition, then all make a second, and so on. Each transition is based upon the current state of the cell as well as the states of its neighbors.

Here we use cellular automata to model what is called the Game of Life. A two-dimensional board of cells is given. Each cell either contains an organism (it's alive), or it is empty (it's dead). For this problem, each interior cell has eight neighbors, located above, below, left, right, and along the four diagonals. Cells in the corner have three neighbors, those on the edges have five.

The Game of Life is played as follows. First, the board is initialized. Second, every cell examines its state and the state of its neighbors, then makes a state transition according to the following rules:

- A live cell with zero or one live neighbors dies from loneliness.

- A live cell with two or three live neighbors survives for another generation.

- A live cell with four or more live neighbors dies due to overpopulation.

- A dead cell with exactly three live neighbors becomes alive.

This process is repeated for some number of generations (steps).

Figure 9.4 outlines a program for simulating the Game of Life. The processes interact using the heartbeat paradigm. On each iteration a cell sends a message to each of its neighbors and receives a message from each. It then updates its local state according to the above rules. As usual with a heartbeat algorithm, the processes do not execute in lockstep, but neighbors never get an iteration ahead of each other.

For simplicity, we have programmed each cell as a process, although the board could be divided into strips or blocks of cells. We have also ignored the special cases of edge and corner cells. Each process cell[i,j] receives

```
chan exchange[1:n,1:n](int row, column, state);

process cell[i = 1 to n, j = 1 to n] {
  int state;    # initialize to dead or alive
  declarations of other variables;
  for [k = 1 to numGenerations] {
    # exchange state with 8 neighbors
    for [p = i-1 to i+1, q = j-1 to j+1]
      if (p != q)
        send exchange[p,q](i, j, state);
    for [p = 1 to 8] {
      receive exchange[i,j](row, column, value);
      save value of neighbor's state;
    }
    update local state using rules in text;
  }
}
```

Figure 9.4   The Game of Life.

messages from element `exchange[i,j]` of the matrix of communication channels, and it sends messages to neighboring elements of `exchange`. (Recall that our channels are buffered and that `send` is nonblocking.) The reader might find it instructive to implement this program and to display the states of the cells on a graphical display.

9.3 Pipeline Algorithms

Recall that a filter process receives data from an input port, processes it, and sends results to an output port. A *pipeline* is a linear collection of filter processes. We have already seen the concept several times, including Unix pipes (Section 1.6), a sorting network (Section 7.2), and as a way to circulate values among processes (Section 7.4). The paradigm is also useful in parallel computing, as we show here.

We always use some number of worker processes to solve a parallel computing problem. Sometimes we can program the workers as filters and connect them together into a parallel computing pipeline. There are three basic structures for such a pipeline, as shown in Figure 9.5: (1) open, (2) closed, and (3) circular. The W_1 to W_n are worker processes. In an *open* pipeline, the input source and output destination are not specified. Such a pipeline can be "dropped down"

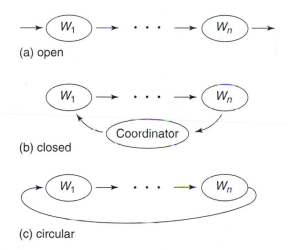

Figure 9.5   Pipeline structures for parallel computing.

anywhere that it will fit. A *closed* pipeline is an open pipeline that is connected to a *Coordinator* process, which produces the input needed by the first worker and consumes the results produced by the last worker. The Unix command "`grep pattern file | wc`" is an example of an open pipeline that can be put in various places; when it is actually executed on a shell command line, it becomes part of a closed pipeline, with the human user being the coordinator. A pipeline is *circular* if the ends are closed on each other; in this case data circulates among the workers.

In Section 1.8 we introduced two distributed implementations of matrix multiplication $a \times b = c$, where all of a, b, and c are dense $n \times n$ matrices. The first solution simply divided the work up among n workers, one per row of a and c, but each process needed to store all of b. The second solution also used n workers, but each needed to store only one column of b. That solution actually employed a circular pipeline, with the columns of b circulating among the workers.

Here we examine two additional distributed implementations of dense matrix multiplication. The first employs a closed pipeline; the second employs a mesh of circular pipelines. Each has interesting properties relative to the prior solutions, and each illustrates a pattern that has other applications.

9.3.1 A Distributed Matrix Multiplication Pipeline

For simplicity, we will again assume that each matrix has size $n \times n$, and we will employ n worker processes. Each worker will produce one row of c. However, initially the workers do not have any part of a or b. Instead, we will connect the workers in a closed pipeline through which they acquire all data items and pass all results. In particular, the coordinator process sends every row of a and every column of b down the pipeline to the first worker; eventually, the coordinator receives every row of c from the last worker.

Figure 9.6 (a) contains the actions of the coordinator process. As indicated, the coordinator sends rows `a[0,*]` to `a[n-1,*]` to channel `vector[0]`, which is the input channel for worker 0. Then the coordinator sends columns `b[*,0]` to `b[*,n-1]` to worker 0. Finally, the coordinator receives the rows of results (it will get these from worker `n-1`). However, the results arrive in the order `c[n-1,*]` to `c[0,*]` for reasons explained below.

Each worker process has three execution phases. First, it receives rows of `a`, keeping the first one it receives and passing the others on. This phase distributes the rows of `a` among the workers, with `Worker[i]` saving the value of `a[i,*]`. Second, workers receive columns of `b`, immediately pass them on to the next worker, then compute one inner product. This phase is repeated n times by each worker, after which time it will have computed $c[i,*]$. Third, each worker sends its row of c to the next worker, and then receives and passes on rows of c from previous workers in the pipeline. The last worker sends its row of c and others it receives to the coordinator. These are sent to the coordinator in order $c[n-1,*]$ to $c[0,*]$, because that is the order in which the last worker sees them; this also decreases communication delays and means that the last worker does not need to have local storage for all of c.

Figure 9.6 (b) shows the actions of the worker processes. The comments indicate the three phases. The extra details are the bookkeeping to distinguish between the last worker and others in the pipeline.

This solution has several interesting properties. First, messages chase each other down the pipeline: first the rows of a, then the columns of b, and finally the rows of c. There is essentially no delay between the time that a worker receives a message and the time it passes it along. Thus messages keep flowing continuously. When a worker is computing an inner product, it has already passed along the column it is using, and hence another worker can get it, pass it along, and start computing its own inner product.

Second, it takes a total of n message-passing times for the first worker to receive all the rows of a and pass them along. It takes another $n-1$ message-passing times to fill the pipeline—namely, to get every worker its row of a. However, once the pipeline is full, inner products get computed about as fast as messages can flow. This is because, as observed above, the columns of b

```
chan vector[n](double v[n]);   # messages to workers
chan result(double v[n]);      # rows of c to coordinator

process Coordinator {
  double a[n,n], b[n,n], c[n,n];
  initialize a and b;
  for [i = 0 to n-1]           # send all rows of a
    send vector[0](a[i,*]);
  for [i = 0 to n-1]           # send all columns of b
    send vector[0](b[*,i]);
  for [i = n-1 to 0]           # receive rows of c
    receive result(c[i,*]);    # in reverse order
}
```

Figure 9.6 (a)   Matrix multiplication pipeline: Coordinator process.

```
process Worker[w = 0 to n-1] {
  double a[n], b[n], c[n];  # my row or column of each
  double temp[n];             # used to pass vectors on
  double total;        # used to compute inner product

  # receive rows of a; keep first and pass others on
  receive vector[w](a);
  for [i = w+1 to n-1] {
    receive vector[w](temp); send vector[w+1](temp);
  }

  # get columns and compute inner products
  for [j = 0 to n-1] {
    receive vector[w](b);  # get a column of b
    if (w < n-1)     # if not last worker, pass it on
      send vector[w+1](b);
    total = 0.0;
    for [k = 0 to n-1]      # compute one inner product
      total += a[k] * b[k];
    c[j] = total;          # put total into c
  }

  # send my row of c to next worker or coordinator
  if (w < n-1)
    send vector[w+1](c);
  else
    send result(c);
  # receive and pass on earlier rows of c
  for [i = 0 to w-1] {
    receive vector[w](temp);
    if (w < n-1)
      send vector[w+1](temp);
    else
      send result(temp);
  }
}
```

Figure 9.6 (b)   Matrix multiplication pipeline: Worker processes.

immediately follow the rows of **a**, and they get passed as as soon as they are received. If it takes longer to compute an inner product than to send and receive a message, then the computation time will start to dominate once the pipeline is full. We leave to the reader the interesting challenges of devising analytical performance equations and conducting timing experiments.

Another interesting property of the solution is that it is trivial to vary the number of columns of **b**. All we need to change are the upper bounds on the loops that deal with columns. In fact, the same code could be used to multiply **a** by any stream of vectors, producing a stream of vectors as results. For example, **a** could represent a set of coefficients of linear equations, and the stream of vectors could be different combinations of values for variables.

The pipeline can also be "shrunk" to use fewer workers. The only change needed is to have each worker store a strip of the rows of **a**. We can still have the columns of **b** and rows of **c** pass through the pipeline in the same way, or we could send fewer, but longer messages.

Finally the closed pipeline used in Figure 9.6 can be opened up and the workers can be placed into another pipeline. For example, instead of having a coordinator process that produces the vectors and consumes the results, the vectors could be produced by other processes—such as another matrix multiplication pipeline—and the results can be consumed by yet another process. To make the worker pipeline fully general, however, all vectors would have to be passed along the entire pipeline (even rows of **a**) so that they would come out the end and hence would be available to some other process.

9.3.2 Matrix Multiplication by Blocks

The performance of the previous algorithm is determined by the length of the pipeline and the time it takes to send and receive messages. The communication network on some high-performance machines is organized as a two-dimensional mesh or in an arrangement called a *hypercube*. These kinds of interconnection networks allow messages between different pairs of neighboring processes to be in transit at the same time. Moreover, they reduce the distance between processors relative to a linear arrangement, which reduces message transmission time.

An efficient way to multiply matrices on meshes and hypercubes is to divide the matrices into rectangular blocks, and to employ one worker process per block. The workers and data are then laid out on the processors as a two-dimensional grid. Each worker has four neighbors, above and below, and to the left and right of it. The workers on the top and bottom of the gird are considered to be neighbors, as are the workers on the left and right of the grid.

Again the problem is to compute the matrix product of two $n \times n$ matrices a and b, storing the result in matrix c. To simplify the code, we will use one worker per matrix element and index the rows and columns from 1 to n. (At the end of the section, we describe how to use blocks of values.) Let Worker[1:n,1:n] be the matrix of worker processes. Matrices a and b are distributed initially so that each Worker[i,j] has the corresponding elements of a and b.

To compute c[i,j], Worker[i,j] needs to multiply every element in row i of a by the corresponding element in column j of b and sum the results. But the order in which the worker performs these multiplications does not matter! The challenge is to find a way to circulate the values among the workers so that each gets every pair of values that it needs.

First consider Worker[1,1]. To compute c[1,1], it needs to get every element of row 1 of a and column 1 of b. Initially it has a[1,1] and b[1,1], so it can multiply them. If we then shift row 1 of a to the left one column and shift column 1 of b up one row, Worker[1,1] will have a[1,2] and b[2,1], which it can multiply and add to c[1,1]. If we repeat this n-2 more times, shifting the elements of a left and the elements of b up, Worker[1,1] will see all the values it needs.

Unfortunately, this multiply and shift sequence will work correctly only for workers handling elements on the diagonal. Other workers will see every value they need, but not in the right combinations. However, it is possible to rearrange a and b before we start the multiply and shift sequence. In particular, first shift row i of a circularly left i columns and row j of b circularly up j rows. (It is not at all obvious why this particular initial placement works; people came up with it by examining small matrices and then generalizing.) The following display illustrates the result of the initial rearrangement of the values of a and b for a 4×4 matrix:

$$a_{1,2}, b_{2,1} \qquad a_{1,3}, b_{3,2} \qquad a_{1,4}, b_{4,3} \qquad a_{1,1}, b_{1,4}$$

$$a_{2,3}, b_{3,1} \qquad a_{2,4}, b_{4,2} \qquad a_{2,1}, b_{1,3} \qquad a_{2,2}, b_{2,4}$$

$$a_{3,4}, b_{4,1} \qquad a_{3,1}, b_{1,2} \qquad a_{3,2}, b_{2,3} \qquad a_{3,3}, b_{3,4}$$

$$a_{4,1}, b_{1,1} \qquad a_{4,2}, b_{2,2} \qquad a_{4,3}, b_{3,3} \qquad a_{4,4}, b_{4,4}$$

After this initial rearrangement of values, each worker has two values, which it stores in local variables aij and bij. Each worker next initializes variable cij to aij*bij and then executes n-1 shift/compute phases. In each, values in aij are sent left one column; values in bij are sent up one row; and

```
chan left[1:n,1:n](double);   # for circulating a left
chan up[1:n,1:n](double);     # for circulating b up

process Worker[i = 1 to n, j = 1 to n] {
  double aij, bij, cij;
  int LEFT1, UP1, LEFTI, UPJ;
  initialize above values;

  # shift values in aij circularly left i columns
  send left[i,LEFTI](aij); receive left[i,j](aij);
  # shift values in bij circularly up j rows
  send up[UPJ,j](bij); receive up[i,j](bij);
  cij = aij * bij;

  for [k = 1 to n-1] {
    # shift aij left 1, bij up 1, then multiply and add
    send left[i,LEFT1](aij); receive left[i,j](aij);
    send up[UP1,j](bij); receive up[i,j](bij);
    cij = cij + aij*bij;
  }
}
```

Figure 9.7   Matrix multiplication by blocks.

new values are received, multiplied together, and added to `cij`. When the workers terminate, the matrix product is stored in the `cij` in each worker.

Figure 9.7 contains the code for this matrix multiplication algorithm. The workers share n^2 channels for circulating values left and another n^2 for circulating values up. These are used to form $2n$ intersecting circular pipelines. Workers in the same row are connected in a circular pipeline through which values flow to the left; workers in the same column are connected in a circular pipeline through which values flow up. The constants **LEFT1**, **UP1**, **LEFTI**, and **UPJ** in each worker are initialized to the appropriate values and used in **send** statements to index the arrays of channels.

The program in Figure 9.7 is obviously inefficient (unless it were to be implemented directly in hardware). There are way too many processes and messages, and way too little computation per process. However, the algorithm can readily be generalized to use square or rectangular blocks. In particular, each worker can be assigned blocks of **a** and **b**. The workers first shift their block of **a** left **i** blocks of columns and their block of **b** up **j** blocks of rows. Each worker then initializes its block of the result matrix **c** to the inner products of its new blocks of a and b. The workers then execute n-1 phases of shift a left one block, shift b up one block, compute the new inner products, and add them to c. We leave the details to the reader (see the exercises at the end of this chapter).

An additional way to improve the efficiency of the code in Figure 9.7 is to execute both sends before either receive when shifting values. In particular, change the code from send/receive/send/receive to send/send/receive/receive. This will decrease the likelihood that receive blocks. It also makes it possible to transmit messages in parallel if that is supported by the hardware interconnection network.

9.4 Probe/Echo Algorithms

Trees and graphs are used in many applications, such as Web searches, databases, games, and expert systems. They are especially important in distributed computing since the structure of many distributed computations is a graph in which processes are nodes and communication channels are edges.

Depth-first search (DFS) is one of the classic sequential programming paradigms for visiting all the nodes in a tree or graph. In a tree, the DFS strategy for each node is to visit the children of that node and then to return to the parent. This is called depth-first search since each search path reaches down to a leaf before the next path is traversed; for example, the path in the tree from the root to the leftmost leaf is traversed first. In a general graph—which may have cycles—the same approach is used, except we need to mark nodes as they are visited so that edges out of a node are traversed only once.

This section describes the probe/echo paradigm for distributed computations on graphs. A *probe* is a message sent by one node to its successor; an *echo* is a subsequent reply. Since processes execute concurrently, probes are sent in parallel to all successors. The probe/echo paradigm is thus the concurrent programming analog of DFS. We first illustrate the probe paradigm by showing how to broadcast information to all nodes in a network. We then add the echo paradigm by developing an algorithm for constructing the topology of a network.

9.4.1 Broadcast in a Network

Assume that we have a network of nodes (processors) connected by bidirectional communication channels. Each node can communicate directly only with its neighbors. Thus the network has the structure of an undirected graph.

Suppose one source node s wants to *broadcast* a message to all other nodes. (More precisely, suppose a process executing on s wants to broadcast a message to processes executing on all the other nodes.) For example, s might be the site of the network coordinator, who wants to broadcast new status information to all other sites.

If every other node is a neighbor of s, broadcast would be trivial to implement: node s would simply send a message directly to every other node. However, in large networks, each node is likely to have only a small number of neighbors. Node s can send the message to its neighbors, but they would have to forward it to their neighbors and so on. In short, we need a way to send a probe to all nodes.

Assume that node s has a local copy of the network topology. (We later show how to compute it.) The topology is represented by a symmetric Boolean matrix; entry `topology[i,j]` is true if nodes `i` and `j` are connected and it is false otherwise.

An efficient way for s to broadcast a message is first to construct a *spanning tree* of the network, with itself as the root of the tree. A spanning tree of a graph is a tree whose nodes are all those in the graph and whose edges are a subset of those in the graph. Figure 9.8 contains an example, with node s on the left. The solid lines are the edges in a spanning tree; the dashed lines are the other edges in the graph.

Given spanning tree t, node s can broadcast a message m by sending m together with t to all its children in t. Upon receiving the message, every node examines t to determine its children in the spanning tree, then forwards both m and t to all of them. The spanning tree is sent along with m since nodes other than s would not otherwise know what spanning tree to use. The full algorithm is given in Figure 9.9. Since t is a spanning tree, eventually the message will reach every node; moreover, each node will receive it exactly once, from its parent in t. We use a separate `Initiator` process on node s to start the broadcast. This makes the `Node` processes on each node identical.

The broadcast algorithm in Figure 9.9 assumes that the initiator node knows the entire topology, which it uses to compute a spanning tree that guides the

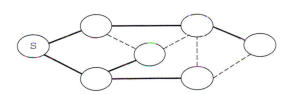

Figure 9.8   A spanning tree of a network of nodes.

```
type graph = bool [n,n];
chan probe[n](graph spanningTree; message m);

process Node[p = 0 to n-1] {
  graph t; message m;
  receive probe[p](t, m);
  for [q = 0 to n-1 st q is a child of p in t]
    send probe[q](t, m);
}

process Initiator {  # executed on source node S
  graph topology = network topology;
  graph t = spanning tree of topology;
  message m = message to broadcast;
  send probe[S](t, m);
}
```

Figure 9.9 Network broadcast using a spanning tree.

broadcast. Suppose instead that every node knows only who its neighbors are. We can still broadcast a message m to all nodes as follows. First, node s sends m to all its neighbors. Upon receiving m from one neighbor, a node forwards m to all its *other* neighbors. If the links defined by the neighbor sets happen to form a tree rooted at s, the effect of this approach is the same as before. In general, however, the network will contain cycles. Thus, some node might receive m from two or more neighbors. In fact, two neighbors might send the message to each other at about the same time.

It would appear that all we need to do in the general case is ignore multiple copies of m that a node might receive. However, this can lead to message pollution or to deadlock. After receiving m for the first time and sending it along, a node cannot know how many times to wait to receive m from a different neighbor. If the node does not wait at all, extra messages could be left buffered on some of the probe channels. If a node waits some fixed number of times, it might deadlock unless at least that many messages are sent; even so, there might be more.

We can solve the problem of unprocessed messages by using a fully symmetric algorithm. In particular, after a node receives m for the first time, it sends m to all its neighbors, including the one from whom it received m. Then the node receives redundant copies of m from all its other neighbors; these it ignores. The algorithm is given in Figure 9.10.

```
chan probe[n](message m);

process Node[p = 1 to n] {
  bool links[n] = neighbors of node p;
  int num = number of neighbors;
  message m;
  receive probe[p](m);
  # send m to all neighbors
  for [q = 0 to n-1 st links[q]]
    send probe[q](m);
  # receive num-1 redundant copies of m
  for [q = 1 to num-1]
    receive probe[p](m);
}

process Initiator {   # executed on source node S
  message m = message to broadcast;
  send probe[S](m);
}
```

Figure 9.10   Broadcast using neighbor sets.

The broadcast algorithm using a spanning tree causes `n-1` messages to be sent, one for each parent/child edge in the spanning tree. The algorithm using neighbor sets causes two messages to be sent over every link in the network, one in each direction. The exact number depends on the topology of the network, but in general the number will be much larger than `n-1`. For example, if the network topology is a tree rooted at the initiator process, `2(n-1)` messages will be sent; for a complete graph in which there is a link between every pair of nodes, `2n(n-1)` messages will be sent. However, the neighbor-set algorithm does not require the initiator node to know the topology or to compute a spanning tree. In essence, a spanning tree is constructed dynamically; it consists of the links along which the first copies of `m` are sent. Also, the messages are shorter in the neighbor-set algorithm since the spanning tree need not be sent in each message.

Both broadcast algorithms assume that the topology of the network does not change. In particular, neither works correctly if there is a processor or communication link failure while the algorithm is executing. If a node fails, it cannot receive the message being broadcast. If a link fails, it might or might not be possible to reach the nodes connected by the link. The Historical Notes at the end of this chapter describe papers that address the problem of implementing a fault-tolerant broadcast.

9.4.2 Computing the Topology of a Network

The efficient broadcast algorithm in Figure 9.9 required knowing the topology of the network. Here we show how to compute it. Initially, every node knows its local topology—namely, its links to its neighbors. The goal is to gather all the local topologies, because their union is the network topology.

The topology is gathered in two phases. First, each node sends a probe to its neighbors, as happened in Figure 9.10. Later, each node sends an echo containing local topology information back to the node from which it received the first probe. Eventually, the initiating node has gathered all the echoes, and hence has gathered the topology. It could then, for example, compute a spanning tree and broadcast the topology back to the other nodes.

For now assume that the topology of the network is acyclic. Since a network is an undirected graph, this means the structure is a tree. Let node s be the root of this tree, and let s be the initiator node. We can then gather the topology as follows. First s sends a probe to all its children. When these nodes receive a probe, they send it to all their children, and so on. Thus probes propagate through the tree. Eventually they will reach leaf nodes. Since these have no children, they begin the echo phase. In particular, each leaf sends an echo containing its neighbor set to its parent in the tree. After receiving echoes from all of its children, a node combines them and its own neighbor set and echoes this information to its parent. Eventually the root node will receive echoes from all its children. The union of these will contain the entire topology since the initial probe will reach every node and every echo contains the neighbor set of the echoing node together with those of its descendants.

The full probe/echo algorithm for gathering the network topology in a tree is shown in Figure 9.11. The probe phase is essentially the broadcast algorithm from Figure 9.10, except that probe messages indicate the identity of the sender. The echo phase returns local topology information back up the tree. In this case, the algorithms for the nodes are not fully symmetric since the instance of Node[p] executing on node s needs to know to send its echo to the Initiator.

To compute the topology of a network that contains cycles, we generalize the above algorithm as follows. After receiving a probe, a node sends the probe to its other neighbors; then the node waits for an echo from those neighbors. However, because of cycles and because nodes execute concurrently, two neighbors might send each other probes at about the same time. Probes other than the first one can be echoed immediately. In particular, if a node receives a subsequent probe while waiting for echoes, it immediately sends an echo containing a null topology (this is sufficient since the local links of the node will be contained in the echo it will send in response to the first probe). Eventually a node will

```
type graph = bool [n,n];
chan probe[n](int sender);
chan echo[n](graph topology)    # parts of the topology
chan finalecho(graph topology)  # final topology

process Node[p = 0 to n-1] {
  bool links[n] = neighbors of node p;
  graph newtop, localtop = ([n*n] false);
  int parent;    # node from whom probe is received
  localtop[p,0:n-1] = links;   # initially my links

  receive probe[p](parent);
  # send probe to other neighbors, who are p's children
  for [q = 0 to n-1 st (links[q] and q != parent)]
    send probe[q](p);

  # receive echoes and union them into localtop
  for [q = 0 to n-1 st (links[q] and q != parent)] {
    receive echo[p](newtop);
    localtop = localtop or newtop;  # logical or
  }
  if (p == S)
    send finalecho(localtop);    # node S is root
  else
    send echo[parent](localtop);
}

process Initiator {
  graph topology;
  send probe[S](S)   # start probe at local node
  receive finalecho(topology);
}
```

Figure 9.11   Probe/echo algorithm for gathering the topology of a tree.

receive an echo in response to every probe. At this point, it sends an echo to the node from which it got the first probe; the echo contains the union of the node's own set of links together with all the sets of links it received.

The general probe/echo algorithm for computing the network topology is shown in Figure 9.12. Because a node might receive subsequent probes while waiting for echoes, the two types of messages have to be merged into one channel. (If they came in on separate channels, a node would have to use **empty** and

```
type graph = bool [n,n];
type kind = (PROBE, ECHO);
chan probe_echo[n](kind k; int sender; graph topology);
chan finalecho(graph topology);

process Node[p = 0 to n-1] {
  bool links[n] = neighbors of node p;
  graph newtop, localtop = ([n*n] false);
  int first, sender; kind k;
  int need_echo = number of neighbors - 1;
  localtop[p,0:n-1] = links;    # initially my links

  receive probe_echo[p](k, first, newtop);  # get probe
  # send probe on to to all other neighbors
  for [q = 0 to n-1 st (links[q] and q != first)]
    send probe_echo[q](PROBE, p, ∅);

  while (need_echo > 0) {
    # receive echoes or redundant probes from neighbors
    receive probe_echo[p](k, sender, newtop);
    if (k == PROBE)
      send probe_echo[sender](ECHO, p, ∅);
    else  # k == ECHO {
      localtop = localtop or newtop;  # logical or
      need_echo = need_echo-1;
    }
  }
  if (p == S)
    send finalecho(localtop);
  else
    send probe_echo[first](ECHO, p, localtop);
}

process Initiator {
  graph topology;   # network topology
  send probe_echo[source](PROBE, source, ∅);
  receive finalecho(topology);
}
```

Figure 9.12   Probe/echo algorithm for computing the topology of a graph.

polling to decide which kind of message to receive. Alternatively, we could use rendezvous, with probes and echoes being separate operations.)

The correctness of the algorithm results from the following facts. Since the network is connected, every node eventually receives a probe. Deadlock is avoided since every probe is echoed—the first one just before a `Node` process terminates, the others while they are waiting to receive echoes in response to their own probes. (This avoids leaving messages buffered on the `probe_echo` channels.) The last echo sent by a node contains its local neighbor set. Hence, the union of the neighbor sets eventually reaches `Node[S]`, which sends the topology to `Initiator`. As with the algorithm in Figure 9.10, the links along which first probes are sent form a dynamically computed spanning tree. The network topology is echoed back up this spanning tree; the echo from each node contains the topology of the subtree rooted at that node.

9.5 Broadcast Algorithms

In the previous section, we showed how to broadcast information in a network that has the structure of a graph. In most local area networks, processors share a common communication channel such as an Ethernet or token ring. In this case, each processor is directly connected to every other one. In fact, such communication networks often support a special network primitive called `broadcast`, which transmits a message from one processor to all others. Whether supported by communication hardware or not, message broadcast provides a useful programming technique.

Let `T[n]` be an array of processes, and let `ch[n]` be an array of channels, one per process. Then a process `T[i]` broadcasts a message `m` by executing

```
broadcast ch(m);
```

Execution of `broadcast` places one copy of `m` on each channel `ch[i]`, including that of `T[i]`. The effect is thus the same as executing

```
co [i = 1 to n]
   send ch[i](m);
```

Processes receive both broadcast and point-to-point messages using the `receive` primitive.

Messages broadcast by the same process are queued on the channels in the order in which they are broadcast. However, `broadcast` is not atomic. In particular, messages broadcast by two processes `A` and `B` might be received by other processes in different orders. (See the Historical Notes for papers that discuss how to implement atomic broadcast.)

We can use `broadcast` to disseminate information—for example, to exchange processor state information in local area networks. We can also use it to solve many distributed synchronization problems. This section develops a broadcast algorithm that provides a distributed implementation of semaphores. The basis for distributed semaphores—and many other decentralized synchronization protocols—is a total ordering of communication events. We thus begin by showing how to implement logical clocks and how to use them to order events.

9.5.1 Logical Clocks and Event Ordering

The actions of processes in a distributed program can be divided into local actions, such as reading and writing variables, and communication actions, such as sending and receiving messages. Local actions have no direct effect on other processes. However, communication actions affect the execution of other processes since they transmit information and are synchronized. Communication actions are thus the significant *events* in a distributed program. We use the term *event* below to refer to execution of `send`, `broadcast`, and `receive` statements.

If two processes A and B are executing local actions, we have no way of knowing the relative order in which the actions are executed. However, if A sends (or broadcasts) a message to B, then the send action in A must happen before the corresponding receive action in B. If B subsequently sends a message to process C, then the send action in B must happen before the receive action in C. Moreover, since the receive action in B happens before the send action in B, there is a total ordering between the four communication events: the send by A happens before the receive by B, which happens before the send by B, which happens before the receive by C. *Happens before* is thus a transitive relation between causally related events.

Although there is a total ordering between causally related events, there is only a partial ordering between the entire collection of events in a distributed program. This is because unrelated sequences of events—for example, communications between different sets of processes—might occur before, after, or concurrently with each other.

If there were a single central clock, we could totally order communication events by giving each a unique timestamp. In particular, when a process sends a message, it could read the clock and append the clock value to the message. When a process receives a message, it could read the clock and record the time at which the receive event occurred. Assuming the granularity of the clock is such that it "ticks" between any send and the corresponding receive, an event that happens before another will thus have an earlier timestamp. Moreover, if processes have unique identities, then we could induce a total ordering—for example, by using the smallest process identity to break ties if unrelated events in two processes happen to have the same timestamp.

Unfortunately, it is unrealistic to assume the existence of a single, central clock. In a local area network, for example, each processor has its own clock. If these were perfectly synchronized, then we could use the local clocks for timestamps. However, physical clocks are never perfectly synchronized. Clock synchronization algorithms exist for keeping clocks fairly close to each other (see the Historical Notes), but perfect synchronization is impossible. Thus we need a way to simulate physical clocks.

A *logical clock* is a simple integer counter that is incremented when events occur. We assume that each process has a logical clock that is initialized to zero. We also assume that every message contains a special field called a *timestamp*. The logical clocks are incremented according to the following rules.

Logical Clock Update Rules. Let `A` be a process and let `lc` be a logical clock in the process. `A` updates the value of `lc` as follows:

(1) When `A` sends or broadcasts a message, it sets the timestamp of the message to the current value of `lc` and then increments `lc` by 1.

(2) When `A` receives a message with timestamp `ts`, it sets `lc` to the maximum of `lc` and `ts+1` and then increments `lc` by 1.

Since `A` increases `lc` after every event, every message sent by `A` will have a different, increasing timestamp. Since a receive event sets `lc` to be larger than the timestamp in the received message, the timestamp in any message subsequently sent by `A` will have a larger timestamp.

Using logical clocks, we can associate a clock value with each event as follows. For a send event, the clock value is the timestamp in the message—i.e., the local value of `lc` at the start of the send. For a receive event, the clock value is the value of `lc` after it is set to the maximum of `lc` and `ts+1` but before it is incremented by the receiving process. The above rules for updating logical clocks ensure that if event a happens before event b, then the clock value associated with a will be smaller than that associated with b. This induces a partial ordering on the set of causally related events in a program. If each process has a unique identity, then we can get a total ordering between all events by using the smaller process identity as a tiebreaker in case two events happen to have the same timestamp.

9.5.2 Distributed Semaphores

Semaphores are normally implemented using shared variables. However, we could implement them in a message-based program using a server process (active monitor), as shown in Section 7.3. We can also implement them in a decentralized way without using a central coordinator. Here, we show how.

A semaphore s is usually represented by a nonnegative integer. Executing P(s) waits until s is positive then decrements the value; executing V(s) increments the value. In other words, at all times the number of completed P operations is at most the number of completed V operations plus the initial value of s. Thus, to implement semaphores, we need a way to count P and V operations and a way to delay P operations. Moreover, the processes that "share" a semaphore need to cooperate so that they maintain the semaphore invariant s >= 0 even though the program state is distributed.

We can meet these requirements by having processes broadcast messages when they want to execute P and V operations and by having them examine the messages they receive to determine when to proceed. In particular, each process has a local message queue mq and a logical clock lc, which is updated according to the Logical Clock Update Rules. To simulate execution of a P or V operation, a process broadcasts a message to all the user processes, including itself. The message contains the sender's identity, a tag (POP or VOP) indicating which kind of operation, and a timestamp. The timestamp in every copy of the message is the current value of lc.

When a process receives a POP or VOP message, it stores the message in its message queue mq. This queue is kept sorted in increasing order of the timestamps in the messages; sender identities are used to break ties. Assume for the moment that every process receives all messages that have been broadcast in the same order and in increasing order of timestamps. Then every process would know exactly the order in which POP and VOP messages were sent and each could count the number of corresponding P and V operations and maintain the semaphore invariant.

Unfortunately, **broadcast** is not an atomic operation. Messages broadcast by two different processes might be received by others in different orders. Moreover, a message with a smaller timestamp might be received after a message with a larger timestamp. However, different messages broadcast by one process will be received by the other processes in the order they were broadcast by the first process, and these messages will also have increasing timestamps. These properties follow from the facts that (1) execution of **broadcast** is the same as concurrent execution of **send**—which we assume provides ordered, reliable delivery—and (2) a process increases its logical clock after every communication event.

The fact that consecutive messages sent by every process have increasing timestamps gives us a way to make synchronization decisions. Suppose a process's message queue `mq` contains a message `m` with timestamp `ts`. Then, once the process has received a message with a larger timestamp from every other process, it is assured that it will *never* see a message with a smaller timestamp. At this point, message `m` is said to be *fully acknowledged*. Moreover, once `m` is fully acknowledged, then all other messages in front of it in `mq` will also be fully acknowledged since they all have smaller timestamps. Thus the part of `mq` containing fully acknowledged messages is a *stable prefix*: no new messages will ever be inserted into it.

Whenever a process receives a `POP` or `VOP` message, we will have it broadcast an acknowledgement (`ACK`) message. These are broadcast so that every process sees them. The `ACK` messages have timestamps as usual, but they are not stored in the message queues. They are used simply to determine when a regular message in `mq` has become fully acknowledged. (If we did not use `ACK` messages, a process could not determine that a message was fully acknowledged until it received a later `POP` or `VOP` message from every other process; this would slow the algorithm down and would lead to deadlock if some user did not want to execute `P` or `V` operations.)

To complete the implementation of distributed semaphores, each process uses a local variable `s` to represent the value of the semaphore. When a process gets an `ACK` message, it updates the stable prefix of its message queue `mq`. For every `VOP` message, the process increments `s` and deletes the `VOP` message. It then examines the `POP` messages in timestamp order. If `s > 0`, the process decrements `s` and deletes the `POP` message. In short, each process maintains the following predicate, which is its loop invariant:

DSEM: `s >= 0` $\wedge$ `mq` is ordered by timestamps in messages

The `POP` messages are processed in the order in which they appear in the stable prefix so that every process makes the same decision about the order in which `P` operations complete. Even though the processes might be at different stages in handling `POP` and `VOP` messages, each one will handle fully acknowledged messages in the same order.

The algorithm for distributed semaphores appears in Figure 9.13. The user processes are regular application processes. There is one helper process for each user, and the helpers interact with each other in order to implement the `P` and `V` operations. A user process initiates a `P` or `V` operation by communicating with its helper; in the case of a `P` operation, the user waits until its helper says it can proceed. Each helper broadcasts `POP`, `VOP`, and `ACK` messages to the other helpers and manages its local message queue as described above. All messages to

```
type kind = enum(reqP, reqV, VOP, POP, ACK);
chan semop[n](int sender; kind k; int timestamp);
chan go[n](int timestamp);

process User[i = 0 to n-1] {
  int lc = 0, ts;
  ...
  # ask my helper to do V(s)
  send semop[i](i, reqV, lc); lc = lc+1;
  ...
  # ask my helper to do P(s), then wait for permission
  send semop[i](i, reqP, lc); lc = lc+1;
  receive go[i](ts); lc = max(lc, ts+1); lc = lc+1;
}

process Helper[i = 0 to n-1] {
  queue mq = new queue(int, kind, int);   # message queue
  int lc = 0, s = 0;           # logical clock and semaphore
  int sender, ts; kind k;   # values in received messages
  while (true) {    # loop invariant DSEM
    receive semop[i](sender, k, ts);
    lc = max(lc, ts+1); lc = lc+1;
    if (k == reqP)
      { broadcast semop(i, POP, lc); lc = lc+1; }
    else if (k == reqV)
      { broadcast semop(i, VOP, lc); lc = lc+1; }
    else if (k == POP or k == VOP) {
      insert (sender, k, ts) at appropriate place in mq;
      broadcast semop(i, ACK, lc); lc = lc+1;
    }
    else {   # k == ACK
      record that another ACK has been seen;
      for (all fully acknowledged VOP messages in mq)
        { remove the message from mq; s = s+1; }
      for (all fully acknowledged POP messages in mq st s > 0) {
        remove the message from mq; s = s-1;
        if (sender == i)     # my user's P request
          { send go[i](lc); lc = lc+1; }
      }
    }
  }
}
```

Figure 9.13   Distributed semaphores using a broadcast algorithm.

helpers are sent or broadcast to the `semop` array of channels. As shown, every process maintains a logical clock, which it uses to place timestamps on messages.

We can use distributed semaphores to synchronize processes in a distributed program in essentially the same way we used regular semaphores in shared variable programs (Chapter 4). For example, we can use them to solve mutual exclusion problems, such as locking files or database records. We can also use the same basic approach—broadcast messages and ordered queues—to solve additional problems; the Historical Notes and the Exercises describe several applications.

When broadcast algorithms are used to make synchronization decisions, every process must participate in every decision. In particular, a process must hear from every other in order to determine when a message is fully acknowledged. This means that broadcast algorithms do not scale well to interactions among large numbers of processes. It also means that such algorithms must be modified to cope with failures.

9.6 Token-Passing Algorithms

This section describes token passing, yet another process interaction paradigm. A *token* is a special kind of message that can be used either to convey permission or to gather global state information. We illustrate the use of a token to convey permission by a simple, distributed solution to the critical section problem. Then we illustrate gathering state information by developing two algorithms for detecting when a distributed computation has terminated. The next section presents an additional example (see also the Historical Notes and the Exercises).

9.6.1 Distributed Mutual Exclusion

Although the critical section problem arises primarily in shared-variable programs, it also arises in distributed programs whenever there is a shared resource that at most one process at a time can use—for example, a communication link to a satellite. Moreover, the critical section problem is often a component of a larger problem, such as ensuring consistency in a distributed file or database system.

One way to solve the critical section problem is to employ an active monitor that grants permission to access the critical section. For many problems, such as implementing locks on files, this is the simplest and most efficient approach. A second way to solve the problem is to use distributed semaphores, implemented

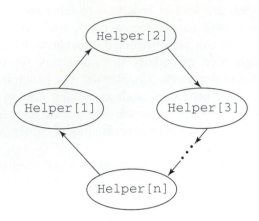

Figure 9.14   A token ring of helper processes.

as shown in the previous section. That approach yields a decentralized solution in which no one process has a special role, but it requires exchanging a large number of messages for each semaphore operation since each **broadcast** has to be acknowledged.

Here we solve the problem in a third way by using a token ring. The solution is decentralized and fair, as is a solution using distributed semaphores, but it requires the exchange of far fewer messages. Moreover, the basic approach can be generalized to solve other synchronization problems.

Let **User[1:n]** be a collection of application processes that contain critical and noncritical sections. As usual, we need to develop entry and exit protocols that these processes execute before and after their critical section. In addition, the protocols should ensure mutual exclusion, avoid deadlock and unnecessary delay, and ensure eventual entry (fairness).

Since the user processes have other work to do, we do not want them also to have to circulate the token. Thus we will employ a collection of additional processes, **Helper[1:n]**, one per user process. These helper processes form a ring, as shown in Figure 9.14. One token circulates between the helpers, being passed from **Helper[1]** to **Helper[2]** and so on to **Helper[n]**, which passes it back to **Helper[1]**. When **Helper[i]** receives the token, it checks to see whether its client **User[i]** wants to enter its critical section. If not, **Helper[i]** passes the token on. Otherwise, **Helper[i]** tells **User[i]** it may enter its critical section, then waits until **User[i]** exits; at this point **Helper[i]** passes the token on. Thus the helper processes cooperate to ensure that the following predicate is always true:

DMUTEX: **User[i]** is in its CS $\Rightarrow$ **Helper[i]** has the token $\wedge$
there is exactly one token

```
chan token[1:n](), enter[1:n](), go[1:n](), exit[1:n]();

process Helper[i = 1 to n] {
  while (true) {      # loop invariant DMUTEX
    receive token[i]();            # wait for token
    if (not empty(enter[i])) {  # does user want in?
      receive enter[i]();          # accept enter msg
      send go[i]();                # give permission
      receive exit[i]();           # wait for exit
    }
    send token[i%n + 1]();       # pass token on
  }
}

process User[i = 1 to n] {
  while (true) {
    send enter[i]();              # entry protocol
    receive go[i]();
    critical section;
    send exit[i]();               # exit protocol
    noncritical section;
  }
}
```

Figure 9.15   Mutual exclusion with a token ring.

The program is shown in Figure 9.15. The token ring is represented by an array of **token** channels, one per helper. For this problem, the token itself carries no data, so it is represented by a null message. The other channels are used for communication between the users and their helpers. When a helper holds the token, it uses **empty** to determine whether its user wishes to enter its critical section; if so, the helper sends the user a **go** message, and then waits to receive an **exit** message.

The solution in Figure 9.15 is fair—assuming as usual that processes eventually exit critical sections. This is because the token continuously circulates, and when **Helper[i]** has it, **User[i]** is permitted to enter if it wants to do so. As programmed, the token moves continuously between the helpers. This is in fact what happens in a physical token-ring network. In a software token ring, however, it is probably best to add some delay in each helper so that the token moves more slowly around the ring. (See Section 9.7 for another token-based exclusion algorithm in which tokens do not circulate continuously.)

This algorithm assumes that failures do not occur and that the token is not lost. Since control is distributed, however, it is possible to modify the algorithm to cope with failures. The Historical Notes describe algorithms for regenerating a lost token and for using two tokens that circulate in opposite directions.

9.6.2 Termination Detection in a Ring

It is simple to detect when a sequential program has terminated. It is also simple to detect when a concurrent program has terminated on a single processor: Every process is blocked or terminated, and no I/O operations are pending. However, it is not at all easy to detect when a distributed program has terminated. This is because the global state is not visible to any one processor. Moreover, even when all processors are idle, there may be messages in transit between processors.

There are several ways to detect when a distributed computation has terminated. This section develops a token-passing algorithm, assuming that all communication between processes goes around a ring. The next section generalizes the algorithm for a complete communication graph. Additional approaches are described in the Historical Notes and the Exercises.

Let `T[1:n]` be the processes (tasks) in some distributed computation, and let `ch[1:n]` be an array of communication channels. For now, assume that the processes form a ring and that all communication goes around the ring. In particular, each process `T[i]` receives messages only from its own channel `ch[i]` and sends messages only to the next channel `ch[i%n + 1]`. Thus `T[1]` sends messages only to `T[2]`, `T[2]` sends only to `T[3]`, and so on, with `T[n]` sending messages to `T[1]`. As usual we also assume that messages from every process are received by its neighbor in the ring in the order in which they were sent.

At any point in time, each process is active or idle. Initially, every process is active. It is idle if it has terminated or is delayed at a receive statement. (If a process is temporarily delayed while waiting for an I/O operation to terminate, we consider it still to be active since it has not terminated and will eventually be awakened.) After receiving a message, an idle process becomes active. Thus a distributed computation has terminated if the following two conditions hold:

> *DTERM*: every process is idle $\wedge$ no messages are in transit

A message is in transit if it has been sent but not yet delivered to the destination channel. The second condition is necessary because when the message is delivered, it could awaken a delayed process.

Our task is to superimpose a termination-detection algorithm on an arbitrary distributed computation, subject only to the above assumption that the processes in the computation communicate in a ring. Clearly termination is a property of the global state, which is the union of the states of individual processes plus the contents of message channels. Thus the processes have to communicate with each other in order to determine if the computation has terminated.

To detect termination, let there be one token, which is passed around in special messages that are not part of the computation proper. The process that holds the token passes it on when it becomes idle. (If a process has terminated its computation, it is idle but continues to participate in the termination-detection algorithm.)

Processes pass the token using the same ring of communication channels that they use in the computation itself. When a process receives the token, it knows that the sender was idle at the time it sent the token. Moreover, when a process receives the token, it has to be idle since it is delayed receiving from its channel and will not become active again until it receives a regular message that is part of the distributed computation. Thus, upon receiving the token, a process sends the token to its neighbor, then waits to receive another message from its channel.

The question now is how to detect that the entire computation has terminated. When the token has made a complete circuit of the communication ring, we know that every process was idle at some point. But how can the holder of the token determine if all other processes are still idle and that there are no messages in transit?

Suppose one process, `T[1]` say, initially holds the token. When `T[1]` becomes idle, it initiates the termination-detection algorithm by passing the token to `T[2]`. After the token gets back to `T[1]`, the computation has terminated if `T[1]` has been *continuously idle* since it first passed the token to `T[2]`. This is because the token goes around the same ring that regular messages do, and messages are delivered in the order in which they are sent. Thus, when the token gets back to `T[1]`, there cannot be any regular messages either queued or in transit. In essence, the token has "flushed" the channels clean, pushing all regular messages ahead of it.

We can make the algorithm and its correctness more precise as follows. First, associate a color with every process: `blue` (cold) for idle and `red` (hot) for active. Initially all processes are active, so they are colored `red`. When a process receives the token, it is idle, so it colors itself `blue`, passes the token on, and waits to receive another message. If the process later receives a regular message, it colors itself `red`. Thus a process that is `blue` became idle, passed the token on, and has remained idle since passing the token.

Second, associate a value with the token indicating how many channels are empty if `T[1]` is still idle. Let `token` be this value. When `T[1]` becomes idle, it

Global invariant *RING:*
```
T[1] is blue ⇒ ( T[1] ... T[token+1] are blue ∧
                 ch[2] ... ch[token%n + 1] are empty )
```

actions of `T[1]` when it first becomes idle:
```
color[1] = blue; token = 0; send ch[2](token);
```

actions of `T[2]`, ..., `T[n]` upon receiving a regular message:
```
color[i] = red;
```

actions of `T[2]`, ..., `T[n]` upon receiving the token:
```
color[i] = blue; token++; send ch[i%n + 1](token);
```

actions of `T[1]` upon receiving the token:
```
         if (color[1] == blue)
    announce termination and halt;
         color[1] = blue; token = 0; send ch[2](token);
```

Figure 9.16   Termination detection in a ring.

colors itself **blue**, sets **token** to 0, and then sends the token to `T[2]`. When `T[2]` receives the token, it is idle and `ch[2]` might be empty. Hence, `T[2]` colors itself **blue**, increments **token** to 1, and sends the token to `T[3]`. Each process `T[i]` in turn colors itself **blue** and increments **token** before passing it on.

These token-passing rules are listed in Figure 9.16. As indicated, the rules ensure that predicate *RING* is a global invariant. The invariance of *RING* follows from the fact that if `T[1]` is **blue**, it has not sent any regular messages since sending the token, and hence there are no regular messages in any channel up to where the token resides. Moreover, all these processes have remained idle since they saw the token. Thus if `T[1]` is still **blue** when the token gets back to it, all processes are **blue** and all channels are empty. Hence `T[1]` can announce that the computation has terminated.

9.6.3 Termination Detection in a Graph

In the previous section, we assumed all communication goes around a ring. In general, the communication structure of a distributed computation will form an arbitrary directed graph. The nodes of the graph are the processes in the computation; the edges represent communication paths. There is an edge from one process to another if the first process sends to a channel from which the second receives.

Here we assume that the communication graph is *complete*—namely, that there is one edge from every process to every other. As before, there are **n** processes `T[1:n]` and channels `ch[1:n]`, and each process `T[i]` receives from its private input channel `ch[i]`. However, now any process can send messages to `ch[i]`.

With these assumptions, we can extend the previous termination-detection algorithm as described below. The resulting algorithm is adequate to detect termination in any network in which there is a direct communication path from each processor to every other. It can readily be extended to arbitrary communication graphs and multiple channels (see the Exercises).

Detecting termination in a complete graph is more difficult than in a ring because messages can arrive over any edge. For example, consider the complete graph of three processes shown in Figure 9.17. Suppose the processes pass the token only from `T[1]` to `T[2]` to `T[3]` and back to `T[1]`. Suppose `T[1]` holds the token and becomes idle; hence it passes the token to `T[2]`. When `T[2]` becomes idle, it in turn passes the token to `T[3]`. But before `T[3]` receives the token, it could send a regular message to `T[2]`. Thus, when the token gets back to `T[1]`, it cannot conclude that the computation has terminated even if it has remained continuously idle.

The key to the ring algorithm in Figure 9.16 is that *all* communication goes around the ring, and hence the token flushes out regular messages. In particular, the token traverses every edge of the ring. We can extend that algorithm to a complete graph by ensuring that the token traverses every edge of the graph, which means that it visits every process multiple times. If *every* process has remained continuously idle since it first saw the token, then we can conclude that the computation has terminated.

As before, each process is colored **red** or **blue**, with all processes initially **red**. When a process receives a regular message, it colors itself **red**. When a process receives the token, it is blocked waiting to receive the next message on its

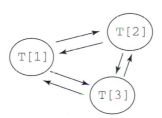

Figure 9.17   A complete communication graph.

input channel. Hence the process colors itself **blue**—if it is not already **blue**—and passes the token on. (Again, if a process terminates its regular computation, it continues to handle token messages.)

Any complete directed graph contains a cycle that includes every edge (some nodes may need to be included more than once). Let **c** be a cycle in the communication graph, and let **nc** be its length. Each process keeps track of the order in which its outgoing edges occur in **c**. Upon receiving the token along one edge in **c**, a process sends it out over the next edge in **c**. This ensures that the token traverses every edge in the communication graph.

Also as before, the token carries a value indicating the number of times in a row the token has been passed by idle processes and hence the number of channels that might be empty. As the above example illustrates, however, in a complete graph a process that was idle might become active again, even if **T[1]** remains idle. Thus, we need a different set of token-passing rules and a different global invariant in order to be able to conclude that the computation has terminated.

The token starts at any process and initially has value 0. When that process becomes idle for the first time, it colors itself **blue** and then passes the token along the first edge in cycle **c**. Upon receiving the token, a process takes the actions shown in Figure 9.18. If the process is **red** when it receives the token—

Global invariant *GRAPH:*
      token has value V $\Rightarrow$
      (the last V channels in cycle **c** were empty $\wedge$
       the last V processes to receive the token were **blue**)

actions of **T[i]** upon receiving a regular message:
      color[i] = red;

actions of **T[i]** upon receiving the token:
      if (token == nc)
    announce termination and halt;
      if (color[i] == red)
        { color[i] = blue; token = 0; }
      else
        token++;
    set **j** to index of channel for next edge in cycle **c**;
      send ch[j](token);

Figure 9.18 Termination detection in a complete graph.

and hence was active since last seeing it—the process colors itself `blue` and sets the value of `token` to `0` before passing it along the next edge in `c`. This effectively reinitiates the termination-detection algorithm. However, if the process is `blue` when it receives the token—and hence has been continuously idle since last seeing the token—the process increments the value of `token` before passing it on.

The token-passing rules ensure that predicate *GRAPH* is a global invariant. Once the value of `token` gets to `nc`, the length of cycle `c`, then the computation is known to have terminated. In particular, at that point the last `nc` channels the token has traversed were empty. Since a process only passes the token when it is idle—and since it only increases `token` if it has remained idle since last seeing the token—all channels are empty and all processes are idle. In fact, the computation had actually terminated by the time the token started its last circuit around the graph. However, no process could possibly know this until the token has made another complete cycle around the graph to verify that all processes are still idle and that all channels are empty. Thus the token has to circulate a minimum of two times around the cycle after any activity in the computation proper: first to turn processes `blue`, and then again to verify that they have remained `blue`.

9.7 Replicated Servers

The final process-interaction paradigm we describe is replicated servers. A server, as usual, is a process that manages some resource. A server might be replicated when there are multiple distinct instances of a resource; each server would then manage one of the instances. Replication can also be used to give clients the illusion that there is a single resource when in fact there are many. We saw an example of this earlier in Section 8.4, where we showed how to implement replicated files.

This section illustrates both uses of replicated servers by developing two additional solutions to the dining philosophers problem. As usual there are five philosophers and five forks, and each philosopher requires two forks in order to eat. This problem can be solved in three ways in a distributed program. Let *PH* be a philosopher process and let *W* be a waiter process. One approach is to have a single waiter process that manages all five forks—the *centralized* structure shown in Figure 9.19 (a). The second approach is to distribute the forks, with one waiter managing each fork—the *distributed* structure shown in Figure 9.19 (b). The third approach is to have one waiter per philosopher—the *decentralized* structure shown in Figure 9.19 (c). We presented a centralized solution earlier in Figure 8.6. Here, we develop distributed and decentralized solutions.

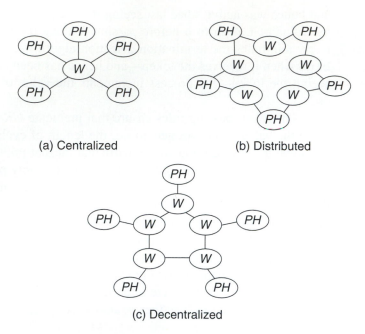

(a) Centralized   (b) Distributed

(c) Decentralized

Figure 9.19   Solution structures for the dining philosophers.

9.7.1 *Distributed Dining Philosophers*

The centralized dining philosopher's solution shown in Figure 8.6 is deadlock-free but it is not fair. Moreover, the single waiter process could be a bottleneck because all philosophers need to interact with it. A distributed solution can be deadlock-free, fair, and not have a bottleneck, but at the expense of a more complicated client interface and more messages.

Figure 9.20 contains a distributed solution programmed using the multiple primitives notation of Section 8.3. (This leads to the shortest program; however, the program can readily be changed to use just message passing or just rendezvous.) There are five waiter processes; each manages one fork. In particular, each waiter repeatedly waits for a philosopher to get the fork then to release it. Each philosopher interacts with two waiters to obtain the forks it needs. However, to avoid deadlock, the philosophers cannot all execute the identical program. Instead, the first four philosophers get their left fork then the right, whereas the last philosopher gets the right fork then the left. The solution is thus very similar to the one using semaphores in Figure 4.7.

```
module Waiter[5]
  op getforks(), relforks();
body
  process the_waiter {
    while (true) {
      receive getforks();
      receive relforks();
    }
  }
end Waiter

process Philosopher[i = 0 to 4] {
  int first = i, second = i+1;
  if (i == 4) {
    first = 0; second = 4; }
  while (true) {
    call Waiter[first].getforks();
    call Waiter[second].getforks();
  eat;
    send Waiter[first].relforks();
    send Waiter[second].relforks();
  think;
  }
}
```

Figure 9.20   Distributed dining philosophers.

The distributed solution in Figure 9.20 is fair because the forks are requested one at a time and invocations of **getfork** are serviced in the order they are called. Thus each call of **getforks** is serviced eventually, assuming philosophers eventually release forks they have acquired.

9.7.2 Decentralized Dining Philosophers

We now develop a decentralized solution that has one waiter per philosopher. The process interaction pattern is similar to that in the replicated file servers in Figures 8.14 and 8.15. The algorithm employed by the waiter processes is another example of token passing, with the tokens being the five forks. Our solution can be adapted to coordinate access to replicated files or to yield an efficient solution to the distributed mutual exclusion problem (see the Exercises).

```
module Waiter[t = 0 to 4]
  op getforks(int), relforks(int);  # for philosophers
  op needL(), needR(),               # for waiters
     passL(), passR();
  op forks(bool,bool,bool,bool);  # for initialization
body
  op hungry(), eat();        # local operations
  bool haveL, dirtyL, haveR, dirtyR;  # status of forks
  int left = (t-1) % 5 ;        # left neighbor
  int right = (t+1) % 5;         # right neighbor

  proc getforks() {
    send hungry();  # tell waiter philosopher is hungry
    receive eat();  # wait for permission to eat
  }
  process the_waiter {
    receive forks(haveL, dirtyL, haveR, dirtyR);
    while (true) {
      in hungry() ->
          # ask for forks I don't have
          if (!haveR) send Waiter[right].needL();
          if (!haveL) send Waiter[left].needR();
          # wait until I have both forks
          while (!haveL or !haveR)
            in passR() ->
                haveR = true; dirtyR = false;
            [] passL() ->
                haveL = true; dirtyL = false;
            [] needR() st dirtyR ->
                haveR = false; dirtyR = false;
                send Waiter[right].passL();
                send Waiter[right].needL()
            [] needL() st dirtyL ->
                haveL = false; dirtyL = false;
                send Waiter[left].passR();
                send Waiter[left].needR();
            ni
          # let philosopher eat, then wait for release
          send eat(); dirtyL = true; dirtyR = true;
          receive relforks();
      [] needR() ->
          # neighbor needs my right fork (its left)
          haveR = false; dirtyR = false;
          send Waiter[right].passL();
```

```
          [] needL() ->
              # neighbor needs my left fork (its right)
              haveL = false; dirtyL = false;
              send Waiter[left].passR();
          ni
        }
    }
end Waiter

process Philosopher[i = 0 to 4] {
  while (true) {
    call Waiter[i].getforks();
    eat;
    call Waiter[i].relforks();
    think;
  }
}

process Main {  # initialize the forks held by waiters
  send Waiter[0].forks(true, true, true, true);
  send Waiter[1].forks(false, false, true, true);
  send Waiter[2].forks(false, false, true, true);
  send Waiter[3].forks(false, false, true, true);
  send Waiter[4].forks(false, false, false, false);
}
```

Figure 9.21   Decentralized dining philosophers.

Each fork is a token that is held by one of two waiters or is in transit between them. When a philosopher wants to eat, he asks his waiter to acquire two forks. If the waiter does not currently have both forks, the waiter interacts with neighboring waiters to get them. The waiter then retains control of the forks while the philosopher eats.

The key to a correct solution is to manage the forks in such a way that deadlock is avoided. Ideally, the solution should also be fair. For this problem, deadlock could result if a waiter needs two forks and cannot get them. A waiter certainly has to hold on to both forks while his philosopher is eating. But when the philosopher is not eating, a waiter should be willing to give up his forks. However, we need to avoid passing a fork back and forth from one waiter to another without its being used.

The basic idea for avoiding deadlock is to have a waiter give up a fork that has been used, but to hold onto one that it just acquired. Specifically, when a philosopher starts eating, his waiter marks both forks as "dirty." When another waiter wants a fork, if it is dirty and not currently being used, the first waiter cleans the fork and gives it up. The second waiter holds onto the clean fork until it has been used. However, a dirty fork can be reused until it is needed by the other waiter.

This decentralized algorithm is given in Figure 9.21. (It is colloquially called the "hygienic philosophers" algorithm because of the way forks are cleaned.) The solution is programmed using the multiple primitives notation described in Section 8.3, because it is convenient to be able to use all of remote procedure call, rendezvous, and message passing.

When a philosopher wants to eat, he calls the **getforks** operation exported by his table module. The **getforks** operation is implemented by a procedure to hide the fact that getting forks requires sending a **hungry** message and receiving an **eat** message. When a waiter process receives a **hungry** message, it checks the status of the two forks. If it has both, it lets the philosopher eat, then waits for the philosopher to release the forks.

If the waiter process does not have both forks, it has to acquire those it needs. The **needL**, **needR**, **passL**, and **passR** operations are used for this. In particular, when a philosopher is hungry and his waiter needs a fork, that waiter sends a need message to the waiter who has the fork. The other waiter accepts the need message when the fork is dirty and not being used, and then passes the fork to the first waiter. The **needL** and **needR** operations are invoked by asynchronous **send** rather than synchronous **call**, because deadlock can result if two waiters call each other's operations at the same time.

Four variables in each waiter are used to record the status of the forks: **haveL**, **haveR**, **dirtyL**, and **dirtyR**. These variables are initialized by having the **Main** process call the **forks** operation in the **Waiter** modules. Initially, waiter zero holds two dirty forks, waiters one to three each hold one dirty fork, and waiter four holds no fork.

In order to avoid deadlock, it is imperative that the forks be distributed asymmetrically *and* that they all be dirty. For example, if every waiter initially has one fork and all philosophers want to eat, each waiter could give up the fork he has and then hold on to the one he gets. If any fork is initially clean, then the waiter that holds it will not give it up until *after* his philosopher has eaten; if the philosopher terminates or never wants to eat, another philosopher could wait forever to get the fork.

The program avoids starvation by having waiters give up forks that are dirty. In particular, if one waiter wants a fork that another holds, he will eventually get it. If the fork is dirty and not in use, the second waiter immediately passes it to the first waiter. If the fork is dirty and in use, eventually the other philosopher will quit eating, and hence the other waiter will pass the fork to the first waiter. If the fork is clean, it is because the other philosopher is hungry, the other waiter just got the fork, or the other waiter is waiting to get a second fork. By similar reasoning, the other waiter will eventually get the second fork, because there is no state in which every waiter holds one clean fork and wants a second. (This is another reason why asymmetric initialization is imperative.)

Historical Notes

All the paradigms described in this chapter were developed between the mid-1970s and the mid-1980s. During that decade, there was a plethora of activity refining, analyzing, and applying the various paradigms. Now the focus is more on using them. Indeed, many problems can be solved in more than one way, hence using more than one paradigm. We describe some of these below; additional examples are given in the Exercises and in Chapter 11.

The manager/worker paradigm was introduced by Gentleman [1981], who called it the administrator/worker paradigm. Carriero and Gelernter have called the same idea a distributed bag of tasks. They present solutions to several problems in Carriero et al. [1986] and Carriero and Gelernter [1989]; the solutions are programmed using their Linda primitives (Section 7.7). Finkel and Manber [1987] use a distributed bag of tasks to implement backtracking algorithms. The manager/worker paradigm is now commonly used in parallel computations, where the technique is sometimes called a work pool, processor farm, or work farm. Whatever the term, the concept is the same: several workers dynamically dividing up a collection of tasks.

Heartbeat algorithms are routinely used in distributed parallel computations, especially for grid computations (see Section 11.1). The author of this book created the term *heartbeat algorithm* in the late 1980s because that phrase seems to characterize the actions of each process: pump (send), contract (receive), prepare for the next cycle (compute), then repeat. Per Brinch Hansen [1995] calls it the cellular automata paradigm, although that term seems better to describe a kind of application than a programming style. In any event, people do not usually use any name to refer to the now canonical send/receive/compute programming style—or they just say that processes exchange information.

In Section 9.2 we presented heartbeat algorithms for the region-label problem from image processing and for the Game of Life, which was invented by mathematician John Conway in the 1960s. Image processing, cellular automata, and the related topic of genetic algorithms are covered in some detail by

Wilkinson and Allen [1999]. Brinch Hansen [1995] also describes cellular automata. Fox et al. [1988] cover numerous applications and algorithms, many of which are programmed using the heartbeat style.

The concept of a software pipeline goes back at least as far as the introduction of Unix in the early 1970s. The concept of a hardware pipeline goes back even farther, to the early vector processors in the 1960s. However, the use of pipelines as a general parallel computing paradigm is more recent. Pipeline and ring (closed pipeline) algorithms have now been developed to solve many problems. Examples can be found in most books on parallel computing. A few good sources are Brinch Hansen [1995], Fox et al. [1988], Quinn [1994], and Wilkinson and Allen [1999]. Hardware pipelines are covered in detail in Hwang [1993]. The behavior of both software and hardware pipelines is similar, so their performance can be analyzed in similar ways.

The concept of a probe/echo paradigm was invented simultaneously by several people. The most comprehensive early work is offered by Chang [1982], who presents algorithms for several graph problems, including sorting, computing biconnected components, and knot (deadlock) detection. (Chang called them echo algorithms; we use the term probe/echo to indicate that there are two distinct phases.) Dijkstra and Scholten [1980] and Francez [1980] use the same paradigm—without giving it a name—to detect termination of a distributed program.

We used the network topology problem to illustrate the use of a probe/echo algorithm. The problem was first described by Lamport [1982] in a paper that showed how to derive a distributed algorithm in a systematic way by refining an algorithm that uses shared variables. That paper also showed how to deal with a dynamic network in which processors and links might fail and then recover. McCurley and Schneider [1986] systematically derive a heartbeat algorithm for solving the same problem.

Several people have investigated the problem of providing reliable or fault-tolerant broadcast, which is concerned with ensuring that every functioning and reachable processor receives the message being broadcast and that all agree upon the same value. For example, Schneider et al. [1984] present an algorithm for fault-tolerant broadcast in a tree, assuming that a failed processor stops executing and that failures are detectable. Lamport et al. [1982] show how to cope with failures that can result in arbitrary behavior—so-called Byzantine failures.

Logical clocks were developed by Lamport [1978] in a now classic paper on how to order events in distributed systems. (Marzullo and Owicki [1983] describe the problem of synchronizing physical clocks.) Schneider [1982] developed an implementation of distributed semaphores similar to the one in Figure 9.13; his paper also shows how to modify this kind of algorithm to deal with failures. The same basic approach—broadcasted messages and ordered queues—can also be used to solve additional problems. For example, Lamport [1978] presents an algorithm for distributed mutual exclusion, and Schneider [1982] presents a distributed implementation of the guarded input/output commands of CSP described in Section 7.6. The algorithms in these papers do not assume that messages are totally ordered. However, for many problems it helps if broadcast is atomic—namely, that every process sees messages that have been broadcast in exactly the same order. Two key papers on the use and implementation of reliable and atomic communication primitives are Birman and Joseph [1987] and Birman et al. [1991].

Section 9.6 showed how to use token-passing to implement distributed mutual exclusion and termination detection, and Section 8.4 showed how to use tokens to synchronize access to replicated files. Chandy and Misra [1984] use token passing to achieve fair conflict resolution, and Chandy and Lamport [1985] use tokens to determine global states in distributed computations.

The token-passing solution to the distributed mutual exclusion problem given in Figure 9.15 was developed by LeLann [1977]. That paper also shows how to bypass some node on the ring if it should fail and how to regenerate the token if it should become lost. LeLann's method requires knowing maximum communication delays and process identities. Misra [1983] later developed an algorithm that overcomes these limitations by using two tokens that circulate around the ring in opposite directions.

The distributed mutual exclusion problem can also be solved using a broadcast algorithm. One way is to use distributed semaphores. However, this requires exchanging a large number of messages since every message has to be acknowledged by every process. More efficient, broadcast-based algorithms have been developed by Lamport, Ricart and Agrawala, Maekawa, and Suzuki and Kasami. These are described and compared in Raynal [1986] and Maekawa et al. [1987].

The token-passing algorithm for detecting termination in a ring is based on an algorithm in Dijkstra et al. [1983]. The algorithm for a complete communication graph first appeared in Misra [1983], which also describes how to modify the algorithm to detect termination in an arbitrary graph. The termination-detection problem can also be solved using other paradigms. For example, Dijkstra and Scholten [1980] and Francez [1980] present probe/echo algorithms for different variations on the problem. Rana [1983] and Morgan [1985] show how to use logical clocks and timestamps. Chandrasekaran and Venkatesan [1990] present a message-optimal algorithm that combines the probe/echo and token-passing paradigms. See Raynal [1988] for a description and comparison of these and other algorithms.

Deadlock detection in a distributed system is similar to termination detection. Several people have also developed probe/echo and token-passing algorithms for this problem. For example, Chandy et al. [1983] give a probe/echo algorithm. Knapp [1987] surveys deadlock detection algorithms in distributed database systems.

Section 8.4 described how to implement replicated files using tokens or weighted voting. Distributed semaphores can also be used, as described by Schneider [1980]; his approach can be made fault tolerant using the techniques described in Schneider [1982]. To make token or lock algorithms fault tolerant, one can regenerate the token or lock as described in LeLann [1977] and Misra [1983]. When there are multiple tokens and a server crashes, the other servers need to hold an election to determine which one will get the lost tokens. Raynal [1988] describes several election algorithms.

Several times we have mentioned the issue of coping with failures, and several of the above papers show how to make specific algorithms fault tolerant. However, a full treatment of fault-tolerant programming is beyond the scope of this book. Schneider and Lamport [1985] give an excellent overview of fault-tolerant programming and describe several general solution paradigms. Jalote [1994] is devoted to fault tolerance in distributed systems.

Bacon [1998] and Bernstein and Lewis [1993] each contain several chapters on distributed systems and aspects of fault tolerance. Both these books also describe transactions and recovery in distributed database systems, one of the main applications that invariably requires fault tolerance. An excellent source for the state of the art (as of 1993) on all aspects of distributed systems is a collection of papers edited by Sape Mullender [1993] and written by an all-star cast of experts.

References

Bacon, J. 1998. *Concurrent Systems: Operating Systems, Database and Distributed Systems: An Integrated Approach*, 2nd ed. Reading, MA: Addison-Wesley.

Bernstein, A. J., and P. M. Lewis. 1993. *Concurrency in Programming and Database Systems*. Boston: Jones and Bartlett.

Birman, K. P., and T. A. Joseph. 1987. Reliable communication in the presence of failures. *ACM Trans. on Computer Systems* 5, 1 (February): 47–76.

Birman, K. P., A. Schiper, and A. Stephenson. 1991. Lightweight, causal, and atomic group multicast. *ACM Trans. on Computing Systems* 9, 3 (August): 272–314.

Brinch Hansen, P. 1995. *Studies in Computational Science.* Englewood Cliffs, NJ: Prentice-Hall.

Carriero, N., and D. Gelernter. 1989. How to write parallel programs: A guide to the perplexed. *ACM Computing Surveys* 21, 3 (September): 323–58.

Carriero, N., D. Gelernter, and J. Leichter. 1986. Distributed data structures in Linda. *Thirteenth ACM Symp. on Principles of Prog. Langs.*, January, pp. 236–42.

Chandrasekaran, S., and S. Venkatesan. 1990. A message-optimal algorithm for distributed termination detection. *Journal of Parallel and Distributed Computing* 8, 245–92.

Chandy, K. M., L. M. Haas, and J. Misra. 1983. Distributed deadlock detection. *ACM Trans. on Computer Systems* 1, 2 (May): 144–56.

Chandy, K. M., and Lamport, L. 1985. Distributed snapshots: Determining global states of distributed systems. *ACM Trans. on Computer Systems* 3, 1 (February): 63–75.

Chandy, K. M., and Misra, J. 1984. The drinking philosophers problem. *ACM Trans. on Prog. Languages and Systems* 6, 4 (October): 632–46.

Chang, E. J.-H. 1982. Echo algorithms: depth parallel operations on general graphs. *IEEE Trans. on Software Engr.* 8, 4 (July): 391–401.

Dijkstra, E. W., W. H. J. Feijen, and A. J. M. van Gasteren. 1983. Derivation of a termination detection algorithm for distributed computation. *Information Processing Letters* 16, 5 (June): 217–19.

Dijkstra, E. W., and C. S. Scholten. 1980. Termination detection in diffusing computations. *Information Processing Letters* 11, 1 (August): 1–4.

Finkel, R., and U. Manber. 1987. DIB—a distributed implementation of backtracking. *ACM Trans. on Prog. Languages and Systems* 9, 2 (April): 235–56.

Fox, G. C., M. A. Johnson, G. A. Lyzenga, S. W. Otto, J. K. Salmon, and D. W. Walker. 1988. *Solving Problems on Concurrent Processors, Volume I: General Techniques and Regular Problems.* Englewood Cliffs, NJ: Prentice-Hall.

Francez, N. 1980. Distributed termination. *ACM Trans. on Prog. Languages and Systems* 2, 1 (January): 42–55.

Gentleman, W. M. 1981. Message passing between sequential processes: the reply primitive and the administrator concept. *Software—Practice and Experience* 11, 435–66.

Hwang, K. 1993. *Advanced Computer Architecture: Parallelism, Scalability, Programmability.* New York: McGraw-Hill.

Jalote, P. 1994. *Fault Tolerance in Distributed Systems.* Englewood Cliffs, NJ: Prentice-Hall.

Knapp, E. 1987. Deadlock detection in distributed databases. *ACM Computing Surveys* 19, 4 (December): 303–28.

Lamport, L. 1978. Time, clocks, and the ordering of events in distributed systems. *Comm. ACM* 21, 7 (July): 558–65.

Lamport, L. 1982. An assertional correctness proof of a distributed algorithm. *Science of Computer Prog.* 2, 3 (December): 175–206.

Lamport, L., R. Shostak, and M. Pease. 1982. The Byzantine generals problem. *ACM Trans. on Prog. Languages and Systems* 3, 3 (July): 382–401.

LeLann, G. 1977. Distributed systems: Towards a formal approach. *Proc. Information Processing 77*, North-Holland, Amsterdam, pp. 155–60.

Maekawa, M., A. E. Oldehoeft, and R. R. Oldehoeft. 1987. *Operating Systems: Advanced Concepts.* Menlo Park, CA: Benjamin/Cummings.

Marzullo, K., and S. S. Owicki. 1983. Maintaining the time in a distributed system. *Proc. Second ACM Symp. on Principles of Distr. Computing*, August, pp. 295–305.

McCurley, E. R., and F. B. Schneider. 1986. Derivation of a distributed algorithm for finding paths in directed networks. *Science of Computer Prog.* 6, 1 (January): 1–9.

Misra, J. 1983. Detecting termination of distributed computations using markers. *Proc. Second ACM Symp. on Principles of Distr. Computing*, August, pp. 290–94.

Morgan, C. 1985. Global and logical time in distributed algorithms. *Information Processing Letters* 20, 4 (May): 189–94.

Mullender, S., ed. 1993. *Distributed Systems*, 2nd ed. Reading, MA: ACM Press and Addison-Wesley.

Quinn, M. J. 1994. *Parallel Computing: Theory and Practice.* New York: McGraw-Hill.

Rana, S. P. 1983. A distributed solution of the distributed termination problem. *Information Processing Letters* 17, 1 (July): 43–46.

Raynal, M. 1986. *Algorithms for Mutual Exclusion.* Cambridge, MA: MIT Press.

Raynal, M. 1988. *Distributed Algorithms and Protocols.* New York: Wiley.

Schneider, F. B. 1980. Ensuring consistency in a distributed database system by use of distributed semaphores. *Proc. of Int. Symp. on Distributed Databases,* March, pp. 183–89.

Schneider, F. B. 1982. Synchronization in distributed programs. *ACM Trans. on Prog. Languages and Systems* 4, 2 (April): 125–48.

Schneider, F. B., D. Gries, and R. D. Schlichting. 1984. Fault-tolerant broadcasts. *Science of Computer Prog.* 4: 1–15.

Schneider, F. B., and L. Lamport. 1985. Paradigms for distributed programs. In *Distributed Systems: Methods and Tools for Specification, An Advanced Course,* Lecture Notes in Computer Science, vol. 190. Berlin: Springer-Verlag, pp. 431–80.

Wilkinson, B., and M. Allen. 1999. *Parallel Programming: Techniques and Applications Using Networked Workstations and Parallel Computers.* Englewood Cliffs, NJ: Prentice-Hall.

Exercises

9.1   Section 9.1 described one way to represent sparse matrices and showed how to multiply two sparse matrices using a distributed bag of tasks.

(a) Suppose matrix **a** is represented by rows as described. Develop code to compute the transpose of **a**.

(b) Implement and experiment with the program in Figure 9.1. First use input matrices that you have generated by hand and for which you know the result. Then write a small program to generate large matrices, perhaps using a random number generator. Measure the performance of the program for the large matrices. Write a brief report explaining tests you ran and the results you observe.

9.2   Section 3.6 presented a bag-of-tasks program for multiplying dense matrices.

(a) Construct a distributed version of that program. In particular, change it to use the manager/worker paradigm.

(b) Implement your answer to (a), and implement the program in Figure 9.1. Compare the performance of the two programs. In particular, generate some large, sparse matrices and multiply them together using both programs. (The programs will, of course, represent the matrices differently.) Write a brief report explaining your tests and comparing the time and space requirements of the two programs.

9.3 The adaptive quadrature program in Figure 9.2 uses a fixed number of tasks. (It divides the interval from **a** to **b** into a fixed number of subintervals.) The algorithm in Figure 3.21 is fully adaptive; it starts with just one task and generates as many as are required.

(a) Modify the program in Figure 9.2 to use the fully adaptive approach. This means that workers will never calculate an area using a recursive procedure. You will have to figure out how to detect termination!

(b) Modify your answer to (a) to use a *threshhold* **T** that defines the maximum size of the bag of tasks. After this many tasks have been generated, when a worker gets a task from the bag, the manager should tell the worker to solve a task recursively and hence not to generate any more tasks.

(c) Implement the program in Figure 9.2 and your answers to (a) and (b), then compare the performance of the three programs. Conduct a set of experiments, then write a brief report describing the experiments you ran and the results you observed.

9.4 Quicksort is a recursive sorting method that partitions an array into smaller pieces and then combines them. Develop a program to implement quicksort using the manager/worker paradigm. Array **a[1:n]** of integers is local to the manager process. Use **w** worker processes to do the sorting. When your program terminates, the result should be stored in administrator array **a**. Do not use any shared variables. Explain your solution and justify your design choices.

9.5 The eight-queens problem is concerned with placing eight queens on a chess board in such a way that none can attack another. Develop a program to generate all 92 solutions to the eight-queens problem using the manager/worker paradigm. Have an administrator process put eight initial queen placements in a shared bag. Use **w** worker processes to extend partial solutions; when a worker finds a complete solution, it should send it to the administrator. The program should compute all solutions and terminate. Do not use any shared variables.

9.6 Consider the problem of determining the number of words in a dictionary that contain unique letters—namely, the number of words in which no letter appears more than once. Treat upper and lower case versions of a letter as the same letter. (Most Unix systems contain one or more online dictionaries, for example in **/usr/dict/words**.)

Write a distributed parallel program to solve this problem. Use the manager/workers paradigm and w worker processes. At the end of the program, the manager should print the number of words that contain unique letters, and also print all those that are the longest. If your workers have access to shared memory, you may have them share a copy of the dictionary file, but if they execute on separate machines, they should each have their own copy.

9.7 *The Traveling Salesman Problem (TSP).* This is a classic combinatorial problem—and one that is also practical, because it is the basis for things like scheduling planes and personnel at an airline company.

Given are n cities and a symmetric matrix dist[1:n,1:n]. The value in dist[i,j] is the distance from city i to city j—e.g., the airline miles. A salesman starts in city 1 and wishes to visit every city exactly once, ending back in city 1. The problem is to determine a path that minimizes the distance the salesman must travel. The result is to be stored in a vector bestpath[1:n]. The value of bestpath is to be a permutation of integers 1 to n such that the sum of the distances between adjacent pairs of cities, plus the distance back to city 1, is minimized.

(a) Develop a distributed parallel program to solve this problem using the manager/workers paradigm. Make a reasonable choice for what constitutes a task; there should not be too many, nor too few. You should also discard tasks that cannot possibly lead to a better result than you currently have computed.

(b) An exact TSP solution has to consider every possible path, but there are n! of them. Consequently, people have developed a number of heuristics. One is called the *nearest neighbor* algorithm. Starting with city 1, first visit the city, say c, nearest to city 1. Now extend the partial tour by visiting the city nearest to c. Continue in this fashion until all cities have been visited, then return to city 1. Write a program to implement this algorithm.

(c) Another TSP heuristic is called the *nearest insertion* algorithm. First find the pair of cities that are closest to each other. Next find the unvisited city nearest to either of these two cities and insert it between them. Continue to find the unvisited city with minimum distance to some city in the partial tour, and insert that city between a pair of cities already in the tour so that the insertion causes the minimum increase in the total length of the partial tour. Write a program to implement this algorithm.

(d) A third traveling salesman heuristic is to partition the plane of cities into strips, each of which contains some bounded number B of cities. Worker processes in parallel find minimal cost tours from one end of the strip to the others.

In odd-numbered strips the tours should go from the top to the bottom; in even-numbered strips they should go from the bottom to the top. Once tours have been found for all strips, they are connected together.

(e) Compare the performance and accuracy of your programs for parts (a) through (d). What are their execution times? How good or bad is the approximate solution that is generated? How much larger a problem can you solve using the approximate algorithms than the exact algorithm? Experiment with several tours of various sizes. Write a report explaining the tests you conducted and the results you observed.

(f) There are several additional heuristic algorithms and local optimization techniques for solving the traveling salesman problem. For example, there are techniques called cutting planes and simulated annealing. Start by finding good references on the TSP. Then pick one or more of the better algorithms, write a program to implement it, and conduct a series of experiments to see how well it performs (both in terms of execution time and how good a solution it generates).

9.8   Figure 9.3 contains a program for the region-labeling problem.

(a) Implement the program using the MPI communication library.

(b) Modify your answer to (a) to get rid of the separate coordinator process. *Hint:* Use MPI's global communication primitives.

(c) Compare the performance of the two programs. Develop a set of sample images, then determine the performance of each program for those images and different numbers of workers. Write a report that explains and analyzes your results.

9.9   Section 9.2 describes the region-labeling problem. Consider a different image processing problem called *smoothing*. Assume images are represented by a matrix of pixels as in Section 9.2. The goal now is to smooth an image by removing "spikes" and "rough edges." In particular, start with the input image, then modify the image by unlighting (setting to 0) all lit pixels *that do not have at least d neighbors*. Each pixel in the original image should be considered independently, so you will need to place the new image in a new matrix. Now use the new image and repeat this algorithm, unlighting all (new) pixels that do not have at least d neighbors. Keep going *until there are no changes between the current and new image*. (This means that you cannot know in advance how many times to repeat the smoothing algorithm.)

(a) Write a parallel program for solving this problem; use the heartbeat paradigm. Your program should use w worker processes. Divide the image into w equal-sized strips and assign one worker process to each strip. Assume **n** is a multiple of **w**.

(b) Test your program for different images, different numbers of workers, and different values of **d**. Write a brief report explaining your tests and results.

9.10 Figure 9.4 contains a program for the Game of Life. Modify the program to use **w** worker processes, and have each worker manage either a strip or block of cells. Implement your program using a distributed programming language or a sequential language and a subroutine library such as MPI. Display the output on a graphical display device. Experiment with your program, then write a brief report explaining your experiments and the results you observe. Does the game ever converge?

9.11 The Game of Life has very simple organisms and rules. Devise a more complicated game that can be modeled using cellular automata, but do not make it too complicated! For example, model interactions between sharks and fish, between rabbits and foxes, or between coyotes and roadrunners. Or model something like the burning of trees and brush in a forest fire.

Pick a problem to model and devise an initial set of rules; you will probably want to use randomness to make interactions probabilistic rather than fixed. Then implement your model as a cellular automaton, experiment with it, and modify the rules so that the outcome is not trivial. For example, you might strive for population balance. Write a report describing your game and the results you observe.

9.12 Section 9.4 describes a probe/echo algorithm for computing the topology of a network. This problem can also be solved using a heartbeat algorithm. Assume as in Section 9.4 that a process can communicate only with its neighbors, and that initially each process knows only about those neighbors. Design a heartbeat algorithm that has each process repeatedly exchange information with its neighbors. When the program terminates, *every* process should know the topology of the entire network. You will need to figure out what the processes should exchange and how they can tell when to terminate.

9.13 Suppose n^2 processes are arranged in a square grid. Each process can communicate only with the neighbors to the left and right, and above and below. (Processes on the corners have only two neighbors; others on the edges of the grid have three neighbors.) Every process has a local integer value **v**. Write a heartbeat algorithm to compute the sum of the n^2 values. When your program terminates, each process should know the sum.

9.14   Section 9.3 describes two algorithms for distributed matrix multiplication.

(a) Modify the algorithms so that each uses w worker processes, where w is much smaller than n. (Pick values of w and n that make the arithmetic easy.)

(b) Compare the performance, on paper, of your answers to (a). For given values of w and n, what is the total number of messages required by each program? Some of the messages can be in transit at the same time; for each program, what is the best case for the longest chain of messages that cannot be overlapped? What are the sizes of the messages in each program? What are the local storage requirements of each program?

(c) Implement your answers to (a) using a programming language or a subroutine library such as MPI. Compare the performance of the two programs for different size matrices and different numbers of worker processes. (An easy way to tell whether your programs are correct is to set both source matrices to all ones; then every value in the result matrix will be n.) Write a report describing your experiments and the results you observe.

9.15   Figure 9.7 contains an algorithm for multiplying matrices by blocks.

(a) Show the layout of the values of a and b after the initial rearrangement for n = 6 and for n = 8.

(b) Modify the program to use w worker processes, where w is an even power of two and a factor of n. For example, if n is 1024, then w can be 4, 16, 64, or 256. Each worker is responsible for one block of the matrices. Give *all* the details for the code.

(c) Implement your answer to (b), for example using C and the MPI library. Conduct experiments to measure its performance for different values of n and w. Write a report describing your experiments and results. (You might want to initialize a and b to all ones, because then the final value of every element of c will be one.)

9.16   We can use a pipeline to sort n values as follows. (This is not a very efficient sorting algorithm, but what the heck, this is an exercise.) Given are w worker processes and a coordinator process. Assume that n is a multiple of w and that each worker process can store at most n/w + 1 values at a time. The processes form a closed pipeline. Initially, the coordinator has n unsorted values. It sends these one at a time to worker 1. Worker 1 keeps some of the values and sends others on to worker 2. Worker 2 keeps some of the values and sends others on to worker 3, and so on. Eventually, the workers send values back to the coordinator. (They can do this directly.)

(a) Develop code for the coordinator and the workers so that the coordinator gets back *sorted* values. Each process can insert a value into a list or remove a value from a list, but it may not use an internal sorting routine.

(b) How many messages are used by your algorithm? Give your answer as a function of n and w. Be sure to show how you arrived at the answer.

9.17   Given are n processes, each corresponding to a node in a connected graph. Each node can communicate only with its neighbors. A spanning tree of a graph is a tree that includes every node of the graph and a subset of the edges.

Write a program to construct a spanning tree on the fly. Do not first compute the topology. Instead, construct the tree from the ground up by having the processes interact with their neighbors to decide which edges to put in the tree and which to leave out. You may assume processes have unique indexes.

9.18   Extend the probe/echo algorithm for computing the topology of a network (Figure 9.12) to handle a dynamic topology. In particular, communication links might fail during the computation and later recover. (Failure of a processor can be modeled by failure of all its links.) Assume that when a link fails, it silently throws away undelivered messages.

Define any additional primitives you need to detect when a failure or recovery has occurred, and explain briefly how you would implement them. You might also want to modify the **receive** primitive so that it returns an error code if the channel has failed. Your algorithm should terminate, assuming that eventually failures and recoveries quit happening for a long enough interval that every node can agree on the topology.

9.19   Given are n processes. Assume that the **broadcast** primitive sends a message from one process to all n processes and that **broadcast** is both reliable and totally ordered. That is, every process sees all messages that are broadcast and sees them *in the same order*.

(a) Using this **broadcast** primitive (and **receive**, of course), develop a fair solution to the distributed mutual exclusion problem. In particular, devise entry and exit protocols that each process executes before and after a critical section. Do not use additional helper processes; the n processes should communicate directly with each other.

(b) Discuss how one might implement atomic broadcast. What are the problems that have to be solved? How would you solve them?

9.20   Consider the following three processes, which communicate using asynchronous message passing:

```
chan chA(...), chB(...), chC(...);

process A { ...
  send chC(...); send chB(...); receive chA(...);
  send chC(...); receive chA(...); }

process B { ...
  send chC(...); receive chB(...);
  receive chB(...); send chA(...); }

process C { ...
  receive chC(...); receive chC(...);
  send chA(...); send chB(...); receive chC(...); }
```

Assume that each process has a logical clock that is initially zero, and that it uses the logical clock update rules in Section 9.5 to add timestamps to messages and to update its clock when it receives messages.

What are the final values of the logical clocks in each process? Show your work; the answer may not be unique.

9.21 Consider the implementation of distributed semaphores in Figure 9.13.

(a) Assume there are four user processes. User one initiates a **v** operation at time **0** on its logical clock. Users two and three both initiate **P** operations at time **1** on their logical clocks. User four initiates a **v** operation at time **10** on its logical clock. Develop a trace of *all* the communication events that occur in the algorithm and show the clock values and timestamps associated with each. Also trace the contents of the message queues in each helper.

(b) In the algorithm, both user processes and helper processes maintain logical clocks, but only the helper processes interact with each other and have to make decisions based on a total ordering. Suppose the users did not have logical clocks and did not add timestamps to messages to their helpers. Would the algorithm still be correct? If so, clearly explain why? If not, develop an example that shows what can go wrong.

(c) Suppose the code were changed so that users broadcast to all helpers when they wanted to do a **P** or **v** operation. For example, when a user wants to do a **v**, it would execute

```
broadcast semop(i, VOP, lc)
```

and then update its logical clock. (A user would still wait for permission from its helper after broadcasting a **POP** message). This would simplify the program by getting rid of the first two arms of the **if/then/else** statement in the helpers. Unfortunately, it leads to an incorrect program. Develop an example that shows what can go wrong.

9.22 The solution to the distributed mutual exclusion problem in Figure 9.15 uses a token ring and a single token that circulates continuously. Assume instead that every `Helper` process can communicate with every other—i.e., the communication graph is complete. Design a solution that does not use circulating tokens. In particular, the `Helper` processes should be idle except when some process `User[i]` is trying to enter or exit its critical section. Your solution should be fair and deadlock-free. Each `Helper` should execute the same algorithm, and the regular processes `User[i]` should execute the same code as in Figure 9.15. (*Hint:* Associate a token with every pair of processes—namely, with every edge of the communication graph.)

9.23 Figure 9.16 presents a set of rules for termination detection in a ring. Variable `token` counts the number of idle processes. Is the value really needed, or do the colors suffice to detect termination? In other words, what exactly is the role of `token`?

9.24 *Drinking Philosophers Problem* [Chandy and Misra 1984]. Consider the following generalization of the dining philosophers problem. An undirected graph `G` is given. Philosophers are associated with nodes of the graph and can communicate only with neighbors. A bottle is associated with each edge of `G`. Each philosopher cycles between three states: tranquil, thirsty, and drinking. A tranquil philosopher may become thirsty. Before drinking, the philosopher must acquire the bottle associated with every edge connected to the philosopher's node. After drinking, a philosopher again becomes tranquil.

Design a solution to this problem that is fair and deadlock-free. Every philosopher should execute the same algorithm. Use tokens to represent the bottles. It is permissible for a tranquil philosopher to respond to requests from neighbors for any bottles the philosopher may hold.

9.25 You have been given a collection of processes that communicate using asynchronous message passing. A *diffusing computation* is one in which one main process starts the computation by sending messages to one or more other processes [Dijkstra and Scholten 1980]. After first receiving a message, another process may send messages.

Design a signaling scheme that is superimposed on the computation proper and that allows the main process to determine when the computation has terminated. Use a probe/echo algorithm as well as ideas from Section 9.6. (*Hint:* Keep counts of messages and signals.)

9.26 The distributed termination detection rules in Figure 9.18 assumes that the graph is complete and that each process receives from exactly one channel. Solve the following exercises as separate problems.

(a) Extend the token-passing rules to handle an arbitrary connected graph.

(b) Extend the token-passing rules to handle the situation in which a process receives from multiple channels (one at a time, of course).

9.27 Consider the following variation on the rules in Figure 9.18 for termination detection in a complete graph. A process takes the same actions upon receiving a regular message. But a process now takes the following actions when it receives the token:

```
if (color[i] == blue)
  token = blue;
else
  token = red;
color[i] = blue;
set j to index of channel for next edge in cycle c;
send ch[j](token);
```

In other words, the value of **token** is no longer modified or examined. Using this new rule, is there a way to detect termination? If so, explain when the computation is known to have terminated. If not, explain why the rules are insufficient.

9.28 Figure 8.15 shows how to implement replicated files using one lock per copy. In that solution, a process has to get every lock when it wants to update the file. Suppose instead that we use **n** tokens and that a token does not move until it has to. Initially, every file server has one token.

(a) Modify the code in Figure 8.15 to use tokens instead of locks. Implement **read** operations by reading the local copy and **write** operations by updating all copies. When a client opens a file for reading, its server needs to acquire one token; for writing, the server needs all **n** tokens. Your solution should be fair and deadlock-free.

(b) Modify your answer to (a) to use weighted voting with tokens. In particular, when a client opens a file for reading, its server has to acquire any **readWeight** tokens; for writing, the server needs **writeWeight** tokens. Assume that **readWeight** and **writeWeight** satisfy the conditions at the end of Section 8.4. Show in your code how you maintain timestamps on files and how you determine which copy is current when you open a file for reading.

(c) Compare your answers to (a) and (b). For the different client operations, how many messages do the servers have to exchange in the two solutions? Consider the best case and the worst case (and define what they are).

10

Implementations

This chapter describes ways to implement the various language mechanisms described in Chapters 7 and 8: asynchronous and synchronous message passing, RPC, and rendezvous. We first show how to implement asynchronous message passing using a kernel. We then use asynchronous messages to implement synchronous message passing and guarded communication. Next we show how to implement RPC using a kernel, rendezvous using asynchronous message passing, and finally rendezvous (and multiple primitives) in a kernel. The implementation of synchronous message passing is more complex than that of asynchronous message passing because both send and receive statements are blocking. Similarly, the implementation of rendezvous is more complex than that of RPC or asynchronous message passing because rendezvous has both two-way communication and two-way synchronization.

The starting point for the various implementations is the shared-memory kernel of Chapter 6. Thus, even though programs that use message passing, RPC, or rendezvous are usually written for distributed-memory machines, they can readily execute on shared-memory machines. It so happens that the same kind of relationship is true for shared-variable programs. Using what is called a *distributed shared memory*, it is possible to execute shared-variable programs on distributed-memory machines, even though they are usually written to execute on shared-memory machines. The last section of this chapter describes how to implement a distributed shared memory.

10.1 Asynchronous Message Passing

This section presents two implementations of asynchronous message passing. The first adds channels and message-passing primitives to the shared-memory kernel of Chapter 6. This implementation is suitable for a single processor or a shared-memory multiprocessor. The second implementation extends the shared-memory kernel to a distributed kernel that is suitable for a multicomputer or a networked collection of separate machines.

10.1.1 Shared-Memory Kernel

Each channel in a program is represented in a kernel by means of a *channel descriptor*. This contains the heads of a message list and a blocked list. The message list contains queued messages; the blocked list contains processes waiting to receive messages. At least one of these lists will always be empty. This is because a process is not blocked if there is an available message, and a message is not queued if there is a blocked process.

A descriptor is created by means of the kernel primitive `createChan`. This is called once for each `chan` declaration in a program, before any processes are created. An array of channels is created either by calling `createChan` once for each element or by parameterizing `createChan` with the array size and calling it just once. The `createChan` primitive returns the name (index or address) of the descriptor.

The send statement is implemented using the `sendChan` primitive. First, the sending process evaluates the expressions and collects the values together into a single message, stored typically on the sending process's execution stack. Then `sendChan` is called; its arguments are the channel name (returned by `create-Chan`) and the message itself. The `sendChan` primitive first finds the descriptor of the channel. If there is at least one process on the blocked list, the oldest process is removed from that list and the message is copied into the process's address space; that process's descriptor is then inserted on the ready list. If there is no blocked process, the message has to be saved on the descriptor's message list. This is necessary because send is nonblocking, and hence the sender has to be allowed to continue executing.

Space for the saved message can be allocated dynamically from a single buffer pool, or there can be a communication buffer associated with each channel. However, asynchronous message passing raises an important implementation issue—what if there is no more kernel space? The kernel has two choices: halt the program due to buffer overflow or block the sender until there is enough buffer space. Halting the program is a drastic step since free space could soon become available, but it gives immediate feedback to the programmer that messages are being produced faster than they are being consumed, which usually indicates an error. On the other hand, blocking the sender violates the non-blocking semantics of **send** and complicates the kernel somewhat since there is an additional cause of blocking; then again, the writer of a concurrent program cannot assume anything about the rate or order in which a process executes. Operating system kernels block senders, and swap blocked processes out of memory if necessary, since they have to avoid crashing. However, halting the program is a reasonable choice for a high-level programming language.

The receive statement is implemented by the **receiveChan** primitive. Its arguments are the name of the channel and the address of a message buffer. The actions of **receiveChan** are the dual of those of **sendChan**. First the kernel finds the descriptor for the appropriate channel, then it checks the message list. If the message list is not empty, the first message is removed and copied into the receiver's message buffer. If the message list is empty, the receiver is inserted on the blocked list. After receiving a message, the receiver unpacks the message from the buffer into the appropriate variables.

A fourth primitive, **emptyChan**, is used to implement the function **empty(ch)**. It simply finds the descriptor and checks whether the message list is empty. In fact, if the kernel data structures are not in a protected address space, the executing process could simply check for itself whether the message list is empty; a critical section is not required since the process only needs to examine the head of the message list.

Figure 10.1 contains outlines of these four primitives. These primitives are added to the single-processor kernel in Figure 6.2. The value of **executing** is the address of the descriptor of the currently executing process, and **dispatcher** is a procedure that schedules processes on the processor. The actions of **send-Chan** and **receiveChan** are very similar to the actions of P and V in the semaphore kernel in Figure 6.5. The main difference is that a channel descriptor contains a message list, whereas a semaphore descriptor merely contains the value of the semaphore.

The kernel in Figure 10.1 can be turned into one for a shared-memory multiprocessor using the techniques described in Section 6.2. The main requirements are to store kernel data structures in memory accessible to all processors, and to use locks to protect critical sections of kernel code that access shared data.

```
int createChan(int msgSize) {
  get an empty channel descriptor and initialize it;
  set return value to the index or address of the descriptor;
  dispatcher();
}

proc sendChan(int chan; byte msg[*]) {
  find descriptor of channel chan;
  if (blocked list empty) {   # save message
    acquire buffer and copy msg into it;
    insert buffer at end of message list;
  }
  else {   # give message to a receiver
    remove process from blocked list;
    copy msg into the process's address space;
    insert the process at end of ready list;
  }
  dispatcher();
}

proc receiveChan(int chan; result byte msg[*]) {
  find descriptor of channel chan;
  if (message list empty) {   # block receiver
    insert executing at end of blocked list;
    store address of msg in descriptor of executing;
    executing = 0;
  }
  else {   # give receiver a stored message
    remove buffer from message list;
    copy contents of buffer into msg;
  }
  dispatcher();
}

bool emptyChan(int chan) {
  bool r = false;
  find descriptor of channel chan;
  if (message list empty)
    r = true;
  save r as the return value;
  dispatcher();
}
```

Figure 10.1   Asynchronous message passing in a single-processor kernel.

10.1.2 Distributed Kernel

We now show how to extend the shared-memory kernel to support distributed execution. The basic idea is to replicate the kernel—placing one copy on each machine—and to have the different kernels communicate with each other using network communication primitives.

Each channel is stored on a single machine in a distributed program. For now, assume that a channel can have any number of senders but that it has only one receiver. Then the logical place to put a channel's descriptor is on the machine on which the receiver executes. A process executing on that machine accesses the channel as in the shared-memory kernel. However, a process executing on another machine cannot access the channel directly. Instead, the kernels on the two machines need to interact. Below we describe how to change the shared-memory kernel and how to use the network to implement a distributed program.

Figure 10.2 illustrates the structure of a distributed kernel. Each machine's kernel contains descriptors for the channels and processes located on that machine. As before, each kernel has local interrupt handlers for supervisor calls (internal traps), timers, and input/output devices. The communication network is a special kind of input/output device. Thus each kernel has network interrupt handlers and contains routines that write to and read from the network.

As a concrete example, an Ethernet is typically accessed as follows. An Ethernet controller has two independent parts, one for writing and one for reading. Each part has an associated interrupt handler in the kernel. A write interrupt is triggered when a write operation completes; the controller itself takes care of

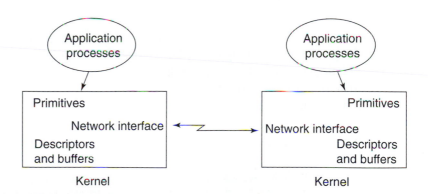

Figure 10.2   Distributed kernel structure and interaction.

network access arbitration. A read interrupt is triggered on a processor when a message for that processor arrives over the network.

When a kernel primitive—executing on behalf of an application process—needs to send a message to another machine, it calls kernel procedure `netWrite`. This procedure has three arguments: a destination processor, a message kind (see below), and the message itself. First, `netWrite` acquires a buffer, formats the message, and stores it in the buffer. Then, if the writing half of the network controller is free, an actual write is initiated; otherwise the buffer is inserted on a queue of write requests. In either case `netWrite` returns. Later, when a write interrupt occurs, the associated interrupt handler frees the buffer containing the message that was just written; if its write queue is not empty, the interrupt handler then initiates another network write.

Input from the network is typically handled in a reciprocal fashion. When a message arrives at a kernel, the network read interrupt handler is entered. It first saves the state of the executing process. Then it allocates a new buffer for the next network input message. Finally, the read handler unpacks the first field of the input message to determine the kind and then calls the appropriate kernel primitive.[1]

Figure 10.3 contains outlines for the network interface routines. These include the network interrupt handlers and the `netWrite` procedure. The `netRead_handler` services three kinds of messages: `SEND`, `CREATE_CHAN`, and `CHAN_DONE`. These are sent by one kernel and serviced by another, as described below. The kernel's dispatcher routine is called at the end of `netWrite_handler` to resume execution of the interrupted process. However, the dispatcher is not called at the end of `netRead_handler` since that routine calls a kernel primitive—depending on the kind of input message—and that primitive in turn calls the dispatcher.

For simplicity, we assume that network transmission is error-free and hence that messages do not need to be acknowledged or retransmitted. We also ignore the problem of running out of buffer space for outgoing or incoming messages; in practice, the kernels would employ what is called *flow control* to limit the number of buffered messages. The Historical Notes section cites literature that describes how to address these issues.

Since a channel can be stored either locally or remotely, a channel name now needs to have two fields: a machine number and an index or offset. The

---

[1] An alternative approach to handling network input is to employ a daemon process that executes outside the kernel. In this case, the interrupt handler simply sends the message to a channel from which the daemon repeatedly receives. Using a daemon decreases execution time in the read interrupt handler but increases the time it takes to process network input. On the other hand, it simplifies the kernel since it removes the details of processing network messages.

```
type mkind = enum(SEND, CREATE_CHAN, CHAN_DONE);
bool writing = false;        # status of network write
other variables for the write queue and transmission buffers;

proc netWrite(int dest; mkind kind; byte data[]) {
   acquire buffer; format message and store it in the buffer;
   if (writing)
      insert the message buffer on the write queue;
   else {
      writing = true;
      start transmitting the message on the network;
   }
}


netWrite_handler: {   # entered with interrupts inhibited
   save state of executing;
   free the current transmission buffer;
   writing = false;
   if (write queue not empty) { # start another write
      remove first buffer from the queue; writing = true;
      start transmitting the message on the network;
   }
   dispatcher();
}


netRead_handler: {    # entered with interrupts inhibited
   save state of executing;
   acquire new buffer; prepare network controller for next read;
   unpack first field of input message to determine kind;
   if (kind == SEND)
      remoteSend(channel name, buffer);
   else if (kind == CREATE_CHAN)
      remoteCreate(rest of message);
   else  # kind == CHAN_DONE
      chanDone(rest of message);
}
```

Figure 10.3   Network interface routines.

machine number indicates where the descriptor is stored; the index indicates where to find the descriptor in that machine's kernel. We also need to augment the `createChan` primitive so that it has an additional argument indicating the machine on which the channel is to be created. Within `createChan`, the kernel checks this argument. If the creator and channel are on the same machine, the kernel creates the channel as in Figure 10.1. Otherwise the kernel blocks the executing process and transmits a `CREATE_CHAN` message to the remote machine. That message includes the identity of the executing process. Eventually the local kernel will receive a `CHAN_DONE` message indicating that the channel has been created on the remote machine. This message contains the channel's name and indicates the process for which the channel was created. As shown in Figure 10.3, when `netRead_handler` receives this message, it calls a new kernel primitive, `chanDone`, which unblocks the process that asked to have the channel created and returns the channel's name to it.

On the other side of the network, when a kernel daemon receives a `CREATE_CHAN` message, it calls the `remoteCreate` primitive. That primitive creates the channel then sends a `CHAN_DONE` message back to the first kernel. Thus, to create a channel on a remote machine, we have the following sequence of steps:

- An application process invokes the local `createChan` primitive.

- The local kernel sends a `CREATE_CHAN` message to the remote kernel.

- The read interrupt handler in the remote kernel receives the message and calls the remote kernel's `remoteCreate` primitive.

- The remote kernel creates the channel and then sends a `CHAN_DONE` message back to the local kernel.

- The read interrupt handler in the local kernel receives the message and calls `chanDone`, which awakens the application process.

The `sendChan` primitive also needs to be changed in a distributed kernel. However, `sendChan` is much simpler than `createChan` since the `send` statement is asynchronous. In particular, if the channel is on the local machine, `sendChan` takes the same actions as in Figure 10.1. If the channel is on another machine, `sendChan` transmits a `SEND` message to that machine. At this point, the executing process can continue. When the message arrives at the remote kernel, that kernel calls the `remoteSend` primitive, which takes essentially the same actions as the (local) `sendChan` primitive. The only difference is that the incoming message is already stored in a buffer, and hence the kernel does not need to allocate a new one.

Figure 10.4 contains outlines for the primitives of the distributed kernel. The `receiveChan` and `emptyChan` primitives are the same as in Figure 10.1 as long as each channel has only one receiver and the channel is stored on the same machine as the receiver. However, if this is not the case, then additional messages are needed to communicate between the machine on which a `receiveChan` or `empty` primitive is invoked and the machine on which the channel is stored. This communication is analogous to that for creating a channel—the local kernel sends a message to the remote kernel, which executes the primitive and then sends the result back to the local kernel.

```
type chanName = rec(int machine, index);

chanName createChan(int machine) {
  chanName chan;
  if (machine is local) {
    get an empty channel descriptor and initialize it;
    chan = chanName(local machine number, address of descriptor);
  } else {
    netWrite(machine, CREATE_CHAN, executing);
    insert descriptor of executing on delay list;
    executing = 0;
  }
  dispatcher();
}

proc remoteCreate(int creator) {
  chanName chan;
  get an empty channel descriptor and initialize it;
  chan = chanName(local machine number, address of descriptor);
  netWrite(creator, CHAN_DONE, chan);
  dispatcher();
}

proc chanDone(int creator; chanName chan) {
  remove descriptor of process creator from the delay list;
  save chan as return value for creator;
  insert the descriptor of creator at the end of the ready list;
  dispatcher();
}
```

```
proc sendChan(chanName chan; byte msg[*]) {
  if (chan.machine is local)
    same actions as sendChan in Figure 10.1;
  else
    netWrite(chan.machine, SEND, msg);
  dispatcher();
}


proc remoteSend(chanName chan; int buffer) {
  find descriptor of channel chan;
  if (blocked list empty)
    insert buffer on message list;
  else {
    remove process from blocked list;
    copy message from buffer to the process's address space;
    insert the process at the end of the ready list;
  }
  dispatcher();
}


proc receiveChan(int chan; result byte msg[*]) {
  same actions as receiveChan in Figure 10.1;
}


bool emptyChan(int chan) {
  same actions as emptyChan in Figure 10.1;
}
```

Figure 10.4   Distributed kernel primitives.

10.2 Synchronous Message Passing

Recall that with synchronous message passing, both **send** and **receive** are blocking primitives. In particular, whichever process tries to communicate first has to wait until the other one is ready. This avoids the need for potentially unbounded queues of buffered messages, but requires that the sender and receiver exchange control signals in order to synchronize.

Below we show how to implement synchronous message passing using asynchronous message passing, then we show how to implement the input, output, and guarded communication statements of CSP using a clearinghouse process. The second implementation can also be adapted to implement Linda's tuple space (Section 7.7). The Historical Notes at the end of this chapter give references for decentralized implementations; see also the exercises at the end of this chapter.

10.2.1 *Direct Communication Using Asynchronous Messages*

Assume that you have been given a collection of **n** processes that communicate using synchronous message passing. The sending side in a communication names the intended receiver, but the receiving side can accept a message from any sender. In particular, a source process **s** sends a message to a destination process **D** by executing

```
synch_send(D, expressions);
```

The destination process waits to receive a message from any source by executing

```
synch_receive(source, variables);
```

Once both processes arrive at these statements, the identity of the sender and the values of the expressions are transmitted as a message from process **s** to process **D**; these values are then stored in **source** and **variables**, respectively. The receiver thus learns the identity of the sender.

We can implement the above primitives using asynchronous message passing by employing three arrays of channels: **sourceReady**, **destReady**, and **transmit**. The first two are used to exchange control signals, the third is used for data transmission. The channels are used as shown in Figure 10.5. A receiving process waits for a message on its element of the **sourceReady** array; the message identifies the sender. The receiver then tells the sender to go ahead. Finally, the message itself is transmitted.

The code in Figure 10.5 handles sending to a specific destination while receiving from any source. If both sides always have to name each other, then we could get rid of the **sourceReady** channels in Figure 10.5 and have the receiver simply send a signal to the source when the receiver is ready for a message. The remaining sends and receives are sufficient to synchronize the two processes. On the other hand, if a process doing a receive has the option of either naming the source *or* accepting messages from any source, the situation is more complicated. (The MPI library supports this option.) This is because we either have to have one channel for each communication path and poll the channels, or the receiving process has to examine each message and save the ones it is not yet ready to accept. We leave to the reader modifying the implementation to handle this case (see the exercises at the end of this chapter).

shared variables:

```
chan sourceReady[n](int);        # source ready
chan destReady[n]();             # destination ready
chan transmit[n](byte msg[*]);   # data transmission
```

Synchronous send executed by source process `S`:

```
gather expressions into a message buffer b;
send sourceReady[D](S);     # tell D that I am ready
receive destReady[S]();     # wait for D to be ready
send transmit[D](b);        # send the message
```

Synchronous receive executed by destination process `D`:

```
int source; byte buffer[BUFSIZE];
receive sourceReady[D](source); # wait for any sender
send destReady[source]();       # tell source I'm ready
receive transmit[D](buffer);    # get the message
unpack the buffer into the variables;
```

Figure 10.5   Synchronous communication using asynchronous messages.

10.2.2 Guarded Communication Using a Clearinghouse

You are again given a collection of `n` processes, but assume now that they communicate and synchronize using the input and output statements of CSP (Section 7.6). Recall that these have the forms

```
Source?port(variables);        # input statement

Destination!port(expressions);  # output statement
```

The statements *match* when the input statement is executed by process `Destination`, the output statement is executed by process `Source`, the `port` names are identical, there are as many expressions as variables, and they have the same types.

CSP also introduced guarded communication, which provides nondeterministic communication order. Recall that a guarded communication statement has the form

```
B; C -> S;
```

where `B` is an optional Boolean expression (guard), `C` is an input or output statement, and **s** is a statement list. Guarded communication statements are used within **if** and **do** statements to choose among several possible communications.

The key to implementing input, output, and guarded statements is to pair up processes that want to execute matching communication statements. We will use a "clearinghouse" process to play the role of matchmaker. Suppose regular process P_i wants to execute an output statement with P_j as destination and that P_j wants to execute an input statement with P_i as source. Assume that the port name and the message types also match. These processes interact with the clearinghouse and each other as illustrated in Figure 10.6. Both P_i and P_j send a message to the clearinghouse; this message describes the desired communication. The clearinghouse saves the first of these messages. When it receives the second, it retrieves the first and determines that the two processes want to execute matching statements. The clearinghouse then sends replies to both processes. After getting the reply, P_i sends the expressions in its output statement to P_j, which receives them into the variables in its input statement. At this point, each process starts executing the code following its communication statement.

To realize the program structure in Figure 10.6, we need channels for each communication path. One channel is used for messages from regular processes to the clearinghouse; these contain templates to describe possible matches. We also need one reply channel for each regular process; these will be used for messages back from the clearinghouse. Finally, we need one data channel for each regular process that contains input statements; these will be used by other regular processes.

Let each regular process have a unique identity that is an integer between **1** and **n**. These will be used to index reply and data channels. Reply messages specify a direction for a communication and the identity of the other process. A message on a data channel is sent as an array of bytes. We assume that the message itself is self-describing—namely, that it contains tags that allow the receiver to determine the types of data in the message.

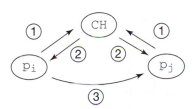

Figure 10.6   Interaction pattern with clearinghouse process.

When regular processes reach input, output, or guarded communication statements, they send *templates* to the clearinghouse. These are used to select matching pairs of statements. Each template has four fields:

```
direction, source, destination, port
```

The direction is `OUT` for an output statement and `IN` for an input statement. Source and destination are the identities of the sender and intended receiver (for output) or intended sender and receiver (for input). The port is an integer that uniquely identifies the port and hence the data types in the input and output statements. There must be one of these for each different kind of port in the source program. This means every explicit port identifier needs to be assigned a unique integer value, as does every anonymous port. (Recall that port names appear in the source program; hence numbers can be assigned statically at compile time.)

Figure 10.7 contains declarations of the shared data types and communication channels and the code that regular processes execute when they reach output and input statements. For unguarded communication statements, a process sends a single template to the clearinghouse, then waits for a reply. The clearinghouse will send a reply when it finds a match, as discussed below. After getting its reply, the source process sends the expressions in the output statement to the destination process, which stores them in the variables in the input statement.

When a process uses a guarded communication statement, it first needs to evaluate each guard. For each guard that is true, the process constructs a template and inserts it into set `t`. After evaluating all guards, the process sends `t` to the clearinghouse and then waits for a reply. (If `t` is empty, the process just continues.) When the process receives a reply, it will indicate which other process has been paired with this one and the direction in which communication is to occur. If the direction is `OUT`, the process sends a message to the other one; otherwise it waits to receive data from the other. The process then selects the appropriate guarded statement and executes it. (We assume that `direction` and `who` are sufficient to determine which guarded communication statement was the one matched by the clearinghouse; in general, ports and types will also be required.)

Figure 10.8 contains the clearinghouse process `CH`. Array `pending` contains one set of templates for each regular process. If `pending[i]` is not empty, then regular process `i` is blocked while waiting for a matching communication statement. When `CH` receives a new set `t`, it first looks at one of the templates to determine which process `s` sent `t`. (If the direction in a template is `OUT`, then the source is `s`; if the direction is `IN`, then the destination is `s`.) The clearinghouse then compares elements of `t` with templates in `pending` to see if there is a match. Because of the way we have constructed templates, two match if the

```
type direction = enum(OUT, IN);
type template =
      rec(direction d; int source; int dest; int port);
type Templates = set of template;

chan match(Templates t);
chan reply[1:n](direction d; int who);
chan data[1:n](byte msg[*]);
```

output statement not in a guard:

```
  Templates t = template(OUT, myid, destination, port);
  send match(t);
  receive reply[myid](direction, who);
  # direction will be OUT and who will be destination
  gather expressions into a message buffer;
  send data[who](buffer);
```

input statement not in a guard:

```
  Templates t = template(IN, source, myid, port);
  send match(t);
  receive reply[myid](direction, who);
  # direction will be IN and who will be myid
  receive data[myid](buffer);
  unpack the buffer into local variables;
```

guarded input or output statement:

```
  Templates t = ∅;    # set of possible communications
  for [ boolean expressions in guards that are true ]
     insert a template for the input or output statement into set t;
  send match(t);          # send matches to clearinghouse
  receive reply[myid](direction, who);
  use direction and who to determine which guarded
          communication statement was the one that matched;
  if (direction == IN)
    { receive data[myid](buffer);
      unpack the buffer into local variables; }
  else        # direction == OUT
    { gather expressions into a message buffer;
      send data[who](buffer); }
  execute appropriate guarded statement S;
```

Figure 10.7   Protocols for regular processes.

```
# global types and channels as declared in Figure 10.7

process CH {
    Templates t, pending[1:n] = ([n] ∅);
    ## if pending[i] != ∅, then process i is blocked
    while (true) {
        receive match(t);   # get a new set of templates
        look at some template in t to determine sender s;
        for [ each template in t ] {
            if (there is a matching pair in some pending[i]) {
                if (s is the source) {
                    send reply[s](OUT, i);
                    send reply[i](IN, s);
                } else {      # s is the destination
                    send reply[s](IN, i);
                    send reply[i](OUT, s);
                }
                pending[i] = ∅;
                break;    # get out of the for loop
            }
        }
        if (no matching pair was found)
            pending[s] = t;
    }
}
```

Figure 10.8   Centralized clearinghouse process.

directions are opposite, the ports are identical, and the source and destination are identical. If CH finds a match with some process i, it sends replies to both s and i; the replies tell each process the identity of the other and the direction in which they are to communicate. In this case, CH then clears pending[i] since process i is no longer blocked. If CH does not find a match for any template in t, it saves t in pending[s], where s is the sending process.

An example will help clarify how these protocols work. Suppose we have two processes A and B that want to exchange data by executing the following guarded communication statements:

```
process A {
   int a1, a2;
   if B!a1 -> B?a2;
   [] B?a2 -> B!a1;
   fi
}

process B {
   int b1, b2;
   if A!b1 -> A?b2;
   [] A?b2 -> A!b1;
   fi
}
```

When A starts executing its if statement, it builds a set with two templates:

```
{ (OUT, A, B, p2), (IN, B, A, p1) }
```

Here we assume that p1 is the identity of A's port and p2 is the identity of B's port. Process A then sends these templates to the clearinghouse.

Process B takes similar actions and sends the following set of templates to the clearinghouse:

```
{ (OUT, B, A, p1), (IN, A, B, p2) }
```

When the clearinghouse gets the second set of templates, it sees that there are two possible matches. It picks one, sends replies to A and B, and then throws away both sets of templates. Processes A and B now execute the matching pair of communication statements selected by the clearinghouse. Next they proceed to the communication statements in the bodies of the selected guarded statements. For these, each process sends one template to the clearinghouse, waits for a reply, and then communicates with the other process.

If the matchmaking done by the clearinghouse process always looks at pending in some fixed order, some blocked processes might never get awakened. However, a simple strategy will provide fairness—assuming the application program is deadlock free. Let start be a integer that indicates where to start searching. When CH receives a new set of templates, it first examines pending[start], then pending[start+1], and so on. Once process start gets the chance to communicate, CH increments start to the next process whose pending set is not empty. In this way, start will continually cycle around the processes—assuming process start is not blocked forever—and thus each process will periodically get the chance to be checked first.

10.3 RPC and Rendezvous

This section shows how to implement RPC in a kernel, rendezvous using asynchronous message passing, and multiple primitives—including rendezvous—in a kernel. The RPC kernel illustrates how to handle two-way communication in a kernel. The implementation of rendezvous using message passing shows the extra communication that is required to support rendezvous-style synchronization. The multiple primitives kernel shows how to implement all of the various communication primitives in a single, unified way.

10.3.1 RPC in a Kernel

Since RPC supports only communication, not synchronization, it has the simplest implementation. Recall that, with RPC, a program consists of a collection of modules that contain procedures and processes. The procedures (operations) declared in the specification part of a module can be invoked by processes executing in other modules. All parts of a module reside on the same machine, but different modules can reside on different machines. (We are not concerned here with how a programmer specifies where a module is located; one such mechanism was described in Section 8.7.)

Processes executing in the same module interact by means of shared variables, and they synchronize using semaphores. We assume that each machine has a local kernel that implements processes and semaphores as described in Chapter 6, and that the kernels contain the network interface routines given in Figure 10.3. Our task here is to add kernel primitives and routines to implement RPC.

There are three possible relations between a caller and a procedure:

- They are in the same module, and hence on the same machine.

- They are in different modules but are on the same machine.

- They are on different machines.

In the first case, we can use a conventional procedure call. There is no need to enter a kernel if we know at compile time that the procedure is local. The calling process can simply push value arguments on its stack and jump to the procedure; when the procedure returns, the calling process can pop results off the stack and continue.

For intermodule calls, we can uniquely identify each procedure by a (`machine`, `address`) pair, where `machine` indicates where the procedure body is stored and **address** is the entry point of the procedure. We can then implement call statements as follows:

```
if (machine is local)
    execute a conventional call to address;
else
    rpc(machine, address, value arguments);
```

To use a conventional procedure call, the procedure must be guaranteed to exist. This will be the case if procedure identities cannot be altered and if modules cannot be destroyed dynamically. Otherwise, we would have to enter the local kernel to verify that the procedure exists before making a conventional call.

To execute a remote call, the calling process needs to send value arguments to the remote machine, then block until results are returned. When the remote machine receives a **CALL** message, it creates a process to execute the procedure body. Before that process terminates, it calls a primitive in the remote kernel to send results back to the first machine.

Figure 10.9 contains kernel primitives for implementing RPC; it also shows the new network read interrupt handler. The routines use the **netWrite** procedure of the distributed kernel for asynchronous message passing (Figure 10.3), which in turn interacts with the associated interrupt handler.

The following events occur in processing a remote call:

- The caller invokes the **rpc** primitive, which sends the caller's identity, procedure address, and value arguments to the remote machine.

- The remote kernel's read interrupt handler receives the message and calls **handle_rpc**, which creates a process to service the call.

- The server process executes the body of the procedure, then invokes **rpcReturn** to send results back to the caller's kernel.

- The read interrupt handler in the caller's kernel receives the return message and calls **handleReturn**, which unblocks the caller.

In the **handle_rpc** primitive, we assume that there is a list of previously created descriptors for processes that will service calls. This speeds up handling a remote call since it avoids the overhead of dynamic storage allocation and descriptor initialization. We also assume that each server process is coded so that its first action is to jump to the appropriate procedure and its last action is to call kernel primitive **rpcReturn**.

declarations of network buffers, free descriptors, delay list

```
netRead_handler: {   # entered with interrupts inhibited
  save state of executingP;
  acquire new buffer; prepare network controller for next read;
  unpack first field of input message to determine kind;
  if (kind == CALL)
    handleRPC(caller, address, value arguments);
  else  # kind == RETURN
    handleReturn(caller, results);
}
```

```
proc rpc(int machine, address; byte args[*]) {
  netWrite(machine, CALL, (executing,address,args));
  insert descriptor of executing on delay list;
  dispatcher();
}
```

```
proc handle_rpc(int caller, address; byte args[*]) {
  acquire free process descriptor; save identity of caller in it;
  put address in a register for the process;
  unpack args and push them onto the stack of the process;
  insert process descriptor on ready list;
  dispatcher();
}
```

```
proc rpcReturn(byte results[*]) {
  retrieve identity of caller from descriptor of executing;
  netWrite(caller's machine, RETURN, (caller, results));
  put descriptor of executing back on free descriptor list;
  dispatcher();
}
```

```
proc handleReturn(int caller; byte results[*]) {
  remove descriptor of caller from delay list;
  put results on caller's stack;
  insert descriptor of caller on ready list;
  dispatcher();
}
```

Figure 10.9   Kernel routines for implementing RPC.

10.3.2 *Rendezvous Using Asynchronous Message Passing*

We now see how to implement rendezvous using asynchronous message passing. Recall that there are two partners in a rendezvous: the caller, which invokes an operation using a call statement, and the server, which services the operation using an input statement. In Section 7.3 we showed how to simulate a caller (client) and server using asynchronous message passing (see Figures 7.4 and 7.5). Here we extend that simulation to implement rendezvous.

The key to implementing rendezvous is implementing input statements. Recall that an input statement contains one or more guarded operations. Execution of **in** delays a process until there is an acceptable invocation—one serviced by the input statement and for which the synchronization expression is true. For now we will ignore scheduling expressions.

An operation can be serviced only by the process that declares it, so we can store pending invocations in that process. There are two basic ways we can store invocations: have one queue per operation or have one queue per process. (There is in fact a third choice that we will use in the next section for reasons that are explained there.) We will employ one queue per process since that leads to a simpler implementation. Also, many of the examples in Chapter 8 employed a single input statement per server process. However, a server might use more than one input statement, and these might service different operations. In this case, we might have to look at invocations that could not possibly be selected by a given input statement.

Figure 10.10 illustrates an implementation of rendezvous using asynchronous message passing. Each process **c** that executes call statements has a **reply** channel from which it receives results from calls. Each process **s** that executes input statements has an **invoke** channel from which it receives invocations. Each server process also has a local queue, **pending**, that contains invocations that have not yet been serviced. An invocation message contains the caller's identity, the operation being called, and the value arguments from the call statement.

To implement an input statement, server process **s** first looks through pending invocations. If it finds one that is acceptable—the invocation statement services that operation and the synchronization expression is true—then **s** removes the oldest such invocation from **pending**. Otherwise, **s** receives new invocations until it finds one that is acceptable, saving those that are not yet acceptable. Once **s** has found an acceptable invocation, it executes the body of the guarded operation, and then sends a reply to the caller.

Recall that a scheduling expression affects which invocation is selected if more than one is acceptable. We can implement scheduling expressions by shared channels:

```
chan invoke[1:n](int caller, opid; byte values[*]);
chan reply[1:n](byte results[*]);
```

call statement in process C to operation serviced by process S:

```
send invoke[S](C, opid, value arguments);
receive reply[C](result variables);
```

input statement in process S:

```
queue pending;  # pending invocations
examine queue of pending invocations;
if (some invocation is acceptable)
   remove oldest acceptable invocation from pending;
else   # get another invocation and check it
   while (true) {
      receive invoke[S](caller, opid, values);
      if (this invocation is acceptable)
         break;
      else
         insert (caller, opid, values) in pending;
   }
execute the appropriate guarded operation;
send reply[caller](result values);
```

Figure 10.10   Rendezvous using asynchronous message passing.

extending the implementation in Figure 10.10 as follows. First, a server process needs to know about all pending invocations in order to schedule them. These are the invocations in **pending** and others that might be queued in its **invoke** channel. So, before looking at **pending**, server S needs to execute

```
while (not empty(invoke[S])) {
   receive invoke[S](caller, opid, values);
   insert (caller, opid, values) in pending;
}
```

Second, if the server finds an acceptable invocation in **pending**, it needs to look through the rest of **pending** to see if there is another invocation of the same operation that is also acceptable and that minimizes the value of the scheduling expression. If so, the server removes that invocation from **pending** and services it instead of the first one. The loop in Figure 10.10 does not need to change, however. If `pending` does not contain an acceptable invocation, the first one that the server receives is trivially the one that minimizes the scheduling expression.

10.3.3 Multiple Primitives in a Kernel

We now develop a kernel implementation of the multiple primitives notation described in Section 8.3. This combines aspects of the distributed kernels for message passing and RPC and the implementation of rendezvous using asynchronous message passing. It also illustrates one way to implement rendezvous in a kernel.

With the multiple primitives notation, operations can be invoked in two ways: by synchronous call statements or by asynchronous send statements. Operations can also be serviced in two ways: by procedures or by input statements (but not by both). Thus the kernel needs to know how each operation is invoked and serviced. We assume that a reference to an operation is represented by a record with three fields. The first indicates how the operation is serviced. The second identifies the machine on which the operation is serviced. For an operation serviced by a `proc`, the third field gives the entry point of the procedure as in the kernel for RPC. For an operation serviced by input statements, the third field gives the address of an operation descriptor (see the next page).

With rendezvous, each operation is serviced by the process that declares it. Hence in the implementation of rendezvous we employed one set of pending invocations per server process. With the multiple primitives notation, however, an operation can be serviced by input statements in more than one process in the module that declares it. Thus server processes in the same module potentially need to share access to pending invocations. We could employ one pending set per module, but then all processes in the module would compete for access to the set even if they do not service the same operation. This would lead to delays waiting to access the set and to unnecessary overhead examining invocations that could not possibly be acceptable. Consequently, we will employ multiple sets of pending invocations, one per operation class as defined below.

An *operation class* is an equivalence class of the transitive closure of the relation "serviced by the same input statement." For example, if operations `a` and `b` appear in an input statement, they are in the same class. If `a` and `c` appear in a different input statement—which would have to be in the same module—then `c` is also in the same class as `a` and `b`. In the worst case, every operation in a module is in the same class. In the best case, each operation is in its own class (e.g., if each is serviced by receive statements).

A reference to an operation that is serviced by input statements contains a pointer to an operation descriptor. This in turn contains a pointer to an operation-class descriptor. Both descriptors are stored on the machine on which the operation is serviced. The class descriptor contains the following information:

lock — used for mutually exclusive access
pending list — pending invocations of operations in the class
new list — invocations that arrive while the class is locked
access list — processes waiting for the lock
waiting list — processes waiting for new invocations to arrive

The lock is used to ensure that at most one process at a time is examining pending invocations. The other fields are used as described below.

The call and send statements are implemented as follows. If an operation is serviced by a procedure on the same machine, then a call statement is turned into a direct procedure call. A process can determine this by looking at the fields of the operation reference defined above. If an operation is on another machine or it is serviced by input statements, then a call statement executes the **invoke** primitive on the local machine. Independently of how an operation is serviced, a send statement executes the **invoke** primitive.

Figure 10.11 contains the code for the **invoke** primitive and two kernel routines it uses. The first argument indicates the kind of invocation. For a **CALL** invocation, the kernel blocks the executing process until the invocation has been serviced. Then the kernel determines whether the operation is serviced locally or on a remote machine. If it is serviced remotely, the kernel sends an **INVOKE** message to the remote kernel. The **localInvoke** routine gets executed by the kernel that services the operation.

```
type howInvoked = enum(CALL, SEND);
type howServiced = enum(PROC, IN);
type opRef = rec(howServiced how; int machine, opid);

proc invoke(howInvoked how; opRef op; byte values[*]) {
  if (how == CALL)
    insert executing on call delay list;
  if (op.machine is local)
    localInvoke(executing, how, op, values);
  else {    # machine is remote
    netWrite(machine, INVOKE, (executing,how,op,values));
    dispatcher();
  }
}
```

```
proc localInvoke(int caller; howInvoked inv;
                  opRef op; byte values[*]) {
  if (op.how == PROC) {
    get free process descriptor;
    if (inv == CALL)
      save identity of caller in the descriptor;
    else      # inv == SEND
      record that there is no caller (set caller field to zero);
    set program counter for the process to op.address;
    push values onto process stack; insert descriptor on ready list;
  }
  else {      # op.how == IN
    look up class descriptor for the operation;
    if (inv == CALL)
      append(opclass, caller, op.opid, values);
    else      # inv == SEND
      append(opclass, 0, op.opid, values);
  }
  dispatcher();
}


proc append(int opclass, caller, opid; byte values[*]) {
  if (opclass is locked) {
    insert (caller, opid, values) into new invocations list;
    move processes (if any) from wait list to access list;
  }
  else {    # opclass not locked
    insert (caller, opid, values) into pending list;
    if (wait list not empty) {
      move first process to ready list;
      move other processes to access list;
      set the lock;
    }
  }
}
```

Figure 10.11   Invocation primitives.

The `localInvoke` routine checks to see if an operation is serviced by a procedure. If so, it grabs a free process descriptor and dispatches a server process to execute the procedure, as happened in the RPC kernel. The kernel also records in the descriptor whether the operation was called. This information is used later to determine whether there is a caller that needs to be awakened when the procedure returns.

If an operation is serviced by an input statement, `localInvoke` examines the class descriptor. If the class is locked—because a process is executing an input statement and examining pending invocations—the kernel saves the invocation in the list of new invocations and moves any processes waiting for new invocations to the access list of the class. If the class is not locked, the kernel saves the invocation in the pending set and then checks the waiting list. (The access list is empty whenever the class is not locked.) If some process is waiting for new invocations, one waiting process is awakened, the lock is set, and any other waiting processes are moved to the access list.

When a process finishes executing a procedure, it calls kernel primitive `procDone`, shown in Figure 10.12. This primitive frees the process descriptor and then awakens the caller if there is one. The `awakenCaller` routine is executed by the kernel on which the caller resides.

For input statements, a process executes the code shown in Figure 10.13. That code then calls the input statement primitives shown in Figure 10.14. A process first acquires exclusive access to the class descriptor of the operation and

```
proc procDone(byte results[*]) {
    put executing back on free descriptor list;
    look up identity of caller  (if any) in process descriptor;
    if (caller is local)
        awakenCaller(caller, results);
    else if (caller is remote)
        netWrite(caller's machine, RETURN, (caller, results));
    dispatcher();
}

proc awakenCaller(int caller; byte results[*]) {
    remove descriptor of caller from call delay list;
    put results on caller's stack; insert descriptor on ready list;
}
```

Figure 10.12   Return primitives.

```
startIn(opclass);
while (true) {
  # loop until find an acceptable invocation
  search pending list of opclass  for acceptable invocation;
  if  (found one)
     break;  # exit the loop
  waitNew(opclass);
}
remove the invocation from pending list of opclass;
execute the appropriate guarded operation;
inDone(opclass, caller, result values);
```

Figure 10.13   Input statement code executed by a process.

then searches pending invocations for one that is acceptable. If no pending invocation is acceptable, the process calls `waitNew` to delay until there is a new invocation. This primitive might return immediately if a new invocation arrives while the process is searching the pending list, and hence the class descriptor is locked.

Once a process finds an acceptable invocation, it executes the appropriate guarded operation and then calls `inDone`. The kernel awakens the caller, if there is one, and then updates the class descriptor. If new invocations arrive while the input statement is executing, they are moved to the pending set, and any processes waiting for new invocations are moved to the access list. Then, if some process is waiting to access the class, one waiting process is awakened; otherwise, the lock is cleared.

This implementation of input statements handles the most general case. It can be optimized for the following, fairly frequent special cases:

- If all operations in a class are serviced by just one process, then the access list is not needed since the server will never have to wait to acquire the lock. (The lock itself is still needed, however, so that the `append` routine can determine whether to insert a new invocation in the new or pending lists.)

- If an operation is in a class by itself and is serviced by receive statements or by input statements that do not contain synchronization or scheduling expressions, then pending invocations are serviced in FIFO order, as they are with message passing. To handle this case, we can add a kernel primitive to delay the server until there is a pending invocation and then return it

```
proc startIn(int opclass) {
   if (opclass locked)
      insert executing on access list for opclass;
   else
      set the lock;
   dispatcher();
}

proc waitNew(int opclass) {
   look up descriptor of operation class opclass;
   if (new invocations list not empty)
      move new invocations to pending list;
   else {
      insert executing on wait list of opclass;
      if (access list empty)
         clear the lock;
      else
         move first process from access list to ready list;
   }
   dispatcher();
}

proc inDone(int opclass, caller; byte results[*]) {
   if (caller is local)
      call awakenCaller(caller, results);
   else if (caller is remote)
      netWrite(caller's machine, RETURN, (caller,results));
   if (new invocations list of opclass not empty) {
      move invocations from new to pending list;
      move processes (if any) from waiting list to access list;
   }
   if (access list of opclass not empty)
      move first descriptor to ready list;
   else
      clear the lock;
   dispatcher();
}
```

Figure 10.14   Input statement primitives.

to the server. There is no need for the server to lock the class and then search the pending list.

- If an operation is effectively a semaphore—it has no parameters or return value, is invoked by `send`, and is serviced by `receive`—then it can be implemented by a semaphore.

These optimizations lead to significant performance improvements.

10.4 Distributed Shared Memory

As noted in the introduction to this chapter, shared-memory machines are usually programmed using shared variables, and distributed-memory machines are usually programmed using message passing (or RPC or rendezvous). However, it is straightforward to support message passing on shared-memory machines, as we showed in Section 10.1. It is also possible—although less straightforward—to support shared variables on distributed-memory machines. Here we summarize how this is done; the Historical Notes and References give pointers to detailed descriptions.

Recall that in a shared-memory multiprocessor, every processor can access every memory location (see Section 1.2). Because memory access time is much larger than the cycle time of processors, multiprocessors employ caches to improve performance. Each processor has one or more levels of cache that contain copies of the memory locations most recently referenced by the code executed by that processor. A cache is organized as a collection of cache lines, each of which contains one or more contiguous words of memory. The hardware implements memory consistency protocols to keep the contents of caches consistent with each other and with primary memory.

A *distributed shared memory* (DSM) is a software implementation of these same concepts on a distributed-memory machine. In particular, a DSM provides a virtual address space that is accessible to every processor. This address space is typically organized as a set of pages, which are distributed among the local memories of the processors. There might be one copy of each page, or it might be replicated, with copies on more than one processor. When a process references an address on a nonlocal page, it has to acquire a copy of the page. A *page consistency protocol* is used to manage the movement of pages and their contents.

The rationale for providing a DSM is that most programmers find it easier to write concurrent programs using shared variables rather than message passing. This is due in part to the fact that shared variables are a familiar concept in sequential programming. However, a DSM introduces overhead to service page faults, to send and receive pages, and to wait for a remote page to arrive. The challenge is to minimize the overhead.

Below we describe how a DSM is implemented; the implementation itself is another example of a distributed program. Then we describe some of the common page consistency protocols and how they support data access patterns in application programs.

10.4.1 Implementation Overview

A DSM is a software layer that lies between an application program and an underlying operating system or special purpose kernel. Figure 10.15 shows the overall structure. The address space of each processor (node) consists of both shared and private sections. The shared variables in an application program are stored in the shared section. The code and private data of the processes are stored in the private section. Thus, we can think of the shared section as containing the heap for the program, with the private sections containing the code segments and process stacks. The private section of each node also contains a copy of the DSM software and the node's operating system or communication kernel.

The DSM implements and manages the shared section of the address space. This is a linear array of bytes that is conceptually replicated on each node. The shared section is divided into individually protected units, each of which resides on one or a few of the nodes. Most commonly, the units are fixed-size pages, although they could be variable-size pages or individual data objects. Here we will assume fixed-size pages. The pages are managed in a way analogous to a paged virtual memory on a single processor. In particular, a page is either resident (present) or not. If present, it is read only or readable and writable.

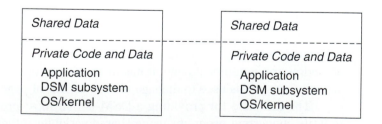

Figure 10.15   Structure of a distributed shared memory system.

Each shared variable in an application is mapped into an address in the shared section, and hence it has the same address on all nodes. The pages in the shared section are initially distributed among the nodes in some fashion. For now, we will assume that there is exactly one copy of each page and that it is both readable and writable on the node that has the copy.

When a process references a shared variable on a resident page, it accesses the variable directly. However, when it references a shared variable on a non-resident page, a page fault occurs. The page fault is handled by the DSM software, which determines where the page is located and sends a message to that node requesting the page. The second node marks the page as no longer resident and sends it back to the first node. When the first node receives the page, it updates the page's protection, then returns to the application process. As in a virtual memory system, the application process reissues the instruction that caused the page fault; the reference to the shared variable now succeeds.

To illustrate the above points, consider the following simple example:

```
int x = 0, y = 0;

process P1 {
    x = 1;
}

process P2 {
    y = 1;
}
```

Two nodes have been given. Process `P1` executes on the first node and `P2` on the second. Assume that the shared variables are stored on a single page that initially resides on the first node. This scenario is shown at the top of Figure 10.16.

The processes could execute in parallel or in either order, but assume that `P1` executes first and assigns to `x`. Because the page containing `x` is currently located on node `1`, the write succeeds and the process terminates. Now `P2` executes. It attempts to write `y`, but the page containing `y` is not resident, so the write causes a page fault. The fault handler on node `2` sends a request for the page to node `1`, which sends the page back to node `2`. After receiving the page, node `2` restarts process `P2`; the write to `y` now succeeds. So in the final state, the page is resident on the second node and both variables have been updated.

When a DSM is implemented on top of a Unix operating system, protection for shared pages is set using the `mprotect` system call. The protection for a resident page is set to `READ` or to `READ` and `WRITE`; the protection for a nonresident page is set to `NONE`. When a nonresident page is referenced, a segmentation violation signal (`SIGSEGV`) is generated. The page-fault handler in the DSM catches

	Node 1	Node 2
initial state	x = 0, y = 0	
1.	write **x**, no fault	
2.		write **y**, page fault
3.		send request to Node 1
4.	send page to Node 2	
5.		receive page
6.		write **y**, no fault
final state		x = 1, y = 1

Figure 10.16   Page fault handling in a DSM.

this signal. It sends a page-request message using UNIX communication primitives (or customized ones). The arrival of a message at a node generates an IO signal (**SIGIO**). The handler for IO signals determines the type of message (page request or reply) and takes the appropriate action. The signal handlers need to execute as critical sections because a new signal could occur while one is being handled—for example, a request for a page could arrive while a page fault is being handled.

A DSM can be either single-threaded or multithreaded. A single-threaded DSM supports only one application process per node. When that process incurs a page fault, it delays until the fault has been resolved. A multithreaded DSM supports more than one application process per node; so when one process causes a page fault, another can be executed while the first is waiting for the fault to be resolved. It is easier to implement a single-threaded DSM because there are fewer critical sections. However, a multithreaded DSM has a much better chance to mask the latency of a remote page reference, and hence is likely to have much better performance.

10.4.2 Page Consistency Protocols

The performance of an application executed on top of a DSM is affected by the efficiency of the DSM itself. This includes whether the DSM is able to mask page access latency as well as the efficiency of the signal handlers and especially the communication protocols. The performance of an application is also greatly dependent upon how pages are managed—namely, upon what *page consistency protocol* is employed. Below we describe three of the possibilities: migratory, write invalidate, and write shared.

In the example in Figure 10.16, we assumed there was exactly one copy of the page. When another node needs it, the copy moves. This is called the *migratory protocol*. The contents of the page are obviously consistent at all times because there is only one copy. However, what happens if two processes on different nodes merely want to read variables on the page? Then, the page will keep bouncing between them in a process called *thrashing*.

The *write invalidate protocol* allows pages to be replicated when they are being read. Each page has an owner. When a process tries to read a remote page, it acquires a read-only copy from the owner. The owner's copy is also at that time marked as read-only. When a process tries to write into a page, it gets a copy (if necessary), invalidates the other copies, and then writes into the page. In particular, the page fault handler on the node doing the write (1) contacts the owner, (2) gets back the page and ownership of it, (3) sends invalidate messages to nodes that have copies (they set the protection on their copy to `NONE`), (4) sets the protection on its copy to `READ` and `WRITE`, and then (5) resumes the application process.

The write invalidate protocol is very efficient for pages that are read-only (after they are initialized) and for pages that are infrequently modified. However, it leads to thrashing when *false sharing* occurs. Consider again the scenario in Figure 10.16. Variables `x` and `y` are not shared by the two processes, but they reside on the same page and that page is shared. Hence, the page would move between the two nodes in Figure 10.16 in the same way with the write invalidate protocol as it does with the migratory protocol.

False sharing can be eliminated by placing variables such as `x` and `y` on different pages; this can be done statically at compile time or dynamically at run time. Alternatively, false sharing can be tolerated by using the *write shared protocol*, a process that allows multiple concurrent writers to a page. For example, when process `P2` executing on node 2 in Figure 10.16 writes into `y`, node `2` gets a copy of the page from node `1` and both nodes have permission to write into it. Obviously, the copies will become inconsistent. At application-specified synchronization points, such as barriers, the copies are merged into a single copy. If there was false sharing on the page, the merged copy will be correct and consistent. However, if there was true sharing on the page, the merged copy will be some nondeterministic combination of the values that were written. To handle this, each node keeps a list of the changes it makes to a write-shared page; these lists are then used to make a merged copy that reflects a possible interleaving of the writes made by different processes.

Historical Notes

Implementations of communication primitives have existed as long as the primitives themselves. The Historical Notes of Chapters 7 through 9 mention several papers that describe new primitives; many of those papers also describe how to implement them. Two good general references are Bacon [1998] and Tanenbaum [1992]. These books describe communication primitives and implementation issues in general and also give case studies of important operating systems.

In the distributed kernel in Section 10.1, we assumed that network transmission was error free and we ignored buffer management and flow control. Books on computer networks describe how to handle these issues—for example, see Tanenbaum [1988] or Peterson and Davie [1996].

The centralized implementation of synchronous message passing (Figures 10.6 to 10.8.) was developed by this author. Several people have developed decentralized implementations that do not have a centralized coordinator. Silberschatz [1979] assumes processes form a ring. Van de Snepscheut [1981] considers hierarchical systems. Bernstein [1980] presents an implementation that works for any communication topology. Schneider [1982] presents a broadcast algorithm that essentially replicates the pending sets of our clearinghouse process (Figure 10.8). Schneider's algorithm is simple and fair, but it requires a large number of messages since every process has to acknowledge every broadcast. Buckley and Silberschatz [1983] give a fair, decentralized algorithm that is a generalization of Bernstein's; it is more efficient than Schneider's but is much more complex. (All the above algorithms are described in Raynal [1988].) Bagrodia [1989] describes yet another algorithm that is simpler and more efficient than Buckley and Silberschatz's.

In Section 10.3, we presented implementations of rendezvous using asynchronous message passing and a kernel. The performance of rendezvous is in general quite poor relative to other synchronization mechanisms because it is more complex. However, in many cases it is possible to transform programs so that rendezvous is replaced by less expensive mechanisms such as procedures and semaphores. For example, Roberts et al. [1981] show how to transform many instances of Ada's rendezvous mechanisms. McNamee and Olsson [1990] present a more extensive set of transformations and analyze the speed-up that is gained, which is up to 95 percent in some cases.

The concept of a distributed shared memory (DSM) was invented by Kai Li in a doctoral dissertation at Yale University supervised by Paul Hudak. Li and Hudak [1989] describe that work, which introduced the write invalidate page consistency protocol. Li made a landmark contribution because at the time practically everyone believed that it was impossible to simulate shared memory using message passing with anything close to reasonable performance. DSMs are now fairly commonplace and are even supported by many supercomputer manufacturers.

Two of the more important recent DSM systems are Munin and Tread-Marks, which were developed at Rice University. Carter, Bennett, and Zwaenepoel [1991] describe the implementation and performance of Munin, which introduced the write shared protocol. Amza et al. [1996] describe Tread-Marks; Lu et al. [1997] compare the performance of PVM and TreadMarks. Tanenbaum [1995] gives an excellent overview of DSMs, including Li's work, Munin, and others. For even more recent work, see the special issue on DSMs in *Proceedings of IEEE* (March 1999).

References

Amza, C., A. L. Cox, S. Dwarkadas, P. Keleher, H. Lu, R. Rajamony, W. Yu, and W. Zwaenepoel. 1996. TreadMarks: Shared memory computing on networks of workstations. *IEEE Computer* 29, 2 (February): 18–28.

Bacon, J. 1998. *Concurrent Systems: Operating Systems, Database and Distributed Systems: An Integrated Approach*, 2nd ed. Reading, MA: Addison-Wesley.

Bagrodia, R. 1989. Synchronization of asynchronous processes in CSP. *ACM Trans. on Prog. Languages and Systems* 11, 4 (October): 585–97.

Bernstein, A. J. 1980. Output guards and non-determinism in CSP. *ACM Trans. on Prog. Languages and Systems* 2, 2 (April): 234–38.

Buckley, G. N., and A. Silberschatz. 1983. An effective implementation for the generalized input-output construct of CSP. *ACM Trans. on Prog. Languages and Systems* 5, 2 (April): 223–35.

Carter, J. B., J. K. Bennett, and W. Zwaenepoel. 1991. Implementation and performance of Munin. *Proc. 13th ACM Symposium on Operating Systems Principles*, October, pp. 152–64.

Li, K., and P. Hudak. 1989. Memory coherence in shared virtual memory systems. *ACM Trans. on Computer Systems* 7, 4 (November): 321–59.

Lu, H., S. Dwarkadas, A. L. Cox, and W. Zwaenepoel. 1997. Quantifying the performance differences between PVM and TreadMarks. *Journal of Par. and Distr. Computation* 43, 2 (June): 65–78.

McNamee, C. M., and R. A. Olsson. 1990. Transformations for optimizing interprocess communication and synchronization mechanisms. *Int. Journal of Parallel Programming* 19, 5 (October): 357–87.

Peterson, L. L., and B. S. Davie. 1996. *Computer Networks: A Systems Approach.* San Francisco: Morgan Kaufmann.

Raynal, M. 1988. *Distributed Algorithms and Protocols.* New York: Wiley.

Roberts, E. S., A. Evans, C. R. Morgan, and E. M. Clarke. 1981. Task management in Ada—a critical evaluation for real-time multiprocessors. *Software—Practice and Experience* 11: 1019–51.

Schneider, F. B. 1982. Synchronization in distributed programs. *ACM Trans. on Prog. Languages and Systems*, 2 (April): 125–48.

Silberschatz, A. 1979. Communication and synchronization in distributed programs. *IEEE Trans. on Software Engr.* SE-5, 6 (November): 542–46.

Tanenbaum, A. S. 1988. *Computer Networks*, 2nd ed. Englewood Cliffs, NJ: Prentice-Hall.

Tanenbaum, A. S. 1992. *Modern Operating Systems.* Englewood Cliffs, NJ: Prentice-Hall.

Tanenbaum, A. S. 1995. *Distributed Operating Systems.* Englewood Cliffs, NJ: Prentice-Hall.

van de Snepscheut, J. L. A. 1981. Synchronous communication between asynchronous components. *Inf. Proc. Letters* 13, 3 (December): 127–30.

Exercises

10.1 Consider the distributed kernel in Figures 10.3 and 10.4.

(a) Extend the implementation to allow a channel to have multiple receivers. In particular, change the `receiveChan` and `emptyChan` primitives so that a process on one machine can access a channel stored on another machine.

(b) Modify the kernel so `sendChan` is what is called *semisynchronous*. In particular, when a process invokes `sendChan`, it should delay until the message has been queued on the channel (or given to a receiver)—even if the channel is stored on another machine.

(c) Add termination detection code to the kernel. Ignore pending I/O; hence a computation has terminated when all ready lists are empty and the network is idle.

10.2 The implementation of synchronous message passing in Figure 10.5 assumes that both the source and destination processes name each other. It is more common for a destination process to be able either to specify the source or to accept a message from any source. Assume processes are numbered from 1 to n and that 0 is used by a receiving process to specify that it wants a message from any source; in the latter case, the input statement sets **source** to the identity of the process that sent the output message.

Modify the communication protocols in Figure 10.5 to handle this situation. As in the figure, you are to use asynchronous message passing as a foundation for implementing the above form of synchronous message passing.

10.3 Develop a kernel implementation of the synchronous message passing primitives **synch_send** and **synch_receive** defined at the start of Section 10.2. First develop a single-processor kernel. Then develop a distributed kernel having the structure shown in Figure 10.2. You may borrow any routines you might need from Figures 10.3 and 10.4.

10.4 Assume that you have been given the processes **P[1:n]**, each initially having one value **a[i]** of an array of n values. The following program uses synchronous message passing; it is written in the CSP notation described in Section 7.6. In the program, each process sends its value to all the others. When the program terminates, every process has the entire array of values.

```
process P[i = 1 to n] {
   int a[1:n];   # a[i] assumed to be initialized
   bool sent[1:n] = ([n] false);
   int recvd = 0;
   do [j = 1 to n] (i != j and not sent[j]);
           P[j]!a[i] -> sent[j] = true;
   [] [j = 1 to n] (i != j and recvd < n-1);
           P[j]?a[j] -> recvd = recvd+1;
   od
}
```

The quantifiers in the arms of the **do** statement indicate that there are n copies of each arm, one for each value of quantifier variable **j**.

(a) Provide a trace of one possible sequence of messages that would be sent if this program is implemented using the centralized clearinghouse process of Figure 10.8. Assume n is three. how the messages that would be sent by the processes and by the clearinghouse, and show the contents at each stage of the clearinghouse's pending set of templates.

(b) What is the *total* number of messages sent to *and* from the clearinghouse in your answer to (a)? What is the total number as a function of n for larger values of n?

10.5 The algorithm in Figure 9.13 gives a fair, decentralized implementation of semaphores. It uses **broadcast**, timestamps, and totally ordered message queues.

(a) Using the same kind of algorithm, develop a fair, decentralized implementation of synchronous message passing. Assume both input and output statements can appear in guards. (*Hint:* Generalize the centralized implementation in Section 10.2 by replicating the clearinghouse's pending set of templates.)

(b) Illustrate the execution of your algorithm for the program containing processes **A** and **B** near the end of Section 10.2.

10.6 The kernel in Figures 10.11 to 10.14 implements the multiple primitives notation defined in Section 8.3.

(a) Suppose a language has just the rendezvous mechanisms defined in Section 8.2. In particular, operations are invoked only by **call** and serviced only by **in** statements. Also, each operation is serviced only by the one process that declares it. Simplify the kernel as much as possible so that it implements just this set of mechanisms.

(b) In Ada, the equivalent of the **in** statement is further restricted as follows: Synchronization expressions cannot reference formal parameters, and there are no scheduling expressions. Modify your answer to (a) to implement this restricted form of **in** statement.

10.7 Consider the Linda primitives defined in Section 7.7.

(a) Develop an implementation of the primitives by modifying the centralized clearinghouse process in Figure 10.8. Also show the actions that regular processes would take for each of the Linda primitives (as in Figure 10.7).

(b) Develop a distributed kernel implementation of the Linda primitives. The level of detail should be comparable to that in Figures 10.3 and 10.4.

10.8 Figure 10.16 illustrates the actions of a DSM that uses the migratory page consistency protocol. In the example, there are two processes. The first executes on Node 1 and writes variable **x**; the second process executes on Node 2 and writes variable **y**. Both variables are stored on the same page, and that page is initially stored on Node 1.

(a) Develop a trace of the actions of a DSM that uses the write invalidate protocol. Assume that the process that writes **x** executes first.

(b) Repeat (a) assuming that the process that writes y executes first.

(c) Develop a trace of the actions of a DSM that uses the write shared protocol. Assume that the process that writes x executes first.

(d) Repeat (c) assuming that the process that writes y executes first.

(e) Repeat (c) assuming that the processes execute concurrently.

(f) When a DSM uses the write shared protocol, a page becomes inconsistent if two or more processes write into it. Assume that pages are made consistent at barrier synchronization points. Extend your answer to part (e) to include a barrier after the two writes, then extend your trace with actions the nodes should take to make consistent the two copies of the page.

Part 3

Parallel Programming

The term *concurrent program* refers to any program that contains multiple processes. Part 1 described how to write concurrent programs in which processes communicate using shared variables and synchronize using busy waiting, semaphores, or monitors. Part 2 described how to write concurrent programs in which processes communicate and synchronize using message passing, RPC, or rendezvous. The latter type of concurrent program is called a *distributed program*, because the processes are usually distributed among processors that do not share memory.

In Part 3 we examine *parallel programs*, which are a different subset of concurrent programs. The distinguishing attribute of a parallel program is that it is written to solve a problem in less time than would be taken by a sequential program. In other words, the main goal is to reduce execution time. One reason for writing parallel programs is to solve larger problems in the same amount of time. Another reason is to solve more instances of the same problem in the same amount of time. For example, a program that forecasts weather has to finish in a timely fashion and should ideally be as accurate as possible. One way to increase accuracy is to use a more detailed weather model; another way is to run a given model multiple times with varying initial conditions. In both cases, implementing the model as a parallel program can make it possible to get results in time for them to be useful.

A parallel program can be written using either shared variables or message passing. The choice is usually dictated by the type of architecture on which the program will execute. In particular, a parallel program that is to be executed on a shared-memory multiprocessor is typically written using shared variables for communication, while a parallel program that is to be executed on a multicomputer or network of machines is typically written using message passing.

527

We have already seen several examples of parallel programs, including matrix multiplication, adaptive quadrature, data parallel algorithms, prime number generation, and image processing. (The exercises at the end of each chapter describe many others.) We now examine the important topic of high-performance computing, which is concerned with using parallel machines to solve *large* problems in science and engineering.

Chapter 11 describes three important classes of scientific applications: (1) grid computations for approximating solutions to partial differential equations, (2) particle computations for modeling systems of interacting bodies, and (3) matrix computations for solving systems of linear equations. For each, we describe a representative problem and develop parallel programs that use shared variables as well as message passing.

The programs in Chapter 11 are written using the language mechanisms and programming techniques described in Parts 1 and 2. Chapter 12 describes additional languages, compilers, libraries, and tools for parallel high-performance computing. Specific topics include the OpenMP library for shared-memory parallelism, parallelizing compilers, data parallel and functional languages, abstract models, the High-Performance Fortran (HPF) programming language, and the Globus toolkit for scientific metacomputations.

Before examing specific applications, we first define a few key concepts that pervade parallel programming: speedup, efficiency, sources of overhead, and challenges that have to be overcome to achieve good performance.

Speedup and Efficiency

As noted, the goal of parallel programming is to solve a problem faster, but what exactly does this mean? The *performance* of a program is its total execution time. Let T_1 be the execution time for solving some problem using a sequential program executed on a single processor. Let T_p be the execution time for solving the *same* problem using a parallel program that is executed on p processors. Then the *speedup* of the parallel program is defined as

Speedup $= T_1 / T_p$

For example, if the execution time for the sequential program is 600 seconds and the execution time for the parallel program on 10 processors is 60 seconds, then the speedup of the parallel program is 10. This is called *linear* (or perfect) speedup because the program is 10 times faster using 10 processors. The more typical case is that the speedup on p processors is less than p; this is called *sublinear speedup*. Occasionally, speedup is actually *superlinear*—namely, greater than p; this can happen when a program's data is too large to fit into the cache of a single processor but when divided up is able to fit into the caches of p processors.

Efficiency is the dual of speedup—a measure of how well a parallel program utilizes extra processors. It is defined as follows:

$$\text{Efficiency} \;=\; \text{Speedup}\,/\,p \;=\; T_1\,/\,(p * T_p)$$

If a program has linear speedup, its efficiency will be 1.0. An efficiency of less than 1.0 means that the speedup is sublinear; an efficiency of greater than 1.0 means that speedup is superlinear.

Speedup and efficiency are relative measures. They depend on the number of processors, the problem size, and the algorithm that is used. For example, the efficiency of a parallel program often decreases as the number of processors increases; for example, it might be close to 1.0 for small numbers of processors but decrease as p increases. Similarly, a parallel program might be quite efficient for solving large problems, but not for solving small problems. A parallel program is said to *scale* if its efficiency is constant for a broad range of numbers of processors and problem sizes. Finally, speedup and efficiency depend on the algorithm that is used. For example, a parallel program might be efficient relative to one sequential algorithm, but not relative to a different sequential algorithm. Thus one has to be careful to consider whether a parallel program is efficient simply because it performs well relative to a poor sequential program. A better metric is *absolute efficiency* (or absolute speedup), in which T_1 is the execution time using the best-known sequential algorithm.

Speedup and efficiency depend on total execution times. A typical program has three phases: (1) input, (2) compute, and (3) output. Suppose that in a sequential program, the input and output phases each take 10 percent of the execution time and that the compute phase takes the remaining 80 percent. Further suppose that the input and output phases are inherently sequential—namely, that they cannot be made faster by using a parallel program. Then the *best* speedup that a parallel program can achieve is only *five*! Consequently, no matter how many processors are used, the input and output phases will still remain at this level. For example, if they each take 10 seconds—and hence the compute phase takes 80 seconds—the minimum time for *any* parallel program will be more than 20 seconds even if the compute phase is reduced to nearly zero seconds. Thus the speedup is limited by 100 / 20, or five.

The above limit on speedup follows from what is called *Amdahl's Law* (named after its inventor). This law states that the amount of improvement that can be achieved by speeding up part of a computation is limited by the fraction of time taken by that part:

$$\text{Speedup}_{\text{overall}} = \text{Execution time}_{\text{old}} / \text{Execution time}_{\text{new}}$$

$$= 1 / (1 - \text{Fraction}_{\text{part}} + \text{Fraction}_{\text{part}} / \text{Speedup}_{\text{part}})$$

In our example, the fraction of the part that can be parallelized is 80 percent (or 0.8). Hence, if the speedup of the compute phase is infinite, the overall speedup is still only $1 / (1 - 0.8)$, which is five. However, the overall speedup on p processors will actually be less. For example, if the speedup of the computational part on 10 processors is a perfect 10, then the overall speedup will be $1 / (0.2 + 0.8 / 10)$, which is approximately 3.57.

Fortunately, for many applications the input and output phases take only a negligible fraction of the total execution time. Moreover, high-performance machines invariably provide hardware support for high-speed, parallel IO. Thus the overall performance of a parallel computation will in general be determined by how well we are able to parallelize the computational phase.

Overheads and Challenges

Suppose we are given a sequential program that solves some problem and have the task of writing a parallel program to solve the same problem. First we have to parallelize the various parts of the algorithm. In particular, we have to decide how many processes to employ, what each one does, and how they will communicate and synchronize. Obviously, the parallel program has to be correct, meaning that it computes the same results and is free of synchronization errors such as race conditions and deadlocks. In addition, we want to achieve the best possible performance—namely, to have the program, if possible, get speedup that scales with both the number of processors and with the problem size. Rarely is it possible to get perfect, scalable speedup, but we want at least to get "reasonable" speedup—where reasonable means informally that performance improves enough to make it worth using multiple processors. For example, even a modest speedup of two on a four-processor machine would make it possible to solve a problem that is twice as large in the same amount of time.

The most important determinant of performance is the algorithm that is employed. Thus we must start with a good algorithm in order to get good performance. We address this topic for each of the applications described in Chapter 11. In fact, sometimes the best parallel algorithm for solving a problem is different than the best sequential algorithm. For now, however, assume that we are given a good sequential algorithm and want to parallelize it.

The overall execution time of a parallel program is the sum of the computation time itself and overheads introduced by parallelism, communication, and synchronization. Any parallel program has to do the same total amount of work as a sequential program solving the same problem. Thus our first programming challenge is to parallelize the computation and assign the processes to processors so as to *balance the computational load*. In particular, let T_{comp} be the computation time of the sequential program. To achieve perfect speedup on p processors, we need to balance the load so that the time taken by each processor is close to T_{comp}/p. If one processor is assigned more load than another, then the second processor will be *idle* part of the time. Thus the total computation time—and hence performance—will be determined by the time taken by the processor that does the most work.

There are three sources of *overhead* in a parallel program in addition to any overhead in the sequential components: (1) process creation and scheduling, (2) communication, and (3) synchronization. These cannot be eliminated, so our second challenge is to minimize them. Unfortunately, the overheads are interdependent, so minimizing one may cause another to increase.

A parallel program has multiple processes that have to be created and scheduled for execution. The standard way to minimize these overheads is to create exactly one process per processor. This is the smallest number of processes that can actually utilize p processors. Moreover, if there is only one process per processor, then there will never be context switching overhead to switch a processor from executing one process to executing another. However, this means that whenever a process has to delay, its processor will be idle. If there were more processes, one could execute. Also, when processes have different amounts of work, it is much easier to balance computational load if there are more processes than processors. Finally, some applications are most easily programmed using recursive or fine-grained processes. Thus there are tradeoffs between the numbers of processes, load balancing, and process creation/scheduling overheads.

The second source of overhead is interprocess communication. This is especially true in programs that use message passing, because sending a message requires taking actions in the sender's and receiver's kernels and transferring the message on the network. The kernel overheads are unavoidable, so to minimize them it is important to minimize the number of messages. Message transfer times are also unavoidable, but they can be *masked* if a processor has other work to do while a message is in transit.

Communication can also introduce overheads even in programs that use shared variables and execute on shared-memory machines. This is because these machines employ caches and use hardware protocols to keep the caches consistent with each other and with primary memory. Moreover, large shared-memory machines have nonuniform memory access times. To minimize memory access overheads, the programmer needs to divide up the data so that each processor works on different parts, and place each part in a memory unit close to where it is used, especially if it is being written. Second, the programmer needs to avoid using shared variables as much as possible. Third, the programmer needs to avoid *false sharing*, which occurs when two variables are stored in the same cache line, are being accessed by different processors, and at least one of the processors is writing into its variable.

Synchronization is the final source of overhead, and it too is usually unavoidable. When processes are working together to solve a problem, they invariably have to synchronize. The common types of synchronization in parallel programs are critical sections, barriers, and message passing. To minimize overhead, we want to limit how often synchronization is required, use efficient synchronization protocols, and minimize delays (which can lead to idle time). For example, instead of accumulating a global result in a single shared variable that has to be protected by a critical section, we might use one variable per processor and have each processor—after a barrier, for example—compute the global value for itself. The extra computation time will typically be much less than the overhead introduced by critical sections. Alternatively, we might send a message as early as possible in a message-passing program to increase the likelihood that it will have arrived by the time another process wants to receive it; this will decrease and perhaps eliminate delays in the receiving process. We will illustrate the use of these and similar techniques in the examples in Chapter 11.

To summarize, the starting point for writing a parallel program is to pick a good algorithm. Then choose a parallelization strategy—namely, to decide how many processes to use and how the data will be divided among them to balance the computational load. Third, add communication and synchronization so that the processes correctly work together to solve the problem. While designing the program, keep the above sources of overhead in mind. Finally, after the program has been written and tested for correctness, measure and tune its performance to minimize overheads. By tuning performance we mean optimizing the program—by hand and by using compiler optimizations—to minimize its total execution time and hence to maximize its performance. We give some hints in the next two chapters on how to do this. The notes at the end of Chapter 12 also describe software systems that can be used to measure and visualize performance.

Scientific Computing

The two traditional modes of scientific discovery are *theory* and *experimentation*. For example, theoretical physics is concerned with devising models that explain physical phenomena, and experimental physics is concerned with examining physical phenomena, often to confirm or refute theoretical hypotheses. There is now a third mode of discovery, *computational modeling*, which uses computers to simulate phenomena and to address "what if?" questions. For example, a computational physicist might develop a program to simulate nuclear fusion or stellar evolution.

Computational modeling was made possible by the invention of high-performance computers in the 1960s. In fact, it is probably more appropriate to say that high-performance computers came about *because* of the needs of scientists and engineers. In any event, the fastest, largest machines have always been used to support scientific computing. This began with early vector processors and now includes massively parallel machines having tens or hundreds of processors. Computational modeling is currently used in all scientific and engineering fields for a dizzying array of applications—from developing new drugs, modeling the climate, and designing airplanes and cars to determining where to drill for oil and studying the movement of pollutants in aquifers.

Despite the plethora of scientific computing applications, and the corresponding plethora of computational models, three fundamental techniques are used again and again: (1) grid computations, (2) particle computations, and (3) matrix computations. Grid computations arise in numerical solutions to partial differential equations and in other applications (such as image processing) that divide a spatial region into a set of points. Particle computations arise in models that simulate the interactions of individual particles, such as molecules or stellar objects. Matrix computations arise whenever one is dealing with systems of simultaneous equations.

This chapter presents examples of grid, particle, and matrix computations. For each, we describe possible algorithms and develop a sequential program. We then develop parallel programs, first using shared variables and then using message passing. We also describe how to optimize the programs to improve performance.

11.1 Grid Computations

Partial differential equations (PDEs) are used to model a variety of different kinds of physical systems: weather, airflow over a wing, turbulence in fluids, and so on. Some simple PDEs can be solved directly, but in general it is necessary to approximate the solution at a finite number of points using iterative numerical methods. Here we show how to solve one specific PDE—Laplace's equation in two dimensions—by means of a grid computation that employs what is called a finite-difference method. Although we focus on this specific problem, the same programming techniques are used in grid computations for solving other PDEs and in other applications such as image processing.

11.1.1 Laplace's Equation

Laplace's equation is an example of what is called an elliptic partial differential equation. The equation for two dimensions is the following:

$$\frac{\partial^2 \Phi}{\partial x^2} + \frac{\partial^2 \Phi}{\partial y^2} = 0$$

Function Φ represents some unknown potential, such as heat or stress.

Given a spatial region and values for points on the boundaries of the region, the goal is to approximate the steady-state solution for points in the interior. We can do this by covering the region with an evenly spaced grid of points, as shown in Figure 11.1. Each interior point is initialized to some value. The steady-state values of the interior points are then calculated by repeated iterations. On each iteration the new value of a point is set to a combination of the old and/or new values of neighboring points. The computation terminates either after a given number of iterations or when every new value is within some acceptable difference **EPSILON** of every old value.

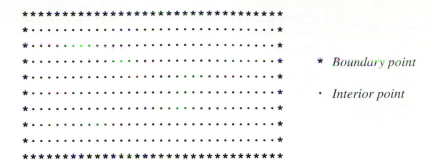

Figure 11.1   Approximating Laplace's equation using a grid.

There are several iterative methods for solving Laplace's equation, including Jacobi iteration, Gauss-Seidel, successive over-relaxation (SOR), and multigrid. We first show how to program Jacobi iteration—using both shared variables and message passing—because it is the simplest method and can be parallelized readily. Then we show how to program the other methods, which converge more rapidly. The algorithms for the other methods are somewhat more complex than Jacobi iteration, but their parallel programs have similar communication and synchronization patterns.

11.1.2 *Sequential Jacobi Iteration*

In Jacobi iteration, the new value for each grid point is set to the average of the old values of the four points left, right, above, and below it. This process is repeated until the computation terminates. Below we develop a simple sequential program, then we make a sequence of code optimizations that will improve the program's performance.

Assume that the grid is an $n \times n$ square and that it is surrounded by a square of boundary points. We need one matrix to represent the grid and its boundary and another for the set of new values:

```
real grid[0:n+1,0:n+1], new[0:n+1,0:n+1];
```

The boundaries of both matrices are initialized to the appropriate boundary conditions, and the interior points are initialized to some starting value such as zero. (For the first algorithm following, the new matrix would not need to store boundary values, but we will need them later.)

Assume for now that we want to terminate the computation when every new value on an iteration is within `EPSILON` of its prior value. Then the main computational loop for Jacobi iteration is as follows:

```
while (true) {
  # compute new values for all interior points
  for [i = 1 to n, j = 1 to n]
    new[i,j] = (grid[i-1,j] + grid[i+1,j] +
                grid[i,j-1] + grid[i,j+1]) / 4;
  iters++;
  # compute the maximum difference
  maxdiff = 0.0;
  for [i = 1 to n, j = 1 to n]
    maxdiff = max(maxdiff, abs(new[i,j]-grid[i,j]));
  # check for termination
  if (maxdiff < EPSILON)
    break;
  # copy new to grid to prepare for next updates
  for [i = 1 to n, j = 1 to n]
    grid[i,j] = new[i,j];
}
```

Above `maxdiff` is a real and `iters` is an integer that counts the number of update phases. The code assumes that arrays are stored in row-major order; if arrays are stored in column-major order (as in Fortran), then the `for` loops should iterate over `j` then `i` rather than `i` then `j`.

Although the above code is correct, it is not very efficient. However, we can greatly improve its performance. We do so below by examining each part and considering how to program that part more efficiently.

The assignment in the first `for` loop is executed n^2 times per update phase. The adds are needed, but the division by `4` can be replaced by a multiply by `0.25`. This will improve performance because it takes fewer machine cycles to execute a multiply than a divide; given that the operation is executed so many times, the improvement will be noticeable. This specific optimization is called *strength reduction*, because it replaces a "strong" (expensive) operation by a weaker one. (In fact, for integer values, divide by four could be replaced by an even weaker operation: shift right by 2.)

We next consider the part of the code that computes the maximum difference. This code is executed on every iteration of the while loop, but only once does it result in breaking out of that loop. It will be *much* more efficient to replace the while loop by a definite loop that iterates a fixed number of times. In essence, we switch the roles of `iters` and `maxdiff`: Instead of counting the number of iterations and using `maxdiff` to terminate the computation, we use `iters` to control the number of iterations to compute the maximum difference just once *after* the main computation loop. Applying this and the first optimization, our program is

```
for [iters = 1 to MAXITERS] {
  # compute new values for all interior points
  for [i = 1 to n, j = 1 to n]
    new[i,j] = (grid[i-1,j] + grid[i+1,j] +
                grid[i,j-1] + grid[i,j+1]) * 0.25;
  # copy new to grid to prepare for next updates
  for [i = 1 to n, j = 1 to n]
    grid[i,j] = new[i,j];
}
# compute the maximum difference
maxdiff = 0.0;
for [i = 1 to n, j = 1 to n]
  maxdiff = max(maxdiff, abs(new[i,j]-grid[i,j]));
```

Above **MAXITERS** is a constant or command-line argument. Although this code is not exactly the same as the original code, it still implements Jacobi iteration. If the programmer runs the new code and finds that the final value of **maxdiff** is too large, it is trivial to run the program again with a larger value for **MAXITERS**. A few conditioning runs should be sufficient to select a good value of **MAXITERS** to use for production runs of the code.

The second version of the code is much more efficient than the first, but we can still do quite a bit better. Now consider the loop that copies **new** to **grid**. We cannot just get rid of this code and update the grid points in place, because Jacobi iteration depends on using old values to compute new values. But the copy loop takes significant time. It would be much more efficient to use pointers to reference the matrices and to swap the pointers after each update phase. Equivalently, we can combine the two matrices into a single, three-dimensional matrix:

```
real grid[0:1][0:n+1,0:n+1];
int old = 0, new = 1;
```

Variables `old` and `new` are used to index the first dimension of `grid`.

With this change in representation, we can code the main loop as follows:

```
for [iters = 1 to MAXITERS] {
  # compute new values for all interior points
  for [i = 1 to n, j = 1 to n]
    grid[new][i,j] = (grid[old][i-1,j] +
          grid[old][i+1,j] + grid[old][i,j-1] +
          grid[old][i,j+1]) * 0.25;
  # swap roles of the grids
  old = 1-old; new = 1-new;
}
```

To swap the roles of the grids, all we have to do is swap the values of `old` and `new`. However, getting rid of the copy loop has a price: Each reference to `grid` in the update loop has an extra index and this will result in extra machine instructions to compute addresses of values in `grid`. Still, the extra execution time required for these instructions should be less than the execution time saved by getting rid of the copy loop.

The above tradeoff between getting rid of the copy loop and using more expensive array indexing can be avoided by using a fourth optimization: *loop unrolling*. The idea is to repeat the body one or more times and to make a corresponding reduction in the number of times the loop iterates. For example, if we unroll the outer loop above twice, we get

```
for [iters = 1 to MAXITERS by 2] {
  # compute new values for all interior points
  for [i = 1 to n, j = 1 to n]
    grid[new][i,j] = (grid[old][i-1,j] +
          grid[old][i+1,j] + grid[old][i,j-1] +
          grid[old][i,j+1]) * 0.25;
  # swap roles of the grids
  old = 1-old; new = 1-new;
  # compute new values for all interior points
  for [i = 1 to n, j = 1 to n]
    grid[new][i,j] = (grid[old][i-1,j] +
          grid[old][i+1,j] + grid[old][i,j-1] +
          grid[old][i,j+1]) * 0.25;
  # swap roles of the grids
  old = 1-old; new = 1-new;
}
```

Loop unrolling by itself has little effect on performance, but it often enables other

```
real grid[0:n+1,0:n+1], new[0:n+1,0:n+1];
real maxdiff = 0.0;
initialize the grids, including the boundaries;
for [iters = 1 to MAXITERS by 2] {
    # compute new values for all interior points
    for [i = 1 to n, j = 1 to n]
        new[i,j] = (grid[i-1,j] + grid[i+1,j] +
                    grid[i,j-1] + grid[i,j+1]) * 0.25;
    # compute new values again for interior points
    for [i = 1 to n, j = 1 to n]
        grid[i,j] = (new[i-1,j] + new[i+1,j] +
                    new[i,j-1] + new[i,j+1]) * 0.25;
}
# compute the maximum difference
for [i = 1 to n, j = 1 to n]
    maxdiff = max(maxdiff, abs(grid[i,j]-new[i,j]));
print the final grid and maximum difference;
```

Figure 11.2   Optimized sequential program for Jacobi iteration.

optimizations.[1] For example, in the previous code there is no longer *any* need to swap the roles of the grids. Instead, we can simply recode the second update loop to read from the new grid produced by the first update loop, and to assign values to the old grid. But then why bother having one, three-dimensional matrix? We can go back to using two separate matrices!

Figure 11.2 contains the optimized program for Jacobi iteration. To summarize, we have optimized the original code in four ways: (1) we have replaced divide by multiply; (2) we have used definite iteration to terminate the computation and computed the maximum difference just once; (3) we have combined the two matrices into a single matrix with an extra dimension to get rid of the need to swap matrices; and (4) we have unrolled the loop twice then recoded the loop body to get rid of the extra index and the swap statements. For this problem we could actually have gone directly from the second to the fourth optimizations. However, the third optimization is often useful.

We could also optimize the program in Figure 11.2 in two additional ways. Because we compute new values for points twice in the body of the outer **for**

---

[1] Performance will get worse if a loop is unrolled so many times that the instructions in the loop body no longer fit in the instruction cache of a processor.

loop, we could delete the multiply by `0.25` from the first compute loop and instead multiply by `0.0625` in the second compute loop. This gets rid of half of the multiplies. We could also optimize the program by *inlining* the function calls in the final loop, which computes the maximum difference. In particular, replace the calls of `max` and `abs` by the bodies of those functions, as follows:

```
temp = grid[i,j]-new[i,j];
if (temp < 0)
  temp = -temp;
if (temp > maxdiff)
  maxdiff = temp;
```

This gets rid of the overhead of two function calls. It also exploits the fact that `maxdiff` is used as a reduction variable (it is both an argument to `max` and where the result is stored). Here, function inlining will lead to only a slight performance improvement, because the maximum difference is computed only once in the program. However, inlining can be very effective when a function is called in an inner loop that is executed repeatedly.

11.1.3 Jacobi Iteration Using Shared Variables

We now consider how we might parallelize Jacobi iteration. We presented a data parallel program earlier in Figure 3.19. That program used one process per grid point, which is the granularity of parallelism that is possible for this problem. Although that program would execute efficiently on a synchronous multiprocessor (SIMD machine), it has far too many processes to be efficient on a conventional MIMD multiprocessor. This is because each process does very little work, so the context switching overhead would dominate execution time. In addition, each process would need its own stack, so the program would not fit in memory if the grid is very large. Hence the parallel program would perform much worse than a sequential program.

Suppose that we have `PR` processors and that the dimensionality of the grid, `n`, is much larger than `PR`. For an efficient parallel program, we want to divide the computation equally among the processors. That is easy for this problem, because updating each grid point involves the same amount of work. Hence, we want to use `PR` processes and have each of them be responsible for the same number of grid points. We could divide the grid either into `PR` rectangular blocks or into `PR` rectangular strips. We will use strips because that is slightly easier to program. It is also likely to be slightly more efficient, because long strips have somewhat better data locality than shorter blocks, and this will lead to better use of the data cache.

Assuming for simplicity that **n** is a multiple of **PR** and also that arrays are stored in memory in row-major order, we can assign each process a horizontal strip of size **n/PR** × **n**. Each process updates its strip of points. However, because the processes share the points on the edges of the strips, we need to use barrier synchronization after each update phase to ensure that every process has completed one update phase before any process begins the next one.

Figure 11.3 contains a parallel program for Jacobi iteration using shared variables. It uses the single program, multiple data (SPMD) style in which each process executes the same code but operates on different parts of the data. Here, each worker process first initializes its strips of the two grids, including the boundaries. The body of each worker process is adapted from the code in Figure 11.2. Barrier synchronization is implemented by a shared procedure that implements one of the algorithms in Section 3.4. For maximal efficiency, this should be a symmetric barrier such as a dissemination barrier.

Figure 11.3 also illustrates an efficient way to compute the maximum differences between all pairs of final values of the grid points. In particular, we have each worker compute the maximum difference for points in its strip—using a *local* variable **mydiff**—and then store this value in an array of maximum differences. After another barrier, every worker could then, in parallel, compute the maximum of the values in **maxdiff[*]**; alternatively, we could have just one worker do this computation. By using a local variable in each process, we (1) avoid having to use a critical section to protect access to a single global variable, and (2) avoid cache conflicts that could result from false sharing of the **maxdiff** array.

The program in Figure 11.3 would probably be slightly more efficient if we had inlined the calls of the **barrier** procedure. However, inlining the code by hand would make the program harder to read. We can get the best of both worlds by using a compiler that supports the inlining optimization.

11.1.4 *Jacobi Iteration Using Message Passing*

Now consider how we might implement Jacobi iteration on a distributed-memory machine. We could employ an implementation of distributed shared memory (Section 10.4) and simply use the program in Figure 11.3. This option is not widely available, however, and is not likely to produce the best performance. It is much more common, and invariably more efficient, to write a parallel program that uses message passing.

One way to develop a message-passing version of a parallel program is to modify a shared-variable program: First distribute the shared variables among the

```
real grid[0:n+1,0:n+1], new[0:n+1,0:n+1];
int HEIGHT = n/PR;    # assume PR evenly divides n
real maxdiff[1:PR] = ([PR] 0.0);

procedure barrier(int id) {
  # efficient barrier algorithm from Section 3.4
}

process worker[w = 1 to PR] {
  int firstRow = (w-1)*HEIGHT + 1;
  int lastRow = firstRow + HEIGHT - 1;
  real mydiff = 0.0;
  initialize my strips of grid and new, including boundaries;
  barrier(w);
  for [iters = 1 to MAXITERS by 2] {
    # compute new values for my strip
    for [i = firstRow to lastRow, j = 1 to n]
      new[i,j] = (grid[i-1,j] + grid[i+1,j] +
                       grid[i,j-1] + grid[i,j+1]) * 0.25;
    barrier(w);
    # compute new values again for my strip
    for [i = firstRow to lastRow, j = 1 to n]
      grid[i,j] = (new[i-1,j] + new[i+1,j] +
                       new[i,j-1] + new[i,j+1]) * 0.25;
    barrier(w);
  }
  # compute maximum difference for my strip
  for [i = firstRow to lastRow, j = 1 to n]
    mydiff = max(mydiff, abs(grid[i,j]-new[i,j]));
  maxdiff[w] = mydiff;
  barrier(w);
  # maximum difference is the max of the maxdiff[*]
}
```

Figure 11.3   Jacobi iteration using shared variables.

processes, then add send and receive statements when processes need to communicate. Another way is to examine the process interaction paradigms in Sections
9.1 to 9.3—bag of tasks, heartbeat, and pipeline—to see if one can be used.
Often, as here, we can employ both methods.

Starting with the program in Figure 11.3, we can again use **PR** worker processes and have each update a strip of grid points. We distributed the **grid** and

new arrays so that the strips are local to the appropriate worker. We also have to replicate the rows on the edges of the strips, because workers cannot read data local to other processes. In particular, each worker needs to store not only the points in its strip but also the points on the edges of neighboring strips. Each worker executes a sequence of update phases; after each update, a worker exchanges the edges of its strip with its neighbors. This is exactly the interaction pattern of a heartbeat algorithm (Section 9.2). The exchanges replace the barrier synchronization points in Figure 11.3.

We also need to distribute the computation of the maximum difference after each process finishes updating its strip of the grid. As in Figure 11.3, we can readily have each worker compute the maximum difference for its strip. Then we can have one worker collect all the values. We can program this using either process-to-process messages or collective communication as in MPI (Section 7.8).

Figure 11.4 gives a message-passing program for Jacobi iteration. It uses a heartbeat algorithm for each of the two update phases, so neighboring workers exchange edges twice per iteration of the main computational loop. The first exchange is programmed as

```
if (w > 1)   send up[w-1](new[1,*]);
if (w < PR)  send down[w+1](new[HEIGHT,*]);
if (w < PR)  receive up[w](new[HEIGHT+1,*]);
if (w > 1)   receive down[w](new[0,*]);
```

All workers but the first send the top row of their strip to the neighbor above; all workers but the last send the bottom row of their strip to the neighbor below. Each worker then receives edges from its neighbors; these become the boundaries of its strip. The second exchange is identical, except that **grid** is used instead of **new**.

After the appropriate number of iterations, each worker computes the maximum difference for its strip, and the first worker collects these values. As noted at the end of the program, the global maximum difference is the final value of **mydiff** in the first worker.

The program in Figure 11.4 can be optimized for better performance. First, for this and many grid computations, it is not necessary to exchange edges after every update phase. Here, for example, we could exchange edges after every other update. This will cause the values of edge points to "jump" somewhat, but as long as the algorithm converges, it will still produce a correct result. Second, we can reprogram the remaining exchange to do local computation between the sends and receives. In particular, we can have each worker (1) send its edges to neighbors, (2) update the interior points of its strip, (3) receive edges from

```
chan up[1:PR](real edge[0:n+1]);
chan down[1:PR](real edge[0:n+1]);
chan diff(real);

process worker[w = 1 to PR] {
  int HEIGHT = n/PR;    # assume PR evenly divides n
  real grid[0:HEIGHT+1,0:n+1], new[0:HEIGHT+1,0:n+1];
  real mydiff = 0.0, otherdiff = 0.0;
  initialize grid and new, including boundaries;
  for [iters = 1 to MAXITERS by 2] {
    # compute new values for my strip
    for [i = 1 to HEIGHT, j = 1 to n]
      new[i,j] = (grid[i-1,j] + grid[i+1,j] +
                      grid[i,j-1] + grid[i,j+1]) * 0.25;
    exchange edges of new -- see text;
    # compute new values again for my strip
    for [i = 1 to HEIGHT, j = 1 to n]
      grid[i,j] = (new[i-1,j] + new[i+1,j] +
                      new[i,j-1] + new[i,j+1]) * 0.25;
    exchange edges of grid -- see text;
  }
  # compute maximum difference for my strip
  for [i = 1 to HEIGHT, j = 1 to n]
    mydiff = max(mydiff, abs(grid[i,j]-new[i,j]));
  if (w > 1)
    send diff(mydiff);
  else        # worker 1 collects differences
    for [i = 1 to w-1] {
      receive diff(otherdiff);
      mydiff = max(mydiff, otherdiff);
    }
  # maximum difference is value of mydiff in worker 1
}
```

Figure 11.4   Jacobi iteration using message passing.

neighbors, and (4) update the edges of its strip. This will greatly increase the likelihood that neighboring edges will have arrived before they are needed and hence that receive statements will not need to delay. Figure 11.5 presents a program with these optimizations. We leave it to the reader to compare the performance and results of the two message-passing programs.

```
chan up[1:PR](real edge[0:n+1]);
chan down[1:PR](real edge[0:n+1]);
chan diff(real);

process worker[w = 1 to PR] {
  int HEIGHT = n/PR;    # assume PR evenly divides n
  real grid[0:HEIGHT+1,0:n+1], new[0:HEIGHT+1,0:n+1];
  real mydiff = 0.0, otherdiff = 0.0;
  initialize grid and new, including boundaries;
  for [iters = 1 to MAXITERS by 2] {
    # compute new values for my strip
    for [i = 1 to HEIGHT, j = 1 to n]
      new[i,j] = (grid[i-1,j] + grid[i+1,j] +
                    grid[i,j-1] + grid[i,j+1]) * 0.25;
    # send edges of new to neighbors
    if (w > 1)
      send up[w-1](new[1,*]);
    if (w < PR)
      send down[w+1](new[HEIGHT,*]);
    # compute new values for interior of my strip
    for [i = 2 to HEIGHT-1, j = 1 to n]
      grid[i,j] = (new[i-1,j] + new[i+1,j] +
                    new[i,j-1] + new[i,j+1]) * 0.25;
    # receive edges of new from my neighbors
    if (w < PR)
      receive up[w](new[HEIGHT+1,*]);
    if (w > 1)
      receive down[w](new[0,*]);
    # compute new values for edges of my strip
    for [j = 1 to n]
      grid[1,j] = (new[0,j] + new[2,j] +
                    new[1,j-1] + new[1,j+1]) * 0.25;
    for [j = 1 to n]
      grid[HEIGHT,j] = (new[HEIGHT-1,j] +
                    new[HEIGHT+1,j] + new[HEIGHT,j-1] +
                    new[HEIGHT,j+1]) * 0.25;
  }
  compute maximum difference as in Figure 11.4;
}
```

Figure 11.5   Optimized Jacobi iteration using message passing.

11.1.5 Red/Black Successive Over-Relaxation (SOR)

Jacobi iteration converges quite slowly. Intuitively this is because the value of any one point takes a long time to influence the value of points far away. For example, it takes `n/2` update phases before the boundary values have any influence on the center of the grid.

The Gauss-Seidel (GS) scheme converges more rapidly and also uses less space. It computes new values for points using a combination of old and new values of neighboring points. The idea is to sweep across the grid from left to right and top to bottom, in much the same way that a TV image is displayed on a picture tube. In particular, new points are computed *in place* by

```
for [i = 1 to n, j = 1 to n]
  grid[i,j] = (grid[i-1,j] + grid[i,j-1] +
               grid[i+1,j] + grid[i,j+1]) * 0.25;
```

Thus each new value depends on the just computed values above and to the left of it and the previous values to the right and below it. By updating points in place, we do not not need a second matrix.

Successive over-relaxation (SOR) is a generalization of Gauss-Seidel. With SOR, new points are computed in place by

```
for [i = 1 to n, j = 1 to n]
  grid[i,j] = omega * (grid[i-1,j] + grid[i,j-1] +
              grid[i+1,j] + grid[i,j+1]) * 0.25
            + (1-omega) * grid[i,j];
```

Variable `omega` is called the relaxation parameter; its value is chosen to be in the range $0 < omega < 2$. If `omega` is `1`, then SOR simplifies to Gauss-Seidel. If it is `0.5`, then the new value of a grid point is half of the average of its neighbors plus half of its old value. The choice of an appropriate value for `omega` depends on the PDE being solved and the boundary conditions.

Although GS and SOR converge faster than Jacobi iteration and require half the storage, it is difficult to parallelize these algorithms directly. This is because they use both old and new values to update a point. Stated differently, GS and SOR are able to update points in place exactly because they employ a sequential update order. (The loops in both algorithms have what are called data dependencies. They can be parallelized using what are called wave fronts. Both topics are discussed in Section 12.2.)

Fortunately, it is possible to parallelize GS and SOR by changing the algorithms slightly (they will still converge). First, color the points using a red/black scheme as with a checkerboard. In particular, starting with the upper-left point, color every other point red and the remaining points black, so that red points have black neighbors and black points have red neighbors. Second, replace the single loop in the update phase by two nested loops: the first updates the red points; the second updates the black points.

The red/black scheme can be parallelized because red points have black neighbors and black points have red neighbors. Hence, all red points can be updated in parallel because their new values depend only on old values for black points. Similarly, black points can be updated in parallel. However, barrier synchronization is required after each update phase to ensure that all red points have been updated before we starting updating black points, and vice versa.

Figure 11.6 contains a parallel program for red/black Gauss-Seidel using shared variables. (The only difference for red/black SOR would be the expression used to update points.) We again assume that there are `PR` worker processes and that `n` is a multiple of `PR`. We also again divide the grid into horizontal strips and assign one strip to each worker.

The structure of the program is identical to that for the Jacobi iteration program in Figure 11.3. Moreover, the maximum difference is computed in the same way. However, each compute phase updates only half as many points as the corresponding compute phase in the parallel Jacobi iteration program. To compensate, the outermost for loop is executed twice as many times. This means there are twice as many barriers, so the overhead from barrier synchronization will be a larger portion of the total execution time. On the other hand, the algorithm will produce better results for the same value of `MAXITERS`, or comparable results for smaller values of `MAXITERS`. The reader might find it instructive to explore these tradeoffs.

The red/black method can also be programmed using message passing. The program will have the same structure as the corresponding program for Jacobi iteration (Figures 11.4 or 11.5). Each worker is again responsible for updating the points in its strip, and neighboring workers need to exchange edges after each update phase. The red and black points on edges can be exchanged separately, but fewer messages will be needed if they are exchanged at the same time.

We have assumed that individual points are colored red or black. Consequently, i and j are incremented in steps of two in all the update loops. This results in poor cache utilization: The entire strip is accessed in each update phase, but any one point is only read or written, not both.[2] We can improve performance by coloring blocks of points, which is analogous to a checkerboard with multiple

---

[2] The generated machine code will also be slower because there are more branch instructions. In addition, incrementing by two might be slower than incrementing by one.

```
real grid[0:n+1,0:n+1];
int HEIGHT = n/PR;    # assume PR evenly divides n
real maxdiff[1:PR] = ([PR] 0.0);

procedure barrier(int id) {
  # efficient barrier algorithm from Section 3.4
}

process worker[w = 1 to PR] {
  int firstRow = (w-1)*HEIGHT + 1;
  int lastRow = firstRow + HEIGHT - 1;
  int jStart;
  real mydiff = 0.0;
  initialize my strip of grid, including boundaries;
  barrier(w);
  for [iters = 1 to MAXITERS] {
    # compute new values for red points in my strip
    for [i = firstRow to lastRow] {
      if (i%2 == 1) jStart = 1;      # odd row
      else jStart = 2;               # even row
      for [j = jStart to n by 2]
        grid[i,j] = (grid[i-1,j] + grid[i,j-1] +
                     grid[i+1,j] + grid[i,j+1]) * 0.25;
    }
    barrier(w);
    # compute new values for black points in my strip
    for [i = firstRow to lastRow] {
      if (i%2 == 1) jStart = 2;      # odd row
      else jStart = 1;               # even row
      for [j = jStart to n by 2]
        grid[i,j] = (grid[i-1,j] + grid[i,j-1] +
                     grid[i+1,j] + grid[i,j+1]) * 0.25;
    }
    barrier(w);
  }
  # compute maximum difference for my strip
  perform one more set of updates, keeping track of the maximum
       difference between old and new values of grid[i,j];
  maxdiff[w] = mydiff;
  barrier(w);
  # maximum difference is the max of the maxdiff[*]
}
```

Figure 11.6   Red/black Gauss-Seidel using shared variables.

points in each square. Better yet, we can color strips of points. For example, divide each worker's strip in half (horizontally), and color the top half red and the bottom half black. As in Figure 11.6, each worker repeatedly updates red points then black points, with barriers after each update phase. Now, however, only half as many points are accessed in each update phase, and each is both read and written.

11.1.6 Multigrid Methods

When approximating a PDE using a grid computation, the granularity of the grid affects the computation time and detail of a solution. Coarse grids can be solved more rapidly but provide less detail; fine grids increase detail but take longer to solve. Simulations of physical systems evolve the system through several time steps and hence require solving a grid computation at every step. This accentuates the tradeoff between computation time and solution detail.

Weather forecasting is a representative application. A weather model starts with current conditions (temperature, pressure, wind velocity, etc.) and then steps through time to predict future conditions. Suppose we want to prepare a forecast for the continental United States (excluding Alaska) using a grid with a resolution of one mile. Then we would need about 3000×1500 (4.5 million) grid points, and we would need to solve this size problem for each time step! To include the significant influence of the oceans, we would need an even larger grid. However, with a grid this large the weather might already have happened before the forecast is completed! If we use a coarser grid, with a resolution say of 10 miles, then we can complete a simulation more rapidly but might entirely miss local storms.

Two approaches are used to solve large problems fast enough for the results to be useful. One is to use an *adaptive grid* (also called an adaptive mesh). With this approach, the granularity of the grid varies. It is coarse where the solution is relatively uniform and fine when greater detail is required. Moreover, the granularity can vary over time to adapt to changes as a simulation is run. For example, the weather over flat terrain and under centers of high pressure tends to be uniform, whereas it varies near mountains and changes rapidly on the edges of fronts.

Multigrid is the second approach to solving large problems rapidly. The idea is to use grids of different granularities and to switch between them to increase the rate of convergence of the finest grid. Multigrid methods employ what is called a *coarse grid correction*, which has the following steps:

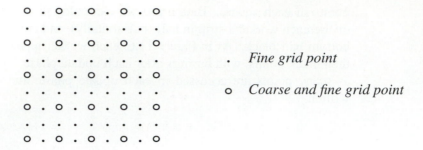

Figure 11.7 Fine and coarse grids, including boundary points.

- Start with a fine grid and update points for a few iterations using one of the relaxation methods (Jacobi, Gauss-Seidel, SOR).

- Restrict the result to a coarser grid in which the points are twice as far apart. Corresponding boundary points have the same values in both grids. A *restriction operator* is used to assign values to the interior points in the coarse grid based on the values of nearby fine grid points.

- Compute a solution on the coarse grid to the desired degree of accuracy.

- Interpolate the coarse grid back to the fine grid. This is done using an *interpolation operator* that assigns values to interior points on the fine grid based on the values of points on the coarse grid.

- Update points on the fine grid for a few iterations.

There are many variations on this basic method, as we shall see.

As a concrete example, consider the overlapping grids in Figure 11.7. The fine grid contains 81 points (both the dots and the circles). The coarse grid contains 25 points (just the circles). The corners of both grids are the same—because the grids cover the same spatial region—but the points in the coarse grid are twice as far apart as those in the fine grid.

There are many possible restriction operators for initializing points in the coarse grid. A representative one is specified by the matrix:

$$\begin{bmatrix} 0 & 1/8 & 0 \\ 1/8 & 1/2 & 1/8 \\ 0 & 1/8 & 0 \end{bmatrix}$$

This means that each coarse grid point gets half its initial value from the corresponding fine grid point and the other half from the sum of one-eighth of the values of each of the four nearest neighbors of the fine grid point. Let `coarse[x,y]` be a fine grid point, and let `fine[i,j]` be the corresponding fine grid point. Then `coarse[x,y]` is updated as follows:

```
coarse[x,y] = fine[i,j] * 0.5  +  (fine[i-1,j] +
       fine[i,j-1] + fine[i,j+1] + fine[i+1,j]) * 0.125;
```

Other possibilities for the restriction operator are to use different weights (as long as they add to one) or to include more neighbors.

There are also many possible interpolation operators for going from the coarse grid back to the fine grid. A representative one—called bilinear interpolation—is specified by the matrix:

$$\begin{bmatrix} 1/4 & 1/2 & 1/4 \\ 1/2 & 1 & 1/2 \\ 1/4 & 1/2 & 1/4 \end{bmatrix}$$

This means that the value of a coarse grid point is copied into the corresponding fine grid point, half of its value is copied into the four immediate neighbors of that fine grid point, and a quarter of its value is copied into the other four nearest neighbors. Thus, a fine grid point that is between two coarse grid points gets half its value from each of the coarse grid points. A fine grid point that is in the center of a square of four coarse grid points gets one quarter of its value from each of the coarse grid points.

Using the above interpolation operator, we can initialize the interior points of the fine grid as follows. First, assign coarse grid points to corresponding fine grid points:

```
fine[i,j] = coarse[x,y];
```

Second, update the other fine grid points in the *columns* that were just updated. One such assignment is

```
fine[i-1,j] = (fine[i-2,j] + fine[i,j]) * 0.5;
```

Finally, update the rest of the fine grid points—those in columns of all dots in Figure 11.7—with the averages of their neighbors in the same row. One such assignment is

```
fine[i-1,j-1] = (fine[i-1,j-2] + fine[i-1,j]) * 0.5;
```

This will give points in the same rows as coarse grid points a value that is the average of the nearest coarse grid points and will give points in other rows a value that is an average of an average, hence a quarter of the sum of the four closest coarse grid points.

There are several kinds of multigrid methods. Each uses a different pattern of coarse grid corrections. The simplest method uses a single correction: start with a fine grid and iterate a few times, restrict down to a coarse grid and solve the problem, then interpolate back up to a fine grid and iterate a few more times. This pattern is called a two-level *V* cycle.

Figure 11.8 illustrates three general multigrid patterns using four grid sizes. If the distance between points in the finest grid is h, the distances between points in the other grids are $2h$, $4h$, and $8h$, as shown. A general *V cycle* has multiple levels: Start with the finest grid and iterate a few times, restrict to a coarser grid and iterate a few times, and so on until you are at the coarsest grid. Now solve the problem. Then interpolate to a finer grid and iterate a few times, and so on until you have iterated a few times on the finest grid.

A *W cycle* improves accuracy by going down and up multiple times. The extra relaxations are done on the coarser grids, and again the problem is always solved exactly on the coarsest grid.

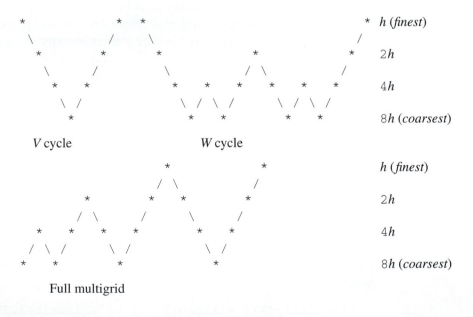

Figure 11.8   Patterns for multigrid methods.

The *full multigrid method* visits the various grids the same number of times as with a W cycle, but it yields even more accurate results. This is because it uses the coarser grids several times before it first uses the finest grid, and hence it yields much better initial values for the finest grid. The full multigrid method involves a recurring sequence of steps: (1) make an initial guess for the coarsest grid, then solving that grid exactly; (2) move up to a finer grid and iterate a few times, then restrict back to the coarsest grid and again solve it exactly; (3) repeat this process, going up to one higher level each time until reaching the finest level, then go through a full V cycle.

Multigrid methods converge much more rapidly than the basic iterative methods. However, they are much harder to program because they require extensive bookkeeping—in particular, managing multiple size grids and continually restricting and interpolating between them.

Given a sequential program that implements multigrid, we can divide each grid into strips and then parallelize restriction, updates, and interpolation in much the same way that we parallelized Jacobi iteration and Gauss-Seidel. Again we would need to use barriers after each phase in a shared-variable program, and we would have to exchange edges after each phase in a message-passing program. It is, however, a challenge to get good speedup in a parallel multigrid program. The extra bookkeeping adds overhead, as do the extra synchronization points. In addition, the way in which multigrid gets a good result in less time than a simple iterative scheme is to do just a few iterations on all but the coarsest grid. The net result is that overhead becomes a larger percentage of total execution time. Still, reasonable speedup can be achieved. This is especially true on very large grids, which are exactly what multigrid methods are intended to handle.

11.2 Particle Computations

Grid computations are used to model continuous systems that can be characterized using partial differential equations. Particle computations are used to model discrete systems consisting of particles that exert forces on each other. Examples are charged particles interacting due to electrical or magnetic forces, molecules interacting due to chemical bonding, and astronomical bodies interacting due to gravity. Here we examine a representative application called the gravitational n-body problem. After defining the problem, we develop sequential and parallel programs that use a complete $O(n^2)$ algorithm, then we describe two approximate $O(n \log_2 n)$ methods: Barnes-Hut and Fast Multipole.

11.2.1 *The Gravitational N-Body Problem*

Suppose we are given a huge collection of astronomical bodies, such as the stars, clouds of dust, and dark matter in a galaxy. The problem is to simulate the evolution of the galaxy.

Each body has a mass and an initial position and velocity. Gravity causes the bodies to accelerate and to move. The motion of an *n*-body system is simulated by stepping through discrete instants of time. At each time step, we calculate the forces on every body and then update their velocities and positions. A simulation of the gravitational *n*-body problem thus has the following structure:

```
initialize bodies;
for [time = start to finish by DT] {
   calculate forces;
   move bodies;
}
```

The value of **DT** (delta time) is the length of a time step.

From Newtonian physics, the *magnitude* of the gravitational force between two bodies *i* and *j* is

$$F = \frac{G\, m_i\, m_j}{r^2}$$

The *m*'s are the masses of the two bodies, and *r* is the distance between them. Gravity is an extremely weak force, so the value of the gravitational constant *G* is the very small number $6.67 \cdot 10^{-11}$.

For simplicity, we will assume the bodies are all on the same spatial plane, and hence that we have only a two-dimensional problem. Let the positions of two bodies be $(p_i \cdot x, p_i \cdot y)$ and $(p_j \cdot x, p_j \cdot y)$. Then the Euclidean distance between them is given by

$$\sqrt{(p_i \cdot x - p_j \cdot x)^2 + (p_i \cdot y - p_j \cdot y)^2}$$

If two bodies come close to each other (a near collision), then *r* will be very small. This will lead to numerical instability in calculating forces, but we ignore the problem here.

The *direction* of the force on body *i* exerted by body *j* is given by a unit vector that points from *i* to *j*. The direction of the force on body *j* due to body *i* is given by a unit vector that points in the opposite direction. Thus, the magnitudes of the forces of each body on the other are the same, but the directions are opposite. The *total force* on a body is the sum of the forces exerted by every other body. (Vector sums are commutative, so the force vectors can be added in any order.)

The gravitational forces on a body cause it to accelerate and move. The relation between force, mass, and acceleration is described by the famous equation

$F = ma$

Thus the acceleration of a body i is the total force on the body divided by its mass. During a small time interval dt, the acceleration a_i on body i is approximately constant, so the change in velocity is approximately

$dv_i = a_i \, dt$

The change in position of the body is the integral of its velocity and acceleration over the time interval dt, which is approximately

$$dp_i = v_i \, dt + \frac{a_i}{2} \, dt^2 = (v_i + \frac{dv_i}{2}) \, dt$$

This formula employs what is called a *leapfrog* scheme, in which half of the change in position is due to the old velocity and half is due to the new velocity.

Figure 11.9 gives a sequential program for solving the *n-body* problem. The program uses a straightforward $O(n^2)$ algorithm as indicated by the for loop in `calculateForces`. In particular, for each body, we calculate the forces exerted on it by every other body. We exploit the symmetry of the forces of two bodies on each other by examining each pair of bodies just once. In particular, the second quantifier, `j`, in the main computational loop ranges from `i+1` to `n`.

The program in Figure 11.9 can be made somewhat more efficient. For example, we can use strength reduction to replace divides and exponentiations by multiplies. We can also compute some of the expressions once rather than multiple times. Inlining the two procedures would also help a small amount, but at the expense of making the program somewhat harder to understand.

11.2.2 Shared-Variable Program

Now consider how we might parallelize the *n*-body program. As usual, our first task is to decide how to divide up the work. Assume that there are `PR` processors, and hence that we will want to use `PR` worker processes. For realistic problems, `n` will be much larger than `PR`. For now also assume that `PR` evenly divides `n`.

The majority of the computation in the sequential program occurs in the for loop in `calculateForces`. For Jacobi iteration, we simply divided the work up by strips, with each worker responsible for `n/PR` rows of the grid. This led to a balanced computational load, because Jacobi iteration has the same amount of computation for each grid point.

```
type point = rec(double x, y);
point p[1:n], v[1:n], f[1:n];    # position, velocity,
double m[1:n];                   # force and mass for each body
double G = 6.67e-11;
initialize the positions, velocities, forces, and masses;

# calculate total force for every pair of bodies
procedure calculateForces() {
  double distance, magnitude; point direction;
  for [i = 1 to n-1, j = i+1 to n] {
    distance = sqrt( (p[i].x - p[j].x)**2 +
                     (p[i].y - p[j].y)**2 );
    magnitude = (G*m[i]*m[j]) / distance**2;
    direction = point(p[j].x-p[i].x, p[j].y-p[i].y);
    f[i].x = f[i].x + magnitude*direction.x/distance;
    f[j].x = f[j].x - magnitude*direction.x/distance;
    f[i].y = f[i].y + magnitude*direction.y/distance;
    f[j].y = f[j].y - magnitude*direction.y/distance;
  }
}

# calculate new velocity and position for each body
procedure moveBodies() {
  point deltav;    # dv = f/m * DT
  point deltap;    # dp = (v + dv/2) * DT
  for [i = 1 to n] {
    deltav = point(f[i].x/m[i] * DT, f[i].y/m[i] * DT);
    deltap = point( (v[i].x + deltav.x/2) * DT,
                    (v[i].y + deltav.y/2) * DT);
    v[i].x = v[i].x + deltav.x;
    v[i].y = v[i].y + deltav.y;
    p[i].x = p[i].x + deltap.x;
    p[i].y = p[i].y + deltap.y;
    f[i].x = f[i].y = 0.0;    # reset force vector
  }
}

# run the simulation with time steps of DT
for [time = start to finish by DT] {
  calculateForces();
  moveBodies();
}
```

Figure 11.9   Sequential program for solving the *n*-body problem.

The corresponding division here would be to assign each worker a contiguous block of bodies: worker 1 handles the first n/PR bodies, worker 2 handles the next n/PR bodies, and so on. However, this will lead to a very imbalanced workload. Worker 1 needs to calculate the forces between body 1 and every other body, then between body 2 and all the other bodies except for 1, and so on. On the other hand, the last worker has relatively little to do because the only forces it needs to calculate—those that are not being calculated by earlier workers—are only the ones between the last n/PR bodies.

As a concrete example, suppose n is 8 and PR is 2. Hence, we employ two workers, named black (B) and white (W). Figure 11.10 shows three ways to assign the bodies to workers. With blocks the first four bodies are assigned to worker B, the last four to worker W. Thus, the number of pairs of forces calculated by B is $7 + 6 + 5 + 4$ (22). On the other hand, the number of pairs of forces calculated by W is $3 + 2 + 1$ (6).

The computational load will be more balanced if we assign bodies to workers in an alternating pattern: body 1 to worker B, body 2 to W, body 3 to B, and so on. This allocation pattern is called *stripes*, because of the analogy with the pattern of stripes on a Zebra. (It is also called a *cyclic allocation*, because the pattern keeps repeating.) The workloads resulting from a striped allocation are 16 pairs of forces for B and 12 for W.

An even better way to balance the load is to use a scheme similar to one commonly used to select teams for pickup games of sports: assign body 1 to worker B, bodies 2 and 3 to W, bodies 4 and 5 to B and so on. We call this allocation pattern *reverse stripes*, because the stripes keep reversing order: black, white; then white, black; then black, white; and so on. For the example in Figure 11.10, the resulting workloads are perfectly balanced: 14 pairs of forces for each worker.

Each of these allocation strategies can readily be generalized to any number PR of workers. The block strategy is trivial. For stripes we would use PR

Pattern	1 2 3 4 5 6 7 8	*Workload*
blocks	B B B B W W W W	B = 22, W = 6
stripes	B W B W B W B W	B = 16, W = 12
reverse stripes	B W W B B W W B	B = 14, W = 14

Figure 11.10   Patterns for assigning bodies to workers.

different colors and assign the first color to body 1, the second to body 2, and so on, repeating the cycle until every body is colored. To use reverse stripes, we would reverse the order of the colors whenever we started a new cycle (i.e., after all `PR` bodies have been colored).

For this or any problem with a similar pattern of loop indices in the main computational loop, allocating data by reverse stripes will yield the most balanced computational load. However, stripes are much easier to program than reverse stripes—and will yield a nearly balanced workload, especially for large values of `n`—so we will use them here.

The next issue to address is what synchronization is required. Are there any critical sections? Do we need barrier synchronization? Here, the answer to both questions is "yes."

Let us first consider the procedure `calculateForces`. The for loop considers each pair of bodies `i` and `j`. While one worker is calculating the forces between bodies `i` and `j`, another worker will be calculating the forces between bodies `i'` and `j'`. Some of these values could be the same; for example, `j` in one worker could be the same as `i'` in the second worker. Consequently, the workers could interfere when updating the force vector `f`. In particular, the four assignment statements that update `f` constitute a critical section of code.

One way to protect the critical section would be to use a single lock variable. However, this would be quite inefficient, because the critical section is executed frequently by every worker. At the other extreme, we could use an array of lock variables, one per body. This would almost eliminate conflicts for locks, but at the expense of using a lot more storage. An intermediate choice would be to have one lock for each block of `B` bodies, but this too would result in conflicts for locks.

The best way to get good performance is, if possible, to avoid locking overhead entirely by getting rid of critical sections. Here, we can do so in either of two ways. One approach is to have each worker take complete responsibility for the bodies assigned to it. By this we mean that the worker responsible for body `i` calculates all forces on body `i` but does *not* update the force vector for any other body `j`. Instead, the worker responsible for body `j` calculates all forces on `j`, including the force exerted by body `i`. This approach is programmed by having index variable `j` in the for loop in `calculateForces` range from `1` to `n` rather than from `i+1` to `n`, and by eliminating the assignments to `f[j]`. However, this means that we do not take advantage of the symmetry of the forces between a pair of bodies, and hence that we do twice as many force calculations.

The second way to get rid of critical sections is to change the force vector into a force matrix, with one row for each worker. In particular, when worker `w` calculates the force between bodies `i` and `j`, it updates two entries in *its* row of the force matrix. Later, when a worker wants to calculate the new position and velocity for a body, it first sums the forces on the body calculated by every worker.

Both approaches to getting rid of critical sections involve the use of *replication*. The first technique replicates work, the second replicates data. This is yet another instance of a time/space tradeoff. Since the reason for writing a parallel program is to decrease execution time, the better choice is to use more space (as long as the program will still fit into the available memory).

The remaining issue to consider is whether barriers are needed, and if so, where. Here, the values of new velocities and positions computed in `moveBodies` depend on the forces computed in `calculateForces`. Thus, we cannot move the bodies until all forces have been computed. Similarly, forces depend on positions and velocities, so we cannot recompute forces until all bodies have been moved. Thus we need barrier synchronization points after each call of `calculateForces` and each call of `moveBodies`.

To summarize, we have described three ways to assign bodies to workers. Using a pattern of stripes leads to a fairly well-balanced computational load that is easy to program. We have also described the critical section problem, ways to use locks, and ways to avoid them. The most efficient approach is to eliminate critical sections by having each worker update its own private force vector. Finally, independent of how we distribute the workload or handle critical sections, we need barriers after calculating forces and moving bodies.

Figure 11.11 contains a parallel program that incorporates these choices. The basic structure of the program is identical to that of the sequential program (Figure 11.9). We add a third procedure, `barrier`, to implement barrier synchronization. We also replace the single main loop for the simulation by `PR` worker processes so that each execute the simulation loop. The `barrier` procedure is called after calculating forces and after moving bodies; all the procedure calls now have an argument, `w`, that identifies the worker making the call. The bodies of the procedures that calculate forces and move bodies are changed as described above. Finally, the main loops in these procedures are changed to increment `i` by `PR` rather than by one; this is all that is needed to assign bodies to workers by stripes. As with the sequential program, we could further optimize the code in Figure 11.11 to make it somewhat more efficient.

11.2.3 Message-Passing Programs

Now consider how to solve the *n*-body problem using message passing. We need to devise some method for distributing the computation among worker processes

```
type point = rec(double x, y); double G = 6.67e-11;
point p[1:n], v[1:n], f[1:PR,1:n];  # position, velocity,
double m[1:n];                       # force and mass for each body
```
initialize the positions, velocities, forces, and masses;

```
procedure barrier(int w) {
  # efficient barrier algorithm from Section 3.4
}

# calculate forces for bodies assigned to worker w
procedure calculateForces(int w) {
  double distance, magnitude; point direction;
  for [i = w to n by PR, j = i+1 to n] {
    distance = sqrt( (p[i].x - p[j].x)**2 +
                     (p[i].y - p[j].y)**2 );
    magnitude = (G*m[i]*m[j]) / distance**2;
    direction = point(p[j].x-p[i].x, p[j].y-p[i].y);
    f[w,i].x = f[w,i].x + magnitude*direction.x/distance;
    f[w,j].x = f[w,j].x - magnitude*direction.x/distance;
    f[w,i].y = f[w,i].y + magnitude*direction.y/distance;
    f[w,j].y = f[w,j].y - magnitude*direction.y/distance;
  }
}

# move the bodies assigned to worker w
procedure moveBodies(int w) {
  point deltav;    # dv = f/m * DT
  point deltap;    # dp = (v + dv/2) * DT
  point force = (0.0, 0.0);
  for [i = w to n by PR] {
    # sum the forces on body i and reset f[*,i]
    for [k = 1 to PR] {
      force.x += f[k,i].x; f[k,i].x = 0.0;
      force.y += f[k,i].y; f[k,i].y = 0.0;
    }
    deltav = point(force.x/m[i] * DT, force.y/m[i] * DT);
    deltap = point( (v[i].x + deltav.x/2) * DT,
                    (v[i].y + deltav.y/2) * DT);
    v[i].x = v[i].x + deltav.x;
    v[i].y = v[i].y + deltav.y;
    p[i].x = p[i].x + deltap.x;
    p[i].y = p[i].y + deltap.y;
    force.x = force.y = 0.0;
  }
}
```

```
process Worker[w = 1 to PR] {
  # run the simulation with time steps of DT
  for [time = start to finish by DT] {
    calculateForces(w);
    barrier(w);
    moveBodies(w);
    barrier(w);
  }
}
```

Figure 11.11   Shared-variable program for the *n*-body problem.

so that the workload is balanced. We also need to minimize communication overhead or at least to make it small relative to the amount of useful work. These are challenging issues because the *n*-body problem involves calculating forces between every pair of bodies, and hence every worker process needs to interact with all the others.

A useful starting point is to consider whether we can use any of the three process interaction paradigms at the start of Chapter 9: manager/workers (distributed bag of tasks), heartbeat, and pipeline. There are well-defined tasks and load balancing is an issue, so the manager/workers paradigm is appropriate. We can also use a heartbeat algorithm by dividing up the bodies and having workers exchange information; however, it is not sufficient to have each worker just exchange information with one or two neighbors. Finally, we can also use a pipeline algorithm and have bodies flow from worker to worker. Below we describe how to solve the *n*-body problem using each of these paradigms, then we discuss the tradeoffs between them.

Manager/Workers Program

First consider using the manager/workers paradigm (Section 9.1). With this approach the manager maintains a bag of tasks; workers repeatedly get a task, do it, then return the result to the manager. For the *n*-body problem, there are two phases. In the first, the tasks are to calculate the forces between every pair of bodies. In the second, the tasks are to move the bodies. The majority of the computation—and the part that can be imbalanced—is calculating forces. Hence it makes sense to use dynamic tasks for the force calculations but to use static tasks (one per worker) for moving bodies.

Suppose there are `PR` processors and that we want to use `PR` worker processes. (Hence, the manager will execute on the same processor as one of the workers.) Assume for simplicity that `n` is a multiple of `PR`. When using the manager/workers paradigm, we want to have at least twice as many tasks as workers to balance the load, but we do not want too many tasks or the workers will spend too much time communicating with the manager. One way to divide up the force calculations for the `n` bodies is as follows:

Divide the bodies into `PR` blocks of size `n/PR`. The first block contains the first `n/PR` bodies, the second the next `n/PR` bodies, and so on.

Form pairs (i, j) for each different combination of block numbers. There will be `PR*(PR+1)/2` such pairs—the sum of the integers from `1` to `PR`.

Let each pair represent a task—for example, the task for pair (i, j) is to calculate the forces between the bodies in block i and those in block j.

As a concrete example, suppose `PR` is four. Then the ten tasks are the pairs

$$(1, 1) \quad (1, 2) \quad (1, 3) \quad (1, 4) \quad (2, 2) \quad (2, 3) \quad (2, 4) \quad (3, 3) \quad (3, 4) \quad (4, 4)$$

The manager process initializes the bag with the pairs defining the tasks. Workers repeatedly get a task from the manager and calculate the forces specified by the task. To do so, a worker needs to know the positions, velocities, and masses of the bodies in one or two blocks. The manager could send these along with the task, but we can greatly reduce the length of messages by having each worker keep its own copy of the data for each body. Similarly, we can get rid of the need to send results to the manager if each worker keeps track of the forces it has calculated for each body.

After calculating all forces—namely when the bag of tasks is empty—the workers need to exchange forces and then move the bodies. The simplest static assignment of work for the move-bodies phase is to have each worker move the bodies in one block: worker 1 moves block 1, worker 2 moves block 2, and so on. Hence, each worker `w` needs the force vectors for the bodies in block `w`. We could use the manager to collect and disseminate the forces calculated by each worker, but it will be more efficient if each worker sends the forces for a block of bodies directly to the worker that will move those bodies. Alternatively, if we have global communication primitives—such as those in the MPI library—the workers can use them to broadcast and reduce (add) the values in the force vectors. After each worker moves its block of bodies, the workers need to exchange the new positions and velocities of the bodies. Again we could use point-to-point messages or global communication to effect this exchange.

Figure 11.12 contains an outline of the code for a manager/workers program. The outer loop in each process executes once for each time step in the simulation. The inner loop in the manager process iterates `numTasks+PR` times, where `numTasks` is the number of tasks in the bag. On the last `PR` iterations, the bag will be empty, so the manager sends the pair (0, 0) as a "bag is empty" sentinel. When each of the `PR` workers gets this sentinel, it breaks out of the loop that calculates forces.

Heartbeat Program

A heartbeat algorithm (Section 9.2) is the message-passing analog of a shared-variable algorithm that has computational phases followed by barriers. The shared-variable program in Figure 11.11 has this structure, so we can modify it as follows to use message passing: (1) each worker is assigned a subset of the bodies; (2) every worker first calculates the forces for its set of bodies then exchanges forces with the other workers; (3) every worker moves its bodies; (4) the workers exchange the new positions and velocities of the bodies. This pattern is repeated for each time step in the simulation.

We can assign bodies to worker processes using any of the allocation patterns described in Figure 11.10: blocks, stripes, or reverse stripes. If we use a stripes or reverse stripes allocation, then the computational load will be much more balanced than if we use fixed-size blocks. However, each worker would need to have its own copy of the position, velocity, force, and mass vectors. Moreover, each worker would need to exchange entire vectors with every other worker after each phase. This leads to a large number of long messages.

If we assign blocks of bodies to workers, we will use about half as many messages and they will be shorter. (We will also need less local storage in the workers.) To see why, consider the example of four workers and ten tasks described in the previous section. With a block assignment, worker 1 handles the first four tasks: (1, 1), (1, 2), (1, 3), and (1, 4). Namely, it handles all force calculations involving the bodies in block 1. To do so, it needs positions and velocities for the bodies in blocks 2, 3, and 4, and it needs to return forces for those blocks. However, worker 1 never needs to tell another worker the position or velocity of its bodies and it never needs to get force information from any other worker. At the other extreme, worker 4 is responsible only for the task (4, 4). It does not need to know the position or velocity of any other body and it does not need to send forces to any other worker.

If the blocks are all the same size, then the workload will be unbalanced, which would more than offset any gain from sending fewer messages. However,

```
chan getTask(int worker), task[1:PR](int block1, block2);
chan bodies[1:PR](int worker; point pos[*], vel[*]);
chan forces[1:PR](point force[*]);

process Manager {
    declare and initialize local variables;
    for [time = start to finish by DT] {
        initialize the bag of tasks;
        for [i = 1 to numTasks+PR ] {
            receive getTask(worker);
            select next task; use (0, 0) to signal bag is empty;
            send task[worker](block1, block2);
        }
    }
}

process Worker[w = 1 to PR] {
    point p[1:n], v[1:n], f[1:n];   # position, velocity
    double m[1:n];                  # force and mass for each body
    declare other local variables; initialize all local variables;
    for [time = start to finish by DT] {
        while (true) {
            send getTask(w); receive task[w](block1, block2);
            if (block1 == 0) break;   # bag is empty
            calculate forces between bodies in block1 and block2;
        }
        for [i = 1 to PR st i != w]      # exchange forces
            send forces[i](f[*]);
        for [i = 1 to PR st i != w] {
            receive forces[w](tf[*]);
            add values in tf to those in f;
        }
        update p and v for my block of bodies;
        for [i = 1 to PR st i != w]      # exchanges bodies
            send bodies[i](w, p[*], v[*]);
        for [i = 1 to PR st i != w] {
            receive bodies[w](worker, tp[*], tv[*]);
            move bodies of worker from tp and tv to p and v;
        }
        reinitialize f to zeros;
    }
}
```

Figure 11.12   Manager/workers program for the n-body problem.

there is no reason that the blocks have to have the same size, as we saw with the shared-variable program. Moreover, bodies can be moved in linear time, so using variable-sized blocks will cause relatively little load imbalance in the move-bodies phase.

Figure 11.13 gives an outline of the code for a heartbeat program that assigns variable-sized blocks of bodies to each worker. As can be seen, the

```
chan bodies[1:PR](int worker; point pos[*], vel[*]);
chan forces[1:PR](point force[*]);

process Worker[w = 1 to PR] {
    int blockSize = size of my block of bodies;
    int tempSize = maximum number of other bodies in messages;
    point p[1:blockSize], v[1:blockSize], f[1:blockSize];
    point tp[1:tempSize], tv[1:tempSize], tf[1:tempSize];
    double m[1:n];
    declarations of other local variables;
    initialize all local variables;
    for [time = start to finish by DT] {
        # send my bodies to lower numbered workers
        for [i = 1 to w-1]
            send bodies[i](w, p[*], v[*]);
        calculate f for my block of bodies;
        # receive bodies from and send forces back to
        # higher numbered workers
        for [i = w+1 to PR] {  # get bodies from others
            receive bodies[w](other, tp[*], tv[*]);
            calculate forces between my block and other block;
            send forces[other](tf[*]);
        }
        # get forces from lower numbered workers
        for [i = 1 to w-1] {
            receive forces[w](tf[*]);
            add forces in tf to those in f;
        }
        update p and v for my bodies;
        re-initialize f to zeros;
    }
}
```

Figure 11.13   Heartbeat program for the n-body problem.

message-passing parts of the code are not symmetric: Different workers send different numbers of messages and they do so at different times. However, we have turned this to an advantage by overlapping communication and computation. In particular, each worker sends messages and then does local computation before receiving messages and processing them.

Pipeline Program

Finally, consider how we might solve the *n*-body problem using a pipeline algorithm (Section 9.3). Recall that in a pipeline, information flows in one direction from process to process. A pipeline can be open, circular, or closed (see Figure 9.5). Here we need to have information about bodies circulate from worker to worker, so we need to use either a circular or closed pipeline. We do not need to use a coordinator process—except perhaps to initialize the workers and gather final results—so a circular pipeline is sufficient for the computation itself.

To get an idea about how to use a circular pipeline, assume for now that every worker is assigned a block of bodies, and that it computes just the forces on its own bodies. (In other words, for now we will do redundant computations; later we will exploit the symmetry of the forces between a pair of bodies.) Each worker needs to see every other body in order to compute the forces from those bodies. Thus, it is sufficient to have the workers circulate blocks of bodies. We can do so as follows:

```
send p and v for my block of bodies to the next worker;
compute the forces among my block of bodies;
for [i = 1 to PR-1] {
    receive p and v for a block of bodies from the previous worker;
    send that block of bodies to the next worker;
    calculate the forces of the new block on bodies in my block;
}
receive back my block of bodies;
move my bodies;
re-initialize forces on my bodies to zeros;
```

Each worker executes this code for every time step of the simulation. (The last send and receive are not needed above, but we will need them below.)

The problem with the above approach is, of course, that we do twice as many force calculations as necessary. Hence, we want to examine each pair of bodies just once and pass the forces calculated so far along with each set of bodies. In order to balance the computational load, we need either to assign different

```
chan bodies[1:PR](int owner; point p[*], v[*], f[*]);

process Worker[w = 1 to PR] {
  int owner, setSize = n/PR, next = w%PR + 1;
  point p[1:setSize], v[1:setSize], f[1:setSize];
  point tp[1:setSize], tv[1:setSize], tf[1:setSize];
  double m[1:n];
  declarations of other local variables;
  initialize my block of bodies and other variables;
  for [time = start to finish by DT] {
    send bodies[next](w, p[*], v[*], f[*]);
    compute the forces among my block of bodies;
    for [i = 1 to PR-1] {
      receive bodies[w](owner, tp[*], tv[*], tf[*]);
      calculate the forces between my bodies and the new ones;
      send bodies[next](owner, tp[*], tv[*], tf[*]);
    }
    # get back my bodies (owner will equal w)
    receive bodies[w](owner, tp[*], tv[*], tf[*]);
    add forces in tf to those in f;
    update p and v for my set of bodies;
    re-initialize forces on my bodies to zeros;
  }
}
```

Figure 11.14   Pipeline program for the *n*-body problem.

numbers of bodies to each worker—as in the heartbeat program—or to assign bodies by stripes or reverse stripes—as in the shared variable program. Here we can use one of the striped assignment patterns, and that will result in the most balanced workload.

Figure 11.14 gives the code for a circular pipeline that uses either of the striped allocation patterns. Each message contains the positions, velocities, and forces so far for a set of bodies. We have not shown the bookkeeping details that are required to keep track of exactly which bodies are in each set; however, this can be determined from the identity of the owner of the set. Each set of bodies circulates around the pipeline until it gets back to its owner, who then moves those bodies.

Comparison

The three message-passing programs differ in several ways: ease of programming, load balancing, numbers of messages, and the amount of local data. Ease of programming is a subjective measure, because it depends on how familiar the programmer is with each style. However, based on length and complexity, the pipeline program is the simplest. It is the shortest program, in part because it has the most regular communication pattern. The managers/workers program is also fairly straightforward, although it requires an extra process. The heartbeat program is the most complex—although not overly so—because it has variable-sized blocks of bodies and an asymmetric communication pattern.

The workload for all three programs will be reasonably well balanced. The managers/workers program dynamically divides up the work, so it will approximately balance the workload even if processors have different speeds or even if some of the processors are also executing other programs. On a dedicated, homogeneous architecture, the pipeline program will have a reasonably balanced workload with a stripes allocation pattern and an almost perfectly balanced workload with a reverse stripes pattern. The heartbeat program uses variable-sized blocks, so it will not have a perfectly balanced load, but it will be close; moreover, the asymmetric communication pattern and overlapping of communication and computation will mask some of the imbalance of force calculations.

Each program sends (and receives) $O(\text{PR}^2)$ messages in each time step. However, the actual numbers of messages differ, as do their sizes, as shown in Table 11.1. The heartbeat algorithm has the fewest messages. The pipeline algorithm has `PR` more messages, but they are the shortest. The manager/workers algorithm has the most messages, but it is the program that could immediately

Program/Phase	Number of Messages	Bodies per Message
Manager/workers		
Get task	`2 * (numTasks+PR)`	`2`
Exchange forces	`PR * (PR-1)`	`n`
Exchange bodies	`PR * (PR-1)`	`2 * n`
Heartbeat		
Exchange bodies	`PR * (PR-1) / 2`	`2 * n`
Exchange forces	`PR * (PR-1) / 2`	`n`
Pipeline		
Circulate bodies	`PR * PR`	`3 * n * PR`

Table 11.1 Comparison of message-passing programs for *n*-body problem.

benefit from using group communication operations to exchange values between workers.

Finally, the programs differ in the amount of local storage in each worker process. In the manager/worker program, every worker has a copy of information on every body; it also needs temporary storage for messages that can have up to 2 n values. In the heartbeat program, each worker has storage for its block of bodies, and temporary storage for the largest block it could receive from another worker. In the pipeline program, each worker needs storage for its set of bodies and temporary storage for one other set of bodies, where the size of a set is `n/PR`. Hence, the pipeline program requires the smallest amount of space per worker.

On balance, the pipeline program is the most attractive for this specific problem: it is somewhat easier to program, will have an approximately balanced load, requires the least local storage, and has a nearly minimal number of messages. Moreover, the pipeline program will execute more efficiently on some communication networks, because each worker communicates with only two neighbors. However, the differences between the programs are relatively minor, so any one would be reasonable to consider. We leave to the reader the interesting task of implementing all three programs and experimentally comparing their performance.

11.2.4 *Approximate Methods*

Force calculations are the dominant part of n-body computations. Indeed, they account for more than 95 percent of the execution time for realistic applications in which n is very large. Because each body interacts with every other one, there are $O(n^2)$ force calculations per time step. However, the magnitude of the gravitational force is inversely proportional to the square of the distance between two bodies. Thus, if two bodies are far apart, the force between them is negligible.

As a concrete example, the motion of the earth is affected by other bodies in our solar system, especially the sun and moon and to a lesser extent other planets. The gravitational force exerted on our solar system by other bodies is negligible, but it is large enough to cause the solar system to move within the Milky Way galaxy.

Newton discovered these facts and showed that a group of bodies could be treated as a single body with respect to other bodies that are far away. In particular, a group of bodies B can be approximated by a single body b that has the total mass of all the bodies in B and is located at the center of mass of B. Then the force between a distant body i and all the bodies in B can be approximated by the force between i and b.

Newton's insight leads to approximate methods for *n*-body simulations. The first to be widely used is called the Barnes-Hut algorithm. More recently, simulations employ the even faster Fast Multipole Method (FMM). Both these methods are instances of what are called *tree codes*, because the underlying data structure is a tree of bodies. The execution time of the Barnes-Hut algorithm is $O(n \log n)$; for uniform distributions of bodies, the execution time of FMM is $O(n)$. Below we briefly describe how these methods work; see the Historical Notes at the end of this chapter for papers that provide details.

The basis for hierarchical methods is a tree-structured representation of physical space. The root of the tree represents a *cell* that contains all the bodies. The tree is constructed recursively by subdividing cells. For a two-dimensional space, first divide the root cell into four equal-sized cells, then divide each of these into four more cells. This process is repeated until every cell contains at most some fixed number of bodies. The tree that results is called a *quadtree*, because each nonleaf node has four children. The shape of the tree adapts to the distribution of bodies, because the tree will have more levels in regions having more bodies. (For a three-dimensional space, parent cells are divided into eight smaller cells; the data structure is then an *octree*.)

Figure 11.15 illustrates the subdivision of a two-dimensional space into cells and the corresponding quadtree. Each group of four equal-sized cells is numbered clockwise from top left to bottom left and is represented in the tree in that order. Each leaf node represents a cell containing either no bodies or one body.

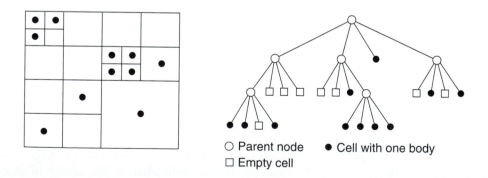

○ Parent node   ● Cell with one body
□ Empty cell

Figure 11.15   Cells and quadtree for a two-dimensional space.

Barnes-Hut Algorithm

Each time step in the n^2 algorithm has two computational phases: calculating forces and moving bodies. The Barnes-Hut algorithm adds two preprocessing phases. There are thus four computations per time step, as follows:

1. Construct a quadtree representing the current distribution of the bodies.

2. Compute the total mass and the center of mass for each cell and store these values in the corresponding node in the quadtree. This is done by making an upward pass through the tree—from the leaf nodes to the root node.

3. Calculate the forces using the information in the tree. In particular, for each body start at the root of the tree and recursively perform the following test for each node that is visited: If the center of mass of the cell is far enough away, approximate the entire subtree by that cell; otherwise, visit the four subcells. A user-defined parameter is used to determine when a cell is far enough away.

4. Move the bodies as before.

The tree is reconstructed in each time step because the bodies move and hence their distribution changes. However, the movement will in general be small, so a refinement of the basic algorithm would be to recompute the tree only if some body moves outside of its current cell. In any event, the center of mass for each cell needs to be recomputed in each time step.

The number of nodes in the quadtree is $O(n \log n)$, so phases (1) and (2) have this time complexity. Calculating forces is also $O(n \log n)$, because the tree traversal for a body descends deeply only for cells that are physically close to the body. Moving bodies is as usual the fastest phase, with a time complexity of $O(n)$.

The Barnes-Hut algorithm does not take advantage of the symmetry of the forces between a pair of bodies. Instead, each body is considered separately in the force calculation phase. (The bookkeeping gets horrendous if we try to keep track of which pairs of forces have already been computed.) Still, the reduced time complexity of the algorithm makes it far more efficient than the $O(n^2)$ algorithm.

The Barnes-Hut algorithm is harder to parallelize efficiently than the basic algorithm. The extra problems are that (1) the spatial distribution of bodies is in general nonuniform and hence the tree is imbalanced, (2) the tree has to be reconstructed at each time step because the bodies move, and (3) the tree is a connected data structure that is harder to distribute (and use) than simple arrays.

These problems make it harder to balance the workload and to reduce storage requirements. For example, each processor should be assigned an equal number of bodies, but this will not correspond to any regular subdivision of the space into cells. Moreover, the processors need to work together to construct the tree and they might need to use the entire tree when calculating forces. Researchers who have made n-body simulations their life's work have developed clever methods for solving these problems (see the Historical Notes at the end of this chapter). Indeed, it is now possible to simulate the evolution of systems containing hundreds of millions of bodies and to get efficient speedup on thousands of processors.

Fast Multipole Method

The Fast Multipole Method (FMM) is a refinement of Barnes-Hut that requires far fewer force calculations. Barnes-Hut considers only body/body and body/cell interactions. FMM computes cell/cell interactions as well. In particular, if an internal cell of the quadtree is far enough away from another internal cell, then FMM computes the force between the two cells and propagates this information to all descendents of both cells.

The second key difference between FMM and Barnes-Hut is the way in which the two methods control the accuracy of force approximations. Barnes-Hut represents each cell by a single point located at the cell's center of mass, and it uses the distance between a body and this point to determine when to approximate the force. FMM represents the distribution of the mass in a cell using a series expansion with multiple terms (this is called a *multipole expansion*), and it considers two cells to be far enough apart if they are farther apart than the length of the sides of the larger cell. Thus FMM uses approximations far more frequently than does Barnes-Hut, but it compensates by having a more accurate characterization of the distribution of mass within a cell.

The phases in a time step of FMM are the same as those in Barnes-Hut, but the second and third phases are realized differently as described above. By computing cell-cell interactions and approximating many more forces, the time complexity of FMM is $O(n)$ for uniform distributions of bodies in space. The Fast Multipole Method is difficult to parallelize, but it can be parallelized efficiently using the same kinds of techniques that are used for Barnes-Hut.

11.3 Matrix Computations

Grid and particle computations are fundamental techniques for scientific computing. Matrix computations are a third. We have already seen how to multiply dense and sparse matrices. Here we show how to use matrices to solve systems of linear equations. This type of problem is central to many scientific and engineering applications, as well as economic modeling and many others. (In fact, Laplace's equation in Section 11.1 can be characterized by a large system of equations; however, the system is very sparse, so it is usually solved using an iterative grid computation.)

We first illustrate what is called Gaussian elimination. Then we describe a more general method called LU decomposition and develop a sequential program. Finally, we develop parallel programs for LU decomposition, first using shared variables and then using message passing. The exercises consider additional matrix computations, including matrix inversion.

11.3.1 Gaussian Elimination

Consider the following set of three equations in three unknowns:

$$a + b + c = 6$$
$$2a - b + c = 3$$
$$-a + b - c = -2$$

The standard way to solve for a, b, and c is to rewrite one of the equations in terms of one of the variables, say a, and then to substitute the value of a in the other two equations. This produces two equations in two unknowns. We can then repeat the process—rewriting one of the two new equations in terms of one of the remaining variables, say b, and then substituting the value of b in the second new equation. We can then solve for the value of c, use that value to solve for b, and finally solve for a.

Gaussian elimination is a systematic method for solving any size system of linear equations. For the above three equations, it works as follows. First, multiply the first equation by 2, then subtract it from the second equation. This eliminates the a term from the second equation. Second, multiply the first equation by -1, then subtract it from the third equation (or equivalently, add the first equation to the third). This eliminates the a term from the third equation. After these two steps, we have three equations:

$$a + b + c = 6$$

$$-3b - c = -9$$

$$2b = 4$$

In this example, c is also eliminated from the third equation, but this will not generally be the case.

Now repeat the above process for the last two equations. In particular, multiply the second equation by $2/3$ and add it to the third equation. This eliminates b from the third equation (and reintroduces c). The final set of equations is

$$a + b + c = 6$$

$$-3b - c = -9$$

$$-2/3c = -2$$

The above steps are called the *forward elimination* phase of Gaussian elimination, because they systematically eliminate one variable at a time from the remaining equations. In the second phase, you can use *backward substitution* to solve for each variable, starting with the last equation and working up to the first. In particular, solving for the one variable in the last equation results in $c = 3$. Next substitute 3 for c in the second equation and solve for b, getting $b = 2$. Finally, substitute the values of b and c in the first equation and solve for a, getting $a = 1$. Thus the solution to this system of equations is $a = 1$, $b = 2$, and $c = 3$.

Solving a system of linear equations is equivalent to solving the matrix equation $A\ x = b$, where A is a square matrix of coefficients, b is a column vector of right-hand sides, and x is a column vector of variables. In particular, row i of A contains the coefficients for the variables in equation i, and element i of b contains the right-hand side of equation i.

Gaussian elimination is implemented by a series of transformations to the matrix A and the vector b. These reduce A to *upper triangular form*—namely, a matrix having all zeros below the diagonal. For the above system of equations, the initial value of A is

```
 1   1   1
 2  -1   1
-1   1  -1
```

The corresponding values for b are $(6, 3, -2)$. The forward elimination phase starts with the leftmost column and transforms A and b as follows. First, compute the multiplier $A[2,1]/A[1,1]$ and subtract this multiple of the first row of

A and first element of b from the second row of A and second element of b. Second, compute the multiplier A[3,1]/A[1,1] and subtract this multiple of the first row of A and first element of b from the third row of A and third element of b. After these two steps, the first column of A will contain zeros in rows two and three. The last forward elimination step for this simple example computes the multiplier A[3,2]/A[2,2] and subtracts this multiple of the second row of the new A and second element of the new b from the third row of A and third element of b. The final value of A will be

```
1   1    1
0  -3   -1
0   0  -2/3
```

The corresponding final values of b will be (6, -9, -2).

Gaussian elimination can be used to solve most systems of n equations in n unknowns.[3] However, each forward elimination step requires calculating multipliers of the form A[k,i]/A[i,i]. Element A[i,i] is called the *pivot element* for column i. If the pivot element is zero, we will get a "divide by zero" exception. Moreover, if the pivot element is very small, then each multiplier will be very large; this can make the algorithm numerically unstable.

Both problems can be solved by using what is called *partial pivoting*. In particular, for each column i, choose as the pivot element the value A[k,i], which has the largest absolute value. Then swap rows k and i before doing the elimination step. The swap can be implemented by swapping elements of an indirection vector, rather than by actually swapping the rows themselves.

11.3.2 LU Decomposition

Gaussian elimination transforms the equation A x = b into an equivalent equation U x = y, where U is an upper triangular matrix. To perform the transformation, we calculate a sequence of multipliers. Rather than throw them away, suppose that we save the multipliers in a third matrix L. In particular, let L be a *lower triangular* matrix that has ones on the main diagonal and zeros above the diagonal. Every other element L[j,i] is the multiplier A[j,i]/pivot, where pivot is the value of the pivot element used for column i. When we are done, the matrix product of L and U will be exactly equal to the original matrix A

---

[3] The equations must be independent, meaning that one equation cannot be derived from the others. More precisely, A must be a nonsingular matrix.

(except for possible round-off errors). As a concrete example, for the above system of equations we have

```
  1     0   0       1   1    1          1   1   1
  2     1   0       0  -3   -1     =    2  -1   1
 -1  -2/3   1       0   0  -2/3        -1   1  -1

       L                 U          =      A
```

This transformation of A into triangular matrices L and U is called the *LU decomposition* of A. The main reason for performing an LU decomposition is that once we have computed L and U, we can readily solve $A \; x \; = \; b$ for different right-hand sides b.[4] In particular, each system can be written as $L \; U \; x \; = \; b$. This represents two triangular systems: $L \; y \; = \; b$ and $U \; x \; = \; y$. We can use forward substitution to solve the first system for y, and then use back substitution to solve the second system for x.

Another attribute of the LU decomposition is that we do not need extra storage for either matrix. In particular, as we transform A, we can store both L and U in place of previous elements of A. This is clearly true for U, because the transformed value of A is U. The multipliers in L are calculated exactly as we eliminate elements of A, so they can be stored in place of what would be zeros in A. Finally, all the diagonal elements of L are ones, so we do not need to store them.

Figure 11.16 gives a sequential program that computes the LU decomposition of matrix A. We store the result in a separate matrix LU to make the code somewhat easier to read; this also preserves A should we need it later. The program uses partial pivoting to avoid dividing by zero or small numbers. The indices of the pivot rows are stored in vector ps. Initially, $ps[i]$ is i; elements of ps are swapped each time a nondiagonal element is chosen as the pivot. Thus, ps always contains a permutation of 1 to n. During the elimination phase, rows of A and LU are accessed using $ps[i]$ instead of simply i.

Figure 11.17 gives a sequential program for solving $A \; x \; = \; b$ given an LU decomposition of A. The first loop solves $L \; y \; = \; b$ for y; the second loop solves $U \; x \; = \; y$ for x. The program stores the intermediate result y in vector x, because this simplifies the back substitution phase.

11.3.3 Shared-Variable Program

Now consider how we might parallelize the programs in Figures 11.16 and 11.17 to use PR processors and hence PR worker processes. First consider the LU

---

[4] Another way to solve for multiple right-hand sides would be first to compute the inverse of A, and then to multiply A^{-1} by each vector b. An exercise at the end of the chapter describes how to compute A^{-1}. However, computing the LU decomposition of a matrix takes less time than inverting the matrix.

```
double A[1:n,1:n], LU[1:n,1:n];  # assume A initialized
int ps[1:n];                     # pivot row indices
double pivot; int pivotRow;      # pivot value and row
double mult; int t;              # temporaries

# initialize ps and LU
for [i = 1 to n] {
  ps[i] = i;
  for [j = 1 to n]
    LU[i,j] = A[i,j];
}

# perform Gaussian elimination with partial pivoting
for [k = 1 to n-1] {         # iterate down main diagonal
  pivot = abs(LU[ps[k],k]); pivotRow = k;
  for [i = k+1 to n] {    # select pivot in column k
    if (abs(LU[ps[i],k]) > pivot) {
      pivot = abs(LU[ps[i],k]); pivotRow = i;
    }
  }
  if (pivotRow != k) {    # swap rows by swapping indices
    t = ps[k]; ps[k] = ps[pivotRow]; ps[pivotRow] = t;
  }
  pivot = LU[ps[k],k];          # get actual value of pivot
  for [i = k+1 to n] {          # for all rows in submatrix
    mult = LU[ps[i],k]/pivot;   # calculate multiplier
    LU[ps[i],k] = mult;         #    and save it
    for [j = k+1 to n]          # eliminate across columns
      LU[ps[i],j] = LU[ps[i],j] - mult*LU[ps[k],j];
  }
}
```

Figure 11.16   Sequential program for LU decomposition of a matrix.

decomposition in Figure 11.16. There are two main phases: initialize ps and LU, then perform Gaussian elimination. The loop bodies in the initialization phase are independent, so they can be divided among the workers using any allocation pattern that assigns each worker the same number of data elements.

The outer loop (on k) in the Gaussian elimination phase has to be executed sequentially by each worker, because LU decomposition proceeds iteratively down the main diagonal and decomposes the submatrix LU[k:n,k:n]. The body of the outer loop has two phases: select a pivot element and make it the

```
double LU[1:n,1:n]; int ps[1:n];   # see Figure 11.16
double sum, x[1:n], b[1:n];

# forward substitution to solve L y = b, storing y in x
for [i = 1 to n] {
  sum = 0.0;
  for [j = 1 to i-1]
    sum = sum + LU[ps[i],j] * x[j];
  x[i] = b[ps[i]] - sum;
}

# backward substitution to solve U x = y for x
for [i = n to 1 by -1] {
  sum = 0.0;
  for [j = i+1 to n]
    sum = sum + LU[ps[i],j] * x[j];
  x[i] = (x[i] - sum) / LU[ps[i],i];
}
```

Figure 11.17   Solving A x = b given an LU decomposition of A.

pivot row, then reduce the rows below the pivot row. There are three ways to select the pivot:

- Have each process examine all the elements in LU[k:n,k] and select the maximum. If each process keeps its own copy of the pivot indices ps, then no barrier is required after this phase.

- Have one process examine the elements in LU[k:n,k], select the maximum, and exchange the pivot row and row k. This requires a barrier synchronization point.

- Have each process examine a subset of the elements in LU[k:n,k], select the maximum of that subset, and then coordinate with the other workers to select the pivot. This also requires a barrier synchronization point and, depending on how it is coded, private copies of ps.

For smaller values of n, the first approach is likely to be faster, because no barrier is required. For large values of n, the third approach is likely to be faster. The crossover point depends on the overhead of a barrier relative to the computation time to select the maximum element.

Once a pivot has been selected, the rows below the pivot row can be eliminated in parallel. For each row, we first calculate and store a multiplier mult and then iterate across the columns to the right of the column containing the pivot element. As LU decomposition proceeds, the submatrix we are eliminating gets smaller and smaller, and hence the amount of work in each elimination phase gets less and less. Thus we should assign the LU matrix to workers by stripes or reverse stripes, so that each worker has something to do during all but the last few iterations of the main loop. Again we will use stripes because it is easier to program than reverse stripes and leads to a reasonably balanced load.

Figure 11.18 presents an outline of a parallel program for LU decomposition using shared variables. The two main changes from the sequential program are that (1) initialization and elimination use stripes of rows, and (2) there are barriers after initialization, after each selection of a pivot (if necessary), and after each elimination step. In addition, each worker will probably need to have its

```
double A[1:n,1:n], LU[1:n,1:n];  # assume A initialized
int ps[1:n];                      # pivot row indices

procedure barrier(int id) { ... }  # see Chapter 3

process Worker(w = 1 to PR) {
  double pivot, mult;
  declarations of other local variables, such as a copy of ps;
  for [i = w to n by PR]
    initialize ps and my stripes of LU;
  barrier(w);

  # perform Gaussian elimination with partial pivoting
  for [k = 1 to n-1] {        # iterate down main diagonal
    find maximum pivot element — see text;
    if necessary, swap pivot row and row k, then call barrier(w);
    pivot = LU[ps[k],k];       # get actual value of pivot
    for [i = k+1 to n st (i%PR == 0)] {  # for my stripe
      mult = LU[ps[i],k]/pivot;  # calculate multiplier
      LU[ps[i],k] = mult;        #    and save it
      for [j = k+1 to n]      # eliminate across columns
        LU[ps[i],j] = LU[ps[i],j] - mult*LU[ps[k],j];
    }
    barrier(w);
  }
}
```

Figure 11.18   Outline of a shared-variable program for LU decomposition.

own private copy of the pivot indices, because that makes it easier to swap rows without requiring synchronization.

Now consider how we might parallelize the forward- and backward-substitution steps in Figure 11.17. Unfortunately, each phase has nested loops, and each inner loop depends on values calculated in previous iterations of the corresponding outer loop. By its very nature, forward substitution calculates elements of **y** one at a time, and backward substitution calculates elements of **x** one at a time.

It is possible to reprogram the loops to introduce independence. For example, in the forward substitution phase we could unroll the inner loops and then rewrite the calculations to compute each value **x[i]** in terms only of **LU** and **b**. This is tedious to do by hand but can be automated in a compiler (see Section 12.2).

Another way to get parallelism is to use what is called *wave front synchronization*. In particular, in the forward substitution phase assign iterations to workers by stripes. Since the calculation of **x[i]** depends on previous values in **x[1:i-1]**, associate a flag (or semaphore) with each element of **x**. When a process finishes computing **x[i]**, it sets the flag for that element. When a process wants to read the value of **x[i]**, it first waits for the flag for that element to be set. For example, the code executed by worker **w** for forward elimination would be as follows:

```
for [i = w to n by PR] {   # for my stripe of x[*]
   sum = 0.0;              # local value
   for [j = 1 to i-1] {
      wait for flag of x[j] to be set;
      sum = sum + LU[ps[i],j] * x[j];
   }
   x[i] = b[ps[i]] - sum;
   set flag of x[i];
}
```

The wave fronts are the settings of flags as new elements are calculated. (The term *wave front* is more commonly used with matrices; there a *wave* typically consists of a diagonal line that sweeps across the matrix.)

Wave fronts are effective if the synchronization overhead is low relative to the amount of computation. Here there is very little computation per element, so the synchronization would have to be programmed using simple flags and busy waiting. This should lead to a small performance improvement for this application.

11.3.4 Message-Passing Program

Now consider how we might implement LU decomposition using message passing. Again, the three approaches to consider are manager/workers, heartbeat, and pipeline. All three paradigms could be used, but when the shared-variable program for an application uses barriers, the most straightforward way to get a distributed program is to use a heartbeat algorithm. Below we develop an outline of a heartbeat program for LU decomposition. The exercises at the end of this chapter examine the other two paradigms.

As usual for a distributed program, we first need to decide how to distribute the data in order to balance the computational load. Since LU decomposition works on smaller and smaller submatrices, the amount of work decreases as elimination proceeds. Hence, we want to assign rows by stripes rather than by strips, as we did in the shared-variable program. If we assume there are `PR` worker processes, then we can assign each worker every `PR`th row of `LU`, for a total of `n/PR` rows per worker.

The first step in LU decomposition is to initialize the local rows of `LU` and of the pivot indices `ps`. Each worker can execute this step in parallel. A barrier is not needed after the initialization step, because there are no shared variables.

The main step in LU decomposition is repeatedly to select a pivot element and pivot row, then to eliminate all rows below the pivot row. Each worker can select the maximum element in column `k` of its `n/PR` rows of `LU`. However, the workers need to interact in order to select the global maximum. We could have one worker play the role of a coordinator, gathering the maximum value from each other worker, selecting the best, and then broadcasting that value to the other workers. Alternatively, if we have global communication primitives such as those in the MPI library, we can use a reduction primitive to compute the pivot value.

After the pivot value is selected, the worker that owns the pivot row needs to broadcast that row to the other workers, because they need it for the elimination phase. After receiving the pivot value and pivot row, each worker can proceed to eliminate the rows it owns that are below the pivot row.

Figure 11.19 contains an outline of a message-passing program for LU decomposition. The various steps in the program are as described above. No explicit barriers are needed, because the message exchanges required to select a pivot value and pivot row also constitute a barrier. The variable `myRow` is used in the elimination phase to map the global row index `i` (which ranges from 1 to `n`) into the index of the appropriate row in the local array of rows.

When the program in Figure 11.19 terminates, the results of the LU decomposition reside in the local arrays in the various workers. To solve a system of declarations of channels;

```
process Worker(w = 1 to PR) {
   double LU[1:n/PR,1:n/PR];     # my rows of LU
   int ps[1:n/PR];               # pivot row indices
   double pivot, mult, pivotRow[n];
   int myRow;
   declarations of other local variables;
   initialize ps and my rows of LU;
   # perform Gaussian elimination with partial pivoting
   for [k = 1 to n-1] {        # iterate down main diagonal
      find maximum pivot element in column k of my rows;
      exchange pivot with other workers;
      select global maximum and update ps;
      if (owner of pivot row)
         broadcast pivotRow to other workers;
      else
         receive pivotRow;
      # eliminate my rows of LU using pivot and pivotRow
      for [i = k+1 to n st (i%PR == 0)] { # for my stripe
         myRow = i/PR;                     # convert row index
         mult = LU[ps[myRow],k]/pivot;  # compute multiplier
         LU[ps[myRow],k] = mult;        #    and save it
         for [j = k+1 to n]        # eliminate across columns
            LU[ps[myRow],j] = LU[ps[myRow],j] -
                              mult * pivotRow[j];
      }
   }
}
```

Figure 11.19   Outline of a message-passing program for LU decomposition.

equations, we need to perform forward and backward substitutions, a process that requires accessing all of the elements of the LU decomposition. One approach would be to have a single process gather all the rows of LU and then to execute the code in Figure 11.17. A second approach would be to use a circular pipeline to implement a message-passing version of wave front synchronization.

With a circular pipeline, the first worker calculates x[1] then passes it to the second worker. The second worker calculates x[2] and passes on both x[1] and x[2] to the third worker. The last worker calculates x[PR] and passes this plus the previous values of x to the first worker. This process continues until `x[n]` has been calculated. We can then use the same circular pipeline for backward substitution, computing the final values for `x[n]`, `x[n-1]`, to `x[1]` and passing them along the pipeline.

The pipeline algorithm for forward and backward substitution is relatively straightforward to program, employs parallelism, and does not require gathering all of `LU`. However, because it requires a large number of messages, it might well be less efficient than using a single process.

Historical Notes

The history of scientific computing coincides with the history of computing. The earliest machines were developed to solve scientific computations, and Fortran—the first high-level language—was developed specifically to express numerical computations. Scientific computing has also been synonymous with high-performance computing, with the largest scientific computations pushing the limits of the fastest machines.

Textbooks on numerical analysis cover the mathematical foundations of scientific computing, and advanced texts cover methods for solving differential equations and matrix equations. Forsythe and Moler [1967] is a clear, timeless book that contains very clear descriptions of linear algebraic systems and algorithms for solving them; that book served as the main source for the material in Section 11.2. Van Loan [1997] gives an introduction to (nonparallel) scientific computing, including linear and nonlinear systems of equations. Mathews and Fink [1999] describe numerical methods for numerous applications, including integration, systems of equations, and differential equations. The latter two books use MATLAB to illustrate algorithms.

Several books on parallel computing provide more details on the algorithms described in this chapter, describe related algorithms, and cover additional topics. Fox et al. [1988] cover finite-difference and finite-element methods for solving PDEs, matrix and particle computations, and Monte Carlo (randomized) methods. Their emphasis is on message-passing algorithms for hypercube machines, but the algorithms can be adapted to other distributed-memory architectures. Bertsekas and Tsitsiklis [1989] cover direct and iterative methods for linear and nonlinear problems, dynamic programming, network flow problems, and asynchronous iterative methods. Kumar et al. [1994] and Quinn [1994] describe grid and matrix computations, sorting, searching, and graph algorithms, and Fast Fourier transforms. Wilkinson and Allen [1999] describe how Jacobi iteration can be represented as a system of linear equations, and they include chapters on image processing and searching and optimization.

Multigrid methods were developed by several researchers beginning in the 1970s. They continue to be studied and refined due to their importance in solving large grid computations. Briggs [1987] contains an excellent introduction to the topic. Hackbrush [1985] is one of several books that cover multigrid methods in detail.

The gravitational *n*-body problem has also been studied for decades. Barnes and Hut [1986] have written the classic paper on a hierarchical tree code for solving the problem. John Salmon in his doctoral dissertation at Cal Tech did some of the important early work on parallel hierarchical *n*-body methods. Warren and Salmon [1992] describe simulations of up to 17.5 million bodies. Warren, Salmon, and Becker [1997] describe a simulation with over 322 million bodies that was run for 437 time steps on more than a thousand processors! Both of the above papers won Gordon Bell prizes for outstanding sustained performance on massively parallel machines.

Greengard [1987] and Greengard and Rokhlin [1987] describe the Fast Multipole Method and its application to evaluating potential fields in particle simulations. Singh, Hennessy, and Gupta [1995] provide excellent summaries of the Barnes-Hut algorithm and the Fast Multipole Method, describe how they can be implemented on large-scale multiprocessors, and evaluate the architectural implications of the two methods. Blackston and Suel [1997] describe portable and efficient parallel implementations of Barnes-Hut, the Fast Multipole Method, and another algorithm called Anderson's Method.

References

Barnes, J., and P. Hut. 1986. A hierarchical $O(N \log N)$ force-calculation algorithm. *Nature* 324, 446–49.

Bertsekas, D. P., and J. N. Tsitsiklis. 1989. *Parallel and Distributed Computation: Numerical Methods.* Englewood Cliffs, NJ: Prentice-Hall.

Blackston, D., and T. Suel. 1997. Highly portable and efficient implementations of parallel adaptive *n*-body methods. *Proc. Supercomputing '97*, November, online at `http://www.supercomp.org/sc97/proceedings`.

Briggs, W. L. 1987. *A Multigrid Tutorial.* Philadelphia: SIAM Publications.

Forsythe, G., and C. B. Moler. 1967. *Computer Solution of Linear Algebra Systems.* Englewood Cliffs, NJ: Prentice-Hall.

Fox, G. C., M. A. Johnson, G. A. Lyzenga, S. W. Otto, J. K. Salmon, and D. W. Walker. 1988. *Solving Problems on Concurrent Processors,* vol. 1, *General Techniques and Regular Problems.* Englewood Cliffs, NJ: Prentice-Hall.

Greengard, L. 1987. *The Rapid Evaluation of Potential Fields in Particle Systems.* New York: ACM Press.

Greengard, L., and V. Rokhlin. 1987. A fast algorithm for particle simulation. *Journal of Computational Physics* 73: 325.

Hackbrush, W. 1985. *Multigrid Methods with Applications.* New York: Springer Verlag.

Kumar, V., A. Grama, A. Gupta, and G. Karypis. 1994. *Introduction to Parallel Computing: Design and Analysis of Algorithms.* Menlo Park, CA: Benjamin/Cummings.

Mathews, J. H., and K. D. Fink. 1999. *Numerical Methods Using MATLAB*, 3rd ed. Upper Saddle River, NJ: Prentice-Hall.

Quinn, M. J. 1994. *Parallel Computing: Theory and Practice.* New York: McGraw-Hill.

Singh, J. P., J. L. Hennessy, and A. Gupta. 1995. Implications of hierarchical n-body methods for multiprocessor architectures. *ACM Trans. on Computer Systems* 13, 2 (May): 141–202.

Warren, M. S., and J. K. Salmon. 1992. Astrophysical n-body simulations using hierarchical tree data structures. *Proc. Supercomputing '92*, November, 570–76.

Warren, M. S., J. K. Salmon, and D. J. Becker. 1997. Pentium Pro inside: I. A treecode at 430 Gigaflops on ASCI Red; II. Price/performance of $50/Mflop on Loki and Hyglac. *Proc. Supercomputing '97*, November, online at `http://www.supercomp.org/sc97/proceedings`.

Wilkinson, B., and M. Allen. 1999. *Parallel Programming: Techniques and Applications Using Networked Workstations and Parallel Computers.* Upper Saddle River, NJ: Prentice-Hall.

Van Loan, C. F. 1997. *Introduction to Scientific Computing.* Upper Saddle River, NJ: Prentice-Hall.

Exercises

11.1   The start of the subsection on sequential Jacobi iteration gives a simple sequential program. The section describes four optimizations that produce the program in Figure 11.2 and then describes two more optimizations.

(a) Construct a set of experiments to measure the individual and cumulative effects of the six optimizations. Start by measuring the execution time of the main computational loop in Jacobi iteration for various grid sizes—such as 64 × 64, 128 × 128, and 256 × 256. Pick values of EPSILON and/or iters so that the computation takes a few minutes. (This should be long enough that you will be able to see the effects of improvements.) Then add the optimizations one at a time and measure the performance improvement of each. Write a short report describing your results and conclusions.

(b) Construct experiments to evaluate the six optimizations independently and in various combinations rather than by adding them one at a time as in part (a). Which optimizations appear to be the most fruitful? Does the order in which they are applied matter?

(c) Consider other ways the program might be optimized. Your goal is to get this one program to run as fast as you can. Describe and measure the effect of each additional optimization that you can think of.

11.2 Implement and measure the performance of the shared-variable program for Jacobi iteration in Figure 11.3. Use a variety of grid sizes and numbers of processors. Then optimize the program in any way you can think of and measure the resulting performance. Write a report that describes all the changes you have made, presents performance results, and gives your conclusions.

11.3 Implement and measure the performance of the unoptimized and optimized Jacobi iteration programs using message passing (Figures 11.4 and 11.5). Use a variety of grid sizes and numbers of processors. Then optimize the programs in any additional ways you can think of and measure the resulting performance. Write a report that describes all the changes you have made, presents performance results, and gives your conclusions.

11.4 Implement and measure the performance of a message-passing version of the red/black Gauss-Seidel program shown in Figure 11.6. Make your program as efficient as possible. What kinds of speedup do you get for various grid sizes and numbers of processors?

11.5 Consider the multigrid methods described in Section 11.1 and illustrated in Figures 11.7 and 11.8.

(a) Write a sequential program that implements a single V cycle. Use three levels and hence four grid sizes. Use grid sizes that make the arithmetic easy. For example, if the smallest grid has a width—from boundary to boundary—of 16, then it will have 15 interior points. The widths of the other grids would then be 32, 64, and 128.

(b) Parallelize your answer to (a) to produce a parallel program that uses shared variables.

(c) Modify your answer to (b) to use message passing instead of shared variables. You will probably want to use the heartbeat paradigm, as in Figure 11.5.

(d) Measure the performance of your programs from (b) and (c) for various grid sizes and numbers of processors. What kinds of speedup do you get? Write a report that describes and analyzes your results.

(e) Modify your programs from (a) through (c) to use a single W cycle rather than a V cycle. Remeasure the performance of each program. How does performance compare with your results from part (d)?

(f) Modify your programs to use the full multigrid method, then re-measure their performance. How does it compare to your results from part (d)?

11.6   Section 11.1 describes three methods for solving Laplace's equation: Jacobi iteration, red/black Gauss-Seidel, and multigrid. Implement sequential and parallel versions of these methods. Use shared variables and/or message passing for the parallel programs, depending on the hardware available to you. Measure the execution times of the various programs and the speedups of the parallel programs. Write a report that presents and analyzes your results. Also describe how difficult it was to write each program; this is subjective, of course, so be precise about what kinds of problems you ran into and how you overcame them.

11.7   Figures 11.9 and 11.11 to 11.14 present five programs for solving the gravitational *n*-body problem in two dimensions.

(a) Implement each program. Distribute the bodies uniformly around or inside a circle, and give them masses that are small enough to reduce the likelihood that two bodies ever "collide." (This would manifest itself in your program by arithmetic overflow when you divide by `distance**2`.) You might also want to play around with the value of `G`.

(b) Run a set of experiments to measure the performance of your programs for various (large) numbers of bodies and various numbers of processors. Write a report that presents and analyzes your results.

(c) Modify the programs to use three dimensions and then repeat part (b).

11.8   Consider the Barnes-Hut algorithm described at the end of Section 11.2. Write sequential, shared-variable, and message-passing programs. For the message-passing program, pick one of the manager/worker, heartbeat, or pipeline paradigms. Then run a set of experiments to measure the performance of your programs for various (large) numbers of bodies and various numbers of processors. Write a report that presents and analyzes your results. What speedups do you observe?

11.9 Your task is to model the motion of disks on a frictionless billiard table or bubbles bouncing around in zero gravity inside a box. Treat each object as a particle. Give the particles initial positions and velocities, then model their motion as they bounce off the walls and off each other. Assume perfect, frictionless motion and perfect rebounds. Implement your model first as a sequential program then as a parallel program. Ideally use a graphical output device to display the results.

11.10 Consider the following system of equations:

```
e + f +  g +  h  =   10
e     -  g       =   -2
2e - f + 4g - 3h =    0
     f +  g -  h  =    1
```

Set the system up as a matrix problem A x = b.

(a) Perform Gaussian elimination on A and b. Show how A and b change as you first eliminate e from three equations, then f from two of the remaining equations, and so on. Then go through the back-substitution phase to compute the values of x.

(b) Perform the LU decomposition of A. Show how the matrix changes each time you select a pivot row. Then solve the system of equations by first using forward elimination to solve L y = b and then using backward substitution to solve U x = y.

11.11 Consider the sequential program for LU decomposition in Figure 11.16.

(a) Implement the program. Then add code to the program to confirm that your implementation is correct—namely, that L × U is equal to A.

(b) Modify the program so that the LU decomposition is computed in place—namely, that it is stored in matrix A as described in the text.

11.12 Consider the outlines of the shared and distributed programs for LU decomposition in Figures 11.18 and 11.19.

(a) Develop implementations of the two programs using a high-level language such as SR or a message-passing library such as MPI.

(b) Conduct a set of performance experiments with your programs. Use various large matrix sizes and run your programs on various numbers of processors. Calculate the speedup of each program.

(c) Design, implement, and measure the performance of a pipeline algorithm for LU decomposition.

(d) Design, implement, and measure the performance of a manager/workers algorithm for LU decomposition.

(e) Compare the performance of the three message-passing programs—heartbeat, pipeline, and manager/workers. Construct a table similar to Table 11.1, and determine the speedup for each program for different size matrices and different numbers of processors.

11.13 LU decomposition has a lot of communication and synchronization overhead. Implement a parallel program for LU decomposition using either shared variables or message passing. Then construct a set of experiments to determine how much computation is required in order for your program to be scalable—i.e., to have an efficiency that stays close to 1.0 as the number of processors increases. Write a report describing your experiments and results.

11.14 The *inverse* of a nonsingular matrix A is a matrix A^{-1} such that $A \times A^{-1} = I$, where I is the identity matrix—i.e., a matrix with ones on the diagonal and zeros elsewhere. The columns of A^{-1} are the solutions of the following linear systems:

$$A \; x_1 = e_1, \; A \; x_2 = e_2, \; \ldots, \; A \; x_n = e_n$$

Each e_i is a unit vector that has a one in the ith position and zeros elsewhere.

(a) Write a sequential program to compute the inverse of input matrix A. First compute the LU decomposition of A (see Figure 11.16). Then solve the n equations above (see Figure 11.17).

(b) Parallelize your answer to (a) using either shared variables or message passing. (*Hint:* The n equations are independent.) Evaluate the performance of your program and calculate its speedup for various matrix sizes and numbers of processors.

11.15 Research some scientific computing problem or method—such as the Fast Fourier Transform, the Fast Multipole Method, some nonlinear optimization problem, the conjugant gradient method for solving PDEs, or Monte Carlo methods. Pick an algorithm, write sequential and parallel programs that implement it, then measure the performance of your programs. Write a report describing the problem, algorithm, programs, and performance results.

12

Languages, Compilers, Libraries, and Tools

The focus of this book has been on writing imperative programs with explicit processes, communication, and synchronization. These are the most common kinds of concurrent programs, and they are what the hardware executes. We have programmed algorithms using a high-level notation in order to make the solutions clear and succinct. The concurrency mechanisms in our notation are similar to those in the SR language; the sequential mechanisms are similar to those in C. This chapter describes additional approaches and tools for high-performance computing.

The most common way to write a parallel program is to use a sequential language and a subroutine library. In particular, the bodies of processes are written in a sequential language such as C or Fortran. Process creation, communication, and synchronization are then programmed by calling library functions. We have already seen the Pthreads library for shared-memory machines and the MPI library for message passing. Section 12.1 shows how to program Jacobi iteration using these libraries. Then we describe OpenMP, an emerging standard for shared-memory programming, and illustrate its use by again programming Jacobi iteration.

A quite different way to develop a parallel program is to employ a parallelizing compiler. Such a compiler automatically finds parallelism in a sequential program and then produces a correctly synchronized parallel program that contains sequential code plus library calls. Section 12.2 gives an overview of parallelizing compilers. The section describes dependence analysis, which is the basis for determining which parts of a program can be executed in parallel, and then describes various program transformations that are used to convert sequential loops into parallel loops. The advantages of parallelizing compilers are that they can be used to parallelize existing application codes and that they free the programmer from having to learn how to write a parallel program. The disadvantages are that it is difficult to parallelize sophisticated algorithms and that it can be hard to achieve optimal performance.

A third way to develop a parallel program is to use a high-level language in which some or all parallelism, communication, and synchronization are implicit. Section 12.3 describes several classes of high-level languages and summarizes important languages from each class. We use Jacobi iteration and other applications described earlier to illustrate the use of each language and to facilitate comparisons between them. We also describe three abstract models that can be used to characterize the execution time of parallel algorithms. The section ends with a case study of High Performance Fortran (HPF), the latest member of the Fortran family of languages for scientific computing. The compilers for languages like HPF employ some of the techniques used by parallelizing compilers, and they produce programs that contain sequential code plus library calls.

Section 12.4 describes software tools that aid the development, evaluation, and use of parallel programs. We first describe tools for performance measurement, visualization, and what is called computational steering. Then we describe *metacomputing*, an emerging approach for harnessing the computational power of diverse machines connected by high-speed networks. For example, the simulation part of a scientific computation might execute on a remote supercomputer and the control and visualization parts might execute on a local graphics workstation. As a specific example, the last part of Section 12.4 describes the new Globus metacomputing infrastructure toolkit.

12.1 Parallel Programming Libraries

A parallel programming library contains subroutines for process creation, process management, communication, and synchronization. The nature of the routines—and especially their implementation—depends on whether the library supports shared-variable programming or message passing.

The Pthreads library is a commonly available standard for writing shared-variable programs in the C language. The MPI and PVM libraries are two common standards for message passing; both have widely used, public domain implementations that support both C and Fortran. OpenMP is a new standard for shared-memory programming that is being implemented by the major vendors of high-performance machines. In contrast to Pthreads, OpenMP is a set of compiler directives and library routines, has a Fortran binding, and provides support for data parallel computations. This section shows how to program Jacobi iteration using the Pthreads and MPI libraries and the OpenMP directives.

12.1.1 Case Study: Pthreads

We introduced the Pthreads library in Section 4.6 and described the routines for using threads and semaphores. In Section 5.5 we described and illustrated the routines for locks and condition variables. We can use these mechanisms to implement Jacobi iterations as shown in Figure 12.1. The program is a straightforward translation of the shared-variable program in Figure 11.3. As usual in a Pthreads program, the main routine initializes thread attributes, reads command-line arguments, initializes global variables, and then creates the workers. After the workers terminate, the main routine prints the results.

Each worker thread is responsible for a contiguous strip of the two grids. For simplicity, we declare a fixed maximum size for each grid. We also assume that the grid size is a multiple of the number of workers. Finally, we have omitted the body of the barrier routine. Figure 5.18 contains one possible Pthreads implementation of a barrier using locks and condition variables. However, if each worker executes on its own processor, it would be far more efficient to use a busy-waiting dissemination barrier (see Section 3.4).

12.1.2 Case Study: MPI

We introduced the MPI library in Section 7.8. Recall that MPI contains a variety of routines for point-to-point and global communication. Here we use some of the routines to program Jacobi iteration as shown in Figure 12.2. The program is similar to the message-passing program in Figure 11.4.

The program in Figure 12.2 contains three functions: `main`, `Coordinator`, and `Worker`. We assume that a total of `numWorkers+1` instances of the program are running. (These are started using a command specific to the MPI implementation that is employed.) Each instance begins by executing the `main` routine, which initializes MPI and reads command-line arguments. Then `main` calls either `Coordinator` or `Worker`, depending on its rank (identity).

Each `Worker` process is responsible for a strip of points. It first initializes its two grids and determines its two neighbors, `left` and `right`. Next, the workers repeatedly exchange the edges of their grids with their neighbors and then update their points. After `numIters` exchange/update cycles, each worker sends the rows of its grid to the coordinator, computes the maximum difference

```
/* Jacobi iteration using Pthreads */

# include <pthread.h>
# include <stdio.h>
# define SHARED 1
# define MAXGRID 258    /* maximum size, with boundaries */
# define MAXWORKERS 16   /* maximum number of workers   */

void *Worker(void *);
void Barrier(int);

int gridSize, numWorkers, numIters, stripSize;
double maxDiff[MAXWORKERS];
double grid[MAXGRID][MAXGRID], new[MAXGRID][MAXGRID];
declarations of other global variables, such as barrier flags;

int main(int argc, char *argv[]) {
  pthread_t workerid[MAXWORKERS];  /* thread ids and */
  pthread_attr_t attr;             /* attributes     */
  int i; double maxdiff = 0.0;

  /* set global thread attributes */
  pthread_attr_init(&attr);
  pthread_attr_setscope(&attr, PTHREAD_SCOPE_SYSTEM);

  /* read command line arguments */
  /* assume gridSize is multiple of numWorkers */
  gridSize = atoi(argv[1]); numWorkers = atoi(argv[2]);
  numIters = atoi(argv[3]);
  stripSize = gridSize/numWorkers;

  initialize grids and flags for barrier;

  /* create the workers, then wait for them to finish */
  for (i = 0; i < numWorkers; i++)
    pthread_create(&workerid[i], &attr, Worker,
                   (void *) i);
  for (i = 0; i < numWorkers; i++)
    pthread_join(workerid[i], NULL);

  compute maxdiff and print results;
}

void *Worker(void *arg) {
  int myid = (int) arg;
  double mydiff;
  int i, j, iters, firstRow, lastRow;
```

```
/* determine first and last rows of my strip */
firstRow = myid*stripSize + 1;
lastRow = firstRow + stripSize - 1;

for (iters = 1; iters <= numIters; iters++) {
  /* update my points */
  for (i = firstRow; i <= lastRow; i++)
    for (j = 1; j <= gridSize; j++)
      new[i][j] = (grid[i-1][j] + grid[i+1][j] +
                   grid[i][j-1] + grid[i][j+1]) * 0.25;
  Barrier(myid);
  /* update my points again */
  for (i = firstRow; i <= lastRow; i++)
    for (j = 1; j <= gridSize; j++)
      grid[i][j] = (new[i-1][j] + new[i+1][j] +
                    new[i][j-1] + new[i][j+1]) * 0.25;
  Barrier(myid);
}
compute the maximum difference in my strip;
maxDiff[myid] = mydiff;
}

void Barrier(int workerid) {
  /* details not shown */
}
```

Figure 12.1   Jacobi iteration using Pthreads.

between pairs of points in its strip, and finally calls `MPI_Reduce` to send `mydiff` to the coordinator.

The `Coordinator` process merely gathers results from the workers. It first receives the rows of the final grid from each worker. Then it calls `MPI_Reduce` to receive and reduce the maximum differences computed by each worker. Note that the arguments in the calls of `MPI_Reduce` are the same in the workers and the coordinator. The next to last argument, `COORDINATOR`, specifies that the reduction is to occur within the coordinator process.

12.1.3 Case Study: OpenMP

OpenMP is a set of compiler directives and library routines that are used to express shared-memory parallelism. The OpenMP Application Program Inter-

```
# include <mpi.h>      /* Jacobi iteration using MPI */
# include <stdio.h>
# define MAXGRID 258   /* maximum grid, with boundaries */
# define COORDINATOR 0  /* rank of Coordinator */
# define TAG 0          /* not used */
static void Coordinator(int,int,int);
static void Worker(int,int,int,int,int);

int main(int argc, char *argv[]) {
  int myid, numIters;
  int numWorkers, gridSize; /* assume gridSize is     */
  int stripSize;            /* multiple of numWorkers */

  MPI_Init(&argc, &argv);              /* initialize MPI */
  MPI_Comm_rank(MPI_COMM_WORLD, &myid);
  MPI_Comm_size(MPI_COMM_WORLD, &numWorkers);
  numWorkers--;  /* one coordinator, rest are workers */
  read gridSize and numIters; compute stripSize;
  if (myid == COORDINATOR)
    Coordinator(numWorkers, stripSize, gridSize);
  else
    Worker(myid,numWorkers,stripSize,gridSize,numIters);
  MPI_Finalize();  /* clean up MPI */
}

static void Coordinator(int numWorkers,
                    int stripSize, int gridSize) {
  double grid[MAXGRID][MAXGRID];
  double mydiff = 0.0, maxdiff = 0.0;
  int i, worker, startrow, endrow;
  MPI_Status status;

  /* get final grid values from Workers */
  for (worker = 1; worker <= numWorkers; worker++) {
    startrow = (worker-1)*stripSize + 1;
    endrow = startrow + stripSize - 1;
    for (i = startrow; i <= endrow; i++)
      MPI_Recv(&grid[i][1], gridSize, MPI_DOUBLE, worker,
          TAG, MPI_COMM_WORLD, &status);
  }
  /* reduce differences from Workers */
  MPI_Reduce(&mydiff, &maxdiff, 1, MPI_DOUBLE,
          MPI_MAX, COORDINATOR, MPI_COMM_WORLD);
  print results;
}
```

```
static void Worker(int myid, int numWorkers,
          int stripSize, int gridSize, int numIters) {
  double grid [2][MAXGRID][MAXGRID];
  double mydiff, maxdiff;
  int i, j, iters;
  int current = 0, next = 1; /* current and next grids */
  int left, right;           /* neighboring workers    */
  MPI_Status status;

  initialize my grids; determine left and right neighbors;

  for (iters = 1; iters <= numIters; iters++) {

    /* exchange my boundaries with my neighbors */
    if (right != 0)  MPI_Send(&grid[next][stripSize][1],
       gridSize, MPI_DOUBLE, right, TAG, MPI_COMM_WORLD);
    if (left != 0)  MPI_Send(&grid[next][1][1], gridSize,
                MPI_DOUBLE, left, TAG, MPI_COMM_WORLD);
    if (left != 0)  MPI_Recv(&grid[next][0][1], gridSize,
       MPI_DOUBLE, left, TAG, MPI_COMM_WORLD, &status);
    if (right != 0) MPI_Recv(&grid[next][stripSize+1][1],
        gridSize, MPI_DOUBLE, right, TAG,
        MPI_COMM_WORLD, &status);

    /* update my points */
    for (i = 1; i <= stripSize; i++)
      for (j = 1; j <= gridSize; j++)
        grid[next][i][j] = (grid[current][i-1][j] +
          grid[current][i+1][j] + grid[current][i][j-1] +
          grid[current][i][j+1]) * 0.25;
    current = next;  next = 1-next;  /* swap grids */
  }

  /* send my rows of final grid to the coordinator */
  for (i = 1; i <= stripSize; i++) {
    MPI_Send(&grid[current][i][1], gridSize, MPI_DOUBLE,
         COORDINATOR, TAG, MPI_COMM_WORLD);
  }
  compute mydiff;
  /* reduce mydiff with Coordinator */
  MPI_Reduce(&mydiff, &maxdiff, 1, MPI_DOUBLE,
         MPI_MAX, COORDINATOR, MPI_COMM_WORLD);
}
```

Figure 12.2   Jacobi iteration using MPI.

faces (APIs) were developed by a group representing the major vendors of high-performance computing hardware and software. A Fortran interface was defined in late 1997; a C/C++ interface was defined in late 1998; efforts to standardize both are underway. The interfaces support the same functionality, but they are expressed differently due to linguistic differences between Fortran, C, and C++.

The majority of the OpenMP interface is a set of compiler directives. The programmer adds these to a sequential program to tell the compiler what parts of the program to execute concurrently and to specify synchronization points. The directives can be added incrementally, so OpenMP provides a path for parallelizing existing software. These attributes are in contrast to Pthreads and MPI, which are library routines that are linked with and called from a sequential program and which require the programmer to manually divide up the work.

Below we describe and illustrate the use of OpenMP for Fortran programs. We first present a sequential program for Jacobi iteration. Then we add OpenMP directives to the program to express parallelism. At the end of the section, we briefly summarize additional directives and the C/C++ interface.

Figure 12.3 contains an outline of a sequential program that implements Jacobi iteration. The syntax is somewhat peculiar because the program is written using Fortran's fixed-format conventions. In particular, comment lines begin with a `c` in column 1 and declarations and statements begin in column 7. Additional comments begin with the `!` symbol. All comments extend to the end of the line.

The sequential program has two routines: `main` and `jacobi`. The `main` routine reads in values for `n` (the grid size including boundaries) and `maxiters` (the maximum number of iterations) and then calls `jacobi`. The data values are stored in a common area and hence passed implicitly from `main` to `jacobi`. This permits `jacobi` to allocate storage dynamically for `grid` and `new`.

The `jacobi` routine implements the sequential algorithm given earlier in Figure 11.2. The main difference between the code in Figure 12.3 and that in Figure 11.2 is due to the difference in syntax between our pseudo-C and Fortran. In Fortran, the lower bound for each dimension of an array is one, so the interior points of the grids are in rows and columns `2` to `n-1`. In addition, Fortran stores matrices in column-major order, so the nested `do` loops iterate first over columns and then over rows.

OpenMP employs a fork/join execution model. Initially there is a single thread of execution. When the compiler encounters one of the `parallel` directives, it inserts code to fork a number of subthreads. Together, the main thread and the subthreads comprise what is called the set of *worker threads*. The actual number of worker threads is chosen by the compiler (the default) or is specified

```
      program main              ! the main program
      integer n,maxiters        ! common data
      common /idat/ n,maxiters
      read values for n and maxiters (not shown)
      call jacobi()
      stop
      end

      subroutine jacobi()       ! implements Jacobi iteration
      integer n,maxiters        ! repeat declaration of common
      common /idat/ n,maxiters
      integer i,j,iters
      double precision grid(n,n), new(n,n)
      double precision maxdiff,tempdiff
      initialize grid and new (see text)
c main loop:  update grids maxiters times
      do iters = 1,maxiters,2    ! go from 1 to maxiters by 2
        do j = 2,n-1             ! update points in new
          do i = 2,n-1
            new(i,j) = (grid(i-1,j) + grid(i+1,j) +
                        grid(i,j-1) + grid(i,j+1)) * 0.25
          enddo
        enddo
        do j = 2,n-1             ! update points in grid
          do i = 2,n-1
            grid(i,j) = (new(i-1,j) + new(i+1,j) +
                         new(i,j-1) + new(i,j+1)) * 0.25
          enddo
        enddo
      enddo

c compute maximum difference
      maxdiff = 0.0
      do j = 2,n-1
        do i = 2,n-1
          tempdiff = abs(grid(i,j)-new(i,j))
          maxdiff = max(maxdiff,tempdiff)
        enddo
      enddo
      return
      end
```

Figure 12.3   Sequential Jacobi iteration in Fortran.

by the user, either statically by means of an environment variable or dynamically by calling an OpenMP library routine.

To parallelize a program using OpenMP, the programmer first identifies the parts of the program that can be executed in parallel—such as loops—and surrounds them by **parallel** and **end parallel** directives. Each worker thread executes this code, working on different subsets of the iteration space (for data parallel loops) or perhaps calling different routines (for task parallel programs). Second, the programmer inserts additional directives to synchronize execution. Thus, the compiler takes responsibility for forking threads and assigning them work (for loops), but the programmer is responsible for ensuring that there is sufficient synchronization.

As a concrete example, the following sequential code initializes the interior points of **grid** and **new** to zeros:

```
do j = 2,n-1
  do i = 2,n-1
    grid(i,j) = 0.0
    new(i,j) = 0,0
  enddo
enddo
```

This code can be parallelized by surrounding it by three OpenMP compiler directives as follows:

```
!$omp parallel do
!$omp& shared(n,grid,new), private(i,j)
      do j = 2,n-1
        do i = 2,n-1
          grid(i,j) = 0.0
          new(i,j) = 0,0
        enddo
      enddo
!$omp end parallel do
```

Each compiler directive begins with !$omp. The first one above specifies the start of a parallel **do** loop. The second directive is a clause that modifies the first one; this is indicated by the & character appended to !$omp. The clause above says that n, **grid**, and **new** are shared variables and that i and j are private to each worker thread. The last directive indicates the end of the parallel **do** loop; it also introduces an implicit barrier synchronization point.

For this specific example, the compiler will divide up the iterations of the *outer* **do** loop (on j) and assign them to the workers in some implementation-dependent manner. The programmer can add a `schedule` clause to control how work is assigned; the types of scheduling supported include block, strip (cyclic), and dynamic (bag of tasks). Each worker will execute the inner `do` loop (on `i`) for the columns that are assigned to it.

Figure 12.4 shows one way to parallelize the body of `jacobi` using the OpenMP directives. First the main thread forks workers to initialize the grids, as shown above. Second, the main thread initializes `maxdiff`. We have moved the initialization of `maxdiff` because we want it to be initialized by one thread before it is used to compute the maximum difference. (We could instead have used a `single` directive, as discussed below.)

After initializing shared variables, we use a `parallel` directive to fork the worker threads. The two clauses specify which variables are shared and which are private. Each worker executes the main computational loop. Within the loop, we have added `do` directives to specify that the iterations of the outer loops that update `new` and `grid` are to be divided among the workers. The ends of these loops are marked by `end do` directives, which also provide implicit barriers.

After the main loop terminates (at the same time in each worker), we use another `do` directive to compute the maximum difference in parallel. Within this section, we want to use `maxdiff` as a reduction variable, so we add a `reduction` clause to the `do` directive. The semantics of a reduction variable are that every update is an atomic action, in this case using the `max` function. In fact, OpenMP implements a reduction variable by using private variables within each worker; the values of the private variables are merged atomically into a single value at the implicit barrier at the end of the parallelized loop.

The program in Figure 12.4 illustrates a few of the most important OpenMP directives. There are several additional directives for parallelization, synchronization, and controlling the data environment. For example, the following directives can be used to exert more control over how statements are synchronized:

`critical`	Execute a block of statements as a critical section.
`atomic`	Execute a single statement atomically.
`single`	Execute a block of statements in a single worker thread.
`barrier`	Execute a barrier among all worker threads.

OpenMP also defines a few library routines that allow a program to query and control its execution environment. For example, there are routines to set the number of worker threads, adjust the number dynamically, and determine the identity of a thread.

```
                    subroutine jacobi()
                    declarations of common, shared, and private variables
                    initialize grid and new in parallel (see text)
                    maxdiff = 0.0                    ! initialize in main thread

c start worker threads; each executes the main loop
!$omp parallel
!$omp& shared(n,maxiters,grid,new,maxdiff)
!$omp& private(i,j,iters,tempdiff)

                    do iters = 1,maxiters,2
!$omp do          ! divide up the iterations of the outer loop
                    do j = 2,n-1
                      do i = 2,n-1
                        new(i,j) = (grid(i-1,j) + grid(i+1,j) +
                               grid(i,j-1) + grid(i,j+1)) * 0.25
                      enddo
                    enddo
!$omp end do    ! implicit barrier

!$omp do          ! divide up the iterations of the outer loop
                    do j = 2,n-1
                      do i = 2,n-1
                        grid(i,j) = (new(i-1,j) + new(i+1,j) +
                               new(i,j-1) + new(i,j+1)) * 0.25
                      enddo
                    enddo
!$omp end do    ! implicit barrier
                    enddo    !  end of main computational loop

c compute maximum difference into a reduction variable
!$omp do          ! divide up the iterations of the outer loop
!$omp& reduction(max: maxdiff)    ! use a reduction variable
                    do j = 2,n-1
                      do i = 2,n-1
                        tempdiff = abs(grid(i,j)-new(i1,j))
                        maxdiff = max(maxdiff,tempdiff) ! atomic update
                      enddo
                    enddo
!$omp end do    ! implicit barrier
!$omp end parallel    ! end of parallel section
                    return
                    end
```

Figure 12.4   Parallel Jacobi iteration using OpenMP.

The OpenMP interface for C/C++ provides the same functionality as the Fortran interface. The differences are due to linguistic differences between C/C++ and Fortran. For example, the parallel directive has the following form:

> `pragma omp parallel` clauses

The keyword `pragma` indicates a compiler directive. Since C uses `for` loops rather than `do` loops for definite iteration, the equivalent of the `do` directive is

> `pragma omp for` clauses

There are no `end` directives in the C/C++ interface. Instead, braces are placed around blocks of code to indicate the extent of directives.

12.2 Parallelizing Compilers

The focus of this text is on how to write explicitly parallel programs—namely, programs in which the programmer must identify the processes, divide the data among them, and program all required communication and synchronization. An explicitly parallel program is what is ultimately required before a program can be executed by a multiple processor machine. However, there are other approaches to writing parallel programs. This section describes parallelizing compilers, which take sequential programs as input and convert them to parallel programs. The next section describes higher-level approaches, including data parallel and functional languages.

Parallelizing a program requires identifying tasks that are independent of each other and hence that can be carried out at the same time. Some programs are *embarrassingly parallel*, meaning that they have a huge number of independent tasks; examples are matrix multiplication and computing Mandelbrot sets. Most programs, however, do not have completely independent parts. Instead, at times the parts need to synchronize. For example, in a producer/consumer program, the processes need to synchronize when communicating with each other. As another example, in a grid computation processes need to perform barrier synchronization after each update phase.

The goal of a parallelizing compiler is to take a sequential program and produce a correct parallel program. To do so, it performs what is called *dependence analysis*. In particular, the compiler determines which parts of the sequential program are independent—and hence are candidates for parallel execution—and which parts are dependent on each other—and hence require either sequential execution or some other form of synchronization. Since most of the computation in a sequential program is inside loops, especially nested loops, a parallelizing compiler concentrates on ways to parallelize loops.

This section defines the different kinds of data dependences and summarizes how compilers perform dependence analysis. It then describes some of the common program transformations that are used to convert sequential loops to parallel loops. The Historical Notes at the end of this chapter describe sources for detailed information.

Parallelizing compilers have become sophisticated and are now quite good at producing efficient, shared-variable parallel programs. This is especially true for scientific programs that have many loops and many time-consuming numerical calculations. However, it is far more difficult to produce good message-passing programs, because there are many choices for program structure and communication, as we saw in Chapter 11. Moreover, it is difficult to parallelize sophisticated sequential algorithms, such as multigrid and Barnes-Hut.

12.2.1 Dependence Analysis

Suppose a sequential program contains two statements, S_1 and S_2, and that S_1 occurs before S_2. A *data dependence* exists between the two statements if they read or write a common memory location in such a way that their execution order must be preserved. There are three important types of data dependence:[1]

1. *Flow dependence.* Statement S_2 is flow dependent on S_1 if S_2 reads a location that S_1 writes. (This is also called *true dependence*.)

2. *Antidependence.* Statement S_2 is antidependent on S_1 if S_2 writes a location that S_1 reads.

3. *Output dependence.* Statement S_2 is output dependent on S_1 if S_2 writes a location that S_1 also writes.

We will say simply that S_2 *depends on* S_1 if there is a data dependence, but we do not care which type it is.

As an example, consider the following sequence of statements:

```
S₁: a = b + d;
S₂: c = a * 3;
S₃: a = b + c;
S₄: e = a / 2;
```

---

[1] A fourth type is input dependence, which occurs when two statements read from the same location. Input dependence does not restrict the order in which statements are executed.

Statement S_2 is flow dependent on S_1, because it reads a. Statement S_3 is anti-dependent on S_2, because it writes a; S_3 is also output dependent on S_1, because they both write a. Finally, statement S_4 is flow dependent on S_3, because it reads a. (S_4 is also flow dependent on S_1, but S_1 has to be executed before S_3.) Because of these dependencies, the four statements have to be executed in the listed order; they cannot be rearranged without altering the results.

It is straightforward to determine data dependences for straight-line code that references only scalar variables. It is much harder to determine dependences for loops and array references, which usually occur together. This is because array references have subscripts, and subscripts usually reference loop indices; hence array subscripts have different values in different loop iterations. In fact, the general problem of computing all data dependencies in a program is unsolvable because of array aliasing that can result from the use of pointers or function calls within subscript expressions. Even if pointers are not allowed—as occurs in Fortran—and subscript expressions are linear functions, the problem is NP hard, meaning that there is unlikely to be any efficient algorithm for it.

To see the issues raised by loops and arrays, consider again the code from Figure 11.17 for the forward substitution phase of solving a system of equations:

```
for [i = 1 to n] {
 S₁: sum = 0.0;
      for [j = 1 to i-1]
 S₂:    sum = sum + LU[ps[i],j] * x[j];
 S₃: x[i] = b[ps[i]] - sum;
}
```

Within each iteration of the outer loop, S_2 depends on S_1, and S_3 depends on both S_1 and S_2. The inner loop contains a single statement, so there is no dependence within that loop. However, the inner loop *carries* a dependence from S_2 to itself, because S_2 both reads and writes sum. Similarly, the outer loop carries a dependence: S_2 depends on S_3, because the value written into x[i] on one iteration of the outer loop is read on every subsequent iteration.

Dependence testing is the problem of determining whether there is a data dependence between any pair of subscripted references. The general setting for the problem is a nested loop with the form

```
for [i₁ = l₁ to u₁] { ...
    for[iₙ = lₙ to uₙ] {
   S₁: a[f₁, ..., fₙ] = ...;
   S₂: ... = a[g₁, ..., gₙ];
    } ... }
```

There are n nested loops and hence n index variables. The l_j and u_j are functions that define the lower and upper bounds of the n index variables. The innermost loop contains two statements that reference elements of an n-dimensional array a; the first writes into a, and the second reads a. The f_j and g_j in the two statements are function calls that take the index variables as arguments; they return values for the subscripts.

We can thus ask the dependence-testing question for the above loop: Are there values of the index variables such that $f_1 = g_1$, $f_2 = g_2$, and so on? The answer will determine when *S2* depends on *S1* in the same loop iteration, and when there are loop-carried dependences between the statements.

Dependence testing can be represented as a special system of linear equations having the following form:

$$A_1 \ x = b_1 \quad \text{and} \quad A_2 \ x \leq b_2$$

The coefficients in matrices A_1 and A_2 are determined by the f and g functions in the program. The values in vectors b_1 and b_2 are determined by the bounds on the index variables. A solution to the first equation is an assignment of values to the index variables that makes the array references overlap. The second equation ensures that the values of the index variables are within the bounds defined by the l and u functions. Solving the above problem is similar to solving two linear equations—as shown in Section 11.3—but it differs in two critical ways: (1) the solution must be a vector of integers not reals, and (2) there is a less-than-or-equals relation in the second equation. These differences are what makes the problem NP hard even when subscript expressions are linear functions and do not contain pointers. (Dependence testing in this case is equivalent to a special case of what is called integer linear programming.)

Although dependence testing is hard—and in the worst case unsolvable—there are a number of efficient tests that work for special cases. In fact, it is possible to determine whether two array references overlap for almost all loops that occur in practice. For example, there are efficient tests when all loop bounds are constant or when the bounds for inner loops depend only on those for outer loops. The forward substitution loop for Gaussian elimination shown above meets these constraints: the bounds for i are constant, one bound for j is constant, and the other bound for j depends on the value of i. If a compiler cannot, however, determine whether two array references are disjoint, then it pessimistically assumes that there is a dependency.

12.2.2 Program Transformations

Dependence testing is the first step in a parallelizing compiler. The second step is to use the results to parallelize loops. Below we use a series of examples to illustrate how this is done.

As a first example, assume that function **f** has no side effects, and consider the following nested loop:

```
for [i = 1 to n]
  for [j = 1 to n]
    a[i,j] = a[i,j] + f(i,j);
```

There are no data dependences, because no array references overlap. Hence, the assignments to **a** can be executed in any order. When a parallelizing compiler encounters this kind of statement, it will most likely parallelize the outer loop as follows:[2]

```
co [i = 1 to n]
  for [j = 1 to n]
    a[i,j] = a[i,j] + f(i,j);
```

This would result in **n** processes, each of which assigns to a row of **a**.

If the matrix is stored in memory in column-major order rather than in row-major order, it would be more efficient to update columns in parallel. However, it would be inefficient simply to parallelize the inner loop instead of the outer loop in the sequential program. (We would repeatedly create and destroy processes, and each would consist of only a single assignment statement.) Instead, we should first *interchange* the two **for** loops to produce an equivalent program:

```
for [j = 1 to n]
  for [i = 1 to n]
    a[i,j] = a[i,j] + f(i,j);
```

Now we can parallelize the outer loop using a **co** statement.

Loop interchange is one type of program transformation used by parallelizing compilers. Below we describe several more of the most useful transformations: privatization, scalar expansion, loop distribution, loop fusion, unroll and jam, loop unrolling, strip mining, loop blocking, and loop skewing. These are summarized in Figure 12.5. They are used to expose parallelism, break dependences, and optimize memory usage, as described below.

---

[2] We use **co** to specify parallel loops. Other languages use a similar kind of statement such as **parallel do** or **for all**.

Loop interchange	Interchange outer and inner loops
Privatization	Give each process a copy of a variable
Scalar expansion	Replace a scalar by an array
Loop distribution	Split one loop into two separate ones
Loop fusion	Combine two loops into one
Unroll and jam	Combine interchange, strip mining, unrolling
Loop unrolling	Replicate loop body and do fewer iterations
Strip mining	Divide iterations of one loop into two nested loops
Loop blocking (*tiling*)	Divide iteration space into rectangular blocks
Loop skewing	Alter loop bounds to expose wavefront parallelism

Figure 12.5   Program transformations used by parallelizing compilers.

Consider the standard sequential program for forming the matrix product **c** of two $n \times n$ matrices **a** and **b**:

```
for [i = 1 to n]
  for [j = 1 to n] {
    sum = 0.0;
    for [k = 1 to n]
      sum = sum + a[i,k] * b[k,j];
    c[i,j] = sum;
  }
```

The three statements in the body of the second loop (on **j**) depend on each other, so they have to be executed sequentially. The two outer loops are independent in their uses of the matrices, because **a** and **b** are only read and each element of **c** is distinct. However, all three loops carry dependencies because **sum** is a single scalar variable. We could parallelize either or both of the outer loops if we *privatize* **sum**—namely, give each process its own copy. Privatization is thus a dependency-breaking transformation.

A different way to parallelize the matrix multiplication program is to use *scalar expansion*, which replaces a single variable by an array. In particular, we can replace **sum** by **c[i,j]**. Here this transformation also allows us to get rid of the last assignment statement, so we get the program

```
for [i = 1 to n]
  for [j = 1 to n] {
    c[i,j] = 0.0;
    for [k = 1 to n]
      c[i,j] = c[i,j] + a[i,k] * b[k,j];
  }
```

The two outer loops no longer carry dependencies, so we can now parallelize the i loop, interchange and parallelize the j loop, or parallelize both loops.[3]

The innermost loop above depends on the initialization of c[i,j]. However, the elements of c can be initialized in any order as long as each element is initialized before we start using it. We can use another transformation, *loop distribution*, to separate the initialization from the inner-product computation. Loop distribution takes independent statements in the body of a single loop (or loop nest) and places them in separate loops with identical headers, as in

```
for [i = 1 to n]      # initialize c[*,*]
  for [j = 1 to n]
    c[i,j] = 0.0;

for [i = 1 to n]      # compute inner products
  for [j = 1 to n]
    for [k = 1 to n]
      c[i,j] = c[i,j] + a[i,k] * b[k,j];
```

Now we can use co to parallelize each outer loop (on i). Alternatively, we can combine the outer loops and use co once, as long as we introduce a barrier synchronization point between the inner loops, as follows:

```
co [i = 1 to n] {
  for [j = 1 to n]
    c[i,j] = 0.0;
  BARRIER;
  for [j = 1 to n]
    for [k = 1 to n]
      c[i,j] = c[i,j] + a[i,k] * b[k,j];
}
```

The tradeoff between these two approaches is whether it is cheaper to create

---

[3] For this application, it would be more efficient to use privatization than scalar expansion. First, sum could be stored in a register. Second, the references to c[i,j] in the above code would probably result in false sharing and hence very poor cache performance.

processes twice or to create them once and employ a barrier; barrier synchronization will usually be more efficient than process creation.

The above example of loop distribution increases the number of processes and makes each finer-grained in the sense that it does less work. Loop distribution is more commonly used to break dependencies and hence to expose parallelism. For example, suppose a loop has the form

```
for [i = 1 to n] {
  a[i] = ...;
  ... =  ... + a[i-1];
}
```

Here, the second statement depends on the result of the first statement from the previous iteration. If the statements are otherwise independent, we could distribute the loop so that the first assignment is executed by the first loop and the second is executed by the second loop, as follows:

```
for [i = 1 to n]
  a[i] = ...;
for [i = 1 to n]
  ... =  ... + a[i-1];
```

Then both loops could be parallelized (assuming there are no other dependencies).

Loop fusion is the dual of loop distribution. It takes loops that have the same header and independent bodies and combines (fuses) them into a single loop. Loop fusion is used to decrease the number of processes and to make them coarser-grained—namely, to give them more work.

Unroll and jam is another transformation that changes dependences. It also brings accesses to the same memory location closer together, and hence can improve performance by enabling reuse of registers or cache memory and by increasing the effectiveness of instruction-level parallelism (ILP) on multiple-issue processors. Consider again the matrix multiplication loops that compute inner products:

```
for [i = 1 to n]
  for [j = 1 to n]
    for [k = 1 to n]
      c[i,j] = c[i,j] + a[i,k] * b[k,j];
```

Unroll and jam uses *loop unrolling* to unroll the outermost loop, then jams (fuses) the resulting loops together so that the innermost loop contains multiple statements. If we apply unroll and jam to the above code, with one unrolling of the outer loop, we get

```
for [i = 1 to n by 2]   # half as many iterations
  for [j = 1 to n]
    for [k = 1 to n] {
      c[i,j] = c[i,j] + a[i,k] * b[k,j];
      c[i+1,j] = c[i+1,j] * b[k,j];
    }
```

In short, every time around the outermost loop, we compute two inner products. These are stored in `c[i,j]` and `c[i+1,j]`, which will be in adjacent memory locations if matrices are stored in row-major order.

Strip mining is a simple transformation that divides a single loop into two loops; the outer loop iterates once per strip, and the inner loop iterates over a strip. For example, unrolling the outer loop once in the matrix multiply program is equivalent to strip mining with a strip width of two:

```
for [i = 1 to n by 2]    # half as many iterations
  for [I = i to i+1]      # strip of two iterations
    for [j = 1 to n]
      for [k = 1 to n]
        c[I,j] = c[I,j] + a[I,k] * b[k,j];
```

Note that the assignment statement now uses `I` rather than `i`. Strip mining adjusts the granularity of loops and is used in combination with other transformations as described below.

The unroll and jam transformation is equivalent to strip mining the outer loop, interchanging the strip mined loop to the innermost position, then completely unrolling the innermost loop. For the above example, we would interchange the loop on `I` to the innermost position as follows:

```
for [i = 1 to n by 2]    # half as many iterations
  for [j = 1 to n]
    for [k = 1 to n]
      for [I = i to i+1]  # strip of two iterations
        c[I,j] = c[I,j] + a[I,k] * b[k,j];
```

If we now unroll the innermost loop—and hence replace `I` by its two values, `i` and `i+1`—we get the same program as for unroll and jam.

Loop blocking (or *tiling*) is another transformation that can improve memory locality and hence cache usage on a shared-memory machine or data layout on a distributed-memory machine. Consider the following code which sets matrix b to the transpose of matrix a:

```
for [i = 1 to n]
  for [j = 1 to n]
    b[i,j] = a[j,i];
```

Assuming that arrays are stored in row-major order, access to the elements of b has a *stride* of 1, meaning that each element of b is next to the previously referenced element of b. However, access to the elements of a has a stride of n, the length of a row. Thus, if cache lines contain more than one value, we are loading other values when we reference a but are not yet using them.

The loop-blocking transformation divides the iteration space into squares or rectangles, typically the width of a cache line. If a cache line contains w values of a or b, the matrix transpose code above would be changed to

```
for [i = 1 to n by W]          # for every W'th row
  for [j = 1 to n by W]        # and column, use a
    for [I = i to min(i+W-1, n)]  # block of width W
      for [J = j to min(j+W-1, n)]
        b[I,J] = a[J,I];
```

The two innermost loops now access a square of $w \times w$ elements at a time. Note that loop blocking is essentially a combination of strip mining and loop interchange.

Loop skewing is the final transformation we consider here. It is used to expose parallelism, especially along wave fronts. A wave-front computation is one in which updates to an array propagate like a wave. We saw this earlier with the forward and backward substitution phases of LU decomposition. Another example of a wave-front computation is the Gauss-Seidel method for solving PDEs (Section 11.1):

```
for [i = 1 to n]
  for [j = 1 to n]
    a[i,j] = (a[i-1,j] + a[i,j-1] +
              a[i+1,j] + a[i,j+1]) * 0.25;
```

Each new value of a depends on two values computed by previous iterations and two values that are not updated until future iterations. Figure 12.6 (a) illustrates these dependences; the dashed lines indicate the wave fronts.

Loop skewing does not change the computation being performed; it merely alters the loop bounds so that the wave fronts become columns rather than

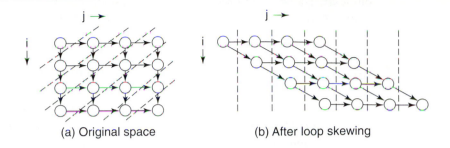

Figure 12.6   Data dependences for Gauss-Seidel iteration.

diagonals, as illustrated in Figure 12.6 (b). Skewing is accomplished by adding a multiple of the outer loop's index variable to the bounds of the inner loop's index variable, and then subtracting the same quantity from every use of the inner loop's index variable in the body of the inner loop. The multiple is called the *skew factor*. Using a skew factor of 1, the Gauss-Seidel code above becomes

```
for [i = 1 to n]
   for [j = i+1 to i+n]    # add i to previous bounds
      a[i,j-i] = (a[i-1,j-i] + a[i,j-i-1] +
                  a[i+1,j-i] + a[i,j-i+1]) * 0.25;
```

This exposes parallelism because there are no longer any dependences within each column of the iteration space. However, to utilize the parallelism on the `i` loop, we have to interchange the above loops. (As written above, the outer loop carries dependences.)

Interchanging skewed loops is somewhat tricky, because the bounds of the inner loop depend on the index variable in the outer loop. However, as long as the bounds of the original loops are independent, we can then compute the bounds for the interchanged, skewed loops as follows. Let `LI` and `UI` be the lower and upper bounds of the original outer loop; let `LJ` and `UJ` be the lower and upper bounds of the original inner loop; and let `f` be the skew factor. Then the bounds of the skewed loops after interchange are

```
for [j = (f*LI + LJ) to (f*UI + UJ)]
   for [i = max(LI, ceil((j-UJ)/f)) to
                 min(UI, ceil((j-LJ)/f))]
```

Applying the formulas to the Gauss-Seidel code, we get

```
for [j = 2 to n+n]
  for [i = max(1, j-n) to min(n, j-1)]
    a[i,j-i] = (a[i-1,j-i] + a[i,j-i-1] +
                a[i+1,j-i] + a[i,j-i+1]) * 0.25;
```

Now the inner loop can be parallelized. We can use either a co statement to create processes every time around the outer loop, or we can create the processes once and have them use flags to synchronize the waves. Neither approach is as efficient as being able to parallelize an outer loop, but wave-front parallelism is useful when n is large or when a machine directly supports fine-grained parallelism.

12.3 *Languages and Models*

Most high-performance parallel programs are written using a sequential language—usually C or Fortran—plus a library. There are several reasons for this. First, programmers are already familiar with a sequential language and have experience using it to write scientific codes. Second, libraries are available on the commonly used parallel computing platforms. Third, the goal of high-performance computing is performance, and libraries are close to the hardware, so they give the programmer low-level control.

However, there are several advantages to using a high-level language that contains mechanisms for both sequential and parallel programming. First, a language provides a higher level of abstraction that can help guide the programmer in solving a problem. Second, the sequential and parallel mechanisms can be integrated with each other, so that they work well together and so that similar things are expressed in similar ways. These two attributes make programs easier to write and to understand, and they also make them shorter. Third, a high-level language provides type checking to guard against many low-level errors. This also makes programs shorter and it can make them more robust, because it frees the programmer from having to check—or forgetting to check—the validity of data types. The challenges for a language designer are to develop a good set of abstractions, a powerful and clean set of mechanisms, *and* an efficient implementation.

Many different parallel programming languages have been developed. Figure 12.7 lists several that are widely used and/or that contain important ideas. The languages in the figure are grouped into classes based on their underlying programming model: shared variables, message passing, coordination, data parallel, and functional. The languages in the first three classes are used to write imperative programs in which processes, communication, and synchronization

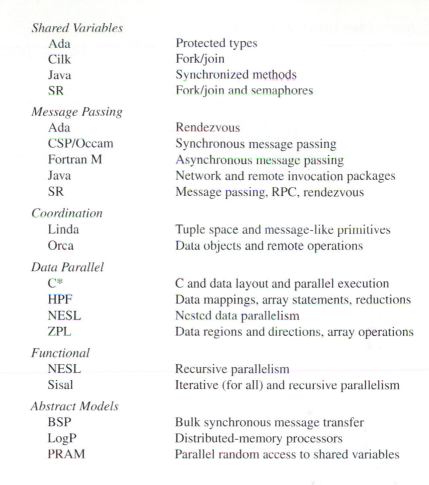

Shared Variables
Ada	Protected types
Cilk	Fork/join
Java	Synchronized methods
SR	Fork/join and semaphores

Message Passing
Ada	Rendezvous
CSP/Occam	Synchronous message passing
Fortran M	Asynchronous message passing
Java	Network and remote invocation packages
SR	Message passing, RPC, rendezvous

Coordination
Linda	Tuple space and message-like primitives
Orca	Data objects and remote operations

Data Parallel
C*	C and data layout and parallel execution
HPF	Data mappings, array statements, reductions
NESL	Nested data parallelism
ZPL	Data regions and directions, array operations

Functional
NESL	Recursive parallelism
Sisal	Iterative (for all) and recursive parallelism

Abstract Models
BSP	Bulk synchronous message transfer
LogP	Distributed-memory processors
PRAM	Parallel random access to shared variables

Figure 12.7   Languages and models for parallel programming.

are programmed explicitly. With data parallel languages, synchronization is implicit; with functional languages, both concurrency and synchronization are implicit. The last group in Figure 12.7 contains three abstract models that can be used to compare algorithms and predict performance.

Some of the languages listed in Figure 12.7 were described in earlier chapters. This section summarizes the novel aspects of the languages and models that have not yet been described, concluding with a more detailed description of High Performance Fortran (HPF). The Historical Notes at the end of the chapter give references for further information on specific languages and describe books and survey papers that contain broad overviews of languages and models.

12.3.1 *Imperative Languages*

The languages in the first three classes in Figure 12.7 are used to write imperative programs in which the programmer explicitly updates and synchronizes access to the program state—namely, the values of variables. All these languages contain some means to specify processes, tasks, or threads. They differ in how one programs communication and synchronization. One choice is to use shared variables for communication and shared locks, flags, semaphores, or monitors for synchronization. A second choice is to use messages for both communication and synchronization. Some languages support one choice or the other; some support both and hence let the programmer choose depending on the problem being solved or the machine architecture on which the program will run. A third choice is to provide a shared data space and message-like operations on it (see the discussion of coordination languages below).

We have already presented case studies of many of the languages that support explicit parallel programming. Three of those languages—Ada, Java, and SR—are listed twice in Figure 12.7, because they support both shared variables and message passing. Ada (Section 8.6) provides tasks, protected types to program monitors, and rendezvous for writing distributed programs. Java provides threads and synchronized methods for programming monitors (Section 5.4), a predefined language package for message passing using sockets and datagrams (Section 7.9), and another package for remote method invocation (Section 8.5). SR (Section 8.7) provides processes, a **co** statement for recursive parallelism, semaphores for shared-variable synchronization, and a variety of message-passing mechanisms: asynchronous, synchronous, remote procedure call (RPC), and rendezvous. A fourth language pair, CSP/Occam (Section 7.6), supports synchronous message passing but not shared variables.

Below we summarize Cilk, an interesting language for shared-variable programming, and Fortran M, another language for message passing.

Cilk

This language extends C with five simple mechanisms for parallel programming. Cilk is especially suited for recursive parallelism, although it also supports task and data parallelism. Cilk is designed to run efficiently on symmetric, shared-memory multiprocessors.

A novel aspect of Cilk is that it adds mechanisms to C in such a way that if they are removed, the remaining—*elided*—program is a syntactically and semantically correct C program. The five Cilk mechanisms are indicated by the keywords `cilk`, `spawn`, `synch`, `inlet`, and `abort`. The `cilk` keyword is prepended to the declaration of a C function to indicate that the function is a Cilk procedure. A `cilk` procedure is forked as a process by executing a `spawn` statement. The spawned threads execute in parallel with their parent, the calling thread. The parent uses `synch` to wait for the threads to terminate and return results. Thus a sequence of `spawn` calls followed by a `synch` is essentially a `co/oc` statement.

The following example illustrates an (inefficient) implementation of a recursive parallel program for computing the nth Fibonacci number:

```
cilk int fib(int n) {
  if (n < 2)
    return n;
  else {
    int x, y;
    x = spawn fib(n-1);
    y = spawn fib(n-2);
    synch;
    return (x + y);
  }
}
```

Notice how deleting the three Cilk mechanisms—`cilk`, `spawn`, and `synch`—from the above program results in a legal C function.

An `inlet` is a C function internal to a Cilk procedure. It is used to perform computations such as reductions when spawned calls return. For example, we could add an inlet to function `fib` as follows:

```
cilk int fib(int n) {
  int x = 0;

  inlet void plusReduce (int result)
    { x += result; return; }

  if (n < 2)
    return n;
  else {
    plusReduce(spawn fib(n-1));
    plusReduce(spawn fib(n-2));
    synch;
    return (x);
  }
}
```

When each spawned instance of `fib` returns, the inlet `plusReduce` is called and executed *atomically;* it adds the results from `fib` to reduction variable `x`.

The final Cilk mechanism, `abort`, is used within an inlet; it destroys threads that were spawned by the same parent and that are still executing. One application of `abort` is in a recursive search program in which multiple paths are explored in parallel; the programmer might want to kill off the thread exploring a path when a better solution is found.

A novel aspect of the Cilk implementation is what is called a work-stealing scheduler. Cilk implements two versions of each Cilk procedure: a fast clone that operates much like a regular C function, and a slow clone that has full support for parallelism along with the overheads that entails. When a procedure is spawned, the fast clone executes. If some worker process (which executes Cilk threads) needs work, it steals a procedure from some other worker. At that time, the procedure is converted to the slow clone.

Fortran M

This language is a small set of extensions to Fortran that supports the modular design of message-passing programs. The message-passing mechanisms are similar to those in Chapter 7. Although the language is no longer supported, its functionality has been incorporated into an MPI binding for the HPF language.

A process in Fortran M is like a parameterized procedure, but it has the keyword `process` instead of `procedure`. The `processcall` statement is used to fork a new process. Such calls occur within code regions indicated by the `processes/endprocesses` statement, which is very similar to a `co/oc` statement.

Processes in Fortran M communicate with each other by means of ports and channels; they cannot share variables. A channel is a queue of messages. It is created by means of a `channel` statement, which defines a pair of ports, one for output and one for input. The `send` statement appends a message to an output port. The `endchannel` statement appends an end-of-channel message to an output port. Both statements are nonblocking (asynchronous). The `receive` statement waits for a message on an input port, then removes the message; thus, `receive` is blocking.

Channels can be created and destroyed dynamically, passed as arguments to processes, and passed as values within messages. For example, to enable two processes to communicate with each other, the programmer would create two channels, then create the two processes and pass them the channels as arguments.

One process uses the output port of one channel and the input port of the second channel; the second process uses the other ports of the two channels.

Fortran M is mainly intended for programming task parallelism, in which each process executes a possibly different task. However, the language also provides some support for data-parallel programming by means of distributed arrays. The data distribution statements are similar to those supported by HPF, which is discussed at the end of Section 12.3.

12.3.2 *Coordination Languages*

A coordination language extends a base language with a shared data space and message-like primitives to operate on the data space. Linda (Section 7.7) originated the concept. Recall that Linda extends a sequential base language such as C with an associative memory abstraction called *tuple space* (TS). TS is conceptually shared by all processes. A new tuple is deposited in TS by executing the `out` primitive. A tuple is extracted by means of `in` or examined by means of `rd`. Finally, a process is forked by means of `eval`; when the process terminates, it deposits its return value in TS. Linda thus combines aspects of shared variables and asynchronous message passing: tuple space is shared by all processes, and tuples are deposited and extracted atomically as if they were messages.

Orca

This is a more recent example of a coordination language. Like Linda, it is based on data structures that are conceptually shared but that may be physically distributed. However, in Orca's case the unifying concept is that of a shared data object rather than a shared tuple. In particular, processes on possibly different processors can share passive objects that are instances of abstract types. A process accesses a shared object by calling an operation defined by the object. Operations are implemented by a mechanism that combines aspects of RPC and rendezvous.

A process in Orca creates another process by means of the `fork` primitive. Process parameters may be `value` or `shared`. For a `value` parameter, the parent process creates a copy of the actual parameter and passes it to the child. For a `shared` parameter, the actual parameter must be a variable that is an object of a user-defined type. After the child is created, the parent and child share the object.

Each user-defined type specifies the operations on objects of that type. Each instance of a shared object is a monitor or server process, depending on how it is implemented. In either case, the operations on the object are executed atomically. The implementation of an operation in Orca can also consist of one or more guarded statements. This supports condition synchronization, but by means of Boolean expressions rather than condition variables.

The original version of Orca supported task parallelism only. The language has recently been extended to support data parallelism as well. This is realized by partitioning array-based data objects, distributing the partitions to different processors, and manipulating them using user-defined parallel operations.

12.3.3 Data Parallel Languages

Data parallel languages directly support the data parallel style of programming in which each process executes the same operations on different parts of shared data. Thus data parallel languages are imperative languages. However, although communication is explicit, synchronization is implicit. In particular, there is an implicit barrier after every statement.

The term *data parallel* originated in the mid-1980s with the first Connection Machine, the CM-1, an SIMD-style architecture.[4] The CM-1 consisted of a conventional front-end processor and a special-purpose back end containing thousands of small processors. The front end executed sequential instructions and broadcast parallel instructions to the back end; every back-end processor executed each parallel instruction in lockstep.

To facilitate programming the CM-1, people at Thinking Machines Corporation developed C* (C Star), a data-parallel variant of C. Even though SIMD machines such as the CM-1 are no longer marketed, the data-parallel style of programming lives on, because many applications are most easily programmed in that style. Below we summarize aspects of C* and ZPL, an interesting new language. In the next section we describe NESL, another new language that is both a data parallel and a functional language. Later we give a case study of HPF, the most widely used data-parallel language. Because (most) synchronization is implicit in these languages, their compilers generate the code that is required for synchronization. Stated differently, the compiler—not the programmer—makes use of an underlying library.

C*

The design of the C* language closely mirrors the CM-1 architecture. The language augments C with features for expressing data layouts and parallel

---

[4] The SIMD style of architecture originated much earlier, in the 1960s.

execution. For example, C* contains a `shape` construct for specifying the shape of parallel data structures such as matrices. Parallel execution is specified by means of a `with` statement, which contains a sequence of statements that manipulate a shape in parallel. A `where` statement supports conditional execution of parallel statements. C* also defines a number of reduction operators that atomically combine values.

As a simple example, consider the following code fragment:

```
shape [256] [256] grid;
real: grid a, b;
initialize b;
real sum;
with (grid) {
  a = b;               /* copy b into a in parallel */
  where (a > 0.0)
    sum = (+= a);   /* add positive elements */
}
```

The first line defines a square `shape` named `grid`. The second line declares two matrices of reals having this shape. The body of the `with` statement copies `b` into `a` and then uses a `where` statement and a reduction operator to accumulate the sum of the positive elements of `a`. Both assignment statements inside the `with` statement execute in parallel on all elements of `a` and `b`.

A C* program starts execution on the front-end machine. All sequential statements are executed there. Parallel statements are compiled into instructions that are broadcast one at a time to the back-end processors. The Connection Machine provided hardware support for reduction operators and moving data in parallel between processing elements.

ZPL

This new language is both a data parallel and an array language. Thus expressions such as `A+B` add whole arrays, can be executed in parallel, and end with an implicit barrier. ZPL is a complete language rather than an extension to a base language. However, it compiles to ANSI C, can interface with legacy codes written in Fortran or C, and provides access to scientific libraries.

The novel aspects of ZPL are regions and directions. Together with array expressions, these make it very easy to write programs that manipulate matrices. Below we use Jacobi iteration to illustrate the declaration and use of regions and directions. Note how simple the program is compared to the explicitly parallel program in Figure 11.3 and especially compared to the C/Pthreads and C/MPI programs in Figures 12.1 and 12.2.

A region is simply a set of indices. A direction is used to modify regions or array index expressions. These are declared as follows:

```
region R = [1..n, 1..n];
direction north = [-1, 0]; south = [1, 0];
           east = [0, 1]; west = [0, -1];
```

The region `R` can be used in declarations such as

```
var A, Temp: [R] float;
    error: float;
```

This declares `A` and `Temp` to be $n \times n$ arrays of floating-point numbers and `error` to be a single float. Regions can also be used in array expressions. For example, the following code initializes the interior points of `A` to zeros and the boundaries around `A` to ones:

```
[R]           A := 0.0;
[north of R]  A := 1.0;
[south of R]  A := 1.0;
[east of R]   A := 1.0;
[west of R]   A := 1.0;
```

The region prefixes indicate that the statements apply to entire arrays. Thus the first line makes n^2 assignments. The last four lines make `n` assignments each, and they implicitly extend the size of `A` to include boundary vectors (which means that the actual storage for `A` consists of $(n+2)^2$ values). Each statement can be implemented using parallelism, and each completes before the next is executed. Because the statements are independent, a barrier is not required until after the last statement.

The main loop in Jacobi iteration can be implemented in ZPL as follows:

```
[R]   repeat
        Temp := ( A@north + A@east + A@west +
                  A@south ) / 4;
        error := max<< abs(A-Temp);
        A := Temp;
      until error < EPSILON;
```

Again the region prefix, `[R]`, indicates that the statements in the loop access entire arrays. The first statement assigns every element of `Temp` the average of its four neighbors from `A`; note the use of directions to express the indices of the neighbors. The second statement sets `error` to the maximum of the differences between pairs of values in `A` and `Temp`; the code `max<<` is a reduction operator.

12.3.4 *Functional Languages*

In imperative languages, processes, communication, and synchronization are all explicit. In data parallel languages, synchronization is implicit. In functional languages, everything is implicit!

Functional programming languages—at least the pure ones—do not have a concept of visible program state and hence do not have an assignment operator that changes the state. Instead, they are called *single-assignment languages* because a variable can be bound to a value only once. A program is described as the composition of a set of functions, not as a sequence of statements.

Because there are no side effects in a single-assignment language, every argument to a function call can be evaluated in parallel. Moreover, the body of a called function can be evaluated as soon as all the arguments have been evaluated. Thus, concurrency does not have to be specified; it is there automatically. Processes communicate implicitly by means of arguments and return values. Finally, synchronization follows simply from the semantics of function call and return: a function body cannot execute until the arguments have been evaluated, and the result of a function is not available until the function returns.

On the other hand, single-assignment semantics makes functional programs difficult to implement efficiently. Even if only a single element of an array is updated, conceptually an entire new copy of the array is made, even though only one value differs. It is thus up to the compiler to detect when it is safe to update an array in place rather than make a new copy. This involves doing dependence analysis to determine when array references overlap and when they are disjoint.

Functional languages have simple, yet powerful properties, so they have long been popular for sequential programming. Being based on functions, they support recursive programming especially well. Lisp was one of the first such languages; Haskell and ML are two others that are currently popular. The implementations of these can employ parallelism. Each of these languages also has variants that give the programmer some control over how much parallelism to use and where to use it. For example, Multilisp is a variant of Lisp, and Concurrent ML is a variant of Standard ML.

Below we describe two functional languages—NESL and Sisal—that were designed specifically to support parallel programming.

NESL

NESL is a data-parallel functional language, whereas ZPL is a data-parallel array language. The most important new ideas in NESL are (1) nested data parallelism, and (2) a language-based performance model. NESL allows one to apply a function in parallel to each element of a collection of data and to nest parallel calls. The performance model is based on the concepts of work and depth rather than on running time. Informally, the work in a computation is the total number of operations that are executed, and the depth is the longest chain of sequential dependences.

The sequential aspects of NESL are based on ML, a functional language, and SETL, a concise language for programming with sets. To illustrate the language, consider the following function, which implements the quicksort algorithm:

```
function Quicksort(S) =
  if ( #S <= 1) then S
  else
    let a  = S[rand( #S )];
        S1 = {e in S | e < a};
        S2 = {e in S | e == a};
        S3 = {e in S | e > a};
        R  = {Quicksort(v); v in [S1,S3]};
    in R[0] ++ S2 ++ R[1];
```

Sequences are the basic data type in NESL, so the argument to the function is a sequence S. The `if` statement returns S if the length of S is at most 1. Otherwise, the function body makes five assignments: (1) a is assigned a random element of S, (2) sequence S1 is assigned all values in S that are less than a, (3) sequence S2 is assigned all values in S that are equal to a, (4) sequence S3 is assigned   all
values in S that are greater than a, and (5) sequence R is assigned the result of calling `Quicksort` recursively.

The last four of the assignment statements above use the apply-to-each operator { ... } to compute values in parallel. For example, the expression in the assignment to S1 means "in parallel find all elements e of S for which e is less than a." The expression in the assignment to R means "in parallel call `Quicksort(v)` for v in S1 and v in S3; this is an instance of nested data parallelism. The results of the recursive calls are sequences. The final line in the above function concatenates the first result R[0], the sequence S2, and the second result R[1].

Sisal

The first functional language developed specifically for writing scientific programs was Sisal (Streams and Iteration in a Single Assignment Language). Its main concepts are functions, arrays, iteration, and streams. Functions are used as usual for recursion and program structuring. Sisal's arrays and iteration constructs are used for iterative parallelism; these are examined below. Streams are sequences of values that are accessed in order; they are used for pipelined parallelism and input/output. Although Sisal is no longer supported by its developers at Lawrence Livermore Labs, it introduced important ideas and remains in use.

The `for` statement in Sisal is the primary mechanism for expressing iterative parallelism. It can be used when iterations are independent. As an example, the following code uses two loops to set `C` to the matrix product of `A` and `B`:

```
C := for i in 1, n cross j in 1, n
        Element := for k in 1, n
          returns value of sum A[i,k] * B[k,j]
        end for
      returns array of Element
    end for;
```

The word `cross` indicates that the outer loop is executed, in parallel, for each cross-product (combination) of the `n` values for `i` and `n` values for `j`. The body of the outer loop is another loop that returns the inner product of `A[i,*]` and `B[*,j]`; the keyword `sum` is a reduction operator. The outer loop returns an array of elements—namely, those computed by the n^2 instances of the inner loop. Notice how the loops are on the right-hand sides of the two assignment statements; this syntax reflects the single-assignment semantics of a functional language.

Sisal also provides another looping construct, `for initial`, that is used when there is a loop-carried dependency. It allows one to write an imperative loop in a functional style. For example, the loop that follows produces a vector `x[1:n]` that contains all partial sums of the vector `y[1:n]`. (This parallel prefix problem was considered earlier in Section 3.5.)

```
for initial
    i := 1; x := y[1];
while i < n repeat
    i := old i + 1;
    x := old x + y[i];
  returns array of x
end for;
```

The first part initializes two new variables and constitutes the first iteration. The `while` part repeatedly adds `1` to the old value of `i` and produces a new value `x` that is the sum of the last value of `x` and `y[i]`. The loop returns an array that contains the newly computed values of `x`.

The implementation of Sisal is based on a dataflow model. In particular, an expression can be computed as soon as its operands have been evaluated. In the matrix multiplication loop above, matrices `A` and `B` are given and fixed, so every product can be computed. The sums of products can be computed as the products are finished. Finally, the array of elements can be constructed as inner products are computed. Each value thus flows to the operators that need it, and operators produce output values once they have all their input values. This dataflow execution model also applies to function calls: arguments are independent, so they can be evaluated in parallel, and the function body can be evaluated as soon as the arguments have been evaluated.

12.3.5 Abstract Models

The usual ways to evaluate the performance of a parallel program are to measure its execution time, or alternatively to count every operation. Measurements of execution time obviously depend on the generated machine code and the underlying hardware. Operation counts depend on knowing which ones can be executed in parallel and which must be executed sequentially and on knowing what overheads are introduced by synchronization. Both approaches provide detailed information, but only relative to one set of assumptions.

A model of parallel computing provides a high-level way to characterize and compare the execution time of different programs. It does so by using abstractions of hardware and execution details. The Parallel Random Access Machine (PRAM) was the first important model for parallel computing; it provides an abstraction of a shared-memory machine. The Bulk Synchronous Parallel (BSP) model bridges the abstractions of both shared and distributed memory. LogP models distributed-memory machines and specifically incorporates the cost of networks and communication. The work/depth model of NESL mentioned above is based on the structure of a program without regard for the hardware on which it might execute. Below we summarize PRAM, BSP, and LogP.

PRAM

The PRAM is an idealized model of a synchronous, shared-memory machine. In the model, every processor executes instructions in lockstep. If the processors execute the same instruction, PRAM is thus an abstract SIMD machine; however, processors are allowed to execute different instructions. The basic instructions are memory read and write plus the usual arithmetic and logical operations.

The PRAM model is idealized in the sense that every processor can *simultaneously* access any memory location. For example, every PRAM processor can simultaneously read the same memory location *or* write into the same memory location. This is obviously not true of an actual parallel machine, because memory modules serialize access to the same memory location. Moreover, memory access times are not uniform on real machines, because of caches and because memory modules may be organized as a hierarchy.

The basic PRAM model supports concurrent reading and concurrent writing (CRCW). Two more realistic variants of the PRAM model have also been proposed:

- *Exclusive Read, Exclusive Write (EREW)*: Each memory location can be accessed by at most one processor at a time.

- *Concurrent Read, Exclusive Write (CREW)*: Each memory location can be read simultaneously but written by at most one processor at a time.

Although these models are more restrictive and hence more realistic, they still cannot be realized in practice. Even so, PRAM and its submodels have been useful in analyzing and comparing parallel algorithms.

BSP

The Bulk Synchronous Parallel (BSP) model is a so-called bridging model that separates synchronization from communication and that incorporates the effects of a memory hierarchy and of message passing. The BSP model has three components:

- *processors* that have local memory and execute at the same speed;

- a *communication network* that enables each processor to communicate with every other processor; and

- a mechanism for *synchronizing* all processors at regular intervals.

The parameters of the model are the number of processors, their speed, the cost of a communication, and the synchronization period.

A BSP computation consists of a sequence of *supersteps*. In each superstep, every processor executes a computation that accesses its local memory and sends messages to other processors. The messages are requests to get a copy of (read) or to update (write) remote data. At the end of a superstep, the processors perform a barrier synchronization and *then* honor the requests they received during the superstep. The processors then proceed to the next superstep.

In addition to being an interesting abstract model, BSP is also now a programming model. In particular, the Oxford Parallel Applications Center has implemented a communication library and set of profiling tools that are based on the BSP model. The library consists of about 20 functions that support BSP-style message passing and remote memory access.

LogP

As a more recent model that addresses the characteristics of distributed-memory machines, LogP incorporates more details about the performance attributes of the communication network than BSP, and processors are asynchronous rather than synchronous. The components of the model are processors, local memory, and an interconnection network. The parameters of the model—from which it gets its name—are the following:

- L, an upper bound on the *latency* (delay) in transmitting a one-word message from one processor to another;

- o, the *overhead* incurred by a processor when sending a message (during this time the processor cannot perform other operations);

- g, the minimum time interval, or *gap*, between consecutive message sends or receives at a processor; and

- P, the number of processor/memory pairs.

All times are measured in multiples of the cycle time of the processors. Messages are assumed to be small. Moreover, the network is assumed to have a finite capacity of at most $\lceil L/g \rceil$ messages in transit at a time from any one processor to any other.

The LogP model specifies the performance attributes of the communication network, but not its structure. It thus allows one to model the communication in an algorithm. However, LogP does not model local computation time. This choice was made in order to keep the model simple and because there is already a good deal known about the local (sequential) execution time of algorithms on processors.

12.3.6 *Case Study: High-Performance Fortran (HPF)*

High-Performance Fortran (HPF) is the latest member of the long-evolving Fortran family of languages. The first version of HPF was designed in 1992 by a number of people from academia, industry, and government laboratories. The second version was published in early 1997. Several compilers currently exist, and HPF programs can run on all major high-performance machines.

HPF is a data parallel language that extends Fortran 90, a sequential language that provides a variety of operations on entire arrays and slices of arrays. The design of HPF was heavily influenced by Fortran D, an earlier data-parallel dialect of Fortran. The most important components of HPF are data parallel array assignments, compiler directives to control data distribution, and statements for writing and synchronizing parallel loops. We describe each of these topics below, then present a complete subroutine for Jacobi iteration.

Array Assignments

HPF, like Fortran 90, allows a variety of operations to be applied to entire arrays; these operations include assignment, addition, multiplication, and so on. The array operations can also be applied to comparable-size slices—so-called conformable sections—of arrays. For example, if `new` and `grid` are $n \times n$ matrices, then the following code implements the main computational loop in Jacobi iteration:

```
do iters = 1, MAXITERS
  new(2:n-1, 2:n-1) =
       ( grid(1:n-2,2:n-1) + grid(3:n,2:n-1) +
         grid(2:n-1,1:n-2) + grid(2:n-1,3:n) ) / 4
  grid = new
end do
```

Both array assignments have data parallel semantics: the right-hand side is evaluated first, then all values are assigned to the left-hand side. The first assignment sets every interior point in `new` to the average of its four neighbors in `grid`. The second copies `new` back into `grid`. In fact, the loop body above could have been coded as

```
grid(2:n-1, 2:n-1) =
     ( grid(1:n-2,2:n-1) + grid(3:n,2:n-1) +
       grid(2:n-1,1:n-2) + grid(2:n-1,3:n) ) / 4
```

The same array can appear on both sides, because of the data-parallel semantics of array assignment. However, the compiler-generated code would have to use a temporary matrix such as **new** to implement the above statement.

An array assignment can be preceded by a **WHERE** clause to specify conditional array operations, such as increment only those elements that are positive. HPF also provides a number of reduction operators, which apply an operation atomically to all elements of an array and then return a scalar. Finally, HPF provides a number of so-called intrinsic functions that work on entire arrays. For example, **TRANSPOSE(a)** computes the transpose of array **a**. Another function, **CSHIFT**, is commonly used to perform a circular shift of data in an array; the right-hand side of the last assignment to **grid** above is essentially a collection of shifted versions of **grid**.

Data Mapping

The data-mapping directives in HPF enable the programmer to control how data is laid out, especially for a distributed-memory machine. Hence, they enable the programmer to control data locality. The directives are recommendations to an HPF compiler. They are not imperatives that have to be followed but rather hints that the programmer believes will lead to better performance. In fact, the program will compute the same results if all data mapping directives are removed; it just might not do so as efficiently.

The main directives are **PROCESSORS**, **ALIGN**, and **DISTRIBUTE**. A **PROCESSORS** directive specifies the shape and size of a virtual machine of processors. An **ALIGN** directive specifies a one-to-one correspondence between elements of two arrays, meaning that they should be aligned with each other and distributed in the same fashion. A **DISTRIBUTE** directive specifies how an array—and any arrays aligned with it—should be mapped onto a virtual machine specified earlier by a **PROCESSORS** directive; the two choices are **BLOCK** (strips) and **CYCLIC** (stripes).

As an example, suppose **position** and **force** are vectors, say in an *n*-body simulation, and consider the following code:

```
!HPF$ PROCESSORS pr(8)
!HPF$ ALIGN position (:) WITH force (:)
!HPF$ DISTRIBUTE position(CYCLIC) ONTO pr
```

The first directive specifies an abstract machine of eight processors. The second aligns corresponding elements of **position** and **force** with each other. The third directive says that **position** is to be mapped in a cyclic (striped) fashion onto the processors; by transitivity, `force` will also be striped on the processors in the same way.

HPF provides additional data-mapping directives. A `TEMPLATE` is an abstract index space that can be used as a target for alignment directives and as a source for a distribute directive. The `DYNAMIC` directive indicates that an array can have its alignment or distribution changed at run time by a `REALIGN` or `REDISTRIBUTE` directive.

Parallel Loops

Array assignments in HPF have data-parallel semantics, and hence they can be executed concurrently. HPF also provides two mechanisms for specifying concurrent loops.

The `FORALL` statement specifies that a loop body is to be executed in parallel. For example, the following loop computes in parallel all new values for a grid:

```
FORALL (i=2:n-1, j=2:n-1)
  new(i,j) = (grid(i-1,j) + grid(i+1,j) +
              grid(i,j-1) + grid(i,j+1)) / 4
```

The effect in this case is the same as the array assignment given earlier. However, the loop body in a `FORALL` statement can consist of more than one statement. The loop indices can also include a mask to specify a predicate that the index values must satisfy; this provides functionality similar to that provided by the `WHERE` statement, and it precludes having to surround the loop body by an `if` statement.

The `INDEPENDENT` directive is the second HPF mechanism for writing parallel loops. This is placed in front of a `do` loop to indicate that the programmer is asserting that the loop bodies are independent and hence can be executed in parallel. For example, in

```
!HPF$ INDEPENDENT
      do i = 1,n
        A(Index(i)) = B(i)
      end
```

the programmer is asserting that the `Index(i)` are all distinct (there are no aliases) and that `A` and `B` do not have overlapping storage. If `B` is a function rather than an array, the programmer could also use the `PURE` directive to assert that `B` has no side effects.

Example: Jacobi Iteration

Figure 12.8 contains a complete HPF subroutine for Jacobi iteration. It employs several of the mechanisms described above. The first three directives specify that matrices `grid` and `new` are to be aligned with each other and to be laid out by blocks (strips) on `PR` processors. (The value of `PR` would have to be a compile-time constant.) The body of the computational loop updates all grid points in parallel, then copies `new` to `grid`, also in parallel. When the main loop terminates, the last assignment computes the maximum difference between pairs of values in `grid` and `new`. There are implicit barriers after the `FORALL` statement, the array copy statement, and the array reduction statement.

The reader might find it instructive to compare this program with the explicitly parallel program in Figure 11.3 and with the program that uses the OpenMP library in Figure 12.4. The code is much shorter because of the data-parallel semantics of HPF. On the other hand, the HPF compiler has to produce explicitly parallel code such as that in Figures 11.3 or 12.4. This is not especially difficult to do for this application and for a shared-memory machine. However, it is much harder to produce good code for a distributed-memory machine. For example, the explicit message passing program for Jacobi iteration in Figure 11.5 is quite

```
      subroutine Jacobi(n)
      integer n                   ! size including boundaries
      integer i, j, iters
      real grid(n,n), new(n,n), maxdiff

!HPF$ PROCESSORS pr(PR)          ! use PR processors
!HPF$ ALIGN grid(i,j) WITH new(i,j)
!HPF$ DISTRIBUTE grid(BLOCK) ONTO pr

      initialize grid and new, including boundaries
      do iters = 1, MAXITERS
        FORALL (i=2:n-1, j=2:n-1)
          new(i,j) = (grid(i-1,j) + grid(i+1,j) +
                      grid(i,j-1) + grid(i,j+1)) / 4
        grid = new               ! copies array in parallel
      end do

      maxdiff = MAXVAL(ABS(grid-new))   ! reduction
      end
```

Figure 12.8   Jacobi iteration in High-Performance Fortran.

different than the above program. The HPF compiler has to distribute the data among the processors and to generate the message passing code. The **ALIGN** and **DISTRIBUTE** directives give it guidance on how to do so.

12.4 Parallel Programming Tools

The previous sections of this chapter described the roles of libraries, compilers, and languages for writing parallel programs for scientific applications. Many additional software tools have been developed to aid in the development, evaluation, and use of parallel programs. These include suites of benchmark programs; libraries for classes of applications such as adaptive grids, linear algebra, sparse matrices, and irregular computations; and low-level tools such as debuggers, parallel random number generators, and parallel input/output libraries.

This section describes two additional kinds of software tools: those that aid in measuring and visualizing the performance of applications, and those that support the construction of geographically distributed metacomputations. The last section gives a case study of one of the newest and most ambitious tool kits: the Globus metacomputing infrastructure. The Historical Notes at the end of the chapter give pointers to detailed information on all these kinds of tools.

12.4.1 Performance Measurement and Visualization

The goal of parallel computing is to solve problems faster. It is fairly easy to calculate the total elapsed time of a computation. It is much more difficult to determine *where* the computation spent its time, and hence to determine performance bottlenecks. Performance measurement and visualization tools help solve this problem.

Pablo was one of the first performance measurement tools for parallel computations, especially those running on distributed-memory machines. The Pablo project dates from the early days of hypercube machines and continues to evolve to include more functionality and to support modern architectures. Pablo is a performance analysis infrastructure that allows the programmer to instrument an application at multiple hardware and software levels. The system then performs real-time data reduction and presents the results to the user in a number of ways. Static graphics are used to present tables, charts, diagrams, and histograms. Dynamic graphics are used to observe temporal evolutions such as computation and communication phases and process interaction patterns. The dynamic graphics are based on time-stamped traces of events that can be displayed in real time or stored and played back later.

Paradyn is a more recent tool for measuring the performance of parallel programs. The novel aspect of Paradyn is that instrumentation is dynamic; it is inserted automatically and refined as the program executes. To employ Paradyn, the application programmer need only link the application program with the Paradyn library. As the program runs, the Paradyn system starts looking for high-level problems such as excessive blocking for synchronization or I/O or excessive memory delays. If problems are found, Paradyn automatically inserts additional instrumentation to find causes of the problem (instrumentation is inserted by modifying the binary program). Paradyn presents results to the user in the paradigm of a performance consultant, which in turn is based on a search model that tries to answer three questions: Why is the program performing poorly? Where is the performance problem? When does the problem occur? The user can guide the search for answers to these questions or let Paradyn conduct a fully automatic search.

Both Pablo and Paradyn use graphics to enable the programmer to visualize performance aspects of program execution. Many applications themselves use graphics packages to enable the programmer to "see" results as they are computed. For example, an *n*-body simulation might display the bodies as they move, or a fluid-flow simulation might use flow lines and colors to enable the programmer to visualize patterns and rates of flow. Another class of visualization tools goes further and allows the programmer to *steer* the application—namely, to alter program variables as the computation is executing and thus to affect its future behavior. Autopilot is an example of a recently developed tool for computational steering. Virtue is a related tool that implements an immersive environment (virtual reality), using real-time performance data from Autopilot. Autopilot and Virtue are implemented on top of portions of the Pablo toolkit. They also use the Globus toolkit (described below) for wide-area communication.

12.4.2 *Metacomputers and Metacomputing*

Most parallel computations run on a single multiple-processor machine or on a cluster of machines on a local network. Ideally, the processors are not running any other application and the network is isolated from other traffic. On local area networks, most machines are idle much of the time—for example at night. These idle cycles could be productively employed by some long-running parallel applications—especially those implemented using the manager/workers paradigm (Section 9.1). Condor—a software system that is named after the very large vulture—supports this use by hunting for and taking over idle machines.

A *metacomputer* is a more general and more integrated collection of computing resources. In particular, a metacomputer is a set of computers that are linked by high-speed networks and by a software infrastructure to present the illusion of a single computing resource. Because the concept originated in the context of high-performance computing, the term metacomputer is often synonymous with *networked virtual supercomputer*. An emerging vision is to build multiple regional, national, and international *computational grids*, which will provide pervasive and dependable computing power in much the same way that power grids provide pervasive and dependable electrical power.

A metacomputer or computational grid is constructed by a layer of software that connects computers and communication networks in order to provide the illusion of a single virtual computer. Another layer of software on top of this infrastructure provides a *metacomputing* environment that enables applications to employ the functionality of the metacomputer. The nature and roles of these layers are similar to those in conventional operating systems, which implement a virtual machine on top of hardware resources and provide a set of tools used by application programmers.

Metacomputing is motivated by the desires of some users to have access to resources that are not available within a single computing environment. Several types of applications have this characteristic:[5]

- distributed supercomputing, which is concerned with solving problems that are too large for the capabilities of a single supercomputer or that can benefit from executing different parts on different computer architectures;

- desktop supercomputing, which enables a user sitting at a workstation to visualize and possibly steer a computation executing on a remote supercomputer or to access remote databases, perhaps using them as input into the application program;

- smart instruments, which are applications that connect users with remote instruments such as telescopes or electron microscopes, which are in turn connected with a program running on a remote supercomputer; and

- collaborative environments, which connect multiple users at different locations with each other, with virtual environments, and with simulations running on supercomputers.

Building such a metacomputing environment is obviously far from trivial. Several challenging problems have to be addressed, among them: different sites are

---

[5] This list was compiled by Foster and Kesselman [1997], the leaders of the Globus project described in the next section.

autonomous, users are concerned about security, computer architectures are different and evolving, there is not a single persistent name space, components can fail, languages and operating systems are not interoperable, and so on.

Legion was one of the first software systems to support metacomputing. The project was begun in 1993 and continues to evolve. Legion uses an object-oriented philosophy and implementation to address the above kinds of problems. In particular, Legion defines a number of classes that encompass the components and functionality of the system. Every component—including machines, file systems, and libraries as well as components of application programs—is then encapsulated within an object that is an instance of one of the Legion classes. The Legion vision is to support a worldwide virtual computer and all the above kinds of applications.

Schooner is a more modest instance of a metacomputing system. It supports desktop supercomputing applications. A key aspect of Schooner is an interface specification language that is machine- and language-independent; it is used to generate interface code that binds software and hardware components in an application. The other key aspect of Schooner is a runtime system that supports both static and dynamic configuration of the components in an application. For example, if a remote host becomes overloaded while an application is running, or another host becomes available, the user can dynamically reconfigure the application to adapt to this change.

12.4.3 Case Study: The Globus Toolkit

Globus is a new, extremely ambitious project to construct a comprehensive set of tools for building metacomputing applications. The project leaders are Ian Foster of Argonne National Labs and Carl Kesselman of USC's Information Sciences Institute. Their collaborators literally span the globe.

The goal of the Globus project is to provide a basic set of tools that can be used to construct portable, high-performance services, which in turn support metacomputing applications. Globus thus builds upon and vastly extends the services provided by earlier systems such as PVM, MPI, Condor, and Legion. The project is also concerned with developing ways to allow high-level services to observe and guide the operation of the low-level mechanisms.

The components of the Globus toolkit are depicted in Figure 12.9. The toolkit modules execute on top of a metacomputer infrastructure and they are used to implement high-level services. The metacomputer infrastructure, or testbed, is realized by software that connects computers together. Two instances of such an infrastructure have been built by the Globus group. The first, the

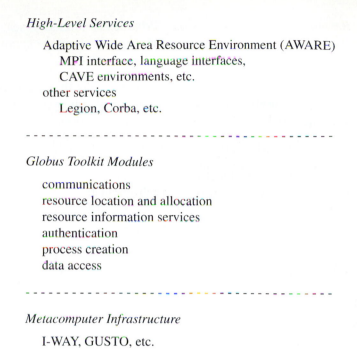

High-Level Services

    Adaptive Wide Area Resource Environment (AWARE)
        MPI interface, language interfaces,
        CAVE environments, etc.
    other services
        Legion, Corba, etc.

- -

Globus Toolkit Modules

    communications
    resource location and allocation
    resource information services
    authentication
    process creation
    data access

- -

Metacomputer Infrastructure

    I-WAY, GUSTO, etc.

Figure 12.9   The components and structure of the Globus toolkit.

I-WAY networking experiment, was built in 1996; it connected 17 sites in North America and was used by 60 groups to develop applications in each of the four classes described in the previous section. The second metacomputer infrastructure, GUSTO (Globus Ubiquitous Supercomputing Testbed), was built in 1997 as a prototype for a computational grid consisting of about 15 sites. GUSTO in fact won a major award for advancing high performance distributed computing.

The Globus toolkit consists of several modules, as listed in Figure 12.9.

- *Communications module*: Provides efficient implementations of many of the communication mechanisms described in Part 2, including message passing, multicast, remote procedure call, and distributed shared memory. It is based on the Nexus communication library.

- *Resource location and allocation module*: Provides mechanisms that allow applications to specify their resource requirements, locate resources that meet those requirements, and acquire access to them.

- *Resource information module*: Provides a directory service that enables applications to obtain real-time information about the status and structure of the underlying metacomputer.

- *Authentication module*: Provides mechanisms that are used to validate the identity of users and resources. These mechanisms are in turn used as building blocks for services such as authorization.

- *Process creation module*: Initiates new computations, integrates them with ongoing computations, and manages termination.

- *Data access module*: Provides high-speed remote access to persistent storage, databases, and parallel file systems. The module uses the mechanisms of the Nexus communication library.

The Globus toolkit modules are being used to help implement high-level application services. One such service is what is called an Adaptive Wide Area Resource Environment (AWARE). It will contain an integrated set of services, including "metacomputing enabled" interfaces to an implementation of the MPI library, various programming languages, and tools for constructing virtual environments (CAVEs). The high-level services will also include those developed by others, including the Legion metacomputing system mentioned earlier and implementations of CORBA, the Common Object Request Broker Architecture.

The Globus toolkit is new and evolving, so details will change as more applications are developed and more services are supported. The interested reader should visit the Globus Web site at `www.globus.org` for information on the current status and latest accomplishments of the project.

Historical Notes

Manufacturers of parallel machines have long provided parallel programming libraries. With few exceptions, however, each vendor's library differs from the others. Standard libraries began to emerge in the 1990s to facilitate the development of portable codes. The Pthreads library was introduced in Chapter 4; the Historical Notes in that chapter give sources of further information. The MPI library was introduced in Chapter 7; the Historical Notes in that chapter describe implementations of MPI and its close relative the PVM library. Information on OpenMP—including an online tutorial—can be found on the World Wide Web at `www.openmp.org`.

The seminal work on dependency analysis was done at the University of Illinois by Utpal Banerjee and Michael Wolfe in doctoral dissertations in 1979 and 1982, respectively, that were supervised by David Kuck. Wolfe [1989] describes that and some additional work. Bacon, Graham, and Sharp [1994] give an excellent survey of dependence analysis and compiler transformations for high-performance computing; the paper contains dozens of references. McKinley, Carr, and Tseng [1996] describe experiments using different transformations to improve data locality and recommend a specific order in which optimizations should be performed.

Several of the languages listed in Figure 12.7 were the subjects of case studies in earlier chapters: Ada in Chapter 8; Java in Chapters 5, 7, and 8; SR in Chapter 8; CSP/Occam in Chapter 7; and Linda in Chapter 7. For further information on these languages, see the Historical Notes in those chapters.

Java and Orca are the only object-oriented languages listed in Figure 12.7. Many other object-oriented languages have also been developed for parallel programming. For example, Wilson and Lu [1996] describe over a dozen languages and systems that are based on C++. Foster [1995] contains a nice summary of one of these languages, Compositional C++, as well as summaries of Fortran M, HPF, and the MPI library. Bal, Steiner, and Tanenbaum [1989] survey programming languages for distributed computing, including object-oriented and functional languages.

Because of Java's popularity and widespread availability, many researchers have explored using Java for high-performance parallel computing. The special issues of *Concurrency—Practice and Experience* in June and November of 1997 contain several papers describing specific projects.

Cilk was developed at MIT by Charles Leiserson and his students. The language is now up to version 5. Frigo, Leiserson, and Randall [1998] give an overview of Cilk-5 and describe the implementation. That paper and many more can be found on the Web at `supertech.lcs.mit.edu/cilk/`. That Web site also contains an introduction to the language, the full reference manual, and the software distribution.

Fortran M was developed by Ian Foster of Argonne National Labs and Mani Chandy of the California Institute of Technology. Foster and Chandy [1995] describe the language and give numerous examples illustrating its use (see also Foster [1995]). More information, the software distribution, and current work on an HPF binding for MPI can be found on the Web at `www-fp.mcs.anl.gov/fortran-m/`.

Orca was developed by Henri Bal of the Vrije Universiteit in Amsterdam in a 1989 doctoral dissertation supervised by Andy Tanenbaum. Bal, Kaashoek, and Tanenbaum [1992] describe the original language, which was based on a task-parallel execution model. Ben Hassen, Bal, and Jacobs [1998] describe a new version of Orca that supports both task and data parallelism. Further information is available on the Web at `www.cs.vu.nl/orca/`.

The C* language was developed at Thinking Machines Corporation in the mid-1980s and language manuals were published by that company. Kumar et al. [1994] and Quinn [1994] summarize the language and give sample programs.

ZPL is the creation of Larry Snyder and his students at the University of Washington. The first version of the language was defined in the early 1990s, but the roots of the ZPL project extend back into the 1980s. Chamberlain et al. [1998] describe the language and argue that it simplifies programming data parallel computations, is portable, and has good performance. The Web site for the ZPL project is located at `www.cs.washington.edu/research/zpl/`. The site contains the software distribution, an overview of the language, and several papers, theses, and dissertations.

Guy Blelloch and colleagues developed NESL at Carnegie Mellon University. Blelloch [1996] describes the language and its work and depth performance model. The NESL Web site at `www.cs.cmu.edu/~scandal/nesl.html` provides the software distribution, a library of parallel algorithms, an interactive tutorial, and more.

As noted in the text, Sisal was the first functional language to be designed specifically to support scientific computing. It was developed by a group at the Lawrence Livermore National Laboratory. The first definition of Sisal appeared in 1985; the language was based on Val, an earlier data flow language. Feo, Cann, and Oldehoeft [1990] give an overview of the language and describe its implementation and performance. A second version of Sisal was created in the mid-1990s, but the project died not long after that. There is a Web page at `www.llnl.gov/sisal/`, but it is no longer maintained.

Section 12.3 mentioned three additional functional programming languages: Lisp, Haskell, and ML. Hudak [1989] survey these and other functional languages and describe parallel functional programming. Haskell includes features to control parallelism; Multilisp and Concurrent ML are concurrent programming variants of Lisp and ML, respectively. Information on these languages can be found by using a Web search engine such as `www.yahoo.com`.

The PRAM model was created by Fortune and Wyllie [1978] when they were graduate students at Cornell University. PRAM is described and illustrated in most textbooks on parallel algorithms, such as Kumar et al. [1994] and Quinn [1994]. The BSP model was created by Valiant [1990]; current information can be found on the Web at `www.bsp-worldwide.org/`. Culler et al. [1996] describe the LogP model. Skillicorn and Talia [1998] survey dozens of models and languages for parallel computing. Juurlink and Wijshoff [1998] provide a quantitative comparison of three models: (1) BSP; (2) E-BSP, an extension of BSP that deals with unbalanced communication patterns; and (3) BPRAM, a message-passing variant of PRAM.

Current information on High-Performance Fortran (HPF) can be found on the HPF home page at `dacnet.rice.edu/Depts/CRPC/HPFF/index.cfm`. That page provides links to online tutorials, the language specification, other publications, and implementations. Brinch Hansen [1998] contains an evaluation of HPF; Offner [1998] examines and rebuts Brinch Hansen's criticisms. The dHPF compiler group at Rice University is one of the key groups developing new program analysis and code generation techniques for data parallel languages in general and HPF in particular; their home page is located at `www.cs.rice.edu/~dsystem/dhpf/`.

Section 12.4 described a number of parallel programming tools. Information on the Pablo project, including the Autopilot and Virtue visualization tools, can be found at `www-pablo.cs.uiuc.edu/`. Miller et al. [1995] give an overview of the Paradyn performance measurement tool; the project's home page is located at `http://www.cs.wisc.edu/~paradyn/`. Foster [1995] describes additional tools for performance analysis, visualization, and random number generation.

Grimshaw et al. [1998] give an overview of metacomputers and metacomputing. Grimshaw and Wulf [1997] describe Legion, one of the most important examples of a metacomputing system; the project's home page is at `legion.virginia.edu`. Homer and Schlichting [1994] describe the Schooner system for distributed scientific computing; more information can be found at `www.cs.arizona.edu/schooner/`.

The November 1997 issue of *Communications of the ACM* contains several articles that describe computational grids, how they can be implemented, and how they can be used. Foster and Kesselman [1999] is the definitive source for current information. Chapters 1 and 2 describe computational grids in detail; the other 20 chapters describe applications, programming tools, grid services, and hardware and software infrastructures. The chapters are written by the experts who are working to make grids a reality. The Globus toolkit discussed at the end of Section 12.4 is described in Chapter 11 of the above book; it was first described in Foster and Kesselman [1997]. The Web page for the Globus project is located at `www.globus.org`.

There are also several general repositories of parallel computing information on the Web. For example, the Netlib repository of mathematical software, papers, and databases is located at `www.netlib.org/`. The Parallel Tools Consortium is a group of researchers, developers, and users who are creating tools to support parallel computing; the consortium's home page is at `www.ptools.org`. Nan Schaller's parallel computing page at `www.cs.rit.edu/~ncs/ parallel.html` contains a well-organized set of links. The IEEE Computer Society's ParaScope site at `computer.org/parascope/` contains an ever-growing set of links to parallel computing journals, conferences, vendors, sites, and projects. The information at the ParaScope site is quite comprehensive, but if you are looking for something, it helps to know its name.

References

Bacon, D. F., S. L. Graham, and O. J. Sharp. 1994. Compiler transformations for high-performance computing. *ACM Computing Surveys* 26, 4 (December): 345–420.

Bal, H. E., J. G. Steiner, and A. S. Tanenbaum. 1989. Programming languages for distributed computing systems. *ACM Computing Surveys* 21, 3 (September): 261–322.

Bal, H. E., M. F. Kaashoek, and A. S. Tanenbaum. 1992. Orca: A language for parallel programming on distributed systems. *IEEE Trans. Softw. Eng. 18*, 3 (March): 190–205.

Ben Hassen, S., H. E. Bal, and C. J. H. Jacobs. 1998. A task- and data-parallel programming language based on shared objects. *ACM Trans. on Programming Lang. and Systems* 20, 6 (November): 1131–70.

Blelloch, G. E. 1996. Programming parallel algorithms. *Comm. of the ACM* 39, 3 (March): 85–97.

Brinch Hansen, P. 1998. An evaluation of High Performance Fortran. *ACM SIGPLAN Notices* 33, 3 (March): 57–64.

Chamberlain, B. L., S.-E. Choi, E. C. Lewis, C. Lin, L. Snyder, and W. D. Weathersby. 1998. The case for high level parallel programming in ZPL. *IEEE Computational Science and Engr.* 5, 3: 76–86.

Culler, D. E., et al. 1996. LogP: A practical model of parallel computation. *Comm. of the ACM* 39, 11 (November): 78–85.

Feo, J. T., D. C. Cann, and R. R. Oldehoeft. 1990. A report on the Sisal language project. *Journal of Parallel and Dist. Comp.* 10: 349–66.

Fortune, S., and J. Wyllie. 1978. Parallelism in random access machines. *Proc. 10th ACM Symp. on Theory of Computing*, pp. 114–18.

Foster, I. 1995. *Designing and Building Parallel Programs*. Reading, MA: Addison-Wesley.

Foster, I. T., and K. M. Chandy. 1995. Fortran M: A language for modular parallel programming. *Journal of Parallel and Dist. Comp.* 26: 24–35.

Foster, I., and C. Kesselman. 1997. Globus: A metacomputing infrastructure toolkit. *Int. Journal of Supercomputing Applications* 11, 2: 115–28.

Foster, I., and C. Kesselman, eds. 1999. *The Grid: Blueprint for a New Computing Infrastructure.* San Francisco: Morgan Kaufmann.

Frigo, M., C. E. Leiserson, and K. H. Randall. 1998. The implementation of the Cilk-5 multithreaded language. *Proc. 1998 ACM SIGPLAN Conference on Programming Language Design and Implementation (PLDI),* June: 212–23.

Grimshaw, A. S., and W. A. Wulf. 1997. The Legion vision of a worldwide virtual computer. *Comm. of the ACM* 40, 1 (January): 39–45.

Grimshaw, A., A. Ferrari, G. Lindahl, and K. Holcomb. 1998. Metasystems. *Comm. of the ACM* 41, 11 (November): 47–55.

Homer, P., and R. Schlichting. 1994. A software platform for constructing scientific applications from heterogeneous resources. *Journal of Parallel and Distributed Computing* 21, 3 (June): 301–15.

Hudak, P. 1989. Conception, evolution, and application of functional programming languages. *ACM Computing Surveys* 21, 3 (September): 359–411.

Juurlink, B. H. H., and H. A. G. Wijshoff. 1998. A quantitative comparison of parallel computational models. *ACM Trans. on Computer Systems* 16, 3 (August): 271–318.

Kumar, V., A. Grama, A. Gupta, and G. Karypis. 1994. *Introduction to Parallel Computing: Design and Analysis of Algorithms.* Menlo Park, CA: Benjamin/Cummings.

McKinley, K. S., S. Carr, and C.-W. Tseng. 1996. Improving data locality with loop transformations. *ACM Trans. of Programming Lang. and Systems* 18, 4 (July): 4214–53.

Miller, B. P., et al. 1995. The Paradyn parallel performance measurement tool. *IEEE Computer* 28, 11 (November): 37–46.

Offner, C. D. 1998. Per Brinch Hansen's concerns about High Performance Fortran. *ACM SIGPLAN Notices* 33, 8 (August): 34–39.

Quinn, M. J. 1994. *Parallel Computing: Theory and Practice.* New York: McGraw-Hill.

Skillicorn, D. B., and D. Talia. 1998. Models and languages for parallel computation. *ACM Computing Surveys* 30, 2 (June): 123–69.

Valiant, L. G. 1990. A bridging model for parallel computation. *Comm. of the ACM* 33, 8 (August): 103–11.

Wilson, G. V., and P. Lu, eds. 1996. *Parallel Programming Using C++*. Cambridge, MA: MIT Press.

Wolfe, M. 1989. *Optimizing Supercompilers for Supercomputers*. Cambridge, MA: MIT Press.

Exercises

12.1 Section 12.1 presented implementations of Jacobi iteration using the Pthreads, MPI, and OpenMP libraries.

(a) Develop parallel programs to solve the *n*-body problem using Pthreads, MPI, and OpenMP. Use shared variables for the Pthreads and OpenMP programs, and use message passing for the MPI program. Write the sequential parts of your program in C for Pthreads and in either C or Fortran for MPI and OpenMP.

(b) Develop parallel programs to implement LU decomposition using Pthreads, MPI, and OpenMP. Use shared variables for the Pthreads and OpenMP programs, and use message passing for the MPI program. Write the sequential parts of your program in C for Pthreads and in either C or Fortran for MPI and OpenMP.

12.2 For each of the following sequential programs, identify all instances of (1) flow dependencies, (2) anti-dependencies, and (3) output dependencies. Indicate which are within loop bodies and which are carried by loops.

(a) The Jacobi iteration program in Figure 11.2.

(b) The *n*-body program in Figure 11.9.

(c) The LU decomposition program in Figure 11.16.

(d) The forward and backward substitution program in Figure 11.17.

12.3 Figure 12.5 lists several types of program transformations that are used by parallelizing compilers. For each transformation and for each of the following sequential programs, determine whether you could apply the transformation and, if so, show how to do so. Consider each transformation independently.

(a) The Jacobi iteration program in Figure 11.2.

(b) The *n*-body program in Figure 11.9.

(c) The LU decomposition program in Figure 11.16.

(d) The forward and backward substitution program in Figure 11.17.

12.4 Repeat the previous exercise, but now apply multiple transformations to each program. Assume you are going to be generating code for an eight-processor shared-memory machine and that the problem size **n** is a multiple of eight. Your goal is to produce a final program that would be fairly easy to turn into a parallel program with a balanced computational load, good data locality, and small synchronization overhead. For each program (1) pick a sequence of transformations, (2) show how the program changes as each one is applied, and (3) explain either why you think the final code will result in a good parallel program or why you cannot get a good parallel program from the given sequential program.

12.5   The Gauss-Seidel algorithm has what is called *wave-front parallelism*, as explained at the end of Section 12.2.

(a) Develop a parallel program for Gauss-Seidel. Use shared variables for communication and use the **co** statement to program both concurrency and the wave-front synchronization.

(b) Develop a second parallel program for Gauss-Seidel. Again use shared variables, but this time create the processes once and use flag variables for wave-front synchronization.

(c) Evaluate and compare the performance of your answers to (a) and (b). Is one always better, or is each sometimes better than the other?

12.6   Section 12.3 gave brief synopses of several parallel programming languages.

(a) Pick one language, gather references on it, and then write a full "case study." The level of detail should be comparable to that of the case studies in the text on Linda, CSP, Ada, and SR.

(b) Pick one language, gather information on it, and acquire and install the software implementation (if necessary). Then write programs in the language for Jacobi iteration, the *n*-body problem, and LU decomposition. You might also wish to write one or more recursive parallel programs. Write a report that explains the language, your programs, and your experience writing them. How easy or hard was the language to learn? How easy or hard was it to use? How well or poorly do your programs perform?

(c) Repeat part (b) for a second language. In addition to reporting your experiences with each language, describe how they compare. Which did you prefer and why?

12.7   Acquire and install an HPF compiler (if necessary). Implement and test the program for Jacobi iteration in Figure 12.8. Then implement and test programs for the *n*-body problem and LU decomposition. Run your programs on both shared- and distributed-memory machines if possible. Write a report that describes the programs, your experience writing them, and their performance.

12.8   Section 12.4 describes several parallel programming tools and toolkits. The Historical Notes above give pointers to many others. Gather detailed information on some tool and acquire and install it. Then experiment with the tool on new programs and on programs you have previously written. Write a report describing the tool, your programs, your experiments, and your experience using the tool. How easy was the tool to use? What did you learn by using it?

Glossary

Assertion

A predicate that characterizes a program state. When an assertion is placed before a statement in a program, it specifies that the predicate must be true every time the program is ready to execute that statement.

At-Most-Once Property

An attribute of an assignment statement $x = e$ in which either (1) x is not read by another process and e contains at most one reference to a variable changed by another process, or (2) x is not written by another process and e contains no references to variables changed by other processes. Such an assignment statement will appear to execute as an atomic action.

Atomic Action

A sequence of one or more statements that appears to execute as a single, indivisible action. A *fine-grained atomic action* is one that can be implemented directly by a single machine instruction. A *coarse-grained atomic action* is implemented using critical section protocols.

Bag-of-Tasks Paradigm

A parallel computing method in which tasks are placed in a bag shared by worker processes. Each worker repeatedly takes a task, executes it, and possibly generates new tasks that it puts into the bag. The computation has terminated when the bag is empty and the workers are idle.

Barrier

A synchronization point that all processes must reach before any are allowed to proceed.

Broadcast Algorithm

A method for disseminating information or making decisions in a distributed program. For decision making, each process broadcasts requests and acknowledgments to all other processes and maintains an ordered message queue that it uses to decide when its request is the oldest.

Busy Waiting

An implementation of synchronization in which a process repeatedly executes a loop waiting for a Boolean condition B to be true. This is often programmed as `while (!B) skip;`. When a process is busy waiting, it is also said to be *spinning*.

Client/Server Program

A process interaction pattern in a distributed program. A server process manages a resource and implements operations on that resource. A client makes a request of the server by invoking one of its operations.

Concurrent Program

A program containing two or more processes. Each process is a sequential program; see also **Distributed Program** and **Parallel Program**.

Condition Synchronization

A type of synchronization that involves delaying a process until some Boolean condition B is true. This is implemented by having one process wait for an event that is signaled by another process.

Conditional Atomic Action

An atomic action that must delay until the state satisfies some Boolean condition B. This is programmed as ⟨`await (B) S;`⟩.

Context Switch

The act of switching a processor from executing one process to executing another. This is called a context switch because the state of each process is called its context. A context switch is performed in a kernel by a routine that is called a dispatcher or scheduler.

Covering Condition

A synchronization technique used with monitors. A process signals a condition variable when it is possible that waiting processes might be able to proceed.

Critical Section

A sequence of statements that must be executed with mutual exclusion with respect to critical sections in other processes that reference the same shared variables. Critical section protocols are used to implement coarse-grained atomic actions.

Data Parallel Program

A program is one in which each processes executes the same actions—usually at the same time—on different parts of shared data.

Deadlock

A state in which two or more processes are waiting for each other, in a so-called deadly embrace.

Distributed Program

A program in which processes communicate using message passing, remote procedure call, or rendezvous. Usually the processes execute on different processors.

Distributed Shared Memory (DSM)

A software implementation of a shared address space on a distributed-memory multiprocessor or a network of processors.

Exclusion of Configurations

A method for proving safety properties such as mutual exclusion and absence of deadlock. Process P_1 cannot be in a state satisfying assertion A_1 at the same time process P_2 is in a state satisfying assertion A_2 if $(A_1 \wedge A_2)$ == `false`.

Fairness

An attribute of a scheduler or algorithm that guarantees that every delayed process gets a chance to proceed; see also **Scheduling Policy**.

False Sharing

A situation in which two processes reference different variables that are stored in the same cache line or DSM page and at least one of the processes writes into its variable.

Filter Process

A process that receives (reads) from one or more input channels, computes a function of the input, and sends (writes) results to one or more output channels. A filter process is both a producer and a consumer, and it can be used in a pipeline.

Global Invariant

A predicate that is true in every visible program state—namely, before and after every atomic action.

Heartbeat Algorithm

A process interaction paradigm in distributed programs. Each process repeatedly executes three phases: (1) send messages to other processes, (2) receive messages from others, and (3) compute with local data and data received in messages.

History

The sequence of states, or actions, resulting from one execution of a program; a history is also called a *trace*.

Independent Statements

Two statements in different processes that do not write into the same variables and that do not read variables written by the other. Independent statements will not interfere with each other if they are executed in parallel.

Interacting Peers

A process interaction pattern in distributed programs in which processes are equals—executing the same code and interacting with each other to exchange information.

Interference

The result of two processes reading and writing shared variables in an unpredictable order and hence with unpredictable results; see also **Noninterference**.

Iterative Parallelism

A type of parallelism in which each process executes a loop that manipulates a part of the program's data. Often results from parallelizing loops in sequential programs.

Kernel

A collection of data structures and primitive operations—uninterruptible procedures—that manages processes, schedules them on processors, and implements high-level communication and synchronization operations such as semaphores or message passing.

Livelock

A situation in which a process is spinning while waiting for a condition that will never become true. Livelock is the busy-waiting analog of deadlock.

Liveness Property

A property of a program that asserts that something good will eventually happen—namely, that the program eventually reaches a good state. Termination and eventual entry into a critical section are examples of liveness properties.

Load Balancing

The act of assigning each process (and processor) in a parallel program an approximately equal amount of work.

Lock

A variable that is used to protect a critical section. A lock is set when some process is executing in a critical section; otherwise it is clear.

Loop Invariant

A predicate that is true before and after every execution of the statements in a loop.

Manager/Workers Paradigm

A distributed implementation of the bag-of-tasks paradigm. A manager process implements the bag and gathers results; workers interact with the manager to get tasks and to return results.

Metacomputer

A set of computers linked by high-speed networks and a software infrastructure that presents the illusion of a single computing resources. Sometimes called a *networked virtual supercomputer*.

Multiple Instruction, Multiple Data (MIMD) Multiprocessor

A hardware architecture in which there are multiple independent processors and each executes a separate program; also called an *asynchronous multiprocessor*.

Multicomputer

A MIMD multiprocessor with distributed memory. Hypercube machines are examples of multicomputers.

Multithreaded Program

A program containing multiple processes or threads. Synonymous with concurrent program, although multithreaded program often means that there are more threads than processors and hence that the threads take turns executing on the processors.

Mutual Exclusion

A type of synchronization that ensures that statements in different processes cannot execute at the same time; see also **Critical Section**.

Nested Monitor Call

A call from one monitor to a second monitor. When a process makes a nested call, the call is said to be *open* if the process releases exclusion in the first monitor. The call is said to be *closed* if the process retains exclusion in the first monitor.

Noninterference

A relation between an atomic action a in one process and a critical assertion c in another process. Execution of a does not interfere with c if it leaves c true, assuming that c is already true.

Parallel Program

A concurrent program in which each process executes on its own processor, and hence the processes execute in parallel. (However, the phrase parallel program is sometimes used to mean any concurrent program.)

Partial Correctness

A property of a program that computes the desired result, assuming the program terminates.

Passing the Baton

A synchronization technique that is used with semaphores. When one process decides that another process should be awakened, it signals a semaphore on which that process is waiting. This signal has the effect of passing a baton to the second process; the baton conveys permission to execute with mutual exclusion.

Pipeline

A set of processes that are connected in a series so that the output produced by one process is the input consumed by the next process. A pipeline is (1) *open* if the ends are not connected to other processes, (2) *circular* if the ends are closed on each other to form a circle, and (3) *closed* if it is circular and there is an extra coordinator process that produces input for the first worker process in the pipeline and that consumes the output of the last worker process.

Postcondition

An assertion that is true when statement s finishes execution.

Precondition

An assertion that is true when statement s starts execution.

Probe/Echo Algorithm

A process interaction paradigm in distributed programs. A *probe* is used to disseminate information from one process to all others; an *echo* is used to gather information.

Producers and Consumers Interaction

An interaction between two processes in which one process produces data that is consumed by the other; see also **Filter Process** and **Pipeline**.

Proof Outline

A program interspersed with enough assertions to convince the reader that the program is correct. A complete proof outline has an assertion before and after every statement.

Race Condition

A situation in a shared-variable concurrent program in which one process writes a variable that a second process reads, but the first process continues execution— namely, races ahead—and changes the variable again before the second process sees the result of the first change. This usually leads to an incorrectly synchronized program.

Recursive Parallelism

A type of parallelism that results from making recursive calls in parallel. Often results from parallelizing sequential programs that use the divide-and-conquer paradigm to solve smaller and smaller problems.

Replicated Servers Paradigm

A process interaction pattern in distributed programs in which there are multiple instances of a server process. Each server manages a part or a copy of some shared resource; the servers interact to ensure that the resource is kept in a consistent state.

Safety Property

A property of a program that asserts that nothing bad will ever happen—namely, that the program never enters a bad state. Partial correctness, mutual exclusion, and absence of deadlock are examples of safety properties.

Scheduling Policy

A policy that determines which action gets to execute next—namely, the order in which processes execute. A scheduling policy is (1) *unconditionally fair* if unconditional atomic actions eventually get to execute, (2) *weakly fair* if conditional atomic actions eventually get to execute if the delay condition becomes true and remains true, and (3) *strongly fair* if conditional atomic actions eventually get to execute if the delay condition is infinitely often true.

Single Instruction, Multiple Data (SIMD) Multiprocessor

A hardware architecture in which there is a single instruction stream that is executed in lockstep by every processor, which operates on its own local data; also called a *synchronous multiprocessor*.

Single Program, Multiple Data (SPMD)

A programming style in which one process is coded. A copy of the process executes on every processor; each copy has its own private data. Usually there is a way for each process to determine its own identity—which is sometimes called its rank.

Speedup

The ratio T_1/T_p of the execution time T_1 of a sequential program on one processor to the execution time T_p of a parallel program on p processors.

Spin Lock

A Boolean variable that is used in conjunction with busy waiting to protect a critical section. A process that wants to enter a critical section spins until the lock is clear.

State of a Program

The value of every program variable at a point in time.

Symmetric Multiprocessor (SMP)

A shared-memory multiprocessor architecture in which processors are identical and every processor can access every memory word in the same amount of time.

Synchronization

An interaction between processes that controls the order in which the processes execute; see also **Mutual Exclusion** and **Condition Synchronization**.

Task Parallel Program

A program in which each process executes a separate task, and hence each process is a different sequential program.

Thread

A sequential program that has its own thread of control—or context—and hence that can execute concurrently with other threads. Threads compete for time on the same processor or they may execute in parallel on separate processors.

Token-Passing Algorithm

A process interaction pattern in distributed programs in which tokens are used to convey permission or to gather information about the global state.

Total Correctness

A property of a program that computes the desired result and terminates.

Triple

A programming logic formula having the form { P } S { Q }, where P and Q are predicates and S is a statement list. The interpretation of a triple is as follows: If execution of S starts in a state satisfying P and if S terminates, then the final state will satisfy Q.

Unconditional Atomic Action

An atomic action that does not have a delay condition. This is programmed as ⟨ S; ⟩ and might be implemented as a single machine instruction.

Index